$\mathscr{A}$MERICA

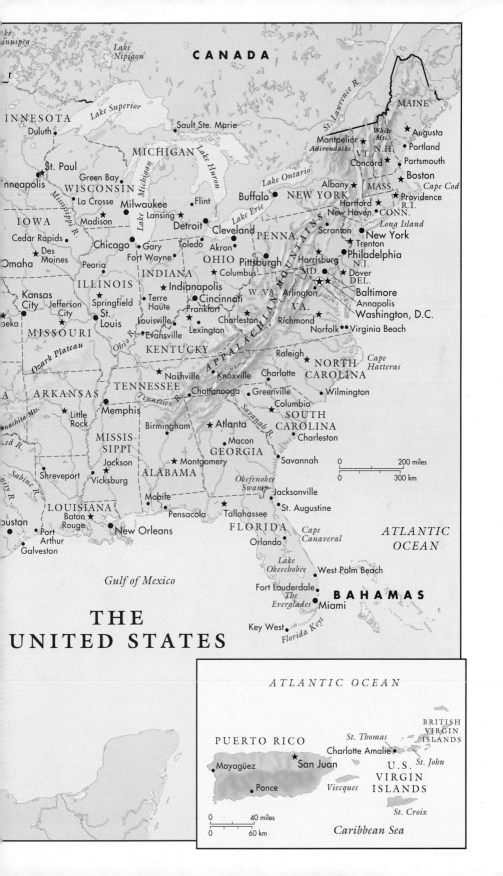

THE
UNITED STATES

THE
WORLD

ARCTIC OCEAN

15°E 30°E 45°E 60°E 75°E 90°E 105°E 120°E 135°E 150°E 165°E 180°

90°N (North Pole)

80°N

70°N

60°N

Arctic Circle

50°N

40°N

30°N

20°N

10°N

Tropic of Cancer

Equator 0°

10°S

Tropic of Capricorn

20°S

30°S

40°S

50°S

60°S

Antarctic Circle

70°S

80°S

90°S (South Pole)

NORWAY SWEDEN FINLAND
DENMARK
GERMANY POLAND BELARUS
CZECH. UKRAINE
SWITZER- SLOVAKIA
LAND AUS. HUNG. MOLD.
ITALY ROMANIA
ALBANIA BULGARIA
GREECE
MALTA
TUNISIA
LIBYA
EGYPT

RUSSIA
Moscow

EST.
LAT.
LITH.

KAZAKHSTAN

MONGOLIA

ASIA
CHINA

Beijing
Tianjin
Shanghai

NORTH
KOREA
SOUTH
KOREA

JAPAN

Seoul
Tokyo

NORTH PACIFIC
OCEAN

East
China
Sea

GEORGIA
TURKEY ARMENIA AZER-
BAIJAN
CYPRUS
SYRIA
LEBANON
ISRAEL IRAQ IRAN
JORDAN
KUWAIT BAHRAIN

UZBEKI-
STAN
TURKMENI-
STAN
TAJIKI-
STAN

KYRGYZ-
STAN

Teheran
AFGHANI-
STAN

PAKISTAN

NEPAL
New
Delhi
Karachi

BHUTAN

BANGLA-
DESH

Hong Kong

TAIWAN

QATAR
UNITED
ARAB
EMIRATES

SAUDI
ARABIA

OMAN

INDIA

Calcutta

Bombay

MYANMAR
(BURMA)

LAOS
Bangkok
THAILAND

VIETNAM

South
China
Sea

PHILIPPINES

Manila

TRUST TERRITORY
OF THE PACIFIC ISLANDS
(U.S.)

WAKE
ISLAND
(U.S.)

GUAM
(U.S.)

NIGER CHAD SUDAN
ERITREA YEMEN
DJIBUTI

Cairo

Arabian
Sea

Bay of Bengal

CAMBODIA

NIGERIA

CENTRAL
AFRICAN
REPUBLIC
ETHIOPIA

SRI
LANKA

BRUNEI

MALAYSIA

FEDERATED STATES
OF MICRONESIA

CAMEROON
EQUATORIAL
GUINEA
GABON CONGO
RINCIPE
SÃO TOME

MALDIVES

SOMALIA

UGANDA
RWANDA
BURUNDI
KENYA

ZAIRE

TANZANIA

SEYCHELLES

Equator

SINGAPORE

Jakarta

INDONESIA

PAPUA
NEW GUINEA

SOLOMON
ISLANDS

KIRIBATI

NAURU

TUVALU

ANGOLA
ZAMBIA
MALAWI
MOZAMBIQUE

COMOROS

MADAGASCAR

MAURITIUS

INDIAN OCEAN

VANUATU

FIJI

NAMIBIA ZIMBABWE
BOTSWANA
SWAZILAND
SOUTH
AFRICA LESOTHO

AUSTRALIA

AUSTRALIA

SOUTH

PACIFIC

OCEAN

NEW
ZEALAND

ANTARCTICA

15°E 30°E 45°E 60°E 75°E 90°E 105°E 120°E 135°E 150°E 165°E 180°

EUROPE

AFRICA

RIA

0   1000   2000   3000 miles

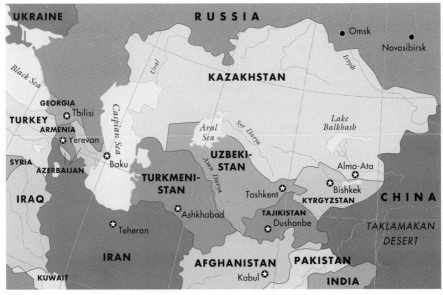

UKRAINE

RUSSIA

Omsk
Novosibirsk

Black Sea

Ural

Irtysh

KAZAKHSTAN

GEORGIA
Tbilisi

TURKEY
ARMENIA
Yerevan

SYRIA

AZERBAIJAN
Baku

Caspian Sea

Aral
Sea

Syr Darya

Lake
Balkhash

UZBEKI-
STAN

Alma-Ata

CHINA

IRAQ

TURKMENI-
STAN

Amu Darya

Tashkent

Bishkek
KYRGYZSTAN

TAJIKISTAN
Dushanbe

TAKLAMAKAN
DESERT

Ashkhabad

Teheran

IRAN

AFGHANISTAN
Kabul

PAKISTAN

INDIA

KUWAIT

AMERICA

AMERICA

A NARRATIVE HISTORY

BRIEF FOURTH EDITION

VOLUME II

GEORGE BROWN TINDALL
DAVID E. SHI

W · W · NORTON & COMPANY · NEW YORK · LONDON

The text of this book is composed in Fairfield Light
with the display set in Torino
Composition by Compset Inc.
Manufacturing by R. R. Donnelley
Book design by Antonina Krass
Cover painting by Richard A. Chase, *Erecting the Outer Drive Bridge*
(aka *Erecting the Lakeshore Drive Bridge*), c. 1936.
Courtesy of the Chicago Historical Society.

The Library of Congress has cataloged the one-volume edition as follows:

Tindall, George Brown.
    America : a narrative history / George Brown Tindall, David E.
Shi.—Brief 4th ed.
        p.   cm
    Includes bibliographical references and index.
    ISBN 0-393-97063-9 (pbk.)
    1. United States—History.   I. Shi, David E.   II. Title.
E178.1.T55   1997
973—dc20   96–25530

ISBN 0-393-97067-1

W. W. Norton & Company, Inc., 500 Fifth Avenue, New York, N.Y. 10110
http://www.wwnorton.com

W. W. Norton & Company Ltd., 10 Coptic Street, London WC1A 1PU

4 5 6 7 8 9 0

FOR BRUCE AND BLAIR

FOR
JASON AND JESSICA

CONTENTS

List of Maps • *xv*
Preface • *xvii*

17 | RECONSTRUCTION: NORTH AND SOUTH   532

THE BATTLE OVER RECONSTRUCTION   532   •   RECONSTRUCTING THE
SOUTH   543   •   BLACKS IN THE RECONSTRUCTED SOUTH   546
•   THE GRANT YEARS   555   •   FURTHER READING   563

PART FIVE / **GROWING PAINS**

18 | NEW FRONTIERS: SOUTH AND WEST   569

THE NEW SOUTH   570   •   THE NEW WEST   582   •   FURTHER READING   599

19 | THE RISE OF BIG BUSINESS   602

THE POST-CIVIL WAR ECONOMY   602   •   ENTREPRENEURS   609
•   ADVANCES FOR LABOR   615   •   FURTHER READING   629

20 | THE EMERGENCE OF MODERN AMERICA   631

AMERICA'S MOVE TO TOWN   632   •   THE NEW IMMIGRATION   635
•   EDUCATION AND THE PROFESSIONS   644   •   THEORIES OF SOCIAL
CHANGE   647   •   REALISM IN FACT AND FICTION   649   •   THE SOCIAL
GOSPEL   654   •   EARLY EFFORTS AT URBAN REFORM   657   •   FURTHER
READING   661

21 | GILDED-AGE POLITICS AND AGRARIAN REVOLT 663

PARADOXICAL POLITICS 663 • CORRUPTION AND REFORM 666 • THE PROBLEMS OF FARMERS 678 • AGRARIAN REVOLT 680 • FURTHER READING 693

$\mathscr{P}$ART SIX / **MODERN AMERICA**

22 | THE COURSE OF EMPIRE 699

TOWARD THE NEW IMPERIALISM 699 • STEPS TO WORLD POWER 702 • THE SPANISH-AMERICAN WAR 704 • IMPERIAL RIVALRIES IN EAST ASIA 716 • AN AMERICAN ORIGINAL 717 • ROOSEVELT'S FOREIGN POLICY 720 • FURTHER READING 726

23 | PROGRESSIVISM: ROOSEVELT, TAFT, AND WILSON 727

ELEMENTS OF REFORM 727 • THE FEATURES OF PROGRESSIVISM 731 • ROOSEVELT'S PROGRESSIVISM 734 • ROOSEVELT'S SECOND TERM 738 • FROM ROOSEVELT TO TAFT 740 • WILSON'S PROGRESSIVISM 744 • THE LIMITS OF PROGRESSIVISM 755 • FURTHER READING 756

24 | WILSON AND THE GREAT WAR 758

WILSON AND FOREIGN AFFAIRS 758 • THE GREAT WAR AND AMERICA 762 • AMERICA'S ENTRY 770 • "THE DECISIVE POWER" 777 • THE FIGHT FOR PEACE AT HOME AND ABROAD 781 • LURCHING FROM WAR TO PEACE 787 • FURTHER READING 793

25 | THE MODERN TEMPER 794

REACTION IN THE TWENTIES 794 • SOCIAL TENSIONS 801 • THE CULTURE OF MODERNISM 808 • FURTHER READING 814

26 | REPUBLICAN RESURGENCE AND DECLINE   815

PROGRESSIVISM TRANSFORMED   815   •   "NORMALCY"   816
•   THE NEW ERA   824   •   PRESIDENT HOOVER, THE ENGINEER   832
•   FURTHER READING   842

27 | FRANKLIN D. ROOSEVELT AND THE NEW DEAL   843

FROM HOOVERISM TO THE NEW DEAL   844   •   RECOVERY THROUGH
REGULATION   851   •   LAUNCHING THE SECOND NEW DEAL   858
•   SECOND-TERM SETBACKS AND INITIATIVES   868   •   THE LEGACY OF
THE NEW DEAL   873   •   CULTURE IN THE THIRTIES   875   •   FURTHER
READING   880

28 | FROM ISOLATION TO GLOBAL WAR   882

POSTWAR ISOLATIONISM   882   •   WAR CLOUDS   887   •   THE STORM
IN EUROPE   894   •   THE STORM IN THE PACIFIC   900   •   FURTHER
READING   905

29 | THE WORLD AT WAR   907

AMERICA'S EARLY BATTLES   907   •   MOBILIZATION AT HOME   909
•   THE ALLIED DRIVE TOWARD BERLIN   920   •   LEAPFROGGING TO
TOKYO   930   •   A NEW AGE IS BORN   934   •   FURTHER READING   945

*P*ART SEVEN / **THE AMERICAN AGE**

30 | THE FAIR DEAL AND CONTAINMENT   951

DEMOBILIZATION UNDER TRUMAN   952   •   THE COLD WAR   957   •   HARRY
GIVES 'EM HELL   966   •   THE COLD WAR HEATS UP   970   •   FURTHER
READING   980

31 | THROUGH THE PICTURE WINDOW: SOCIETY AND CULTURE, 1945–1960   981

PEOPLE OF PLENTY   982   •   A CONFORMING CULTURE   991   •   CRACKS IN THE PICTURE WINDOW   995   •   A PARADOXICAL ERA   1002   •   FURTHER READING   1003

32 | CONFLICT AND DEADLOCK: THE EISENHOWER YEARS   1005

"TIME FOR A CHANGE"   1005   •   CIVIL RIGHTS IN THE FIFTIES   1020 •   A SEASON OF TROUBLES   1025   •   ASSESSING THE EISENHOWER YEARS 1031   •   FURTHER READING   1033

33 | NEW FRONTIERS: KENNEDY AND JOHNSON   1035

THE NEW FRONTIER   1036   •   FOREIGN FRONTIERS   1043   •   LYNDON JOHNSON AND THE GREAT SOCIETY   1048   •   FROM CIVIL RIGHTS TO BLACK POWER   1056   •   THE TRAGEDY OF VIETNAM   1060   •   SIXTIES CRESCENDO   1066   •   FURTHER READING   1069

34 | REBELLION AND REACTION IN THE 1960S AND 1970S   1071

THE ROOTS OF REBELLION   1071   •   NIXON AND VIETNAM   1087 •   NIXON AND MIDDLE AMERICA   1092   •   NIXON TRIUMPHANT   1096 •   WATERGATE   1098   •   AN UNELECTED PRESIDENT   1102   •   THE CARTER INTERREGNUM   1104   •   FURTHER READING   1109

35 | A NEW GILDED AGE   1111

THE REAGAN RESTORATION   1111   •   REAGAN'S SECOND TERM   1122 •   THE BUSH YEARS   1133   •   FURTHER READING   1147

36 | CULTURAL POLITICS   1149

AMERICA'S CHANGING FACE: THE 1990 CENSUS   1152   •   BUSH TO CLINTON 1158   •   DEMOCRATIC RESURGENCE   1163   •   THE REPUBLICAN AGENDA 1175   •   FURTHER READING   1184

APPENDIX

THE DECLARATION OF INDEPENDENCE   A1   •   ARTICLES OF CONFEDERATION
A6   •   THE CONSTITUTION OF THE UNITED STATES   A14   •   PRESIDENTIAL
ELECTIONS   A34   •   ADMISSION OF STATES   A38   •   POPULATION OF THE
UNITED STATES   A39   •   IMMIGRATION TO THE UNITED STATES, FISCAL YEARS
1820–1990   A40   •   IMMIGRATION BY REGION AND SELECTED COUNTRY OF
LAST RESIDENCE, FISCAL YEARS 1820–1989   A42   •   PRESIDENTS,
VICE-PRESIDENTS, AND SECRETARIES OF STATE   A49   •   CHRONOLOGY
OF SIGNIFICANT EVENTS   A52

ILLUSTRATION CREDITS   A59

INDEX   A61

MAPS

Indian Wars	586
Spanish-American War: The Pacific, 1898	708
Spanish-American War: The Caribbean, 1898	709
U.S. Interests in the Caribbean	721
Europe at War	762
The Western Front, 1918	778
Europe After Versailles	784
The Tennessee Valley Authority	857
Aggression in Europe	890
Japanese Expansion Before Pearl Harbor	900
War in Europe and Africa, 1942–1945	922–23
The War in the Pacific, 1942–1945	932–33
Occupation of Germany and Austria	963
The Korean War, 1950	973
The Korean War, 1950–1953	973
Postwar Alliances: The Far East	1019
Postwar Alliances: Europe, North Africa, the Middle East	1026
Vietnam, 1966	1061
Election, 1968	1068
The Post Cold War West	1141
The Gulf War, 1990–1991	1144

PREFACE

Just as history is never complete, neither is a historical textbook. We have learned much from the responses of readers and instructors to the first three editions of Brief *America*. Perhaps the most important and reassuring lesson is that our original intention has proved valid: to provide a compelling narrative history of the American experience, a narrative animated by human characters, informed by analysis and social texture, and guided by the unfolding of events. Readers have also endorsed the book's unique format. *America* is designed to be read and to carry a moderate price.

In a significant attempt to help students grasp the major themes and developments throughout the text, without compromising its intellectual integrity, Brief *America* now contains a new pedagogical program. Students will receive additional guidance when reading the text from new part openers, which lay out the major ideas emphasized in upcoming chapters. Chapter organizers appear on the first page of each chapter and present key idea statements that serve as a guide through the narrative. "Making Connections" boxes appear on the final page of each chapter (except the last) to link significant events in the current chapter to issues in surrounding chapters. The new pedagogical program with the larger format and the new two-color design result in an attractive, easy-to-read text that instructors and students should find inviting.

The revisions that set off the Brief Fourth Edition of *America: A Narrative History* highlight frontiers: the experiences of men and women on America's frontiers and the significance of frontiers in shaping the nation's history. Frontiers can be understood in many ways. In announcing that the American frontier had closed in 1893, the historian Frederick Jackson Turner described the frontier as the source of American democratic values and institutions. For Turner the frontier was the place where Americans reinvented themselves, made better lives, tamed the wilderness, and set it on the path to civilized development. The frontier experience forged the distinctive American character and the independence, acquisitiveness, and boldness often attributed to it. Turner's frontier incorporated images already being conjured in American popular culture: savage Indians, virtuous settlers, gritty desperadoes, and gallant mothers and wives.

Turner's "frontier thesis" dominated the teaching of American history for almost half a century. Yet his uncritical celebration of the dramatic process of westward expansion overlooked many tragedies and failures along the way. It also was highly selective. His cast of characters was made up almost exclusively of white males. He left out many other important actors: Indians, women, Hispanics, Asians, and African Americans, among others.

Despite the flaws in Turner's version of the frontier, the concept itself remains viable. Many historians still find the frontier a useful frame for understanding important aspects of the American experience (not to mention other societies as well). In tracing the significance of the frontier experience in the development of American society and culture, we adopt an expansive definition and an inclusive treatment of its participants.

America has had many frontiers. They were places of fast-paced change. The unsettled conditions in many areas helped alter social relations, including those between women and men. Frontiers also served as crossroads where ethnic and racial groups formed new configurations, often with violent overtones. And the frontier exists in the minds of Americans as a powerful metaphor for change, for the chance to start anew.

There is much that is new in the Brief Fourth Edition of *America*. The frontier theme surfaces in fresh treatments of the Spanish Southwest in the colonial period and the ways Native Americans and Spanish settlers reacted and adapted to each other (Chapters 1 and 4). In Chapter 1 there are new discussions of Indian cultures and societies in the colonial Atlantic region. The French empire in America and its interactions with the Native Americans receive fresh attention in Chapter 3. There are new sections detailing Anglo-Indian relations (Chapters 1, 3, and 4), and expanded treatments of the old Southwest (Chapters 13 and 14), the mining frontier (Chapters 15 and 18), the Civil War in the

West (Chapter 16), and the development of the West in the late nineteenth century (Chapter 18). This edition of *America* also provides more extensive coverage of the West in the twentieth century, with new discussions of the West during the Great Depression of the 1930s and World War II, and the particular experiences of Hispanics.

This Brief Fourth Edition, like its predecessor, integrates more social history into the narrative of American experience, detailing the folkways and contributions of those groups often underrepresented in historical treatments—women, blacks, and ethnic Americans. New sections have been added dealing with the Salem witch trials, Andrew Jackson, Clara Barton, Woodrow Wilson, Eleanor Roosevelt, the D-Day invasion, the social impact of the GI Bill, the "black power" movement, cultural conservatism, and the Clinton administration. This edition also features new material about religious life in general and revivalism in particular.

In preparing this Brief Fourth Edition of *America* we have benefitted from the insights and suggestions of many people. The following scholars provided close readings of the manuscript at various stages: Holly Mayer (Duquesne University), Jean B. Lee (University of Wisconsin, Madison), Elizabeth Leonard (Colby College), Bruce Field (Northern Illinois University), Virginia DeJohn Anderson (University of Colorado), Fred Anderson (University of Colorado), Charles Eagles (University of Mississippi), and David Parker (Kennseaw College). Once again we thank our friends at W. W. Norton, especially Margaret Farley, Mary Kelly, Kate Nash, and Steve Forman, for their care and attention along the way.

—George B. Tindall
—David E. Shi

AMERICA

17 ∽ RECONSTRUCTION:

NORTH AND SOUTH

CHAPTER ORGANIZER

This chapter focuses on:

- the different approaches to Reconstruction

- congressional efforts to reshape southern society

- the role of African Americans in the early postwar years

- national politics in the 1870s

THE BATTLE OVER RECONSTRUCTION

In the spring of 1865 the wearying war was over. At the frightful cost of 620,000 lives and the destruction of the southern economy and much of its landscape, American nationalism emerged triumphant, and some 4 million slaves emerged free. But peace had come only on the battlefields. "Cannon conquer," recognized a northern editor, "but they do not necessarily convert." Now the North faced the imposing task of "reconstructing" a ravaged and resentful South. A few northerners thought the task relatively simple. The poet and professor James Russell Lowell wrote a friend in April 1865: "I worry a little about reconstruction, but am inclined to think that matters will very much settle themselves."

He was wrong. A tangle of difficult issues confronted northern politicians. Should the Confederate leaders be tried for treason? How were new governments to be formed? How and at whose expense was the South's economy to be rebuilt? What was to be done with the freed slaves? Were they to be given land? social equality? education? voting rights? Such complex questions required careful planning, but policy makers did not have the luxury of time or the benefits of consensus.

FORCED DOMESTICITY   The defeat of the Confederacy transformed much of southern society. The freeing of slaves, the destruction of property, and the free-fall in land values left many among the former planter elite destitute and homeless. Amanda Worthington, a plantation mistress from Mississippi, saw her whole world destroyed. In the fall of 1865, she assessed the damage: "None of us can realize that we are no longer wealthy—yet thanks to the yankees, the cause of all unhappiness, such is the case. As long as I thought we would conquer in our just cause, I cared nothing for the loss of property for I felt as if we would be rich if we had *Our Rights & Our Country* left us—but now they are lost too, & *we have* suffered *in vain. In vain!* There is where the bitterness lies!"

Genteel southerners now found themselves forced to rebuild lives and families without the help of slaves. Women accustomed to relying on slaves for their every need were unprepared for the tasks at hand. Those who still had some money after the war often recruited former slaves to work as domestic servants. Now, however, they had to pay for the services. "It seems humiliating to be compelled to bargain and haggle with our servants about wages," wrote one exasperated woman.

BITTER IN DEFEAT   After the Civil War many former Confederates were so embittered by defeat and so resistant to the idea of living under northern rule that they abandoned their native region rather than submit to "Yankee rule." Some migrated to Canada, Europe, Mexico, South America, and Asia. Others preferred the western territories and states. Still others moved north, settling in northern and midwestern cities on the assumption that their educational and economic opportunities would be better among the victors.

Most of those who chose to remain in the South returned to find their farms and homes and communities transformed. One Confederate army captain reported that on his father's plantation "Our negroes are living in great comfort. They were delighted to see me with overflowing affection. They waited on me as before, gave me breakfast, splendid dinners, etc. But they firmly and respectfully informed me: 'We own this land now. Put it out of your head that it will ever be yours again.'"

As Union troops fanned out across the defeated South, it was readily apparent that many former Confederates resented and resisted their presence. People cursed and spat upon the troops as they marched into town. Acts of sabotage kept the federal forces on the alert. Fervent southern nationalists, both men and women, planted in their children a similar hatred of Yankees and a defiance of northern rule. One mother said that she trained her children to "fear God, love the South, and live to avenge her."

LINCOLN'S PLAN AND CONGRESS'S RESPONSE The problem of reconstruction arose early in the Civil War, as Union forces advanced into the South and were forced to create new local governments. Lincoln in 1862 named military governors for Tennessee, Arkansas, and Louisiana, and by the end of the following year he had formulated a plan for regular civilian governments in those states and any others that might be liberated from the Confederacy.

Acting under his pardon power, President Lincoln issued in 1863 a Proclamation of Amnesty and Reconstruction, under which any Rebel state could form a Union government whenever a number equal to 10 percent of those who had voted in 1860 took an oath of allegiance to the Constitution and Union and received a presidential pardon. Participants also had to swear support for laws and proclamations dealing with emancipation. Excluded from the pardon, however, were certain groups: civil, diplomatic, and high military officers of the Confederacy; judges, congressmen, and military officers of the United States who had left their posts to aid the rebellion; and those accused of failure to treat captured black soldiers and their officers as prisoners of war.

Under this plan loyal governments appeared in Tennessee, Arkansas, and Louisiana, but Congress refused to recognize them. In the absence of any specific provisions for reconstruction in the Constitution, politicians disagreed as to where authority properly rested. Lincoln claimed the right to direct reconstruction under the presidential pardon power, and also under the Constitutional obligation to guarantee each state a republican form of government.

A few conservative and most moderate Republicans supported Lincoln's program of immediate restoration. A small but influential group known as Radical Republicans, however, desired to see a sweeping transformation of southern society that would include making the freedmen full-fledged citizens. The Radicals hoped to reconstruct southern society so as to mirror the North's emphasis on small-scale competitive capitalism. This meant thwarting the efforts of the old planter class to reestablish a caste system and keep the freed blacks in a state of peonage.

The Radicals were talented, earnest men who maintained that Congress, not the president, should supervise the reconstruction program. To this end they helped pass in 1864 the Wade-Davis Bill, sponsored by Senator Benjamin Wade of Ohio and Representative Winter Davis of Maryland. In contrast to Lincoln's 10 percent plan, the Wade-Davis Bill required that a majority of white male citizens declare their allegiance and that only those who swore an "ironclad" oath that they had always remained loyal to the Union could vote or serve in the state constitutional conventions. The conventions, moreover, would have to abolish slavery, deny political rights to high-ranking civil and military officers of the Confederacy, and repudiate Confederate war debts. Passed during the closing days of the 1864 session, the bill went unsigned by Lincoln, and this "pocket veto" provoked the bill's sponsors to issue the Wade-Davis Manifesto, a blistering statement that accused the president of usurping power and attempting to use readmitted states to ensure his reelection.

By early 1865 Lincoln and the Radical Republicans were embroiled in an increasingly heated debate about the direction of reconstruction policy. A few Radicals argued that what the freed blacks needed most was land. But the several proposals for land confiscation and distribution never materialized. Even most dedicated abolitionists shrank from the measures of land reform that might have given the freed slaves more self-support and independence. Citizenship and legal rights were one thing, wholesale confiscation quite another. Instead of land or material help the freedmen more often received age-old advice: work hard and lead sober, honest, and frugal lives. Frederick Douglass, the black abolitionist, suggested that after the war the former slave was left "free from the individual master but a slave of society. He had neither money, property, nor friends. He was free from the old plantation, but he had nothing but the dusty road under his feet. . . . He was turned loose, naked, hungry, and destitute to the open sky." According to a former Confederate general, recently freed blacks had "nothing but freedom."

In March 1865 Congress did establish within the War Department the Bureau of Refugees, Freedmen, and Abandoned Lands, to provide "such issues of provisions, clothing, and fuel" as might be needed to relieve "destitute and suffering refugees and freedmen and their wives and children." The Freedmen's Bureau would also take over abandoned and confiscated land for rental in forty-acre tracts to "loyal refugees and freedmen," who might buy the land at a fair price within three years. But such lands were limited, and by the end of 1865 all confiscated lands were returned to the original owners. Bureau agents were also entrusted with negotiating labor contracts (something new for both freed slaves and planters), providing medical care, and setting up schools. White intransigence and the failure of the bureau to grasp the intensity of white racial prejudice increasingly thwarted the efforts of the Freedmen's Bureau to protect and assist the former slaves.

And Congress was not willing to strengthen the powers of the bureau to deal with such problems. Beyond such temporary measures of relief, no program of reconstruction ever incorporated much more than basic constitutional and legal rights for freedmen. These were important in themselves, of course, but their scope was uncertain, to be settled more by the course of events than by any clear-cut commitment to equality.

Lincoln issued his final statement on reconstruction in his last public address, on April 11, 1865. Speaking from the White House balcony, he dismissed the theoretical question of whether the Confederate states had technically remained in the Union as "good for nothing at all—a mere pernicious abstraction." These states were simply "out of their proper practical relation with the Union," and the object was to get them "into their proper practical relation" as quickly as possible. At a cabinet meeting Lincoln proposed to get state governments in operation before Congress met in December. He worried that Congress might push through a harsher reconstruction program. Lincoln wanted "no persecution, no bloody work," no dramatic restructuring of southern social and economic life.

That evening Lincoln went to Ford's Theater and his rendezvous with death. Shot in the head by John Wilkes Booth, a crazed actor and Confederate zealot, the president died the next morning. Pursued into Virginia, Booth was trapped and shot in a burning barn. His last words were: "Tell mother I die for my country. I thought I did for the best." Three collaborators were tried and hanged, along with Mrs. Mary Surratt, at whose boardinghouse they had plotted. Three others received life sentences, including a Maryland doctor who set the leg Booth had broken when he jumped from Lincoln's box onto the stage. The doctor achieved lasting fame by making common a once obscure expression. His name was Mudd.

JOHNSON'S PLAN   Lincoln's death suddenly elevated to the White House Andrew Johnson of Tennessee, a man whose state remained in legal limbo and whose party affiliation was unclear. He was a War Democrat who had been put on the Union ticket in 1864 as a gesture of unity. Of humble origins like Lincoln, Johnson had moved as a youth from his birthplace in Raleigh, North Carolina, to Greenville, Tennessee, where he became proprietor of a tailor shop. Self-educated with the help of his wife, he had made himself into an effective, salty orator, and he won election as mayor, congressman, governor, and senator, then as military governor of Tennessee before he became vice-president. In the process Johnson had become an advocate of the small farmers against the large planters. He also shared the racial attitudes of most white yeomen. "Damn the negroes," he exclaimed to a friend during the war, "I am fighting those traitorous aristocrats, their masters."

Some of the Radicals at first thought Johnson, unlike Lincoln, to be one of them. Johnson had, for example, asserted that treason "must be made infamous and traitors must be impoverished." Ben Wade loved such harsh talk. "Johnson, we have faith in you," he pledged. "By the gods, there will be no trouble now in running this government." But Wade would soon find him as untrustworthy as Lincoln, if for different reasons. Johnson's very loyalty to the Union sprang from a strict adherence to the Constitution. Given to dogmatic abstractions that were alien to Lincoln's temperament, he nevertheless arrived by a different route at similar objectives. The states should be brought back into their proper relation to the Union, not by ignoring as a pernicious abstraction the theoretical question of their status, but because the states and the

Union were indestructible. By May 1865 he was arguing that "there is no such thing as reconstruction. Those states have not gone out of the Union. Therefore reconstruction is unnecessary."

Johnson's plan to restore the Union thus closely resembled Lincoln's. A new Proclamation of Amnesty (May 29, 1865) added to the list of those Lincoln had excluded from pardon everybody with taxable property worth more than $20,000. These wealthy planters and merchants were the people Johnson believed had led the South into secession. But those in the excluded groups might make special applications for presidential pardon, and before the year was out Johnson had issued some 13,000 such pardons.

In each of the Rebel states not already organized by Lincoln, Johnson named a native Unionist provisional governor with authority to call a convention elected by loyal voters. Lincoln's 10 percent requirement was omitted. Johnson called upon the conventions to invalidate the secession ordinances, abolish slavery, and repudiate all debts incurred to aid the Confederacy. Each state, moreover, was to ratify the Thirteenth Amendment, which ended slavery. Like Lincoln, Johnson endorsed a limited black suffrage. He reminded the provisional governor of Mississippi, for example, that the state conventions might "with perfect safety" extend suffrage to those blacks with education or with military service so as to "disarm the adversary"—the adversary being "radicals who are wild upon Negro franchise."

The state conventions for the most part met Johnson's requirements. But a northern visitor found in the South "an utter absence of national feeling . . . and a desire to preserve slavery . . . as much and as long as possible." Southern whites accepted the situation because they thought so little had changed after all. Emboldened by Johnson's indulgence, they ignored his advice to move cautiously in restoring their political and social traditions. Suggestions of black suffrage were scarcely raised in the conventions, and promptly squelched when they were.

SOUTHERN INTRANSIGENCE When Congress met in December 1865, for the first time since the end of the war, it had only to recognize the new state governments functioning in the South. But there was the rub: the "new" governments were remarkably like the old. Among the new members presenting themselves to Congress were Georgia's Alexander H. Stephens, late vice-president of the Confederacy, four

Confederate generals, eight colonels, six cabinet members, and a host of lesser Rebels. The Congress forthwith denied seats to all members from the eleven former Confederate states. It was too much to expect, after four bloody years, that Unionists would welcome ex-Confederates back like prodigal sons.

Furthermore, the new southern legislatures, in passing repressive Black Codes regulating the freedom of blacks, baldly revealed that they intended to preserve the trappings of slavery as nearly as possible. As one southerner stressed, the "ex-slave was not a free man; he was a free Negro," and the Black Codes were intended to highlight the distinction. They extended to blacks certain new rights, but also insisted that the freed slaves be set aside as a separate caste subject to special restraints.

The details of the Black Codes varied from state to state, but some provisions were common. Existing black marriages, including common-law marriages, were recognized, and testimony of blacks was accepted in legal cases involving them—in six states in all cases. Blacks could hold property. They could sue and be sued in the courts. On the other hand, blacks in Mississippi could not own farm lands, and in South Carolina they could not own city lots. Blacks were required to enter into annual labor contracts, with provision for punishment in case of

According to a former Confederate general, recently freed blacks had "nothing but freedom."

violation. Dependent children were subject to compulsory apprenticeship and corporal punishment by masters. Vagrant blacks were punished with severe fines and could be sold into private service if unable to pay. To many people it indeed seemed that slavery was on the way back in another guise.

THE RADICALS   Faced with such evidence of southern intransigence, moderate Republicans drifted more and more toward the Radical camp. Having excluded southern members, the new Congress set up a Joint Committee on Reconstruction, with nine members from the House and six from the Senate, to gather evidence and submit proposals. As a parade of witnesses testified to the Rebels' impenitence, initiative on the committee fell to determined Radicals: Benjamin Wade of Ohio, George W. Julian of Indiana, Henry Wilson of Massachusetts—and most conspicuously of all, Thaddeus Stevens of Pennsylvania and Charles Sumner of Massachusetts. Stevens, a crusty old bachelor with a chiseled face, thin, stern lips, and brooding eyes, was the domineering floor leader in the House. Driven by a genuine, if at times fanatical, idealism, he angrily insisted that the "whole fabric of southern society *must* be changed."

Sumner, Stevens's counterpart in the Senate, agreed. Now recovered from "Bully" Brooks's 1856 assault, Sumner strove to see the South *reconstructed* rather than simply restored. This put him at odds with Johnson. After visiting the White House, Sumner found the president "harsh, petulant, and unreasonable." He was especially disheartened by Johnson's "prejudice, ignorance, and perversity" regarding the treatment of blacks. Sumner and other Radicals now grew determined to take matters into their own hands. He argued that "Massachusetts could govern Georgia better than Georgia could govern herself." The southern plantations, seedbeds of aristocratic pretension and secession, he later added, "must be broken up, and the freedmen must have the pieces."

Most of these Radical Republicans had long been connected with the antislavery cause, and they approached the question of black rights with a sincere humanitarian impulse. Few, however, could escape the bitterness bred by the long and bloody war or remain unaware of the partisan advantage that would come to the Republican party from "Negro suffrage." But they reasoned that their party, after all, could best guarantee the fruits of victory and that granting suffrage could best guarantee black rights. Stevens reflected the mixed motives of the Radicals when he proclaimed: "I am for negro suffrage in every rebel state. If it be just, it should not be denied; if it be necessary, it should be adopted; if it be a punishment to traitors, they deserve it."

The growing conflict of opinion over reconstruction policy brought about an inversion in constitutional reasoning. Secessionists—and Johnson—were now arguing that their states had in fact remained in the Union, and some Radicals were contriving arguments that they had left the Union after all. Stevens argued that the Confederate states had indeed seceded and were now conquered provinces, subject to the absolute will of the victors. Sumner maintained that the southern states, by their acts of secession, had in effect committed suicide and reverted to the status of unorganized territories subject to the will of Congress. But most congressmen embraced the "forfeited rights theory," which held that the states continued to exist, but by the acts of secession and war had forfeited "all civil and political rights under the Constitution." And Congress was the proper authority to determine conditions under which such rights might be restored.

JOHNSON'S BATTLE WITH CONGRESS   A long year of political battling remained, however, before this idea triumphed. By the end of 1865, Radical views had gained only a slight majority in Congress, insufficient to override presidential vetoes. But the critical year 1866 saw the gradual waning of Johnson's power and influence, much of this self-induced. Johnson first challenged Congress in February, when he vetoed a bill to extend the life of the Freedmen's Bureau. For the moment Johnson's prestige remained sufficiently intact that the Senate upheld his veto.

Three days after the veto, however, Johnson undermined his already weakening prestige by launching an intemperate assault on Radical leaders during an impromptu speech on Washington's Birthday. From that point forward, moderate Republicans backed away from the president, and Radical Republicans went on the offensive. Johnson was now "an alien enemy of a foreign state," Stevens declared.

In mid-March 1866, Congress passed the Civil Rights Act. A direct response to the Black Codes, this bill declared that "all persons born in the United States . . . excluding Indians not taxed," were citizens entitled to "full and equal benefit of all laws." The grant of citizenship to native-born blacks, Johnson claimed, went beyond anything formerly held to be within the scope of federal power. It would, moreover, "foment discord among the races." He vetoed the measure, but this time, in April 1866, Congress overrode the presidential veto. Then in July it enacted a revised Freedmen's Bureau Bill, again overturning a veto. From that point on Johnson's support steadily eroded.

THE FOURTEENTH AMENDMENT   To remove all doubt about the validity of the new Civil Rights Act, the Joint Committee recommended a new constitutional amendment, which passed Congress in 1866 and was ratified in 1868. The Fourteenth Amendment, however, went far beyond the Civil Rights Act, and it would have significant and unforeseen effects long thereafter. The first section asserted four principles: it reaffirmed state and federal citizenship for all persons—regardless of race—born or naturalized in the United States, and it forbade any state (the word "state" was important in later litigation) to abridge the "privileges and immunities" of citizens; to deprive any person (again an important term) of life, liberty, or property without "due process of law"; or to deny any person "the equal protection of the laws." The amendment also voided all Confederate debts.

The last three of these clauses have been the subject of long and involved lawsuits resulting in applications not foreseen at the time. The "due-process clause" has come to mean that state as well as federal power is subject to the Bill of Rights, and it has been used to protect corporations, as legal "persons," from "unreasonable" regulation by the states. Other provisions of the amendment had less far-reaching effects. One section specified that the debt of the United States "shall not be questioned," but declared "illegal and void" all debts contracted in aid of the rebellion. Another section specified the power of Congress to pass laws enforcing the amendment.

Johnson's home state was among the first to ratify the Fourteenth Amendment. In Tennessee, which had harbored probably more Unionists than any other Confederate state, the government had fallen under Radical control. But the rest of the South steadfastly resisted the Radical challenge to Johnson's program. In 1866 bloody race riots in Memphis and New Orleans added fuel to the flames. Both incidents sparked indiscriminate massacres of blacks by local police and white mobs. The rioting, Radicals argued, was the natural fruit of Johnson's policy.

RECONSTRUCTING THE SOUTH

THE TRIUMPH OF CONGRESSIONAL RECONSTRUCTION As 1866 drew to an end, the upcoming congressional elections promised to be a referendum on the growing split between Johnson and the Radicals. Johnson embarked on a speaking tour of the Midwest, a "swing around the circle," which provoked undignified shouting contests between the president and his audiences. Subjected to attacks on his integrity, Johnson responded in kind. In Cleveland he described the Radicals as "factious, domineering, tyrannical" men. Once, while Johnson was speaking from an observation car, the engineer mistakenly pulled the train out of the station, making the president appear quite the fool. Such incidents tended to confirm his image as a "ludicrous boor," which Radical papers eagerly projected. When the election returns came in, the Republicans had well over a two-thirds majority in each house, a comfortable margin with which to override any presidential vetoes.

The Congress actually enacted a new program even before new members took office. On March 2, 1867, two days before the old Congress expired, it passed three basic laws of congressional reconstruction over Johnson's vetoes: the Military Reconstruction Act, the Command of the Army Act, and the Tenure of Office Act.

This cartoon appeared at the time of the 1866 congressional elections. It shows "King Andy I" approving the execution of Radical leaders in Congress.

The first of the three acts prescribed conditions under which new southern state governments should be formed. The other two sought to block obstruction by the president. The Army Act required that all orders from the president, as commander-in-chief, go through the headquarters of the general of the army, then Ulysses S. Grant. The Radicals trusted Grant, who was already leaning their way. The Tenure of Office Act required the consent of the Senate for the president to remove any officeholder whose appointment the Senate had to confirm in the first place. In large measure it was intended to retain Secretary of War Edwin M. Stanton, the one Radical sympathizer in Johnson's cabinet. The Military Reconstruction Act, often hailed or denounced as the triumphant victory of "Radical" Reconstruction, actually fell short of a thoroughgoing transformation. Diluted by moderate Republicans, the Military Reconstruction Act boiled down to little more than a requirement that southern states accept black suffrage and ratify the Fourteenth Amendment.

Tennessee, which had already ratified the Fourteenth Amendment, was exempted from the application of the act. The other ten southern states were divided into five military districts, and the commanding officer of each was authorized to keep order and protect the "rights of persons and property." The Johnson governments remained intact for the time being, but new constitutions were to be framed "in conformity with the Constitution of the United States," in conventions elected by male citizens twenty-one and older "of whatever race, color, or previous condition." Each state constitution had to provide the same universal male suffrage. Then, once the constitution was ratified by a majority of voters and accepted by Congress, and once the state legislature had ratified the Fourteenth Amendment, and once the amendment became part of the Constitution, any given state would be entitled to representation in Congress. Persons excluded from officeholding by the proposed amendment were also excluded from participation in the process. Before the end of 1867 new elections had been held in all the states but Texas.

Having clipped the president's wings, the Republican Congress moved a year later to safeguard its program from possible interference by the Supreme Court. On March 27, 1868, Congress simply removed the power of the Supreme Court to review cases arising under the Military Reconstruction Act, which Congress clearly had the constitutional right to do under its power to define the Court's appellate jurisdiction. The Court accepted this curtailment of its authority on the same day it affirmed the notion of an "indestructible Union" in *Texas v. White* (1868). In that case it also acknowledged the right of Congress to reframe state governments, thus endorsing the Radical point of view.

THE IMPEACHMENT AND TRIAL OF JOHNSON (1868) Congress's move to restrain the Supreme Court preceded by just two days the trial of the president in the Senate on an impeachment brought in by the House. Johnson, though hostile to the congressional program, had gone through the motions required of him. He continued, however, to pardon former Confederates in wholesale lots and transferred several of the district military commanders who had displayed Radical sympathies. Nevertheless a lengthy investigation by the House Judiciary Committee, extending through most of the year 1867, failed to convince the House that grounds for impeachment existed.

Johnson himself provided the occasion for impeachment when he deliberately violated the Tenure of Office Act in order to test its constitutionality. Secretary of War Stanton had become a thorn in the president's side, refusing to resign despite his disagreements with Johnson's reconstruction policy. On August 12, 1867, during a congressional recess, Johnson suspended Stanton and named General Grant in his place. When the Senate refused to confirm Johnson's action, however, Grant returned the office to Stanton. On February 24, 1868, the House voted impeachment.

Of the eleven articles of impeachment, eight focused on the charge that Johnson had unlawfully removed Stanton and had failed to give the Senate the name of a successor. Article 9 accused the president of issuing orders in violation of the Army Act. The last two articles in effect charged him with criticizing Congress by "inflammatory and scandalous harangues." Article 11 also accused Johnson of "unlawfully devising and contriving" to violate the Reconstruction Acts, contrary to his obligation to execute the laws. At the very least, it stated, Johnson had tried to obstruct Congress's will while observing the letter of the law.

The Senate trial opened on March 5, 1868, and continued until May 26, with Chief Justice Salmon P. Chase presiding. On May 16 enough Republican senators joined their pro-Johnson colleagues to prevent conviction by the narrowest of margins—one vote. These Republicans had broken ranks with their party largely because they feared the consequences of removing a president essentially for political rather than criminal reasons, and they opposed the economic and social agenda of the Radicals. Impeachment of Johnson was in the end a great political mistake, for the failure to remove the president damaged Radical morale and support. Nevertheless, the Radical cause did gain something. To blunt the opposition, Johnson agreed not to obstruct the process of Reconstruction, and thereafter Radical Reconstruction began in earnest.

REPUBLICAN RULE IN THE SOUTH   In June 1868 Congress agreed that seven states had met the conditions for readmission, all but Virginia, Mississippi, and Texas. Congress rescinded Georgia's admission, however, when the state legislature expelled twenty-eight black members and seated some former Confederate leaders. The military commander of Georgia then forced the legislature to reseat the black members and remove the Confederates, and the state was compelled to ratify the Fifteenth Amendment before being admitted in July 1870. Mississippi, Texas, and Virginia had returned earlier in 1870, under the added requirement that they too ratify the Fifteenth Amendment. This amendment, ratified in 1870, forbade the states to deny any citizen the vote on grounds of race, color, or previous condition of servitude.

Long before the new governments were established, partisan Republican groups began to spring up in the South, promoted by the Union League, an organization founded in 1862 to rally support for the Union. League representatives enrolled blacks and loyal whites as members, initiated them into the secrets and rituals of the order, and instructed them "in their rights and duties." These Union Leagues became a powerful source of Republican political strength in the South and as a result drew the ire of unreconstructed whites.

BLACKS IN THE RECONSTRUCTED SOUTH

To focus solely on what white Republicans did to reconstruct the defeated South creates the false impression that the freed slaves were simply pawns in the hands of others. Such a stereotype appeared early. "The Negroes are to be pitied," wrote South Carolinian Julius J. Fleming, a white teacher, minister, and public official. "They do not understand the liberty which has been conferred upon them."

In fact, however, southern blacks were active agents in affecting the course of Reconstruction. Although many of them found themselves liberated but destitute after the fighting ended, the mere promise of freedom raised their hopes about achieving a biracial democracy, equal justice, and economic opportunity. "Most anyone ought to know that a man is better off free than as a slave, even if he did not have anything," said the Reverend E. P. Holmes, a black Georgia preacher and former domestic servant. "I would rather be free and have my liberty."

Participation in the Union army or navy gave many freedmen a training ground in leadership. Black military veterans would form the core of the first generation of African-American political leaders in the postwar South. Military service provided many former slaves the first opportunities to learn to read and write. "A large portion of the regiment have been going to school during the winter months," wrote a black sergeant from Virginia in 1865. Army life also alerted them to alternative social choices and to new opportunities for advancement and respectability. "No negro who has ever been a soldier," reported a northern official after visiting a black unit, "can again be imposed upon; they have learnt what it is to be free and they will infuse their feelings into others." Fighting for the Union cause also instilled a fervent sense of nationalism. "We are Americans," announced a gathering of Virginia blacks, "we know no other country, we love the land of our birth." Another Virginia freedman explained that the United States was "now *our* country—made emphatically so by the blood of our brethren."

The pent-up desire among former slaves for freedom from white control led them to establish independent black churches after the war, churches that would serve as the foundation of African-American community life. In war-ravaged Charleston, South Carolina, the first new building to appear after the war was a black church on Calhoun Street; by 1866 ten more had been built. Blacks preferred Baptist churches over other denominations, in part because of their decentralized structure that allowed each congregation to worship in its own way. By 1890 there were over 1.3 million black Baptists in the South, nearly three times as many as any other black denomination. For many former slaves, churches were the first institutions they owned and controlled. In addition to forming viable new congregations, freed blacks organized thousands of fraternal, benevolent, and mutual-aid societies, clubs, lodges, and associations. Memphis, for example, had over two hundred such organizations; Richmond boasted twice that number.

The freed slaves, both women and men, also hastened to reestablish and reaffirm families. Marriages that had been prohibited were now legitimized through the assistance of the Freedmen's Bureau. By 1870 a preponderant majority of former slaves lived in two-parent households. One white editor in Georgia, lamenting the difficulty of finding black women to serve as house servants, reported that "every negro woman wants to set up house keeping" for herself and her family. To do so they often chose to be sharecropping farmers. With little money or technical training, freed slaves faced the prospect of becoming wage laborers. Yet in order to retain as much autonomy over their productive energies and those of their children on both a daily and seasonal basis, many husbands and wives chose sharecropping. This enabled mothers and wives to devote more of their time to domestic needs while still contributing to family income.

Black communities in the postwar South also quickly sought to establish schools. The antebellum planter elite had denied education to blacks because they feared that literate slaves would organize uprisings. After the war the white elite feared education programs would encourage both poor whites and blacks to leave the South in search of better social and economic opportunities. Economic leaders wanted to protect the competitive advantage afforded by the region's low-wage labor market.

The general resistance among the former slaveholding class to new education initiatives forced the freed slaves to rely on northern assistance or to take their own initiative. A Mississippi Freedmen's Bureau agent noted in 1865 that when he told a gathering of some 3,000 former slaves that they "were to have the advantages of schools and education, their joy knew no bounds. They fairly jumped and shouted in gladness." Black churches and individuals helped raise the money and often built the schools and paid the teachers. Soldiers who had acquired some reading and writing skills often served as the first teachers, and the students included adults. A Florida teacher reported that a sixty-year-old former slave woman in her class was so excited by literacy that she "spells her lesson all the evening, then she dreams about it, and wakes up thinking about it."

BLACKS IN SOUTHERN POLITICS   The new role of blacks in politics caused the most controversy, then and afterward. If largely illiterate and inexperienced in the rudiments of politics, they were little different from millions of whites enfranchised in the age of Jackson or immigrants herded to the polls by political bosses in New York and other cities after the war. Some freedmen frankly confessed their disadvantages. Beverly Nash, a black delegate in the South Carolina convention of 1868, told his colleagues: "I believe, my friends and fellow-citizens, we are not prepared for this suffrage. But we can learn. Give a man tools and let him commence to use them, and in time he will learn a trade. So it is with voting."

Several hundred black delegates participated in the statewide political conventions. Most had been selected by local political meetings or by churches, fraternal societies, Union Leagues, and black army units, although a few simply appointed themselves. "Some bring credentials," explained a North Carolina black leader, "others had as much as they could to bring themselves, having to escape from their homes stealthily at night" to avoid white assaults. The black delegates "ranged all colors and apparently all conditions," but free mulattoes from the cities played the most prominent roles. At Louisiana's Republican state convention, for instance, nineteen of the twenty black delegates had been born free.

By 1867, however, former slaves began to gain political influence, and this led to debates that revealed emerging tensions within the black community. Some southern blacks resented the presence of northern brethren, while others complained that few ex-slaves were represented in leadership positions. Northern blacks and the southern free black elite, most of whom were urban dwellers, tended to oppose efforts to confiscate and redistribute land to the rural freedmen, and many insisted that political equality did not mean social equality. As an Alabama black leader stressed, "We do not ask that the ignorant and degraded shall be put on a social equality with the refined and intelligent." In general, however, unity rather than dissension prevailed, and blacks focused on common concerns such as full equality under the law.

Brought suddenly into politics in times that tried the most skilled of statesmen, many blacks nevertheless served with distinction. Yet the derisive label "black Reconstruction" used by later critics exaggerates black political influence, which was limited mainly to voting, and overlooks the large numbers of white Republicans, especially in the moun-

A lithograph depicting five of the major black political figures of the Reconstruction period: Hiram Revels (top left) and Blanche K. Bruce (center) served in the U.S. Senate, Joseph H. Rainey (bottom left), John R. Lynch (bottom right), and James T. Rapier (top right) in the House of Representatives.

tain areas of the upper South. Only one of the new conventions, South Carolina's, had a black majority, 76 to 41. Louisiana's was evenly divided racially, and in only two other conventions were more than 20 percent of the members black: Florida's, with 40 percent, and Virginia's, with 24 percent. The Texas convention was only 10 percent black, and North Carolina's 11 percent—but that did not stop a white newspaper from calling it a body consisting of "baboons, monkeys, mules . . . and other jackasses."

In the new state governments, any black participation was a novelty. Although some 600 blacks—most of them former slaves—served as state legislators, no black man was ever elected governor and few served as judges, although in Louisiana, Pinckney B. S. Pinchback, a northern black and former Union soldier, won the office of lieutenant-governor and served as acting governor when the white governor was indicted for corruption. Several blacks were elected lieutenant-governors, state treasurers, or secretaries of state. There were two black senators in Congress, Hiram Revels and Blanche K. Bruce, both from Mississippi, and fourteen black members of the House during Reconstruction. Among these were some of the ablest congressmen of the time.

REPUBLICANS IN THE SOUTH   The top positions in southern state governments went for the most part to white Republicans, whom the opposition soon labeled "carpetbaggers" and "scalawags," depending on their place of birth. Northern opportunists who allegedly came south with all their belongings in carpetbags to reap political spoils were more often than not Union veterans who had arrived as early as 1865 or 1866, drawn south by the hope of economic opportunity. Others were lawyers, businessmen, editors, teachers, social workers, or preachers who came on missionary endeavors.

The "scalawags," or southern white Republicans, were even more reviled and misrepresented. A Nashville editor called them the "merest trash that could be collected in a civilized community, of no personal credit or social responsibility." Most "scalawags" had opposed secession, forming a Unionist majority in many mountain counties as far south as Georgia and Alabama, and especially in the hills of eastern Tennessee. Though many were indeed crass opportunists who indulged in corruption at the public's expense, several were quite distinguished figures. They included former Confederate general James A. Longstreet, who decided after Appomattox that the Old South must change its ways. To that end, he became a successful cotton broker in New Orleans, joined the Republican party, and supported the Radical reconstruction program. Others were former Whigs who found the Republican party's expansive industrial and commercial program in keeping with Henry Clay's earlier American System.

THE REPUBLICAN RECORD   The new state constitutions were objectionable to adherents of the old order more because of their origin than because of their content, excepting their provisions for black suffrage and civil rights. Otherwise the documents were in keeping with other state constitutions of the day, their provisions often drawn from the basic laws of northern states. Most remained in effect for some years after the end of Radical control, and later constitutions incorporated many of their features. Conspicuous among Radical innovations were such steps toward greater democracy as requiring universal manhood suffrage, reapportioning legislatures more nearly according to population, and making more state offices elective.

Given the hostile circumstances in which the Radical governments arose and operated, they made a surprisingly good record. In most of the South they established the first state school systems, however inadequate and ill supported at first. Some 600,000 black pupils were in schools by 1877. State governments under the Radicals also gave more attention than ever before to poor relief and to public institutions for the disadvantaged and handicapped, such as orphanages, asylums, institutions for the deaf, dumb, and blind of both races. Public roads, bridges, and buildings were repaired or rebuilt. Blacks achieved new rights and opportunities that would never again be taken away, at least in principle: equality before the law, and the right to own property, carry on business, enter professions, attend schools, and learn to read and write.

Yet several of these Republican regimes also practiced systematic corruption. In Louisiana, the carpetbag governor acknowledged the situation: "Why," he said, "down here everybody is demoralized. Corruption is the fashion." Public money and public credit were often voted to privately owned corporations, notably railroads, under conditions that invited influence peddling. Contracts were let at absurd prices, and public officials took their cut. Taxes and public debt rose in every state. Still, the figures of taxation and debt hardly constitute an unqualified indictment of Radical governments, since they then faced unusual and inflated costs for the physical reconstruction of public works in the South. Corruption was not invented by the Radical regimes, nor did it die with them. In Mississippi, the Republican governments of Reconstruction were quite honest compared to their Democratic successors.

WHITE TERROR   The case of Mississippi suggests that whites were hostile to Republican regimes less because of their corruption than their inclusion of blacks. Most white southerners remained unreconstructed, so conditioned by slavery that they were unable to conceive of blacks as citizens or even free agents. White women in the postwar South were as violently opposed as men to northern rule. "I have always been down on Reconstruction," declared Ella Cooper, "and never should one Southern man accept it with my consent. I opposed it to the last. They can force it on us, but I say 'never accept it.'" In some places hostility to the new regimes took the form of white terror. Efforts to oust Republican rule focused largely on violence. Said one unreconstructed Mississippian, "Carry the election peaceably if we can, forcibly if we must."

This Thomas Nast cartoon chides the Ku Klux Klan and the White League for promoting conditions "worse than slavery" for southern blacks after the Civil War.

The prototype of terrorist groups was the Ku Klux Klan, first organized in 1866 by some young men of Pulaski, Tennessee, as a social club with the costumes, secret ritual, and mumbo-jumbo common to fraternal groups. At first a group of pranksters, they soon began to intimidate blacks and white Republicans, and the KKK spread rapidly across the South in answer to the Union League. Klansmen rode about the countryside hiding under masks and robes, spreading horrendous rumors, harassing assertive blacks, and occasionally running amok, wreaking violence and destruction.

In Mississippi Klansmen mutilated a black Republican leader in front of his family. Three white "scalawag" Republicans were murdered in Georgia in 1870. That same year, an armed mob of whites assaulted a Republican political rally in Alabama, killing four blacks and wounding fifty-four. In South Carolina the Klan was especially active. Virtually the entire white male population of York County joined the Klan, and they were responsible for eleven murders and hundreds of whippings. In 1871 some 500 masked men laid siege to the Union County jail and eventually lynched eight black prisoners. Although most Klansmen were poor farmers and tradesmen, middle-class whites—planters, merchants, bankers, lawyers, doctors, even ministers—also joined the group and participated in its brutalities.

Congress struck back with three Enforcement Acts (1870–1871) to protect black voters. The first of these measures levied penalties on persons who interfered with any citizen's right to vote. A second placed the election of congressmen under surveillance by federal election supervisors and marshals. The third (the Ku Klux Klan Act) outlawed the characteristic activities of the Klan—forming conspiracies, wearing disguises, resisting officers, and intimidating officials. President Grant, in 1871, singled out nine counties in upcountry South Carolina as an example, and pursued mass prosecutions that brought an abrupt halt to Klan terrorism. The program of federal enforcement broke the back of the Klan, whose activities declined steadily as recalcitrant southerners resorted to more subtle methods of racial intimidation.

CONSERVATIVE RESURGENCE   The Klan in fact could not take credit for the overthrow of Republican control in any state. Perhaps its most important effect was to weaken the morale of blacks and Republicans in the South and strengthen in the North a growing weariness with the whole "southern question." Americans had other fish to fry anyway. Western expansion, Indian wars, industrial development, and political controversy over the tariff and the currency distracted attention from southern outrages. Republican control in the South gradually loosened as "Conservative" parties—Democrats used that name to mollify former Whigs—mobilized the white vote. Scalawags, and many carpetbaggers, drifted away from the Radical ranks under pressure from their white neighbors. Few of them had joined the Republicans out of concern for black rights in the first place. And where persuasion failed to work, Democrats were willing to use chicanery. As one enthusiastic Democrat boasted, "the white and black Republicans may outvote us, but we can outcount them."

Such factors led to the collapse of Republican control in Virginia and Tennessee as early as 1869, in Georgia and North Carolina in 1870. Reconstruction lasted longest in the Deep South states with the heaviest black population, where whites abandoned Klan hoods for barefaced intimidation in paramilitary groups like the Mississippi Rifle Club and the South Carolina Red Shirts. In overwhelmingly black Yazoo County, Mississippi, vengeful whites used violence to reverse the political bal-

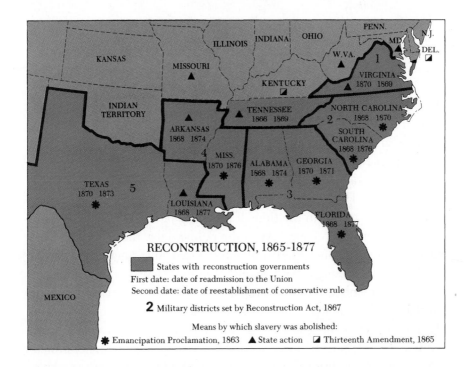

RECONSTRUCTION, 1865-1877

States with reconstruction governments
First date: date of readmission to the Union
Second date: date of reestablishment of conservative rule

2 Military districts set by Reconstruction Act, 1867

Means by which slavery was abolished:
✸ Emancipation Proclamation, 1863   ▲ State action   ◩ Thirteenth Amendment, 1865

ance of power. In the 1873 elections the Republicans cast 2,449 votes and the Democrats 638; two years later the Democrats polled 4,049 votes, the Republicans 7. By 1876 Radical regimes survived only in Louisiana, South Carolina, and Florida, and these all collapsed after the elections of that year.

THE GRANT YEARS

GRANT'S ELECTION   Ulysses S. Grant, who presided over the collapse of Republican rule in the South, brought to the presidency less political experience than any man who had ever occupied the office, except perhaps Zachary Taylor, and arguably less political judgment than any other. But in 1868 the rank-and-file voter could be expected to support "the Lion of Vicksburg" because of his brilliant record as a war leader. Both parties wooed him, but his falling-out with President Johnson pushed him toward the Republicans and built trust in him among the Radicals. They were, as Thad Stevens said, ready to "let him into the church."

When the Republicans gathered in Chicago, they named Grant their unanimous choice. The platform endorsed Radical Reconstruction, cautiously defending black suffrage as a necessity in the South but a matter each northern state should settle for itself. It also urged payment of the nation's war debt in gold rather than in the new "greenback" paper currency printed during the war. More important than the platform were the great expectations of a soldier-president and his slogan: "Let us have peace."

The Democrats took an opposite position on both Reconstruction and the debt. The Republican Congress, the platform charged, had "subjected ten states, in the time of profound peace, to military despotism and Negro supremacy." As to the public debt, the party endorsed Representative George H. Pendleton's "Ohio idea" that, since most bonds had been bought with depreciated greenbacks, they should be paid off in greenbacks unless they specified payment in gold. With no conspicuously available candidate in sight, the convention turned to Horatio Seymour, war governor of New York and chairman of the convention. The Democrats made a closer race than expected, attesting to the strength of traditional party loyalties. While Grant swept the electoral college by 214 to 80, his popular majority was only 307,000 out of a total of over 5.7 million votes. More than 500,000 black voters accounted for Grant's margin of victory.

Grant had proven himself a great leader in the war, but in the White House he seemed blind to the political forces and influence peddlers around him. Shy and withdrawn, he was uncomfortable around intellectuals and impatient with idealists. Grant preferred watching horse races to reading about complex issues. Although personally honest, he was dazzled by men of wealth and unaccountably loyal to greedy subordinates who betrayed his trust. In the formulation of policy he passively followed the lead of Congress. This approach endeared him at first to party leaders, but it left him at last ineffective and caused others to grow disillusioned with his leadership. At the outset Grant consulted nobody on his cabinet appointments. Some of his choices indulged personal whims; others simply reflected bad judgment. Secretary of State Hamilton Fish of New York turned out to be a fortunate exception; he masterfully guided foreign policy throughout the Grant presidency.

THE GOVERNMENT DEBT   Financial issues dominated the political agenda during Grant's presidency. After the war the Treasury had assumed that the $400 million worth of greenbacks issued during the conflict would be retired from circulation. Congress in 1866 granted the Treasury discretion to do so gradually. Many agrarian and debtor groups resisted this contraction, believing that a larger money supply would mean rising farm prices and easier-to-pay debts. They were joined by a large number of Radicals who thought a combination of high tariffs and inflation would generate more rapid economic growth. In 1868 "soft money" supporters in Congress halted the retirement of greenbacks, leaving $356 million outstanding. There matters stood when Grant took office.

The "sound" or "hard" money advocates, mostly bankers, merchants, and other creditors, claimed that Grant's election was a mandate to save the country from the Democrats' "Ohio idea." Quite influential in Republican circles, they also had the benefit of a deeply ingrained popular assumption that hard money was morally preferable to paper currency. Grant agreed, and in his inaugural address he endorsed payment of the national debt in gold as a point of national honor.

SCANDAL AND REFORM   Within less than a year of his election Grant fell into a cesspool of scandal. In the summer of 1869 two brilliant, if crass, young railroad entrepreneurs, the crafty Jay Gould and the flamboyant Jim Fisk, connived with the president's brother-in-law to corner the gold market. Gould concocted an argument that the government should refrain from selling gold on the market because the resulting rise in gold prices would raise temporarily depressed farm prices. Grant apparently smelled a rat from the start, but was seen in public with the speculators. As the rumor spread on Wall Street, gold rose from $132 to $163 an ounce. Finally, on "Black Friday," September 24, 1869, Grant ordered the Treasury to sell a large quantity of gold, and the bubble burst. Fisk got out by repudiating his agreements and hiring thugs to intimidate his creditors. "Nothing is lost save honor," he said.

The plot to corner the gold market was only the first of several scandals that rocked the Grant administration. In 1872 the public first learned about the financial buccaneering of the Crédit Mobilier, a construction company that had milked the Union Pacific Railroad for exorbitant fees to line the pockets of insiders who controlled both firms. Rank-and-file Union Pacific shareholders were left holding the bag. This chicanery had transpired before Grant's election in 1868, but it

The People's Handwriting on the Wall. *An 1872 engraving comments on the corruption engulfing Grant.*

now touched a number of prominent Republicans who had been given shares of Crédit Mobilier stock in exchange for favorable votes. Of thirteen Congressmen involved, only two were censured.

Even more odious disclosures soon followed, and some involved the president's cabinet. Grant's secretary of war, it turned out, had accepted bribes from merchants at army posts in the West who traded with Indians. He was impeached, but resigned in time to elude trial. Post-office contracts, it was revealed, went to carriers who offered the highest kickbacks. In St. Louis a "Whiskey Ring" bribed tax collectors to bilk the government of millions in revenue. Grant's private secretary was enmeshed in that scheme, taking large sums of money and other valuables in return for inside information. There is no evidence that Grant himself participated in any of the fraud, but his poor choice of associates earned him widespread censure.

Long before Grant's first term ended, a reaction against the Radical Reconstruction measures, and against incompetence and corruption in the administration, had incited mutiny within the Republican ranks. Open revolt broke out first in Missouri, where Carl Schurz, a German immigrant and war hero, led a group that elected a governor with Democratic help in 1870 and sent Schurz to the Senate.

In 1872 the Liberal Republicans (as they called themselves) held a clamorous national convention in Cincinnati, which produced a compromise platform condemning the party's "vindictive" southern policy and favoring civil service reform, but which remained silent on the protective tariff. The delegates stampeded toward an anomalous presidential candidate: Horace Greeley, editor of the *New York Tribune,* a strong protectionist and enthusiastic reformer. During his long journalistic career he had promoted vegetarianism, brown bread, free-thinking, socialism, and spiritualism. His image as a visionary eccentric was complemented by his open hostility to Democrats, whose support the Liberals needed. One reporter suggested that there had been "too much brains and not enough whiskey" at the convention. The Democrats nevertheless swallowed the pill and gave their nomination to Greeley as the only hope of beating Grant.

The 1872 election result surprised no one. Republican regulars duly endorsed Radical Reconstruction and the protective tariff. Grant still had seven carpetbag states in his pocket, generous support from business and banking interests, and the stalwart support of the Radicals. Above all he still evoked the glory of Vicksburg and Appomattox. Greeley, despite an exhausting tour of the country—still unusual for a presidential candidate—carried only six southern and border states and none in the North. Devastated by his crushing defeat and the simultaneous death of his wife, Greeley entered a mental sanitarium and died three weeks later.

PANIC AND REDEMPTION   A paralyzing economic panic followed close upon the public scandals besetting the Grant administration. Contraction of the money supply brought about by the Treasury's postwar withdrawal of greenbacks and the reckless overexpansion of the railroads into sparsely settled areas helped precipitate a financial crisis. During 1873 some twenty-five strapped railroads defaulted on their interest payments. Caught short, the prominent investment firm of Jay Cooke and Company went bankrupt on September 18, 1873. The ensuing stampede of selling forced the stock market to close for ten days. The Panic of 1873 set off a depression that lasted for six years, the longest and most severe that Americans had yet suffered, marked by widespread bankruptcies, chronic unemployment, and a drastic slow-down in railroad building.

Hard times and corruption hurt Republicans in the midterm elections of 1874, allowing the Democrats to win control of the House of Representatives and gain in the Senate. The new Democratic House immediately launched inquiries into the Grant scandals and unearthed further evidence of corruption in high places. The panic meanwhile focused attention once more on greenback currency. Since greenbacks were valued less than gold, they had become the chief circulating medium. Most people spent greenbacks first and held their gold or used it to settle foreign accounts, which drained much gold out of the country. To relieve this deflationary spiral and stimulate business, therefore, the Treasury reissued $26 million in greenbacks previously withdrawn.

For a time the advocates of paper money were riding high. But Grant vetoed an attempt to issue more greenbacks in 1874, and in his annual message he called for their gradual withdrawal. Congress obliged the president by passing the Resumption Act of 1875. The resumption of paying gold to customers who turned in their greenbacks began on January 1, 1879, after the Treasury had built a gold reserve for the purpose and reduced the value of greenbacks in circulation. This act infuriated those promoting an inflationary monetary policy and provoked the formation of the National Greenback party. The much debated "money question" would remain one of the most divisive issues in American politics until the end of the century.

THE COMPROMISE OF 1877   Grant yearned to run again in 1876, but the recent scandals precluded any challenge to the two-term tradition. James G. Blaine of Maine, former Speaker of the House, emerged as the Republican front-runner, but he too bore the taint of scandal. Letters in the possession of James Mulligan of Boston linked Blaine to some dubious railroad dealings. Newspapers soon published these "Mulligan Letters," and Blaine's candidacy was dealt a body blow.

The Republican convention in Cincinnati therefore eliminated Blaine and several other hopefuls in favor of Ohio's favorite son, Rutherford B. Hayes. Three times governor of Ohio and an advocate of hard money, Hayes had a sterling character and had been a civil service reformer. But his chief virtue, as Henry Adams put it, was "that he is obnoxious to no one."

The Democratic convention in St. Louis was abnormally harmonious from the start. The nomination went on the second ballot to Samuel J. Tilden, millionaire corporation lawyer and reform governor of New York, who had directed a campaign to overthrow first the corrupt Tweed Ring in New York City and then another ring in Albany that had bilked the state of millions.

The campaign generated no burning issues. Both candidates favored the trend toward restoring conservative rule in the South. During one of the most corrupt elections ever, both candidates favored civil service reform. In the absence of strong differences, Democrats waved the Republicans' dirty linen. In response, Republicans waved the bloody shirt, which is to say that they engaged in verbal assaults on former Confederates and the spirit of rebellion, linking the Democratic party with Secession and with the outrages committed against both black and white Republicans in the South. As one Republican speaker insisted, "Every man that tried to destroy this nation was a Democrat. . . . The man that assassinated Abraham Lincoln was a Democrat. . . . Soldiers, every scar you have on your heroic bodies was given you by a Democrat!"

Early election returns pointed to a Tilden victory. Tilden had 184 electoral votes, just one short of a majority, but Republicans claimed nineteen doubtful votes from Florida, Louisiana, and South Carolina, while Democrats laid a counterclaim to one of Oregon's three votes. The Republicans had clearly carried Oregon, but the outcome in the South was less certain, and given the fraud and intimidation perpetrated on both sides, nobody will ever know the truth of the matter. In all three of the disputed southern states, rival canvassing boards sent in different returns. The Constitution offered no guidance in this unprecedented situation. Even if Congress were empowered to sort things out, the Democratic House and the Republican Senate proved unable to reach an agreement.

The impasse dragged on for months, and there was even talk of public violence. Finally, on January 29, 1877, the two houses decided to set up a special Electoral Commission. It had fifteen members, five each from the House, the Senate, and the Supreme Court. The decision on each contested state went by a vote of 8 to 7, along party lines, in favor of Hayes. After much debate and threat of filibuster by Democrats, the

House voted on March 2 to accept the report and declare the Republican Hayes the victor by an electoral vote of 185 to 184.

Critical to this outcome was the defection of southern Democrats who had made several informal agreements with the Republicans. On February 26, 1877, a bargain was struck between prominent Ohio Republicans and powerful southern Democrats. The Republicans promised that, if elected, Hayes would withdraw federal troops from Louisiana and South Carolina, letting the Republican governments there collapse. In return the Democrats pledged to withdraw their opposition to Hayes, to accept in good faith the Reconstruction amendments, and to refrain from partisan reprisals against Republicans in the South.

With this agreement in hand, southern Democrats could justify deserting Tilden. This so-called Compromise of 1877 brought a final "redemption" from the "Radicals" and a return to "home rule," which actually meant rule by native white Democrats. Other, more informal promises bolstered the secret agreement. Hayes's friends pledged more support for Mississippi levees and other internal improvements, including federal subsidy for a transcontinental railroad along a southern route. Southerners extracted a further promise that Hayes would name a white southerner as postmaster-general, the cabinet position with the most patronage jobs at hand. In return, southerners would let Republicans make James A. Garfield Speaker of the new House.

THE END OF RECONSTRUCTION   After Hayes took office, most of these promises were either renounced or forgotten. In 1877, Hayes withdrew federal troops from the state houses in Louisiana and South Carolina, and the Republican governments there soon collapsed— along with much of Hayes's claim to legitimacy. Hayes chose a Tennessean as postmaster-general. But after southern Democrats failed to permit the choice of Garfield as Speaker, Hayes expressed doubt about any further subsidy for railroad building, and none was voted.

As to southern promises regarding the civil rights of blacks, only a few Democratic leaders remembered them for long. Over the next three decades those rights crumbled under the pressure of white rule in the South and the force of Supreme Court decisions narrowing the application of the Fourteenth and Fifteenth Amendments. Radical Reconstruction never offered more than an uncertain commitment to racial equality before the law. Yet it left an enduring legacy, the Thirteenth,

Fourteenth, and Fifteenth Amendments—not dead but dormant, waiting to be warmed back into life. If Reconstruction did not provide social equality or substantial economic opportunities for blacks, it did create the opportunity for future transformation. It was a revolution, sighed North Carolina Governor Jonathan Worth, and "nobody can anticipate the action of revolutions."

MAKING CONNECTIONS

- The political, economic, and racial policies of the Bourbons, the conservatives who overthrew the Republican governments in the southern states, are described in Chapter 18.

- Several of the political scandals mentioned in this chapter were related to the railroads, a topic discussed in greater detail in Chapter 19.

- This chapter ends with the election of Rutherford B. Hayes; for a discussion of Hayes's administration, see Chapter 21.

FURTHER READING

Reconstruction has long been "a dark and bloody ground" of conflicting interpretations. The best synthesis is Eric Foner's *Reconstruction: America's Unfinished Revolution, 1863–1877* (1988).*

More specialized works give closer scrutiny to the aims of the principal political figures. For a study of Andrew Johnson, see Hans L. Trefousse's *Andrew Johnson: A Biography* (1989). Why Johnson was impeached is detailed in Hans L. Trefousse's *Impeachment of a President* (1975).

Scholars have been fairly sympathetic to the aims and motives of the Radical Republicans. See, for instance, Richard Nelson Current's

*These books are available in paperback editions.

Those Terrible Carpetbaggers: A Reinterpretation (1988).* The ideology of the Radicals is explored in Michael Les Benedict's *A Compromise of Principle: Congressional Republicans and Reconstruction* (1974).

The intransigence of southern white attitudes is examined in Michael Perman's *Reunion without Compromise* (1973).* Allen W. Trelease's *White Terror* (1971)* covers the various organizations that practiced vigilante tactics, chiefly the Ku Klux Klan. The difficulties former planters had in adjusting to the new labor system are documented in James L. Roark's *Masters without Slaves* (1977).*

Numerous works have appeared on the freed blacks' experience in the South. Start with Leon F. Litwack's *Been in the Storm So Long* (1979).* The situation of freed slave women, which was often quite different from that of freed slave men, is discussed in Jacqueline Jones's *Labor of Love, Labor of Sorrow: Black Women, Work and the Family from Slavery to Present* (1985) and Dorothy Sterling's *We Are Your Sisters* (1984).*

The politics of corruption outside the South is depicted in William S. McFeely's *Grant: A Biography* (1981).* The political maneuvers of the election of 1876 and the resultant crisis and compromise are explained in C. Vann Woodward's *Reunion and Reaction* (1951)* and William Gillette's *Retreat from Reconstruction, 1869–1879* (1979).*

*These books are available in paperback editions.

PART FIVE

GROWING
PAINS

The northern victory in 1865 restored the Union and in the process helped to accelerate America's transformation into a modern nation-state. A distinctly national consciousness began to displace the sectional emphases of the antebellum era. During and after the Civil War, the Republican-led Congress pushed through legislation to foster industrial and commercial development and western expansion. In the process, the United States abandoned the Jeffersonian dream of a decentralized agrarian republic and began to forge a dynamic new industrial outlook generated by an increasingly national market.

After 1865, many Americans turned their attention to the unfinished business of settling a continent and completing an urban-industrial revolution begun before the war. Huge new national corporations based upon mass production and mass marketing began to dominate the economic order. As the prominent sociologist William Graham Sumner remarked, the process of industrial development "controls us all because we are all in it. It creates the conditions of our own existence, sets the limits of our social activity, and regulates the bonds of our social relations."

The industrial revolution was not only an urban phenomenon; it transformed rural life as well. Those who got in the way of the new emphasis on large-scale, highly mechanized commercial agriculture and ranching were brusquely pushed aside. Farm folk, as one New Englander stressed, "must understand farming as a business; if they do not it will go hard with them." The friction between new market forces and traditional folkways generated political revolts and social unrest during the last quarter of the nineteenth century. Fault lines appeared throughout the social order, and they unleashed tremors that exerted what one writer called "a seismic shock, a cyclonic violence" upon the body politic.

The clash between tradition and modernity came to a climax during the decade of the 1890s, one of the most strife-ridden in American history. A deep depression, agrarian unrest, and labor violence provoked fears of a class war. This turbulent situation transformed the presidential election campaign of 1896 into a clash between two rival visions of America's future. The Republican candidate, William McKinley, campaigned on behalf of modern urban-industrial values. By contrast, William Jennings Bryan, the nominee of both the Democratic and Populist parties, was an eloquent defender of America's rural past. McKinley's victory proved to *be a watershed in American political and social history. By 1900 the United States would emerge as one of the world's greatest industrial powers, and it would thereafter assume a new leadership role in world affairs.*

18   NEW FRONTIERS:

SOUTH AND WEST

CHAPTER ORGANIZER

This chapter focuses on:

- the economic and political policies of the states in the post-Reconstruction South

- race relations in the New South

- the farmers', miners', and cowboys' frontiers

- late-nineteenth-century Indian policy

*A*fter the Civil War the West and the South provided enticing opportunities for pioneers and entrepreneurs alike. Before 1860 most Americans had viewed the region between the Mississippi River and California as a barren landscape unfit for human habitation or cultivation, an uninviting land suitable only for Indians and animals. Half of the state of Texas, for instance, was still not settled at the end of the Civil War. After 1865, however, the federal government encouraged western settlement and economic exploitation. The construction of transcontinental railroads, the military conquest of the Indians, and a liberal land distribution policy combined to help lure thousands of pioneers and expectant capitalists westward.

Although the first great wave of railroad building occurred in the 1850s, the most spectacular growth took place during the quarter century after the Civil War. From about 35,000 miles of track in 1865, the network grew to nearly 200,000 miles by 1897. The transcontinental rail lines led the way, and they helped populate the plains and the Far West. During the century after the Civil War, fourteen new states were created out of America's western territories.

Meanwhile, southern rail lines were rebuilt and supplemented with new branch lines. The defeated South, although not a frontier in the literal sense of the term, offered capitalists and entrepreneurs a fertile new ground for investment and industrial development. Proponents of a "New South" after 1865 argued that the region must abandon its single-minded preoccupation with agriculture and pursue industrial and commercial development. As a result, the South as well as the West experienced dramatic social and economic changes during the last third of the nineteenth century. By 1900 these new "frontiers" had been transformed in ways that few could have predicted.

THE NEW SOUTH

A FRESH VISION   After the Civil War many southerners looked back wistfully to the plantation life that had characterized their region before the firing on Fort Sumter. A few prominent leaders, however, insisted that the postwar South must liberate itself from such paralyzing nostalgia and create a new society of small farms, thriving industries, and bustling cities. The major prophet of this "New South" was Henry W. Grady, the thirty-six-year-old editor of the *Atlanta Constitution*. During the 1880s, Grady set forth the vision that inspired a generation of southerners: "The Old South rested everything on slavery and agriculture, unconscious that these could neither give nor maintain healthy growth. The New South presents a perfect democracy . . . a social system compact and closely knitted, less splendid on the surface, but stronger at the core—a hundred farms for every plantation, fifty homes for every palace—and a diversified industry that meets the complex need of this complex age."

It was a compelling vision, and other advocates of this New South Creed soon emerged. In the aftermath of the Civil War these men, and their Yankee patrons, preached the gospel of industry with evangelical fervor. The Confederacy, they reasoned, had lost because it relied too much on King Cotton. In the future the South must follow the North's example and industrialize. From that central belief flowed certain implications: that a more diversified and efficient agriculture would be a foundation for economic growth, that more widespread education, especially vocational training, would promote material success. By the late 1870s, with Reconstruction over and the Panic of 1873 forgotten, a mood of progress permeated the editorials and the speeches of the day.

ECONOMIC GROWTH   The first and chief accomplishment of the New South movement was an expansion of the area's textile production, which began in the 1880s and overtook its older New England competitors by the 1920s. From 1880 to 1900 the number of cotton mills in the South grew from 161 to 400, and the number of mill workers (among whom women and children outnumbered the men) increased fivefold.

Tobacco growth also increased significantly, entering a new era with the development of two new varieties of the weed: burley, which first appeared in southern Ohio, and bright leaf, which was grown on otherwise infertile soils and cured by a charcoal process discovered by a slave in 1839. Knowledge of the bright-leaf type remained chiefly local until, in what seemed a misfortune, Union soldiers swarmed over central North Carolina in 1865.

White Oak Cotton Mills, Greensboro, North Carolina. *These women are measuring, sewing, and finishing denim.*

One victim of their looting was John Ruffin Green, whose bright-leaf tobacco factory was ransacked by soldiers loitering around Durham Station. Within a few weeks orders began to pour in to Green's factory for the Best Flavored Spanish Smoking Tobacco "that did not bite." With this revival, Green adopted as his trademark a bull's head similar to that on Colman's mustard, made in Durham, England. It did not take long for Green and his successors to make the image of Bull Durham ubiquitous, so much so that years later Mark Twain, who was not above embellishing a good story, claimed that when he visited Egypt he never saw the pyramids because they were obscured by Bull Durham signs.

Even more important in the rise of tobacco and the city of Durham was the Duke family, who inhabited a nearby farm. At the end of the Civil War, the story goes, old Washington Duke had fifty cents obtained from a Yankee soldier in exchange for a souvenir Confederate five-dollar bill. He took a load of tobacco, and with the help of his three sons, beat it out with hickory sticks, stuffed it in bags, hitched up two mules to his wagon, and set out across the state, selling bright leaf as he went. By 1872 the Dukes had a factory producing 125,000 pounds of tobacco annually, and Washington Duke prepared to settle down and enjoy success.

His son Buck (James Buchanan Duke), however, had the same entrepreneurial drive that animated the Carnegies and Rockefellers of that day. Buck Duke recognized early that the tobacco industry was "half smoke and half ballyhoo," so he poured large sums into advertising schemes. Duke also undersold competitors in their own markets, and cornered the supply of ingredients. Eventually his competitors were ready to take the hint that they join forces, and in 1890 Duke brought most of them into the American Tobacco Company, which controlled nine-tenths of the nation's cigarette production. In 1911 the Supreme Court found the company in violation of the antitrust laws and ordered it broken up, but by then Duke had found new worlds to conquer in hydroelectric power and aluminum.

Systematic use of other natural resources helped revitalize the area along the Appalachian mountain chain from West Virginia to Alabama. Coal production in the South (including West Virginia) grew from 4.6 million tons in 1875 to 49.3 million tons by 1900. At the southern end of the mountains, Birmingham, Alabama, sprang up during the 1870s as a major steel producing center and soon tagged itself the "Pittsburgh of the South."

Industrial growth created a need for wood-framed housing, and after 1870 lumbering became a thriving industry in the South. By the turn of the century it had surpassed textiles in value. Tree cutting seemed to know no bounds, despite the resulting ecological devastation. In time the industry would be saved only by the warm climate, which fostered quick renewal, and the rise of scientific forestry.

Two forces that would impel an even greater industrial revolution were already on the southern horizon at the turn of the century: petroleum in the Southwest and hydroelectric power in the Southeast. In 1901 the Spindletop oil gusher in Texas brought a huge bonanza. Electrical power proved equally profitable, and local power plants dotted the South by the 1890s. Richmond, Virginia, had the nation's first electric streetcar system in 1888, and Columbia, South Carolina, boasted the first electrically powered cotton mill in 1894. The greatest advance would begin in 1905 when Buck Duke's Southern Power Company set out to electrify entire river valleys in the Carolinas.

AGRICULTURE, OLD AND NEW   At the turn of the century, however, most of the South remained undeveloped, at least by northeastern standards. Despite the optimistic rhetoric of New South spokesmen, the typical southerner was less apt to be tending a loom or forge than, as the saying went, facing the eastern end of a westbound mule. King Cotton survived the Civil War and expanded over new acreage even as its export markets leveled off. Louisiana cane sugar, probably the most war-devastated of all crops, also flourished again by the 1890s.

The majority of southern farmers were not flourishing, however. Sharecropping and tenancy grew increasingly prevalent in the aftermath of emancipation. By 1890 most southern farms were worked by people who did not own the land. High tenancy rates in the Deep South belied the rosy rhetoric of New South prophets: South Carolina, 61 percent; Georgia, 60 percent; Alabama, 58 percent; Mississippi, 62 percent; and Louisiana, 58 percent.

How did the system work? The sharecropper, who had nothing to offer the landowner but his or her labor, tilled the land in return for supplies and a share of the crop, generally about half. Tenant farmers,

Black sharecroppers, ca. 1880–1890.

hardly better off, might have their own mule, a plow, and credit with the country store. They were entitled to claim a larger share, commonly three-fourths of the cash crop and two-thirds of the subsistence crop, which was mainly corn. The system was horribly inefficient, for the tenant lacked incentive to care for the land, and the owner had little chance to supervise the work. In addition the system bred a morbid suspicion on both sides. The folklore of the rural South was replete with tales of tenants who remained stubbornly shiftless and improvident and landlords who kept books with crooked pencils.

The crop lien system was equally flawed. At best, it supplied credit where cash was scarce. Country merchants furnished supplies in return for liens (or mortgages) on farmers' crops. To a few tenants and small farmers who seized the chance, such credit offered a way out, but to most it offered only a hopeless cycle of perennial debt. The merchant, who assumed great risks, generally charged interest that ranged, according to one journalist, "from 24 percent to grand larceny." The merchant, like the planter (often the same man), required his farmer clients to grow a cash crop that could be readily sold at harvest time. Thus, for all the New South ballyhoo about diversification, the routines of tenancy and sharecropping were geared to a staple crop, usually cotton. The resulting stagnation of rural life held millions, white and black, in bondage to privation and ignorance.

THE BOURBON REDEEMERS   In post–Civil War politics, despite the South's formal democracy, habits of deference still prevailed. After Reconstruction ended in 1877, a planter-merchant elite, collectively known as Bourbons, dominated southern politics. Like the French Bourbons, the royal family which, Napoleon once said, forgot nothing and learned nothing in the ordeal of revolution, the southern Bourbons were said to have forgotten nothing and learned nothing in the ordeal of the Civil War.

The word functioned mainly as a hateful epithet, and few could glory in it. *Bourbon* came to signify the leaders of the Democratic party, whether they were real reactionaries or, more commonly, champions of an industrial New South who, if they had forgotten nothing, had at least learned something. They may have worshipped at the shrine of the old order, but they embraced a new order of economic development.

These Bourbons of the New South perfected a political alliance with northeastern conservatives and an economic alliance with northeastern capitalists. They generally pursued a policy of laissez-faire, except for the tax exemptions and other favors they offered to business. They avoided political initiatives, making the transition from Republican rule to Bourbon rule less abrupt than is often assumed. The Bourbons' favorable disposition toward the railroads was not unlike that of the Radicals. And despite their reputation for honesty, Bourbon officeholders were occasionally caught with their fingers in the till.

The Bourbons focused on cutting back the size and cost of government. This spelled austerity for public services, including the school systems started during Reconstruction. In 1871 the south Atlantic states were spending $10.27 per pupil; by 1880 the figure was down to $6.00, and in 1890 it stood at only $7.63. Illiteracy rates at the time ran at about 12 percent of the white population and 50 percent of the black population.

The Bourbons' urge to economize led them to adopt the degrading system of convict leasing. The destruction of prisons and the poverty of state treasuries combined with the demand for cheap labor on the railroads, in the mines, and in lumber camps, to make the leasing of convict labor a way for southern states to avoid expenses and even bring in revenue. The burden of detaining criminals grew after the war because freed slaves, who had been subject to the discipline of masters, were now subject to the criminal law. Convict leasing, in the absence of state supervision, allowed inefficiency, neglect, and disregard for human life to proliferate.

The Bourbons scaled down not only state expenditures but also the public debt, and by a simple means—they repudiated a vast amount of debt that had been issued by the Radical state regimes. The corruption and extravagance of Radical rule were commonly advanced as justification for the process, but repudiation did not stop with Reconstruction debts. Altogether nine states repudiated more than half of what they owed to bondholders and various other creditors.

There are elements of diversity in the Bourbon record, however. These scrimping regimes did respond to the demand for commissions to regulate the rates charged by railroads for commercial transport. They established boards of agriculture, boards of public health, agricultural experiment stations, agricultural and mechanical colleges, teacher-training schools and women's colleges, even state colleges for African Americans. Nor will any simplistic interpretation encompass the variety of Bourbon leaders. The Democratic party was then a mongrel coalition that threw Old Whigs, Unionists, secessionists, businessmen, small farmers, hillbillies, planters, and even some Republicans together in alliance against the Reconstruction Radicals. Democrats therefore, even those who willy-nilly bore the Bourbon label, often marched to different drummers, and the Bourbon regimes never achieved complete unity in philosophy or government.

Perhaps the ultimate paradox of the Bourbons' rule was that these paragons of white supremacy tolerated a lingering black voice in politics and showed no haste about raising legal barriers of racial separation. Blacks sat in the state legislature of South Carolina until 1900, of Georgia until 1908, and of Virginia until 1890; some of these black representatives were Democrats. The South sent black congressmen to Washington in every election until 1900 except one, though they always represented gerrymandered districts into which most of the black voters had been thrown. Under the Bourbons the disfranchisement of black voters remained inconsistent, a local matter brought about mainly by fraud and intimidation, though it occurred often enough to ensure white control of the southern states.

A like flexibility applied to other areas of race relations. The color line was drawn less strictly than it would be in the twentieth-century

South. In some places, to be sure, racial segregation appeared before the end of Reconstruction, especially in schools, churches, hotels and rooming houses, and private social relations. In places of public accommodation such as trains, depots, theaters, and soda fountains, however, segregation was more sporadic.

DISFRANCHISING BLACKS During the 1890s the attitudes of patrician benevolence that permitted such moderation eroded swiftly. One reason for this was that, despite signs of progress, many whites claimed that blacks, loosed from the restraints of slavery, were "retrogressing" toward bestiality, especially the younger blacks born after emancipation.

Another reason was political. The rise of Populism, a farm-based protest movement that culminated in the creation of a third political party in the 1890s, divided the white vote to such an extent that in some places the black vote became the balance of power. Some Populists courted black votes. In response the Bourbons revived the race issue, which they exploited with seasoned finesse, all the while controlling for their ticket a good part of the black vote in plantation areas. Nevertheless the Bourbons soon insisted that the black vote be eliminated completely from southern elections. It was imperative, the Louisiana governor told the state legislature in 1894, that "the mass of ignorance, vice and venality without any proprietary interest in the State" be denied the vote. Some farm leaders hoped that disfranchisement of blacks would make it possible for whites to divide politically without raising the specter of "Negro domination."

But since the Fifteenth Amendment made it illegal to disfranchise blacks as such, racists accomplished their purpose indirectly with devices such as poll taxes (or head taxes) and literacy tests. Some opposed such devices because they also ensnared poor whites, and this led to the creation of loopholes through which illiterate whites could slip.

Mississippi led the way to near-total disfranchisement of blacks. The state called a constitutional convention in 1890 for the express purpose of changing the suffrage provisions of the old Radical constitution of 1868. The resulting Mississippi plan set the pattern that seven more states would follow over the next twenty years. First, a residence requirement—two years in the state, one year in the election district—struck at those tenant farmers who were in the habit of moving yearly in search of a better chance. Second, voters were disqualified if convicted of certain crimes, many of them petty. Third, all taxes, including a poll tax, had to be paid by February 1 of election year, which left plenty of time to lose the receipt before the fall vote. This proviso fell most heavily on the poor, most of whom were black. Fourth and finally, all voters had to be literate. The alternative, designed as a loophole for whites otherwise disqualified, was an "understanding" clause. The voter, if unable to read the Constitution, could qualify by "understanding" it—to the satisfaction of the registrar. Fraud was thus institutionalized by "legal" disfranchisement.

In other states, variations on the Mississippi plan added a few flourishes. In 1898 Louisiana invented the "grandfather clause," which allowed illiterates to qualify if their fathers or grandfathers had been eligible to vote on January 1, 1867, when blacks were still excluded. By 1910 Georgia, North Carolina, Virginia, Alabama, and Oklahoma had all adopted the grandfather clause. Every southern state, moreover, adopted a statewide Democratic primary which became the only meaningful election outside isolated areas of Republican strength. With minor exceptions, the Democratic primaries excluded black voters altogether. The effectiveness of these measures can be seen in a few sample figures: Louisiana in 1896 had 130,000 black voters registered, and in 1900 5,320. Alabama in 1900 had 121,159 literate black males over twenty-one, according to the census; only 3,742 were registered to vote.

SEGREGATION SPREADS   What came to be called "Jim Crow" segregation followed hard on disfranchisement and in some states came first. The symbolic target at first was the railway train. In the 1880s it was still common practice for American trains to have first- and second-class cars, which afforded a degree of racial segregation by the difference in fares. In 1885, nevertheless, novelist George Washington Cable noted that in South Carolina blacks "ride in first class cars as a right" and "their presence excites no comment." From 1875 to 1883, in fact, any racial segregation violated a federal Civil Rights Act, which forbade discrimination in places of public accommodation. But in 1883 the Supreme Court ruled on seven *Civil Rights Cases* involving discrimination against blacks by corporations or individuals. The Court held, with only one dissent, that the force of federal law could not extend to individual action because the Fourteenth Amendment, which provided that "no State" could deny citizens the equal protection of the laws, stood as a prohibition only against state, not individual, action.

This left as an open question the validity of state laws *requiring* separate public facilities under the rubric of "separate but equal," a slogan popular with the New South prophets. In 1888 Mississippi required railway passengers, under penalty of law, to occupy the car set aside for their race. When Louisiana followed suit in 1890, the law was challenged in the case of *Plessy v. Ferguson,* which the Supreme Court decided in 1896.

The test case originated in New Orleans when Homer Plessy, an octoroon (a person of one-eighth black ancestry), refused to leave a white car when asked to do so. He was convicted, and the case rose on appeal to the Supreme Court. The Court ruled that segregation laws "have been generally, if not universally recognized as within the competency of state legislatures in the exercise of their police power."

Very soon the principle of statutory racial segregation extended into every area of southern life, including street railways, hotels, restaurants, hospitals, recreations, sports, and employment. If an activity was overlooked by the laws, it was not overlooked in custom and practice. The editor of the *Richmond Times* expressed the prevailing view in 1900: "It is necessary that this principle be applied in every relation of Southern life. God Almighty drew the color line and it cannot be obliterated. The negro must stay on his side of the line and the white man must stay on his side, and the sooner both races recognize this fact and accept it, the better it will be for both."

Violence accompanied the so-called Jim Crow laws that mandated segregated facilities. From 1890 to 1899 lynchings in the United States averaged 187 per year, 82 percent of which occurred in the South; from 1900 to 1909 they averaged 93 per year, 92 percent in the South. Whites constituted 32 percent of the victims during the first period, only 11 percent in the latter. A young Episcopal priest in Montgomery remarked that extremists had proceeded "from an undiscriminating attack upon the Negro's ballot to a like attack upon his schools, his labor, his life."

WASHINGTON AND DU BOIS   A few brave souls, black and white, spoke out against such attitudes, but by and large blacks had to accom-

Booker T. Washington.

modate to them as best they could. Some blacks even began to make a virtue of necessity, and their chief spokesman was Booker T. Washington, the black prophet of the New South Creed. Born in Virginia of a slave mother and a white father, Washington had fought extreme adversity to get an education at Hampton Institute, one of the postwar missionary schools, and then, in 1881, to build at Tuskegee, Alabama, a leading college for blacks.

Washington argued that black Americans should not antagonize whites by demanding social or political equality; instead they should concentrate on establishing an economic base for their advancement. In his speech at the Atlanta Cotton States and International Exposition in 1895, which propelled him to fame and was later labeled the "Atlanta Compromise," Washington advised fellow blacks to begin "at the bottom of life" and stress their opportunities rather than their grievances: "Cast down your bucket where you are—cast it down in making friends . . . of the people of all races by whom we are surrounded. Cast it down in agriculture, mechanics, in commerce, in domestic service, and in the professions." He conspicuously omitted politics and implied an endorsement of segregation: "In all things that are purely social we can be as separate as the five fingers, yet one as the hand in all things essential to mutual progress."

Some people bitterly criticized Washington, in his lifetime and after, for making a bad bargain: the sacrifice of broad education and of civil rights for the dubious acceptance of white conservatives. W. E. B. Du

W. E. B. Du Bois.

Bois led blacks in this criticism of Washington. A native of Great Barrington, Massachusetts, the son of free blacks, Du Bois once said defiantly that he was born "with a flood of Negro blood, a strain of French, a bit of Dutch, but thank God! no 'Anglo-Saxon.'" Du Bois first experienced southern racial practices as an undergraduate at Fisk University in Nashville. Later he earned a Ph.D. in history from Harvard and afterward attended the University of Berlin. In addition to an active career in racial protest, he left a distinguished record as a teacher and scholar. Trim and dapper in appearance, sporting a goatee, cane, and gloves, he possessed a combative, fiery spirit. Not long after he began his teaching career at Atlanta University in 1897, he began to assault Washington's accommodationist philosophy of black progress and put forward his own program of "ceaseless agitation."

Washington, Du Bois argued, preached "a gospel of Work and Money to such an extent" that it overshadowed "the higher aims of life." The education of blacks, he maintained, should not be merely vocational but should nurture leaders willing to challenge segregation and discrimination through social protest and political action. He believed in work, "but work is not necessarily education. Education is the development of power and ideal." He demanded that disfranchisement and legalized segregation cease and that the laws of the land be enforced. And he provided the formula for attaining such goals: "By voting where we may vote, by persistent, unceasing agitation, by hammering at the truth, by sacrifice and work." Du Bois minced no words in criticizing Washington's "Atlanta Compromise" philosophy: "We refuse to surrender the leadership of this race to cowards and trucklers."

THE NEW WEST

For vast reaches of western America the great epics of Civil War and Reconstruction were remote events hardly touching the lives of Indians, Mexicans, Asians, and white trappers, miners, cowboys, traders, and Mormons scattered through the plains and mountains. There the march of Manifest Destiny continued its inexorable course, propelled by a lust for land and a passion for profits. On one level, the settlement of the West beyond the Mississippi constitutes a colorful drama of determined pioneers overcoming all obstacles to secure their visions of freedom and opportunity amid the region's awesome vastness.

Of course, this romantic vision of western history has long gripped the American imagination. On another level, however, the colonization of the Far West involved short-sighted greed and irresponsible behavior, a story of reckless exploitation that nearly exterminated the culture of Native Americans, scarred the land, and decimated its wildlife. The history of the West seen from this perspective is not a grand success story but a tale of hardship, frustration, and failure. Both images of the process of western settlement are accurate in some respects.

In the second tier of trans-Mississippi states—Iowa, Kansas, Nebraska—and in western Minnesota, the last frontier of farmers pressed out onto the Great Plains. From California the miners' frontier scattered enclaves east through the mountains at one new strike after another. From Texas the nomadic cowboys migrated northward into the plains and across the Rockies into the Great Basin. Now there were two frontiers of settlement, east and west, and even a third in the south; in another generation there would be none. After one great final rush the occupation of the continent would be complete, less than three centuries after the first English beachhead at Jamestown.

As settlement moved west, the environment gradually altered. The Great Plains were arid, and the scarcity of water and timber rendered obsolete the axe, the log cabin, the rail fence, and the usual methods of tilling the soil. For a long time the region had been called the Great American Desert, a barrier to cross on the way to the Pacific, unfit for human habitation and therefore, to white Americans, the perfect refuge for Indians. But that pattern changed in the last half of the nineteenth century as a result of new finds of gold, silver, and other minerals, completion of transcontinental railroads, destruction of the buffalo, the rise of the range-cattle industry, and the dawning realization that the arid region need not be a sterile desert. With the use of what water was available, techniques of dry farming and irrigation could make the land fruitful after all.

THE MIGRATORY STREAM   During the second half of the nineteenth century, an unrelenting stream of migrants flowed into the largely Indian and Hispanic West. Newspaper editors described western migration as a "flood tide." Millions of Anglo-Americans, African Americans, Mexicans, and European and Chinese immigrants transformed the patterns of western society and culture. Most of the settlers were relatively prosperous white, native-born farming families. Because of the expense of transportation, land, and supplies, the very poor could not afford to relocate. Three-quarters of the western migrants were men.

The largest number of foreign immigrants came from northern Eu-

An American family on their way west.

rope and Canada. In the northern plains, Germans, Scandinavians, and Irish were especially numerous. Not surprisingly, these foreign settlers tended to cluster together according to ethnic and kinship ties. Norwegians and Swedes, for example, often gravitated toward others from the same home province or parish to form cohesive rural communities. Settlers from northern Europe soon represented large segments of state populations. In the new state of Nebraska in 1870, a quarter of the 123,000 residents were foreign-born. In North Dakota in 1890, 45 percent of the residents were immigrants. Compared to European immigrants, those from China and Mexico were much less numerous but nonetheless significant. More than 200,000 Chinese arrived in California between 1876 and 1890.

In the aftermath of the collapse of Radical Republican rule in the South, thousands of blacks began migrating west from Kentucky, Tennessee, Louisiana, Mississippi, and Texas. Many headed for Kansas. Some 6,000 southern blacks arrived in Kansas in 1879 alone, and as many as 20,000 may have come the following year. They came to be known as Exodusters, making their exodus out of the South in search of a haven from racism and poverty. These Exodusters usually became farmers, ranchers, and cowboys. By 1890, some 520,000 blacks lived west of the Mississippi River. As many as 25 percent of the cowboys who participated in the Texas cattle drives were African Americans. The

Nicodemus, Kansas: a colony founded by Southern blacks in the 1860s.

army units assigned to the western frontier included the all-black "Buffalo Soldiers," eighteen of whom won Congressional Medals of Honor while fighting Indians in the West.

MINING THE WEST Miners were also ethnically diverse. Every race and nationality was represented in the mining communities. The miners' frontier was in fact not so much a frontier as a scattering of settlements in places unsuitable for farming, such as steep mountainsides, remote highlands, and barren deserts. The California miners of '49 set the typical pattern in which the disorderly rush of prospectors was quickly followed by the arrival of the camp followers, a motley array of saloonkeepers, prostitutes, card sharps, hustlers, and assorted desperadoes, out to mine the miners. An era of lawlessness eventually gave way to vigilante rule and, finally, to a stable community and more subtle forms of exploitation.

The drama of the 1849 gold rush was reenacted time and again in the following three decades. Though the California fever had passed by 1851, and no big strikes were made for seven years, new finds in Colorado and Nevada revived hopes for riches. While nearly 100,000 early rushers were crowding around Pikes Peak in Colorado in 1859, miners discovered the Comstock Lode at Gold Hill, Nevada. The lode produced gold and silver, and within twenty years had yielded more than $300 million from shafts that reached hundreds of feet into the mountainside. In both Arizona and Montana, the most important mineral proved to be neither gold nor silver, but copper.

The growing demand for orderly government in the West led to the hasty creation of new territories, and eventually the admission of a host of new states. In 1861 Nevada became a territory and in 1864 the state of Nevada was admitted in time to give its three electoral votes to Lincoln. After Colorado was admitted in 1876, however, no new states entered for over a decade because of the party divisions in Congress. Democrats were reluctant to create states out of territories that were heavily Republican. After the sweeping Republican victory of 1888, however, Congress admitted the Dakotas, Montana, and Washington in 1889, and Idaho and Wyoming in 1890, completing a tier of states from coast to coast. Utah entered in 1896 (after the Mormons abandoned the practice of polygamy), Oklahoma in 1907, and in 1912 Arizona and New Mexico finally rounded out the forty-eight continental states.

THE INDIAN WARS   As the frontier pressed in from east and west, relentless greed and duplicity pursued the Indians into what was supposed to be their last refuge. Perhaps 250,000 Indians in the Great Plains and mountain regions lived mainly off the buffalo herds that provided food and, from their hides, clothing and shelter. No sooner was Andrew Jackson's removal policy complete than the onrush of white migration in the 1840s began to crowd the Indians' lands. From the early 1860s until the late 1870s, the frontier raged with Indian wars, and intermittent outbreaks continued through the 1880s.

In Colorado, where Cheyenne and Arapaho chiefs accepted a treaty banishing them westward, protesting braves began sporadic raids on the trains and mining camps. In 1864 the territorial governor persuaded most of the warring Indians to gather at Fort Lyon on Sand Creek, where they were promised protection. Despite this promise, Colonel J. M. Chivington's militia fell upon an Indian camp that was flying a white flag of truce, and slaughtered 450 peaceful Indians—men, women, and children. One general called it the "foulest and most unjustifiable crime in the annals of America."

The Battle of Little Bighorn in a pictograph by an Oglala Sioux, Amos Bad Heart Bull, 1876.

With other scattered battles erupting, in 1865 a congressional committee began to gather evidence on the grisly Indian wars and massacres. Its 1867 *Report on the Condition of the Indian Tribes* led to an act to establish an Indian Peace Commission charged with removing the causes of Indian wars in general. Congress decided this was best accomplished at the expense of the Indians, by persuading them to take up life on out-of-the-way reservations. This solution continued the persistent encroachment on Indian hunting grounds.

In 1867 a conference at Medicine Creek Lodge, Kansas, ended with the Kiowa, Comanche, Arapaho, and Cheyenne reluctantly accepting lands in western Oklahoma. The following spring the Sioux agreed to settle within the Black Hills reservation in Dakota Territory. But Indian resistance in the southern plains continued until the Red River War of 1874–1875. In a winter campaign of relentless pursuit, General Philip Sheridan, the hard-charging Civil War cavalryman, scattered the Indians and finally forced them to terms in the spring of 1875.

By then trouble was brewing once again in the north. In 1874, General George A. Custer led an exploring expedition into the Black Hills, accompanied by gold seekers. Miners were soon filtering into the Sioux hunting grounds despite promises that the army would keep them out. The army had done little to protect the Indian lands. When ordered to move against wandering bands of Sioux hunting on the range according to their treaty rights, the army moved vigorously. After several indecisive encounters, Custer found the main encampment of Sioux and their Cheyenne allies on the Little Big Horn River. Separated from the main body of his men, Custer and 200 soldiers were surrounded by 2,500 warriors and annihilated.

Instead of following up their victory, the Indians threw away their advantage in celebration and renewed hunting. The army regained the offensive, and the Sioux were forced to give up their hunting grounds and the gold fields in return for payments. In response to the peace commission that imposed this settlement, Chief Spotted Tail said: "Tell your people that since the Great Father promised that we should never be removed, we have been moved five times. . . . I think you had better put the Indians on wheels and you can run them about wherever you wish."

In the Rockies and westward the same story of hopeless resistance was repeated. In Idaho the peaceful Nez Perces finally refused to surrender lands along the Salmon River. Chief Joseph tried to avoid war, but when some unruly braves started a fight, he directed a masterful campaign against overwhelming odds, one of the most spectacular feats in the history of Indian warfare. After a 1,500-mile retreat through mountains and plains, he was finally caught thirty miles short of the Canadian border, and exiled to Oklahoma. A generation of Indian wars

Chief Joseph of the Nez Perce tribe.

virtually ended in 1886 with the capture of Geronimo, a chief of the Chiricahua Apaches, who had fought encroachments in the Southwest for fifteen years.

Over the long run the collapse of Indian resistance resulted as much from the killing off of the buffalo herds on which they subsisted as from direct suppression. White hunters felled buffaloes for sport, sometimes firing from train windows merely for the pleasure of seeing the large animals die. In the 1870s a systematic slaughter of the buffalo served the demand of fashionable easterners for buffalo robes and overcoats. By the mid-1880s the herds were near extinction.

Most frontier folk had little tolerance for moralizing on the Indian question, but Easterners who were far removed from frontier dangers took a different view. The slaughter of Indians was immensely unpopular. In his annual message of 1877 President Hayes echoed the protest: "Many, if not most, of our Indian wars have had their origin in broken promises and acts of injustice on our part." Politicians and religious leaders spoke out against mistreatment of Indians, but the most effective voice was a woman's. Helen Hunt Jackson, a novelist and poet, focused attention on the Indian cause in *A Century of Dishonor* (1881), a book that aroused public indignation and calls for new legislation.

INDIAN POLICY   As a result of such outcries, Indian policy gradually became more benevolent. Well-intentioned reformers sought to "Americanize" the Indians by dealing with them as individuals rather than as

Geronimo, a chief of the Chiricahua Apaches.

tribes. The fruition of reform efforts came in the Dawes Severalty Act of 1887, which proposed to introduce the Indians to individual land ownership and agriculture. The Dawes Act permitted the president to divide the lands of any tribe and grant 160 acres to each head of family and lesser amounts to others. To protect an Indian's property, the government held it in trust for twenty-five years, after which the owner won full title and became a citizen. In 1901 citizenship was extended to the Five Civilized Tribes of Oklahoma, and in 1924 to all Indians.

But the more it changed, the more Indian policy remained the same. Despite the best of intentions, the Dawes Act struck a double blow at the Indians. It created new chances for more land spoliation, and it disrupted what remained of the traditional cultures. Those lands not distributed to Indian families were sold, while others were lost to land sharks because of the Indians' inexperience with private ownership, or simply their powerlessness in the face of fraud. Between 1887 and 1934 Indians lost an estimated 86 million of their 130 million acres. Most of what remained was unsuited for agriculture.

CATTLE AND COWBOYS   While the West was being taken from the Indians, cattle entered the grasslands where the buffalo had roamed. The cowboy enjoyed his brief heyday, fading then into the folklore of the Wild West. From colonial times, especially in the South, cattle raising had been a common enterprise just beyond the fringe of settlement. In many cases the early slaves took care of the livestock. Later, in the West, black cowboys were still a common sight, although they were lost from view in the novels and "horse operas" that pictured a lily-white frontier. Much of the romance of the open-range cattle industry derived from its Mexican roots. The Texas longhorns and the cowboys' horses had in large part descended from stock brought over by the Spaniards, and many of the industry's trappings had been worked out in Mexico first: the cowboy's saddle, his chaps (*chaparejos*) to protect the legs, his spurs, and his lariat.

For many years wild cattle competed with the buffalo in the Spanish borderlands. Natural selection and contact with "Anglo" scrub cattle produced the Texas longhorns: lean and rangy, they were noted more for speed and endurance than for providing a choice steak. They had little value, moreover, because the largest markets for beef were too far away.

At the end of the Civil War, perhaps as many as 5 million roamed the grasslands of Texas, still neglected—but not for long. In the upper Mississippi Valley, where herds had been depleted by the war, cattle prices ranged from $30 to $50 a head, while the Texas cattle could be had just for the effort of rounding them up.

So the cattle drives after the Civil War took on a scale far greater than before. In 1866 a large Texas herd set out for Sedalia, Missouri, the western terminus of the Missouri-Pacific Railroad. But that route proved unsuitable because it was subject to raids by postwar bushwhackers (bandits), obstructed by woodlands, and opposed by Arkansas and Missouri farmers. New opportunities arose as railroads pushed farther west where cattle could be driven through relatively vacant lands. Joseph G. McCoy, an Illinois livestock dealer, realized the possibilities and encouraged railroad executives to run a line from the prairies to Chicago, the meat-packing center.

The Kansas-Pacific Railroad liked McCoy's vision, and with its help he made Abilene, Kansas, the western terminus of a new line. In 1867, the first shipment of Texas cattle went to Chicago. As the railroads moved west, so did the cowtowns and the trails.

The flush times of the cowtowns soon passed, however, and many reverted to sleepy villages. The long cattle drives played out because they were economically unsound. The dangers of the trail, the wear and tear on men and cattle, the charges levied on drives that crossed Indian territory, and the advance of farms across the trails combined to persuade cattlemen that they could best function near the railroads. As railroads spread out into Texas and the plains, the cattle business spread with them over the High Plains as far as Montana and on into Canada.

In the absence of laws governing the open range, cattlemen at first worked out their own arrangements when rights and uses conflicted. But in 1873 Joseph Glidden, an Illinois farmer, invented the first effective barbed wire, which ranchers used to fence off their claims at relatively low cost. Five years later an eastern promoter, John W. "Bet-a-Million" Gates, one of the early agents for Glidden, gave a persuasive demonstration of the barbed wire in San Antonio. Skeptical cattlemen discovered that their meanest longhorns shied away from the fence which, as Gates put it, was light as air, stronger than whiskey, and cheaper than dirt. Orders poured in, and Gates eventually put together a virtual monopoly in the American Steel and Wire Company. The coming of barbed wire was the crucial factor in ending the open, free range. Thereafter the cowboy settled into a more sedentary existence.

RANGE WARS   The growth of the cattle industry placed a premium upon land. Conflicting claims over land and water rights provoked violent disputes between ranchers and farmers. Ranchers often tried to drive off neighboring farmers, and farmers in turn tried to sabotage the cattle barons, cutting their fences and spooking their herds. The cattle ranchers also clashed with sheepherders over access to grasslands. A strain of ethnic and religious prejudice heightened the tension between ranchers and herders. In the Southwest shepherds were usually Mexican-Americans; in Idaho and Nevada they were Basques or Mormons. Many Anglo-American cattlemen and cowboys viewed these ethnic and religious groups as un-American and inferior. This helped them rationalize the use of violence against the sheepherders.

There also developed a perennial tension over grassland use between large and small cattle ranchers. The large ranchers fenced in huge tracts of public lands, leaving the smaller ranchers with too little pasture. To survive, the smaller ranchers cut the fences. In central Texas this practice sparked the Fence-Cutters' War of 1883–1884. Several ranchers were killed and dozens wounded before the state ended the conflict by passing legislation outlawing fence cutting.

An even more violent confrontation between large and small ranchers occurred in Wyoming when members of the Wyoming Stock Association organized an assault against small ranchers, who they charged were rustling their stock. In Johnson County, Wyoming, in 1889, the cattle barons lynched James Averell, a small rancher, and Ella Watson, a prostitute embroiled in the dispute. The vigilantes were brought to trial, but the case was dismissed when the four witnesses to the hanging refused to testify.

Two years later, in 1891, the large ranchers grew bolder. They organized a "lynching bee" to eliminate rustlers in Johnson County and hired gunmen from Texas to do their bidding. On Tuesday, April 5, 1892, two dozen Texan mercenaries and an equal number of ranchers who dubbed themselves "regulators" set out to wipe out the rustlers. After killing two men, the vigilante group headed north, only to find itself surrounded by a band of small ranchers who had been alerted to their arrival. The timely arrival of federal cavalry troops prevented a massacre. The cattle kings thereupon turned to a bounty hunter, Tom Horn, who murdered "rustlers" until he himself was caught, convicted, and hanged.

FARMERS AND THE LAND   Among the legendary figures of the West, the sodbusters projected an unromantic image in contrast to the cowboys, the cavalry, and the Indians. After 1860, on paper at least, the land laws offered favorable terms to the farmer. Under the Homestead Act of 1862 a farmer could either realize the old dream of free land simply by staking out a claim and living on it for five years, or by buying the land at $1.25 an acre after six months. But the land legislation of earlier days was predicated upon an entirely different environment from that of the Plains, and the laws never completely adjusted to the fact that much of the land was suited only for cattle. Cattlemen were forced to obtain land by gradual acquisition from homesteaders or land-grant railroads.

The unchangeable fact of aridity, rather than land laws, shaped institutions in the New West. Where farming was impossible the cattlemen simply established dominance by control of the water, regardless of the laws. Belated legislative efforts to develop irrigable lands finally achieved a major success when the Newlands Reclamation Act (after the aptly named Senator Francis G. Newlands of Nevada) of 1901 set up the Bureau of Reclamation. The proceeds of public land sales in sixteen states created a fund for irrigation works, and the Reclamation Bureau set about building such major projects as Boulder (later Hoover) Dam on the Nevada-Arizona line, Roosevelt Dam in Arizona, and Elephant Butte Dam and Arrowrock Dam in New Mexico.

But the stubborn problem of too little water remained, rendering much of the West's land useless for field crops. The area in which rainfall averaged ten to twenty inches per year was marginal, but with the techniques of "dry farming," it could support such crops as sorghum, kaffir corn, and Turkey wheat. Certain varieties of spring and winter wheat grew at the times of greatest rainfall. The eastern Plains from Minnesota and North Dakota down to Texas emerged as the wheat belt, the new breadbasket of the nation, and behind wheat the corn belt and corn-hog combination edged westward.

The lands of the New West, as on previous frontiers, passed to their ultimate owners more often from private hands than directly from the government. Much of the 274 million acres claimed under the Homestead Act passed quickly to cattlemen or speculators, and thence to settlers. The land-grant railroads got some 200 million acres of the public domain in the twenty years from 1851 to 1871, and sold much of this land to build population centers and traffic along the lines. The New West of cattlemen and farmers was in fact largely the product of the railroads.

The first arrivals on the sod-house frontier faced a grim struggle against danger, adversity, and monotony. Though land was relatively cheap, horses, livestock, wagons, wells, fencing, seed, and fertilizer were not. Freight rates and interest rates on loans seemed criminally high. As in the South, indebtedness soon became a chronic condition that led strapped farmers to embrace virtually any plan to inflate the money supply. The virgin land itself, although fertile, resisted planting; the heavy sod broke many a plow and wearied many a back. Since wood was almost nonexistent on the prairies, pioneer families came to rely on buffalo chips (dried dung) for fuel. Farmers and their families also fought a constant battle with the elements: tornadoes, hailstorms, droughts, prairie fires, blizzards, and pests. Swarms of locusts would cloud the horizon, occasionally covering the ground six inches deep and

The Shores family. *Black homesteaders near Westerville, Nebraska, in 1887.*

consuming everything in their path. A Wichita newspaper reported in 1878 that the grasshoppers devoured "everything green, stripping the foliage off the bark and from the tender twigs of the fruit trees, destroying every plant that is good for food or pleasant to the eyes, that man has planted."

PIONEER WOMEN   The West remained a largely male society throughout the nineteenth century. In Texas, for example, the ratio of men to women in 1890 was 110 to 1. Women continued to face traditional legal barriers and social prejudice. A wife could not sell property without her husband's approval. In Texas women could not sue except for divorce, nor could they serve on juries, act as lawyers, or witness a will.

But the fight for survival in the trans-Mississippi West made husbands and wives more equal partners than their eastern counterparts. Prairie life also allowed women more independence than could be had by those living domestic lives back east. One woman declared that she insisted on leaving out of their marriage vows the phrasing about "obeying" her husband. "I had served my time of tutelage to my parents as all children are supposed to. I was a woman now and capable of being the other half of the head of the family." Similar examples of strong-willed femininity abound. Explained one Kansas woman: "The outstanding fact is that the environment was such as to bring out and develop the dominant qualities of individual character. Kansas women of that day learned at an early age to depend on themselves—to do whatever work there was to be done, and to face danger when it must be faced, as calmly as they were able." Their goal, she added, was to carve out a new world, to "develop from wild prairie to comfortable homes."

Indeed, as the railroads arrived from Chicago bearing lumber from the wooded regions to the north, farm families could leave their dugouts or sod homes and build frame houses. New machinery helped open fresh opportunities for farmers. In 1868 James Oliver of Indiana made a successful chilled-iron plow. With further improvements his "sod buster" was ready for mass production by 1878, easing the task of breaking the shallow but tough grass roots of the Plains. Improvements and new inventions lightened the burden of labor but added to the capital outlay of the farmer.

To get a start on a family homestead required a minimum investment of $1,000. And while the overall value of farm lands and farm products increased in the late nineteenth century, the small farmers did not keep up with the march of progress. Their numbers grew but decreased in proportion to the population at large. Wheat, like cotton in the antebellum period, provided the great export crop that evened America's balance of payments and spurred economic growth. But for a variety of reasons few small farmers prospered. And by the decade of the 1890s many were in open revolt against the "system" that thwarted their efforts and denied their dreams.

A VIOLENT CULTURE   Although often exaggerated in Hollywood films, the western frontier during the second half of the nineteenth century was indeed a scene of pervasive violence. Guns, rifles, and knives were everywhere evident, and people readily used them to resolve their disputes. The brutal requirements for self-preservation on the frontier or in the mining communities led to a change in the long-standing premise of English common law that required a person to flee or retreat in the face of a violent threat. In 1876 a court ruled that a "true man" was no longer obligated "to fly" from an assailant. A popular folk song expressed the prevailing attitude:

> Wake up, wake up darlin' Corrie
> And go and get my gun
> I ain't no hand for trouble
> But I'll die before I run.

The need to protect one's family or homestead in the face of threats and the frontier's obsessive preoccupation with masculine honor helped nourish what came to be called the Code of the West. It stressed the need for a man to stand and fight when threatened or wronged, and this spawned a reckless preoccupation with individual courage. As the famous frontier marshal James Butler ("Wild Bill") Hickok explained, "Meet anyone face to face with whom you disagree," and "if you meet him face to face and took the same risk as he did, you could get away with almost anything [including killing], as long as the bullet was in the front."

Most of the individual violence associated with the "Wild West" occurred in the cattle towns and mining communities, where young single men dominated the populace and liquor was the most popular refreshment. Bodie, California, in the heart of the mining region, developed a reputation as a "shooter's town." Between 1877 and 1883, there were forty-four shootings leaving twenty-nine dead. The courts convicted only one man of murder. A few roughnecks in Bodie preferred weapons other than guns. For several months Man Eater McGowan terrorized the town. He gained his nickname from his tendency to chew on his opponent's appendages. Before being run out of town, he bit the sheriff's leg, broke a pitcher over a waiter's head, and bit or chewed off the noses or ears of a dozen others.

Perhaps the most violent region of the West between the 1860s and 1890s was central Texas, an area bounded by Houston, Fort Worth, Dallas, San Antonio, and San Angelo. This huge territory included a volatile mix of peoples—native Indians, Hispanics, German immigrants, freed slaves, and former Confederate soldiers. Ethnic and racial tensions, range wars, boundary disputes, outlaw activity, and vigilantism generated unrelenting conflict. Gunplay in Texas, while not an everyday occurrence as implied in movies and television shows, was not uncommon. John Wesley Hardin, the West's most prolific gunman, killed more than twenty men in political disputes and community feuds. Once, a drunken Hardin fired a bullet through the wall of his hotel room to silence a snoring guest. The man never snored again.

"THE FRONTIER HAS GONE" American life reached an important juncture in the last decade of the nineteenth century. After the 1890 population count, the superintendent of the census noted that he could no longer locate a continuous frontier line beyond which population thinned out to fewer than two persons per square mile. This fact inspired the historian Frederick Jackson Turner to develop the influential frontier thesis, first outlined in his paper "The Significance of the Frontier in American History," delivered to the American Historical Association in 1893. "The existence of an area of free land," Turner wrote, "its continuous recession, and the advance of American settlement westward, explain American development." The frontier had shaped the national character in striking ways. It was

> to the frontier [that] the American intellect owes its striking characteristics. That coarseness and strength combined with acuteness and acquisi-

tiveness; that practical, inventive turn of mind, quick to find expedients; that masterful grasp of material things, lacking in the artistic but powerful to effect great ends; that restless, nervous energy; that dominant individualism, working for good and for evil, and with all that buoyancy and exuberance which comes with freedom—these are traits of the frontier, or traits called out elsewhere because of the existence of the frontier.

But, Turner ominously concluded in 1893, "the frontier has gone and with its going has closed the first period of American history."

Turner's "frontier thesis" guided several generations of scholars and students in their understanding of the distinctive characteristics of American history. His view of the frontier as the westward-moving source of America's democratic politics, open society, unfettered economy, and rugged individualism, far removed from the corruptions of urban life, gripped the popular imagination as well. But it left much out of the story. Turner's description of the frontier experience exaggerated the homogenizing effect of the physical environment and virtually ignored the roles of women, blacks, Indians, Mormons, Hispanics, and Asians in shaping the diverse human geography of the western United States. Turner also implied that the West would be fundamentally different after 1890 because the frontier experience was essentially over. But in many respects that region has retained the qualities associated with the rush for land, gold, timber, and water rights during the post-Civil War decades. The mining frontier, as one historian has recently written, "set a mood that has never disappeared from the West: the attitude of extractive industry—get in, get rich, get out."

MAKING CONNECTIONS

- The problems of southern and western farmers described in this chapter will set the stage for the rise of the Populists in Chapter 21.

- This is a crucial period in the evolution of race relations in the South, bridging the antebellum period and the twentieth century.

- This chapter closes with the observation that, as of 1890, according to the superintendent of the census and the historian Frederick Jackson Turner, "the frontier has gone." Where would Americans now look to fulfill their expansionist urgings?

FURTHER READING

The concept of the "New South" is explored in Paul M. Gaston's *The New South Creed: A Study in Southern Mythmaking* (1970).* C. Vann Woodward's *Origins of the New South, 1877–1913* (1951)* is also useful. On the development of southern politics since Reconstruction, see Dewey W. Grantham's *The Life and Death of the Solid South: A Political History* (1988). A splendid recent treatment of southern society after the end of Reconstruction is Edward L. Ayers's *Southern Crossing: A History of the American South, 1877–1906* (1995).*

A good survey of industrialization in the South is James C. Cobb's *Industrialization and Southern Society, 1877–1984* (1984). To see how industrialization affected the Appalachian South, see Ronald D Eller's *Miners, Millhands, and Mountaineers* (1982).*

*These books are available in paperback editions.

Developments in southern agriculture are treated in Roger L. Ransom and Richard Sutch's *One Kind of Freedom: The Economic Consequences of Emancipation* (1977).* Also useful is Edward Royce's *The Origins of Southern Sharecropping* (1993).* Nate Shaw's *All God's Dangers* (1974) tells the story of one sharecropper.

C. Vann Woodward's *The Strange Career of Jim Crow* (3rd ed., 1974)* remains the standard on southern race relations. Some of Woodward's points are challenged in Howard N. Rabinowitz's *Race Relations in the Urban South, 1865–1890* (1978),* in Joel Williamson's *A Rage for Order,* 1986,* and in John W. Cell's *The Highest Stage of White Supremacy* (1982).* J. Morgan Kousser's *The Shaping of Southern Politics: Suffrage Restriction and Establishment of the One-Party South, 1880–1910* (1974)* handles disfranchisement.

Two overviews of the transformation of the West are Rodman W. Paul's *The Far West and the Great Plains in Transition, 1859–1908* (1988) and David Alan Johnson's *Founding the Far West: California, Oregon, and Nevada, 1840–1890* (1992). The Turner thesis is best presented by Frederick Jackson Turner himself, in *The Frontier in American History* (1920).*

The best introduction to the history of the Plains Indians remains Wilcomb E. Washburn's *The Indian in America* (1975).* The Indian conflict with the encroaching white settlers is explored in three books by Robert M. Utley, *The Last Days of the Sioux Nation* (1963),* *The Indian Frontier of the American West, 1846–1890* (1984),* and *The Lance and the Shield: The Life and Times of Sitting Bull* (1993). For a presentation of the Native American side of the story, see Peter Nabokov's *Native American Testimony: A Chronicle of Indian-White Relations from Prophecy to the Present, 1492–1992* (1992).

Terry G. Jordan's *Trails to Texas: Southern Roots of Western Cattle Ranching* (1981) finds cowboy origins along the Atlantic seaboard. Gilbert C. Fite's *The Farmer's Frontier, 1865–1900* (1966) and Allan G. Bogue's *From Prairie to Corn Belt* (1963) detail the harsh Great Plains life. The views of important participants are analyzed in Joanna L. Stratton's *Pioneer Women: Voices from the Kansas Frontier* (1981) * and Annette Kolodny's *The Land Before Her* (1984).*

---

*These books are available in paperback editions.

On the western miners, see Rodman W. Paul's *Mining Frontiers of the Far West, 1848–1880* (1963) and Paula Petrik's *No Step Backward: Women and Family on the Rocky Mountain Mining Frontier, 1865–1900* (1987).

For a sense of the directions in which the "new western history" is heading, see Patricia Nelson Limerick's *The Legacy of Conquest: The Unbroken Past of the American West* (1987), Richard White's *"It's Your Misfortune and None of My Own": A New History of the American West* (1991),* Donald Worster's *Under Western Skies: Nature and History in the American West* (1992), and *Under an Open Sky: Rethinking America's Western Past,* edited by William Cronon, George Miles, and Jay Gitlin (1992).

*These books are available in paperback editions.

19 THE RISE OF
BIG BUSINESS

CHAPTER ORGANIZER

This chapter focuses on:

- factors that fueled the growth of the post-Civil War economy

- the methods and achievements of major entrepreneurs

- the rise of large labor unions

THE POST–CIVIL WAR ECONOMY

America's rise as an industrial giant and agricultural cornucopia in the late nineteenth century is a fact of towering visibility. Between 1869 and 1899 the nation's population nearly trebled, farm production more than doubled, and the value of manufactures grew sixfold (in constant dollars). Within three generations after the Civil War, the nation that had long been a predominantly rural society dependent upon household production, governed by the requirements of the land and the rhythms of the seasons, burst forth as the world's preeminent economic power. The United States became a highly structured, increasingly centralized, urban-industrial society buffeted by the imperatives of mass production, mass consumption, and time-clock efficiency. Bigness became the prevailing standard of corporate life, and social tensions worsened with

The Hand of Man, *photogravure by Alfred Stieglitz, 1902.*

the rising scale of business enterprise. The industrial revolution "controls us all," said Yale University sociologist William Graham Sumner, "because we are all in it."

The Industrial Revolution created huge corporations that came to dominate the economy during the late nineteenth century. Why did businesses become so large and concentrated after the Civil War? Such corporate giants were the natural result of the modern capitalist system running its course. An older economy dependent upon small business and craftspeople could not satisfy the rapidly growing national market. Entrepreneurs who recognized this development focused their attention on developing systems of mass production and distribution. To do so, they took advantage of many technological innovations. As the volume of these businesses grew, the owners sought to integrate all the processes of production and distribution into single companies, thus producing even larger firms. Others joined forces with their competitors in an effort to dominate entire industries. This process of industrial combination and concentration, whether the result of natural economic forces or human machinations, transformed the nation's social order. It also provoked widespread dissent and the emergence of an organized labor movement.

BUILDING THE TRANSCONTINENTAL RAILROADS Railroads were the first big business, the first magnet for the great financial markets, and the first industry to develop a large-scale management bureaucracy. The railroads opened the West, connected raw materials to factories and markets, and in so doing created a national market for the nation's goods and produce. At the same time they were themselves gigantic markets for iron, steel, lumber, and other capital goods.

The renewal of railroad building after the Civil War increased the total mileage from 30,600 in 1862 to 53,000 in 1870 and 94,000 by 1880. During the 1880s, the greatest decade of railroad building, mileage leaped to 167,000 and then grew to 199,000 by 1900. Most of this construction filled out the network east of the Mississippi, but the most spectacular exploits were the transcontinental lines built across the plains and mountains. Running through sparsely settled lands, they served the national purpose of binding the country together, and so received generous government aid. In addition to federal land grants the railroads received financial aid in the form of loans and tax breaks from federal, state, and local governments.

Before the Civil War, sectional differences over routes held up the start of a transcontinental line. Secession finally permitted passage of the Pacific Railway Bill, which Lincoln signed into law in 1862. The act authorized a line along a north-central route, to be built jointly by the Union Pacific railroad westward from Omaha and the Central Pacific railroad eastward from Sacramento. As amended in 1864, the act donated to these two corporations huge tracts of adjoining land and granted loans from $16,000 to $48,000 per mile, depending on the difficulty of the terrain.

Both roads began construction during the war, but most of the work was done after 1865. The Union Pacific pushed across the plains at a rapid pace, avoiding the Rockies by going through Evans Pass in Wyoming. The work crews, with large numbers of ex-soldiers and Irish immigrants as laborers, had to cope with bad roads, water shortages, rugged weather, and Indian attacks. Construction of the rail line and bridges was hasty and much of it was so flimsy that it had to be redone later, but the Union Pacific made its rendezvous with the Central Pacific. The Central Pacific was organized by a quartet of Sacramento shopkeepers who made an indelible imprint on their state as the California "Big Four": Charles Crocker, Mark Hopkins, Collis P. Huntington, and Leland Stanford, who was elected governor in 1862.

THE CHINESE CONNECTION   The Central Pacific construction crews were mainly Chinese workers recently arrived from the region around Canton on the southeast coast of China. Made destitute by the mid-century economic and political collapse in south China, and lured first by the California gold rush and then by railroad jobs, thousands of Chinese men migrated to America, raising their numbers in the United States from 7,500 in 1850 to 105,000 in 1880. Most of these "coolie" laborers were single males intent upon accumulating money and then returning to their homeland, where they could afford to marry and buy a parcel of land. Their temporary status and dream of a good life back in China apparently made them more willing than American laborers to endure the dangerous working conditions and low pay of railroad work. Charles Crocker explained: "We can't get enough white labor to build this railroad, and build it we must, so we're forced to hire them." He failed to mention the economic benefit to the railroad of paying the Chinese one-third less than Americans. By 1867 the Central Pacific Railroad's 12,000 Chinese laborers represented 90 percent of its entire work force.

Clearing trees, handling explosives and operating power drills, and working in snowdrifts was dangerous work, and many Chinese died on the job. Fifty-seven miles east of Sacramento, the construction crews encountered the towering Sierras, but they were eventually able to cut through to more level country in Nevada. The Union Pacific had built 1,086 miles to the Central Pacific's 689 when the race ended on the salt plains of Utah near Ogden, at Promontory. There, on May 10, 1869, Leland Stanford drove a gold spike that symbolized the road's completion.

It was twelve years before the next transcontinental was completed, when the Atchison, Topeka and Santa Fe made contact with the Southern Pacific in southern California. These transcontinentals soon sprouted numerous trunk lines that in turn encouraged the building of other transcontinentals. The result was a massive and continuous railroad building boom that lasted into the early 1890s and in turn stimulated the rest of the economy.

The celebration after the last spike was driven at Promontory, Utah, on May 10, 1869, completing the first transcontinental railroad.

FINANCING THE RAILROADS   The building of both the Union Pacific and Central Pacific generated shameless profiteering through construction companies, controlled by insiders, which overcharged the railroad companies. One scandal involved the Crédit Mobilier Company, a construction company that had charged the Union Pacific for exorbitant fees in order to line the pockets of insiders who controlled both firms. Crédit Mobilier, according to a congressional investigation, bought congressmen like sacks of potatoes and charged the Union Pacific $94 million for construction that cost at most $44 million.

Eastern rail lines engaged in similar acts of financial buccaneering, which centered first on the Erie Railroad, the favorite prey of manipulators. Prince of the railroad "robber barons" was Jay Gould, a secretive trickster who mastered the art of buying rundown railroads, making cosmetic improvements, and selling out at a profit, meanwhile using corporate treasuries for personal speculation and judicious bribes. Nearly every enterprise he touched was either compromised or ruined, while Gould built a fortune that amounted to $100 million upon his death.

Few railroad fortunes were built in those freewheeling times by purely ethical methods, but compared to such as Gould, most railroad entrepreneurs were giants of honesty. They at least took some interest in the welfare of their companies, if not always in that of the public. Cornelius Vanderbilt, called "Commodore" by virtue of his early exploits in steamboating, stands out among the railroad barons. Already rich before the Civil War, he decided to give up the hazards of wartime shipping and move his money into land transport. His great achievement was consolidating separate trunk lines into a single powerful rail network led by the New York Central. After the Commodore's death in 1877, his son William Henry extended the Vanderbilt lines to include more than 13,000 miles in the Northeast. This consolidation trend was nationwide. About two-thirds of the nation's railroad mileage fell under the control of only seven major groups by 1900.

ADVANCES IN MANUFACTURING   The story of manufacturing after the Civil War shows much the same pattern of expansion and merger in both old and new industries. The Patent Office, which had recorded only 276 inventions during its first decade of existence, the 1790s, registered 234,956 in the decade of the 1890s. And whether or not necessity was the mother of invention, invention was the mother of new industries—and new departures in old ones. The list of innovations after the Civil War can be extended indefinitely: barbed wire, farm implements, the air brake for trains, steam turbines, gas distribution and electrical devices, the typewriter (1867), vacuum cleaner (1869), and countless others. Before the end of the century the internal combustion engine and the motion picture were laying foundations for new industries of the twentieth century.

These technological advances altered the lives of ordinary people far more than politics or intellectual developments. In no field was this truer than in the applications of electricity to communications and power. Few if any inventions of the times could rival the importance of the telephone, which Alexander Graham Bell patented in 1876 and demonstrated at the Philadelphia Centennial Exposition the same year.

To promote the new device the inventor and his supporters formed the Bell Telephone Association, out of which grew in 1879 the National Bell Telephone Company. Its stiffest competition came from Western Union, which, after turning down a chance to buy Bell's "toy," employed Thomas Edison to develop an improved version. Edison's telephone, with its separate transmitter and receiver, became the prototype of the modern instrument. But Bell had a prior claim on the basic principle, and Western Union, rather than risk a legal defeat, sold its rights and properties for a tidy sum, clearing the way for the creation of a monopoly. In 1885 the Bell interests organized the American Telephone and Telegraph Company. By 1899 it was a huge holding company in control of forty-nine licensed subsidiaries and itself an operating company for long-distance lines.

EDISON'S INVENTIONS   In the rise of electrical industries, the name of Thomas Alva Edison stands above those of other inventors. He started his career at an early age selling papers and candies on trains, soon learned telegraphy, and began making improvements in that and other areas. In 1876 Edison went full-time into the "invention business." He invented the phonograph in 1877, the first successful incandescent light bulb in 1879. Altogether he created or perfected hundreds of new devices and processes, including the storage battery, dictaphone, mimeograph, dynamo, electric transmission, and the motion picture. In 1882, with the backing of financier J. P. Morgan, the Edison Electric Illuminating Company began to supply current to eighty-five customers in New York City, beginning the great electric utility industry. A number of companies making light bulbs merged into the Edison General Electric Company in 1888. Financially secure, Edison retired from business to devote full time once again to invention.

The use of direct current limited Edison's lighting system to a radius of about two miles. To get more distance required an alternating current, which could be transmitted at high voltage and then stepped down by transformers. George Westinghouse, inventor of the air brake, developed the first alternating-current system in 1886 and manufactured the equipment through the Westinghouse Electric Company. Edison considered the new method too dangerous, but just as Edison's instrument supplanted Bell's first telephone, the Westinghouse system won the "Battle of the Currents," and the Edison companies had to switch over. After the invention of the alternating-current motor in 1888, Westinghouse acquired and improved the motor, which worked a revolution by enabling factories to locate wherever they wished. Capable now of using electricity as a power source, they no longer had to cluster around waterfalls and coal supplies.

ENTREPRENEURS

Edison and Westinghouse were rare examples of inventors with the luck and foresight to get rich from the industries they created. Most of the architects of industrial growth—the great captains of industry—were not inventors but pure entrepreneurs, men skilled mainly in organizing and promoting industry. Three post–Civil War entrepreneurs stand out both for their achievements and for their special contributions: John D. Rockefeller, Andrew Carnegie, and J. Pierpont Morgan.

ROCKEFELLER AND THE OIL TRUST   Born in New York state, the son of a pious, uncompromising mother and a carousing, conniving father, John D. Rockefeller learned early the lessons of hard work and shrewd dealing. He moved as a youth to Cleveland, where railroad and ship connections provided a strategic location for servicing the newly discovered oil fields of western Pennsylvania. In economic importance the Pennsylvania oil rush of the 1860s far outweighed the California gold rush of just ten years before. Well before the end of the Civil War, derricks checkered the area around Titusville, and refineries sprang up in Pittsburgh and Cleveland.

Of the two cities, Cleveland had the edge in transportation, and John D. Rockefeller made the most of the fast-growing commercial city's advantages. His desire for personal advancement and material gain was obsessive. While other young men were going off to fight the Civil War, Rockefeller moved aggressively into the oil business. In 1862 he backed a refinery started by his friend, Samuel Andrews, with whom Rockefeller then formed a partnership. The firm expanded, and in 1870 Rockefeller incorporated his various interests as the Standard Oil Company of Ohio, capitalized at $1 million.

Rockefeller's refinery was already the nation's largest, but as he put it, "the butcher, the baker, and the candlestick maker began to refine oil." As a result, "the price went down and down until the trade was ruined." Rockefeller resolved to bring order out of chaos, which is to say he decided to weed out the competition, and soon he hatched an ingenious scheme.

In 1872 the inscrutable Rockefeller created the South Improvement Company, which he made the marketing agent for a large percentage of his oil shipments. By controlling this traffic, he gained clout with the railroads, which gave him large rebates (refunds) on the standard freight rates in order to keep his business. In some cases they even gave him information on competitors' shipments. Rockefeller then approached his Cleveland competitors and offered to buy them out at his own price. Most of them saw the wisdom of this course. By 1879 Standard Oil had come to control 90–95 percent of the oil refining in the country.

Much of Rockefeller's success was based on his determination to "pay nobody a profit." Instead of depending on the products or services of other firms, Standard undertook to make its own barrels, cans, and whatever else it needed. Economists label this *vertical integration*. The company kept large amounts of cash reserves to make it independent of banks in case of a crisis. Rockefeller also set out to control his transportation needs. With Standard owning most of the pipelines leading to railroads, as well as the tank cars and the oil-storage facilities, it was able to dissuade the railroads from servicing eastern competitors. Those rivals who insisted on holding out then faced a giant marketing organization capable of driving them to the wall with price wars.

Eventually, in order to consolidate scattered business interests under more efficient control, Rockefeller and his advisers resorted to the legal device of the trust. Long established in law to enable one or more people to manage property belonging to others, such as children or the mentally incompetent, the trust now was used for another purpose—centralized control of business across state lines. In 1882 all of the thirty-seven stockholders in various Standard Oil enterprises conveyed their stock to nine trustees, getting "trust certificates" in return. The nine trustees were thus empowered to give central direction to all the Standard companies.

The original plan, never fully carried out, was to organize a Standard Oil Company in each state in which the trust did business. But the trust device, widely copied in the 1880s, proved legally vulnerable to prosecution under state laws against monopoly or restraint of trade.

In 1892 the Supreme Court of Ohio ordered the Standard Oil Trust dissolved. For a while the company managed to unify control by the simple device of interlocking directorates, through which the board of directors of one company was made identical or nearly so to the boards of the others. Gradually, however, Rockefeller took to the idea of the holding company, a company that controlled other companies by holding all or at least a majority of their stock. He was convinced that big business was a natural result of capitalism at work. "It is too late," he declared in 1899, "to argue about the advantages of industrial combinations. They are a necessity." That same year Rockefeller brought his empire under the direction of the Standard Oil Company of New Jersey, a holding company. Though less vulnerable to prosecution under state law, some holding companies, as we will see, proved vulnerable to the Sherman Anti-Trust Act of 1890. Meanwhile the term "trust" had become so fixed in the public mind that it was used to describe large combinations under holding companies as well.

CARNEGIE'S GOSPEL OF WEALTH   Andrew Carnegie, like Rockefeller, experienced the untypical rise from poverty to riches that came to be known in those days as "the typical American success story." Born in Scotland, the son of a weaver who fell upon hard times, he migrated with his family to Allegheny, Pennsylvania, in 1848. Then thirteen, he started out as a bobbin boy and engine tender in a textile mill at wages of $1.20 per week. At fourteen he was getting $2.50 per week as a telegraph messenger. He worked hard, and in 1853 he became personal secretary and telegrapher to the district superintendent of the Pennsylvania Railroad. When the superintendent became the president of the line, Carnegie took his place, and the pace of his career accelerated. During the Civil War, Carnegie went to Washington, where he developed a military telegraph system and personally helped evacuate the wounded from Bull Run.

Andrew Carnegie, apostle of "The Gospel of Wealth."

Carnegie kept on moving—from telegraphy to railroading to bridge building, then to iron and steelmaking, and investments. In 1865 he quit the railroad to devote full time to his own interests. These were mainly in iron and bridge building, but the versatile entrepreneur also made money in oil and sold railroad bonds in Europe. In his *Autobiography* Carnegie recalled his growing determination to allow "nothing to interfere for a moment with my business career." He kept his pledge. In 1872 he netted $150,000 on a trip during which he also met Sir Henry Bessemer, inventor of a new process of steelmaking. The process dazzled Carnegie, and he returned to America a converted prophet of steel, exclaiming to a friend: "The day of iron has passed!" The next year Carnegie resolved to concentrate on steel, or as he put it, to put all his eggs in one basket and then watch the basket. As competitors arose, Carnegie picked them off one by one.

Steel was the miracle material of the post–Civil War era not because it was new but because it suddenly was cheap. Until the mid-nineteenth century, the only way to make steel was from wrought iron—itself expensive—and in small quantities. Then in 1856 Bessemer invented what became known as the Bessemer converter, a process by which steel could be produced directly and quickly from pig iron. As the volume of steel rose, its price dropped and its uses increased. In 1860 the United States produced only 13,000 tons of steel. By 1880 production had reached 1,400,000 tons.

Carnegie was never a technical expert on steel. He was a promoter, salesman, and organizer with a gift for finding and using men of expert ability. He always insisted on up-to-date machinery and equipment, and shrewdly used times of recession to expand more cheaply. Carnegie retained a large part of his annual profits during good times to tide the business over during lean years. During business depressions, when construction costs were low and competitors were forced to the wall, Carnegie used his surplus capital to buy them out and expand. He also preached to his employees a philosophy of constant innovation in order to reduce operating costs.

In much of this Carnegie was a typical businessman of the time, if abler and luckier than most. But he stands out from the lot as a thinker who publicized a philosophy for big business, a conservative rationale that became deeply implanted in the conventional wisdom of some

Americans. Carnegie argued that, however harsh their methods at times, the captains of industry were on the whole public benefactors.

Carnegie's best remembered essay was "The Gospel of Wealth," published in 1889. In this basic statement of his philosophy Carnegie drew upon the ideas of the English naturalist, Charles Darwin, and especially on the social implications of Darwinism elaborated by Herbert Spencer, who had invented the phrase "survival of the fittest." In the evolution of society, Carnegie argued, the contrast between the millionaire and the laborer measures the distance society has come. "Not evil, but good, has come to the race from the accumulation of wealth by those who have the ability and energy that produces it." The process had been costly in many ways, but the law of competition was "best for the race, because it insures the survival of the fittest in every department."

Carnegie then delivered a sermon on the proper uses of wealth. The best way to dispense a fortune was to administer it during one's lifetime for the public good: "The man who dies rich dies disgraced." One should first set an example of humble living—in Carnegie's case this included owning a castle in Scotland as well as enjoying an annual income of $40 million—and provide for his dependents, then consider the rest a trust fund for the public good. One should avoid alms-giving, for the "pauper is a social leper." Instead the wealthy should provide means for people to help themselves by supporting universities, libraries, hospitals, parks, halls for meetings and concerts, swimming baths, and church buildings—in that order. To his credit, Carnegie devoted his wealth to many such benefactions and to the cause of world peace. He spent some $60 million on public libraries and another $60 million on higher education. Rockefeller too gave many gifts, mainly to education and medicine, but partly because he was persuaded it would make for good public relations.

Carnegie's gospel of wealth fit perfectly the late nineteenth century's worship of success and respect for the self-made man. The popularity of such attitudes opened up a huge market for inspirational literature touting the ancient verities of thrift, integrity, and hard work. Among the sages of that school none was better known than Horatio Alger, whose very name became a byword for vocational success. A Unitarian minister in New York, he wrote novels for boys with titles such as *Ragged Dick* (1867), *Luck and Pluck* (1869), and *Tattered Tom* (1871).

J. Pierpont Morgan. *This is the famous portrait by the photographer Edward Steichen, done in 1903.*

J. P. MORGAN, THE FINANCIER   J. Pierpont Morgan, who was born to wealth and increased it enormously, was about as far from being a Horatio Alger hero as one could get. Morgan's father was a partner in a London banking house, and his wealth enabled him to send young Pierpont to boarding school in Switzerland and Germany. After a brief apprenticeship, Morgan in 1857 began work in a New York firm that represented his father's bank, and in 1860 he set himself up as its New York agent under the name of J. Pierpont Morgan and Company. This firm, under various names, channeled a great deal of European capital into the country and grew into a financial power in its own right.

As an investment banker, Morgan bought corporate stocks and bonds wholesale and then sold them at a profit, much as other merchants would market, say, hardware, but on a larger scale. The growth of large corporations put Morgan's and other investment firms in an increasingly strategic position in the economy.

Morgan realized that railroads were the key to the times, and he picked up and reorganized one line after another. After the Panic of 1893, when hard times gutted the net worth of many railroads, Morgan took over the Erie, Philadelphia and Reading, the Northern Pacific, and organized the Southern Railway; he already had a hand in the Vanderbilt and Pennsylvania lines. Since the investment business depended on the general good health of client companies, investment bankers became involved in the operation of their clients' firms, demanding places on boards of directors and helping to shape their fiscal dealings. By these means bankers could influence company policies. Eventually people were speaking of the "money trust," the greatest trust of all, with its hand in all kinds of other enterprises.

Morgan's crowning triumph was the consolidation of the steel industry. In 1901 he bought out Carnegie's huge steel and iron holdings. Carnegie set his own price, which came to nearly $500 million, of which Carnegie's personal share was nearly $300 million. After closing the deal, Morgan told the steel king, "Mr. Carnegie, I want to congratulate you on being the richest man in the world." In rapid succession Morgan added other steel mills. Altogether the new United States Steel Corporation, a holding company for these varied interests, was capitalized at $1.4 billion, a total that was heavily watered (valued well above the company's actual assets) but was soon made solid by large profits. The new giant was a marvel of the new century, the first billion-dollar corporation, the climactic event in that age of corporate consolidation. By 1904 there were some 318 industrial trusts in the United States, capitalized at over $7 billion, with nearly 5,300 distinct plants.

ADVANCES FOR LABOR

SOCIAL TRENDS   Accompanying the spread of these giant industrial combinations was a rising standard of living for most people. If the rich were still getting richer, a lot of other people were at least becoming better off. The continuing demand for workers meanwhile was filled by new groups entering the work force at the bottom: immigrants above all, but also growing numbers of women and children. Because of a long-term decline in prices and the cost of living, real wages and earnings in manufacturing went up about 50 percent between 1860 and 1890, and another 37 percent from 1890 to 1914. By latter-day standards, however, working conditions then were dreary indeed. At the turn of the century the average hourly wage in manufacturing was 21.6 cents, and average annual earnings were $490. The average work week was fifty-nine hours, which amounted to nearly six ten-hour days, but that was only an average. Most steelworkers put in a twelve-hour day, and as late as the 1920s, a great many worked a seven-day, or eighty-four-hour, week.

Moreover, although wages were steadily rising, working and living conditions remained precarious. In the crowded tenements of immigrant neighborhoods in the major cities the death rates ran substantially higher than in the countryside. Factories often maintained poor health and safety conditions. In 1913, for instance, there were some 25,000 factory fatalities and some 700,000 injuries that required at least four weeks' disability—more than half the number of American casualties in World War I. In this new industrial world ever-larger numbers of people were dependent on the machinery and factories of owners whom they seldom if ever saw. In the simpler world of small shops, workers and employers could enter into close personal relationships; the larger corporation, on the other hand, was likely run by a bureaucracy in which ownership was separate from management. Much of the social history of the modern world in fact turns on the transition from a world of personal relationships to one of impersonal and contractual relationships.

DISORGANIZED PROTEST   In these circumstances it was far more difficult for workers to organize for mutual benefit than for a few captains of industry to organize for personal profit. Civic officials and business leaders respected property rights more than the rights of labor. Among workers recently removed from an agrarian world, the idea of durable unions was slow to take hold. Immigrant workers represented diverse and frequently antagonistic cultures and spoke many tongues. Many, if not most, saw their jobs as transient, the first rung on the ladder to success. They hoped to move on to a homestead, or to return with their earnings to the old farms of their European homelands. With or without unions, though, workers often staged impromptu strikes protesting long working hours and wage cuts. But such action often led to violence, and three violent incidents of the 1870s colored much of the public's view of labor unions thereafter.

The decade's early years saw a reign of terror in the eastern Pennsylvania coal fields, attributed to an Irish group called the Molly Maguires. Taking their name from an Irish patriot who had directed violent resistance against the British, the group aimed to right perceived wrongs against Irish workers by such methods as intimidation, beatings, and killings. Their terrorism reached its peak in 1874–1875. At trials in

1876, twenty-four of the Molly Maguires were convicted, and the next year twenty of them were hanged. The trials also resulted in a wage reduction in the mines.

THE RAILROAD STRIKE OF 1877   Far more significant, because more widespread, was the Great Railroad Strike of 1877, the first major interstate strike. Wage cuts caused the Great Strike. After the Panic of 1873 and the ensuing depression, the major rail lines in the East had cut wages. In 1877 they made another 10 percent cut, which provoked most of the railroad workers at Martinsburg, West Virginia, to walk off the job and block the tracks. Without organized direction, however, their picketing groups degenerated into a mob that burned and plundered railroad property.

Walkouts and sympathy demonstrations spread spontaneously from Maryland to San Francisco. The strike engulfed hundreds of cities and towns, leaving in its wake over a hundred people killed and millions of dollars in property destroyed. Federal troops finally quelled the violence. The greatest outbreak began at Pittsburgh on July 19, when the Pennsylvania Railroad put on "double-headers" (long trains pulled by two locomotives) in order to reduce crews. Public sympathy for the strikers was so great at first that local militiamen, called out to suppress them, instead joined the workers. Militiamen from Philadelphia managed to disperse one crowd at the cost of twenty-six lives, but then found themselves besieged in the railroad's roundhouse, where they disbanded and shot their way out.

Looting, rioting, and burning went on for another day until the frenzy wore itself out. A reporter described the scene as "the most horrible ever witnessed, except in the carnage of war. There were fifty miles of hot rails, ten tracks side by side, with as many miles of ties turned into glowing coals and tons on tons of iron car skeletons and wheels almost at white heat." Public opinion, sympathetic at first, shifted until it tended to blame the workers for the looting and violence. Eventually the strikers, lacking organized bargaining power, had no choice but to drift back to work. Everywhere the strikes failed.

For many people, the strike raised the specter of a worker-based social revolution like the Paris Commune of 1871, in which disgruntled mobs chanted "Bread or Blood." As a Pittsburgh newspaper warned, "This may be the beginning of a great civil war in this country between labor and capital." Equally disturbing to those in positions of corporate and political power was the presence of many women among the protesters. A Baltimore journalist noted that the "singular part of the disturbances is the very active part taken by the women, who are the wives and mothers of the [railroad]firemen." From the point of view of organized labor, however, the Great Railroad Strike demonstrated potential strength and the need for tighter organization. As the labor leader Samuel Gompers later recalled, "The railroad strike of 1877, was the tocsin that sounded a ringing message of hope for us all."

TOWARD PERMANENT UNIONS Meanwhile, efforts to build a permanent union movement had begun to bear fruit. Earlier efforts, in the 1830s and 1840s, had largely been dominated by reformers with schemes that ranged from free homesteads to utopian socialism. But the 1850s witnessed the beginning of "job-conscious" unions in certain skilled trades. By 1860 there were about twenty such unions, and during the Civil War, because of the demand for labor, these craft unions grew in strength and numbers.

There was no overall federation of these groups until August 1866, when the first National Labor Union convened in Baltimore. Essentially the NLU comprised delegates from labor and reform groups more interested in political and social change than in bargaining with employers. The groups espoused such ideas as the eight-hour day, workers' cooperatives, paper money, and equal rights for women and blacks. But the organization lost momentum after the death of its president in 1869, and by 1872 it had entirely collapsed. The National Labor Union, however, was not a total failure. It was influential in persuading Congress to enact an eight-hour day for federal employees and to repeal the 1864 Contract Labor Law, which allowed employers to bind immigrant laborers by paying for their passage from Europe. That such immigrants were willing to work for low wages made them unpopular with American workers.

THE KNIGHTS OF LABOR Before the National Labor Union collapsed, another labor group of national standing had emerged, the Noble and Holy Order of the Knights of Labor. The name betokened a tendency to copy the forms of fraternal orders and to evoke the aura of medieval guilds. The founder of the Knights of Labor, Uriah S. Stephens, a Philadelphia tailor, was a habitual "joiner" involved with several secret orders, including the Masons. Secrecy, he felt, along with a semireligious ritual, would protect members against retaliation and at the same time create a sense of solidarity.

The Knights of Labor, started in 1869, at first grew slowly, but during the years of depression after 1873, as other unions collapsed, it spread more rapidly. In 1878 its first General Assembly established a national organization. Its preamble and platform endorsed producers' and consumers' cooperatives, hoping to replace the wage-labor system with worker-owned factories. The Knights also called for free homesteads, bureaus of labor statistics, elimination of convict-labor competition, the eight-hour day, and the acceptance of greenbacks as currency in order to enlarge the money supply and ease credit. One plank in the platform, far ahead of the times, called for equal pay for equal work by both sexes.

Throughout their existence the Knights emphasized reform measures and preferred boycotts to strikes as a way to put pressure on employers. They also had a liberal membership policy, welcoming all who had ever worked for wages except lawyers, doctors, bankers, and those who sold liquor. Theoretically it was one big union of all workers regardless of race, color, creed, or sex, skilled and unskilled. Each local assembly was to be formed on such a basis, but in practice some local and district assemblies were organized on a craft basis, such as the telegraphers and cigar makers. Above these stood the General Assembly, a General Executive Board, and at the head of the organization a Grand Master Workman.

Stephens was the first elected to this office, but in 1879 he gave way to Terence V. Powderly, the thirty-year-old mayor of Scranton, Pennsylvania. In many ways Powderly was unsuited to the new job. At once mayor, head of the Knights, county health officer, and part owner and manager of a grocery store, he had too many irons in the fire. He was physically frail, sensitive to criticism, and indecisive at critical moments. Powderly was temperamentally opposed to strikes, and when they did occur, did not always back up the locals. Yet the Knights ironically owed their greatest growth to strikes that occurred under his leadership.

In the mid-1880s membership in the Knights grew rapidly. In 1884 a successful strike against wage cuts in the Union Pacific shops at Denver led many railroad workers to form new assemblies. Then, in 1885, the Knights scored a startling victory over Jay Gould. Late the previous year and early in 1885 Gould had cut wages on several of his railroads. A spontaneous strike on these lines in 1885 spread to Gould's Missouri-Pacific, and as organizers from the Knights of Labor moved in, Gould restored the wage cuts. Such successes allowed the Knights to grow rapidly from about 100,000 members to more than 700,000 in 1886.

But the Knights peaked in 1886 and then went into rapid decline. Jay Gould, taken by surprise in 1885, set a trap for the Knights in 1886. He spoke favorably of unions, expressing his wish that all railroad workers were organized, but in 1886 he provoked another strike by firing a fore-man in the Texas-Pacific shops. When the Knights struck, Gould re-fused arbitration and hired Pinkerton agents to harass strikers and keep the trains running. The Knights had to call off the strike. The organiza-tion was further damaged by an incident in Chicago's Haymarket Square that very night, with which the Knights had little to do but which provoked widespread revulsion against labor groups in general.

ANARCHISM   The tensions between labor and management during the late nineteenth century in both the United States and Europe helped generate interest in the doctrine of anarchism. The anarchists believed that government, any government, was in itself an abusive de-vice used by the rich and powerful to oppress and exploit the working poor. Anarchists dreamed of the eventual disappearance of government altogether, and many of them believed that the transition to this state-less society could be hurried along by promoting revolutionary action among the masses. One favored tactic was the use of dramatic acts of violence against representatives of the government. Many European an-archists emigrated to the United States during the last quarter of the nineteenth century, and they brought with them this belief in the im-pact of "propaganda of the deed."

THE HAYMARKET AFFAIR   On May 3, 1886, Chicago's International Harvester plant was the site of an unfortunate clash between strikers and policemen in which one striker was killed. Leaders of a minuscule anarchist movement in Chicago scheduled an open meeting the follow-ing night at Haymarket Square to protest the killing. Under a light driz-zle the crowd listened to long speeches promoting socialism and anar-chism, and was beginning to break up when a group of policemen arrived and called upon the activists to disperse. At that point someone threw a bomb at the police, killing one and wounding others. The police responded by firing into the crowd. In a trial marked by prejudice and hysteria, seven anarchist leaders were sentenced to death despite the lack of any evidence linking them to the bomb-thrower, whose identity was never established. Of the seven, two were reprieved and some years later pardoned, one committed suicide in prison, and four were hanged. The episode helped stamp in anxious American minds the stereotype of bearded and swarthy alien anarchists and labor radicals. All but one of the group were German-speaking, but that one held a membership card in the Knights of Labor.

Despite his best efforts, Powderly could never dissociate in the public mind the Knights from the anarchists. He clung to leadership until 1893, but after that the union evaporated. By the turn of the century it was but a memory. A number of problems accounted for the Knights' decline: a leadership devoted more to reform than to pragmatic organization, the failure of the Knights' cooperative enterprises, and a preoccupation with politics rather than negotiations with management.

The Knights nevertheless attained some lasting achievements, among them the creation of the Federal Bureau of Labor Statistics and the Foran Act of 1885, which penalized employers who imported contract laborers from abroad. The Knights also spread the idea of unionism and initiated a new type of union organization: the industrial union, an industry-wide union of both the skilled and unskilled.

GOMPERS AND THE AFL   The craft unions opposed the industrial unionism of the Knights. They organized workers who shared special skills, such as typographers or cigar makers. Leaders of the crafts feared that joining with the unskilled would mean a loss of their separate craft identities and a loss of the bargaining power held by skilled workers. In the summer of 1886 delegates from craft unions met at Columbus, Ohio, and organized the American Federation of Labor (AFL). In structure it differed from the Knights in that it was a federation of national craft organizations, each of which retained a large degree of autonomy and exercised greater leverage against management.

Samuel Gompers served as president of the AFL from its start until his death in 1924. Born in London of Dutch-Jewish ancestry, Gompers came to the United States as a teenager, joined the Cigarmakers Union in 1864, and became president of his New York local in 1877. This background was significant. The Cigarmakers tended to be the intellectuals of the labor movement; to relieve the tedium of their task, they hired young men to read aloud as they worked, and debated such weighty topics as socialism and Darwinism. But Gompers and other leaders of the union focused on concrete economic gains, avoiding involvement with utopian ideas or politics. "At no time in my life," Gompers once admitted, "have I ever worked out a definitely articulated economic theory." Adolph Strasser, head of the Cigarmakers, put it more strongly: "We have no ultimate ends," he told a Senate hearing. "We are going on from day to day. We are fighting only for immediate objects—objects that can be realized in a few years."

Such job-consciousness became the policy of the AFL under Gompers, whose lifetime concern was the effectiveness of the federation. Gompers hired organizers to spread unionism and worked as a diplomat to prevent overlapping unions and to settle jurisdictional disputes. The federation represented workers in matters of national legislation and acted as a sounding board for their cause. On occasion it exercised its power to request dues from members for the support of strikes. Gompers, it turned out, was temperamentally more fitted than Powderly for the rough-and-tumble world of unionism. He had a thick hide, liked to talk and drink with workers in the back room, and advocated using the strike to achieve labor's objectives. His preference, though, was to achieve these objectives through agreements with management that included provisos for union recognition in the form of closed shops (which could hire only union members) or union-preference shops (which could hire others only if no union members were available).

The AFL at first grew slowly, but by 1890 it had already surpassed the Knights of Labor in membership. By the turn of the century it claimed 500,000 members in affiliated unions; in 1914, on the eve of World War I, it had 2 million; and in 1920, it reached a peak of 4 million. But even then the AFL embraced less than 15 percent of the nonagricultural workers, and all unions, including the unaffiliated railroad brotherhoods, accounted for little more than 18 percent of these workers. Organized labor's strongholds were in transportation and the building trades. Most of the larger manufacturing industries, including textiles, tobacco, and packinghouses, remained almost untouched.

THE HOMESTEAD STRIKE   Two violent incidents in the 1890s scarred the emerging industrial union movement and set it back for forty years to come—the Homestead Steel Strike of 1892 and the Pullman Strike of 1894. The Amalgamated Association of Iron and Steel Workers, founded in 1876, had by 1891 a membership of more than 24,000 and was probably the largest craft union at that time. But it excluded the unskilled and had failed to organize the larger steel plants. The Homestead Works at Pittsburgh was an important exception. There the union had enjoyed friendly relations with the Carnegie company until H. C. Frick became its president in 1889. A showdown was delayed, however, until 1892, when the union contract came up for renewal. Andrew Carnegie, who had expressed sympathy for unions in the past, had gone to Scotland and left matters in the hands of Frick. Carnegie, however, knew what was afoot: a cost-cutting reduction in the number of workers through the use of labor-saving devices, and a deliberate attempt to smash the union.

As negotiations dragged on, the company announced it would deal with workers as individuals unless an agreement was reached by June 29. A strike, or more properly a lockout of unionists, began on that date. Even before the negotiations ended, Frick had begun barricading the plant and hired as plant guards 300 Pinkerton detectives whose specialty was union-busting. But on the morning of July 6, 1892, when the Pinkertons floated up the Monongahela River on barges, discharged union workers were waiting behind iron breastworks on shore. Who fired the first shot remains unknown, but a battle erupted in which nine workers and seven Pinkertons died. In the end, the Pinkertons surrendered and marched away, to the taunts of crowds in the street. Six days later 8,000 state militiamen appeared at the plant to protect the strikebreakers hired to restore production. The strike dragged on until November, but by then the union was dead at Homestead. Its cause was not helped when an anarchist shot and wounded Frick. Much of the local sympathy for the strikers evaporated.

THE PULLMAN STRIKE   The Pullman Strike of 1894 was perhaps the most notable strike in American history. It paralyzed the economies of twenty-seven states and territories making up the western half of the nation. It grew out of a dispute at the "model" town of Pullman, Illinois, just outside Chicago, which housed workers of the Pullman Palace Car Company in neat brick homes nestled on grassy lots along shaded streets. The town's idyllic appearance, however, was deceptive. Employees were required to live there, pay rents and utility costs higher than in nearby towns, and buy their goods from company stores. With the onset of the depression in 1893, George Pullman laid off 3,000 of 5,800 employees, and cut wages 25 to 40 percent, but not his rents and other charges. When Pullman fired three members of a grievance committee, a strike began on May 11, 1894.

During this tense period the Pullman workers had been joining the American Railway Union, founded the previous year by Eugene V. Debs. The tall, gangly Debs was a charismatic man who led by example and by the electric force of his convictions. A child of working-class immigrants, he quit school in 1869 at age fourteen in order to go to work for an Indiana railroad. There he soon "learned of the hardships of the rail in snow, sleet, and hail, of the ceaseless danger that lurks along the iron highway, the uncertainty of employment, scant wages and altogether trying lot of the workingman, so that from my very boyhood I was made to feel the wrongs of labor." He felt them so deeply that he eagerly

Eugene V. Debs, founder of the American Railway Union and later candidate for president as head of the Socialist Party of America.

accepted an invitation to start a local of the railroad brotherhood, a craft union of skilled workers.

Still, it was not until the Haymarket bombing that Debs came to see an inevitable conflict between labor and management. By the early 1890s he had become a tireless spokesman for labor radicalism, and he launched a crusade to organize *all* railway workers—skilled and un-skilled—into the American Railway Union. His earnest appeal generated a tremendous response, and soon he was in charge of a powerful new labor organization. He quickly turned his attention to the Pullman controversy.

After Pullman refused Debs's plea for arbitration, the union workers in June 1894 stopped handling Pullman cars and by the end of July had tied up most of the railroads in the Midwest. The rail owners then brought strikebreakers from Canada and elsewhere, instructing them to connect mail cars to Pullman cars so that interference with Pullman cars also meant interference with the federal mail. Attorney-General Richard Olney, a former railroad attorney, swore in 3,400 special deputies to keep the trains running. When clashes occurred between these and some of the strikers, lawless elements ignored Debs's plea for an orderly boycott and repeated some of the violent scenes of the 1877 strike.

Finally, on July 3, 1894, President Grover Cleveland answered an appeal from the railroads to send federal troops into the Chicago area, where the strike was centered. Illinois Governor John Peter Altgeld issued a vigorous protest, insisting that the state could keep order, but Cleveland claimed authority and a duty to ensure delivery of the mails. "If it takes every dollar in the Treasury and every soldier in the United States to deliver a postal card in Chicago," he vowed, "that postal card should be delivered."

As strikers clashed with troops and burned hundreds of cars, the federal district court granted an injunction forbidding any interference with the mails or any combination to restrain interstate commerce. On July 13 the union called off the strike, and on the same day the district court cited Debs for violating the injunction and sentenced him to six months in jail. The Supreme Court upheld the decree in the case of *In re Debs* (1895) on broad grounds of national sovereignty: "The strong arm of the national government may be put forth to brush away all obstructions to the freedom of interstate commerce or the transportation of the mails." Debs served his term, during which time he read deeply in socialist literature, and he emerged to devote the rest of his life to that cause.

SOCIALISM AND THE UNIONS   The major American unions, for the most part, never allied themselves with the socialists, as many European labor movements did. But socialist ideas had been abroad in the country at least since the time Robert Owen visited America in the 1820s. The movement gained little notice before the rise of Daniel DeLeon in the 1890s as the dominant figure in the Socialist Labor party. A native of the Dutch West Indies, DeLeon had studied law and lectured for some years at Columbia University. He proposed to organize industrial unions with a socialist purpose, and to build a political party that would abolish the state once it gained power. His ideas seem to have influenced Lenin, leader of Russia's Bolshevik revolution of 1917, but DeLeon preached revolution at the ballot box, not by violence.

Yet Debs was more successful at building a socialist movement in America. To many, DeLeon seemed doctrinaire and inflexible. Debs, however, built his new party by following a method now traditional in the United States: he formed a coalition, one that embraced viewpoints ranging from moderate reform to doctrinaire Marxism. In 1897 Debs announced that he was a Socialist and organized the Social Democratic party from the remnants of the American Railway Union. He received over 4,000 votes as its candidate for president in 1900. In 1901 his followers joined a number of secessionists from DeLeon's party, led by Morris Hillquit of New York, to set up the Socialist Party of America. In 1904 Debs polled over 400,000 votes as the party's candidate for president and more than doubled that to almost 900,000 votes in 1912, or 6 percent of the popular vote.

By 1912 the party seemed well on the way to becoming a permanent fixture in American politics. Thirty-three cities had Socialist mayors. The Socialist party sponsored five English daily newspapers, eight foreign-language dailies, and a number of weeklies and monthlies. Its support was not confined to urban workers and intellectuals. In the Southwest the party built a sizable grassroots following among farmers and tenants. But the party reached its peak in 1912. During World War I it was wracked by disagreements over America's participation, and was

split thereafter. The Great Depression of the 1930s served only to interrupt, not halt, its decline.

THE WOBBLIES   During the years of Socialist party growth there
emerged a parallel effort to revive industrial unionism, led by the Industrial Workers of the World (IWW), dubbed the Wobblies. The chief
base for this group was the Western Federation of Miners, organized at
Butte, Montana, in 1893. Over the next decade the Western Federation
was the storm center of violent confrontation with unyielding bosses
who mobilized private armies against it in Colorado, Idaho, and elsewhere. In June 1905 the founding convention of the IWW drew a variety of people who opposed the AFL's philosophy. Debs participated,
although many of his comrades preferred to work within the AFL.
DeLeon seized this chance to strike back at craft unionism. A radical
manifesto issued from the meetings, arguing that the IWW "must be
founded on the class struggle, and its general administration must be
conducted in harmony with the recognition of the irrepressible conflict
between the capitalist class and the working class."

But the IWW waged class war better than it articulated class ideology. Like the Knights of Labor, it was designed to be "One Big Union,"
including all workers, skilled or unskilled. Its roots were in the mining
and lumber camps of the West, where unstable conditions of employment created a large number of nomadic workers, to whom neither the
AFL's pragmatic approach nor the socialists' political appeal held much
attraction. The revolutionary goal of the Wobblies was an idea labeled
syndicalism by its French supporters: the ultimate destruction of the
state and its replacement by one big union. How it would govern remained vague.

Like other radical groups, the IWW was split by sectarian disputes.
Because of policy disagreements all the major founders withdrew, first
the Western Federation of Miners, then Debs, then DeLeon. William
D. "Big Bill" Haywood of the Western Federation remained, however,
and as its leader he held the group together. Although since embel-
lished in myth, Haywood was indeed an imposing figure. Well over six
feet tall, handsome, broad-shouldered, one-eyed, and rippling with
muscles, he commanded the attention and respect of his listeners. This
thirty-six-year-old hardrock miner, union organizer, and Socialist from
Salt Lake City had nothing but disdain for the AFL and its conservative

labor philosophy. He called Samuel Gompers "a squat specimen of humanity" with "small, snapping eyes, a hard cruel mouth," and "a personality vain, conceited, petulant, and vindictive." Instead of following Gompers's advice to organize only skilled workers, Haywood promoted the concept of one all-inclusive union whose credo would be the promotion of a socialism "with its working clothes on."

But Haywood and the Wobblies were reaching out to the fringe elements that had the least power and influence, chiefly the migratory workers of the West and the ethnic groups of the East. Always ambivalent about diluting their revolutionary principles, they heaped scorn on the usual labor agreements, even when they participated in them. They engaged in spectacular battles with corporate America but scored few victories. The largest was a textile strike at Lawrence, Massachusetts, in 1912; the strikers won wage raises, overtime pay, and other benefits. But the next year a strike of silk workers at Paterson, New Jersey, ended in disaster, and the IWW entered a rapid decline.

The fading of the movement was accelerated by the hysterical opposition it engendered. The *Los Angeles Times,* for instance, declared that "I.W.W. stands for I won't work, and I want whiskey. . . . The average Wobbly, it must be remembered, is a sort of half wild animal." Many of the authorities treated them as such. Bragged one sheriff, "When a Wobbly comes to town, I just knock him over the head with a night stick and throw him in the river. When he comes up he beats it out of town."

Branded as anarchists, bums, and criminals, the IWW was effectively destroyed during World War I, when most of its leaders were jailed for their militant opposition to the war. Big Bill Haywood fled to the Soviet Union, where he married a Russian woman, died in 1928, and was honored by burial in the Kremlin wall. The Wobblies left behind a rich folklore of nomadic working folk and a gallery of heroic agitators such as Elizabeth Gurley Flynn, a dark-haired Irish girl who at age eighteen, ardent and pregnant, chained herself to a lamppost to impede her arrest during a strike. The movement also bequeathed martyrs such as the Swedish singer and labor organizer Joe Hill, framed (so the faithful assumed) for murder and executed by a Utah firing squad. His last words were written to Haywood: "Goodbye, Bill. I die like a true blue rebel. Don't waste any time mourning. Organize." Such intensity of conviction and devotion to a cause ensured that the IWW's ideal of a classless society did not die.

MAKING CONNECTIONS

- The Darwinian ideas implicit in the attitudes of many leading entrepreneurs, especially Andrew Carnegie, are described in greater detail in the next chapter.

- In response to the growth of the railroads, reformers in the 1880s and 1890s began to push for regulation, a trend discussed in Chapter 21.

- The economic and industrial growth discussed in this chapter was an important factor in America's "new imperialism" in the late nineteenth century, as shown in Chapter 22.

- The socialist approach to reform was a significant influence on the Progressive movement, described in Chapter 23.

FURTHER READING

A useful recent survey of the industrial process is Walter Licht's *Industrializing America: The Nineteenth Century* (1995).* Scholarship on the growth of railroads includes George R. Taylor and Irene D. Neu's *The American Railroad Network, 1861–1890* (1956) and Robert W. Fogel's *Railroads and American Economic Growth* (1964).*

On entrepreneurship in the iron and steel sector, see Thomas J. Misa's *A Nation of Steel: The Making of Modern America, 1865–1920* (1995). Harold Livesay's *Andrew Carnegie and the Rise of Big Business* (1975)* treats the titan of the steel mills.

Nathan Rosenberg's *Technology and American Economic Growth* (1972)* documents the growth of invention during the period. For an absorbing biography of the foremost inventor of the era, see Neil Baldwin's *Edison: Inventing the Century* (1995).

---

*These books are available in paperback editions.

Much of the scholarship on labor stresses the traditional values that the work force brought to the factory. Herbert G. Gutman's *Work, Culture, and Society in Industrializing America* (1976)* best introduces these themes. In *The Fall of the House of Labor* (1987), David Montgomery interprets labor-management conflicts over work organization. As for the labor groups, Gerald N. Grob's *Workers and Utopias* (1961) examines the difference in outlook between the Knights of Labor and the American Federation of Labor. To trace the rise of socialism among organized workers, see Nick Salvatore's *Eugene V. Debs: Citizen and Socialist* (1982).*

*These books are available in paperback editions.

20 ∽ THE EMERGENCE OF
MODERN AMERICA

CHAPTER ORGANIZER

This chapter focuses on:

- immigration and the growth of the modern city

- the rise of powerful reform movements

- the impact of Darwinian thought on the social sciences

- literary and philosophical trends of the late nineteenth century

---

The novelist Henry James remarked in 1866 that the "dreadful chill of change" was in the air. During the second half of the nineteenth century, the United States experienced an urban revolution unparalleled in world history. As factories, mines, and mills sprouted across the landscape, cities grew up around them. The late nineteenth century, declared an economist in 1899, was "not only the age of cities, but the age of great cities." Between 1860 and 1910 the urban population grew from 6 million to 44 million. Farmers no longer represented the majority of working Americans. The United States was rapidly losing its rural flavor. Indeed, by 1920, more than half of the population would be living in urban areas.

The mushrooming cities, in turn, served as powerful magnets that lured workers by the millions from the countryside and overseas. This urban-industrial revolution greatly increased the national wealth and transformed the pace and tenor of American life. City people and folks who worked in factories rather than on farms, while differing significantly among themselves, also became distinctively and recognizably urban in demeanor and outlook. The rise of modern metropolitan America also created an array of new social problems. Corporations became so powerful that some of their owners decided that they were above the law. When someone complained to Cornelius Vanderbilt, the railroad tycoon, that he might be violating the law, he is alleged to have replied, "Law? What do I care about the law. Hain't I got the power?"

The Industrial Revolution brought to American shores waves of new immigrants from every part of the globe. By the end of the century, nearly 30 percent of the residents of major cities were foreign-born. These newcomers provided much-needed labor, but their arrival provoked ugly racial and ethnic tensions. Rapid urban development also produced widespread poverty and political corruption. The problems of how to feed, clothe, shelter, and educate the new arrivals taxed the imagination—and patience—of many Americans.

AMERICA'S MOVE TO TOWN

EXPLOSIVE URBAN GROWTH   The frontier was a safety valve, Frederick Jackson Turner said in his influential thesis on American development. Its cheap lands afforded a release for the population pressures mounting in the cities. If there was such a thing as a safety valve in his own time, however, he had it exactly backward. The flow of population toward the city was greater than toward the west, and "country come to town" epitomized the American people better than the occasional city "dude" who turned up in cow country.

Much of the westward migration in fact was itself an urban movement, spawning new towns near the mining digs or at the railheads. The Pacific coast boasted a greater urban proportion of the population than anywhere else; its major concentrations were first around San Francisco Bay and then in Los Angeles, which became a boom town after the arrival of the Southern Pacific and Santa Fe Railroads in the 1880s.

Seattle also grew quickly, first as the terminus of three transcontinental railroad lines, and by the end of the century as the staging area for the Yukon gold rush. Minneapolis, St. Paul, Omaha, Kansas City, and Denver were no longer the mere villages they had been in 1860. The South, too, produced new cities: Durham, North Carolina, and Birmingham, Alabama, which were centers of tobacco and iron manufactures, and Houston, Texas, which handled cotton and cattle, and later, oil. The industrial explosion powered the growth of new cities during this period.

The cities expanded both vertically and horizontally to absorb their huge populations. In either case transportation innovations played an important role: the elevator, the streetcar, and before the end of the century, the first automobiles. In 1889 the Otis Elevator Company installed the first electric elevator, which made possible the erection of taller buildings. Before the Civil War few structures had gone higher than three or four stories. Another support for the vertical city came from the engineers who developed cast-iron and steel-frame construction during the 1800s.

Before the 1890s the chief power sources of urban transport were either animals or steam. Horse- and mule-drawn streetcars had appeared in antebellum cities, but they were slow and cumbersome, and cleaning up after the animals added to their cost. In 1873 San Francisco became the first city to use cable cars that clamped onto a moving underground cable driven by a central power source. Some cities used steam-powered commuter trains or elevated tracks, but by the 1890s electric trolleys were replacing these. Mass transportation received an added boost when around the turn of the century subway systems began to function in Boston, New York, and Philadelphia.

The spread of mass transit made it possible for large numbers of people to become commuters, and a growing middle class (laborers often could not afford even the nickel fare) retreated to quieter tree-lined "streetcar suburbs" whence they could travel into the central city for business or entertainment. The pattern of urban growth often became a sprawl, since it took place usually without plan in the interest of a fast buck, and without thought to the need for parks and public services. But some developers had the wit to look ahead. New York in the early 1850s had set up a park commission, which hired Frederick Law Olmsted as superintendent to plan Central Park. By 1870, six years before its official completion, as many as 100,000 people a day visited the 840-

Pedestrians, horse-drawn carts, trolleys, and electric trains all made their way between Brooklyn and Manhattan over the Brooklyn Bridge, completed in 1883.

acre park. Olmsted later planned parks and even new subdivisions in San Francisco, Brooklyn, Chicago, and other cities.

CITY PROBLEMS AND POLITICS   Workers in the big cities often had no choice other than to live in crowded tenements, most of which were poorly designed. In 1900 Manhattan's 42,700 tenements housed almost 1.6 million people, an average of 37 residents per building. Before the day of high-rise apartments this represented an extremely high density, and such unregulated urban growth created immense problems of health and morale.

The sheer size of these cities helped create a new form of politics. Since individuals could hardly provide for themselves such necessary services as transit, paving, water, sewers, street lighting and cleaning, and fire and police protection, they came increasingly to rely on city government support. These services as well as many city problems were handled by local political bosses who traded in patronage favors and graft. Big-city political machines were not altogether sinister in their effects: they provided food and money for the poor, fixed problems at city hall, and generally helped immigrants in their adjustment to a new life. One ward boss in Boston said: "There's got to be in every ward somebody that any bloke can come to—no matter what he's done—and get help. Help, you understand, none of your law and justice, but help." In return the political professionals felt entitled to some reward for having done the grubby work of the local organization.

But whatever the problems of the cities, the wonder of their glittering new arc and electric lights, their streetcars, telephones, vaudeville shows and other amusements, newspapers and magazines, and a thousand other attractions cast a magnetic lure on the youth of the farms. The new cities threw into stark contrast the frustration of unending toil and the isolation and loneliness of country life. In times of rural depression thousands left for the cities in search of the opportunity and personal freedom that Horatio Alger and other writers of success literature dangled before their eyes. The exodus from the countryside was especially evident in the East, where the census documented the shift in population from country to city, and stories began to appear of entire regions where buildings were abandoned and going to ruin, where the wilderness was reclaiming farms that had been wrested from it during the previous 250 years.

Indeed, one of the most persistent subjects of American literature during this period was the migration of rural youth to the city. Where Alger's heroes almost always succeeded, however, a few fictional characters confronted the grinding reality of modern city life. In Theodore Dreiser's *Sister Carrie*, for instance, Carrie Meeber leaves her country village and travels to Chicago, attracted by the beguiling image of the city's throbbing activity and dazzling material opportunities. But once in the city she abruptly discovers that its life is not all excitement and fun. "Amid all the maze, uproar, and novelty," Dreiser wrote, "she felt cold reality taking her by the hand."

THE NEW IMMIGRATION

AMERICA'S PULL Newcomers to the cities arrived not only from the surrounding rural areas but from Europe and Asia as well. They gathered in American cities to live with others of like language, customs,

Steerage Deck of the S.S. *Pennland*, 1893. *These immigrants are about to arrive at New York's Ellis Island.*

and religion, and because they lacked the means to go west and take up farms. Though cities of the South and West (excepting the Far West) drew their populations mainly from the native-born of their regions, American cities as a whole drew more residents from abroad. During the peak decade of immigration, 1900–1910, 41 percent of the urban newcomers arrived from abroad.

This nation of immigrants continued to draw new inhabitants for much the same reasons as always, and from much the same strata of society. Immigrants took flight from famine, cholera, or the lack of economic opportunity in their native lands. They fled racial, religious, and political persecution and compulsory military service.

Yet more immigrants probably *were* pulled by America's promise than were pushed out by conditions at home. American industries, seeking cheap labor, kept recruiters abroad and at American ports. Railroads, eager to sell land and build up the traffic on their lines, distributed tempting propaganda in a medley of languages. Many of the western and southern states set up official bureaus and agents to attract immigrants. Under the Contract Labor Law of 1864 the federal government itself encouraged immigration by allowing companies to recruit foreign workers by paying for their passage.

After the Civil War the tide of immigration rose from just under 3 million in the 1870s to more than 5 million in the 1880s, then fell to a little over 3.5 million in the depression decade of the 1890s, and rose to its high-water mark of 8.8 million in the first decade of the new century.

A NEW WAVE   During the 1880s the continuing search for cheap labor combined with renewed persecutions in eastern Europe to bring a noticeable change in the source of immigration, one fraught with meaning for American social history. Before 1880 immigrants were mainly of Germanic and Celtic origin, hailing from northern and western Europe. But by the 1870s there were signs of a change. The proportion of Latin, Slavic, and Jewish people from southern and eastern Europe rose sharply. After 1890 these groups made up a majority of the newcomers, and by the first decade of the new century they formed 70 percent of the immigrants to this country. Among these new immigrants were Italians, Hungarians, Czechs, Slovaks, Poles, Serbs, Croats, Russians, Romanians, and Greeks—all people of markedly different cultural and language stocks from those of western Europe, and most followers of different religions, including Judaism and Catholicism.

ELLIS ISLAND   As the number of immigrants passing through the Port of New York soared during the late nineteenth century, the state-run Castle Garden receiving center overflowed with corruption. Money-changers cheated new arrivals, railroad agents overcharged them for tickets, and baggage handlers engaged in blackmail. With reports of these abuses filling the newspapers, Congress ordered an investigation of Castle Garden, which resulted in the closure of the facility in 1890. Thereafter the federal government's new Bureau of Immigration took over the business of admitting newcomers to New York City.

To launch this effort, Congress funded the construction of a new reception center on a tiny island off the New Jersey coast, a mile south of Manhattan and some 1,300 feet from the Statue of Liberty. The statue, unveiled in 1886, was a centennial gift from the French government commemorating the Franco-American alliance during the Revolutionary

War. It soon came to be viewed as a symbol of hope for immigrants passing under "Lady Liberty." In the base of the statue, workers had chiseled the poet Emma Lazarus's tribute to the promise of new life in America:

> Give me your tired, your poor,
> Your huddled masses yearning to breathe free,
> The wretched refuse of your teeming shore.
> Send these, the homeless, tempest-tossed to me,
> I lift my lamp beside the golden door!

In 1892 Ellis Island (named after its late-eighteenth-century owner, Samuel Ellis) opened its doors to the "huddled masses" of the world. Before 1954, when it closed, some 12 million people first touched American soil there. Forty percent of Americans today have ancestors who passed through Ellis Island. In 1907, the center's busiest year, more than a million new arrivals filtered through the cavernous Great Hall, an average of about 5,000 per day; in one day alone immigration officials processed some 11,750 arrivals. These were the immigrants who arrived crammed into the steerage compartments of ship hulls. Those immigrants who could afford first- and second-class cabins did not have to visit Ellis Island; they were examined on board ship, and most of them simply walked down the gangway onto the docks in lower Manhattan.

The first Ellis Island Immigration Station—a 400-foot-long barnlike structure made of Georgia pine—burned to the ground in 1897. In its place rose a majestic structure, a 220,000 square-foot Main Building made of fireproof red brick and limestone. Four graceful copper-plated domes towered above the massive roof, giving the building the appearance of a European palace. The enormous dimensions of the Great Hall, with its arching two-story ceiling, must have awed the new arrivals as they sat on benches waiting to be processed.

The prevailing atmosphere at Ellis Island was not comforting. Its bureaucratic purpose was to process immigrants, not welcome them. An army of inspectors, doctors, nurses, and public officials questioned, examined, and documented the newcomers. Inspectors asked probing questions: Have you money, relatives, or a job in the United States? Are you a polygamist? An anarchist? Doctors and nurses poked and prodded, searching for any sign of debilitating handicap or infectious disease. All the while, the immigrant worried: "Will they let me in?" Although some

Immigrants, with identification papers, newly arrived at Ellis Island.

Immigrants waiting in the Registry Room for further inspections.

who were sick or lame were detained for days or weeks, the vast majority of immigrants received stamps of approval and were on their way after three or four hours. Only 2 percent of the newcomers were denied entry altogether, usually because they were criminals, strikebreakers, anarchists, or carriers of some "loathsome or dangerous contagious disease," such as tuberculosis or trachoma, a contagious eye disease resulting in blindness. These luckless folk were then returned to their places of origin, with the steamship companies picking up the tab.

Between 1892 and 1954, 70 percent of all European immigrants circulated through Ellis Island. (Others landed at Boston, Philadelphia, Baltimore, New Orleans, and Galveston.) Among the arrivals at Ellis Island were many youngsters who would distinguish themselves in their new country: songwriter Irving Berlin (Russia), football legend Knute Rockne (Norway), Supreme Court justice Felix Frankfurter (Austria), singer Al Jolson (Lithuania), and comedian Bob Hope (England). But many others found America's opportunities harder to grasp.

MAKING THEIR WAY   Disembarking finally from the ferry onto American soil in Manhattan or New Jersey, the immigrants felt exhilaration, exhaustion, and usually a desperate need for work. Many were greeted by family and friends who had come over before, others by representatives of the many immigrant aid societies or by agents offering the men jobs in mines, mills, and sweatshops. Since most knew little if any English and nothing about American employment practices, the immigrants were easy subjects for exploitation.

In exchange for providing men with a bit of whiskey and a job, obliging recruiters claimed a healthy percentage of their wages. Among Italians and Greeks these agents were known as *padrones,* and they came to dominate the labor market in New York. Other contractors provided train tickets for immigrants to travel inland to jobs in cities such as Buffalo, Pittsburgh, Cleveland, Chicago, Milwaukee, Cincinnati, and St. Louis.

Eager to retain a sense of community and to sustain skills they may have brought with them, the members of ethnic groups tended to cluster in particular vocations. Poles, Hungarians, Slovaks, Bohemians, and Italians used to the pick and shovel flocked to coal mines, just as the Irish, Cornish, and Welsh had done at midcentury; Slavs and Poles comfortable with muscle work gravitated to the steel mills; Greeks preferred working in textile mills; Russian and Polish Jews peopled the needle trades and pushcart markets of New York. The vast majority of women immigrants found work as domestic servants. Others worked in textile mills or urban "sweatshops." A few determined peasants up-rooted from their agricultural heritage made their way west and were able to find work on farms or even a parcel of land for themselves.

Most of the immigrants, however, settled in the teeming cities. Strangers in a new land, they naturally gravitated to neighborhoods pop-ulated by their own kind. These immigrant enclaves—nicknamed Little Italy, Little Hungary, Chinatown, and so on—served as crucial transi-tional communities between the newcomers' Old World past and their New World future. By 1920 Chicago had some seventeen separate Lit-tle Italy colonies scattered across the city representing various home provinces. In such kinship communities the immigrants could practice their religions and native customs, converse in their native tongue, and fill an aching loneliness. But they paid a price for such community soli-darity. When the "new immigrants" moved into an area, older residents typically moved out, taking with them whatever social prestige and po-litical influence they had achieved. The quality of living quickly deteri-orated as housing and sanitation codes went unenforced.

As the number of new arrivals mushroomed during the last quarter of the nineteenth century, cities grew so cramped and land so scarce that designers were forced to build upward. The result was the "dumbbell" tenement house. These structures, usually six to eight stories tall and jammed tightly against one another, derived their name from the fact that housing codes required a two-foot wide air shaft between build-ings, giving the structure the appearance of a dumbbell when viewed from overhead. Twenty-four to thirty-two families would cram into each building, meaning that some city blocks housed almost 4,000 people. The tiny air shaft provided little ventilation; instead, it proved to be a fire hazard, fueling and conveying flames from building to building.

The early tenements were poorly heated and had toilets outside in the yard or alley for communal use. By the end of the century they would feature two toilets on each floor, available to all comers. Shoe-horned into such quarters, families had no privacy, free space, or sun-shine; children had few places to play except in the city streets; infec-tious diseases and noxious odors were rampant. Not surprisingly, the mortality rate for urban immigrants was much higher than that of the general population. In one Chicago ethnic ghetto at the end of the century, three babies of every five died before their first birthday.

THE NATIVIST RESPONSE   Many Americans of longer standing saw the new immigration as a threat, and the undercurrent of nativism so often present in American culture surfaced during the late nineteenth century, mainly in anti-Catholic and anti-Semitic sentiments. But more than religious prejudice underlay hostility toward the latest newcomers. Cultural differences confirmed in the minds of nativists the assumption that the Nordic peoples of the old immigration were superior to the Slavic and Latin peoples of the new immigration. Many of the new immigrants were illiterate, and more appeared so because they could not speak English. Some resorted to crime in order to survive in the new land, and political and social radicals turned up among these immigrant groups in sufficient numbers to encourage nativists to blame labor disputes on alien elements.

A resurgence of nativism in the 1880s led to the creation of the American Protective Association, operated mainly in Protestant strongholds of the upper Mississippi Valley. The movement grew slowly from its start in 1887 until 1893, when keen leaders took advantage of a severe depression to draw large numbers of the frustrated to its ranks. The APA soon vanished with the return of prosperity, but while it lasted it promoted restricted immigration, more stringent naturalization requirements, refusal to employ aliens or Catholics, and the teaching of only the "American" language in the schools.

IMMIGRATION RESTRICTION   The movement to restrict immigration had mixed success beyond the exclusion of certain individuals deemed undesirable. In 1891 Representative Henry Cabot Lodge of Massachusetts took up the cause of excluding illiterates—a measure that would have affected much of the new immigration, even though the language of literacy did not have to be English. Several times during the next twenty-five years Congress passed bills embodying the restriction, but they were vetoed by Presidents Cleveland, Taft, and Wilson. In 1917, however, Congress overrode Wilson's veto.

Proponents of immigration restriction during the late nineteenth century did succeed in excluding the Chinese, who were victims of everything the new European immigrants suffered and color prejudice

The slogan of the Workingmen's party was "The Chinese Must Go!"

as well. By 1880 there were some 75,000 Chinese in California, about one-ninth of the state's population. Railroad owners found them hardworking and submissive. "They prove nearly equal to white men in the amount of labor they perform," one owner wrote, "and are much more reliable. No danger of strikes among them." Many white workers resented the Chinese for accepting lower wages, but their greater sin, a New York editor stressed, was perpetuating "those disgusting habits of thrift, industry, and self-denial."

Exclusion of the Chinese began in 1880, when the urgent need for railway labor had ebbed. A new treaty with China permitted the United States to "regulate, limit, and suspend" Chinese immigration, and in 1882 President Chester Arthur signed a bill authorizing a ten-year suspension. The legislation closing the doors to Chinese immigrants received overwhelming support. One Congressman explained that because the "industrial army of Asiatic laborers" was increasing the tension between workers and management in the American economy, "the gate must be closed." The Chinese Exclusion Act was periodically renewed before being extended indefinitely in 1902. Not until 1943 were such barriers to Chinese immigration finally removed.

The West Coast counterpart to Ellis Island was the Immigration Station on rugged Angel Island, six miles offshore from San Francisco. Opened in 1910, it served as a processing center for tens of thousands of Asian immigrants, most of them Chinese. Although the Chinese Exclusion Act had sharply reduced the flow of Chinese immigrants, it did not stop the influx completely. Those arrivals who could claim a Chinese-American parent were allowed to enter, as were certain officials, teachers, merchants, and students. The powerful prejudice the Chinese immigrants encountered helps explain why over 30 percent of the arrivals at Angel Island were denied entry. Those who appealed such denials were housed in prisonlike barracks for weeks or months. One of the detainees scratched a moving poem on the wall:

> This place is called an island of immortals,
> When, in fact, this mountainous wilderness is a prison.
> Once you see the open net, why throw yourself in?
> It is only because of empty pockets. I can do nothing else.

EDUCATION AND THE PROFESSIONS

THE SPREAD OF SCHOOLS The spread of public education, spurred partly by the determination to "Americanize" immigrant children, helped quicken the emergence of a new America after the Civil War. By the 1870s, America's commitment to public education was well nigh universal. In 1870 there were 7 million pupils in public schools; by 1920 the number had tripled. Despite such progress, educational lead-

History class at Tuskegee Institute, an early leader in vocational education for African Americans.

The campus of Texas A & M College, 1895, with Ross Hall at the right.

ers all too often had to struggle against a pattern of political appointments, corruption, and incompetence in the public schools.

The spread of secondary schools accounted for much of the increased enrollment in public schools. In antebellum America private academies prepared those who intended to enter college. At the beginning of the Civil War there were only about 100 public high schools in the whole country, but their number grew rapidly to about 800 in 1880 and 6,000 at the turn of the century.

HIGHER EDUCATION   American colleges as this time sought to instill discipline, morality, and a curriculum heavy on mathematics and the classics (and in church schools, theology), along with ethics and rhetoric. History, modern languages and literature, and some science courses were tolerated, although laboratory work was usually limited to a professor's demonstration in class. The college teacher was all too apt to be a young man seeking temporary refuge, or a broken-down preacher seeking safe harbor. In 1871 one writer called the typical professor "nondescript, a jack of all trades, equally ready to teach surveying and Latin eloquence, and thankful if his quarter's salary is not docked to whitewash the college fence."

Nevertheless, the increasing demand for higher learning drove the college student population up from 52,000 in 1870 to 157,000 in 1890 and to 600,000 in 1920. During the same years the number of institu- tions rose from 563 to about 1,000. To accommodate the diverse needs of these growing numbers, colleges moved away from rigidly prescribed courses toward an elective system. The new approach allowed students to favor their strong points and colleges to expand their scope. But as Henry Cabot Lodge complained, it also allowed students to "escape without learning anything at all by a judicious selection of unrelated subjects taken up only because they were easy or because the burden imposed by those who taught them was light."

Women's access to higher education improved markedly in this pe- riod. Before the Civil War a few colleges had already gone coeduca- tional, and state universities in the West were commonly open to women from the start. But colleges in the South and East fell in line very slowly. Of the women's colleges, Vassar (1865) was the first to teach by the same standards as the best of the men's colleges. In 1875 two more excellent women's schools appeared in Massachusetts: Wellesley and Smith, the latter being the first to set the same admission requirements as men's colleges. Thereafter the older women's colleges rushed to upgrade their standards in the same way.

The dominant new trend in American higher education after the Civil War was the rise of the graduate school. Heretofore, most profes- sors had a knowledge more broad than deep. With some notable excep- tions they engaged in little research, nor were they expected to advance the frontiers of knowledge. Gradually, however, more and more Ameri- can scholars studied at German universities, where training was more systematic and focused. After the Civil War the German system be- came the basis for the modern American graduate university. By the 1890s the Ph.D. was fast becoming the ticket of admission to the guild of professors.

THE RISE OF PROFESSIONALISM   The Ph.D. revolution, moreover, was but one aspect of a growing emphasis on professionalism, with its imposition of uniform standards, licensing of practitioners, and accred- itation of professional schools. The number of professional schools grew rapidly in fields such as theology, law, medicine, dentistry, phar- macy, and veterinary medicine.

Along with advanced schooling went a movement for licensing prac- titioners in certain fields. During the second half of the nineteenth century, the first state licensing laws were enacted for dentistry, pharmacy, veterinary medicine, accounting, and architecture. Such licensing benefited the public by certifying competence in a given field, but it also benefited members of the profession by controlling the number of practitioners and thereby limiting competition.

THEORIES OF SOCIAL CHANGE

Every field of thought in the postbellum years felt the impact of Charles Darwin's *On the Origin of Species* (1859), which argued that existing species, including humanity itself, had evolved through a long process of "natural selection" from less complex forms of life. Those species that adapted to survival by reason of quickness, shrewdness, or other advantages reproduced their kind, while others died away. The idea of species evolution shocked people with conventional religious views by contradicting a literal interpretation of the creation stories in Genesis. Heated arguments arose among scientists and clergymen. Some of the faithful rejected Darwin's doctrine, while others found their faith severely shaken. Most of the faithful, however, eventually came to reconcile science and religion, viewing evolution as a natural process designed by God.

SOCIAL DARWINISM   Though Darwin's theory applied only to biological phenomena, other thinkers drew broader inferences from it. The temptation to apply evolutionary theory to the social world proved irresistible. Darwin's fellow Englishman Herbert Spencer became the first major prophet of what came to be called social Darwinism, and he exerted an important influence on American thought. Spencer argued that human society and institutions, like species, passed through the process of natural selection, which resulted in what he called the "survival of the fittest."

If, as Spencer believed, society naturally evolved for the better, then individual freedom was inviolable, and any governmental interference with the process of social evolution was a serious mistake. Social Darwinism thus implied a hands-off governmental policy; it decried the regulation of business, the proposals for a graduated income tax, sanitation and housing regulations, and even protection against medical quacks. Such initiatives, no matter how well intended, would only help the "unfit" survive and thereby impede progress. The only acceptable charity was voluntary, and even that was of dubious value. Spencer warned that "fostering the good-for-nothing at the expense of the good, is an extreme cruelty."

For Spencer and his many supporters, successful businessmen and corporations were the engines of social progress. If small businesses were crowded out by trusts and monopolies, that too was part of the evolutionary process. John D. Rockefeller told his Baptist Sunday school class that the "growth of a large business is merely a survival of the fittest."

The ideas of Darwin and Spencer were quickly popularized in America. Their most powerful advocate was William Graham Sumner, a professor at Yale who preached the gospel of natural selection to his classes and in writings such as *What Social Classes Owe to Each Other* and "The Absurd Effort to Make the World Over."

REFORM DARWINISM   The influence of Darwin and Spencer over the American mind did not go without challenge. Reform found its major philosopher in an obscure civil servant, Lester Frank Ward, who had fought his way up from poverty and never lost his empathy for the underdog. Ward's book *Dynamic Sociology* (1883) singled out one product of evolution that Spencer and others had neglected, the human brain. Humans, unlike animals, had a mind that could plan for and shape the future. Far from being the helpless pawn of powerful evolutionary forces, Ward argued, humanity could actively shape the process of evolution. The competition extolled by Sumner, Spencer, and other social Darwinists was in fact highly wasteful, and so was the natural competitive process: plant or cattle breeding, for instance, could actually improve on the results of natural selection.

Ward's reform Darwinism challenged Sumner's conservative social Darwinism, holding that cooperation, not competition, would better promote progress. Government could become the agency of progress by striving to ameliorate poverty, which impeded the development of the mind, and to promote the education of the masses. "Intelligence, far more than necessity," Ward wrote, "is the mother of invention," and "the influence of knowledge as a social factor, like that of wealth, is proportional to the extent of its distribution." Intellect, rightly informed by science, could plan successfully. In the benevolent "sociocracy" of the future, Ward argued, legislatures would function mainly to sanction decisions worked out in the sociological laboratory.

Realism in Fact and Fiction

HISTORY AND THE SOCIAL SCIENCES   The pervasive effect of Darwinism in late nineteenth-century American intellectual circles was comparable to the effect of romanticism in the first part of the century. Like the earlier reaction against the Enlightenment's praise of reason, the trend in social thought now was turned against abstract logic and toward concrete reality. Oliver Wendell Holmes, Jr., in *The Common Law* (1881), expressed the realistic impulse when he wrote that the "life of the law has not been logic; it has been experience." And experience was history. "The law embodies the story of a nation's development through many centuries," Holmes wrote, "and it cannot be dealt with as if it contained only the axioms and corollaries of a book of mathematics."

In the milieu of Darwinism, the study of history flourished. The historian, like the biologist, studied the process of development, but in the origins and the evolution of society. Under the influence of German scholarship and the new emphasis on science, history aspired to become "scientific." This meant examining documents and manuscripts critically, using external and internal evidence to determine validity and relevancy. The ideal of the scientific historian was to reproduce history with perfect objectivity, a noble if unreachable goal.

PRAGMATISM   Around the turn of the century the evolutionary idea found expression in a philosophical principle set forth in mature form by William James in his book *Pragmatism: A New Name for Some Old Ways of Thinking.* James, a professor of philosophy and psychology at Harvard, shared Lester Frank Ward's concern with the role of ideas in the process of evolution. Truth, to James, arose from the testing of new ideas, the value of which lay in their practical consequences. Similarly, scientists could test the validity of their ideas in the laboratory and judge their import by their applications. Pragmatism thus reflected a quality often looked upon as genuinely American: the inventive, experimental spirit focusing on tangible results.

John Dewey, who would become the chief philosopher of pragmatism after James, preferred the term "instrumentalism," by which he meant that ideas were instruments of practical use, especially for promoting social reform. Dewey, unlike James, threw himself into movements for the rights of labor and women, the promotion of peace, and the reform of education. He believed that education was the process through which society would gradually progress toward greater social equality and harmony. Dewey became the prophet of what was later labeled "progressive education," which emphasized the teaching of history, geography, and science in order to enlarge the child's personal experience. Dewey also pointed out that social conditions had so changed that schools now had to find ways to inculcate values once derived from participation in family and community activities.

THE LOCAL COLORISTS Writers of American fiction in this period also sought new ways to capture concrete reality, present and past. What came to be called the local color movement expressed the nostalgia of a people for places where old values and folkways survived. Sarah Orne Jewett depicted the down-easters of her native Maine most enduringly in the stories and sketches collected in *The Country of the Pointed Firs* (1896). Jewett's creative glance was always backward and affectionate, as she identified more with her forebears than her peers. She looked upon her parents' "generation as the one to which I really belong—I who was brought up with grandfathers and granduncles and aunts for my best playmates." She told another writer that her head was always full of old women and old houses, and when the two came together the result was a richly textured fiction marked by the essential dignity of a bygone day.

This local color impulse was not limited to New England. Once the passions of war and Reconstruction were spent, the South became for many northern readers an inexhaustible gallery of quaint types and picturesque settings. George Washington Cable exploited the local color of the quaint Louisiana Creoles and Cajuns in *Old Creole Days* (1879), *The Grandissimes* (1880), and other books. Joel Chandler Harris, a white newsman and columnist, wove authentic African-American folk tales into the unforgettable stories of Uncle Remus.

CLEMENS, HOWELLS, AND JAMES   The best of the local colorists could find universal truths in local life, and Samuel Langhorne Clemens (Mark Twain) transcended them all. A native of Missouri, Clemens was forced to work from the time he was twelve, becoming first a printer and then a Mississippi riverboat pilot. When the Civil War shut down the river traffic, he briefly joined a Confederate militia company, then left with his brother for Nevada, where he wrote for a local newspaper. He moved on to California in 1864 and first gained widespread notice with his tall tale of the gold country, "The Celebrated Jumping Frog of Calaveras County" (1865). With the success of *Roughing It* (1871), an account of his western years, he moved to Hartford, Connecticut, and was able to set up as a full-time author and hilarious lecturer.

Clemens was the first significant American writer born and raised west of the Appalachians. His early writings accentuated his western background, but for his greatest books he drew heavily upon his boyhood in the border slave state of Missouri and the tall-tale tradition of southwestern humor. In *The Adventures of Tom Sawyer* (1876) he evoked the prewar Hannibal, Missouri, where his own boyhood was cut so short. Its story of childhood adventures is firmly etched on the American memory. *Life on the Mississippi* (1882), based on articles written eight years before, drew upon what Clemens remembered as his happiest days as a young riverboat pilot before the war. His pseudonym, "Mark Twain," was in fact derived from a phrase that referred to the depth of the river.

Clemens's masterpiece, *The Adventures of Huckleberry Finn* (1884), created unforgettable characters in Huck Finn, his shiftless father, the runaway slave Jim, the Widow Douglas, the "King," and the "Duke." Huck Finn embodied the instinct of every red-blooded American boy to "light out for the territory" whenever polite society set out to civilize him. Huck's effort to help his friend Jim escape bondage expressed well the moral dilemmas imposed by slavery on everyone. Many years later another great American writer, Ernest Hemingway, would claim that "All modern literature comes from one book by Mark Twain, called *Huckleberry Finn*."

One of Clemens's foremost supporters was his close friend William Dean Howells. During the half century after the Civil War, Howells dominated the American literary scene. As editor of the influential *Atlantic Monthly* and later a columnist and critic for *Harper's Monthly,* Howells preached and practiced the new doctrine of realism, a literary rebellion against romantic idealism that sought to portray with scientific accuracy the contemporary social scene. He wrote that realism "was nothing more or less than the truthful treatment of . . . the motives, the impulses, the principles that shape the life of actual men and women."

To this end Howells wrote novels, plays, travel books, criticism, essays, biography, and autobiography. Amid the varied output of a long and productive life, *The Rise of Silas Lapham* (1885) stands out as his most famous novel. In it Howells presented a sympathetic portrayal of a newly rich manufacturer from the West, and one of the earliest fictional treatments of an American businessman.

The third major literary figure of the times, Henry James, moved in a world far different from that of Clemens or Howells. Brother of the pragmatist philosopher William James and son of wealthy parents, Henry spent most of his adult life as a voluntary expatriate in London, where he produced elegant novels that for the first time explored the international society of Americans in Europe. In works such as *Portrait of a Lady* (1881), *The Ambassadors* (1903), and *The Golden Bowl* (1904), James explored the tensions that developed between direct, innocent, and idealistic Americans (most often young women) and sophisticated, devious Europeans. Unlike Clemens, James typically wrote of the cosmopolitan upper class, and his stories turned less on plot than on moral dilemmas. His intense exploration of the inner selves of his characters brought him the title of "father of the psychological novel."

LITERARY NATURALISM   Realism grew into a powerful literary movement during the 1880s, but during the 1890s it took on a new character in the writings of the so-called naturalists. This group of younger writers sought to integrate scientific determinism into literature. Having grown up in the era of Darwin and Spencer, they viewed humankind as prey to natural forces and internal drives without control or full knowledge of them. Frank Norris thus pictured in *McTeague* (1899) the descent of a San Francisco dentist and his wife into madness, driven by greed, violence, and lust. Stephen Crane in *Maggie: A Girl of the Streets* (1893) and *The Red Badge of Courage* (1895) portrayed people caught up in environmental situations beyond their control. *Maggie* depicted a tenement girl driven to prostitution and death amid scenes so grim and sordid that Crane had to finance publication himself. *The Red Badge of Courage,* his masterpiece, told the story of a young man going through his baptism of fire in the Civil War, and evoked fear, nobility, and courage amid the ungovernable carnage of war.

Two of the naturalists, Jack London and Theodore Dreiser, achieved a degree of popular success. London was both a professed socialist and a believer in the German philosopher Friedrich Nietzsche's doctrine of the superman. In adventure stories such as *The Call of the Wild* (1903) and *The Sea Wolf* (1904) he celebrated the triumph of brute force and the will to survive.

Theodore Dreiser did not celebrate the overwhelming power of social and biological forces; he dissected them for the reader. The result was powerfully disturbing to readers accustomed to more genteel fare. Dreiser shocked the public probably more than the others with protagonists who sinned without remorse and without punishment. *Sister Carrie* (1900), for example, showed Carrie Meeber surviving illicit lovers and going on to success on the stage.

SOCIAL CRITICISM   Behind their dogma of determinism, several of the naturalists harbored intense outrage at human misery. Their indignation was shared by an increasing number of journalists and social critics who addressed themselves more directly to protest and reform. One of the most influential of these reformers was Henry George, a journalist who vowed to seek out the cause of poverty in the midst of the industrial progress he saw around him. The basic social problem, George reasoned, was the unearned increment in wealth that came to those who owned the land. He wrote down the fruit of his thought in *Progress and Poverty* (1879), a thick, rambling, and difficult book whose earnest moralism and sympathetic tone helped it sell about 2 million copies in several languages.

George held that everyone had a basic right to the use of the land, since it was provided by nature to all. Nobody had a right to the increasing value that accrued from the land, since that was created by the community, not by its owner. Labor and capital, on the other hand, did have a just claim on the wealth they produced. He proposed simply to tax the unearned increment in the value of the land, or the rent.

George's "single-tax" idea was intended to free capital and labor from paying tribute for the land, and to put to use lands previously held out of production by speculators. George's idea provoked much discussion and actually affected local tax policy here and there, but his influence on the thinking of the day came less from his "single-tax" panacea than from the paradox he posed in his title *Progress and Poverty,* and his plea for social cooperation and equality.

The journalist and freelance writer Henry Demarest Lloyd, son of a minister, addressed himself to what many found a more vital issue than Henry George's, not the monopoly in land but in industry. His best-known book, *Wealth Against Commonwealth* (1894), drew on more than a decade of studying the Standard Oil Company. Lloyd, like George and Lester Frank Ward, saw the key to social progress in cooperation rather than competition. Economic activities in their cooperative aspects demonstrated a civilizing process, he argued. The cooperative principle should be applied "to all toils in which private sovereignty has become through monopoly a despotism over the public." Where monopoly had developed, it should be transferred to public operation in the public interest. In 1903, just before his death, Lloyd joined the Socialist party.

Thorstein Veblen brought to his social criticism a background of formal training in economics and a purpose of making economics more an evolutionary or historical science. By all accounts he taught miserably, even inaudibly, and seldom held a job for long, but he wrote brilliantly. In his best known work, *The Theory of the Leisure Class* (1899), he examined the pecuniary values of the affluent and introduced phrases that have since become commonplace in our language: "conspicuous consumption" and "conspicuous leisure." With the advent of industrial society, Veblen argued, the showy display of money and property became the conventional basis of status. For the upper classes, moreover, it became necessary to spend time casually as evidence of the ability to afford a life of leisure.

THE SOCIAL GOSPEL

While novelists, journalists, and commentators were writing about the rising social tensions and injustices of late-nineteenth-century

America, more and more people were addressing these problems through direct social action. Some reformers focused on legislative solutions to social problems; others stressed philanthropy or organized charity. A few militants promoted socialism or anarchism. Whatever the method or approach, however, social reformers were on the march at the turn of the century, and their activities gave to American life a new urgency and energy.

RISE OF THE INSTITUTIONAL CHURCH The churches responded slowly to the mounting social criticism, for American Protestantism had become one of the main props of the established order. The Reverend Henry Ward Beecher, for instance, pastor of the fashionable Plymouth Congregational Church in Brooklyn, preached material success, social Darwinism, and the unworthiness of the poor.

As the middle classes moved out to the streetcar suburbs, their churches followed. In the years 1868–1888, for instance, seventeen Protestant churches abandoned the areas south of Fourteenth Street in Manhattan. In the center of Chicago 60,000 residents had no church, Protestant or Catholic. Where churches became prosperous they fell under the spell of complacent respectability and do-nothing social Darwinism. Some prominent clergymen expressed open disdain for the lower classes. De Witt Talmage, an outspoken Presbyterian minister in Brooklyn, stressed that he wanted no working men stinking up his church. "If you are going to kill the church thus with bad smells, I will have nothing to do with this work of evangelization." Not surprisingly, more and more working-class people felt out of place in churches where affluence was both worshipped and flaunted.

But gradually some religious leaders realized that Protestantism was in danger of losing its working-class constituency unless it reached out to the urban poor. Two organizations were created expressly for that purpose. The Young Men's Christian Association had entered the United States from England in the 1850s and grew rapidly after 1870; the Salvation Army, founded in London in 1876, entered the United States four years later. Individual urban churches also began to develop institutional features that were more social than strictly religious in function. Church buildings acquired gymnasiums, libraries, lecture rooms, and other facilities in an effort to attract working-class people back to organized religion.

A Salvation Army group in Flint, Michigan, 1894.

RELIGIOUS REFORMERS   Some church reformers who feared that Christianity was becoming irrelevant to the needs and aspirations of the working poor began preaching what came to be called the social gospel. One of the earliest, Washington Gladden of Columbus, Ohio, managed to profess the social gospel from the pulpit of a middle-class Congregational church. The new gospel in fact expressed the social conscience of the middle class. Gladden maintained that true Christianity resided not in rituals, dogmas, or even in the mystical experience of God, but in the principle that "Thou shalt love thy neighbor as thyself." Christian law should therefore govern the workplace, with laborer and employer united in serving each other's interest. The "law of greed and strife," he insisted, "is not a natural law; it is unnatural; it is a crime against nature; the law of brotherhood is the only natural law." He thus argued for labor's right to organize, supported maximum-hours laws and factory inspections, and endorsed antitrust legislation.

THE CATHOLIC CHURCH   In the post–Civil War years Catholic social thought was initially quite conservative. Papal decrees declared erroneous such current ideas as progress, liberalism, rationalism, and so-

cialism, and warned American Catholics against supporting the new social movements. The Vatican's outlook altered drastically in 1891, when
Pope Leo XIII issued his encyclical, *Rerum novarum* ("Of modern
things"). This new expression of Catholic social doctrine upheld private
property as a natural right but condemned capitalism where it had imposed poverty and degradation on workers. It also affirmed the right of
Catholics to join labor unions and socialist movements insofar as these
were not antireligious. But American Catholics for the most part remained isolated from organized reform movements until the twentieth
century, though they themselves were among the most abused victims
of urban slums.

EARLY EFFORTS AT URBAN REFORM

THE SETTLEMENT HOUSE MOVEMENT While preachers of the social gospel dispensed inspiration, other dedicated reformers attacked
the problems of the slums from residential and community centers
called settlement houses. By 1900 perhaps a hundred settlement houses
existed in America, some of the best known being Jane Addams and

Jane Addams.

Ellen Starr's Hull House in Chicago and Lillian Wald's Henry Street Settlement in New York.

The settlement houses were staffed mainly by idealistic middle-class young people, a majority of them college-trained women who had few other outlets for meaningful work. Settlement workers sought to broaden the horizons and improve the lives of slum dwellers in diverse ways. At Hull House, for instance, workers sought to draw the neighborhood children into clubs, kindergartens, and a nursery, which served the infant children of working mothers. Settlement houses were also meant to provide workingmen an alternative to the saloon as a place of recreation and an alternative to the political boss as a source of social services. Their programs gradually expanded to include health clinics, lectures, music and art studios, employment bureaus, men's clubs, training in skills such as bookbinding, gymnasiums, and savings banks.

Addams and other settlement house leaders realized, however, that the spreading slums made their work as effective as bailing out the ocean with a teaspoon. They therefore organized political support for housing laws, public playgrounds, juvenile courts, mothers' pensions, workers' compensation laws, and legislation against child labor. Julia Lathrop, another Hull House staffer, was appointed in 1912 the first head of the federal Children's Bureau, an agency designed to scrutinize the use and abuse of child labor.

THE WOMEN'S SUFFRAGE MOVEMENT   Settlement house workers, insofar as they were paid, made up but a fraction of all gainfully employed women. With rapid population growth in the late nineteenth century the number of employed women steadily increased, as did their percentage of the labor force. The greatest leaps forward came in the decades of the 1880s and the 1900s, both of which were also peak decades of immigration, a correlation that can be explained by the immigrants' need for income. The number of employed women doubled from 1880 to 1900 and then doubled again by 1910. Through all those years domestic work remained the largest category of employment for women; teaching and nursing also remained among the leading fields. The main change was that clerical work (bookkeeping, stenographic work, and the like) and sales jobs became increasingly available to women.

These changes in occupational status had little connection with the women's rights movement, which increasingly focused on the issue of suffrage. Immediately after the Civil War, Susan B. Anthony, a seasoned veteran of the movement, demanded that the Fourteenth Amendment guarantee the vote for women as well as black males. She made little impression on the defenders of masculine prerogative, however, who insisted that women belonged solely in the home. "Their mission is at home, by their blandishments and their love to assuage the passions of men as they come in from the battle of life. . . ." said a New Jersey senator.

In 1869 the unity of the women's movement disintegrated in a manner reminiscent of the antislavery rift three decades before. The question once again was whether the movement should concentrate on one overriding issue or broaden its focus. Anthony and Elizabeth Cady Stanton founded the National Woman Suffrage Association to promote a woman suffrage amendment to the Constitution, but they looked upon suffrage as but one among many feminist causes to be promoted. Later that same year, Lucy Stone, Julia Ward Howe, and other leaders formed the American Woman Suffrage Association, which focused single-mindedly on the vote as the first and basic reform.

The long struggle for state legislation on the suffrage issue focused the women's cause ever more on the primary objective of the vote. In 1890, after three years of negotiation, the rival groups united as the National American Woman Suffrage Association, with Elizabeth Cady Stanton as president for two years, followed by Susan B. Anthony until 1900. The work thereafter was carried on by a new generation led by Anna Howard Shaw and Carrie Chapman Catt. Over the years the movement slogged its way to some local and some partial victories, as a few states granted woman suffrage in school board or municipal elections. In 1869 the Territory of Wyoming granted full suffrage to women, and after 1890 retained woman suffrage as a new state. Three other western states soon followed suit, but not until New York acted in 1917 did a state east of the Mississippi adopt universal suffrage.

Despite the focus on the vote, women did not confine their public work to that issue. In 1866 a Young Women's Christian Association, a parallel to the YMCA, appeared in Boston and spread elsewhere. The New England Women's Club, started in 1868 by Julia Ward Howe and others, was an early example of the women's clubs that then proliferated to the extent that a General Federation of Women's Clubs tied

Carrie Chapman Catt, a leader in the women's suffrage movement.

them together in 1890. Many women's clubs confined themselves to "literary" and social activities, but others became deeply involved in charities and reform. The New York Consumers League, formed in 1890, and the National Consumers League, formed nine years later, sought to make the buying public, chiefly women, better aware of degrading labor conditions.

GROWTH OF THE WELFARE STATE   Even without the support of voting women in most places, the states groped toward rudimentary measures to regulate big business and labor conditions in the public interest. By the end of the century nearly every state had provided for the regulation of railroads, if not always effectively, and had moved to supervise banks and insurance companies. Between 1887 and 1897, by one count, the states and territories passed more than 1,600 laws relating to conditions of work that limited the hours of labor, provided special protection for women, limited or forbade child labor, required regular wage payments in cash, called for factory inspections, and outlawed blacklisting or the importation of "Pinkerton men." Still, the effect of the effort was limited by poor enforcement and by conservative judges who ruled that the Constitution protected employers from many such attempts at state regulation.

As the turn of the century neared, opinion in the country stood poised between conservative rigidities and a growing sense that new conditions impose new personal and governmental responsibilities. The last two decades of the nineteenth century had already seen a slow erosion of free-market values that had found their most secure home in the courts. There emerged instead a concept of the general-welfare state, which called upon the government to act on behalf of the whole society rather than allow rugged individualism to run rampant. The conflict between this notion and laissez-faire values spilled over into the new century, but by the mid-twentieth century, after the Progressive Movement and the New Deal, the nation would be firmly committed to the premises of the general-welfare state.

MAKING CONNECTIONS

- As the next chapter shows, the presidential election of 1896 was in many ways a contest between the new urban values discussed in this chapter and those of a more traditional rural American society.

- The reform impulse you've read about in this chapter finds voice again in the discussion of the Progressive movement in Chapter 23.

- The nativist thinking discussed in this chapter fueled the immigration restriction laws enacted in the 1920s (Chapter 25).

FURTHER READING

Surveys of urbanization include Eric H. Monkkonen's *America Becomes Urban* (1988) and Charles N. Glaab and A. Theodore Brown's *A History of Urban America* (3rd ed., 1983).* Gunther P. Barth discusses the emergence of a new urban culture in *City People: The Rise of*

Modern City Culture in Nineteenth Century America (1980).* On city planning, see Stanley K. Schultz's *Constructing Urban Culture: American Cities and City Planning, 1800–1920* (1989).

Immigration has an extensive scholarship. General surveys include Leonard Dinnerstein and David M. Reimer's *Ethnic Americans: A History of Immigration and Assimilation* (2nd ed., 1982)* and Alan M. Kraut's *The Huddled Masses* (1982).* John Bodnar presents a synthesis of the urban immigrant experience in *The Transplanted: A History of Immigrants in Urban America* (1985).

For trends in higher education, consult Laurence Veysey's *The Emergence of the American Univeristy* (1965).* Burton J. Bledstein's *The Culture of Professionalism: The Middle Class and the Development of Higher Education in America* (1976)* is particularly insightful. For the growth of urban leisure and sports, see Stephen A. Riess's *City Games: The Evolution of American Urban Society and the Rise of Sports* (1989).

Richard Hofstadter's *Social Darwinism in American Thought* (rev. ed., 1955)* and Cynthia E. Russett's *Darwin in America* (1976)* examine the impact of the theory of evolution. On the rise of realism in thought and the arts during the second half of the nineteenth century, see David Shi's *Facing Facts: Realism in American Thought and Culture* (1995).*

John L. Thomas's *Alternative America: Henry George, Edward Bellamy, Henry Demarest Lloyd, and the Adversary Tradition* (1983) and Nick Salvatore's *Eugene V. Debs: Citizen and Socialist* (1982)* provide the best introductions to the social critics of the time.

William L. O'Neill's *Everyone Was Brave: The Rise and Fall of Feminism in America* (1969) and Eleanor Flexner's *Century of Struggle: The Women's Rights Movement in the United States* (rev. ed., 1975)* present good introductions to the condition of women in the late nineteenth century.

*These books are available in paperback editions.

21 GILDED-AGE POLITICS AND AGRARIAN REVOLT

CHAPTER ORGANIZER

This chapter focuses on:

- political developments in the Gilded Age

- problems, both real and perceived, affecting American farmers

- the rise of the agrarian revolt and the Populists

- the significant election of 1896

PARADOXICAL POLITICS

In 1873 Mark Twain and Charles Dudley Warner created an enduring label for the post–Civil War era when they collaborated on a novel entitled *The Gilded Age*. The book depicted an age of widespread political corruption, personal greed, and social vulgarity. Perspectives on the times would eventually change, but generations of political scientists and historians have since reinforced the two novelists' judgment. As a young college graduate in 1879 Woodrow Wilson described the state of the American political system: "No leaders, no principles; no principles, no parties." His contemporary, the historian Henry Adams, shared his view. "The period," he groused, "was poor in purpose and barren in results." Indeed, the real movers and shakers of the Gilded Age were not the men who sat in the White House or the Congress but the captains of industry who flung railroads across the continent and decorated its cities with their plumed smokestacks and gaudy mansions.

On the national issues of the day the major parties pursued for the most part a policy of evasion. Only the tariff provoked clear-cut divisions between protectionist Republicans and low-tariff Democrats, but there were individual exceptions even on that. On questions of the currency, regulation of big business, farm problems, civil service reform, and immigration the parties differed very little.

Two factors, above all, accounted for the muddled politics of this period. Americans had before them the fearsome lesson of what had happened in 1860, when parties had taken clear-cut stands on a deeply felt moral issue, with bloody consequences. But the more compelling cause of political inertia was the even division between the parties. From 1869 to 1913, from the presidencies of Grant to Taft, Republicans monopolized the White House except during the two nonconsecutive terms of Grover Cleveland, but Republican domination was more apparent than real. Between 1872 and 1896 no president won a majority of the popular vote. And while Republicans usually controlled the Senate, Democrats usually controlled the House. Only during 1881–1883 and 1889–1891 did a Republican president have a Republican Congress. And only between 1893 and 1895 did a Democratic president enjoy a Democratic Congress.

Deferential presidents also contributed to the political stalemate. No chief executive between Lincoln and Theodore Roosevelt could be described as a "strong" president. None seriously challenged the prevailing view that the formulation of public policy belonged to Congress. Senator John Sherman of Ohio expressed the widely held notion that the legislative branch should be primary in a republic: "The President should merely obey and enforce the laws." At the same time, the almost equal strength of the parties in Congress worked against any vigorous new initiatives there, since most bills required bipartisan support to pass both houses and legislators tended to vote along party lines. Under such static conditions, the parties became machines for seeking office and dispensing patronage in the form of government jobs and contracts.

An alliance of business and politics was characteristic of the period. This was not necessarily corrupt, since many a politician favored busi-

The Bosses of the Senate. *This 1889 cartoon bitingly portrays the alliance between big business and politics in this period.*

ness interests out of conviction. Nor was the public as sensitive to conflicts of interest as it would be later. James G. Blaine of Maine, for example, and many of his supporters saw nothing wrong in his accepting stock from an Arkansas railroad after helping it win a land grant from Congress. Railroad passes, free entertainment, and a host of other favors were freely accepted by politicians, editors, and other leaders in positions to influence public opinion.

POLITICS AND THE VOTERS   But if many observers considered this a time of political mediocrity in which the parties refused to face up to such "real issues" as the growth of an unregulated economy and its attendant social injustices, it is nonetheless clear that the voters of the time thought more was at stake. Voter turnout during the Gilded Age was commonly about 70–80 percent, even in the South, where the disfranchisement of blacks was not yet complete. (By contrast, the turnout for the 1992 presidential election was barely 50 percent.) How was it then that leaders who failed to face up to the real issues presided over the most highly organized and politically active electorate in American history?

The answer is partly that the politicians and the voters deeply believed that they *were* dealing with crucial issues: the tariff, monopolies, the currency, civil service reform, and immigration. Yet what most motivated party loyalties and voter turnout in these years were intense cultural conflicts among ethnic and religious groups. The Republican party attracted mainly Protestants of British descent. Their native seat was New England, and their other strongholds were New York and the upper Middle West, both of which were populated with Yankee stock. Legitimate heirs to the abolitionist tradition, Republicans drew to their ranks a host of reformers and moralists, spiritual descendants of the perfectionists who championed the revivals and the reform movements of the antebellum years. The party's heritage of anti-Catholic nativism would also make a comeback in the 1880s. And the Republicans could also rely on the votes of blacks and Union veterans of the Civil War.

The Democrats, by contrast, tended to be a heterogeneous, often unruly coalition embracing southern whites, immigrants and Catholics of any origin, Jews, freethinkers, skeptics, and all those repelled by the "party of morality." As one Chicago Democrat explained, "A Republican is a man who wants you t' go t' church every Sunday. A Democrat says if a man wants to have a glass of beer on Sunday he can have it."

In the Midwest especially, tensions over religious and social issues, such as Sunday closing laws and liquor prohibition, created sharp political allegiances. Republicans pressed nativist causes, calling for restrictions on immigration and on the employment of foreigners, and greater emphasis on the teaching of the "American" language in the schools. Prohibitionism revived along with nativism in the 1880s. Among the immigrants who crowded into the growing cities were many Irish, Germans, and Italians who enjoyed alcoholic beverages. Republicans increasingly saw saloons as the central social evil around which all others revolved, including vice, crime, political corruption, and neglect of families, and they associated these ethnic groups with the problem.

CORRUPTION AND REFORM

While grassroots Republicans and Democrats differed over ethnic and cultural issues, their party leaders squabbled over the so-called "spoils" of office. Each party had its share of corrupt officials willing to buy and sell government appointments or congressional votes, yet each also witnessed the emergence of factions promoting honesty in government. This struggle for clean government soon became one of the foremost issues of the day.

HAYES AND CIVIL SERVICE REFORM   In the aftermath of Reconstruction, Rutherford B. Hayes admirably embodied the "party of morality." Hayes brought to the White House in 1877 a new style of uprightness, a sharp contrast to the graft and corruption of the Grant administration. The son of an Ohio farmer, Hayes became one of the early Republicans, was wounded four times in the Civil War, and was promoted to major-general. Elected governor of Ohio in 1867, he served three terms. Honest and respectable, competent and dignified, he lived in a modest style with his wife, who was nicknamed "Lemonade Lucy" because of her refusal to serve alcohol at White House functions.

Yet Hayes's tenure as president suffered from the manner of his defeat of Tilden in the 1876–1877 election. Snide references to him as "His Fraudulence" dogged his steps and denied him any chance at a second term, which he renounced from the beginning. Hayes's own party was split between so-called Stalwarts and Half-Breeds, led respectively by Senators Roscoe Conkling of New York and James G. Blaine of Maine. The difference between these Republican factions was murkier than that between the parties. The Stalwarts generally supported Grant, a Radical southern policy, and the spoils system. The Half-Breeds took a contrary view on the first two and even vaguely supported civil service reform.

For the most part, the Stalwart and Half-Breed factions were loose alliances designed to advance the careers of Conkling and Blaine. The two men could not abide one another. Blaine once referred to Conkling as displaying a "majestic, supereminent, overpowering, turkey-gobbler strut." He was right. Tall and lordly, with a pointed beard, thick, auburn hair, and upturned jaw and nose, Conkling boasted good looks, fine clothes, and an arrogant manner. He dressed and lived flamboyantly, sporting pastel bow ties, silk scarves, moon-colored vests, and patent leather shoes. Yet for all his sartorial splendor and glamorous facade, he was always a ruthless power broker. Conkling viewed politics as a brute struggle for control, and its arena was no place for faint hearts. Politics "is a rotten business," he declared. "Nothing counts except to win."

Hayes thought otherwise, and he aligned himself with the growing public discontent over the corruption and jobbery that had prevailed under Grant. In promoting the cause of civil service reform, he issued an Executive Order in 1877 that declared that those already in office would be dismissed only for the good of the government and not for political reasons. His cabinet tried to carry out the new policy. Secretary of the Treasury John Sherman revealed that both collector Chester A. Arthur and naval officer Alonzo Cornell were guilty of "laxity" and of using the New York Customs House for political management on behalf of Conkling's organization. Hayes removed Arthur and Cornell, and thereby won Conkling's lasting hatred.

For all his efforts to clean house, Hayes retained a limited vision of government's role. On the economic issues of the day he held to a conservative line that would guide his successors for the rest of the century. His solution to labor troubles, demonstrated during the Great Railroad Strike of 1877, was to send in troops and break the strike. A financial conservative, he denied the demands of farmers and debtors for an expansion of the currency by vetoing the Bland-Allison Act. Passed over his veto, the bill enacted a limited expansion of silver currency through the government's purchase for coinage of $2 million to $4 million worth of silver per month.

GARFIELD AND ARTHUR   With Hayes unavailable for a second term, the Republicans were forced to look elsewhere in 1880. The Stalwarts, led by Conkling, brought Grant forward for a third time, still a strong contender despite the tarnish of his administration's scandals. For two days the Republican convention in Chicago was deadlocked, with Grant holding a slight lead over Blaine and John Sherman. On the thirty-fifth ballot, Wisconsin suddenly switched sixteen votes to former House Speaker (now Senator-elect) James A. Garfield, Sherman's campaign manager. Garfield rose to protest but was ruled out of order, and on the next ballot the convention stampeded to the dark-horse candidate. As a sop to the Stalwarts, the convention tapped Chester A. Arthur, of Custom House notoriety, for vice-president.

The Democrats named Winfield Scott Hancock, a Union commander at Gettysburg, to counterbalance the Republicans' Brigadier-General Garfield and thus ward off "bloody-shirt" attacks on their party as the vehicle of secession. The election turned out to be the closest of the century. Garfield eked out a plurality of only 39,000 votes with 48.5 percent of the vote, but with a comfortable margin of 214 to 155 in the electoral college.

An Ohio native, Garfield had distinguished himself as a soldier during the Civil War, and was mustered out as a general when he entered Congress in 1863. Noted for his oratory and parliamentary skills, he became one of the outstanding leaders in the House and eventually its Speaker.

On July 2, 1881, President Garfield was leaving on a vacation in New England when, as he walked through the Baltimore rail station, a deranged office seeker named Charles Guiteau shot him in the back. "I am a Stalwart," Guiteau shouted to the arresting officers. "Arthur is now President of the United States." Guiteau's announcement would prove crippling to the Stalwarts and his attack fatal to Garfield, who died after a two-month struggle. Garfield had been president for a little over six months.

One of the chief henchmen of Stalwart leader Roscoe Conkling was now president. Little in Chester Arthur's past suggested that he would rise above spoils politics. A native of Vermont and a Phi Beta Kappa graduate of Union College, he had made a political career in appointive offices, most notably as New York's collector of customs from 1871 to 1878.

But Arthur, a wealthy, handsome widower who loved fine wines and sported a lavish wardrobe and billowing sideburns, demonstrated surprising leadership qualities as president. He distanced himself from Conkling and the Stalwarts and established a genuine independence, almost a necessity after Guiteau's announcement. As Arthur noted, "For the vice-presidency I was indebted to Mr. Conkling, but for the presidency of the United States my debt is to the Almighty."

Most startling of all was Arthur's emergence as something of a civil service and tariff reformer. Stalwarts had every reason to expect him to oppose such changes, but instead he allied himself with the reformers. While the assassin Guiteau had unwittingly added a certain urgency to the public support of reform, the defeat of a reform bill in 1882 sponsored by "Gentleman George" Pendleton, Democratic senator from Ohio, aroused public opinion further. The Pendleton Civil Service Act finally passed in January 1883, setting up a three-member Civil Service Commission independent from the regular cabinet departments, the first such federal agency established on a permanent basis. About 14 percent of all government jobs would now be filled on the basis of competitive examinations rather than political connections. What was more, the president could enlarge the class of affected jobs at his discretion, as many later did.

Meanwhile the tariff continued to be the most controversial political issue. The high protective tariff, a heritage of the Civil War, had by the early 1880s raised revenues to the point that the government actually enjoyed a surplus that drew money into the Treasury and out of circulation, thus impeding economic growth. Some argued that lower tariff rates would reduce prices and the cost of living, and at the same time leave more money in circulation. In 1882 Arthur named a special commission to study the problem. The Tariff Commission recommended a 20–25 percent rate reduction, which gained Arthur's support, but Congress's effort to enact the proposal was marred by logrolling (the trading of votes to benefit different legislators' local interests). The result was the "Mongrel Tariff" of 1883, so called because of its diverse percentages for different commodities. Overall the tariff provided for a slight rate reduction, but it actually raised the duty on some articles.

SCURRILOUS CAMPAIGN   When the 1884 election came around, Arthur's record might have commended him to the voters, but it did not please the leaders of his party. The Republicans dumped Arthur and turned to the majestic Senator James G. Blaine of Maine, leader of the Half-Breeds. Blaine was the consummate politician. He never forgot a name or a face, he inspired the party faithful with his oratory, and at the same time he knew how to wheel and deal in the back rooms.

Back in 1876 Blaine had been nominated for the presidency by a Republican official who, in an eloquent flight of oratory, had announced: "Like an armed warrior, like a plumed knight, James G. Blaine marched down the halls of American Congress and threw his shining lance full and fair against the brazen forehead of the defamers of his country and maligners of his honor." To his followers in 1884 Blaine remained the "plumed knight," with a strikingly long, pale face animated by dark eyes and anchored in a silvery beard. But Democratic newspapers portrayed him as the plumed knave. The "maligners of his honor" were those who claimed that Blaine had engaged in corrupt dealings with Arkansas railroad barons, selling his votes on measures favorable to their interests.

Such charges were based on references contained in the so-called Mulligan letters.

During the campaign more letters surfaced with disclosures embarrassing to Blaine. For the reform element of the Republican party, this was too much, and many bolted the ticket. Party regulars scorned the idealists as "goo-goos"—the "good-government" crowd who ignored partisan realities—and one editor jokingly tagged them Mugwumps, after an Algonquian word meaning a great chieftain. To the party regulars, in what soon became a stale joke, Mugwumps were unreliable Republicans who had their "mugs" on one side of the fence and their "wumps" on the other.

The rise of the Mugwumps, however, influenced the Democrats to nominate Stephen Grover Cleveland as a reform candidate. Cleveland had a rapid rise from obscurity to prominence. One of many children in the family of a New York Presbyterian minister, he had been forced by his father's death to go to work at an early age. He got a job as clerk in a law office, read law, passed the bar examination, became an assistant state attorney-general in New York in 1863 and later sheriff of Erie County. Elected mayor of Buffalo in 1881, Cleveland first attracted national attention for effectively battling graft and corruption in that city. In 1882 the Democrats elected him governor, and he continued to build a reform record by fighting New York's corrupt Tammany Hall organization. As mayor and as governor he repeatedly vetoed what he considered special-privilege bills serving selfish interests.

A stocky 250-pound man with a droopy mustache, Cleveland seemed the stolid opposite of Blaine. He possessed little charisma, but impressed the public with his stubborn integrity. Cleveland was a crusader against government and corporate corruption, and as such he drew to him many of those making up the growing chorus of reformers. One supporter said: "We love him for the enemies he has made."

Then the *Buffalo Evening Telegraph* revealed some of bachelor Cleveland's escapades during the early 1870s with a tall, attractive Buffalo widow, Maria Halpin, who managed the cloak department in a department store. Mrs. Halpin had named Cleveland as the father of a boy born to her in 1874. Cleveland took responsibility and provided financial help when the child was placed in an orphanage. When supporters asked Cleveland what to say about the affair, he answered with typical candor: "Tell the truth." The respective personal escapades of Blaine and Cleveland provided the 1884 campaign with some of the most colorful battle cries in American political history. "Blaine, Blaine, James G. Blaine, the continental liar from the state of Maine," Democrats chanted. Republicans countered with "Ma, ma, where's my pa? Gone to the White House, ha, ha, ha!"

Near the end of the campaign Blaine and his supporters committed two fateful blunders. The first occurred at New York's fashionable Delmonico's restaurant, where Blaine attended a lavish fund-raising dinner with a clutch of millionaire bigwigs, including robber barons. Cartoons and accounts of this "Belshazzar's Feast" festooned the opposition press for days. The second fiasco cost Blaine much of the Irish vote when a Protestant minister visiting Republican headquarters in New York insolently referred to the Democrats as the party of "rum, Romanism, and rebellion." A Cleveland campaign worker heard the remark and rushed back to his headquarters. Blaine, who was present, let it pass and perhaps failed to catch the implied insult to Irish Catholics—a fatal oversight, since he had always cultivated Irish-American support with his anti-British talk and public reminders that his mother was Catholic. Democrats spread word that he had let the insult pass, even that he had made it himself.

The two incidents may have tipped the election. The electoral vote in Cleveland's favor stood at 219 to 182, but the popular vote ran far closer; Cleveland's plurality was fewer than 30,000 votes.

CLEVELAND AND THE SPECIAL INTERESTS   For all of Cleveland's hostility to the spoils system and politics as usual, he represented no sharp break with the conservative policies of his Republican predecessors, except in opposing governmental favors to business. He held to a strictly limited view of government's role in both economic and social matters, a rigid philosophy illustrated by his 1887 veto of a bill to aid drought-stricken farmers. Back to Congress it went with a lecture on the need to limit the powers and functions of government—"though the people support the government, the government should not support the people," Cleveland asserted.

Despite his strong convictions, Cleveland had a mixed record on the civil service. He harbored good intentions, but he also headed a party with its first president since Buchanan, and many partisans were eager to gain government jobs. Before his inauguration he repeated his support for the Pendleton Act, and he pledged not to remove able government workers on partisan grounds. But party pressures gradually forced Cleveland's hand. To a friend he remarked: "The damned everlasting clatter for office continues . . . and makes me feel like resigning." When he left office about two-thirds of the federal officeholders were Democrats, but at the same time Cleveland had almost doubled the number of jobs on the civil service list. He thereby satisfied neither Mugwumps nor spoilsmen; indeed, he managed to antagonize both.

Cleveland incurred the wrath of many Union military veterans by his firm stand against expanded pensions. Congress had passed the first Civil War pension law in 1862 to provide for veterans disabled in service and for the widows, orphans, and dependents of veterans. By 1882 the Grand Army of the Republic, an organization of Union veterans and a powerful pressure group, was trying to get pensions paid for any disability, no matter how it was incurred. Meanwhile, many veterans succeeded in getting legislators to pass private pension bills. Insofar as time permitted, Cleveland examined such bills critically and vetoed the dubious ones. Although he signed more than any of his predecessors, he also vetoed more. The issue climaxed in 1887 when Cleveland vetoed a new Dependent Pension bill containing more liberal benefits and qualifications. Cleveland argued that it would become a refuge for frauds rather than a "roll of honor."

About the middle of his term Cleveland set out after new special interests by advocating an important new policy, railroad regulation. Since the late 1860s state after state had adopted regulatory railroad laws, and from the early 1870s Congress had debated federal legislation. In 1886 a Supreme Court decision finally spurred action. In the case of *Wabash Railroad v. Illinois,* the Court ruled that a state could not regulate rates on interstate traffic. Cleveland urged that since this "important field of control and regulation [has] thus been left entirely unoccupied," Congress should act.

It did, and in 1887 Cleveland signed into law an act creating the Interstate Commerce Commission (ICC), the first such independent federal regulatory commission. The law required that all freight and passenger rates be "reasonable and just," and it empowered the ICC to investigate carriers and prosecute violators. Railroads were also forbidden to grant secret rebates to preferred shippers, discriminate against persons, places, and commodities, or enter into pools (agreements to fix rates). The commission's actual powers, however, proved to be weak when first tested in the courts. Though creating the ICC seemed to conflict with Cleveland's fear of big government, it accorded with his wariness of big business. The Interstate Commerce Act, to his mind, was a legitimate exercise of sovereign power. To Jay Gould and other railroad owners, it was a means of defusing growing public outrage while not truly hurting corporations. "Let it go," Gould advised, "or we will get a worse dose next season."

THE TARIFF ISSUE   Cleveland's most dramatic challenge to special interests came in his efforts to spur tariff reform. Why was the tariff such an important and controversial issue? By the late nineteenth century, many observers had concluded that the formation of huge corporate "trusts" was not a natural development of a maturing capitalist system. Instead, they charged that government policies had fostered big business at the expense of small producers and retailers. Among those policies was an excessively high protective tariff. "The mother of all trusts is the tariff bill," proclaimed one leading business executive. By shielding American manufacturers from foreign competition, the tariff, critics argued, made it easier for them to combine into ever-larger entities. High tariff rates also enabled big corporations to restrict production and fix prices. "The heart of the trust problem is in our tariff system of plunder," declared the head of the New England Free Trade League. "The quickest and most certain way of reaching the evils of trusts is not by direct legislation against them, or by constitutional amendment, but by the abolition of tariff duties."

Cleveland agreed. Having decided that the rates were too high and included many inequities, he sought to dramatize the issue near the end of 1887 by devoting his entire annual message to the subject. He did so in full knowledge that he was walking onto a political minefield on the eve of an election year. "What is the use of being elected if you don't stand for something?" he asked skeptical advisers.

Cleveland's message noted that tariff revenues had bolstered the federal surplus, making the Treasury "a hoarding place for money needlessly withdrawn from trade and the people's use." The high tariff pushed up prices for everybody and benefited only a few politically powerful manufacturing interests. The wise solution was to spur Congress to look at the more than 4,000 items on the tariff list with an eye to eliminating as many as possible and lowering all the remaining duties.

The House soon passed a bill calling for modest tariff reductions from an average level of about 47 percent of the value of imported goods to about 40 percent. But the bill stalled in the Republican Senate and finally died a lingering death in committee. If Cleveland's tariff proposal accomplished his purpose of drawing party lines more firmly, it also confirmed the fears of his advisers. The election of 1888 for the first time in years highlighted a sharp difference between the major parties on an issue of substance.

THE ELECTION OF 1888   Cleveland was the nominee of his party, whose platform endorsed "the views expressed by the President in his last message to Congress." The Republicans passed up old warhorses such as Blaine and Sherman and turned to the obscure Benjamin Harrison, who had all the attributes of availability. Grandson of a former president, a flourishing lawyer in Indiana, the diminutive Harrison resided in a pivotal state. He also boasted a good war record, and there was little in his political record to offend any voter. The Republican platform accepted Cleveland's challenge to make the protective tariff the chief issue, and promised generous pensions to veterans.

The campaign thus became the first waged mainly on the tariff issue. As insurance against tariff reduction, manufacturers obligingly larded Harrison's campaign fund, which was used to denounce Cleveland's un-American "free-trade" stance and his pension vetoes.

On the eve of the election Cleveland suffered a devastating blow from a dirty campaign trick. Posing as an English immigrant and using the false name Charles F. Murchison, a California Republican had written British Minister Sir Lionel Sackville-West and asked his advice on how to vote. Sackville-West hinted in reply that he should vote for Cleveland. Published two weeks before the election, the "Murchison letter" aroused a storm of protest against foreign intervention and further linked Cleveland to British free-traders.

Still, the outcome in 1888 was very close. Cleveland won the popular vote by 5,538,000 to 5,447,000, but that was poor comfort. The distribution was such that Harrison, with the key states of Indiana and New York on his side, carried the electoral college by 233 to 168. For the first time since John Quincy Adams's election in 1824, the country had not only a minority president, but one who lacked even a plurality in the popular vote.

REPUBLICAN REFORM UNDER HARRISON   Harrison became a competent and earnest figurehead, overshadowed by his secretary of state, James G. Blaine. His first step was to reward those responsible for his victory. He owed a heavy debt to the old-soldier vote, which he discharged by naming the head of the veterans' group to the office of pension commissioner. "God help the surplus," the new commissioner reportedly exclaimed, and proceeded to approve pensions with such abandon that the secretary of the interior removed him six months and several million dollars later. In 1890 Congress passed, and Harrison signed, the Dependent Pension Act, substantially the same measure that Cleveland had vetoed three years earlier. Any veteran unable to make a living by manual labor for whatever reason was granted a monthly pension. The pension rolls almost doubled by 1893, as did the program's costs.

During the first two years of Harrison's term, the Republicans controlled the presidency and both houses of Congress for the only time in the twenty years between 1875 and 1895. They made the most of their clout. During 1890 several significant pieces of legislation made their way to the White House for Harrison's signature. In addition to the Dependent Pension Act, Congress and the president approved the Sherman Anti-trust Act, the Sherman Silver Purchase Act, the McKinley Tariff, and the admission of the last of the "omnibus states," Idaho and Wyoming, which followed the admission of the Dakotas, Montana, and Washington in 1889.

Both parties had pledged themselves to do something about the growing power of trusts and monopolies. The Sherman Anti-trust Act, named for Senator John Sherman, chairman of the committee that drafted it, forbade contracts, combinations, or conspiracies in restraint of trade or in the effort to establish monopolies in interstate or foreign commerce. A broad consensus put the law through, but its passage turned out to be largely symbolic. During the next decade successive administrations expended little effort on the act's enforcement. From 1890 to 1901 the Justice Department instituted only eighteen antitrust suits, and four of those were against labor unions.

Congress meanwhile debated currency legislation against the backdrop of growing distress in the farm regions of the West and South. Hard-pressed farmers were now agitating for an increased coinage of silver to inflate the currency supply. They sought to raise commodity prices, making it easier for farmers to earn the money with which to pay their debts. The silverite forces were also strengthened, especially in the Senate, by members from those new states that had silver-mining interests. Congress thus passed the Sherman Silver Purchase Act of 1890, replacing the Bland-Allison Act of 1878. It required the Treasury to purchase 4.5 million ounces of silver each month and to issue in payment Treasury notes redeemable in either gold or silver. But the act failed to satisfy the demands of the silverites. Although it doubled the amount of silver purchased, that was still too little to have much inflationary impact on the economy. The stage was thus set for the currency issue to eclipse all others during the financial panic that swept the country three years later.

Republicans took their victory over Cleveland as a mandate not just to maintain the protective tariff but to raise it. Yet the mandate was less than clear, in view of Cleveland's plurality. Passage of the new tariff remained doubtful until its backers struck a bargain with western silverites. Piloted through by the prominent Ohio senator William McKinley, the McKinley Tariff of 1890 raised duties on manufactured goods to an average of about 49.5 percent, the highest to that time.

The absence of a public consensus for higher tariffs became clearly visible in the 1890 elections. The November congressional election returns suggested that the voters had repudiated the Republican-sponsored McKinley tariff with a landslide of Democratic votes. In the new House, Democrats outnumbered Republicans by almost a three to one margin; in the Senate the Republican majority was reduced to eight. One of the election casualties was McKinley himself. But there was more to the election than the tariff. Voters also reacted against the baldly partisan measures of the Harrison administration and its extravagant expenditures on pensions and other programs.

The large Democratic vote in 1890 may have also been a reaction to Republican efforts on a local level to legislate against alcohol and government-supported Catholic schools. In many districts with a high percentage of Catholic constituents, local Democratic legislators had defied the principle of separation of church and state by allocating tax revenues to help support parochial schools. With this assault on drinking and Catholic schools, Republicans were playing a losing game, arousing wets (antiprohibitionists) on the Democratic side. In 1889 Wisconsin Republicans compounded their party's problems by pushing through a law that struck at parochial schools, thus turning large numbers of outraged Catholic immigrants into Democratic activists. In 1890 the Democrats swept state after state.

THE PROBLEMS OF FARMERS

The 1890 election returns reflected even more than a reaction against the Republican tariff, spoils politics, extravagance, and moralizing. The returns revealed a deep-seated unrest in the farming communities of the South and West that was beginning to find voice in the new People's party, a grassroots movement destined to have a fundamental impact on American politics and social thought.

ECONOMIC CONDITIONS For some time farmers had been subject to worsening economic and social conditions. The source of their problem was a long-term decline in commodity prices from 1870 to 1898, the product of domestic increases in production and growing international competition for world markets. Considerations of abstract economic forces, however, puzzled many farmers. How could one speak of overproduction when so many remained in need? Instead, many assumed, there must be a screw loose somewhere in the system.

The railroads and the middlemen who handled the farmers' products became convenient targets. Farmers resented the high railroad rates that prevailed in farm regions with no alternative forms of transportation. Individual farmers could not get the rebates the industrial shippers could extract from railroads, nor could they exert the political influence wielded by the railroad lobbies. In other ways farmers found themselves with little bargaining power either as buyers or sellers. When they went to sell wheat or cotton, the buyer set the price; when they went to buy a plow point, the seller set the price.

High tariffs operated to the farmers' disadvantage because they protected manufacturers against foreign competition, allowing them to raise the prices of factory goods on which farmers depended. Farmers, however, had to sell their wheat, cotton, and other staples in foreign

"*I Feed You All,*" *a poster showing the farmer at the
center of society, first published in* Prairie Farmer
in 1869.

markets, where competition lowered prices. Tariffs inflicted a double
blow on farmers because insofar as they hampered imports, they indirectly hampered exports by making it harder for foreign buyers to get the
necessary American currency or exchange to purchase American crops.

Debt, too, had been a perennial agricultural problem. After the Civil
War farmers grew ever more enmeshed in debt: western farmers incurred mortgages to cover the costs of land and machinery, while southern farmers were forced to use crop liens to the local merchant. As
commodity prices dropped, the debt burden grew because farmers had
to cultivate more wheat or cotton to raise the same amount of money.
By growing more they furthered the vicious cycle of surpluses and price
declines.

AN INADEQUATE CURRENCY   Currency deflation also contributed
to the rising cost of borrowing money: a tight money supply caused
bankers to hike interest rates on loans. Ultimately, the festering farm
discontent focused on the currency issue, magnifying this grievance out
of proportion to all others. The basic problem with the nation's money
supply in the late nineteenth century was that it lacked the flexibility to
grow along with America's expanding economy. From 1865 to 1890 the
amount of currency in circulation per capita decreased about ten percent.

Metallic currency dated from the Mint Act of 1792, which authorized free and unlimited coinage of silver and gold at a ratio of 15 to 1. The ratio meant that the amount of precious metal in a silver dollar weighed fifteen times as much as that in a gold dollar. This reflected the relative values of silver and gold at the time. The phrase "free and unlimited coinage" simply meant that owners of precious metals could have any quantity of their gold or silver coined free, except for a nominal fee to cover costs.

A fixed ratio of values, however, could not reflect fluctuations in the market value of the metals. When gold rose to a market value higher than that reflected in the official ratio, owners ceased to present it for coinage. The country was actually on a silver standard until 1837, when Congress changed the ratio to 16 to 1, which soon reversed the situation. Silver became more valuable in the open market than in coinage, and the country drifted to a gold standard. This state of affairs prevailed until 1873, when Congress passed a general revision of the coinage laws and, without fanfare, dropped the then-unused provision for the coinage of silver.

This occurred, however, just when silver production began to increase, reducing its market value through the growth in supply. Under the old laws this would have induced owners of silver to present it at the mint for coinage. Soon advocates of currency inflation began to denounce the "crime of '73," which they had scarcely noticed at the time. Gradually suspicion grew that bankers and merchants had conspired in 1873 to ensure a scarcity of money. But the silverites had little more legislative success than the advocates of greenback inflation. The Bland-Allison Act of 1878 and the Sherman Silver Purchase Act of 1890 provided for some silver coinage, but too little in each case to offset the overall contraction of the currency.

AGRARIAN REVOLT

Frustrated by the unwillingness of Congress to meet their demands and ease their plight, disgruntled farmers began to organize after the Civil War. Like so many of their counterparts laboring in urban factories, they realized that social change could be provoked only by demonstrations of power, and power lay in numbers. But unlike labor unions, farm organizations faced a more complex array of economic variables affecting their livelihood. They had to deal with more than just management; bankers, middlemen, railroad and grain elevator operators, and the world market all played a role in affecting the agricultural sector.

So too did the unpredictable forces of nature: droughts, blizzards, insects, erosion. Other important obstacles to collective action by farmers included the deeply ingrained tradition of rugged individualism and physical isolation. American farmers had long prided themselves on their self-reliant hardihood, and many balked at sacrificing their independence. Consequently, farm activists discovered that it was often difficult to develop and maintain a cohesive organization. But for all the difficulties, they persevered, and the results were dramatic, if not completely successful.

THE GRANGER MOVEMENT   When the Department of Agriculture sent Oliver H. Kelley, a former Minnesota farmer and post office clerk, on a tour of the postbellum South in 1866, it was the farmers' isolation that most impressed him. Resolving to do something about it, Kelley in 1867 founded the Patrons of Husbandry, better known as the Grange (an old word for granary). In the next few years the Grange mushroomed, reaching a membership as high as 1.5 million by 1874. The Grange started out as a social and educational response to the farmers' isolation, but as it grew it began to promote farmer-owned cooperatives for buying and selling. Their ideal was to free themselves from the conventional marketplace.

The Grange soon became indirectly involved in politics through independent third parties, especially in the Midwest during the early 1870s. The Grangers' chief political goal was state regulation of the rates charged by railroads and warehouses. In five states they brought about the passage of "Granger Laws," which provoked court challenges. In a key case involving warehouse regulation, *Munn v. Illinois* (1877), the Supreme Court affirmed that the state under its "police powers" had the right to regulate property where that property was clothed with a public interest.

The Granger movement gradually declined (but never vanished) as members' energies were drawn off into cooperatives, many of which failed, and into political action. Out of the independent political movements of the time there grew, in 1875, a party known as the Greenback party, which favored expansion of the currency with more paper money. In the 1878 midterm elections it polled over 1 million votes and elected fifteen congressmen. But in 1880 the party's fortunes declined, and it disintegrated after 1884.

FARMERS' ALLIANCES   As the Granger movement waned, another farm organization grew in size and significance: the Farmers' Alliance. In county after county in the South and Midwest, farmers rushed to join the Alliance movement, which promised to address the hardships created by chronic indebtedness, declining prices, and devastating droughts. Many isolated, struggling farmers and their families were attracted also by the sense of community provided by the Alliances, whose gatherings often resembled spiritual camp meetings.

The Alliance movement attracted women and men alike. Alliances welcomed rural white women and men over sixteen years old who displayed a "good moral character," believed in God, and demonstrated "industrious habits." One North Carolina woman in 1891 expressed her appreciation for the "grand opportunities" the Alliance provided women to liberate themselves from traditional domesticity. "Drudgery, fashion and gossip," she declared, "are no longer the bounds of woman's sphere." One of the Alliance publications made the point explicitly: "The Alliance has come to redeem woman from her enslaved condition, and place her in her proper sphere." In the eyes of some agrarian radicals that new sphere entailed greater self-reliance and political, social, and educational equality. Not all Alliance groups, however, embraced such an agenda. As one Alliance official harrumphed, "I think that the ladies are best suited to home affairs." Nevertheless, overall the number of women in the Alliance movement increased rapidly, and many assumed key leadership roles.

THE TEXAS ALLIANCE   The Alliance movement in Texas was one of the largest and most influential. From the start, the organization differed significantly from the earlier Grange movement. Unlike the Grange, which was a national organization that tended to attract larger and more prosperous farmers, the Alliance was a local grassroots organization representing marginal farmers. Like the Grange, the Texas Alliance offered social and recreational opportunities, but it also emphasized political action. In 1884 the Texas Alliance hired S. O. Dawes to serve as a traveling lecturer. He crisscrossed the state, organizing new Alliances and bolstering the energy of old ones. By 1886 the Texas Alliance listed a membership of 100,000 farm folk. That same year, Robert M. Humphreys, a white minister, responded to the appeals of black farmers and organized the Colored Alliance. The white leadership of the Alliance movement in Texas endorsed this development because the Colored Alliance stressed that its objective was economic justice, not social equality.

A devastating drought in Texas in 1886 brought matters to a head. When President Grover Cleveland vetoed a bill to aid Texas farmers, Alliance leaders resolved to challenge the Democratic party at the polls. This fractured the Alliance. Conservative members whose primary allegiance was to the Democratic party left the movement. In 1887 Charles W. Macune, the new Alliance president, announced his intention to exert pressure on Congress to assist southern farmers. In addition, he proposed that Texas farmers create their own Alliance Exchange in an effort to free themselves from their dependence on middlemen and banks. Members of the Exchange would sign joint notes, borrow money from banks, and purchase their goods and supplies from a new corporation created by the Alliance in Dallas. The Exchange would also build its own warehouses to store and market the crops of members. While their crops were being stored, member farmers could obtain credit from the warehouse cooperative so they could buy goods and supplies. But this grand "cooperative" scheme collapsed when the Texas banks refused to accept the joint notes from Alliance members. This led Macune and others to focus their energies on political action.

FARM POLITICS   By 1890 there were two major groups: the northwestern Alliance, organized in 1880, was never effective and by the late 1880s was mostly a paper organization; the southern Alliance proved the more militant, effective, radical, and ultimately the more national in scope of the two. By absorbing existing farm groups and organizing new locals, the Alliance swept the cotton belt and established strong positions in Kansas and the Dakotas. By 1890 it had members from New York to California numbering about 1.5 million. A parallel Colored Farmers Alliance, centered in the Deep South, claimed over 1 million members.

After Reconstruction ended, many black families (called "Exodusters") left the South to farm in Kansas. They laid the groundwork for later organizations such as the Colored Farmers' Alliance.

The Alliance economic program was much more elaborate than that of the Grange, but Alliance agencies and exchanges soon went the way of the Granger cooperatives, victims of discrimination by wholesalers, manufacturers, railroads, and bankers, but above all victims of inexperienced management and overextended credit. As the cooperatives struggled to survive, many southern Alliance supporters endorsed a "subtreasury plan" that would allow farmers to store their crops in new government warehouses and obtain government loans for up to 80 percent of their crops' value at 1 percent interest. Besides credit, the plan allowed farmers to hold their crops for a good price, since they would not have to sell immediately at harvest time to pay off debts. The plan also promoted inflation, because loans to farmers would be made in new legal-tender notes. The plan went before Congress in 1890 but was never adopted. Its defeat as well as setbacks to other proposals convinced many farm leaders that they needed more political power to secure railroad regulation, currency inflation, state departments of agriculture, antitrust laws, and farm credit.

In 1890 Alliance members plunged headlong into politics. In the West, where hard times had descended after the blizzards of 1887, farmers were ready for third-party action, and locally they began calling themselves the "people's party," or, more commonly, Populists. In the South, however, white Alliance members hesitated to bolt the Democratic party, seeking instead to influence or control it. Both approaches gained startling success. Independent parties under various names upset the political balance in western states, almost electing a governor under the banner of the Populist party in Kansas (a Populist was elected governor in 1892) and taking control of one house of the legislature there and both houses in Nebraska. In South Dakota and Minnesota they gained a balance of power in the legislatures, while Kansas and South Dakota sent Populists to the Senate.

The Populists produced colorful leaders, especially in Kansas, where Mary Elizabeth Lease advised farmers "to raise less corn and more hell." Born in Pennsylvania to parents who were political exiles from Ireland, she eventually migrated to Kansas, taught school, raised a family, and finally failed at farming in the mid-1880s. She then studied law for a time, "pinning sheets of notes above her wash tub," and through strenuous effort became one of the state's first female lawyers. At the same time, she took up public speaking on behalf of various causes ranging from Irish nationalism to temperance to women's suffrage. By

Mary Elizabeth Lease, 1890.

the end of the 1880s she had joined the Alliance as well as the Knights of Labor, and soon applied her natural gifts as a fiery speaker to the cause of free silver. A tall, proud, and imposing woman, Lease drew excited and attentive audiences. "The people are at bay," she warned in 1894, "let the bloodhounds of money beware."

"Sockless Jerry" Simpson was an equally colorful farm leader. Born in Canada, Simpson eventually moved to Kansas, where he tried and failed at farming and cattle-raising. Simpson's difficulties led him to the Alliance movement, and in 1890 he campaigned for Congress. A shrewd, witty, and intelligent man with huge, calloused hands and pale blue eyes, Simpson effectively simplified the complex economic and political issues of the day. "Man must have access to the land," he maintained, "or he is a slave." He warned Republicans: "You can't put this movement down by sneers or by ridicule, for its foundation was laid as far back as the foundation of the world. It is a struggle between the robbers and the robbed." His Republican opponent for Congress, a wealthy railroad lawyer, conducted his campaign from a private rail car, and this gave Simpson a perfect foil. Simpson dismissed him as an indulgent pawn of the corporations whose "soft white hands" and "silk hosiery" betrayed his true priorities. His outraged opponent thereupon shouted that it was better to have silk socks than none at all, providing Simpson with an endearing nickname.

"Sockless Jerry" Simpson won a seat in Congress, and so too did many other farmers' advocates. In the South the Alliance won equal if not greater success by forcing the Democrats to nominate candidates pledged to their program. In 1890 the southern states elected four pro-Alliance governors, seven pro-Alliance legislatures, forty-four pro-Alliance congressmen, and several senators. Among the most respected of the southern Alliance leaders was Tom Watson of Georgia. The son of prosperous slaveholders who lost everything during and after the Civil War, he attended Mercer University for two years before running out of funds, and eventually became a successful lawyer and charismatic orator on behalf of the Alliance cause. He took the lead in appealing to black tenants and sharecroppers to join with their white counterparts in ousting the Bourbon white political elite. "You are kept apart," he told black and white farmers, "that you may be separately fleeced of your earnings."

THE POPULIST PARTY   As economic conditions worsened, many insurgents began promoting the formation of a new national political party. In 1891 delegates from farm, labor, and reform organizations met in Cincinnati to discuss the creation of a People's party. Few southerners attended, but many endorsed the third-party idea after their failure to win over the Democratic party to the subtreasury plan. In 1892 a larger meeting at St. Louis proposed a national convention of the People's party at Omaha to adopt a platform and choose national candidates. The stirring platform, written by Ignatius Donnelly of Minnesota, typified the apocalyptic, almost paranoid, style that increasingly characterized both the farmers' movement and its opponents:

> We meet in the midst of a nation brought to the verge of moral, political, and material ruin. Corruption dominates the ballot-box, the Legislatures, the Congress, and touches even the ermine of the bench. The newspapers are largely subsidized or muzzled, public opinion silenced, business prostrated, homes covered with mortgages, labor impoverished, and the land concentrating in the hands of the capitalists. . . . A vast conspiracy against mankind has been organized. . . . If not met and overthrown at once it forebodes terrible social convulsions . . . or the establishment of an absolute despotism.

The platform itself focused on issues of finance, transportation, and land. Its financial program demanded the subtreasury plan, free and unlimited coinage of silver at the 16 to 1 ratio, an increase in the amount of money in circulation, and a graduated income tax. As to transportation, the government should nationalize the railroads, and the telephone and telegraph systems as well. It should also reclaim from railroads and other corporations lands "in excess of their actual needs," and forbid land ownership by illegal aliens. Finally, the platform endorsed the eight-hour day and immigration restriction laws. The party took these positions to win support from the urban workers, whom Populists looked upon as fellow "producers."

The party's platform turned out to be more exciting than its candidate, Iowa's James B. Weaver. Though an able, prudent man, Weaver carried the stigma of his defeat on the Greenback ticket twelve years before. To balance Weaver, a former Union general, the party named a former Confederate general for vice-president.

The Populist party was the startling new feature of the 1892 campaign. The major parties renominated Grover Cleveland and Benjamin Harrison. The tariff remained the chief issue between them. The outcome, however, was different. Both major candidates polled over 5 million votes, but Cleveland carried a plurality of the popular votes and a majority of the electoral college. Weaver gained over 1 million votes and carried Colorado, Kansas, Nevada, and Idaho, for a total of twenty-two electoral votes.

THE DEPRESSION OF 1893   Cleveland's second administration stumbled early amid one of the most devastating business panics in history, set off just before he took office by the failure of the Philadelphia and Reading Railroad and a panic on Wall Street. By 1894 the economy had reached bottom. That year some 750,000 workers went out on strike; millions found themselves unemployed; railroad construction workers, laid off in the West, began tramping east and talked of marching on Washington.

Few of them made it to the capital. One group that did was "Coxey's Army," led by Jacob S. Coxey, a wealthy Ohio quarry owner turned Populist who demanded that the federal government provide unemployed people with meaningful work. Coxey, his wife, and their son, Legal Tender Coxey, rode in a carriage ahead of some 400 hardy protesters who finally straggled into Washington. There Coxey was arrested for walking on the grass, but his army as well as the growing political strength of Populism struck fear into the hearts of many Americans. Critics portrayed Populists as "hayseed socialists" whose election would endanger property rights.

The 1894 congressional elections took place amid this climate of anxiety. The elections amounted to a severe setback for Democrats, who paid politically for the economic downturn, and the Republicans were the chief beneficiaries. The Populists emerged with six senators and seven representatives. They had polled 1.5 million votes for their congressional candidates and still expected the festering discontent to carry them to national power in 1896.

SILVERITES VS. GOLDBUGS   The course of events, however, would dash that hope. In the mid-1890s events conspired to focus all concerns on the currency issue. One of the causes of the 1893 depression had been the failure of a major British bank, which led many British investors to unload their American holdings in return for gold. Soon after Cleveland's inauguration the gold reserve fell below $100 million. To plug this drain on the Treasury the president sought repeal of the Sherman Silver Purchase Act to stop the issuance of silver notes redeemable in gold. Cleveland won the act's repeal in 1893, but at the cost of irreparable division in his own party. One embittered silver Democrat labeled the president a "Benedict Arnold."

Western silver interests raised the agitation for silver coinage to a crescendo, which presented a strategic dilemma for Populists: should the party promote the long list of varied reforms it had originally advocated, or should it try to ride the silver issue into power? The latter seemed the practical choice. Consequently the Populist leaders decided, over the protest of more radical members, to hold their 1896 convention last, confident that the two major parties would at best straddle the silver issue and that the Populists would then reap a harvest of bolting silverite Republicans and Democrats.

THE ELECTION OF 1896   Contrary to these expectations, the major parties took clear and opposing positions on the currency issue. The Republicans, as expected, chose William McKinley on a gold-standard platform. McKinley had a magisterial appearance. His high forehead, sharply cut mouth, and Roman nose looked presidential, and then, as now, looks were important in national politics. On the Democratic side the pro-silver forces gathered to wrest control of the party from Cleveland and the fiscal conservatives. A reporter covering the convention recognized the shift of power: "All the silverites need is a Moses. They have the principle, they have the grit . . . and they have the howl and the hustle." They also soon had their Moses, who emerged this time not from the bullrushes but from the Nebraska plains.

In William Jennings Bryan the silver Democrats found a crusading, charismatic leader. A fervent Baptist and advocate of the free coinage of silver, Bryan was a two-term congressman from Nebraska who had been defeated in the senatorial race in 1894. At the 1896 convention the self-assured Bryan delivered a galvanizing speech that had most of the 20,000 delegates on their feet and many in tears. Much like a revivalist at a camp meeting, he drew the audience with the emotion of his appeal. Bryan spoke for silver and the new West, for the "hardy pioneers"

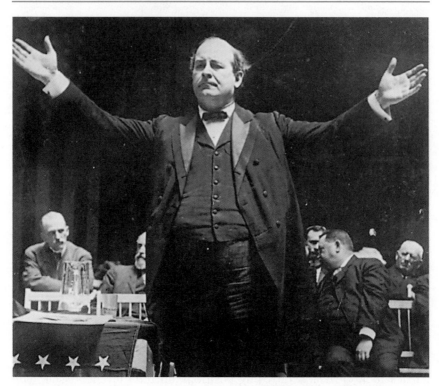

William Jennings Bryan, whose "Cross of Gold" speech at the 1896 Democratic convention roused the delegates and secured him the party's presidential nomination.

and against the "financial magnates" of the urban East. "Burn down your cities and leave our farms [untouched]," he predicted, "and your cities will spring up again as if by magic; but destroy our farms and the grass will grow in the streets of every city in the country." He then directly challenged Republicans as well as Cleveland and the gold Democrats with a compelling metaphor: "You shall not press down upon the brow of labor this crown of thorns. You shall not crucify mankind upon a cross of gold!"

The next day the heroic Bryan was nominated on the fifth ballot, and in the process the Democratic party was fractured beyond repair. Disappointed pro-gold Democrats walked out of the convention and nominated their own candidate, who then announced: "Fellow Democrats, I will not consider it any great fault if you decide to cast your vote for William McKinley."

When the Populists met in St. Louis two weeks later, they faced an impossible choice. "If we fuse [with the Democrats]," one Populist admitted, "all the silver men we have will leave us for the more powerful Democrats." But if they named their own candidate they would divide the silver vote with Bryan and give the election to McKinley. "Sockless Jerry" Simpson advised merger: "I care not for party names; it is substance we are after, and we have it in William J. Bryan." In the end the delegates agreed. They backed Bryan, but chose their own vice-presidential candidate, Georgia's Tom Watson, and invited the Democrats to drop their vice-presidential nominee—an action that Bryan refused to countenance.

The thirty-six-year-old Bryan launched a whirlwind campaign. He crisscrossed the country, exploiting his spellbinding eloquence and radiating honesty, sincerity, and energy. McKinley, meanwhile, conducted a "front-porch campaign," receiving selected delegations of supporters at his home in Canton, Ohio, and giving only prepared responses. His campaign manager, Mark Hanna, shrewdly portrayed Bryan as a radical whose "communistic spirit" would ruin the capitalist system. Many observers agreed with the portrait. The editor of the *New York Tribune* denounced Bryan as a "wretched rattle-pated boy, posing in vapid vanity and mouthing resounding rottenness." A factory owner told his employees: "Men, vote as you please, but if Bryan is elected . . . the whistle will not blow Wednesday morning."

By preying upon such fears, Hanna raised a huge campaign chest and financed an army of Republican speakers who stumped the country in support of McKinley. The Democratic-Populist-Silverite candidates were overwhelmed. McKinley won the popular vote by 7.1 million to 6.5 million and the electoral college vote by 271 to 176.

Bryan carried most of the West and the South below the border states, but garnered little support in the metropolitan centers east of the Mississippi and north of the Ohio and Potomac Rivers. Urban workers simply saw little to gain from the inflation promoted by Bryan and the silverites. Moreover, in the critical midwestern battleground, from Minnesota and Iowa eastward to Ohio, Bryan carried not a single state. Many ethnic voters, normally drawn to the Democrats, were repelled by Bryan's evangelical style. Farmers in the East and Midwest, moreover, were hurting less than those in the wheat and cotton belts. There was less tenancy and a greater diversity of crops in those farm regions, and the prospering farmers therefore saw little attraction in agrarian radicalism.

A NEW ERA   The election of 1896 proved a climactic political struggle between rural and metropolitan America, and metropolitan America
won. Anticipating Bryan's defeat and the collapse of the Populist vision,
Mark Hanna telegraphed McKinley on election night, "God's in his
Heaven, all's right with the world!"

The values of urban-industrial America had indeed taken firm hold of
the political system. As its first important act the McKinley administration called a special session of Congress to raise the tariff again. The
Dingley Tariff of 1897 became the highest to that time. By 1897 prosperity was returning, helped along by inflation of the currency, which
bore out the arguments of greenbackers and silverites. But the inflation
came, in one of history's many ironies, not from silver but from a new
flood of gold onto the market and into the mints. During the 1880s and
1890s new discoveries of gold in South Africa, Canada, and the Yukon
led to spectacular new gold rushes, a return to the gold standard, and an
end to the free silver movement. To compound the irony, most of the
Populist platform, which seemed so radical in 1892, would nevertheless
take effect within two decades.

Amid the new prosperity, the old issues of tariffs and currency policy
gave way to international concerns. "The Spanish War finished us," said
the old Populist Tom Watson. "The blare of the bugle drowned the voice
of the Reformer."

MAKING CONNECTIONS

- This chapter concludes with the suggestion that the Spanish-
  American War, a major event on the horizon, marked the end of
  the reform spirit of the Populists.

- The laissez-faire policies of the Gilded Age were challenged by
  Progressive reform activists, discussed in Chapter 23.

- William Jennings Bryan was one of the most prominent figures
  in American politics and political culture over some thirty
  years.

FURTHER READING

A good overview of the Gilded Age that covers politics in detail is Morton Keller's *Affairs of State: Public Life in Nineteenth Century America* (1977).* Many scholars use the ethnocultural approach to study Gilded-Age politics. See Paul Kleppner's *The Third Electoral System, 1853–1892* (1979) and Richard J. Jensen's *The Winning of the Midwest: Social and Political Conflicts, 1888–1896* (1971).

One of the most controversial works on Populism is Lawrence Goodwyn's *The Populist Moment* (1978).* A new addition to scholarship on the Populists is Jeffrey Ostler's *Prairie Populism: The Fate of Agrarian Radicalism in Kansas, Nebraska, and Iowa, 1880–1892* (1993).

*These books are available in paperback editions.

PART SIX

MODERN AMERICA

The United States entered the twentieth century in a state of flux. Since the election of Thomas Jefferson in 1800, the country had seen itself relentlessly transformed. A rural, agrarian society largely detached from the concerns of international affairs turned into a highly industrialized, urban culture with a growing involvement in world politics and commerce. In other words, the United States in 1900 was on the threshold of modernity.

The prospect of modernity both excited and scared Americans. Old truths and beliefs clashed with unsettling new scientific discoveries and social practices. People debated the legitimacy of Darwinism, the existence of God, the dangers of jazz, and the federal effort to prohibit alcoholic beverages. The automobile, airplane, and radio helped shrink the distances of time and space and accelerate a national consciousness. In the process the United States began to emerge from its isolationist shell. Throughout most of the nineteenth century, policy makers had sought to isolate America from the intrigues and conflicts of the great European powers. As early as 1780, John Adams had warned Congress against involving the United States in the affairs of Europe. "Our business with them, and theirs with us," he wrote, "is commerce, not politics, much less war." George Washington echoed this sentiment in his farewell address upon leaving the presidency, warning Americans to avoid "entangling alliances" with foreign governments.

With only a few exceptions, American statesmen during the nineteenth century had followed such advice. Noninvolvement in foreign wars and nonintervention in the internal affairs of foreign governments formed the pillars of American foreign policy until the end of the century. During the 1890s, however, expanding commercial interests around the world led Americans to extend the horizons of their concerns. Imperialism was the order of the day among the great European powers, and a growing number of American expansionists demanded that the United States also adopt a global ambition and join in the hunt for new territories and markets. Such motives helped spark the Spanish-American War of 1898 and helped to justify the resulting acquisition of American colonies outside the continental United States. Entangling alliances with European powers soon followed.

The outbreak of the Great War in Europe in 1914 posed an even greater challenge to the American tradition of isolation and nonintervention. The prospect of a German victory over the French and British threatened the European balance of power, which had long ensured the security of the United States. By 1917 it appeared that Germany might emerge triumphant and begin to menace the Western Hemisphere. Woodrow Wilson's crusade to use American intervention in World War I to transform the world order in accordance with his idealistic principles severed American foreign policy from its isolationist moorings. It also spawned a prolonged debate about the role of the United States in world affairs, a debate that World War II would resolve for a time on the side of internationalism.

At the same time that the United States was entering the world stage as a great military power, it was also becoming a great industrial power. Cities and factories sprouted across the landscape. An abundance of new jobs served as a magnet attracting millions of immigrants from every corner of the globe. They were not always welcomed, nor were they readily assimilated. Ethnic and racial strife, as well as labor agitation, increased at the turn of the century. In the midst of such social turmoil and unparalleled economic development, American reformers made their first sustained attempt to adapt their political and social institutions to the realities of the industrial age. The worst excesses and injustices of urban-industrial development—corporate monopolies, child labor, political corruption, hazardous working conditions, urban ghettos—were finally addressed in a comprehensive way. During the Progressive Era (1900–1917), local, state, and federal governments sought to rein in the excesses of industrial capitalism and develop a more rational and efficient public policy.

A conservative Republican resurgence challenged the notion of the new regulatory state during the 1920s. Free enterprise and corporate capitalism witnessed a dramatic revival. But the stock market crash of 1929 helped propel the United States and many other nations into the worst economic downturn in history. The unprecedented severity of the Great Depression renewed public demands for federal government programs to protect the general welfare. "This nation asks for action," declared President Franklin D. Roosevelt in his 1933 inaugural address. The plethora of New Deal initiatives and agencies instituted by Roosevelt and his Democratic administration created the framework for a welfare state that has since served as the basis for American public policy.

The New Deal helped revive public confidence and put people back to work, but it did not end the Great Depression. It took a world war to re-

store full employment. The necessity of mobilizing the nation in support of the Second World War also served to accelerate the growth of the federal government. And the incredible scope of the war helped catapult the United States into a leadership role in world politics. The creation of a nuclear bomb to help end the war ushered in a new era of atomic diplomacy that held the fate of the world in the balance. For all of the new creature comforts associated with modern life, Americans in 1945 found themselves living amid an array of new anxieties.

22 ∽ THE COURSE OF EMPIRE

CHAPTER ORGANIZER

This chapter focuses on:

- the circumstances that led to America's "new imperialism"

- the causes of the Spanish-American War

- Theodore Roosevelt's foreign policy in Asia and Latin America

TOWARD THE NEW IMPERIALISM

Throughout most of the late nineteenth century, Americans dis-played what one senator called "only a languid interest" in foreign af-fairs. Indeed, the overriding concerns of the time were industrial devel-opment, western settlement, and domestic politics. Compared to these, foreign relations simply were not important to the vast majority of Americans. After the Civil War an isolationist mood swept across the United States as the country basked in its geographic advantages: wide oceans as buffers on either side, the British navy situated between America and the powers of Europe, and militarily weak neighbors in the Western Hemisphere.

EXPANSION IN THE PACIFIC   Yet the spirit of Manifest Destiny remained alive, if muted, in the decades after Appomattox, and a few key figures sought to lead the United States out of its isolationist shell. For such expansionists Asia especially offered an alluring temptation. Andrew Johnson's secretary of state, William H. Seward, believed that the United States must inevitably exercise commercial domination "on the Pacific ocean, and its islands and continents." Eager for American manufacturers to capture Asian markets, Seward believed the United States first had to remove all foreign interests from the northern Pacific coast and gain access to that region's valuable ports. To that end he cast covetous eyes on the British Crown Colony of British Columbia, sandwiched between Russia's possessions in Alaska and Washington Territory. Late in 1866, while encouraging annexation sentiment among the British Columbians, Seward learned of Russia's desire to sell Alaska because it had become unprofitable. He leapt at the opportunity, and in 1867 the United States bought Alaska for $7.2 million, less than 2 cents an acre. "Seward's folly" of buying the Alaskan "icebox" proved in time to be the biggest bargain for the United States, economically and strategically, since the Louisiana Purchase.

Seward bought Alaska in part because he feared the British would buy it and in part because he knew of the territory's rich mineral deposits, fisheries, and bountiful forests. He also hoped that its purchase would convince the British Columbians to request annexation. For a while that seemed a real possibility, but in 1870 British Columbia decided instead to join the new Confederation of Canada.

SAMOA AND HAWAII   Seward's successors at the State Department never completely lost sight of his expansionist vision, and the Pacific Ocean remained the major field of overseas activity. During the post–Civil War years the United States sought coaling stations and trading posts in this area, and it laid claim to various small islands and coral atolls of the mid-Pacific. Among these islands two inhabited groups occupied especially strategic positions: Samoa and Hawaii (also known as the Sandwich Islands).

American interest in these islands gradually deepened as commercial activity in the Pacific increased, and in 1878 the Samoans signed a treaty with the United States that granted a naval base at Pago Pago.

The following year the German and British governments worked out similar arrangements on other islands of the Samoan group.

In Hawaii the Americans had a clearer field. The islands, a united kingdom since 1795, hosted a sizable settlement of American missionaries and planters, and had long been a popular way station for whalers and traders. They were also strategically more important than Samoa to the United States, since their occupation by another major power might have posed a threat to American sugar interests and even to defense of the continent.

In 1875 the Hawaiians signed a reciprocal trade agreement under which their sugar entered the United States duty free. Twelve years later it was amended to grant the United States exclusive right to a fortified naval base at Pearl Harbor, near Honolulu. These agreements resulted in a boom in sugar growing, and American settlers in Hawaii came to have a dominant position economically. In 1887 the Americans forced Hawaii's king to grant a constitutional government, which they dominated.

Hawaii's political climate changed sharply when the king's sister, Queen Liliuokalani, ascended the throne in 1891 and began efforts to reclaim power. Shortly before that the McKinley Tariff had destroyed Hawaii's favored position in the sugar trade by putting the sugar of all countries on the free list and granting growers in the United States a two-cent bounty. The resultant discontent in Hawaii led the white pop-

Queen Liliuokalani.

ulation to stage a revolt early in 1893. A committee of public safety seized power, and the American minister brought in marines to support the coup. As he cheerfully reported to Washington, "The Hawaiian pear is now fully ripe, and this is the golden hour for the United States to pluck it." Within a month a committee of the new American-dominated government turned up in Washington and, in 1893, signed an annexation treaty.

This occurred just weeks before President Harrison left office, however, and Democratic senators blocked ratification. President Cleveland withdrew the treaty and sent a special commissioner to investigate. He withdrew the American marines and reported that Americans on the islands had acted improperly. Most Hawaiians opposed annexation, said the commissioner, who thought the revolution had been engineered mainly by sugar planters hoping to get the new domestic sugar bounty by annexation to the United States. Cleveland therefore proposed to restore the queen in return for amnesty to the revolutionists. The provisional government refused and on July 4, 1894, proclaimed the Republic of Hawaii, which had in its constitution a standing provision for American annexation, which would happen presumably after Cleveland was succeeded by a president whose sensibilities were less easily offended.

STEPS TO WORLD POWER

The antebellum spirit of expansionism thus had neither died out with the 1850s nor gone completely dormant. It would return full blown in the 1890s with the addition of some new flourishes. European powers from about 1870 on set an example with a new surge of imperialism in Africa and Asia, where they seized territory, established colonies and protectorates, and began a systematic program of economic exploitation and Christian evangelism. Above all, the new imperialism was economic, a quest for markets and raw materials, and to more than one observer the European example seemed to address a new aspect of the American experience. The closing of America's frontier was brought forcefully to public attention by the census of 1890 and by historian Frederick Jackson Turner's classic 1893 essay on the significance of the frontier. Many thought this signaled the end of America's constantly growing domestic market and highlighted a need to seek markets overseas.

Most Americans became increasingly aware of world markets as developments in transportation and communication quickened the pace of commerce and diplomacy. From the first, agricultural exports had been the basis of American economic growth. Now the conviction grew that American manufactures had matured to the point that they could outsell foreign goods in the world market. But should the expansion of markets lead to territorial expansion as well? Or to intervention in the internal affairs of other countries? On such points Americans disagreed, but a small yet growing and vocal group of public officials was ready to entertain the idea of overseas possessions. They included Senators Albert J. Beveridge of Indiana and Henry Cabot Lodge of Massachusetts, Theodore Roosevelt, and not least of all, Captain Alfred Thayer Mahan.

NAVAL POWER   During the 1880s Captain Mahan, a graduate of Annapolis, became a leading advocate of sea power and western imperialism. In 1890 he published *The Influence of Sea Power upon History, 1660–1783,* in which he argued that national greatness and prosperity flowed from sea power. To Mahan, economic development called for a powerful navy, a strong merchant marine, foreign commerce, colonies, and naval bases. Mahan expounded on America's destiny to control the Caribbean, build an isthmian canal, and spread Western civilization in the Pacific. His ideas were widely circulated in popular journals and within the American government. Even before Mahan's writings became influential, a gradual expansion of the navy had begun. In 1880 the nation had fewer than a hundred seagoing vessels, many of them rusting or rotting at the docks. By 1896 eleven powerful new battleships had been built or authorized.

IMPERIALIST THEORY   Meanwhile, certain intellectual currents of the day worked to bolster the new spirit of Manifest Destiny. Applications of the Darwinian idea of natural selection to society and politics afforded a handy argument for imperialism. Among nations as among individuals, expansionists claimed, the fittest survive and prevail. John Fiske, the historian and popular lecturer on Darwinism, developed racial corollaries from Darwin's idea. In *American Political Ideas* (1885) he stressed the superior character of "Anglo-Saxon" institutions and peoples. The English "race," he argued, was destined to dominate the globe in the institutions, traditions, language, even in the blood of the world's peoples.

Josiah Strong, a Congregationalist minister, added the sanction of religion to theories of racial and national superiority. In his book *Our Country: Its Possible Future and Its Present Crisis* (1885), Strong asserted that "Anglo-Saxons" embodied two great ideas: civil liberty and "a pure spiritual Christianity." The Anglo-Saxon was "divinely commissioned to be, in a peculiar sense, his brother's keeper." Expansion to establish foreign missions also found favor in both Protestant and Catholic churches.

These religious, intellectual, and economic factors combined to provide a potent rationale for an expansionist foreign policy. The *Washington Post* made the point explicitly in 1898:

> A new consciousness seems to have come upon us—the consciousness of strength—and with it a new appetite, the yearning to show our strength. . . . We are face to face with a strange destiny. The taste of Empire is in the mouth of the people even as the taste of blood in the jungle.

THE SPANISH-AMERICAN WAR

"CUBA LIBRE" Animated by such expansionist ideas, the United States suddenly in 1898 and 1899 thrust its newly developed power to the far reaches of the Pacific. The occasion for this explosion of imperialism lay neither in the Pacific nor in the quest for bases and trade, but to the south in Cuba. The chief motive was a sense of outrage at another country's imperialism.

Throughout the second half of the nineteenth century, Cubans had repeatedly revolted against Spanish rule, only to be ruthlessly put down. All the while American investments in Cuba, mainly in sugar and mining, were steadily rising. The United States in fact traded more with Cuba than Spain did. The growing economic interest in their island neighbor made more and more Americans sympathetic to the ideal of Cuban independence. When insurrection broke out again on February 24, 1895, public feeling in the United States sided with the rebels, and many Americans extended help to the Cuban Revolutionary party, which organized the revolt and waged an effective propaganda campaign from headquarters in New York.

The insurrectionists waged guerrilla warfare to damage Spain's economic interests on the island, which in turn would excite the concern of American investors. The strategy dictated hit-and-run attacks on trains, railways, and plantations. Such tactics forced people either into the insurgent forces or into garrisoned towns, which in turn might be cut off from food supplies. Revolutionary propaganda of course presented the effort in a different light, and Americans were more than ready to look upon the insurrection in the light of their own War of Independence.

In 1896 Spanish general Valeriano Weyler adopted a policy of gathering Cubans behind Spanish lines, often in detention (*reconcentrado*) centers so that no one could join the insurrections by night and appear peaceful by day. In some of these centers, poor food and unsanitary conditions soon brought a heavy toll of disease and death. The American press promptly christened the Spanish commander "Butcher" Weyler.

Events in Cuba supplied exciting copy for the popular press. Chance had it that William Randolph Hearst's *New York Journal* and Joseph Pulitzer's *New York World* were at the time locked in a monumental struggle for circulation. "It was a battle of gigantic proportions," one journalist wrote, "in which the sufferings of Cuba merely chanced to furnish some of the most convenient ammunition." The sensationalism practiced by both papers came to be called "yellow journalism," and Hearst emerged as the undisputed champion. His *Journal* excelled at invective against "Weyler the brute, the devastator of haciendas, the destroyer of men."

PRESSURE FOR WAR   American neutrality toward events in Cuba changed sharply when McKinley entered office. His platform had endorsed Cuban independence, as well as American control of Hawaii and the construction of an isthmian canal. Spain offered Cuba autonomy (self-government without formal independence) in return for peace. What the Cubans might once have welcomed, however, they now rejected as they sensed their growing power. Spain was impaled on the horns of a dilemma, unable to end the war and unready to give up Cuba.

Early in 1898 events moved rapidly to arouse opinion against Spain. On February 9, Hearst's *New York Journal* released the text of a letter from Spanish minister Depuy de Lôme to a friend in Havana. In the letter, which had been stolen from the post office by a Cuban spy, de Lôme called President McKinley "weak and a bidder for the admiration of the crowd." This was hardly more extreme than what McKinley's assistant secretary of the navy, Theodore Roosevelt, had said about him. As early as 1895 Roosevelt had written: "This country needs a war," and he had since become increasingly frustrated by McKinley's refusal to declare one. The "white-livered" president, Roosevelt groused, had "no more backbone than a chocolate eclair." But that comment had remained private. De Lôme's had not, and he resigned to prevent further embarrassment to his government.

Six days later, during the night of February 15, 1898, the American battleship *Maine* exploded in Havana harbor and sank with a loss of 260 men, most of whom died in their hammocks. Those eager for a war with Spain now demanded an immediate declaration. Roosevelt called the sinking "an act of dirty treachery on the part of the Spaniards." A naval court of inquiry reported in March that an external mine had set off an explosion in the ship's magazine. Lacking hard evidence, the court made no effort to fix the blame, but the yellow press had no need of evidence. The *New York Journal* gleefully reported: "The Whole Country Thrills with War Fever." The jingoistic outcry against Spain reached a crescendo in the words "Remember the Maine! To Hell with Spain!" Few jingoes wrestled with the obvious fact that the Spanish government was determined to *avoid* a confrontation with the United States and therefore had nothing to gain from sinking the *Maine*. What actually happened remains a mystery.

Under the mounting pressure of public excitement, McKinley tried to maintain a steady course. The president, a Civil War veteran, told an aide, "I have been through one war. I have seen the dead piled up, and I do not want to see another." But the frazzled president, besieged by demands that he take a forceful stand, was increasingly swayed by the weight of outraged public opinion and by militants in his own party such as Roosevelt and Lodge. As one congressman remarked, McKinley "keeps his ear to the ground so close that he gets it full of grasshoppers much of the time." On March 9, 1898, the begrudgingly militant president pushed through Congress a $50 million defense appropriation.

Still, he sought to avoid war, as did most business spokesmen. Such caution infuriated Roosevelt. "We will have this war for the freedom of Cuba," he fumed on March 26, "in spite of the timidity of the commercial interests."

The Spanish government, sensing the growing militancy in the United States, announced a unilateral cease-fire in early April 1898. On April 10, the Spanish minister gave the State Department a message that amounted to a surrender: the United States should indicate the nature and duration of the armistice; Cuba would have an autonomous government; and the two countries would submit the question of the *Maine* to arbitration. The United States minister to Spain then cabled from Madrid: "I hope nothing will now be done to humiliate Spain, as I am satisfied that the present government is going . . . as fast and as far as it can." McKinley, he predicted, could win a settlement by August 1 on any terms, including either Cuban independence or cession of Cuba to the United States.

But the message came too late. The following day McKinley sent Congress his war message. He asked for the power to use armed forces in Cuba to abate a nuisance off U.S. shores and to protect American property and trade. On April 20 a joint resolution of Congress went beyond endorsing the use of the armed forces: it declared Cuba independent and demanded withdrawal of Spanish forces. The Teller Amendment, added on the Senate floor, disclaimed any American designs on Cuban territory. McKinley signed the resolution and sent a copy to the Spanish government. On April 22 the president announced a blockade of Cuba, under international law an act of war. Rather than give in to an ultimatum, the Spanish government declared war on April 24. Congress then, determined to be first, declared war the next day but made it retroactive to April 21, 1898.

Why such a rush into war after the American minister had predicted that Spain would cave in before the summer was out? No one knows for sure, but it seems apparent that too much momentum and popular pressure had already built up for a confidential message to change the course of events. Also, leaders of the business community, which tolerates uncertainty poorly, were demanding a quick resolution of the problem. Many lacked faith in the willingness or ability of the Spanish government to carry out a moderate policy in the face of a hostile public opinion. Still, it is fair to ask why McKinley did not take a stand for

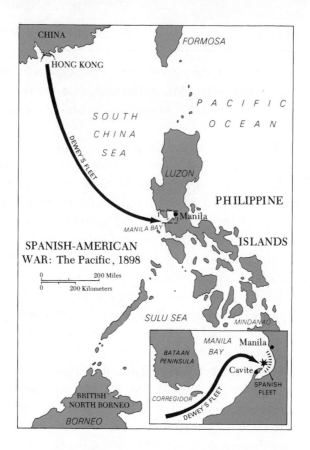

SPANISH-AMERICAN
WAR: The Pacific, 1898

peace, knowing what he did. He might have defied Congress and public opinion, but in the end he deemed the political risk too high. The ultimate blame for war, if blame must be levied, belongs to the American people for letting themselves be whipped up into such a hostile frenzy.

DEWEY TAKES MANILA   The war itself lasted only four months. The American victory marked the end of Spain's once-great New World empire, which had begun with Columbus, and the emergence of the United States as a world power. But if American participation saved many lives by ending the insurrection in Cuba, it also led to American involvement in another insurrection, in the Philippines, and it created a host of commitments in the Caribbean and the Pacific that would haunt American policy makers during the twentieth century.

The war was barely under way before the navy produced a quick, spectacular victory in an unexpected quarter—Manila Bay. While public attention centered on Cuba, Roosevelt focused on the Philippines. As assistant secretary of the navy, he had Commodore George Dewey appointed commander of the small Asiatic squadron and ordered him to engage Spain's ships in the Philippines in case of war. President McKinley had approved those orders.

Arriving late on April 30, 1898, Dewey's squadron destroyed or captured all the Spanish warships in Manila Bay. Dewey, without an occupation force, was now in awkward possession of Manila Bay. Promised reinforcements, he stayed while foreign warships, including a powerful German force, loomed about the scene like watchful vultures. Army troops finally arrived, and with the help of Filipino insurrectionists under Emilio Aguinaldo, Dewey's forces liberated Manila from Spanish control on August 13.

THE CUBAN CAMPAIGN   While these events transpired halfway around the world, the war reached a surprisingly quick climax closer to home. Although the navy was fit, the army could muster only an ill-assorted guard of 28,000 regulars and about 100,000 militiamen. The armed forces suffered badly from both inexperience and maladministration, with the result that far more American troops died from disease than from enemy action. The United States' salvation was that Spanish forces were even worse off and their morale infinitely so.

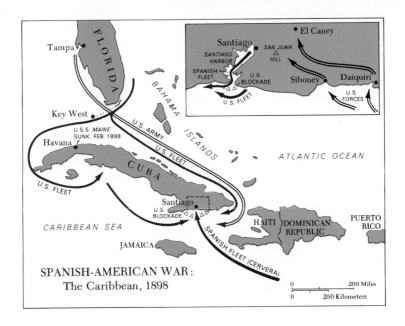

SPANISH-AMERICAN WAR:
The Caribbean, 1898

Lieutenant-Colonel Theodore Roosevelt posing with his "Rough Riders" after the battle of San Juan, 1898.

An invasion force of some 17,000 American troops was hastily assembled at Tampa. One significant element of that force was the so-called "Rough Riders," best remembered because Lieutenant-Colonel Theodore Roosevelt was second in command. Eager to get "in on the fun," and "to act up to my preachings," Roosevelt had quit the Navy Department after war was declared. He ordered a custom-fitted, fawn-colored uniform with yellow trim from Brooks Brothers, grabbed a dozen pairs of spectacles, and rushed to help organize a colorful volunteer regiment of Ivy League athletes, leathery ex-convicts, Indians, and southwestern sharpshooters.

The major land action of the Cuban campaign occurred on July 1. While a much larger American force attacked Spanish positions at San Juan Hill, a smaller unit, including the dismounted Rough Riders—most of whose horses were still in Florida—and two crack black regiments, seized the enemy position atop nearby Kettle Hill. In the midst of the fray, Roosevelt satisfied his blood lust by seeing a Spaniard he shot double up "neatly as a jackrabbit." He later claimed that he "would rather have led that charge than served three terms in the U.S. Senate."

A friend wrote to Roosevelt's wife that her husband was "revelling in victory and gore."

The two battles put American forces atop heights from which they could bring the Spanish fleet under siege. On July 3 the Spanish ships made a gallant run for it, but the aging vessels were little match for the newer American fleet. The casualties were one-sided: 474 Spanish were killed and wounded and 1,750 were taken prisoner, while only one American was killed and one wounded. Santiago, port for the Spanish fleet, surrendered with a garrison of 24,000 on July 17. On July 25, an American force also moved into the Spanish-held island of Puerto Rico.

The next day the Spanish government sued for peace. After discussions lasting two weeks, negotiators signed an armistice on August 12, 1898, less than four months after the war's start and the day before Americans entered Manila. The peace protocol specified that Spain should give up Cuba, and that the United States should annex Puerto Rico and should occupy the city, bay, and harbor of Manila pending disposition of the Philippines.

And so the "splendid little war," as the future secretary of state, John Hay, called it in a letter to his friend Roosevelt, officially ended. It was splendid only in the sense that its cost was relatively slight. Among more than 274,000 Americans who served during the war and the ensuing demobilization, 5,462 died, but only 379 in battle. Most succumbed to malaria, typhoid, dysentery, or yellow fever. At such a cost the United States was launched onto the world stage as a great power, with all the benefits—and burdens—of that new status.

THE DEBATE OVER ANNEXATION   The United States and Spain signed the Treaty of Paris on December 10, 1898. Disposition of the Philippines posed the key question, indeed one of the biggest decisions to face United States foreign policy to that time, and one that caught the country unprepared for sober reflection. McKinley, who claimed that at first he himself could not locate the Philippines on a map within 2,000 miles, gave ambiguous signals to the peace commission, which itself was divided.

There had been no demand for annexation of the Philippines or other Spanish possessions before the war, but Dewey's victory quickly kindled expansionist fever. Businessmen began thinking of the commercial pos-

"Well, I Hardly Know Which to Take First." *At the end of the nineteenth century it seemed that Uncle Sam had developed a considerable appetite for foreign territory.*

sibilities in the nearby continent of Asia, such as oil for the lamps of China and textiles for its millions. "If this be commercialism," cried Senator Mark Hanna, then "for God's sake let us have commercialism." Missionary societies yearned to save the "little brown brother." It was neither the first nor the last time that Americans would get caught up in fantasies of "saving" Asian souls or getting rich there. McKinley pondered the alternatives and later explained his reasoning to a group of Methodists:

> And one night late it came to me this way—I don't know how it was, but it came: (1) that we could not give them [the Philippines]back to Spain—that would be cowardly and dishonorable; (2) that we could not turn them over to France or Germany—our commercial rivals in the Orient—that would be bad business and discreditable; (3) that we could not leave them to themselves—they were unfit for self-government—and they would soon have anarchy and misrule over there worse than Spain's was; and (4) that there was nothing left for us to do but to take them all, and to educate the Filipinos, and uplift and civilize and Christianize them, and by God's grace do the very best we could by them, as our fellowmen for whom Christ also died. And then I went to bed, and went to sleep and slept soundly.

Although these Filipino candidates for conversion were already largely Catholic, the word went forth to take the Philippines for the sake of their souls. Spanish negotiators raised the delicate point that American forces had no claim by right of conquest, and had even taken Manila after the armistice. American negotiators finally offered the Spanish $20 million as compensation for possession of the Philippines as well as Puerto Rico in the Caribbean and Guam in the Pacific.

Meanwhile, Americans had taken other giant steps in the Pacific. Hawaiian annexation, promised in McKinley's platform, failed to get a two-thirds majority in the Senate, but the Spanish-American War demonstrated the islands' strategic importance all the more. The administration therefore convinced Congress to annex Hawaii on July 7, 1898, in the midst of the war. The United States also claimed Wake Island (1898), which would be a vital link in a future trans-Pacific cable line.

The Treaty of Paris had yet to be ratified in the Senate, where most Democrats and Populists, and some Republicans, opposed it. Anti-imperialists argued that acquisition of the Philippines would undermine democracy. They appealed to traditional isolationism, American principles of self-government, the inconsistency of liberating Cuba and annexing the Philippines, the involvement in foreign entanglements that would undermine the logic of the Monroe Doctrine, and the danger that the Philippines would become an Achilles heel, expensive if not impossible to defend. The prospect of incorporating so many alien peoples into American life was not the least of some people's worries. "Bananas and self-government cannot grow on the same piece of land," one senator claimed.

The opposition may have been strong enough to kill the treaty had not the populist Democrat William Jennings Bryan influenced the vote for approval. A formal end to the war, he argued, would open the way for the future independence of Cuba and the Philippines. Ratification finally came on February 6, 1899.

By this time Americans had already clashed with Filipino insurrectionists near Manila. The Filipino rebel leader, Emilio Aguinaldo, had been in exile until Commodore Dewey brought him back to Luzon to make trouble for the Spanish. Since Aguinaldo's forces were almost in control of the islands outside Manila, what followed over the next two years was largely an American war of conquest. Organized Filipino resistance collapsed by the end of 1899, but even after the capture of

Emilio Aguinaldo (seated third from right) and other leaders of the Filipino insurgents.

Aguinaldo in March 1901, sporadic guerrilla action lasted until mid-1902.

It was a sordid little war, with massacres and torture on both sides. American forces soon displayed the same callous outlook that had animated the Spanish in Cuba. One American colonel boasted that he and his men "would rawhide these bullet-headed Asians until they yell for mercy." They must be pacified, he added, in order to make way for the "bandwagon of Anglo-Saxon progress and decency."

Against the backdrop of this nasty guerrilla war the great debate over annexation continued. The treaty debates inspired a number of anti-imperialist groups, which united in 1899 as the American Anti-Imperialist League. The league attracted members representing many shades of opinion; the main thing they had in common was that most belonged to an older generation. Andrew Carnegie footed the bills, but on imperialism at least, labor leader Samuel Gompers was in agreement with him. The usually soft-spoken philosopher William James exploded in opposition: "God damn the United States for its vile conduct in the Philippine Isles!" The selfish proponents of imperialism, he declared, had caused the nation to "puke up its ancient soul."

ORGANIZING THE NEW ACQUISITIONS   Such criticism, however, did not faze the expansionists. Senator Beveridge boasted in 1900: "The Philippines are ours forever. And just beyond the Philippines are China's illimitable markets. We will not retreat from either. . . . The power that rules the Pacific is the power that rules the world. That power will forever be the American Republic."

In the Philippines, McKinley quickly moved toward setting up a civil government. On July 4, 1901, military government ended, and under an act of Congress, Judge William Howard Taft became the civil governor. The Philippine Government Act, passed by Congress on July 1, 1902, made the Philippine Islands an "unorganized territory" and made the inhabitants citizens of the Philippines. In 1934 the Tydings-McDuffie Act offered independence after a tutelary period of ten more years. Independence finally took effect on July 4, 1946.

Puerto Rico had been acquired in part to serve as an American outpost guarding the approaches to the Caribbean and any future isthmian canal. In 1900 the Foraker Act established a civil government on the island. Residents of the island were citizens of Puerto Rico but not of the United States until 1917, when they were granted United States citizenship. In 1952 Puerto Rico became a commonwealth with its own constitution and elected officials, a unique status. Like a state, Puerto Rico is free to change its constitution insofar as it does not conflict with the United States Constitution.

American authorities soon learned that liberated Cuba posed problems at least as irksome as those in the new possessions. After the American forces had restored order, started schools, and improved sanitary conditions, they began turning over the reins of power to the Cubans. The Platt Amendment to the Army Appropriations Bill passed by Congress in 1901, however, sharply restricted the new government's independence. The amendment required Cuba never to impair its independence by treaty with a third power, to maintain its debt within the government's power to repay out of ordinary revenues, and to acknowledge the right of the United States to intervene for the preservation of Cuban independence and the maintenance of "a government adequate for the protection of life, property, and individual liberty." Finally, Cuba was called upon to sell or lease to the United States lands to be used for coaling or naval stations—a proviso that led to an American naval base at Guantanamo Bay, which remains in existence.

IMPERIAL RIVALRIES IN EAST ASIA

CHINA AND THE "OPEN DOOR" During the 1890s not only the United States but also Japan emerged as a world power. Commodore Matthew Perry's voyage of 1853–1854 had opened Japan to Western ways, and the island nation began modernization in earnest after the 1860s. Flexing its new muscles, Japan engaged China's stagnant empire in the Sino-Japanese War (1894–1895) and, as a result, acquired the island of Taiwan (renamed Formosa). China's weakness, demonstrated in the war, led Russia, England, France, and Germany to renew their scramble for "spheres of influence" on that remaining frontier of imperialist expansion.

The possibility that these competing powers would carve up China and erect tariff barriers in their own spheres of influence dimmed the bright prospect of American trade with China. The British had much to lose in a tariff war though, for they already enjoyed substantial trade with China. Fearful of such a development, the British suggested in 1899 that the United States join them in preserving China's commercial and territorial integrity.

The State Department agreed that something must be done, but Secretary of State John Hay preferred to act alone rather than in concert with the British. In its origins and content, then, what came to be known as the Open Door Policy resembled the Monroe Doctrine. In both cases the United States proclaimed unilaterally a hands-off policy that the British had earlier proposed as a joint statement. The policy outlined in Hay's Open Door Note, dispatched in 1899 to London, Berlin, and St. Petersburg, and a little later to Tokyo, Rome, and Paris, proposed to keep China open to trade with all countries on an equal basis. None except Britain accepted Hay's principles, but none rejected them either, so Hay blandly announced that all powers had accepted the policy.

Soon after that a new crisis arose. In 1900 a group of Chinese nationalists known to the Western world as Boxers rose in rebellion against foreign encroachments on China, laying siege to foreign embassies in

Peking. The British, Germans, Russians, Japanese, and Americans quickly mounted a military expedition to relieve the embassy compound. Hay, fearful that the intervention might become an excuse to dismember China, seized the chance to further refine his Open Door Policy. The United States, he declared in a circular letter of July 3, 1900, sought a solution that would "preserve Chinese territorial and administrative integrity" as well as "equal and impartial trade with all parts of the Chinese Empire." Six weeks later, the expedition reached Peking and broke the Boxer Rebellion.

The Open Door Policy, if rooted in the self-interest of American businessmen eager to exploit the markets of China, also tapped the deep-seated sympathies of those who opposed imperialism, especially as it endorsed China's territorial integrity. But it had little more legal standing than a pious affirmation. When the Japanese, concerned about Russian pressure in Manchuria, asked how the United States intended to enforce the policy, Hay replied that the United States was "not prepared" to do so. So it would remain for forty years, a hollow but dangerous commitment, until continued Japanese expansion would bring war with America in 1941.

An American Original

More than any other American political leader of his time, Theodore Roosevelt helped transform the role of the United States in world affairs. The nation had emerged from the Spanish-American War a world power, and he insisted that this entailed major new responsibilities. To ensure that the country accepted such international obligations, Roosevelt stretched both the Constitution and executive power to the limit. In the process he pushed a reluctant nation onto the center stage of world affairs.

ROOSEVELT'S RISE In the fall elections of 1898 Republicans benefited from the euphoria of military victory and increased their majority in Congress. That hardly amounted to a mandate for imperialism, however, since the election preceded most of the debates on the issue. In 1900 the Democrats turned once again to Bryan, who sought to make imperialism the "paramount issue" of the campaign. The Democratic

Roosevelt on the stump, Wyoming, 1903.

platform condemned the Philippine involvement as "an unnecessary war" that had "placed the United States, previously known . . . throughout the world as the champion of freedom, in the false and un-American position of crushing with military force the efforts of our former allies to achieve liberty and self-government." The Republicans welcomed the issue. They renominated McKinley, and named as his running mate Theodore Roosevelt, who had been elected governor of New York after his role in the Spanish-American War.

The trouble with Bryan's idea of a solemn referendum on imperialism was the near impossibility of making any presidential contest so simple. Bryan himself complicated his message by insisting once again on free silver, and the tariff became an issue again too. The Republicans' biggest advantage was probably the return to prosperity, which they were fully ready to take credit for. So those who opposed imperialism but also opposed free silver or tariff reduction faced a bewildering choice.

The outcome was a victory for McKinley greater than his last, by 7.2 million to 6.4 million in the popular vote and by 292 to 155 in the electoral vote. There had been no clear-cut referendum on annexations, but the question was settled nonetheless, although it would take yet another year and a half to subdue the Filipino rebels. The job would be finished, however, under the direction of another president.

On September 6, 1901, while McKinley attended a reception at the Pan-American Exposition in Buffalo, a fanatical anarchist named Leon Czolgosz approached him with a gun and fired at point-blank range. McKinley died six days later, suddenly elevating Theodore Roosevelt to the White House. "Now look," Mark Hanna erupted. "That damned cowboy is President of the United States!"

Six weeks short of his forty-third birthday, Roosevelt was the youngest man ever to take charge of the White House, but he brought to it more experience in public affairs than most and more vitality than any. Born in 1858, the son of a wealthy New York merchant and a Georgia belle, Roosevelt grew up in Manhattan in cultured comfort, visited Europe as a child, spoke German fluently, and graduated Phi Beta Kappa from Harvard in 1880. A sickly, scrawny boy, he built himself up by sheer force of will into a uniquely blended physical and intellectual athlete who became a lifelong preacher and practitioner of the "strenuous life." Boxer, wrestler, and hardy outdoorsman, he was also an omnivorous reader, renowned historian and essayist, and outspoken moralist.

After Harvard, Roosevelt read law briefly and within two years of graduation won election to the New York legislature. That same year he published *The Naval War of 1812*, the first of a number of historical, biographical, and other writings to flow from his pen. He seemingly had the world at his feet—and then disaster struck. In 1884 his beloved mother, only forty-eight years old, died. Eleven hours later, in the same house, his twenty-two-year-old wife died in his arms, soon after giving birth to their only child. That night Roosevelt drew a large cross over the entry in his diary: "The light has gone out of my life." The double funeral was so wrenching that the officiating minister wept throughout his prayer.

In an attempt to recover from this "strange and terrible fate," Roosevelt sold the family house and moved west to take up the cattle business on the Dakota frontier. Adorned in a custom-fitting buckskin shirt, silver spurs, and alligator boots, he told a relative he was "having a glorious time here." The blue-blooded New Yorker came to relish hunting, leading roundups, capturing outlaws, fighting Indians—and reading

Tolstoy by the campfire. Although his western career was brief, he never quite got over being a cowboy.

Back in New York the charming, earnest Roosevelt ran for mayor, and later served six years as civil service commissioner and two years as New York City's police commissioner. In the latter capacity he loved to don a black cloak and broad-brimmed hat and patrol the streets at midnight. When he came upon a sleeping policeman, Roosevelt would rap the man with his nightstick. Such devotion to duty led McKinley to appoint him assistant secretary of the navy in 1897, and Roosevelt did all he could to promote the war with Spain over Cuba. "A just war," he insisted, "is in the long run far better for a man's soul than the most prosperous peace."

As a public servant Roosevelt quickly developed a reputation as a prodigious worker renowned for his pristine integrity and infectious sense of humor. Indeed, Teddy Roosevelt was an American original of seismic magnitude. His glittering spectacles and glistening teeth, along with his captivating grin and overflowing gusto, were a godsend to the cartoonists, who added another trademark when he pronounced the adage "Speak softly, and carry a big stick."

Along with his boundless energy went an unshakable righteousness and a tendency to cast every issue in moral and patriotic terms. He saw the presidency as his "bully pulpit," and he was eager to preach fist-smacking sermons on the virtues of righteousness, honesty, civic duty, and the strenuous life to his national flock. But appearances were deceiving. The boundless energy left a false impression of impulsiveness, and the talk of morality actually cloaked a cautious pragmatism. Roosevelt could get carried away on occasion, but as he said of his foreign policy steps, this was likely to happen only when "I am assured that I shall be able eventually to carry out my will by force."

ROOSEVELT'S FOREIGN POLICY

BUILDING THE PANAMA CANAL   After the Spanish-American War the United States became more deeply involved than ever in the Caribbean area, where one issue overshadowed every other: the Panama Canal. The narrow isthmus of Panama had excited dreams of an interoceanic canal ever since Balboa's crossing in 1513. After America's

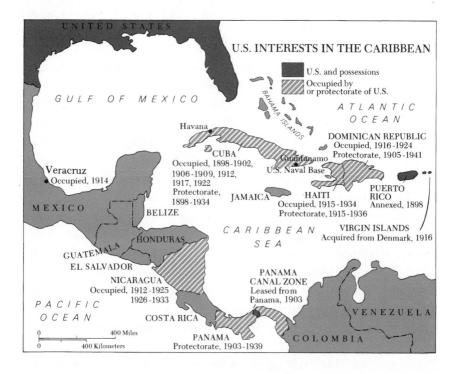

U.S. INTERESTS IN THE CARIBBEAN

■ U.S. and possessions
▨ Occupied by or protectorate of U.S.

victory over Spain, Secretary of State John Hay commenced talks with the British ambassador to gain Britain's consent to an American plan to build a canal. These negotiations led to the Hay-Pauncefote Treaty of 1901, in which Britain gave its consent to the American plan.

Other obstacles remained, however. From 1881 to 1887 a French company had spent nearly $300 million and sacrificed some 20,000 lives to dig less than a third of a canal through Panama. The company now offered to sell its holdings to the United States. Meanwhile Secretary Hay had opened negotiations with Ambassador Thomas Herrán of Colombia to build a canal across Panama, which was then a reluctant province of Colombia. In return for a Canal Zone six miles wide, the United States agreed to pay $10 million in cash and a rental fee of $250,000 a year. The United States Senate ratified the Hay-Herrán Treaty in 1903, but the Colombian Senate held out for $25 million in cash. Incensed by the "foolish and homicidal corruptionists at Bogotá," Theodore Roosevelt flew into a rage punctuated by references to "dagoes" and "contemptible little creatures."

Meanwhile in Panama itself, Colombia's rejection of the treaty heightened the desire for independence. Recognizing this development, an employee of the French canal company then hatched a plot in collusion with the company's representative, Philippe Bunau-Varilla.

He visited Roosevelt and Hay and, apparently with inside information, informed the Panamanian rebels that the U.S.S. *Nashville* would call at Colón in Panama on November 2, 1903.

An army of some 500 Panamanians revolted against Colombian rule the next day. Colombian troops, who could not penetrate the overland jungle, found American ships athwart the sea lanes. On November 4 the rebel commander addressed his victorious forces. "The world is astounded at our heroism. President Roosevelt has made good." A few days later the Roosevelt administration indeed made good on its collusion with the revolutionaries by recognizing Panama's independence, and on November 18 Roosevelt and the new Panamanian ambassador, who happened to be Bunau-Varilla, signed a treaty extending the Canal Zone from six to ten miles in width. For $10 million down and $250,000 a year the United States received "in perpetuity the use, occupation and control" of the zone. "I took Panama," Roosevelt would later boast.

In essence he had. But by needlessly offending Latin American sensibilities, Roosevelt had committed one of the greatest blunders in American foreign policy. Colombia eventually got its $25 million from the Harding administration in 1921, but only after America's interest in Colombian oil had lubricated the wheels of diplomacy. There was no apology, but the payment was made to remove "all misunderstandings growing out of the political events in Panama, November, 1903." The canal itself opened on August 15, 1914, less than two weeks after the outbreak of World War I in Europe. It was a tribute to American engineering and a boon to American commerce and the Panamanian economy.

THE ROOSEVELT COROLLARY   Even without the canal, the United States would have been concerned with the stability of the Caribbean area, and particularly with the activities of any hostile power in the region. A prime excuse for intervention in those days was to force the collection of debts owed to foreigners. In 1904 a crisis over the Dominican Republic's debts gave Roosevelt an opportunity to formulate American policy. In his annual address to Congress in 1904, he set forth what came to be known as the Roosevelt Corollary to the Monroe Doctrine: the principle, in short, was that since the Monroe Doctrine enjoined European intervention in the region, the United States was justified in

The World's Constable. *Theodore Roosevelt, shown here as the world's policeman, wields the "big stick" symbolizing his approach to diplomacy.*

intervening first to forestall the actions of outsiders. Roosevelt suggested that the United States could exercise an "international police power" in its own sphere of influence. As put into practice by mutual agreement with the Dominican Republic in 1905, the Roosevelt Corollary called for the United States to install and protect a collector of customs, who would apply a portion of his revenues to debt payments. The principle, applied peaceably in 1905, became the basis for military interventions later.

THE RUSSO-JAPANESE WAR   In East Asia, meanwhile, the Open Door policy received a serious challenge when tensions between Russia and Japan flared into a fight over China and Korea. On February 8, 1904, war broke out when the Japanese launched a surprise attack that devastated the Russian fleet. The Japanese then occupied Korea and drove the Russians back into Manchuria. But neither side could score a knockout blow, and neither relished a prolonged war. When the Japanese signaled President Roosevelt that they would welcome a negotiated settlement, he agreed to sponsor a peace conference in Portsmouth, New Hampshire. In the Treaty of Portsmouth (1905), the concessions all went to the Japanese. Russia acknowledged Japan's "predominant political, military, and economic interests in Korea" (Japan would annex the kingdom in 1910), and both powers agreed to evacuate Manchuria.

AMERICA'S RELATIONS WITH JAPAN   Japan's show of strength in the war with Russia raised doubts about the security of the Philippines. During the Portsmouth talks Roosevelt sent Secretary of War William Howard Taft to meet with the Japanese foreign minister in Tokyo. The two men arrived at the Taft-Katsura Agreement of July 29, 1905, in which the United States accepted Japanese control of Korea and Japan disavowed any designs on the Philippines. Three years later, the Root-Takahira Agreement, negotiated by Secretary of State Elihu Root and the Japanese ambassador, endorsed the status quo, promised to respect the other's possessions, and reinforced the Open Door Policy by supporting "the independence and integrity of China" and "the principle of equal opportunity for commerce and industry in China."

Behind the diplomatic facade of goodwill, however, lay simmering mutual distrust. For many Americans the Russian threat in East Asia now gave way to distrust of Japan's "yellow peril" (a term coined by Germany's Kaiser Wilhelm II). Racial animosities on the West Coast helped sour relations with Japan. In 1906 the San Francisco school board ordered students of Chinese, Japanese, and Korean descent to attend a separate public school. The Japanese government sharply protested this show of prejudice, and President Roosevelt managed to talk the school board into changing its mind. For its part Japan then agreed to limit sharply its issuance of passports to the United States. This "Gentleman's Agreement" of 1907, the precise terms of which have never been revealed, halted the influx of Japanese immigrants and brought some respite to racial agitations in California.

THE UNITED STATES AND EUROPE   During these years of expansionism abroad, the United States cast its gaze mainly westward and southward. But events in Europe required attention. While Roosevelt was mediating the Russo-Japanese War in 1905, another dangerous crisis began heating up in Morocco, where the Germans and French fought for control. Roosevelt felt that the United States had something at stake in preventing the outbreak of a major war. At the kaiser's behest he talked the French and British into attending an international conference at Algeciras, Spain, with American delegates present. Roosevelt then maneuvered the Germans into accepting his lead. The Act of Algeciras, signed in 1906, affirmed the independence of Morocco and guaranteed an open door for trade there. Roosevelt received the Nobel

Peace Prize in 1906 for his work at Portsmouth and Algeciras. For all his bellicosity on other occasions, he had earned it.

Before Roosevelt left the White House in March 1909, he celebrated America's rise to world power with one great flourish. In 1907 he sent the United States navy, by then second in strength only to the British fleet, on a grand tour around the world. At every port of call the "Great White Fleet" set off rousing celebrations. It was the first such display of American naval might in the Pacific, and many feared the reaction of the Japanese, for whose benefit Roosevelt had in fact staged the show. They need not have worried, for in Japan the flotilla got the greatest welcome of all. Thousands of schoolchildren turned out waving tiny American flags and singing "The Star Spangled Banner" in English. The triumphal procession continued home by way of the Mediterranean and steamed back into American waters in 1909, just in time to close out Roosevelt's presidency on a note of success.

But that note would not resonate for long. In time the mixed consequences of Roosevelt's policies in Latin America and Asia would catch up to the United States.

MAKING CONNECTIONS

- The Spanish-American war marked a turning point in American foreign policy. America's emergence as a global power is a central theme in the twentieth century.

- Theodore Roosevelt's foreign policy displayed an activist approach to the presidency. In the next chapter we see the connections between his foreign policies and his approach to domestic affairs.

Further Reading

A survey of the diplomacy of the era is Robert L. Beisner's *From the Old Diplomacy to the New, 1865–1900* (2nd ed., 1986).* For background to the events of the 1890s, see Walter LaFeber's *The New Empire: An Interpretation of American Expansion, 1860–1898* (1963).* David F. Trask's *The War with Spain in 1898* (1981) is the comprehensive volume on that conflict. See also H. Wayne Morgan's concise *America's Road to Empire: The War with Spain and Overseas Expansion* (1965).* For an account of American involvement in the Philippines from the 1890s to the present, see H. W. Brands's *Bound to Empire: The United States and the Philippines* (1992).

A good introduction to American interest in China is Michael H. Hunt's *The Making of a Special Relationship* (1983).* For American policy in the Caribbean and Central America, see Walter LaFeber's *Inevitable Revolutions* (1983)* and Bruce J. Calder's *The Impact of Intervention* (1984).

*These books are available in paperback editions.

23 ∞ PROGRESSIVISM: ROOSEVELT, TAFT, AND WILSON

CHAPTER ORGANIZER

This chapter focuses on:

- the social bases of progressivism

- the basic elements of progressive reform

- the presidencies of Theodore Roosevelt. William H. Taft, and Woodrow Wilson

- the significance of the election of 1912

ELEMENTS OF REFORM

Theodore Roosevelt's emergence as a national leader coincided roughly with the onset of what historians have labeled the Progressive Era (1900–1917). The rise of the so-called Progressive movement had many causes, the most powerful of which was the devastating depression of the 1890s and its attendant social unrest. The depression brought hard times to the cities and provoked both the fears and consciences of the rapidly growing middle and upper-middle classes. By the turn of the century so many activists were at work seeking to diagnose and heal the worst sores on the body politic that people began to speak of a "Progressive age," an era of fermenting idealism and constructive social, economic, and political change.

Progressivism was a reform movement so varied and comprehensive it almost defies definition. Political progressives saw themselves as engaged in a crusade against the abuses of urban political bosses and corporate robber barons. Their goals were greater democracy, honest government, more effective regulation of business, and greater social justice for working people. One paradox in the movement was that it contained an element of conservatism. In some cases the regulation of business turned out actually to be regulation proposed *by* business leaders, who preferred the stability afforded by a regulated market to the chaos and uncertainty of unrestrained competition.

The Kansas editor William Allen White hinted at another paradox in the movement when he called progressivism just populism that had "shaved its whiskers, washed its shirt, put on a derby, and moved up into the middle class." As White suggested, urban business and professional leaders brought to progressivism a certain respectability that the Populists had lacked. They also brought a more businesslike, efficient approach to reform. While one strand in the complex fabric of progressivism retained the resonant appeal of agrarian democracy and its antitrust traditions, a new emphasis on efficiency and tighter organization soon gained ascendancy. Even farm groups replaced their loose grassroots structures with more centralized and bureaucratic forms of organization. In so doing, they and other progressives may have been trying to find a new sense of identity, no longer derived from the local community, in business and professional groups.

It should be clear, then, that the Progressive movement represented the common spirit of an age rather than a single organized group or party. What reformers shared was a common assumption that the complex social ills and tensions generated by the urban-industrial revolution required new responses, responses that frequently entailed expanding the scope of local, state, and federal government authority.

The "real heart of the movement," declared one reformer, was "to use the government as an agency of human welfare." Governments were now called upon to extend a broad range of direct services: schools, good roads (a movement propelled first by cyclists and then by automobilists), conservation, public health and welfare, care of the handi-

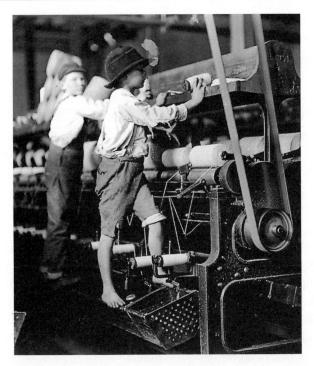

Child workers at a spinning frame, Macon, Georgia, 1909.

capped, farm loans and demonstration agents, among other things. Such initiatives represented the first tentative steps toward what would become known during the 1930s and after as the welfare state.

ANTECEDENTS TO PROGRESSIVISM   Populism was one of the key currents feeding the mainstream of progressivism. The Populist platform of 1892 outlined many reforms that would be accomplished in the Progressive era. After the collapse of the farmers' movement in the aftermath of Bryan's defeats in 1896 and 1900, the focus of the reform spirit increasingly shifted to cities, where middle-class reformers had for years attacked the problems of political bossism and urban development.

The Mugwumps, those gentlemen reformers who had fought the spoils system and promoted a civil service based on merit, supplied the Progressive movement with an important element of its thinking, the good-government ideal. Over the years their ranks had been supplemented and the good-government outlook broadened by leaders who confronted such old and new urban problems as crime, vice, and the efficient provision of gas, electricity, water, sewers, mass transit, and garbage collection.

Finally, another significant force in fostering the spirit of progressivism was the growing prominence of socialist doctrines and their critiques of living and working conditions. The Socialist party of the time, small but earnest and vocal, served as the left wing of progressivism. Still, most progressives found socialist remedies unacceptable, and the main progressive reform impulse grew in part from a desire to counter the growing appeal of socialist doctrines.

THE MUCKRAKERS   Also important in stimulating reform activity were those social critics who publicized festering problems. The writers who thrived on exposing scandal got their name when Theodore Roosevelt compared them to a character in John Bunyan's *Pilgrim's Progress:* "A man that could look no way but downwards with a muckrake in his hands." The "muckrakers" (and Roosevelt was no mean muckraker himself) "are often indispensable to . . . society," Roosevelt said, "but only if they know when to stop raking the muck."

Henry Demarest Lloyd is sometimes cited as the first of the muckrakers for his critical examination of the Standard Oil Company and other monopolies, *Wealth Against Commonwealth* (1894). Lloyd exposed the growth of corporate giants responsible to none but themselves, able to corrupt if not control governments. Lincoln Steffens likewise revealed the prevalence of municipal corruption in a series of articles later collected into a book, *The Shame of the Cities* (1904). Another early muckraker was Jacob Riis, a Danish immigrant who, as an influential New York journalist, exposed slum conditions in *How the Other Half Lives* (1890). The chief outlets for these social critics were the popular middle-class magazines that began to flourish in the 1890s, such as *The Arena* and *McClure's Magazine*. *McClure's* also ran Ida M. Tarbell's *History of the Standard Oil Company* (1904). Tarbell provided a more detailed treatment than the earlier book by Lloyd, but it was all the more damaging in its detail.

Without the muckrakers, progressivism surely would never have achieved the popular support it had. In feeding a growing public appetite for facts about the new urban industrial society, the muckrakers demonstrated one of the salient features of the Progressive movement, and one of its central failures. The progressives were stronger on diagnosis than on remedy, thereby reflecting a naïve faith in the power of democracy. Let the people know, expose corruption, and bring government close to the people, they assumed, and the correction of evils would follow automatically. The cure for the ills of democracy was, to progressive reformers, simply a more enlightened democracy.

THE FEATURES OF PROGRESSIVISM

DEMOCRACY   The most important reform the progressives used to try to democratize government was the direct primary, in which candidates would be nominated by the vote of all party members rather than by a few political bosses. After South Carolina adopted the first statewide primary in 1896, the concept spread within two decades to nearly every other state.

The primary was but one expression of a broad movement for greater public participation in the political process. In 1898 South Dakota became the first state to adopt the initiative and referendum, procedures that allowed voters to enact laws directly. If a designated number of voters petitioned to have a measure put on the ballot (the initiative), the electorate could then vote it up or down (the referendum). In 1910 Oregon instituted the recall, whereby public officials could be removed by petition and vote. By 1920 nearly twenty states had adopted the initiative and referendum and nearly a dozen the recall. The direct election of senators by the people, rather than by the state legislatures, was another progressive political reform. The popular election of senators required a constitutional amendment, and by 1912 the Senate finally agreed to the Seventeenth Amendment, which was ratified by the states in 1913.

EFFICIENCY   A second major theme of progressivism was the "gospel of efficiency." In the business world at the turn of the century and after, Frederick W. Taylor, the original "efficiency expert," developed an array of new scientific management techniques designed to cut costs and enhance productivity. In government, efficiency demanded the reorganization of agencies to prevent overlapping, to establish clear lines of authority, and to fix responsibility.

Two new ideas for making municipal government more efficient gained headway in the first decade of the new century. The commission system was first adopted by Galveston, Texas, in 1901, when local government there collapsed in the aftermath of a devastating hurricane that killed 6,000 people and destroyed half the town. It placed ultimate authority in a board composed of elected administrative heads of city departments—commissioners of sanitation, police, utilities, and so on. By 1914 more than 400 towns and small cities across the country had adopted the commission system. The more durable idea, however, was the city-manager plan, under which a professional administrator ran the government in accordance with policies set by the elected council and mayor. Staunton, Virginia, first adopted the plan in 1908. By 1914 the National Association of City Managers heralded the arrival of a new profession.

By the early twentieth century it was apparent that many functions of government and business now required greater expertise than in pre-industrial America. This principle's most ardent disciple was Progressive governor Robert M. ("Fighting Bob") La Follette of Wisconsin (1901–1906), who established a Legislative Reference Bureau staffed by professors and specialists to provide research, advice, and help in the drafting of legislation designed to curb the power of special interests and promote social justice. This "Wisconsin Idea" of efficient government was widely publicized and copied. La Follette also worked for such reforms as the direct primary, stronger railroad regulation, the conservation of natural resources, and workers' compensation.

Born in a log cabin and educated at the University of Wisconsin, the short, muscular La Follette possessed an abiding faith in grassroots democracy, in the power and judgment of the people. He was more enlightened about modern trends than William Jennings Bryan and equally intense, sincere, and determined. He was also Bryan's equal as an orator; La Follette could talk for hours without taxing himself or his listeners.

Counterparts to La Follette appeared as Progressive governors in other states. As counsel to a legislative committee in New York, Charles Evans Hughes became a national figure by uncovering spectacular insurance frauds, and won the governorship in 1906. Hiram Johnson was elected governor of California in 1910 on the promise of reining in the railroads.

REGULATION   Of all the problems facing American society at the turn of the century, one engaged a greater diversity of reformers and elicited more—and more controversial—solutions than any other: the regulation of giant corporations, which became a third major theme of progressivism. Some progressives advocated a policy of trust-busting in the belief that restoring old-fashioned competition would best prevent economic abuses. The Sherman Anti-Trust Act of 1890 had aimed for this, but the act turned out to be a paper tiger.

Efforts to restore the competition of small firms proved unworkable in part because breaking up large combinations was complex and difficult. Consequently, the main thrust of Progressive reform over the years was toward regulation, rather than dissolution, of big businesses. To some extent regulation and "stabilization" won acceptance among businessmen who, whatever respect they paid to competition in principle, preferred not to face it in practice. In the long run, regulation posed the problem raised in the old maxim: Who will guard the guards? Regulatory agencies often came under the influence or control of those they were supposed to regulate. Railroad executives, for instance, generally had more intimate knowledge of the intricate details involved in their business, giving them the advantage over the outsiders who might be appointed to the Interstate Commerce Commission.

SOCIAL JUSTICE   A fourth important feature of the Progressive spirit was the impulse toward social justice, which motivated diverse actions from private charity drives to campaigns against child labor and liquor. The settlement house movement of the late nineteenth century had spawned a corps of social workers and genteel reformers devoted to the uplift of slum dwellers. But with time it became apparent that social evils extended beyond the reach of private charities and demanded governmental intervention.

Labor legislation was perhaps the most significant reform to emerge from the drive for social justice. The National Child Labor Committee, organized in 1904, led a movement for state laws banning the still widespread employment of young children. Within ten years the committee helped foster new laws in most states banning the labor of underage children (the minimum age varied from twelve to sixteen) and limiting the working hours of older children. Closely linked with the child-labor reform movement was a concerted effort to regulate the hours of work for women. Spearheaded by Florence Kelley, the head of the National Consumers League, this progressive crusade promoted the passage of state laws addressing the distinctive hardships that long working hours imposed on women who were wives and mothers.

The Supreme Court pursued a curiously erratic course in ruling on such state labor laws. In *Lochner v. New York* (1905), the Court voided a ten-hour-day law because it violated workers' "liberty of contract" to accept any terms they chose. Then in *Muller v. Oregon* (1908) the high court upheld a ten-hour law for women largely on the basis of sociological data that attorney Louis D. Brandeis presented regarding the adverse effects of long hours on the health and morals of women. In *Bunting v. Oregon* (1917) the Court accepted a ten-hour day for both men and women, but held out for twenty more years against state minimum-wage laws.

Legislation to protect workers against accidents gained momentum from disasters such as the 1911 fire at the Triangle Shirtwaist Company in New York in which 146 people, mostly young women, died for want of adequate exits. The victims either were trapped on the three upper floors of a ten-story building, or they plunged to the street below. Stricter building codes and factory inspection acts followed.

For many activists the cause of liquor prohibition absorbed the yearnings for reform. The Women's Christian Temperance Union had been battling the sale of alcoholic beverages since 1874, but the most successful political action followed the formation in 1893 of the Anti-Saloon League, an organization that pioneered the strategy of the single-issue pressure group. In 1913 the Anti-Saloon League endorsed a prohibition amendment to the Constitution, adopted by Congress that year. By the time it was ratified six years later, state and local action already had dried up areas occupied by nearly three-fourths of the nation's population.

ROOSEVELT'S PROGRESSIVISM

Theodore Roosevelt brought to the White House in 1901 not only his inexhaustible energy but also an expansive vision of the presidency that was admirably suited to the cause of Progressive reform. In one of his first addresses to Congress, he stressed the need for a new political approach. When the Constitution was first drafted, he explained, the nation's social and economic conditions were quite unlike those at the dawn of the twentieth century. "The conditions are now wholly different and wholly different action is called for."

More than any other president since Lincoln, Roosevelt possessed an activist bent. His was the politics of pure energy. Still, his initial approach to reform was cautious. He sought to avoid the extremes of socialism on the one hand and laissez-faire individualism on the other. A skilled political maneuverer, he cultivated party leaders in Congress and steered away from such meat-grinder issues as the tariff and regulation of the banks. And when he did approach the explosive issue of the trusts, he always took care to reassure the business community. For him, politics was the art of the possible. Unlike the more radical progressives and the doctrinaire "lunatic fringe," as he called them, he would take half a loaf rather than none at all.

THE TRUSTS   Caution characterized Roosevelt's first annual message, but he felt impelled to take up the trust problem in the belief that it might be even more risky to ignore it. The message carefully balanced arguments on both sides of the question. Roosevelt endorsed the "sincere conviction that combination and concentration should be, not prohibited, but supervised and within reasonable limits controlled." In August 1902, he proposed a "square deal" for all, calling for enforcement of existing antitrust laws and stricter controls on big business.

From the outset, however, Roosevelt believed that wholesale trust-busting was too much like trying to unscramble eggs. Effective regulation, he insisted, was better than a futile effort to restore small business, which might be achieved only at a cost to the efficiencies of scale gained in larger operations. Roosevelt nevertheless soon acquired a reputation as a "trustbuster."

Because Congress balked at regulatory legislation, Roosevelt sought to force the issue by a more vigorous prosecution of the Sherman Anti-Trust Act (1890). He chose his target carefully. In the case against the Sugar Trust (*United States v. E.C. Knight and Company*, 1895), the Supreme Court had declared manufacturing a strictly intrastate activity. Most railroads, however, were beyond question engaged in interstate commerce and thus subject to federal authority. Consequently, in

No Lack of Big Game. *A 1905 cartoon shows Roosevelt going after the trusts.*

1902 Roosevelt moved against the Northern Securities Company, a holding company controlling the Great Northern and Northern Pacific railroads. When Roosevelt attacked the new trust, J. P. Morgan invited him to "send your man to my man and they can fix it up." The president refused, and in 1904 the Supreme Court ordered the combination dissolved in *U.S. v. Northern Securities Company.* Roosevelt continued to use his executive powers to enforce the Sherman Act, but he avoided conflict in Congress by drawing back from further proposals for antitrust legislation. Altogether his administration brought about twenty-five antitrust suits.

The most notable victory came in *Swift and Company v. United States* (1905), a decision against the "beef trust" through which most of the packers had avoided competitive bidding in the purchase of livestock. In this decision the Supreme Court put forth the "stream-of-commerce" doctrine, which overturned its previous holding that manufacturing was strictly intrastate. Since both livestock and the meat products of the packers moved in the stream of interstate commerce, the Court reasoned, they were subject to federal regulation. This interpretation of the interstate commerce power would be broadened in later years until few enterprises would remain beyond the reach of federal regulation.

THE 1902 COAL STRIKE   Support for Roosevelt's use of the "big stick" against corporations was strengthened by the stubbornness of mine owners in the anthracite coal strike of 1902. On May 12 the United Mine Workers (UMW) walked off the job in West Virginia and Pennsylvania. They demanded a 20 percent wage increase, a reduction in daily working hours from ten to nine, and formal management recognition of their union. The operators dug in their heels against concessions and shut down the mines in an effort to starve out the miners. As one of them asserted, "The miners don't suffer—why, they can't even speak English."

Facing the real prospect of a national coal shortage, Roosevelt called the parties to a conference at the White House. The mine owners, led by George F. Baer, president of the Reading Railroad, attended but refused even to speak to the UMW leaders. The "extraordinary stupidity and temper" of the "wooden-headed" owners outraged Roosevelt. The president wanted to grab Baer "by the seat of his breeches" and "chuck him out" a White House window.

After the conference ended in an impasse, Roosevelt threatened to take over the mines and run them with the army. When a congressman questioned the constitutionality of such a move, an exasperated Roosevelt grabbed the man by the shoulders and roared: "To hell with the Constitution when the people want coal!" Militarizing the mines would indeed have been an act of dubious legality, but the owners feared that Roosevelt might actually do it and that public opinion would support him.

The coal strike ended in October 1902 with an agreement to submit the issues to an arbitration commission named by the president. The agreement enhanced the prestige of both Roosevelt and the union's leader, although it produced only a partial victory for the miners. By the arbitrators' decision in 1903, the miners won a nine-hour day but only a 10 percent wage increase and no union recognition.

AN EXPANDING STATE   In 1903 Congress strengthened both antitrust enforcement and governmental regulation by creating the Department of Commerce and Labor and by passing the Elkins Act, which made it illegal for corporations to take as well as to give rebates. The Bureau of Corporations, a new federal agency within the new department, had no direct regulatory powers, but it did have a mandate to study and report on the activities of interstate corporations. Its findings could lead to antitrust suits, but its purpose was rather to help corporations correct malpractices and avoid the need for lawsuits. Many companies cooperated, but others held back. When Standard Oil refused to turn over records, the government brought an antitrust suit that resulted in its dissolution in 1911. The Supreme Court ordered the American Tobacco Company broken up at the same time.

ROOSEVELT'S SECOND TERM

Roosevelt's policies built a coalition of progressive- and conservative-minded voters that assured his election in his own right in 1904. The Democrats, having twice lost with Bryan, turned to Alton B. Parker who, as chief justice of New York's state supreme court, had upheld labor's right to the closed shop and the state's right to limit hours of work. Despite Parker's liberal record, party leaders presented him as a safe conservative, and his acceptance of the gold standard as "firmly and irrevocably established" bolstered such a view. Yet the effort to portray their candidate as more conservative than Roosevelt proved a futile gesture for the party that had twice nominated Bryan. Despite Roosevelt's trust-busting, most business leaders, according to the *New York Sun,* preferred the "impulsive candidate of the party of conservatism to the conservative candidate of the party which the business interests regard as permanently and dangerously impulsive." Even J. P. Morgan and E. H. Harriman contributed handsomely to Roosevelt's campaign chest.

An invincible popularity and the sheer force of his personality swept Roosevelt to an impressive victory. Parker carried only the Solid South of the former Confederacy and two border states, Kentucky and Maryland. It was a great personal triumph for Roosevelt. Amid the excitement of election night he announced that he would not run again, a statement he later would regret.

LEGISLATIVE LEADERSHIP   Elected in his own right, Roosevelt approached his second term with heightened confidence and a stronger commitment to progressive reform. In late 1905 he devoted most of his annual message to the need for greater regulation and control of business. This irked his corporate contributors. Said steel baron Henry Frick, "We bought the son of a bitch and then he did not stay put." The independent Roosevelt took aim at the railroads first.

Roosevelt asked Congress to extend the authority of the Interstate Commerce Commission (ICC) and give it effective control over railroad rates. He had to mobilize all the pressure and influence at his disposal to push through the bill introduced by Representative Peter Hepburn of Iowa. Enacted in 1906, the Hepburn Act gave the ICC power to set maximum freight rates. The commission no longer had to go to court to enforce its decisions. The Hepburn Act also extended the ICC's regulatory reach beyond railroads to pipelines, freight companies, sleeping-car companies, bridges, and ferries.

On the very day after passage of the Hepburn Act, a growing movement for the regulation of meat-packers, food processors, and makers of drugs and patent medicines reached fruition. Discontent with abuses in these fields had grown rapidly as a result of the muckrakers' disclosures. The chief chemist of the Agriculture Department, for example, supplied telling evidence of harmful additives used in the preparation of "embalmed meat" and other food products. Others reported on dangerous ingredients in some patent medicines.

Perhaps the most telling blow against such abuses was struck by Upton Sinclair's novel *The Jungle* (1906), which graphically portrayed the filthy conditions in Chicago's meatpacking industry. In the storage rooms, Sinclair wrote, "a man could run his hand over these piles of meat and sweep off handfuls of the dried dung of rats. These rats were nuisances, and the packers would put poisoned bread out for them, they would die, and then rats, bread, and meat would go into the hoppers together." Roosevelt read *The Jungle*—and reacted quickly. He sent two federal agents to Chicago to investigate, and their report confirmed all that Sinclair had said. Soon he and the Congress were hammering out a bill to address the problem.

The Meat Inspection Act of 1906 required federal inspection of meats destined for interstate commerce and empowered officials in the Agriculture Department to impose sanitary standards. The Pure Food and Drug Act, enacted the same day, placed restrictions on the makers of prepared foods and patent medicines, and forbade the manufacture, sale, or transportation of adulterated, misbranded, or harmful foods, drugs, and liquors.

With the achievements of 1903 and 1906, Theodore Roosevelt's campaign for regulatory legislation reached its chief goals and in the process moved the federal government a great distance from the laissez-faire policies that had prevailed before the turn of the century.

CONSERVATION   One of the most enduring legacies of the Roosevelt years was the president's energetic support for the budding conservation movement. Concern for protecting the environment grew with the rising awareness that exploitation of natural resources was despoiling the frontier. As early as 1872 Yellowstone National Park had been set aside as a public reserve, and in 1881, Congress had created a Division of Forestry in the Department of Agriculture. Roosevelt, an ardent hiker, camper, hunter, and bird watcher, was determined to halt the unchecked destruction of the nation's natural resources and wonders by providing a barrier of federal regulation and protection. His appointment of Gifford Pinchot as chief forester resulted in vigorous new scientific management of public lands. Roosevelt added fifty federal wildlife refuges, approved five new national parks, and initiated the system of designating national monuments, such as the Grand Canyon. He also used the Forest Reserve Act (1891) to exclude from settlement or harvest some 172 million acres of timberland. Lumber companies were irate, but Roosevelt held firm, bristling, "I hate a man who would skin the land."

FROM ROOSEVELT TO TAFT

Toward the end of his second term, Roosevelt crowed: "I have had a great time as president." But he was ready to move on, and he held to his 1904 decision not to run again. Instead he sought to have his secretary of war, William Howard Taft, replace him, and the Republican convention ratified the choice on its first ballot in 1908. The Democrats, whose conservative strategy had backfired in 1904, decided to give William Jennings Bryan one more chance. Still vigorous at forty-eight, Bryan retained a faithful following, but once again it was not enough. In the end the voters opted for Roosevelt's chosen successor, leaving Bryan only the southern states plus Nebraska, Colorado, and Nevada. The real surprise of the election was the strong showing of the Socialist party candidate, labor hero Eugene V. Debs. He attracted over 400,000 votes, illustrating the mounting intensity of working-class unrest.

Born to a prominent Cincinnati family, Taft boasted more experience in public service than any president since Van Buren. After graduating second in his class at Yale, he progressed through appointive offices, from assistant prosecutor, tax collector, and judge in Ohio, to solicitor in the Justice Department, federal judge, governor-general in the Philippines, and secretary of war. The presidency was the only elective office he ever held. Later he would be appointed Chief Justice of the Supreme Court (1921–1930), a job more suited to his temperament.

Taft was a jovial man who loved playing golf or poker but detested politics. "Politics, when I am in it," he admitted, "makes me sick." Taft never felt comfortable in the White House. He once observed that whenever someone said "Mr. President," he looked around for Roosevelt. The political dynamo in the family was his wife, Nellie, who had wanted the presidency more than he. One of the major tragedies of Taft's presidency was that Helen "Nellie" Taft suffered a debilitating stroke soon after they entered the White House, and for most of his term, she remained unable to serve as his political adviser.

TARIFF REFORM   Once a student of the social Darwinist William Graham Sumner, Taft had absorbed the laissez-faire views of his mentor and had since differed with orthodox Republican protectionism. Against Roosevelt's advice, he had promised a tariff reduction during the campaign, and true to his word, he called a special session of Congress eleven days after his inauguration. But if in pressing an issue that Roosevelt had skirted Taft seemed bolder, he proved less adroit in shepherding legislation.

A reduced tariff passed the House with surprising ease. But before the Senate passed the bill it made more than 800 changes, most of which raised rates. Outraged by such obvious catering to special interests, a group of ten Progressive Republicans joined the Democrats in an unsuccessful effort to defeat the bill. Taft at first agreed with them, but then, fearful of a party split, he backed the majority and agreed to an imperfect bill. He only made matters worse by calling the tariff the best "that the Republican party ever passed." Temperamentally conservative, inhibited by scruples about interfering too much with the legislative process, Taft drifted into the orbit of the Republican Old Guard and quickly alienated the Progressive wing of his party, whom he tagged "assistant Democrats."

BALLINGER AND PINCHOT   In 1910 Taft's policies drove the wedge deeper between the Republican factions. What came to be known as the Ballinger-Pinchot controversy made Taft appear to be a less reliable custodian of Roosevelt's conservation policies than he actually was. The controversy arose after Taft's secretary of the interior, Richard A. Ballinger, turned over coal-rich government lands in Alaska to a group of investor friends. Apparently without Ballinger's knowledge, this group had already agreed to sell part of the lands to a mining syndicate. When Chief of Forestry Gifford Pinchot revealed the scam, Taft fired him for insubordination. A joint congressional investigation later exonerated Ballinger from all charges of fraud or corruption, but conservationist suspicions created such pressures that he resigned in 1911.

In firing Pinchot, Taft acted on the strictly legal view that his training had taught him to value. But the unsavory circumstances surrounding the incident tarnished Taft's public image. He had been elected to carry out the Roosevelt policies, his opponents said, and he *was* carrying them out—"on a stretcher." And it did not take long for Roosevelt, who was in Europe after completing an African safari ("Let every lion do his duty," J. P. Morgan had wished when Roosevelt left for Africa), to learn of Taft's apparent change of principles.

Events had conspired to cast Taft in a conservative role at a time when Progressive sentiment was riding high. The result was a sharp setback for the president in the congressional elections of 1910, first by the widespread defeat of pro-Taft candidates in the Republican primaries, then by the election of a Democratic majority in the House and of enough Democrats in the Senate that Progressive Republicans could wield the balance of power.

TAFT AND ROOSEVELT   In 1910 Roosevelt had returned from his travels abroad. As news accounts highlighted the Taft "betrayal," his followers urged him to take action. After hesitating for several months, Roosevelt again entered the political arena, having concluded that Taft had "sold the Square Deal down the river." At a speech in Kansas in August 1910, he gave a catchy name to his latest principles, the "New Nationalism," declaring that he intended to put the national interest above any "sectional or personal advantage." Roosevelt then issued a stirring call for an array of new federal regulatory laws and new measures of direct democracy, including the old Populist demands for the initiative, recall, and referendum. His purpose was not to revolutionize American life but to save it from the threat of revolution. "What I have advocated," he explained a few days later, "is not wild radicalism. It is the highest and wisest kind of conservatism."

Thereafter, Roosevelt intensified his criticism of the administration. Equally critical of Taft was Senator Robert La Follette of Wisconsin, who in 1911 helped organize the National Progressive Republican League and soon became its leading candidate for the Republican party nomination. Sensing Taft's weakness, Roosevelt officially threw his hat in the ring in 1912. Even though many of La Follette's supporters rushed to embrace the ex-president, the Wisconsin idealist stubbornly refused to give way to TR. He felt that Roosevelt was not genuinely committed to the sweeping reforms necessary for a truly progressive America.

The rebuke implicit in Roosevelt's decision to run against Taft, his chosen successor, was in many ways undeserved. During Taft's first year in office one political tempest after another left his image irreparably damaged. The three years of solid achievement that followed could not restore its luster or reunite his divided party. Taft had at least attempted tariff reform, which Roosevelt had never dared. And in the end his administration set aside more public lands in four years than TR's had in nearly eight and brought more antitrust suits, by a score of eighty to twenty-five. Taft's reform record was further extended by the establishment of the Bureau of Mines and the Federal Children's Bureau (1912). He also supported both the Sixteenth Amendment (1913), which authorized a federal income tax, and the Seventeenth Amendment (1913), which provided for the popular election of senators.

Despite this record, Roosevelt now hastened Taft's demise. Brusquely pushing aside La Follette's claim to the "progressive" Republican mantle, Roosevelt won most of the Republican primaries in 1912, even in Taft's Ohio. But such popular support was no match for Taft's advantages as president and party leader. The Old Guard's control of the convention machinery ensured their triumph, and the Taft forces proceeded to nominate their man by the same "steamroller" tactics that had nominated Roosevelt in 1904. Outraged at such "naked theft," the

Roosevelt delegates issued a call for a Progressive party convention, which assembled in Chicago on August 5. The new third-party supporters were a curious mixture of social gospel clergymen and laymen, college presidents, professors, journalists, liberal businessmen, and social workers. Roosevelt told the group he felt "fit as a bull moose" in accepting their nomination. Now it was the Democrats' turn.

WILSON'S PROGRESSIVISM

WILSON'S RISE   The emergence of Thomas Woodrow Wilson as the Democratic nominee in 1912 climaxed a political rise even more rapid than that of Cleveland. In 1910, before his election as governor of New Jersey, Wilson had been president of Princeton University, but had never run for public office. Born in Staunton, Virginia, in 1856, the son of a "noble-saintly mother" and a stern Presbyterian minister, he had grown up in Georgia and the Carolinas during the Civil War and Reconstruction. From the beginning he was a reconstructed southerner. As he once stressed, "*because* I love the South, I rejoice in the failure of the Confederacy."

Young Wilson, tall and slender with a long, sharply chiseled face, inherited his father's unquestioning piety, once declaring that "so far as religion is concerned, argument is adjourned." His father also stressed the importance of rhetorical skills: "Learn to think on your feet," he told his son. "Shoot your words straight at the target. Don't mumble and fumble."

Young Wilson soaked up such advice. He also developed a consuming ambition to "serve" humankind. Driven by a sense of destiny and duty, he was resolute, humane, rigid, and self-exacting to a fault. Indeed, Wilson nurtured a righteous commitment to principle. When a friend once insisted that there were two sides to every question, Wilson replied: "Yes, a right side and a wrong side." His fits of tenacious inflexibility would prove to be his Achilles heel.

After college at Princeton and law school at the University of Virginia, Wilson went on to the new Johns Hopkins University in Baltimore, where he studied history and political science. Wilson's dissertation, *Congressional Government,* published in 1885, argued that the president, like the British prime minister, should be the leader of party government, as active in directing legislation as in the administration and enforcement of laws. In calling for a strong presidency, Wilson expressed views closer to those of Roosevelt than those of Taft. He likewise shared Roosevelt's belief that politicians should promote the general welfare rather than narrow special interests. And, like Roosevelt, he was critical of big business, organized labor, socialists, and radical agrarianism.

After teaching at Princeton for twelve years, Wilson was unanimously elected president of the university in 1902. In that position he showed the first evidence of reform views. "We are not put into this world to sit still and know," he stressed in his inaugural address. "We are put into it to act." And act he did. At Princeton he revamped the curriculum, expanded and improved the faculty, introduced the tutorial system, raised admissions standards, and attacked the boisterous and snobbish eating clubs.

His success at Princeton began to attract outside attention. In 1910 New Jersey's Democratic boss offered Wilson his support for the gubernatorial nomination, and Wilson accepted. The party leaders sought a respectable candidate to ward off Progressive challengers, but they discovered too late that the supposedly innocent schoolmaster actually had an iron will of his own. He also had a developing political philosophy. "We are not in the same America as we were ten years ago," he acknowledged in one speech. Elected as a reform candidate, Governor Wilson promoted progressive measures and pushed them through the legislature. He pressured New Jersey lawmakers to enact a workers' compensation law, a corrupt-practices law, measures to regulate public utilities, and ballot reforms. Such strong leadership in a state known as the "home of the trusts" for its lenient corporation laws brought Wilson to national attention.

THE ELECTION OF 1912   In the spring of 1911 a group of southern Democrats in New York opened a Wilson presidential campaign headquarters, and Wilson set forth on strenuous tours into all regions of the country, denouncing special privilege and political bossism. But by convention time, despite a fast start, the Wilson campaign seemed headed for defeat. House Speaker Bennett Champ Clark of Missouri seemed

Democratic candidate Woodrow Wilson speaking from a train platform during the election of 1912.

destined to win the nomination. On the fourteenth ballot, however, Bryan, having decided that party conservatives were behind Clark, went over to Wilson; others followed and Wilson captured the nomination.

No sooner did the campaign open than Roosevelt's candidacy almost ended. While stepping into a car in Milwaukee, he was shot by a crazed fanatic. The bullet went through his overcoat, spectacles case, folded speech, then fractured a rib before lodging just below his right lung. Jolted, he reeled backward, coughed, and then righted himself. "Stand back, don't hurt the man," he yelled at the crowd as they mobbed the attacker. Roosevelt then demanded that he be driven to the auditorium to deliver his speech. His dramatic sense unhampered, he showed the audience his bloodstained shirt and punctured text and vowed: "It takes more than this to kill a bull moose." He apologized for his halting delivery, but, bullet and all, he gave his speech.

Roosevelt was soon shooting verbal bullets at Taft and Wilson. He called Taft a "fathead" with "brains less than those of a guinea pig." Taft, deeply wounded by the sharp rhetoric of his "closest friend," fought back, branding Roosevelt a "demagogue" and "a dangerous egotist." But it quickly became clear that in a three-man race Taft was out of the running. "There are so many people in the country who don't like me," he lamented.

After the initial name-calling, the campaign settled down to a running debate over the competing ideologies of the two front-runners: Roosevelt's "New Nationalism" and Wilson's "New Freedom." The fuzzy ideas that Roosevelt fashioned into his New Nationalism had first been presented systematically in *The Promise of American Life* (1909), a widely influential book by Herbert Croly, a New York journalist. Its central point was that the times required Progressives to give up Jeffersonian prejudices against big government and use the power of government to achieve democratic ends in the public interest.

The old nationalism had been used "by the sinister . . . special interests," TR claimed. His New Nationalism would enable government to achieve social justice, and more specifically to effect such reforms as graduated income and inheritance taxes, workers' compensation for disabling injuries or illnesses, regulation of the labor of women and children, and a stronger Bureau of Corporations. These and more went into the platform of his Progressive party, which called for a federal trade commission with sweeping authority over business and a tariff commission to set rates on a "scientific basis."

Before the end of his administration, Wilson would be swept into the current of such new nationalism too, but initially he adhered to the decentralizing antitrust traditions of his party. Before the start of the campaign Wilson conferred with Louis D. Brandeis, a progressive lawyer from Boston who focused Wilson's thought much as Croly had focused Roosevelt's. Brandeis's design for the New Freedom differed from Roosevelt's New Nationalism in its belief that the federal government should restore competition rather than regulate monopolies. This required eliminating *all* trusts, lowering tariffs, and breaking up the concentration of financial power on Wall Street. Brandeis and Wilson also dreamed of turning over most social programs to the states and cities. In this sense they saw the vigorous expansion of federal power as only a temporary necessity, not a permanent condition. Having restored competition and the diffusion of power and programs, the national government would revert to its aloof heritage. Roosevelt, who was convinced that both corporate concentration and an expanding federal government were permanent developments, dismissed the New Freedom as mere nostalgia.

The Republican schism opened the way for Woodrow Wilson to win by 435 electoral votes to 88 for Roosevelt and 8 for Taft. The Republican Taft and the former Republican Roosevelt were now private citizens. Taft took his loss with grace. When Yale offered him the Kent Chair of Constitutional Law, the rotund ex-president accepted, noting, however, that a "Sofa of Law" might be more appropriate. During the 1920s Chief Justice Taft served on the Supreme Court with distinction. Even his liberal jurist associates afforded him the highest respect. "It's very difficult for me to understand," Louis Brandeis later wrote, "why a man who is so good as Chief Justice . . . could have been so bad as President."

The 1912 election was significant in a number of respects. First, it was a high-water mark for progressivism. The two leading candidates debated the basic issues in a campaign unique for its focus on vital alternatives and for its high philosophical tone. Taft, too, despite his temperament and associations, showed his own progressive instincts. And the Socialist party, the left wing of progressivism, polled over 900,000 votes for Eugene V. Debs, about 6 percent of the total vote, its highest proportion ever.

Second, the election brought the Democrats back into effective national power for the first time since the Civil War. For two years during the second Cleveland administration, 1893–1895, they had held the White House and majorities in both houses of Congress, but they had quickly fallen out of power during the most severe depression in American history to that time. Now they had their chance again.

Third, Wilson's election brought southerners back into the orbit of national and international affairs in a significant way for the first time since the Civil War. Five of Wilson's ten cabinet members were born in the South, and William Jennings Bryan, the secretary of state, was an idol of the southern masses. At the president's right hand, and one of the most influential members of the Wilson circle, was Colonel Edward M. House of Texas. On Capitol Hill southerners, by virtue of their seniority, held most committee chairmanships. As a result, much of the progressive legislation of the Wilson era would bear the names of the southerners who guided the bills through Congress.

WILSONIAN REFORM Wilson's 1913 inaugural address vividly expressed the ideals of social justice that inspired many Progressives. "We have been proud of our industrial achievements," he observed, "but we have not hitherto stopped thoughtfully enough to count the human cost." He promised specifically a lower tariff and a new banking system. "This is not a day of triumph; it is a day of dedication. Here muster, not the forces of party, but the forces of humanity."

Whereas Roosevelt had been a strong president by force of personality, Wilson became a strong president by force of conviction. The president, he argued, must become the dynamic voice in national affairs. Wilson courted popular support, but he also courted members of Congress through personal contacts, invitations to the White House, and visits to the Capitol. He used patronage power to reward friends and punish enemies. Though he might have acted through a bipartisan progressive coalition, he chose instead, as he had argued the president should in *Congressional Government,* to rely on party loyalty.

THE TARIFF   The new president's leadership met its first test on the issue of tariff reform. Wilson summoned Congress into special session and addressed it in person—the first president to do so since John Adams. "The object of the tariff duties henceforth laid must be effective competition," Wilson declared. Congress now acted vigorously on tariff reductions. Only four Democrats bolted the party line as the bill passed the House easily.

The crunch came in the Senate, the traditional graveyard of tariff reform. Swarms of lobbyists got so thick in Washington, Wilson noted, that "a brick couldn't be thrown without hitting one of them." But Wilson turned the tables with a public statement that focused the spotlight on the "industrious and insidious" tariff lobby. In the end Louisiana's two "sugar senators" were the only Democrats to vote against the bill. The Underwood-Simmons Tariff of 1913 reduced the overall average duty from about 37 percent to about 29 percent. The act lowered tariffs but raised internal revenues with the first income tax levied under the newly ratified Sixteenth Amendment.

THE FEDERAL RESERVE ACT   Before the new tariff had cleared the Senate, the administration proposed the first major banking and currency reform since the Civil War. The need for a change had been acknowledged since the brief financial panic of 1907, which threatened to bring on widespread bank failures. The panic revealed what the Populists had long ago pointed out: that the nation's financial fate was determined by huge New York banks and that there was no reliable way to regulate the nation's money supply. Wilson and his advisers wanted a more flexible and decentralized financial system that would expand or contract to meet the nation's fluctuating credit needs.

The Federal Reserve Act, signed into law two days before Christmas 1913, created a new banking system with twelve regional Federal Reserve Banks, each owned by member banks in its district. All national banks became members; state banks could join if they wished. Each member bank had to subscribe 6 percent of its capital to the Federal Reserve Bank and deposit a portion of its reserve there, the amount depending on the size of the community.

These "bankers' banks" dealt chiefly with their members and not at all with individuals. Along with other banking functions, the chief service to member banks was to take over their outstanding loans in exchange for Federal Reserve Notes (paper currency), which member banks might then use to make further loans. This arrangement made it possible to expand both the money supply and bank credit in times of high business activity, or as the level of borrowing increased. A Federal Reserve Board exercised general supervision over the activities of the member banks and adjusted interest rates to fight inflation or stimulate business. It is hard to exaggerate the significance of the passage of the Federal Reserve Act. Through Wilson's skillful leadership, the Congress took a major step in providing the nation with a sound yet flexible currency system and at the same time helped decentralize the money supply.

ANTITRUST LAWS The next major issue confronting Wilson, after tariffs and banking, concerned the antitrust laws. In his campaign Wilson had made trust-busting the central focus of the New Freedom, for the concentration of economic power had continued to grow despite the Sherman Anti-Trust Act and the watchdog agency, the Bureau of Corporations. During the summer of 1914, Wilson decided to make a strong Federal Trade Commission the cornerstone of his antitrust program. Created in 1914, the five-member commission replaced Roosevelt's Bureau of Corporations and assumed new powers to define "unfair trade practices" and to issue "cease and desist" orders when it found evidence of unfair competition.

Having embraced the principle of "controlled competition," Wilson seemed to lose interest in the antitrust bill drafted by Henry D. Clayton (D-Ala.) of the House Judiciary Committee. The Clayton Antitrust Act,

Mr. Wilson Taking Charge of the School. *A cartoon*
depicting the professorial president taking on big business.

passed in 1914, outlawed such practices as price discrimination (charging different customers different prices for the same goods), "tying" agreements that limited the right of dealers to handle the products of competing manufacturers, and corporations' acquisition of stock in competing corporations. In every case, however, conservative forces in the Senate qualified these provisions by tacking on the weakening phrase "where the effect may be to substantially lessen competition" or words of similar effect. In accordance with the president's recommendation, however, corporate officials were made personally responsible for any violations.

Agrarian reformers, in alliance with organized labor, won a stipulation in the Clayton Act that declared farm and labor organizations not to be, per se, unlawful combinations in restraint of trade. Injunctions in labor disputes, moreover, were not to be handed down by federal courts unless "necessary to prevent irreparable injury to property." Though hailed by Samuel Gompers as labor's "Magna Carta," these provisions were actually little more than pious affirmations, as later court decisions would demonstrate. Wilson himself remarked that the act did little more than affirm the right of unions to exist by forbidding their dissolution for being in restraint of trade.

Administration of the antitrust laws generally proved disappointing to the more vehement progressives under Wilson. The Justice Department offered help and advice to business owners interested in arranging matters so as to avoid antitrust prosecutions. The appointment of conservative men to the Interstate Commerce Commission and the Federal Reserve won plaudits from the business world and profoundly disappointed progressives.

SOCIAL JUSTICE   Wilson had in fact never been a strong Progressive of the social-justice persuasion. He had carried out his promises to lower the tariff, reorganize the banking system, and strengthen the antitrust laws, but was not inclined to go much further. The New Freedom was now complete, he wrote late in 1914; the future would be "a time of healing because a time of just dealing."

The sweep of events and the pressures of more far-reaching Progressives pushed Wilson beyond where he intended to go on some points. Yet Wilson retained several social blind spots. Although he endorsed state action for women's suffrage, he declined to support a suffrage amendment because his party platform had not. He withheld support from federal child-labor legislation because he regarded it as a state matter, and he opposed a bill providing federal loans for strapped farmers on the ground that it was "unwise and unjustifiable to extend the credit of the government to a single class of the community."

PROGRESSIVISM FOR WHITES ONLY   Like many other Progressives, Woodrow Wilson showed little interest in the plight of African Americans. In fact, he shared many of the racist attitudes prevalent at the time. Although Wilson never joined the Ku Klux Klan, and he denounced its "reign of terror," he sympathized with its motives to restore white rule in the postwar South and to relieve whites of the "ignorant and hostile" power of the black vote. As a student at Princeton, Wilson had declared that "universal suffrage is the foundation of every evil in this country." He opposed giving the vote to uneducated whites, but he detested the enfranchisement of blacks, arguing that Americans of Anglo-Saxon origin would always resist domination by "an ignorant and inferior race." He believed that white resistance to black rule was "unalterable."

Later, as a politician, Wilson courted black voters, but he rarely consulted African-American leaders and repeatedly avoided opportunities to associate with them in public. Many of the southerners he appointed to his cabinet were uncompromising racists who systematically began segregating the employees in their agencies, even though the agencies had been integrated for over fifty years. Workplaces were segregated by race, as were toilets and drinking fountains. When black leaders protested these actions, Wilson replied that such racial segregation was intended to eliminate "the possibility of friction" in the federal workplace.

PROGRESSIVE RESURGENCE   The need to weld a winning coalition in 1916 pushed Wilson back on the road of reform. Progressive Democrats were restless, and after war broke out in Europe in 1914, further divisions arose over defense and foreign policy. At the same time, the Republicans were repairing their own rift. The Progressive party showed little staying power in the 1914 midterm election, and Roosevelt showed little will to preserve it. Most observers recognized that Wilson could shape a majority only by courting progressives of all parties. In 1916 Wilson scored points with them when he nominated Louis D. Brandeis to the Supreme Court. Conservatives waged a vigorous battle against Brandeis, but Senate progressives rallied to win confirmation of the social-justice champion as the first Jewish member of the Supreme Court.

Wilson meanwhile began to embrace the broad program of farm and labor reforms he had earlier spurned. On the issue of federal farm credit, he reversed himself abruptly, supporting early in 1916 a proposal to set up land banks to sponsor farm loans. With this boost the Federal Farm Loan Act became law. Under the control of a Federal Farm Loan Board, twelve Federal Land Banks, each with a minimum capital of $750,000, paralleled the Federal Reserve Banks and offered low-interest loans to farmers.

The dream of cheap rural credits, sponsored by a generation of Populists, had come to fruition. Democrats never embraced the Populist subtreasury plan, but made a small step in that direction with the Warehouse Act of 1916. This measure authorized federal licensing of private warehouses; federal backing made their receipts for stored produce

A family outside their tumbledown shack, Southern Pines, North Carolina, 1914.

more acceptable to local bankers as collateral for short-term loans. Other concessions to farm demands included the Smith-Lever Act of 1914 and the Smith-Hughes Act of 1917, both of which passed with little controversy. The first provided federal grants-in-aid for farm demonstration agents under the supervision of land-grant colleges to show farmers new planting techniques, fertilizers, and equipment. The second measure funded agricultural and mechanical education in the high schools.

Farmers with automobiles had more than a passing interest as well in the Federal Highways Act of 1916, which provided dollar-matching contributions to states with highway departments that met certain federal standards. The measure authorized distribution of $75 million over five years, and marked a sharp departure from Jacksonian opposition to internal improvements at federal expense, just as the Federal Reserve System departed from Jacksonian banking principles. Although the argument that highways were one of the nation's defense needs had weakened constitutional scruples against the act, it still restricted support to "post roads." A renewal act in 1921 would mark the beginning of a systematic network of numbered U.S. highways.

The progressive resurgence of 1916 broke the logjam on labor reforms as well. Advocates of child-labor legislation persuaded Wilson to overcome doubts of its constitutionality and sign the Keating-Owen Child Labor Act, which excluded from interstate commerce goods manufactured by children under fourteen. But the Supreme Court soon ruled it unconstitutional on the grounds that regulation of interstate commerce could not extend to the conditions of labor. Another important accomplishment was the Adamson Act of 1916, which mandated the eight-hour day for railroad workers.

In Wilson's first term progressive government reached its zenith. A creative time, the age of progressivism at the beginning of the twentieth century set a framework within which American politics and society would still function, by and large, near the end of the century. Progressivism had conquered the old dictum that the government is best which governs least, whatever political rhetoric might be heard to the contrary, and left the more extreme doctrines of limited government as dead as Grover Cleveland. Progressivism, an amalgam of agrarian, business, governmental, and social reform, amounted in the end to a movement for active government on behalf of the public interest.

THE LIMITS OF PROGRESSIVISM

Like all great historic movements, progressivism contained elements of paradox and irony. Despite all the talk of greater democracy at the turn of the century, it was also the age of disfranchisement for southern blacks and xenophobic reactions to "new" immigrants. The initiative and referendum, supposedly democratic reforms, proved subject to manipulation by well-financed publicity campaigns. And much of the public policy of the time came to be formulated by experts and members of appointed boards, not by broad segments of the population. There is a fine irony in the fact that the drive to increase the political role of ordinary people moved parallel with efforts to strengthen executive leadershp and exalt expertise. This age of much-ballyhooed efficiency and bureaucracy, in business as well as government, generated a situation in which more and more key decisions were made by faceless policy makers.

Progressivism was largely a middle-class movement in which the poor and unorganized had little influence. It is surprising that a movement so dedicated to the democratic rhetoric should experience so steady a decline in voter participation. In 1912, the year of the Bull Moose campaign, voting dropped off by almost 7 percent. The new politics of issues and charismatic leaders proved to be less effective in turning out voters than party organizations and bosses had been. And by 1916 the optimism of an age that looked to infinite progress was already confronted by a vast slaughter. Europe had stumbled into war, and America would soon be drawn in. The twentieth century, which had dawned with such bright hopes, held in store episodes of unparalleled horror.

MAKING CONNECTIONS

- Many of the Progressive reforms described in this chapter—particularly business regulation and the growth of the welfare state—provided the seeds for the New Deal reforms of the 1930s (Chapter 27).

- The Progressive impulse carried on after World War I, but was transformed by the new political and social conditions of postwar America. Progressive reforms such as prohibition and women's suffrage were enacted after the war, but the moralistic strain in Progressivism took an ugly turn in the Red Scare and immigration restriction.

- The next chapter shows how Wilson's foreign policy in Latin America and Europe reflected the same moralism that guided his domestic policy.

FURTHER READING

A good introduction to the topic of progressivism can be found in Lewis L. Gould's *Reform and Regulation: American Politics, 1900–1916*

(2nd ed., 1986).* Progressivism has been interpreted in many ways. Robert H. Weibe's *The Search for Order, 1877–1920* (1967)* presents the organizational model for reform. Richard Hofstadter's *The Age of Reform: From Bryan to FDR* (1955)* examines the consensus at the basis of reform. Gabriel Kolko sees reform as a means of social control in *The Triumph of Conservatism* (1963).* Dewey W. Grantham's *Southern Progressivism* (1983)* shows the distinctiveness of reform in that region. A favorable study of progressivism is Alan Dawley's *Struggles for Justice: Social Responsibility and the Liberal State* (1992).

The evolution of government policy toward business is examined in Martin J. Sklar's *The Corporate Reconstruction of American Capitalism, 1890–1916* (1988). On other aspects of the Progressive impulse, see James H. Timberlake's *Prohibition and the Progressive Movement, 1900–1920* (1963) and Ruth Rosen's *The Lost Sisterhood* (1982),* on prostitution. Samuel P. Hays's *Conservation and the Gospel of Efficiency: The Progressive Conservation Movement, 1890–1920* (1959)* and Harold T. Pinkett's *Gifford Pinchot: Private and Public Forester* (1970)* cover conservation and the Ballinger-Pinchot controversy.

*These books are available in paperback editions.

24 WILSON AND THE GREAT WAR

CHAPTER ORGANIZER

This chapter focuses on:

- Wilson's foreign policy toward Mexico

- the causes and early years of the Great War in Europe

- America's entry into and role in the Great War

- Wilson's efforts to promote his peace plan

- the aftermath of the war

WILSON AND FOREIGN AFFAIRS

When Woodrow Wilson was sworn in as president of the United States in 1913, the former college president and professor brought to the office little background in the study or conduct of foreign relations. Wilson admitted as much when he remarked just before taking office that it "would be an irony of fate if my administration had to deal chiefly with foreign affairs." But events in Latin America and Europe were to make the irony all too real. From 1914 on, foreign relations increasingly preoccupied Wilson's attention.

Although lacking in international experience, Wilson did not lack ideas or convictions in this area. He saw himself as a man of destiny who would help create a new world order governed by morality and idealism rather than by greed and crass national interests. He believed that his election had put him on a course charted "by no plan of our conceiving, but by the hand of God who led us into this way." Both he and his secretary of state, William Jennings Bryan, believed that America had been called to promote democracy and moral progress in the world. "When properly directed," Wilson maintained in 1914, "there is no people not fitted for self-government." How to promote such democratic idealism and self-determination abroad, however, remained a thorny issue, as Wilson soon discovered in responding to rapidly changing events in Mexico.

INTERVENTION IN MEXICO   For most of the thirty-five years from 1876 to 1911 President Porfirio Díaz had dominated Mexico. As military dictator he had suppressed opposition and showered favors on his followers and on foreign investors, who piled up holdings in Mexican mines, petroleum, railroads, and agriculture. But eventually the dictator's hold slipped, and in 1910 popular resentment boiled over in revolt. By 1911 revolutionary armies had occupied Mexico City, and Díaz had fled.

The leader of the rebellion, Francisco I. Madero, a charismatic dreamer, proved unable to manage the tough customers attracted to the revolt by the scramble for power. In 1913 General Victoriano Huerta assumed power, and Madero was murdered soon afterward. Wilson challenged the legitimacy of Huerta's violent coup. "I will not recognize a government of butchers," he insisted privately. At the same time he obliquely expressed sympathy with a new revolutionary movement led by Venustiano Carranza and began to put diplomatic pressure on Huerta. "I am going to teach the South American republics to elect good men," he vowed to a visiting British diplomat.

Early in 1914 Wilson removed an embargo on arms to Mexico in order to help Carranza's forces, and he stationed warships off Veracruz to halt foreign arms shipments to Huerta. On April 9, 1914, several American sailors, gathering supplies ashore at Tampico, strayed into a restricted area and were arrested. The local commander quickly released them and sent an apology to the American naval commander. There the incident might have ended, but the naval commander demanded that the Mexicans salute the American flag. Wilson backed him up and won from Congress authority to use force to bring Huerta to terms. Before the Tampico incident could be resolved, Wilson sent a naval force to Veracruz. American marines and sailors went ashore on April 21, 1914, and they forcibly occupied the town at a cost of nineteen killed. The Mexicans lost at least 200 killed.

In Mexico the American occupation aroused the opposition of all factions, and Huerta tried to rally support against foreign invasion. At this juncture Wilson accepted a mediation offer by the ABC powers (Argentina, Brazil, and Chile). In June 1914 they proposed withdrawal of United States forces, the removal of Huerta, and installation of a provisional government. Huerta refused, but the moral effect of the proposal, his isolation abroad, and the growing strength of his foes forced him to leave office in July. In August the Carranzistas entered Mexico City, and in November the Americans left Veracruz. Wilson's "missionary diplomacy" seemed to have worked. "With the retirement of Huerta," one editor predicted, "prospects are bright for the triumph of President Wilson's moral-suasion peace policy." Finally, in October 1915 the United States and several Latin American governments recognized Carranza as president of Mexico.

Still, the troubles south of the border continued. No sooner had the Carranzistas taken power than they began to squabble among themselves for the spoils of office. The most incendiary confrontation occurred between Carranza and his foremost general, Pancho Villa, a moody, violent former bandit who shrewdly claimed to represent "the people" behind the revolution. Such a public stance attracted Wilson's sympathy, and he initially threw American support behind Villa. This turned out to be a colossal blunder. As fighting erupted in 1915 the Villistas suffered several serious defeats. The Wilson administration, confused and frantic, thereupon shifted its stance to that of strict neutrality, with the president announcing that the Mexicans should be allowed to determine their own fate without outside interference.

Critics, however, charged that Wilson was a bungler and a coward. The always militant Theodore Roosevelt, for example, attacked the president's earlier support of the revolution and called for American military intervention to restore order. Responding to such pressure, Wilson warned the two Mexican factions to stop fighting or risk the involvement of American troops. Villa then requested an armistice, but Carranza, sensing his military dominance, rejected Wilson's right to intrude in Mexico's affairs. This led Wilson to grumble that he had "never known a man more impossible to deal with on human principles than this man Carranza."

By the fall of 1915, however, relations between Carranza and Wilson improved, as the United States formally recognized his claim as the *de facto* leader of the Mexican nation. This enraged Villa, and his naturally violent tendencies now came to the fore. In early 1916 Villa's men stopped a train and murdered sixteen American mining engineers in a deliberate attempt to provoke American intervention, discredit Carranza, and build himself up as an opponent of the "Gringos." Two months later, Villa's band of renegades entered Columbus, New Mexico, burned the town, and killed seventeen Americans.

Outraged, Wilson asked Carranza to allow American forces to pursue the attackers into Mexico. He agreed, but grew understandably alarmed when Wilson sent General John J. Pershing and a force of some 11,000 men deep inside Mexico. For nearly a year Pershing's troops chased Villa through northern Mexico but, missing their quarry, they returned home in 1917. Carranza then pressed his own war against the bandits and put through a new liberal constitution in 1917. Mexico was by then well on the way to a more orderly government, almost in spite of Wilson's actions rather than because of them.

The Veracruz incident in April 1914 provoked this comment on Wilson's policy in Mexico.

PROBLEMS IN THE CARIBBEAN   In the Caribbean Wilson found it as hard to act on his ideals as in Mexico. During President Taft's term (1909–1913) refinements of Roosevelt's interventionist policy had earned from its opponents the less exalted—if fairly accurate—title of "dollar diplomacy." The policy so tagged had its origin in China in 1909, when President Taft personally cabled the Chinese government on behalf of American investors interested in an international consortium to finance railroad lines in China. In Latin America "dollar diplomacy" worked differently and with somewhat more success. The idea was to encourage American bankers to help prop up the finances of shaky Caribbean governments.

One of the first applications of Wilsonian idealism to foreign policy came when the president renounced dollar diplomacy. The government, he declared, was not supporting any "special groups or interests." Despite Wilson's public stand against using American force to back up American investments, however, he kept the marines in Nicaragua, where they had been sent by Taft in 1912, to prevent renewed civil war. There they would stay almost continuously through 1933. Then in 1915 Wilson dispatched more marines to Haiti after two successive revolutions and subsequent disorders. The American forces stayed until 1934. Disorders in the Dominican Republic brought American marines to the country in 1916, where they remained until 1924. The presence of American military force in the region only worsened the already prevalent irritation at "Yankee imperialism."

THE GREAT WAR AND AMERICA

Problems in Mexico and Central America loomed larger in Wilson's thinking than the gathering storm in Europe. When the thunderbolt of war struck Europe in the summer of 1914, it came to most Americans, one North Carolinian wrote, "as lightning out of a clear sky." Whatever the troubles in Mexico, whatever disorders and interventions agitated other countries, it seemed unreal that civilized Europe could descend into such an orgy of destruction. But the assassination of Austrian Archduke Franz Ferdinand by a Serbian nationalist, Austria-Hungary's determination to punish Serbia, and Russia's mobi-

EUROPE AT WAR

Central Powers (Triple Alliance)

Allied Powers (Triple Entente)

Neutral countries

lization in sympathy with its Slavic brothers in Serbia suddenly trig-gered a conflict between a European system of alliances: the Triple Al-liance or Central Powers (Germany, Austria-Hungary, and Italy) and the Triple Entente or Allied Powers (France, Great Britain, and Russia). When Russia refused to stop its mobilization, Germany, which backed Austria-Hungary, declared war on Russia on August 1, 1914, and on Russia's ally France two days later. Germany then invaded Belgium to get at France, which brought Great Britain into the war on August 4. Japan, eager to seize German holdings in the Pacific, declared war on August 23, and Turkey entered on the side of the Central Powers a week later. Italy stayed out, however, and struck a bargain under which it joined the Allied Powers in 1915.

AMERICA'S INITIAL REACTIONS Shock in the United States gave way to gratitude that an ocean stood between America and the battle-fields. "Our isolated position and freedom from entangling alliances," said the *Literary Digest*, "inspire our press with cheering assurance that we are in no peril of being drawn into the European quarrel." President Wilson urged the American people to be "neutral in thought as well as in action."

That was more easily said than done, not least for Wilson himself. Americans might want to stay out, but most of them cared deeply which side won. In the 1910 U.S. population of 92 million, more than 32 million were "hyphenated Americans," first- or second-generation immigrants who retained close ties to their old countries. Among the more than 13 million from the countries at war, the 8 million German-Americans were by far the largest group, and the 4 million Irish-Americans harbored a deep-rooted enmity to Britain. These groups instinctively leaned toward the Central Powers.

Old-line Americans, largely of British origin, supported the Allies. If, as has been said, Britain and the United States were divided by a common language, they were united by ties of culture and tradition. Americans identified also with France, which had contributed to American culture and ideas, and to independence itself. Britain and France, if not their ally Russia, seemed the custodians of liberal democracy, while Germany more and more seemed the embodiment of autocracy and militarism. If not a direct threat to the United States, Germany would pose at least a potential threat if it destroyed the balance of power in Europe. High officers of the United States government were pro-British in thought from the outset. Robert Lansing, first counselor of the State Department, Walter Hines Page, ambassador to London, and Colonel Edward House, Wilson's closest adviser, saw in German militarism a potential danger to America.

What effects the propaganda of the warring powers had on American opinion is unclear. The Germans and the British were most active, but German propaganda, which played on American dislike of Russian autocracy and Russian anti-Semitism, fell mainly upon barren ground. Only German- and Irish-Americans responded to a "hate England" theme. From the outset the British had one supreme advantage in this area. Once they had cut the direct telegraph cable from Germany early in the war, nearly all news from the battlefronts had to clear through London.

A STRAINED NEUTRALITY At first the war brought a slump in American exports and the threat of a depression, but by the spring of 1915 the Allies' demand for supplies generated a wartime boom. The Allies bought so much that they soon needed loans to continue their purchases. Early in the war Secretary of State Bryan argued that loans

Helping the President. *Wilson holds to the middle course between Bryan's pacifism and Roosevelt's belligerance in this 1915 cartoon.*

to any warring nation were "inconsistent with the true spirit of neutrality." Technically he was correct, but Wilson, for all his public professions of neutrality, was in fact determined to aid Great Britain. By October 1914 he quietly began approving credits to sustain trade with the Allies. American investors would advance over $2 billion to the Allies before the United States entered the war, and only $27 million to Germany.

The administration nevertheless clung to its official stance of neutrality through two and a half years of warfare in Europe and tried to uphold the traditions of "freedom of the sea," which had guided American policy since the Napoleonic Wars. Trade on the high seas assumed a new importance as the German drive through Belgium and toward Paris finally ground down into the stalemate of trench warfare. In a war of attrition survival depended on access to supplies, and in such a war British naval power counted for a great deal. With the German fleet outnumbered and bottled up almost from the outset, the war in many ways assumed the pattern that in 1812 had led America into war with Britain.

In November 1914 the British declared the whole North Sea a war zone and sowed it with mines. Four months later they further announced that they would seize ships carrying goods of presumed enemy destination, ownership, or origin. British policies of search and seizure caused extended delays in shipping, sometimes running into months. Britain also ordered its ships to stop vessels carrying German goods via neutral ports. When the State Department protested, Britain reminded the United States that this was the same doctrine of continuous voyage on which the United States had acted in the 1860s to keep British goods out of the Confederacy.

NEUTRAL RIGHTS AND SUBMARINES   British actions, which included blacklisting companies that traded with the enemy and censoring the mails, raised some old issues of neutral rights, but the German reaction introduced an entirely new question. In the face of the British blockade, only German submarines could venture out to harass the enemy. On February 4, 1915, in response to the "illegal" British blockade, the German government proclaimed a war zone around the British Isles. Enemy merchant ships in those waters were liable to sinking by submarines, the Germans declared. As the chief advantage of U-boat (*Unterseeboot*) warfare was in surprise, it violated the established international procedure of stopping enemy vessels on the high seas and providing for the safety of passengers and crews. Since the British sometimes flew neutral flags as a ruse, neutral ships in the zone would also be in danger.

The United States pronounced the German policy "an indefensible violation of neutral rights" and warned that Germany would be held to "strict accountability" for any destruction of American lives and property. The administration asked the British to give up flying neutral flags and its blockade of foodstuffs in return for German renunciation of submarine warfare, but nothing came of the effort. On March 28, 1915, one American drowned when the Germans sank a British steamer in the Irish Sea. The following May an American tanker went down with a loss of two lives. The administration was divided on the proper course of action. Bryan wanted to warn American citizens that they entered the war zone at their own risk; his counselor, Robert Lansing, and Colonel House wanted to threaten a possible break in diplomatic relations with Germany.

As Wilson pondered the alternatives, the sinking of the majestic British liner *Lusitania* provoked a crisis. On May 7, 1915, a German U-boat torpedoed the *Lusitania,* which exploded and sank within eighteen minutes. Before the ship's departure from New York, bound for Liverpool, the German embassy had published warnings in the American press against travel to the war zone, but among the 1,198 persons lost were 128 Americans.

Americans were outraged. It was an act of piracy, Theodore Roosevelt declared. To quiet the uproar Wilson stressed: "There is such a thing as a man being too proud to fight. There is such a thing as a nation being so right that it does not need to convince others by force that it is right." Wilson's previous demand for "strict accountability," however, forced him to make a strong response. On May 13 Bryan reluctantly signed a note demanding that the Germans abandon unrestricted submarine warfare, disavow the sinking, and pay reparations. The Germans responded that the passenger ship had been armed (which it was not) and carried a secret cargo of small arms and ammunition (which it did). A second note on June 9 repeated American demands in stronger terms. Bryan, unwilling to risk war on the issue, resigned in protest and joined the peace movement as a private citizen. His successor, Robert Lansing, signed the note.

In response to the uproar over the *Lusitania,* the German government had secretly ordered U-boat captains to avoid sinking large passenger vessels. When, despite the order, two American lives were lost in the sinking of the British liner *Arabic,* bound for New York, the German ambassador demanded and got from Berlin a public assurance, which he delivered on September 1, 1915: "Liners will not be sunk by our submarines without warning and without safety of the lives of non-combatants, provided that the liners do not try to escape or offer resistance." With this "Arabic pledge" Wilson's resolute stand seemed to have won a victory for his policy.

THE DEBATE OVER PREPAREDNESS   The *Lusitania* incident, and more generally the quarrels over neutral commerce, contributed to a growing demand for a stronger American army and navy. After the *Lusi-*

tania sinking the outcry from preparedness advocates grew into a clamor, and Theodore Roosevelt stood at the forefront of the movement. As journalist William Allen White recognized, "Social and industrial justice no longer interested Colonel Roosevelt. He had a war, a war greater than he ever realized it would be, to engage his talents."

In his annual message in 1915, Wilson alerted Congress to his plans for war preparedness. The response was far from unanimous. Progressives and pacifists, and a broad-based antiwar sentiment running through the rural South and West, awakened the traditional American suspicion of standing armies, which dated back to the colonial period. Jane Addams and suffragist Carrie Chapman Catt organized a Women's Peace party. Bryan, La Follette, and other leaders also lent their voices to the peace movement.

Wilson eventually accepted a compromise between advocates of an expanded force under federal control and advocates of a traditional citizen army. The National Defense Act of June 3, 1916, expanded the regular army from 90,000 to 175,000 and permitted a gradual enlargement to 223,000. It also authorized a National Guard of 440,000. The bill for an increased navy had less trouble because of the general feeling expressed by Secretary Josephus Daniels that there was "no danger of militarism from a relatively strong navy such as would come from a big standing army." The Naval Construction Act of August 1916 authorized between $500 and $600 million for a three-year building program.

Forced to relent on preparedness, progressive opponents determined that the financial burden should rest on the wealthy. The income tax became their weapon. Supported by a groundswell of popular support, they wrote into the Revenue Act of 1916 changes that included doubling the basic income tax from 1 to 2 percent. The new taxes on wealth amounted to the most clear-cut victory of radical progressives in the entire Wilson period, a victory that Wilson supported in preparation for the election of 1916.

THE ELECTION OF 1916   Republicans hoped to regain their normal electoral majority, and Roosevelt hoped to be their leader again. But in 1912 he had committed the deadly sin of bolting his party and, what was more, he now expressed a bellicosity on war issues that would scare off voters. Needing somebody who would draw Bull Moose progressives back into the fold, the regulars turned to Justice Charles Evans Hughes, who had made a progressive record as governor of New York from 1907 to 1910. On the Supreme Court since then, he had neither endorsed a candidate in 1912 nor spoken out on foreign policy.

The Democrats, as expected, chose Wilson once again, and in their platform endorsed a program of social legislation, neutrality, and reasonable preparedness. The party further commended women's suffrage to the states, denounced groups that placed the interests of other countries above those of the United States, and pledged support for a postwar League of Nations to enforce peace with collective security measures against aggressors. The Democrats found their most popular issue, however, in Wilson's commitment to neutrality. The peace theme, refined into the slogan "He kept us out of war," became the rallying cry of the campaign, one that had the merit of taking credit without making any promises for the future.

In the end Wilson's twin pledges of peace and progressivism, a unique combination of issues forged in the legislative and diplomatic crucibles of 1916, brought victory. The final vote showed a Democratic sweep of the Far West and South, enough for victory in the electoral college by 277 to 254, and in the popular vote by 9 million to 8.5 million. Wilson also carried many social-justice progressives who in 1912 had supported the Bull Moose campaign.

LAST EFFORTS FOR PEACE   Immediately after the election Wilson began to plan another peace move, but before he was ready the German government announced its readiness to discuss peace terms. Wilson sent identical notes to the belligerent powers, asking each to state its war aims. The Germans responded promptly that they would state theirs only to a conference of the belligerents at a neutral site. In early 1917 the Allies made it plain that they intended to exact reparations, break up the Austro-Hungarian and Ottoman Empires, and destroy German power. Wilson then decided to make one more appeal, in the hope that public opinion would force the hands of the warring governments. Speaking before the Senate, he asserted the right of the United States to share in laying the foundations for a lasting peace. This would have to be a "peace without victory," for only a "peace among equals" could endure.

Although Wilson did not know it, he was already too late. Exactly two weeks before he spoke, German leaders had decided to wage unrestricted submarine warfare. Faced with weakening resources in a war of attrition, the Germans took the calculated risk of provoking American anger in the hope of scoring a quick knockout. On January 31, 1917, Germany announced the new policy, effective the next day: all vessels in the war zone, belligerent or neutral, would be sunk without warning. "Freedom of the seas," said the *Brooklyn Eagle,* "will now be enjoyed by icebergs and fish."

On February 3, 1917, Wilson informed a joint session of Congress that the United States had broken diplomatic relations with the German government. He added that he still did not believe the Germans would do what they said they felt at liberty to do—only overt acts would persuade him that they actually intended to sink neutral ships. In case of such acts, he would take measures to protect American seamen and citizens.

Then, on March 1, news of the so-called Zimmermann Telegram broke in the American press. The British had intercepted and decoded an important message from German Foreign Secretary Arthur Zimmermann to his minister in Mexico. The note instructed the envoy to offer an alliance and financial aid to Mexico in case of war between the United States and Germany. In return for diversionary action against the United States, Mexico would recover "the lost territory in Texas, New Mexico, and Arizona." All this was contingent on war with the United States, but an electrified public read in it an aggressive intent. Later in March another bombshell burst when a revolution overthrew Russia's czarist government and established the provisional government of a Russian Republic. The fall of the czarist autocracy allowed Americans the illusion that all the major Allied powers were now fighting for constitutional democracy. Not until November 1917 was this illusion shattered, when the Bolsheviks seized power in Russia.

AMERICA'S ENTRY

The overt acts of war Wilson awaited came in March 1917, when German submarines sank five American merchant vessels. On March 20 Wilson's cabinet unanimously endorsed a declaration of war, and the following day the president called a special session of Congress. When it met on April 2, Wilson asked Congress to recognize the war that imperial Germany was already waging against the United States, then turned to a discussion of the issues. The German government had revealed itself as a natural foe of liberty, and, Wilson argued, "The world must be made safe for democracy." The war resolution passed the Senate by a vote of 82 to 6 on April 4. The House concurred, 373 to 50, and Wilson signed the measure on April 6. It was Good Friday.

How had it come to this, less than three years after Wilson's proclamation of neutrality? Prominent among the various explanations of America's entrance into the war are the effects of British propaganda and America's deep involvement in trade with the Allies, which some observers then and later credited to the intrigues of war profiteers and munitions makers. Some Americans thought German domination of Europe would be a threat to American security, especially if it meant the destruction or capture of the British navy. Whatever the influence of such factors, they likely would not have been decisive without the issue of submarine warfare. This issue need not have become decisive, either, since such neutrals as Norway, Sweden, and Denmark took relatively heavier losses and yet stayed out of the war. But once Wilson had taken a stand for the traditional rights of neutrals and noncombatants, he was to some extent at the mercy of decisions by the German high command. Wilson was then led step by step into a war over what to a later generation would seem a rather quaint, if noble, set of principles.

AMERICA'S EARLY ROLE   The scope of America's role in the European land war remained unclear for a time. Few on either side of the Atlantic expected more from the United States than a token military effort.

Within a month of America's declaration of war, the British and French requested money for supplies, a request Congress had already anticipated in the Liberty Loan Act of April 24, which added $5 billion to the national debt in "Liberty Bonds." Of this amount, $3 billion could be loaned to the Allied Powers. The United States was also willing to furnish naval support, credits, supplies, and munitions. But to raise and train a large army, equip it, and send it across a submarine-infested ocean seemed out of the question. The United States did agree to send a token force to bolster Anglo-French morale, and on June 26, 1917, the first American contingent, about 14,500 men commanded by General John J. Pershing, began to disembark on the French coast. After reaching Paris, Pershing decided that the war-weary Allies would be

A *Liberty Loan poster with an "honor roll" of ethnic Americans.*

unable to mount an offensive by themselves. He therefore requested that Wilson send a million American troops by the following spring, and the president obliged.

When the United States entered the war the combined strength of the regular army and National Guard was only 379,000; at the end it would be 3.7 million. The need for such large numbers of troops converted Wilson to the idea of conscription. Under the Selective Service Act of May 18, 1917, all men aged twenty-one to thirty (later, from eighteen to forty-five) had to register for service. In the course of the war about 2 million Americans crossed the Atlantic and about 1.4 million saw some combat.

MOBILIZING A NATION Such a total war required complete economic mobilization and more regulation of industry than most progressives had imagined. Still, a lingering lack of coordination among public and private officials made wartime mobilization less efficient than it should have been. It was not the Wilson administration's finest hour.

In 1916 Congress had created a Council of National Defense, which in turn set up more wartime agencies. The United States Shipping

Board, organized in 1917, within two years was constructing more than forty steel and ninety wooden ships monthly. In 1917 Congress created both a Food Administration, headed by Herbert Hoover, a future president, and a Fuel Administration. Hoover, a mining engineer and former head of the Commission for Relief in Belgium, had the responsibility of raising production while reducing civilian use of foodstuffs. "Food will win the war" was the slogan. Hoover directed a propaganda campaign that "Hooverized" the country with "Meatless Tuesdays," "Wheatless Wednesdays," "Porkless Saturdays," the planting of victory gardens, and the use of leftovers. The Fuel Administration introduced the country to Daylight Saving Time and "heatless Mondays."

The War Industries Board (WIB) was established in 1917, and it soon became the most important of all the mobilization agencies. Wilson summoned Bernard Baruch, a brilliant Wall Street investor, to head the board, giving him a virtual dictatorship over the economy. The WIB could allocate raw materials, tell manufacturers what to produce, order construction of new plants, and, with presidential approval, fix prices.

With the high wartime demand for labor, the closing off of foreign immigration, and the movement of 4 million men from the labor force into the armed services, women and blacks and other ethnic minorities were encouraged to enter industries and agricultural activities heretofore dominated by white males. Northern businesses sent recruiting agents into the Deep South to find workers for their factories and mills, and over 400,000 southern blacks began the "Great Migration" northward during the war years, a mass movement that continued unabated through the 1920s. Mexican-Americans followed the same migratory pattern. Recruiting agents and newspaper editors portrayed the North as the "land of promise" for southern blacks suffering from their region's depressed agricultural economy and rising racial intimidation and violence. The African-American newspaper *Chicago Defender* exclaimed: "To die from the bite of frost is far more glorious than at the hands of a mob." By 1930 the number of African Americans living in the North had tripled from 1910 levels.

But the newcomers were not always welcomed above the Mason-Dixon line. Many native white workers resented the new arrivals, and racial tensions sparked riots in cities across the country. In 1917 over forty African Americans and nine whites were killed during a riot over employment in a defense plant in East St. Louis. Two years later the toll of a Chicago race riot was nearly as high, with twenty-three black and fifteen white deaths. In these and other incidents of racial violence the pattern was the same. Whites angered by the influx of blacks into their communities would seize upon an incident to rampage through black neighborhoods, killing, burning, and looting, while white policemen looked the other way or actively encouraged the hooliganism.

American intervention in World War I also had a significant impact on women. Initially, women supported the war effort in traditional ways. They helped organize war-bond and war-relief drives, conserved foodstuffs and war-related materials, supported the Red Cross, and joined the Army nurse corps. But as the scope of the war widened, both government and industry sought to mobilize women workers for service on farms, loading docks, and railway crews, as well as in armaments industries, machine shops, steel and lumber mills, and chemical plants. Many women leaders saw such opportunities as a real breakthrough. "At last, after centuries of disabilities and discrimination," said a speaker at a Women's Trade Union League meeting in 1917, "women are coming into the labor and festival of life on equal terms with men." A black woman who exchanged her job as a live-in servant for work in a

Women taking the place of male workers on the Great Northern Railway, Great Falls, Montana, 1918.

factory declared: "I'll never work in nobody's kitchen but my own any more. No indeed, that's the one thing that makes me stick to this job."

In fact, however, war-generated changes in female employment were limited and brief. About a million women participated in "war work," but most of them were young single women already working outside the home. Most returned to their previous jobs once the war ended. In fact, male-dominated unions encouraged women to revert to their stereotypical domestic roles after the war ended. The Central Federated Union of New York baldly insisted that "the same patriotism which induced women to enter industry during the war should induce them to vacate their positions after the war." The anticipated gains of women in the work force failed to materialize. In fact, by 1920 the 8.5 million working women made up a smaller percentage of the labor force than they had in 1910. Still, one tangible result of women's contributions to the war effort was Woodrow Wilson's decision to endorse female suffrage. In the fall of 1918 he told the Senate that giving women the vote was "vital to the winning of the war."

The wartime emergency placed organized labor in a position to make solid advances in employment and wages, despite the rise in consumer prices. A newly created United States Employment Service placed some 4 million workers in war-related jobs. Labor unions benefited from expanded employment, the increased demand for labor, and government policies favorable to collective bargaining. From 1913 to 1918 AFL membership increased by 37 percent.

The exigencies of winning the war led the government to mobilize more than economic life: the progressive gospel of efficiency suggested mobilizing public opinion as well. On April 14, 1917, eight days after the declaration of war, Wilson established the Committee on Public Information. Its executive director, George Creel, a Denver newsman, sold Wilson on the idea that the best approach to influencing public opinion was "expression, not repression"—propaganda instead of censorship. Creel organized a propaganda machine to convey the Allies' war aims to the people, and above all to the enemy, where it might encourage the forces of moderation. Creel pumped propaganda into Germany that accentuated Wilson's idealism, the size of the American war effort, and offers of an easy peace if the German people would rebel against their government.

CIVIL LIBERTIES   By arousing public opinion to such a frenzy, however, the war effort channeled the zeal of progressivism into grotesque campaigns of "Americanism" and witch-hunting. Wilson had foreseen such consequences. "Once lead this people into war," he told an editor, "and they'll forget there even was such a thing as tolerance." Popular prejudice equated anything German with disloyalty. Schools even dropped German language courses.

While mobs hunted spies and chased rumors, the federal government stalked bigger game, with results often as absurd. The Espionage and Sedition Acts of 1917 and 1918 effectively outlawed criticism of government leaders and war policies. These laws led to more than 1,500 prosecutions and 1,000 convictions. According to one law professor: "It became criminal to advocate heavier taxation instead of bond issues, to state that conscription was unconstitutional though the Supreme Court had not yet held it valid, to say that the sinking of merchant vessels was legal, to urge that a referendum should have preceded our declaration of war, to say that war was contrary to the teachings of Christ."

The impact of these acts fell with most severity upon radicals. In Chicago over 100 leaders of the Industrial Workers of the World went on trial for opposing the war effort. All were found guilty, and the IWW never fully recovered from the blow. The same fate befell the Socialist party. Eugene V. Debs, who had polled over 900,000 votes as the socialist candidate for president in 1912, ardently opposed American intervention, declaring that "I am opposed to every war but one; I am for that war heart and soul, and that is the world-wide revolution." He repeatedly urged men to refuse to serve in the military, even though he knew he could be prosecuted for such remarks under the Espionage Act. "I would a thousand times rather be a free soul in jail than a sycophant and a coward in the streets." He received his wish. Debs was arrested and eventually sentenced to twenty years in prison for encouraging draft resistance. In 1920, still in jail, he polled nearly 1 million votes for president.

In an important decision just after the war, the Supreme Court upheld the Espionage and Sedition Acts. *Schenck v. United States* (1919) sustained the conviction of a man for circulating antidraft leaflets among members of the armed forces. In this case Justice Oliver Wendell Holmes observed: "Free speech would not protect a man in falsely shouting fire in a theater, and causing a panic." The act applied where there was "a clear and present danger" that free speech in wartime might create evils Congress had a right to prevent.

"THE DECISIVE POWER"

American troops played little more than a token role in the European fighting until the end of 1917, when the Allied position turned desperate. In October the Italian lines collapsed in the face of the Austrian offensive. In November the Bolshevik Revolution overthrew the infant Russian Republic, and four months later Lenin's new Soviet government dropped out of the war. With the Central Powers now free to concentrate their forces on the Western Front, the American war effort became a "race for France" to restore the balance of strength in that arena. By March 1918 American troops had assumed responsibility for only 4.5 miles of the Western Front. Anticipating a major German offensive, French Premier Georges Clemenceau appealed to the Ameri-

A gun crew firing on entrenched German positions, 1918.

THE WESTERN FRONT, 1918

—— The Western Front, March 1918
••••• German offensive, spring 1918
⟹ Allied counteroffensive
—— The Western Front, November 1918

cans to accelerate their mobilization: "A terrible blow is imminent," he predicted to an American journalist. "Tell your Americans to come quickly."

THE WESTERN FRONT   The turning point in the western campaign came on July 15, 1918, in the Second Battle of the Marne. On both sides of Reims the Germans commenced their push against the French lines. Within three days they had shot their bolt, and the Allies, mainly with American troops, took the offensive.

Soon the British, French, and American forces began to roll the German front back into Belgium. On September 12, an army of more than 500,000 staged the first strictly American offensive of the war, aimed at German forces at St. Mihiel. Within three days the Germans had pulled back. Two weeks later the massive Meuse-Argonne offensive employed American divisions in a drive toward the rail center at Sédan, which supplied the entire German front. The largest American action of the war, it cost 117,000 American casualties, including 26,000 dead. Through October and early November the battle raged. By the first week of November the Americans were at the outskirts of Sédan and had cut the railroad line. All along the front from Sédan to Flanders the Germans were in retreat. "America," wrote a German commander, "thus became the decisive power in the war."

THE FOURTEEN POINTS   The approaching end of the war brought the question of war aims to the point of decision. Neither the Allies nor the Central Powers, despite Wilson's prodding, had stated openly what they hoped to gain through the bloodletting. Wilson insisted that the Americans had no selfish ends. "We desire no conquest, no dominion," he stressed in his war message. Unfortunately for his purpose, the Bolsheviks later published copies of secret treaties in which the Allies had promised territorial gains in order to win Italy, Romania, and Greece to their side. When an Interallied Conference in Paris late in 1917 failed to agree on a statement of aims, Colonel House advised Wilson to formulate his own.

With advice from a panel of experts, Wilson drew up a statement that would comprise the famous Fourteen Points. These he delivered to a joint session of Congress on January 8, 1918, "as the only possible program" for peace. The first five points called for open diplomacy, freedom of the seas, removal of trade barriers, armaments reduction, and an impartial adjustment of colonial claims based on the interests of the populations involved. Most of the remainder called on the Central Powers to evacuate occupied lands and endorsed self-determination for various nationalities. Point 14, the capstone in Wilson's thinking, championed a general association of nations to guarantee the independence and territorial integrity of all countries, great and small.

Wilson sincerely believed in the Fourteen Points, but they also served important political purposes. One of their aims was to keep Russia in the war by a more liberal statement of purposes—a vain hope, as it turned out. Another was to reassure the Allied peoples that they were involved in a noble cause. A third was to drive a wedge between the governments of the Central Powers and their peoples by the offer of a reasonable peace. But the chaos into which central Europe descended in 1918, as both Germany and Austria-Hungary verged on starvation and experienced socialist uprisings, took matters out of Wilson's hands.

Members of the U.S. 369th Infantry Regiment, which was awarded the Croix de Guerre for bravery at the battle of Meuse-Argonne.

On September 29, 1918, German general Erich Ludendorff advised his government to seek the best peace terms possible. On October 3, a new chancellor made the first German overtures for peace on the basis of the Fourteen Points. The Allies, after a month of diplomatic fencing, accepted the Fourteen Points as a basis of peace but with two significant reservations: they reserved the right to discuss freedom of the seas further, and they demanded reparations for war damages.

Meanwhile German morale plummeted, culminating in a naval mutiny. Germany's allies, Bulgaria, Turkey, and Austria-Hungary, dropped out of the war during the early fall of 1918. On November 9 the kaiser, head of the German Empire, abdicated and a German Republic was proclaimed. Two days later, on November 11, 1918, at 5:00 A.M., an armistice was signed, ceasing the hostilities. Under the armistice the Germans agreed to evacuate occupied territories, pull back behind the Rhine, and surrender their navy, railroad equipment, and other materials. The Germans were assured that the Fourteen Points would be the basis for the peace conference.

INTERVENTION IN RUSSIA   When the war broke out in 1914, czarist Russia was one of the Allied Powers. By 1917 the Russians had suffered some 5.5 million casualties, there were widespread food and ammunition shortages, and the government was in shambles. It gave way to a provisional republican government, which finally succumbed in November 1917 to a revolution led by Vladimir Lenin and his Bolshevik party, who promised the Russian people "Peace, Land, and Bread."

With German troops then deep in Russian territory, and with armies of "White" Russians organizing to resist the Bolsheviks, Lenin concluded a separate peace with the Germans in the Treaty of Brest-Litovsk (March 3, 1918). In an effort to protect stockpiled Allied supplies and encourage the counter-revolutionary Russian "Whites" in prosecuting a civil war against the "Reds," fourteen Allied nations sent troops into eastern Russia. On August 2, 1918, some 8,000 Americans joined the expedition and remained on Russian soil until April 1920.

The Allied intervention in Russia was a colossal failure. The Bolsheviks were able to consolidate their power, defeat the "Whites," and withdraw from World War I. The Russians therefore did not participate in the peace settlement. Even more importantly, Lenin and the Soviets never forgave the West for attempting to thwart their revolution.

THE FIGHT FOR PEACE AT HOME AND ABROAD

DOMESTIC UNREST   Wilson made a fateful decision to attend in person the Paris peace conference, which convened on January 18, 1919, and would last almost six months. A president had never left the country for so long a time, but doing so dramatized all the more Wilson's messianic vision and his desire to ensure his goal of a lasting peace. From one viewpoint it was a shrewd move, for his prestige and determination made a difference in Paris. But he lost touch with developments at home, where his political coalition was already unraveling under the pressures of wartime discontent (a state of war officially existed until 1921). Western farmers complained about the government's control of wheat prices, while Eastern business leaders chafed at revenue policies designed, according to the *New York Sun,* "to pay for the war out of taxes raised north of the Mason and Dixon Line." Labor, despite real gains, groused about inflation and the problems of reconversion to a peacetime economy.

In the midterm elections of 1918, Wilson made matters worse with a partisan appeal for a Democratic Congress to ensure support of his foreign policies. Republicans, who for the most part had supported his war measures, took affront. So too did many voters. In elections held a week before the Armistice, the Democrats lost control of both houses of Congress. With an opposition majority in the new Congress, Wilson further weakened his standing by failing to include a single prominent Republican in the American delegation headed for Paris and the treaty negotiations. Humorist Will Rogers joked that Wilson was telling the Republicans, "I tell you what, we will split 50–50. I will go and you fellows can stay." Former President Taft suggested that Wilson's real intention in going to Paris was "to hog the whole show."

When Wilson reached Europe in December 1918, enthusiastic demonstrations greeted him in Paris. At the conference table, however, Wilson had to deal with some tough-minded statesmen. The Paris conference comprised a body of delegates from all countries that had declared war or broken diplomatic relations with Germany. But it was dominated by the Big Four: the prime ministers of Britain, France, and Italy, and the president of the United States. David Lloyd George of England was a gifted politician fresh from electoral victory on the slogan "Hang the Kaiser." Italy's Vittorio Orlando was there to pick up the spoils promised in the secret Treaty of London (1915). French Premier Georges Clemenceau, a stern realist, insisted on severe measures to weaken Germany and guarantee French security. He scorned Wilson's idealism. "God gave us the Ten Commandments and we broke them," he sneered. "Wilson gave us the Fourteen Points—we shall see."

THE LEAGUE OF NATIONS   Wilson carried the point that his cherished League of Nations must come first in the conference and in the treaty. Whatever compromises he might have to make, whatever mistakes might result, Wilson believed that such a permanent peace agency would maintain international stability.

Wilson presided over the commission set up to work out a charter for the League. Article X of the charter, which he called "the heart of the

League," pledged members to consult on military and economic sanctions against aggressors. The use of arms would be a last resort. The League structure allowed each member an equal voice in the Assembly; the Big Five (Britain, France, Italy, Japan, and the United States) and four other rotating members would make up the Council.

On February 14, 1919, Wilson delivered the finished draft of the League charter and departed the next day for a month-long visit home. Already he faced rumblings of opposition. Republican Henry Cabot Lodge, chairman of the Senate Foreign Relations Committee, claimed that the League was unacceptable "in the form now proposed." His statement of March 4 bore the signatures of thirty-nine Republican senators or senators-elect, more than enough to block ratification.

TERRITORY AND REPARATIONS   Back in Paris, Wilson found it politic to seek amendments to meet the objections at home. These provided that any member nation could withdraw from the League on two years' notice, that domestic affairs remained outside League jurisdiction, and that regional understandings such as the Monroe Doctrine would remain undisturbed. All these went pretty much without saying, but the French exploited Wilson's discomfort to press for territorial concessions and reparations from Germany. Wilson clashed sharply with Clemenceau, but after the president threatened to leave the conference they agreed that the Allies would occupy a demilitarized German Rhineland for fifteen years, and that the League of Nations would administer Germany's Saar Basin. France could use Saar coal mines for fifteen years, after which the region's voters would determine their status.

In other territorial matters Wilson had to compromise his principle of national self-determination. There was in fact no way to make boundaries correspond to ethnic divisions, because the folk wanderings of centuries had left mixed populations scattered through central Europe. In some areas, moreover, national self-determination yielded to other interests such as trade and defense. The result was a reorganized map of central Europe in which portions of the former Austro-Hungarian Empire became independent, most notably Czechoslovakia and Yugoslavia, and portions became attached to Poland, Romania, and Italy. Ethnic and nationalist tensions continued, and would contribute to the crisis that culminated in World War II.

EUROPE AFTER
VERSAILLES

········· 1914 boundaries

New nations

Plebiscite areas

Occupied area

    The discussion of reparations (financial compensation to the victors)
began after the French felt they had already given up a great deal in territorial matters. Britain and France both sought reparations, and the
French wanted enough to cripple Germany's economy. Discussions of
the issue were among the longest and most bitter at the conference.
Despite a pre-Armistice agreement that Germany would be liable only
for civilian damages, Clemenceau and Lloyd George proposed reparations for the entire cost of the war. On this point Wilson made perhaps
his most fateful concessions. He agreed to a clause in the treaty by
which Germany accepted responsibility for starting the war and for its
entire costs. The "war guilt" clause offended all Germans and provided
a source of persistent bitterness. In 1921 a Reparations Commission
estimated that Germany owed the victors $33 billion.

    On May 7, 1919, the victorious powers presented the treaty to the
German delegates, who returned three weeks later with 443 pages of
criticism protesting that the terms violated the Fourteen Points. A few
small changes were made, but when the Germans still refused to sign,
Marshal Ferdinand Foch prepared to move his army across the Rhine.
On June 28 the Germans gave in and signed the treaty at Versailles.

WILSON'S LOSS AT HOME   Wilson returned home with the Versailles Treaty on July 8, 1919. Two days later he called on the Senate to accept "this great duty." The force of Wilson's idealism struck deep, and he returned amid a great clamor of popular support. A third of the state legislatures had endorsed the League, as had thirty-three of forty-eight governors.

Lodge, however, harbored serious reservations. He did not wish the United States to withdraw from world affairs, but he doubted that the Paris negotiators could make "mankind suddenly virtuous by a statute or written constitution." A partisan Republican who nourished an intense dislike for Wilson, Lodge relished a fight. "I never thought I could hate a man as I hate Wilson," he confessed. Lodge knew the undercurrents already stirring up opposition to the treaty: the resentment felt by German, Italian, and Irish groups, the disappointment of liberals at Wilson's compromises on reparations and boundaries, the distractions of demobilization and resulting domestic problems, and the revival of isolationism. Lodge's close friend, Theodore Roosevelt, still a popular figure, lambasted the League, noting that he keenly distrusted a "man who cares for other nations as much as his own."

Others agreed. In the Senate a group of "irreconcilables," fourteen Republicans and two Democrats, opposed American participation in the League on any terms. They were mainly western or midwestern progressives who stood on principle. The irreconcilables would be useful to Lodge's purpose, but he belonged to a larger group of "reservationists." They were ready to compromise with Wilson but insisted on limiting American involvement in the League and its actions. Wilson of course said that he had already amended the covenant to these ends, pointing out that with a veto in the League Council the United States could not be obligated to do anything against its will.

Lodge, who set more store by the old balance of power than by the new idea of collective security, offered a set of amendments, or reservations. Wilson responded by agreeing to interpretive reservations, but to nothing that would reopen the negotiations. He especially opposed the amendments weakening Article X, which provided for collective action by the signatory governments against aggression.

By September, with momentum for the treaty slackening, Wilson decided to go directly to the people. Bold appeals to public opinion had

Three Senators Refuse the Lady a Seat. *Americans reacted against the Senate's defeat of the Versailles peace treaty.*

helped get the New Freedom through Congress—why not the treaty? Against the advice of doctors and friends he set forth on a tour through the Midwest to the West Coast, pounding out speeches on his type-writer between stops. In all he traveled 8,000 miles in twenty-two days, gave thirty-two major addresses, refuted his opponents, and voiced dire warnings.

For a while Wilson seemed to be regaining the initiative, but then his body rebelled. On October 2 he suffered a severe stroke and paralysis on his left side, leaving him an invalid for the rest of his life. For more than seven months his protective wife kept him isolated from all but the most essential business. The illness intensified his stubbornness. He might have done better to have stayed in the White House and secured the best compromise possible, but now he refused to yield anything. As he scoffed to an aide, "Let Lodge compromise."

Lodge was determined to amend the treaty before it was ratified. Be-tween November 7 and 19, the Senate adopted fourteen of Lodge's reservations to the Versailles Treaty, most having to do with the League. Wilson refused to make any compromises or concessions. As a result the Wilsonians found themselves thrown into an unlikely combination with irreconcilables who opposed the treaty under any circumstances. The Senate vote on the treaty with reservations was 39 for and 55 against. On the question of taking the treaty without reservations, irreconcilables and reservationists combined to defeat ratification again, with 38 for and 53 against.

In the face of strong public criticism, however, the Senate voted to reconsider. But the stricken Wilson remained adamant: "Either we should enter the league fearlessly . . . or we should retire as gracefully as possible from the great concert of powers by which the world was saved." On March 19, 1920, twenty-one Democrats deserted Wilson and joined the reservationists, but the treaty once again fell short of a two-thirds majority by a vote of 49 yeas and 35 nays. The real winners were the smallest of the three groups in the Senate, neither the Wilsonians nor the reservationists but the irreconcilables.

Wilson still hoped that he could make the next presidential election a "solemn referendum" on the League of Nations. He deluded himself, as Bryan had in 1900, for presidential elections are determined by many issues. When Congress declared the war at an end by joint resolution on May 20, 1920, Wilson vetoed the action; it was not until after he left office, on July 2, 1921, that a joint resolution officially ended the state of war with Germany and Austria-Hungary. Peace treaties with Germany, Austria, and Hungary were ratified on October 18, 1921, but by then Warren Gamaliel Harding was president of the United States.

Lurching from War to Peace

The Versailles Treaty, for all the time it took in the Senate, was but one issue clamoring for public attention in the turbulent period after the war. On the domestic scene Wilson's leadership was missing. He had been preoccupied by the war and the League, and once broken by his illness became strangely grim and peevish. His rudderless administration floundered through rough waters its last two years.

Demobilization proceeded without plan, indeed without much sense that a plan was needed once the war ended. The War Industries Board closed shop on January 1, 1919, and the sudden cancellation of war contracts left workers and business leaders to cope with reconversion on their own. By April 1919, the armed forces were discharging about 4,000 men daily, and within a year the process was nearly complete.

THE SPANISH FLU   Amid the initial confusion of postwar life many Americans confronted a virulent menace that produced far more casualties than the war itself. It became known as the Spanish flu, and its contagion spread around the globe. Erupting in the spring of 1918 and lasting a year, the pandemic killed more than 22 million people throughout the world, twice as many as the number who had died in World War I. In the United States alone the flu accounted for over 500,000 deaths, five times the number of combat deaths in France. "Never before," a writer in *Science* magazine observed in 1919, had there been "a catastrophe at once so sudden, so devastating and so universal."

American servicemen returning from France brought the flu with them, and it raced through the congested army camps and naval bases. At Fort Riley, Kansas, 522 soldiers contracted the virus and were hospitalized during one week in March 1918. Still, no one seemed alarmed, for the flu remained a common if severe ailment. But then the hospitalized men started dying by the dozens, and it became obvious that this was no ordinary flu virus. Most surprising was the fact that this flu epidemic exacted an unusually high toll among young adults rather than among children and the elderly. In fact, 43,000 American servicemen died of influenza in 1918.

By September 1918 the epidemic had spread to the civilian population. In that month alone 10,000 Americans died from the disease. Municipal health officers began fining people for spitting on the sidewalks or for sneezing without a handkerchief. Millions of people began wearing surgical masks to work. Phone booths were locked up, as were other public facilities such as dance halls, poolrooms, and theaters. Even churches and saloons in many communities were declared off limits. Still the death toll rose. From September 1918 to June 1919 a quarter of the population had contracted the illness.

Yet by the spring of 1919 the pandemic had run its course. It ended as suddenly—and as inexplicably—as it had begun. Although another outbreak occurred in the winter of 1920, the population had grown more resistant to its assaults. No disease, plague, war, famine, or natural catastrophe in world history had killed so many people in such a short time.

THE ECONOMIC TRANSITION   An unforeseen postwar boom eased the country over the difficult economic transition from war to peace.

The boom fed on markets renewed by pent-up demand and wartime savings, and on overseas trade left open because German and British shippers had been weakened by wartime damage. Both farmers and business owners benefited. A record $2 billion cotton crop resulted from a happy mix of high prices and high production in 1919. Reports from the southern countryside marveled at the unaccustomed wealth to be found among tenants and sharecroppers, but a drop in farm prices in 1920 and a general business slump in 1921 ended the euphoria.

The problems of postwar readjustment were worsened by general labor unrest. Prices continued to rise steeply after the war, and discontented workers, released from wartime constraints, were more willing to strike for their demands. In 1919, more than 4 million workers walked out in thousands of disputes, and after a general strike in Seattle, public opinion began to turn hostile.

The most celebrated postwar labor dispute was the Boston Police Strike, which inadvertently launched a presidential career. On September 9, 1919, most of Boston's police force went out on strike, demanding recognition of their union. Governor Calvin Coolidge mobilized the

"Shoeless Joe" Jackson. *The anxieties and illegalities Americans suffered in 1919 touched the national pastime as well, when the World Series was tainted by a scandal involving the Chicago White Sox and their star center fielder, "Shoeless Joe."*

National Guard to arrest looters and restore order. After four days the strikers were ready to return, but the police commissioner fired them all. When Samuel Gompers appealed for their reinstatement, Coolidge responded in words that suddenly turned him into a national figure: "There is no right to strike against the public safety by anybody, anywhere, anytime."

RACIAL FRICTION   The summer of 1919 also brought a season of race riots, North and South. Whites invaded the black section of Longview, Texas, in search of a teacher who had allegedly accused a white woman of a liaison with a black man. They burned shops and houses and ran several blacks out of town. A week later in Washington, D.C., reports of attacks on white women aroused white mobs, and for four days gangs of white and black rioters waged race war in the streets until soldiers and driving rains ended the fighting. These were but preliminaries to the Chicago riot of late July, in which 38 people were killed and 537 injured. The climactic disorders of the summer occurred in the rural area around Elaine, Arkansas, where black tenant farmers tried to organize a union. According to official reports 5 whites and 25 blacks were killed in the violence, but whites told one reporter in the area that more than 100 blacks died. Altogether twenty-five race riots took place in 1919, and more threatened.

THE RED SCARE   Public reaction to the wave of strikes and riots was influenced by the impact of Russia's Bolshevik Revolution. A minority of radicals thought America's domestic turbulence, like that in Russia, was the first scene in a drama of revolution. A much larger public was persuaded that they might be right. After all, Lenin's tiny faction in Russia had exploited confusion to impose its will. Wartime hysteria against all things German was thus readily transformed into a postwar Red Scare.

Fears of revolution might have remained latent except for the actions of a lunatic fringe. In April 1919 the postal services intercepted nearly forty bombs addressed to various prominent citizens. One slipped through and blew off the hands of a Georgia senator's maid. In June another destroyed the front of Attorney-General A. Mitchell Palmer's house in Washington. Such random violence led many Americans to see Red on all sides and to condone attacks on all minorities in retaliation.

Beware the Reefs! *In a* Brooklyn Eagle *cartoon, the ship* Triumphant Democracy *returns from the war to navigate the dangers of "Reaction" and "Bolshevism."*

Soon the government itself was promoting witch-hunts. Attorney-General Palmer harbored a bitter distrust of aliens and a strong desire for the presidency. In June 1919 the Justice Department decided to deport radical aliens, and Palmer set up as the head of the department's new General Intelligence Division the young J. Edgar Hoover, who began to collect an index file on radicals. Raids began on November 7, 1919, when agents swooped down on the Union of Russian Workers in twelve cities. Many of those arrested were deported without a court hearing. On January 2, 1920, police raids in dozens of cities swept up some 5,000 suspects, many taken from their homes without search warrants. About half of those seized were kept in custody. That same month the New York legislature expelled five duly elected Socialist members.

Basking in popular approval, Palmer continued to warn of the Red menace, but like other fads and alarms, the ugly mood of intolerance passed. By the summer of 1920 the Red Scare had begun to evaporate. Communist revolutions in Europe died out, leaving Bolshevism isolated in Russia; bombings tapered off; the strike wave and race riots receded. The attorney-general and his mimics began to seem more threatening to civil liberties than a handful of radicals were to the social order. By September 1920, when a bomb explosion at the corner of Broad and Wall Streets in New York killed thirty-eight people, Americans were ready to take it for what it was, the work of a crazed mind and not the start of a revolution. The Red Scare nevertheless left a lasting mark on American life. Part of its legacy was the continuing crusade for "100 percent Americanism" and restrictions on immigration. It also left a stigma on labor unions and contributed to the anti-union open-shop campaign—the "American Plan," its sponsors called it. But for many thoughtful Americans the chief residue of the Great War and its disordered aftermath was a profound disillusionment.

MAKING CONNECTIONS

- The Red Scare at the end of World War I led to a wave of nativism and immigration restriction, outlined in the next chapter.

- This chapter ends by noting the "profound disillusionment" Americans felt with efforts to reform the world. The political aspect of that disillusionment—the turn to "normalcy" of the 1920s—is discussed in Chapter 26.

- The treaty ending World War I was designed to cripple Germany's military strength. But as Chapter 28 shows, within two decades Adolf Hitler was leading a rebuilt German military force into World War II.

FURTHER READING

A good overview of events covered in this chapter is Robert H. Ferrell's *Woodrow Wilson and World War I, 1917–1921* (1985).* A number of scholars concentrate on the neutrality issue. Arthur S. Link, Wilson's greatest biographer, is sympathetic to the ideals of the president in *Woodrow Wilson: Revolution, War, and Peace* (1979).* For a more critical view, see Ross Gregory's *The Origins of American Intervention in the First World War* (1971).*

Edward M. Coffman's *The War to End All Wars: The American Military Experience in World War I* (1968)* is a detailed presentation of America's military involvement. David M. Kennedy's *Over Here: The First World War and American Society* (1980)* surveys the impact of the war on the home front.

Thomas J. Knock interrelates domestic affairs and foreign relations in his explanation of Wilson's peace-making in *To End All Wars: Woodrow Wilson and the Quest for a New World Order* (1992).*

The problems of the immediate postwar years are chronicled by a number of historians. On the Spanish flu, see Alfred W. Crosby's *America's Forgotten Pandemic: The Influenza of 1918* (1990). Labor tensions are examined in David E. Brody's *Labor in Crisis: The Steel Strike of 1919* (1965) and Francis Russell's *A City in Terror: 1919, the Boston Police Strike* (1975). On racial strife, see William Tuttle, Jr.'s *Race Riot: Chicago and the Red Summer of 1919* (1970).* The fear of Communists is analyzed in Robert K. Murray's *Red Scare: A Study of National Hysteria, 1919–1920* (1955).*

*These books are available in paperback editions.

25 ❦ THE MODERN TEMPER

REACTION IN THE TWENTIES

The "Roaring Twenties" were supposedly years of prosperity, frivolity, and loosening morals. They were that for some Americans, yet for others the period provoked despair and doubt. The war's unprecedented carnage hastened a growing challenge in modern thought to the old values of progress, faith, reason, and optimism. As novelist F. Scott Fitzgerald observed in 1920, "here was a new generation . . . grown up to find all Gods dead, all wars fought, all faiths in man shaken." Such aching disillusionment among what came to be called the "lost generation" was not as widespread as Fitzgerald or others have suggested, but it was a prominent feature of postwar intellectual and social life. Equally visible—and even more potent—was a contrasting mood of defiance against the changes transforming national life. Most Americans remained firmly tied to the old values of church, home, family, farm, and small business, but in the 1920s these ties took on a defensive quality. This mood found expression in a growing tendency to connect American nationalism with nativism, Anglo-Saxon racism, and militant Protestantism.

NATIVISM   In the immediate aftermath of World War I, a wave of strikes, bombings, and race riots convinced many that America was on the verge of revolutionary change. The foreign connections of so many radicals strengthened the suspicion that the seeds of sedition were foreign born. The most celebrated case of the times seemed to prove the connection. It involved two Italian-born anarchists, Nicola Sacco and Bartolomeo Vanzetti. Arrested in 1920 for a robbery and murder in South Braintree, Massachusetts, they were tried by a judge who privately referred to the defendants as "anarchist bastards." The question of the two men's guilt is still disputed. Many then and since have insisted that they were sentenced more for their beliefs and their ethnic origins than for any crime they had committed. The case became a great radical and liberal cause of the 1920s, but despite pleas for mercy and worldwide demonstrations on behalf of the two men, Sacco and Vanzetti were sent to the electric chair in 1927.

The surging postwar nativism brought an end to three centuries of unlimited European immigration dating back to the first colonial settlements. Congress, alarmed at the influx of new foreigners after 1919, passed the Emergency Immigration Act of 1921, which restricted new European arrivals each year to 3 percent of the foreign-born of any nationality as shown in the 1910 census. A new quota law in 1924 reduced the number to 2 percent based on the 1890 census, which included fewer of the "new" immigrants from southern and eastern Europe. This law set a permanent limitation, which became effective in 1929, of slightly over 150,000 immigrants per year based on the "national origins" of the American people as of 1920. In signing the law, President Coolidge pledged: "America must be kept American."

However inexact the quotas, their purpose was clear: to tilt the balance in favor of the old immigration from northern and western Europe, which was assigned about 85 percent of the total. The law completely excluded people from East Asia. Yet it left the gate open to new arrivals from Western Hemisphere countries, so that an ironic consequence

In 1925 the Ku Klux Klan staged a 40,000-man parade down Pennsylvania Avenue in Washington, D.C.

was a great increase in the Hispanic Catholic population. People of Latin American descent (chiefly Mexicans, Puerto Ricans, and Cubans) became the fastest growing ethnic minority in the country.

THE KLAN   During the postwar years the nativist tradition took on a new form, a revived Ku Klux Klan modeled on the group founded during Reconstruction. But now the new Klan was devoted to "100 percent Americanism" rather than the old Confederacy, and restricted its membership to native-born white Protestants. The new Klan was determined to protect its warped notion of the American way of life not only from blacks, but also from Roman Catholics, Jews, and immigrants. America was no melting pot, its founder, the failed Methodist minister William J. Simmons, warned: "It is a garbage can! . . . When the hordes of aliens walk to the ballot box and their votes outnumber yours, then that alien horde has got you by the throat." In going nativist, the Klan had spread far outside the South. Its appeal reached areas as widely scattered as Oregon and Maine, flourishing mainly among the uprooted and insecure native newcomers to the cities and towns. The spooky robes and flaming crosses brought drama into the dreary routine of a thousand communities.

For all its own exotic ritual, the Klan represented a visceral and vicious reflex against the strange and exotic, against shifting moral standards, the declining influence of churches, and the social permissiveness of cities and colleges. In the Southwest the Klan became more than anything else a moral crusade. "It is going to drive the bootleggers forever out of this land," declared a Texan. "It is going to bring clean moving pictures . . . clean literature . . . break up roadside parking . . . enforce the laws . . . protect homes." The Klan used intimidation and floggings to achieve its goals. Estimates of its peak membership, probably inflated, range from 3 million to 8 million, but the Klan's influence decayed as quickly as its numbers grew. For one thing, the Klan suffered from a decline in nativist excitement after passage of the 1924 immigration law. For another, it suffered recurrent factional quarrels and schisms. And its willing use of violence tarnished its moral pretensions.

FUNDAMENTALISM   While the Klan saw a threat mainly in the "alien menace," many adherents of the old-time religion saw threats from modernism in the churches: new ideas that the Bible should be studied in the light of modern scholarship (the "higher criticism"), or that it could be reconciled with scientific theories of evolution. Fearing that such "modernist" notions had infected schools and even pulpits, fundamentalism, grounded in a literal interpretation of the Bible, took on a new militancy.

Among the rural fundamentalist leaders only William Jennings Bryan, the political progressive, had the following, prestige, and eloquence to make the movement a popular crusade. By 1920, Bryan was showing signs of age: paunchy, balding, his face lined with deepening creases, he had lost his commanding physical presence. But he remained as silver-tongued as ever. In 1921 Bryan sparked a drive for laws to prohibit the teaching of evolution in the public schools. He denounced Darwin with the same zeal he had once directed against McKinley. Anti-evolution bills began to appear in legislatures in the Midwest and South, but the only victories came in the South—and there were few of those. Some officials took direct action without legislation. Governor Miriam "Ma" Ferguson of Texas ordered textbooks upholding Darwinism eliminated from state schools. "I am a Christian mother . . ." she declared, "and I am not going to let that kind of rot go into Texas schoolbooks."

The climax came in Tennessee, where in 1925 the legislature outlawed the teaching of evolution in public schools and colleges. A young teacher at a high school in Dayton, Tennessee, John T. Scopes, accepted an offer from the American Civil Liberties Union to defend a test case. It soon was a case heard round the world. Before the opening day of the "monkey trial," the streets of Dayton swarmed with "holy rollers," publicity hounds, curiosity-seekers, professional evangelists and professional atheists, hot-dog and soda-pop hucksters, and a miscellany of reporters. The scene struck H. L. Mencken, the prominent Baltimore satirist, as "genuinely fabulous. I have stored up enough material to last me twenty years."

The two stars of the show were Bryan, who led the prosecution of Scopes for teaching evolution in violation of Tennessee law, and Clarence Darrow, renowned Chicago trial lawyer and confessed agnostic, who defended Scopes by challenging the anti-evolution law. The trial quickly became a debate between fundamentalism and modernism. When the judge (a practicing evangelist) damaged Darrow's

Clarence Darrow (right) shaking hands with John Scopes at the start of the notorious "monkey trial" in Dayton, Tennessee, 1925.

case by ruling out scientific testimony on evolution, most observers assumed the trial was over.

But the defense rebounded by calling Bryan as an expert witness on biblical interpretation. Darrow, who had once supported Bryan, now relentlessly entrapped the elderly statesman in literal-minded interpretations and exposed Bryan's ignorance of biblical history and scholarship. Bryan insisted that a "great fish" actually swallowed Jonah, that Joshua literally made the sun stand still, that the world was created in 4004 B.C.—all, according to Darrow, "fool ideas that no intelligent Christian on earth believes." It was a bitter scene. At one point the two men, their patience exhausted in the broiling summer heat, lunged at one another, shaking their fists, leading the judge to adjourn the court.

The next day the testimony ended. The only issue before the court, the judge ruled, was whether Scopes had in fact taught evolution. He was found guilty, but the Tennessee Supreme Court, while upholding the law, overruled the $100 fine on a legal technicality. The chief prosecutor accepted the higher court's advice against "prolonging the life of this bizarre case" and dropped the issue. With more prescience than he knew, Bryan had described the trial as a "duel to the death." A few days after it closed he died suddenly of a heart condition aggravated by heat and fatigue. After Dayton, the fundamentalists—their fury spent for the moment—went dormant.

PROHIBITION Prohibition offered another example of reforming zeal channeled into a drive for moral righteousness and conformity. American moralists had been campaigning against excessive drink since the eighteenth century. Around 1900, however, the leading temperance organizations, the Women's Christian Temperance Union and the Anti-Saloon League, had converted from efforts to reform individuals to a campaign for legal prohibition. The Anti-Saloon League became one of the most effective pressure groups in American history, mobilizing Protestant churches behind its single-minded battle to elect "dry" candidates.

The 1916 elections finally produced two-thirds majorities in both houses of Congress for a prohibition amendment to the Constitution. Soon the wartime spirit of sacrifice, the need to use grain for food, and wartime hostility to German-American brewers transformed the cause virtually into a test of patriotism. On December 18, 1917, Congress passed and sent to the states the Eighteenth Amendment, which, one year after ratification on January 16, 1919, banned nationwide the manufacture, sale, or transport of intoxicating liquors.

But determined Americans kept drinking. Congress never supplied adequate enforcement, if such were indeed possible given the public thirst, the spotty support of local officials, and the profits to be made in bootlegging. In Detroit the liquor industry during the prohibition era was second in size only to the auto industry. Speakeasies, hip flasks, and cocktail parties were among the social innovations of the prohibition era, along with increased drinking by women.

It would be too much to say that prohibition gave rise to organized crime, for organized vice, gambling, and extortion had long been practiced, and often tied in with the saloons. But prohibition supplied ruthless and flamboyant criminals, such as Al Capone, with an enormous new source of income, while the automobile and the submachine gun provided greater mobility and firepower. Gangland leaders showed remarkable gifts for exploiting loopholes in the law, when they did not simply bribe policemen and politicians.

Capone was by far the most celebrated criminal of the 1920s. In 1927 he pocketed $60 million from his bootlegging, prostitution, and

Al Capone (center) *in 1929.*

gambling empire, and he took pains to flaunt his wealth as well as his open disregard for legal authorities. The son of Italian immigrants, "Scarface" Capone rapidly worked his way up from nightclub bouncer to syndicated crime boss. He wore expensive suits and silk pajamas, rode in a custom-upholstered and bulletproof Cadillac, surrounded himself with an entourage of bodyguards, lavishly supported city charities, and always insisted that he was merely providing the public with the goods and services they demanded. "I've given people light pleasures," he once complained, "and all I get is abuse." He neglected to say that he had also bludgeoned to death several conspiring police lieutenants and ordered the execution of dozens of his criminal competitors. Law-enforcement officials began to smash his bootlegging operations in 1929, but were unable to pin anything on Capone until a Treasury agent infiltrated his gang and uncovered evidence that convicted him later that year for tax evasion. He was sentenced to eleven years in prison.

In the light of the illegal activities of Capone and other organized crime members, it came as no great surprise in 1931 when a commission reported evidence that enforcement of prohibition had broken down. Still, the commission voted to extend prohibition, and President Hoover chose to stand by what he called the "experiment, noble in motive and far-reaching in purpose."

SOCIAL TENSIONS

In many ways the defensive temper of the 1920s and the repressive movements to which it gave rise seem the dominant trends of the decade, but they arose in part as reactions to social and intellectual currents that seemed about to sweep America away from its old moorings. During those years a new cosmopolitan, urban America confronted an old provincial, small-town and farm America, and cultural conflict reached new levels of tension.

The smart set of the sophisticated metropolis developed an active disdain for the old-fashioned values of the hinterlands. Sinclair Lewis's novel *Main Street* (1920) caricatured the stifling life of the prairie town, depicting a "savorless people, gulping tasteless food, and sitting afterward, coatless and thoughtless, in rocking chairs prickly with inane decorations, listening to mechanical music, saying mechanical things about the excellence of Ford automobiles, and viewing themselves as the greatest race in the world." The banality of small-town life became a pervasive theme in much of the literature of the time, and the heartland responded with counterimages of alien cities infested with vice, crime, corruption, and foreigners.

THE NEW MORALITY Much of the shock to traditionalists came from the changes in manners and morals evidenced first among young people, and especially on the college campuses. In *This Side of Paradise* (1920), a novel of student life at Princeton, F. Scott Fitzgerald wrote of "the great current American phenomenon, the 'petting party.'" None of the Victorian mothers, he said, "had any idea how casually their daughters were accustomed to be kissed." From such novels, and also from magazines and movies, many Americans learned about the cities' wild parties, bathtub gin, promiscuity, and speakeasies.

Sex came to be discussed with surprising frankness. Much of the talk derived from a spreading awareness of Dr. Sigmund Freud, the Viennese father of psychoanalysis. When in 1909 Freud visited Clark University in Massachusetts, he was surprised to find himself so well known "even in prudish America." By the 1920s his ideas had begun to percolate into the popular awareness, and the talk spread in society and literature about libido, inhibitions, Oedipus complexes, sublimation, and repression. The writer Sherwood Anderson recalled in his memoirs: "Freud had been discovered at the time and all the young intellectuals were busy analyzing each other and everyone they met."

Freudian themes also penetrated popular culture. Radio singers during the 1920s belted out songs with titles such as "Hot Lips," "I Need Lovin'," and "Burning Kisses." Movie ads promised kisses on screen "where heart, and soul, and sense in concert move, and the blood is lava, and the pulse is ablaze." The new jazz music blended African and European musical traditions into a distinctive brew characterized by improvisation, "blue notes," and polyrhythms. Its leading performers included King Oliver, Jelly Roll Morton, and the great Louis Armstrong. Jazz's syncopated rhythms were immensely popular among young blacks and whites and gave rise to carefree dance steps such as the Charleston and Black Bottom.

In 1919 women's skirts were typically six inches above the ground; by

Margaret Sanger (left) founded the American Birth Control League and in 1916 opened the first public clinic for counseling on contraception.

1927 they were at the knees, and the "flapper," with her bobbed hair, rolled stockings, cigarettes, lipstick, and sensuous dancing, was providing a shocking new model of feminism. The name derived from the way female rebels allowed their galoshes to "flap" about their ankles. Conservative moralists saw the flappers as just another sign of a degenerating society. Others saw in the "new woman" an expression of rugged American individualism. "By sheer force of violence," explained the *New York Times* in 1929, the flapper has "established the feminine right to equal representation in such hitherto masculine fields of endeavor as smoking and drinking, swearing, petting, and upsetting the community peace."

But by 1930 or so the thrill of rebellion was waning; the revolution against Victorian morality had run its course. Its extreme expressions in time aroused doubts that the indulgence of lust equaled liberation. And the much-discussed revolution in morals was also greatly exaggerated.

The twenties "roared" for only a small proportion of the population. F. Scott Fitzgerald reminded Americans in 1931 that the "jazz age" was jazzy only for the "upper tenth of [the]nation." Still, some new folkways had come to stay. In the late 1930s a survey disclosed that among college women almost half had had sexual relations before marriage, but of these three-quarters had had them only with their future spouses.

THE WOMEN'S MOVEMENT   At the same time that many women were embracing new sexual mores, all women were being liberated politically. The suffrage movement, which had been in the doldrums since 1896, sprang back to life in the second decade of the new century. In 1912 Alice Paul, a Quaker social worker, returned from an apprenticeship with the militant suffragists of England to become chair of the National American Woman Suffrage Association's Congressional Committee. By 1917 Paul and her followers were picketing the White House and deliberately inviting arrest, after which they went on hunger strikes in prison.

   In 1915 Carrie Chapman Catt once again became head of the National Suffrage Association and through her gift for organization spurred the final campaigns for voting rights. For several years President Wilson

The march for women's suffrage, 1913.

had evaded the issue of a suffrage amendment, but he supported a plank in the 1916 Democratic platform endorsing state action for woman suffrage. He addressed the National Suffrage Organization that year, and thereafter he worked closely with its leaders. On June 4, 1919, the Senate finally adopted the Nineteenth Amendment by a bare two-thirds majority, and after an agonizing fourteen months, the states finally ratified the women's suffrage amendment on August 21, 1920, the climactic achievement of the Progressive Era.

Women thereafter entered politics in growing numbers, but this did not usher in any basic political change or any sudden release of women from deeply embedded social customs and legal discrimination. The new women voters tended to vote like men on most issues. What was more, the suffrage victory left the broader women's movement prey to a letdown that lasted for a generation. A few years after the triumph, Catt wrote that suffragists were disappointed "because they miss the exaltation, the thrill of expectancy, the vision which stimulated them in the suffrage campaign. They find none of these appeals to their aspiration in the party of their choice."

One group, however, wanted something more. Alice Paul set a new goal, first introduced in Congress in 1923: an Equal Rights Amendment that would eliminate any remaining legal distinctions between the sexes—including the special legislation for the protection of working women put on the books in the previous fifty or so years. It would be another fifty years before Alice Paul would see Congress adopt her amendment in 1972; she did not live, however, to see it fall short of ratification.

The sharp increase in the number of women in the work force during World War I proved ephemeral, but in the longer view a steady increase in the numbers of employed women occurred in the 1920s and, surprisingly, continued through the depression decade of the 1930s. Still these women remained concentrated in traditional occupations: they were mostly domestics, office workers, teachers, clerks, salespeople, dressmakers, milliners, and seamstresses. On the eve of World War II women's work was little more diversified than it had been at the turn of the century, but by 1940 it would be on the eve of a great transformation.

THE "NEW NEGRO" The discriminations that have befallen blacks and women display many parallels, and the loosening of restraints for

"A Negro Family Just Arrived in Chicago from the Rural South," 1922. *Between 1910 and 1930 almost 1 million blacks left the South in the Great Migration north.*

both have frequently coincided. The most significant development in African-American life during these years was known as the Great Migration. Competition for jobs from foreign immigrants was prevented first by the war and then by postwar legal restrictions on immigration. The movement of blacks from the South northward began in 1915–1916, when war industries were depleting the ranks of common labor, leaving openings for blacks. Altogether, between 1910 and 1920 the Southeast lost some 323,000 blacks, or 5 percent of the 1920 native black population, and by 1930 had lost another 615,000 or 8 percent of the native black population. With the migration north, a slow but steady growth in black political influence set in. African Americans were freer to speak and act in a northern setting, and they gained political leverage by concentrating in large cities located in states with many electoral votes.

Along with political activity came a bristling spirit of protest among blacks, a spirit that received cultural expression in a literary and artistic movement labeled the Harlem Renaissance. Claude McKay, a Jamaican immigrant, was the first significant writer of the movement, which sought to rediscover black folk culture. Poems collected in McKay's *Harlem Shadows* (1922) expressed defiance in such titles as "If We Must Die" and "To the White Fiends." Other emergent black writers included Langston Hughes, Zora Neale Hurston, Countee Cullen, and James Weldon Johnson. Perhaps the greatest single creation of the time was Jean Toomer's novel *Cane*, which portrayed the lives of simple blacks in rural Georgia and the sophisticated inhabitants of Washington's African-American middle class.

The spirit of the "New Negro" also found outlet in what came to be called "Negro nationalism," which exalted blackness, black cultural expression, and, at its most extreme, black exclusiveness. The leading spokesman for such views was the flamboyant Marcus Garvey. In 1916 he brought to New York the United Negro Improvement Association, which he had started in his native Jamaica two years before. His organization grew rapidly under the strains of the postwar years. Racial bias, he charged, was so ingrained in whites that it was futile to appeal to their sense of justice. The only hope for blacks was to flee America and build their own republic in Africa.

Garvey, the "Black Moses," quickly enlisted half a million members

Marcus Garvey, founder of the United Negro Improvement Association and a leading spokesman for "Negro nationalism" in the 1920s.

in his association, and claimed as many as 6 million by 1923. As one of his followers remarked, Garvey gave "my people backbone where they had wishbone." At the peak of his popularity, however, Garvey was convicted of mail fraud. He was imprisoned in 1925 and remained so until President Coolidge pardoned and deported him to Jamaica in 1927. Garvey died in obscurity in London in 1940, but the memory of his movement kept alive an undercurrent of racial pride that would reemerge later under the slogan of "black power."

Even more influential in promoting black rights was a new organization, the National Association for the Advancement of Colored People (NAACP). Founded in 1910, it was led by northern white liberals and black leaders such as W. E. B. Du Bois. Although most white Progressives shunned the NAACP, the new group took the Progressive idea that the solution to social problems began with educating the people seriously, and it planned an active press bureau to accomplish this. Its main strategy, however, focused on enforcing the Fourteenth and Fifteenth Amendments. One early victory came with *Guinn v. United States* (1915), in which the Supreme Court struck down Oklahoma's grandfather clause, which had been part of the state's attempt to disfranchise blacks.

In 1919 the NAACP launched a campaign against lynching, still a common atrocity in many parts of the country. An antilynching bill making mob murder a federal offense passed the House in 1922, but lost to a filibuster by southern senators. Yet the continued agitation of the issue did help reduce lynchings, which declined to a third of what they had been the previous decade.

THE CULTURE OF MODERNISM

Changes in the realms of science and social thought were perhaps even more dramatic than those affecting women and blacks in the interwar years. As the twentieth century advanced, the easy faith in progress and reform expressed by Progressives fell victim to a series of frustrations and disasters, including the Great War, the failure of the League of Nations, Woodrow Wilson's physical and political collapse, and the failure of prohibition. Deeper still, startling new findings in physics further shook prevailing assumptions of order and certainty.

SCIENCE AND SOCIAL THOUGHT   Physicists of the early twentieth century altered the image of the cosmos in ways that seemed almost a conspiracy against common sense. The conventional wisdom since Sir Isaac Newton held the universe to be governed by laws that the scientific method could ultimately uncover. A world of such certain order bolstered hopes of infinite progress in human knowledge.

This world of order and certainty disintegrated at the turn of the century when Albert Einstein, a young German physicist working in the Swiss patent office, concluded that space, time, and mass were not absolutes but relative to the location and motion of the observer. Isaac Newton's eighteenth-century mechanics, according to Einstein's relativity theories, worked well enough at relatively slow speeds, but the more nearly one approached the velocity of light (about 186,000 miles per second) the more all measuring devices would change accordingly, so that yardsticks would become shorter, clocks and heartbeats would slow down, even the aging process would ebb.

Certainty dissolved the farther one reached out into the universe and the farther one reached down into the minute world of the atom. The discovery of radioactivity in the 1890s showed that atoms were not irreducible units of matter but that some of them emitted particles of energy. This meant, Einstein noted, that mass and energy were not separate phenomena but interchangeable.

Meanwhile, the German physicist Max Planck had discovered that electromagnetic emissions of energy, whether as electricity or light, came in little bundles that he called quanta. The development of quantum theory suggested that atoms were far more complex than once believed and, as another pioneering German physicist, Werner Heisenberg, stated in his uncertainty principle in 1927, ultimately indescribable. One could never know both the position and the velocity of an electron, Heisenberg concluded, because the very process of observation would inevitably affect the behavior of the particle, altering its position or velocity.

Heisenberg's thesis meant that human knowledge had limits. "The physicist thus finds himself in a world from which the bottom has dropped clean out," a Harvard mathematician wrote in 1929. He had to "give up his most cherished convictions and faith. The world is not a world of reason, understandable by the intellect of man, but as we penetrate ever deeper, the very law of cause and effect, which we had thought to be a formula to which we could force God Himself to sub-scribe, ceases to have any meaning." Hard for the public to grasp, such findings proved too troubling even for Einstein, who spent much of the rest of his life in quest of an explanation that would unify the relativity and quantum theories. "I shall never believe that God plays dice with the world," Einstein asserted.

Just as Enlightenment thinkers drew on Newton's laws of gravitation two centuries before to formulate their views on the laws governing so-ciety, the ideas of relativity and uncertainty in the twentieth century provoked people to deny the relevance of absolute values in any sphere of society, which undermined the concepts of personal responsibility and absolute standards. Anthropologists aided the process by trans-forming the word "culture," which had before meant refinement, into a term for the whole system of ideas, folkways, and institutions within which any group lived. Even the most primitive groups had cultures and, all things being relative, one culture should not impose its value judgments on another. Two anthropologists, Ruth Benedict and Mar-garet Mead, were especially effective in spreading this viewpoint.

MODERNIST LITERATURE   The cluster of scientific ideas associated with Darwin and Einstein helped inspire a revolution in the minds of many intellectuals and creative artists during the early twentieth cen-tury. Some observers now count this new "modernism" as ranking with the Enlightenment or Romanticism in its sweep and significance. The modernist world was one in which, as Karl Marx said, "All that is solid melts into air." Modernism arose out of a widespread recognition that Western civilization was entering an era of bewildering change. New technologies, new modes of transportation and communication, and new scientific discoveries combined to transform the nature of every-day life and to generate dramatic new forms of artistic expression.

The community of belief about the nature of things that was so cen-tral to nineteenth-century art and literature was breaking down by the 1920s. The very perception of reality itself underwent startling revi-sions. "One must never forget," declared Gertrude Stein, "that the real-ity of the twentieth century is not the reality of the nineteenth century, not at all." Where nineteenth-century writers and artists took for granted an accessible public world that could be readily observed and accu-rately represented, self-willed modernists viewed the "real" as something to be created rather than copied, expressed rather than reproduced. As a consequence, they concluded that the subconscious regions of the psyche were more interesting and potent than reason, common sense, and logic.

In the various arts such concerns resulted in abstract painting, which sought to represent the artist's inner mood rather than a recognizable image of an external object, atonal music, free verse in poetry, stream-of-consciousness narrative, and interior monologues in stories and novels. Writers showed an intense concern with new forms in language in an effort to violate expectations and shock their audiences.

The chief American prophets of modernism were emigrés in Europe: Ezra Pound and T. S. Eliot in London and Gertrude Stein in Paris. All were deeply concerned with creating new and often difficult styles of modernist expression. Pound, as foreign editor for *Poetry,* served as the conduit through which many American poets achieved publication in America and Britain. At the same time he became the leader of the Imagist movement, a revolt against the ornamental verbosity of Victorian poetry in favor of the concrete image.

Pound's brilliant protégé was the St. Louis-born Harvard graduate, T. S. Eliot, who in 1915 contributed to *Poetry* his first major poem, "The Love Song of J. Alfred Prufrock," the musings of an ineffectual man who "after tea and cakes and ices" could never find "the strength to force the moment to its crisis." Eliot went to Oxford in 1913 and soon decided to make England his home and poetry his career. Skeptical of the Western notion of social progress through scientific advance and horrified by the slaughter of the Great War, he rejected the nineteenth century's "cheerfulness, optimism, and hopefulness." He rejected as well the traditional notion of poetry as the representation of a beautiful world. The modern poet, he insisted, must "be able to see beneath both beauty and ugliness; to see the boredom, and the horror and the glory." Eliot's *The Waste Land* (1922) made few concessions to readers in its obscure allusions, its juxtaposition of unexpected metaphors, its deep sense of postwar disillusionment and melancholy, and its suggestion of a burned-out civilization. But it became for an alienated younger generation almost the touchstone of the modern temper.

Gertrude Stein, another voluntary exile, settled in Paris in 1903 and became an early champion and collector of modern art. Long regarded as no more than the literary eccentric who wrote "Rose is a rose is a rose

Frankie "Half Pint" Jackson and His Band at the Sunset Cafe, Chicago, 1920s. *Jazz emerged during this period as an especially American expression of the modernist spirit. Black artists bent musical conventions to give fuller rein to improvisation.*

is a rose," she would later be recognized as one of the chief originators of the modernist prose style. At the time she was known chiefly through her influence on such 1920s expatriates as Sherwood Anderson and Ernest Hemingway, whom she told: "All of you young people who served in the war, you are the lost generation."

The earliest chronicler of that generation, F. Scott Fitzgerald, blazed up brilliantly and then quickly flickered out, like all the tinseled, carefree, sad young people of his novels. Successful and famous at age twenty-four with the publication of *This Side of Paradise* (1920), he, along with his wife, Zelda, experienced and depicted the "greatest, gaudiest spree in history," and then both had their crack-ups during the Great Depression. What gave depth to the best of Fitzgerald's work was what a character in *The Great Gatsby* (1925), his finest novel, called "a sense of the fundamental decencies" amid all the surface gaiety—and almost always a sense of impending doom.

Hemingway suffered even more from a psychic wound inflicted by an uncaring world. For him literature was a means of defense, a way to strike back, and in the process find a meaning for himself rather than accept one imposed by society. Hemingway's first novel, *The Sun Also Rises* (1926), pictures a desperate search for life by a group of American expatriates, chasing about frantically from the bistros of Paris to the bullrings of Spain. Young Jake Barnes, emasculated by a war wound, explains his postwar outlook toward the world: "I did not care what it was all about. All I wanted to know was how to live in it." Hemingway's second novel, *A Farewell to Arms* (1929), is based on his own experience as a volunteer in the ambulance corps in northern Italy during World War I. It pursues the love affair of a driver and a nurse who abandon the war for Switzerland, where the young woman dies in childbirth. Hundreds of writers tried to imitate Hemingway's terse style, but few had his gift, which lay less in what he had to say than in the way he said it.

MAKING CONNECTIONS

- The next chapter discusses the growing consumer culture of the 1920s, an economic aspect of the "Roaring Twenties" described here.

- Chapter 27 describes changes in American literary culture wrought by the Great Depression—from the modernism discussed in this chapter to a return of social significance and the cultural "rediscovery of America" in the 1930s.

- The status of women in the workforce remained stable in the 1920s, despite the successes of the women's movement. That status changed, at least temporarily, during World War II. Chapter 29 traces the rise of "Rosie the Riveter."

Further Reading

For a standard survey of the interwar period, start with William E. Leuchtenburg's *The Perils of Prosperity, 1914–1932* (1958).* John Higham's *Strangers in the Land: Patterns of American Nativism, 1860–1925* (1955)* details the story of immigration restriction. Paul Avrich's *Sacco and Vanzetti: The Anarchist Background* (1991)* discusses the case against those accused radicals.

Women's suffrage is treated extensively in Eleanor Flexner's *Century of Struggle: The Women's Rights Movement in the United States* (rev. ed., 1975).* See Charles F. Kellogg's *NAACP* (1967)* for his analysis of the pioneering court cases against racial discrimination. Gilbert Osofsky's *Harlem: The Making of a Ghetto, 1890–1930* (2nd ed., 1971),* Nathan I. Huggins's *Harlem Renaissance* (1971),* and Jervis Anderson's *This Was Harlem: A Cultural Portrait, 1900–1950* (1982)* cover the cultural impact of the Great Migration in New York.

*These books are available in paperback editions.

26 ‍ REPUBLICAN RESURGENCE AND DECLINE

CHAPTER ORGANIZER

This chapter focuses on:

- the conservatism in the presidencies of Harding, Coolidge, and Hoover

- growth in the American economy in the 1920s

- the causes of the Great Depression

PROGRESSIVISM TRANSFORMED

The progressive coalition that reelected Woodrow Wilson in 1916 proved to be quite fragile, and by 1920 it had fragmented. It began to show signs of fissure during the war when radicals and others grew disaffected with America's involvement. After the war Wilson's support continued to erode. Organized labor resented the administration's unsympathetic attitude toward the strikes of 1919–1920, and farmers complained that wartime price controls had discriminated against them. Some intellectuals grew disillusioned with the emphases on grassroots democracy because of the popular support for prohibition and religious fundamentalism. Many among the middle class, meanwhile, lost interest in political activism and channeled their energies into building a new business civilization based upon mass production and mass consumption, greater leisure, and the introduction of labor-saving electrical appliances in the home. Moreover, progressivism's final triumphs at the national level were already pretty much foregone conclusions before the war's end: the Eighteenth Amendment, which imposed national prohibition, was ratified in 1919, and the Nineteenth Amendment, which extended women's suffrage to the entire country, became law a year later.

Progressivism, however, did not completely disappear in the 1920s. Reformers dominated Congress during much of the decade even while the White House was in conservative Republican hands. The Progressive impulse for "good government" and extended public services still remained strong, especially at the state and local levels, where movements for good roads, education, public health, and social welfare all gained momentum during the decade. Much of the Progressive impulse for reform, however, was largely transformed into the drive for moral righteousness and conformity animating the Ku Klux Klan and the fundamentalist and prohibitionist movements.

"NORMALCY"

HARDING'S ELECTION   Amid the postwar confusion, another presidential season approached. Most Americans had grown weary of idealistic crusades and suspicious of leaders sounding the trumpet of reform. In speaking of Wilson's fall from favor, one observer explained: "The moralist unquestionably secures wide popular support—but he also wearies his audience." Wilson himself recognized this fact. "It is only once in a generation," he remarked, "that a people can be lifted above material things. That is why conservative government is in the saddle two-thirds of the time."

When the Republicans met in Chicago in 1920, the Old Guard sought to reclaim its conservative heritage. The regulars found their man in Ohio senator Warren Gamaliel Harding, who had set the tone of his campaign when he told a Boston audience: "America's present need is not heroics, but healing; not nostrums, but normalcy; not revolution, but restoration; not agitation, but adjustment; not surgery, but serenity; not the dramatic, but the dispassionate; not experiment, but equipoise, not submergence in internationality, but sustainment in triumphant nationality." His prose was clumsy, but Harding caught the mood of the times—a longing for "normalcy" and contentment with the status quo. So too did his running mate, Massachusetts governor Calvin Coolidge, who had gained national attention with his stern opposition to the Boston Police Strike.

Harding's promise of a "return to normalcy" reflected his own conservative values and folksy personality. The son of an Ohio farmer, he described himself as not an intellectual or a crusader but "just a plain fellow" who was "old-fashioned and even reactionary in matters of faith and morals." But such a description suggests a certain puritan regimen that Harding never practiced. Far from being an old-fashioned moralist in his personal life, he drank bootleg liquor in the midst of prohibition, smoked and chewed tobacco, relished weekly poker games, and actively sought sexual satisfaction from women other than his austere and matronly wife, whom he called "Duchess." But the general public was unaware of Harding's self-indulgence and weak character. Instead the voters saw him as a handsome, charming, gregarious, and lovable politician. A man of self-confessed limitations in vision, leadership, and intellectual power, he once admitted that "I cannot hope to be one of the great presidents, but perhaps I may be remembered as one of the best loved."

The Democrats hoped that Harding would not be president at all. James Cox, former newsman and former governor of Ohio, won the nomination of an increasingly fragmented party on the forty-fourth ballot. For vice-president the convention named Franklin D. Roosevelt, who as assistant secretary of the navy occupied the same position his Republican cousin Teddy had held before him.

The Democrats suffered from the breakup of the Wilsonian coalition and the conservative postwar mood. In the words of journalist William Allen White, Americans in 1920 were "tired of issues, sick at heart of ideals, and weary of being noble." The country voted overwhelmingly for Harding's promised "return to normalcy." Harding got 16 million votes to 9 million for Cox, who carried no state outside the Solid South. In the minority again, the Democrats had returned to normalcy too.

EARLY APPOINTMENTS AND POLICY   Harding in office had much in common with Ulysses Grant. His cabinet, like Grant's, mixed some of the best men in the party with some of the worst. Charles Evans Hughes became a distinguished secretary of state. Herbert Hoover in the Commerce Department, Andrew W. Mellon in Treasury, and Henry A. Wallace in Agriculture were also efficient and forceful figures. Of the others, Secretary of the Interior Albert B. Fall landed in prison and Attorney-General Harry M. Daugherty only narrowly escaped prosecution. Many lesser offices went to members of the soon notorious "Ohio Gang," headed by Daugherty, a group of Harding's old Ohio friends with whom the president met regularly for poker games lubricated with illegal liquor.

Until he became president, Harding had loved politics. He was the complete party hack, "bloviating" (a verb of his own making, which meant speaking with gaseous eloquence) on the stump, jollying it up in the clubhouse and cloakroom, hobnobbing with the great and near-great in Washington. As president, however, Harding was simply in over his head, and self-doubt overwhelmed him. "I don't think I'm big enough for the Presidency," he confided to a friend. Alice Roosevelt Longworth, Theodore Roosevelt's oldest daughter, recognized Harding's limitations. "Harding wasn't a bad man," she noted. "He was just a slob."

Harding and his friends set about dismantling or neutralizing as many of the social and economic components of progressivism as they could. Harding's four appointments to the Supreme Court were all conservatives, including Chief Justice William Howard Taft, who announced that he had been "appointed to reverse a few decisions." During the 1920s the Taft Court struck down a federal child-labor law and a minimum wage law for women, issued numerous injunctions against striking unions, and passed rulings limiting the powers of federal regulatory agencies.

The Harding administration established a pro-business tone reminiscent of the McKinley White House. Big business, whipping-boy of many progressives, had won renewed respectability by expanding production during the war and by initiating a "New Era" of prosperity after the postwar slump in 1921. To sustain economic growth, Secretary of the Treasury Mellon promoted spending cuts and tax reduction. Mellon insisted that tax cuts should go mainly to the rich, on the Hamiltonian principle that wealth in the hands of the few would promote the general welfare through increased capital investment.

In Congress a group of western Republicans and southern Democrats fought a dogged battle to preserve the graduated scale built into wartime taxes, but Mellon, in office through the 1920s, eventually won out. At his behest Congress first repealed the wartime excess-profits tax and lowered the maximum rate on personal income from 65 to 50 percent. Subsequent revenue acts eventually lowered the maximum rate to 20 percent. The Revenue Act of 1926 extended further benefits to high-income groups by lowering estate taxes and repealing the gift tax. Much of the tax money released to wealthy people by these acts seems to have fueled the speculative excess of the late 1920s as much as it boosted consumer spending and entrepreneurial activity. Mellon, however, did balance the federal budget for a time. Governmental expenditures fell, as did the national debt.

In addition to tax cuts, Mellon favored the time-honored Republican policy of high tariffs. So too did spokesmen for several emerging new industries. Wartime innovations in chemical and metal processing revived the argument for protection of infant industries from foreign competition. The Fordney-McCumber Tariff of 1922 dramatically increased rates on chemical and metal products as a safeguard against the revival of German industries that had previously commanded the field. To please the farmers, the new act further extended the duties on imported farm products.

Higher tariffs, however, had unexpected consequences. During the war the United States had been transformed from a debtor to a creditor nation. In former years foreign capital had flowed into the United States, playing an important role in fueling economic expansion. But the private and public credits given the Allies during the war had reversed the pattern. Mellon now insisted that the European powers must repay all that they had borrowed during the war. The tariff walls erected against imports, however, made it all the harder for other nations to sell in the United States and thereby acquire the dollars with which to repay their war debts. For nearly a decade further extensions of American loans and investments sent more dollars abroad, postponing the reckoning.

Rounding out the Republican economic program was a more lenient attitude toward government regulation of corporations. Neither Harding nor his successor, Coolidge, could dissolve the regulatory agencies created by progressivism, but by naming commissioners who were less than sympathetic to regulation, they rendered these agencies ineffective. Harding named advocates of big business to the Interstate Commerce Commission, the Federal Reserve Board, and the Federal Trade Commission. One senator characterized the new appointments as "the nullification of federal law by a process of boring from within." Senator Henry Cabot Lodge agreed, noting: "We have torn up Wilsonism by the roots."

A CORRUPT ADMINISTRATION   Republican conservatives such as Lodge, Mellon, Coolidge, and Hoover were at least operating out of philosophical conviction. The crass members of Harding's "Ohio Gang," however, used White House connections to line their own pockets. In 1923 Harding learned that the head of the Veterans Bureau was systematically looting medical and hospital supplies. The corrupt administrator resigned and fled to Europe. Harding's general counsel then committed suicide. Not long afterward a close crony of Attorney-General Daugherty also shot himself. The man held no federal appointment, but he had set up an office in the Justice Department from which he peddled influence for a fee. Daugherty himself was implicated in the fraudulent handling of German assets seized after the war. When this was discovered, he refused to testify on the ground that he might incriminate himself. Twice brought to court, he was never indicted; possibly the lack of evidence resulted from his destruction of pertinent records. These were but the most visible among many scandals that touched the Justice Department, the Prohibition Bureau, and other agencies under Harding.

But one major scandal rose above all others. Teapot Dome, like the Watergate break-in fifty years later, became the catchword for an era of government corruption. An oil deposit on federal land in Wyoming, Teapot Dome had been set aside as a reserve to be administered by the Interior Department under Albert B. Fall. He proceeded to let private companies exploit the deposits, arguing that these contracts were in the government's interest. Yet why did Fall act in secret, without allowing competitive bids?

Suspicion grew when Fall's own standard of living suddenly grew lavish. It turned out that he had taken loans of about $400,000 (which

Juggernaut. *This 1924 cartoon shows the dimensions of the Teapot Dome scandal.*

came in "a little black bag") from oil executives. For the rest of his life Fall insisted that the loans were unrelated to the leases, and that he had contrived a good deal for the government, but at best the circumstances revealed his fatal blindness to impropriety.

Harding himself avoided public disgrace. How much he knew of the scandals remains unclear, but he knew enough to become visibly troubled. "My God, this is a hell of a job!" he confided to a journalist. "I have no trouble with my enemies, I can take care of my enemies all right. But my damn friends, my God-damn friends . . . they're the ones that keep me walking the floor nights!" In 1923 Harding left on what would be his last journey, a western speaking tour and a trip to the Alaska territory. Sailing to Alaska, he asked Commerce Secretary Herbert Hoover: "If you knew of a great scandal in our administration, would you for the good of the country and the party expose it publicly or would you bury it?" Hoover replied quickly: "Publish it, and at least get credit for integrity on your side."

But Harding had little time to act. Back in Seattle he suffered a heart attack, recovered briefly, then died in a San Francisco hotel. Not since the death of Lincoln had there been such an outpouring of grief for a "beloved President," for the kindly, ordinary man who found it in his heart (as Wilson had not) to pardon the former Socialist candidate Eugene Debs, who had been jailed for opposing U.S. intervention in World War I. As the funeral train moved toward Washington, then back to Ohio, millions stood by the tracks to honor their lost leader.

Eventually, however, grief yielded to scorn and contempt. For nearly a decade after Harding's death, scandalous revelations concerning administrative officials were paraded before congressional committees and then courts. Harding's extramarital affairs with several mistresses also came to light. As a result of such amorous detours and corrupt associates, Harding's foreshortened administration came to be widely viewed as one of the worst in American history. More recently, however, scholars have suggested that the scandals obscured several real accomplishments. Some historians credit Harding with leading the nation out of the turmoil of the postwar years and creating the foundation for the decade's remarkable economic boom. They also stress that he was a hardworking president who played a far more forceful role in shaping administrative economic and foreign policies than previously believed. Still, even Harding's foremost scholarly defender admits that he lacked good judgment and "probably should never have been president."

"SILENT CAL"   The news of Harding's death came when Vice-President Calvin Coolidge was visiting his father in the mountain village of Plymouth, Vermont, his birthplace. There at 2:47 on the morning of August 3, 1923, by the light of a kerosene lamp, Colonel John Coolidge administered the oath of office to his son. The rustic simplicity of Plymouth, the very name itself, evoked just the image of traditional roots and solid integrity that the country would long for amid the slimy wake of the Harding scandals.

Coolidge brought to the White House a clear conviction that the presidency should revert to its passive stance of the Gilded Age and defer to the leadership of Congress. One editor observed that Coolidge "aspired to become the least President the country ever had; he attained his desire." Coolidge insisted on twelve hours of sleep and an afternoon nap. H. L. Mencken asserted that Coolidge "slept more than any other president, whether by day or by night. Nero fiddled, but Coolidge only snored."

But Americans took to their hearts the unflappability of "Silent Cal," his long midday naps, and the pictures of him fishing, pitching hay, and wearing Indian warbonnets while primly clad in business suit and necktie. His pinched facial expression and dry personality provoked affectionate satire. One wit, commenting on Coolidge's seemingly dour facial expression, suggested that he must have been weaned on a pickle. Another popular story reported that a dinner guest had bet Coolidge she could make him say three words. "You lose," he replied. The image of "Silent Cal," however, has been overdrawn; he may have been a man of few words, but he was not as bland or as dry as critics claimed.

As Herbert Hoover once stressed, Coolidge was a "real conservative, probably the equal of Benjamin Harrison. He was a fundamentalist in religion, in the economic and social order, and in fishing, too." (He used live worms for bait.) Even more than Harding, Coolidge embraced the orthodox creed of business. "The chief business of the American people is business," he intoned. "The man who works there worships there." Where Harding had sought to balance the interests of labor, agriculture, and industry, Coolidge focused on industrial development at the expense of the other two areas. He sought to unleash the free enterprise system and even more than Harding, he sought to end government regulation. His pro-business stance led the *Wall Street Journal* to exult: "Never before, here or anywhere else, has a government been so completely fused with business."

THE 1924 ELECTION   Coolidge successfully distanced himself from the Harding scandals and put two lawyers of undoubted integrity in charge of the prosecutions. He also quietly took control of the Republican party machinery and seized the initiative in the campaign for the 1924 nomination, which he won with only token opposition.

The Coolidge luck held as the Democrats fell victim to continuing internal dissensions, which were enough to prompt Will Rogers's classic statement: "I am a member of no organized political party. I am a Democrat." The party's divisions reflected the deep alienation growing up between the new urban culture of the twenties and the more traditional hinterland, a gap that the Democratic party could not bridge. It took 103 ballots to bestow the party's tarnished nomination on John W. Davis, a Wall Street lawyer from West Virginia who could hardly outdo Coolidge in conservatism.

While the Democrats fumbled, a new farm-labor coalition mobilized a third-party effort. Meeting in Cleveland on July 4, 1924, farm and labor groups reorganized the Progressive party and nominated Wisconsin senator Robert M. La Follette for president. La Follette also won the support of the Socialist party and the American Federation of Labor.

In the campaign Coolidge chose to focus on La Follette, whom he called a dangerous radical who would turn America into a "communistic and socialistic state." The country preferred to "keep cool with Coolidge," who swept both the popular and electoral votes by decisive majorities. Davis took only the Solid South, and La Follette carried only his native Wisconsin.

THE NEW ERA

Business executives interpreted the Coolidge victory as a vindication of their leadership, and Coolidge saw in the surging prosperity of the time a confirmation of his philosophy. In fact, the prosperity and technological achievements of the time had much to do with Coolidge's victory over the Democrats and Progressives. Those in the large middle class who before had formed an important part of the progressive coalition were now absorbed instead into the new corporate and consumer world created by advances in communications, transportation, and business organization. As more and more commentators stressed, the United States seemed to be entering a "new era" of advanced capitalism.

A GROWING CONSUMER CULTURE   The American economy was changing markedly during the 1920s. Dramatic increases in productive efficiency flooded the marketplace with new consumer delights. Goods once available only to the affluent were now made accessible to the working classes: hand cameras, wristwatches, cigarette lighters, vacuum cleaners, washing machines. But such enticing new goods threatened to produce economic havoc unless people abandoned traditional notions of frugality. Hence, business leaders, salesmen, and public relations experts began a concerted effort to eradicate what was left of the original Protestant ethic's emphasis on plain living. "People may ruin themselves by saving instead of spending," warned one economist. A newspaper editorial was even more blunt. It insisted that the American's "first importance to his country is no longer that of citizen but that of consumer. Consumption is a new necessity."

The public had to be taught the joys of consumerism, and the new industry of mass advertising obliged. By portraying impulse buying as a therapeutic measure to help self-esteem, the advertising industry shrewdly helped undermine notions of simple living. In his popular novel *Babbitt,* Sinclair Lewis recognized advertising's impact upon middle-class life: "These standard advertised wares–toothpastes, socks, tires, cameras, instantaneous hot water heaters–were the symbols and proofs of excellence."

Inventions in communications and transportation, such as motion pictures, radio, telephones, and automobiles, not only brought transformations in society but also ignited the decade's economic boom. By 1905 the first movie house opened in Philadelphia, and within three years there were nearly 10,000 nationwide. During the next decade Hollywood became the center of movie production, grinding out serials, features, westerns, and the timeless two-reel comedies of Mack Sennett's Keystone Studios, where slapstick comedians, most notably Charlie Chaplin, perfected their art into a powerful form of social criticism. By the mid-1930s every large American city and most small towns had theaters, and movies replaced oratory as the chief mass entertainment, growing into a multi-million dollar industry.

Radio broadcasting had an even more spectacular growth. The first radio commercial aired in 1922. By the end of that year there were over

A farm family gathered around the radio, Hood River County, Oregon, 1925.

500 stations and some 3 million receivers in action. In 1927 Congress established a Federal Radio Commission to regulate the industry; in 1934 it became the Federal Communications Commission, with authority over other forms of communication as well.

AIRPLANES, AUTOMOBILES, AND THE ECONOMY   Advances in transportation were equally startling. Wilbur and Orville Wright of Dayton, Ohio, owners of a bicycle shop, built and flew the first airplane at Kitty Hawk, North Carolina, on December 17, 1903, but the use of planes advanced slowly until the outbreak of war in 1914. An American aircraft industry developed during the war but foundered in the postwar demobilization. In 1925 the government began to subsidize the industry through airmail contracts and, the following year started a program of federal aid to air transport and navigation, including funds for constructing airports.

Aviation received a psychological boost in 1927 when Charles A. Lindbergh, Jr., flew the first transatlantic solo flight from New York to Paris in thirty-three hours and thirty minutes. The deed, which won him a prize of $25,000, was dramatic. He flew through a dense fog and had at times dropped to within ten feet of the water before sighting the Irish coast and regaining his bearings. The New York City parade honoring Lindbergh surpassed even the celebration of the Armistice in its scope.

Four years later New York City honored another pioneering American aviator—Amelia Earhart. In 1931 she became the first woman to fly solo across the Atlantic Ocean. Born in Kansas in 1897, she made her first solo flight in 1921. Soon thereafter she bought her own plane and began working as a barnstorming stunt pilot at air shows across the country. A tall, thin, grey-eyed young woman with short, tousled blond hair and a "boyish" smile, she looked remarkably like Lindbergh, and after her first transatlantic flight in 1928, as a passenger with two male pilots, reporters dubbed her "Lady Lindy," the "First Lady of the Air." She became aviation editor of *Cosmopolitan* and vice-president of an airline company. Newly emancipated American women looked to the radiant Earhart as an inspiring example of female leadership and courage. Earhart's popularity soared after her own transatlantic solo flight from Newfoundland to Northern Ireland. The fifteen-hour feat led Congress to award her the Distinguished Flying Cross, and she was named Outstanding American Woman of the Year.

Charles Lindbergh in front of the airplane he piloted across the Atlantic, The Spirit of St. Louis.

Caught up in the fervor of the time for such dramatic exploits, Earhart began preparing in 1935 for "just one more long flight." Two years later she and a male navigator left Miami, Florida, and headed east on a round-the-world flight. The trip went smoothly until July 2, 1937, when they attempted the most difficult leg: from New Guinea to a tiny atoll in the Pacific 2,556 miles away. A Coast Guard vessel anchored near the island picked up weakening signals indicating that Earhart's plane was losing fuel. The plane disappeared, and despite extensive searches, no trace of it or the pilots was ever found. It remains the most perplexing and intriguing mystery in aviation history.

The accomplishments of Earhart and Lindbergh helped catapult the aviation industry into prominence. By 1930 there were forty-three American airline companies in operation. But the most significant transportation development of the time was the automobile. The first motor car had been manufactured for sale in 1895, but in 1900 the census did not even give the infant industry a separate listing. The founding of the

Ford Motor Company in 1903 revolutionized the industry. Ford's reliable Model T (the celebrated "tin lizzie") appeared in 1908 at a price of $850 (in 1924 it would sell for $290). Ford aimed "to democratize the automobile. When I'm through everybody will be able to afford one, and about everyone will have one." He was right. In 1916 the number of cars manufactured passed 1 million; by 1920 more than 8 million were registered, and in 1929 more than 23 million. The production of automobiles consumed large portions of the nation's steel, rubber, glass, and textile output, among other materials. It gave rise to a gigantic market for oil products just as the Spindletop gusher (1901) in Texas heralded the opening of vast southwestern oilfields. It quickened the movement for good roads, introduced efficient mass-production assembly-line techniques to other industries, speeded transportation, encouraged the sprawl of suburbs, and sparked real-estate booms in California and Florida.

STABILIZING THE ECONOMY   The efficiency craze, which had been a prominent feature of the progressive impulse, was now powering the wheels of mass production and consumption during the 1920s, and had become a cardinal belief of Republican leaders. Herbert Hoover, who served as secretary of commerce through the Harding-Coolidge years, was himself an engineer who had made a fortune in far-flung mining operations in Australia, China, Russia, and elsewhere. During World War I he was a brilliant manager of the Belgian relief program and the Food Administration. When young Franklin D. Roosevelt met Hoover in 1919, he labeled him "a wonder." Roosevelt then added with what would become prophetic irony: "I wish we could make him President of the United States. There could not be a better one."

As Harding's and Coolidge's dynamic secretary of commerce, Hoover transformed the trifling Commerce Department into the most active agency of two Republican administrations. During a period of governmental retrenchment, he promoted expansion. Hoover sought out new markets for business and sponsored more than a thousand conferences on product design, production, and distribution. He also continued the wartime emphasis on standardization of everything from automobile tires and paving bricks to bedsprings and toilet paper.

Most of all Hoover endorsed the burgeoning trade-association movement. The organization of business trade associations became his favorite instrument for "stabilization" to avoid the waste inherent in competition. Through such associations executives in a given field would gather and disseminate information on everything: sales, purchases, shipments, production, and prices. This information allowed them to lay plans with more confidence, the advantages of which included predictable costs, prices, and markets, as well as more stable employment and wages. Sometimes abuses crept in as trade associations skirted the edge of legality by engaging in price-fixing and other monopolistic practices, but the Supreme Court in 1925 held the practice of sharing information as such to be within the law.

THE BUSINESS OF FARMING   During the Harding and Coolidge administrations, agriculture remained a weak sector in the economy, in many ways as weak as it had been during the 1890s, when cities flourished and agriculture languished. For a brief time after the war the farmers' hopes soared on wings of prosperity. The wartime boom lasted into 1920, and then commodity prices collapsed as European farmers began to resume high levels of production. Low prices persisted into 1923, especially in the wheat and corn belts, and after that improvement was spotty. A bumper cotton crop in 1926 resulted only in a price collapse and an early taste of depression in much of the South, where foreclosures and bankruptcies spread.

Yet in some ways farmers shared the business outlook of the so-called New Era. Many farms, like corporations, were getting larger, more efficient, and more mechanized. By 1930 about 13 percent of all farmers had tractors, and the proportion rose even higher on the western plains. Better plows and other machines were part of the mechanization process that accompanied improved crop yields, fertilizers, and animal breeding.

Farm organizations of the 1920s moved away from the proposed alliance with urban labor that marked the Populist era and toward a new view of farmers as profit-conscious business owners. During the postwar farm depression the idea of marketing cooperatives emerged as the farmer's equivalent to the businessman's trade-association movement. Farm groups formed regional commodity-marketing associations that enabled them to negotiate ironclad contracts with producers for the delivery of their crops over a period of years. These associations also brought order to the marketing of farm products, requiring uniform standards and grades, efficient handling and advertising, and a businesslike organization with professional technicians and executives.

But if concern with marketing co-ops and other businesslike approaches drew farmers farther away from Populist traditions, farm problems still invited political solutions. The most effective political response to the collapse of farm prices of the early 1920s was the formation of the farm bloc, a congressional coalition of western Republicans and southern Democrats that put through an impressive, if fairly moderate, program of legislation from 1921 to 1923. During that period the farm bloc passed bills exempting farm cooperatives from antitrust laws and creating new credit banks that could lend to cooperative producing and marketing associations.

In the spring of 1924 a new panacea appeared when Senator Charles L. McNary of Oregon and Representative Gilbert N. Haugen of Iowa introduced a bill to secure "equality for agriculture in the benefits of the protective tariff." Complex as it would have been in operation, it was simple in conception: in short, the McNary-Haugen plan sought to dump American farm surpluses on the world market in order to raise commodity prices in the home market. The goal was to achieve "parity"–that is, to raise domestic farm prices to a point where farmers would have the same purchasing power relative to other prices that they had enjoyed between 1909 and 1914, a time viewed in retrospect as a golden age of American agriculture.

A McNary-Haugen bill finally passed both houses of Congress in 1927 and again a year later, only to be vetoed both times by President Coolidge. He criticized the measure as an unsound effort at price-fixing, and as un-American and unconstitutional to boot. He was partially right, but in a broader sense McNary-Haugenism did not fail. The debates over the bill catapulted the farm problem into the arena of national debate and defined it as a problem of crop surpluses. The evolution of the McNary-Haugen plan, moreover, revived the political alliance between the South and West, a coalition that became in the next decade a dominant influence on national farm policy. That policy would follow a different procedure, but its chief focus would be on surpluses and its goal would be "parity."

SETBACKS FOR UNIONS   Urban workers shared more than farmers in the affluence of the times. Their annual per-capita earnings rose be-

The Cash Register Chorus *sings of its ties to Coolidge in this 1924 cartoon.*

tween 1921 and 1928 from an average of $1,171 to $1,408. Without a matching rise in living costs, this meant a gain of about 20 percent in real wages. The benefits of this rise, however, were distributed unevenly. Miners and textile workers actually suffered a decline in real wages. In these and other trades the introduction of new production methods and machines eliminated jobs. Still, most workers witnessed a rise in their standard of living during the Coolidge years. "A workman is far better paid in America than anywhere else in the world," a French visitor wrote in 1927, "and his standard of living is enormously higher."

Organized labor, however, did no better than organized agriculture in the 1920s. In fact, unions suffered a setback after the growth years of the war. The Red Scare and strikes of 1919 left the uneasy impression that unions practiced subversion, an idea promoted by the enemies of unions. The brief postwar depression of 1921 weakened the unions further, and they felt the severe impact of open-shop associations that proliferated across the country after the war, led by chambers of commerce and other business groups. While the open shop in theory implied only the right of employers to hire whom they pleased, in practice it frequently meant discrimination against unionists and refusal to recognize unions even in shops where most of the workers were members.

Nor were employers always above the use of strong-arm methods, such as requiring "yellow-dog" contracts that forced workers to agree to stay out of unions, using labor spies, exchanging blacklists, and resorting to intimidation and coercion. Some employers tried to kill the unions with kindness. They introduced programs of "industrial democracy" guided by company unions, or various schemes of "welfare capitalism" such as profit-sharing, bonuses, pensions, health programs, recreational activities, and the like. The benefits of such programs were often considerable. The combined result of prosperity, propaganda, welfare capitalism, and active hostility was a decline in union membership from about 5 million in 1920 to 3.5 million in 1929.

PRESIDENT HOOVER, THE ENGINEER

HOOVER VS. SMITH   On August 2, 1927, while on vacation in the Black Hills of South Dakota, President Coolidge passed out to reporters slips of paper with the curious statement: "I do not choose to run for President in 1928." Exactly what he meant puzzled observers then and since. Apparently he at least half hoped for a convention draft, but his statement cleared the way for Herbert Hoover to mount an active campaign for the Republican nomination. Well before the 1928 Republican convention in Kansas City, Hoover was too far in the lead to be stopped. The platform took credit for prosperity, debt and tax reduction, and the protective tariff that had been in operation since 1922 ("as vital to American agriculture as it is to manufacturing"). It rejected the McNary-Haugen program, but promised a farm board to manage surpluses more efficiently.

The Democratic nomination went to Governor Alfred E. Smith of New York. The Democratic party had had its fill of factionalism in 1924, and all remained fairly harmonious until Smith revealed in his acceptance speech a desire to liberalize prohibition. Hoover by contrast had pronounced the outlawing of alcoholic beverages "a great social and economic experiment, noble in motive and far-reaching in purpose," and he called for improved enforcement.

The two candidates projected sharply different images that obscured the similarity of their platforms. Hoover was the Quaker son of middle America, the successful engineer and businessman, the architect of Republican prosperity, while Smith was the prototype of those things that rural and small-town America distrusted: the son of Irish immigrants, Catholic, a critic of prohibition, and a Tammanyite with an East Side New York twang. Outside the large cities such qualities were handicaps he could scarcely surmount, for all his affability and wit.

In the election Hoover won in the third consecutive Republican landslide, with 21 million popular votes to Smith's 15 million, and an even more top-heavy electoral majority of 444 to 87. Hoover even cracked the Solid South, leaving Smith only a hard core of six Deep South states plus Massachusetts and Rhode Island. The election was above all a vindication of Republican prosperity, but the shattering defeat of the Democrats concealed a major realignment in the making. Smith had nearly doubled the vote for the Democratic candidate of four years before. Smith's image, though a handicap in the hinterlands, swung big cities back into the Democratic column. In the farm states of the West there were signs that some disgruntled farmers had switched over to the Democrats. A coalition of urban workers and unhappy farmers was in the making.

HOOVER IN CONTROL   The milestone year of 1929 dawned with high hopes. Business seemed solid, incomes were rising, and the chief architect of Republican prosperity was about to enter the White House. "I have no fears for the future of our country," Hoover told his inauguration audience. "It is bright with hope."

Forgotten in the rush of later events would be Hoover's credentials as a progressive and humanitarian president. Over the objection of Treasury Secretary Mellon, he announced a plan for tax reductions in the low-income brackets. He shunned corrupt patronage practices, and he refused to countenance "Red hunts" or interference with peaceful picketing of the White House. He also defended his wife's right to invite prominent blacks to the White House, and he sought more money for all-black Howard University.

Hoover also showed greater sympathy than Coolidge for the struggling agricultural sector. To open up glutted markets he proposed higher tariffs on imported farm products. After fourteen months of struggle with competing interests, however, Hoover settled for a general upward revision on manufactures as well as farm goods. The Hawley-Smoot Tariff of 1930 carried duties to an all-time high. Average rates went from about 32 to 40 percent. More than 1,000 economists petitioned Hoover to veto the bill because, they predicted, it would raise prices to consumers, damage the export trade, and thus hurt farmers, promote inefficiency, and provoke foreign reprisals. Events proved them right, but Hoover felt that he had to go along with his party in an election year. This proved to be a disastrous mistake, for it only exacerbated the growing economic depression.

THE ECONOMY OUT OF CONTROL   Depression? Most Americans had come to assume during the 1920s that there would never be another depression. This misguided optimism proved to be an important factor in generating the economic free-fall after 1929. Throughout the 1920s the idea grew that American business had entered a New Era of *permanent* growth. Such naïve talk helped promote an array of get-rich-quick schemes. Speculative mania fueled the Florida real-estate boom, which got under way when the combination of Coolidge prosperity and Henry Ford's "tin lizzies" made Florida an accessible playground.

The Florida real-estate boom collapsed in 1926, but the stock market took up the slack. Until 1927 stock values had risen with profits, but then they began to soar on wings of fanciful speculation. Mellon's tax reductions had released money which, with the help of aggressive brokerage houses, found its way to Wall Street. One could now buy stock on margin—that is, make a small down payment (usually 10 percent) and borrow the rest from a broker who held the stock as security against a down market. If the stock price fell and the buyer failed to provide more cash, the broker could sell the stock to cover his loan.

Gamblers in the market ignored warning signs. By 1927 residential construction and automobile sales were catching up to demand, business inventories rose, and the rate of consumer spending slowed. By mid-1929 production, employment, and other gauges of economic activity were declining. Still the stock market rose, driven by excessive confidence and perennial greed. By 1929 the market had become a fantasy world. Conservative financiers and brokers who counseled caution went unheeded. Hoover worried too, and he sought to discourage speculation, but to no avail. On September 4, stock prices wavered, and the next day they dropped. The Great Bull Market staggered on into October, trending downward but with enough good days to keep hope alive. On October 22 a leading bank president told reporters: "I know of nothing fundamentally wrong with the stock market or with the underlying business and credit structure."

THE CRASH AND ITS CAUSES The next day prices tumbled, and the day after that a wild scramble to unload stocks lasted until word arrived that leading bankers had formed a pool to stabilize prices. For the rest of the week prices steadied, but after a weekend to think the situation over stockholders began to unload their portfolios. On Tuesday, October 29, the most devastating single day in the market's history to that point, the index dropped another 43 points, almost 13 percent. The plunge in prices fed on itself as brokers sold the shares they held for buyers who failed to come up with more cash. During October the value of stocks on the New York Exchange fell by an average of 37 percent.

Business and government leaders initially expressed hope. According to President Hoover, "the fundamental business of the country" was sound. John D. Rockefeller issued his first public statement in decades, admitting that "my son and I have for some days been purchasing sound common stocks." Some speculators who got out of the market went back in for bargains but found themselves caught in a slow, tedious erosion of values. By March 1933, the value of stocks on the New York Exchange was less than 20 percent of the value at the market's 1929 peak.

Caution was now the watchword for consumers and business leaders. Buyers held out for lower prices, orders fell off, wages fell or ceased altogether, and the decline in purchasing power brought further cutbacks in business. From 1929 to 1932 Americans' personal incomes declined by more than half, from $82 million to $40 million. Unemployment continued to rise exponentially, from 1.6 million in 1929 to 12.8 million in 1933, from 3 percent to 25 percent of the labor force. And farmers, already in trouble, faced catastrophe as commodity prices fell by half. More than 9,000 banks closed during the period, factories and mines shut down, entire towns were abandoned, and thousands of farms were sold for debt.

The crash had revealed the fundamental business of the country to be unsound. Too many businesses during the boom years had maintained prices and taken profits while holding down wages and the cost of raw materials. As a result, about one-third of the nation's personal income went to only 5 percent of the population. By plowing profits back into expansion, business brought on a growing imbalance between rising productivity and declining purchasing power. As the demand for goods declined, the rate of investment in new plants and equipment also began to decline. For a time the softness of purchasing power was concealed by greater use of installment buying, and the deflationary effects of high tariffs were concealed by the volume of loans and investments abroad, which supported foreign demand for American goods. But the flow of American capital abroad began to dry up when the stock market became a more attractive investment. Swollen profits and dividends enticed the rich into market speculation. When trouble came, the bloated corporate structure collapsed.

Governmental policies also contributed to the debacle. Mellon's tax reductions brought oversaving, which helped diminish demand for consumer goods. The growing money supply fed the fever of speculation by lowering interest rates. Hostility toward unions discouraged collective bargaining and may have worsened the prevalent imbalances in income. High tariffs discouraged foreign trade. Lax enforcement of antitrust laws encouraged concentration, monopoly, and high prices.

HOOVER'S EFFORTS AT RECOVERY   Not only did the policies of public officials help bring on economic collapse; few public leaders acknowledged the severity of the crisis: all that was needed, they thought, was a slight correction of the market. Those who held to the theory of laissez-faire thought the economy would cure itself. The best policy, Mellon advised, would be to "liquidate labor, liquidate stocks, liquidate the farmers, liquidate real estate." Doing so would "purge the rottenness out of the system." Hoover, however, was unwilling to sit by and let events take their course. In fact he did more than any previous president in such dire economic circumstances. Still, his own philosophy, now hardened into dogma, set strict limits to governmental action, and he refused to set it aside even to meet an emergency.

Hoover believed that the country's main need was confidence. In speech after speech he exhorted the public to keep up hope, and he asked business and labor leaders to keep the mills and shops open, maintain wage levels, and spread the work to avoid layoffs—in short, to let the shock fall on corporate profits rather than on purchasing power. In return, union leaders, who had little choice, agreed to refrain from wage demands and strikes.

While reassuring the American public, Hoover also accelerated the building of public projects in order to provide jobs, but state and local cutbacks more than offset federal spending. At Hoover's demand the Federal Reserve returned to an easier credit policy, and Congress passed a modest tax reduction to put more purchasing power in people's pockets. The high Hawley-Smoot Tariff, proposed at first to help farmers, brought reprisals abroad, devastating foreign trade.

As always, depression hurt the party in power, and the floundering president was easy game. Near the city dumps and along railroad tracks, the dispossessed huddled in shacks of tarpaper and galvanized iron, in old packing boxes and abandoned cars. These squalid settlements were labeled "Hoovervilles." A "Hoover blanket" was a derisive name for a newspaper, a "Hoover flag" was an empty pocket turned inside out. Such scornful labels reflected the quick erosion of Hoover's political support. In 1930 the Democrats gained their first national victory since 1916, winning a majority in the House and enough gains in the Senate to control it in coalition with western agrarians.

"Hoovervilles" of tarpaper shacks sprang up around the country as the depression set in.

In the first half of 1931 economic indicators rose, renewing hope for an upswing. Then, as recovery beckoned, another shock jolted public confidence. In 1931 the failure of Austria's largest bank triggered a financial panic in central Europe. To halt the domino effect of spreading defaults, President Hoover proposed a one-year moratorium on both reparations and war-debt payments. The major European nations accepted the moratorium and later also a temporary "standstill" on settlement of private obligations between banks. The general shortage of exchange drove Europeans to withdraw their gold from American banks and dump their American securities. One European nation after another abandoned the gold standard and devalued its currency. All these foreign developments worsened the collapse of the American economy, which slid into the third bitter winter of depression.

CONGRESSIONAL INITIATIVES   With a new Congress in session, demands for federal action impelled Hoover to stretch his philosophy to its limits. He was ready now to use governmental resources at least to shore up the financial institutions. In 1932 the new Congress set up the Reconstruction Finance Corporation (RFC) with $500 million (and authority to borrow $2 billion more) for emergency loans to banks, life insurance companies, building and loan societies, farm mortgage associations, and railroads. The RFC staved off some bankruptcies, but Hoover's critics charged that it favored business at the expense of workers. The RFC nevertheless remained a key agency through the decade and during World War II.

Further help to the financial structure came with the Glass-Steagall Act of 1932, which eased the availability of commercial loans. It also released about $750 million in gold formerly used to back Federal Reserve Notes, countering the effect of foreign withdrawals and domestic hoarding of gold at the same time that it enlarged the supply of credit. For homeowners the Federal Home Loan Bank Act of 1932 created with Hoover's blessing a series of discount banks for home mortgages. They provided savings and loan associations a service much like that which the Federal Reserve System provided to commercial banks.

Hoover's critics argued that all these measures reflected a dubious "trickle-down" theory. If government could help banks and railroads, asked New York's senator Robert G. Wagner, "is there any reason why we should not likewise extend a helping hand to that forlorn American, in every village and every city of the United States, who has been without wages since 1929?" By 1932 members of Congress were filling the hoppers with bills to provide federal relief for individuals. At that point Hoover might have pleaded "dire necessity," taken the leadership of the relief movement, and salvaged his political fortunes.

Instead he held back and only grudgingly edged toward federal relief. On July 21, 1932, Hoover signed the Emergency Relief and Construction Act, which avoided a direct federal dole (cash payments to individuals) but gave the RFC $300 million for relief loans to the states, authorized loans of up to $1.5 billion for state and local government construction projects, and appropriated $322 million for federal public works.

Relief for farmers had long since been abandoned. In mid-1931 the government quit buying surpluses and helplessly watched prices slide. In 1919 wheat had fetched $2.16 a bushel; by 1932 it had sunk to 38¢. Cotton had reached a high of 41.75¢ a pound in 1919; before the 1932 harvest it went to 4.6¢. Other farm prices declined comparably. Between 1930 and 1934 the titles of nearly a million farms passed from their owners to the mortgage holders.

FARMERS AND VETERANS IN PROTEST   Faced with total loss, some desperate farmers began to defy the law. Angry mobs stopped foreclosures and threatened to lynch judges. In Nebraska farmers burned corn to keep warm; dairy farmers dumped milk into roadside ditches in an effort to raise prices. Like voluntary efforts to reduce acreage, these strikes generally failed, but they vividly dramatized the farmers' frustration and anger.

Fears of organized disorder arose when unemployed World War I veterans converged on Washington in the spring of 1932. The "Bonus Expeditionary Force" grew quickly to more than 15,000. Their purpose was to get immediate payment of the cash bonus to war veterans that Congress had voted in 1924. It took the form of life insurance payable in 1945 (earlier to heirs of deceased veterans). The House approved a bonus bill, but when the Senate voted it down most of the veterans went home. The rest, having no place to go, camped in vacant government buildings and in a shantytown within sight of the Capitol.

The chief of the Washington police gave the squatters a friendly welcome and won their trust, but a fearful White House fretted. Eager to

Unemployed veterans, members of the "Bonus Expeditionary Force," clash with Washington, D.C. police at Anacostia Flats, July 1932.

disperse the destitute veterans, Hoover convinced Congress to vote funds to buy their tickets home. More left, but others stayed even after Congress adjourned, hoping at least to meet with the embattled president. Late in July the administration ordered the shantytown razed. In the ensuing melee, one policeman panicked, fired into the crowd, and killed two veterans. The Secretary of War then dispatched about 700 soldiers under General Douglas MacArthur, aided by junior officers Dwight D. Eisenhower and George S. Patton, Jr. The soldiers easily drove out the unarmed veterans and their families, and burned the shacks. MacArthur self-righteously explained in his report that when dealing with "riotous elements" a show of "obvious strength gains a moral ascendancy." Among the evicted was a New Jersey veteran who had received the Distinguished Service Cross for a wartime exploit that had saved the life of George Patton. The one fatality—from tear gas— was an eleven-week-old boy, born in one of the shanties.

General MacArthur said the "mob," spurred by "the essence of revolution," was about to seize control of the government. The administration insisted that the Bonus Army consisted mainly of Communists and criminals, but neither a grand jury nor the Veterans Administration could find evidence to support the charge. One observer wrote before the incident: "There is about the lot of them an atmosphere of hopelessness, of utter despair, though not of desperation. . . . They have no enthusiasm whatever and no stomach for fighting."

Their mood, and the mood of the country, echoed that of Hoover himself. He worked hard, but took no joy from his labors. "I am so tired," he sometimes sighed, "that every bone in my body aches." Presidential news conferences were more strained and less frequent. When friends urged Hoover to seize the reins of leadership, he replied, "I can't be a Theodore Roosevelt," or "I have no Wilsonian qualities." His gloom and growing sense of futility were conveyed to the country. In a mood more despairing than rebellious, people waited to see what another presidential campaign would bring forth.

MAKING CONNECTIONS

- This chapter discusses setbacks for labor unions during the Republican administrations of the 1920s. In the next chapter, unions win new protections under Franklin Roosevelt's New Deal.

- An element of the "normalcy" discussed in this chapter was American isolationism from global affairs. Chapter 28 discusses that isolationism in the context of the coming of World War II.

- Compare the characteristics of 1920s American society with the postwar society and culture of the 1950s, discussed in Chapter 31.

FURTHER READING

On political developments during the 1920s, see David Burner's *The Politics of Provincialism: The Democratic Party in Transition, 1918–1932* (1968).* William H. Chafe's *The American Woman: Her Changing Social, Economic, and Political Roles* (1972)* is a good introduction to the achievement of female suffrage.

Overviews of the depressed economy of the 1930s are found in C. P. Kindleberger's *The World in Depression* (rev. ed., 1986)* and Peter Fearon's *War, Prosperity and Depression: The U.S. Economy, 1917–1945* (1987). John A. Garraty's *The Great Depression* (1986) describes how people survived the depression. See James N. Gregory's *American Exodus: The Dust Bowl Migration and Okie Culture in California* (1989)* for a discussion of the migratory movement's effect on American culture.

*These books are available in paperback editions.

27 ☙ FRANKLIN D. ROOSEVELT
AND THE NEW DEAL

CHAPTER ORGANIZER

This chapter focuses on:

- the social effects of the Great Depression

- Roosevelt's efforts at relief, recovery, and reform

- the pragmatism of the New Deal

- criticism of the New Deal, from both the right and the left

- how the New Deal greatly expanded the federal government's authority and responsibilities

- the change in cultural direction in the 1930s.

*U*pon arriving in the White House Franklin Roosevelt inherited a nation mired in an unprecedented economic depression. He and a supportive Congress would adopt bold measures that provided the foundation for what came to be called welfare capitalism. A three-pronged strategy guided the New Dealers. They first sought to deal with the financial crisis and provide short-term emergency relief for the jobless. They then tried to promote industrial recovery through increased federal spending and cooperative agreements between management and labor. The third prong of the New Deal strategy involved efforts to raise commodity prices (and thereby farm income) by paying farmers to reduce crops and herds. None of these initiatives worked perfectly, but their combined effect was to restore hope and energy to a nation struggling to overcome the worst depression in its history.

FROM HOOVERISM TO THE NEW DEAL

FDR'S ELECTION   On June 14, 1932, while the Bonus Army was still encamped in Washington, Republicans gathered in Chicago to renominate Hoover. The delegates went through the motions in a mood of defeat. The Democrats, in contrast, converged on Chicago late in June confident that they would nominate the next president. New York governor Franklin D. Roosevelt already had lined up most of the delegates, but he still faced an uphill battle for a two-thirds majority. Among the favorite sons only House Speaker John Nance Garner of Texas had any serious chance, but he released his delegates after the third ballot, and Roosevelt went over the top. Garner's reward was the vice presidency, an office he later pronounced "not worth a pitcher of warm spit."

In a bold gesture, Roosevelt appeared before the convention in person to accept the nomination instead of awaiting formal notification. He told the expectant delegates: "I pledge you, I pledge myself to a new deal for the American people." What the New Deal would be in practice Roosevelt had little idea as yet, but he was much more flexible and willing to experiment than Hoover. What was more, his ebullient personality communicated joy and hope—as did his campaign song, "Happy Days Are Here Again."

Born in New York in 1882, Roosevelt was the only child of a wealthy patrician father and an imperious mother, and a distant cousin of Theodore Roosevelt. He had the advantage of a refined education at prestigious Groton School and Harvard, topped off by the Columbia Law School. Tall, handsome, and athletic, he seemed destined for great achievement. In 1912 he backed Woodrow Wilson, and for both of Wilson's terms he served as his assistant secretary of the navy. Then, in 1920, largely on the strength of his name, he gained the vice-presidential nomination. Political defeat was followed by personal crisis when in

1921 he contracted polio, which left him permanently crippled, unable to stand or walk without braces. But his prolonged struggle with this handicap, eased immeasurably by the untiring efforts of his wife, Eleanor, transformed the once snobbish young aristocrat into one of the century's most outgoing political figures. Justice Oliver Wendell Holmes, Jr., later summed up his qualities: "A second-class intellect—but a first-class temperament."

For seven years Roosevelt fought his way back to health and in 1928 ran for governor of New York and won. Reelected by a whopping majority of 700,000 in 1930, he became the Democratic front-runner for the presidency in 1932. Behind the public facade of a cheery and self-confident politician, Roosevelt was also a shrewd and at times crass manipulator of people and power. Obsessed with gaining the highest office in the land, he was willing to subordinate and utilize all else in his life—family, health, staff, friends—to that end. Roosevelt occasionally inflated his own accomplishments and took credit for those of others, but his own strengths and achievements were considerable. A born leader, he had a talent for surrounding himself with capable people and getting the most out of them. Most important, however, was his bulldog determination to succeed, to overcome all obstacles, to triumph over despair and adversity, and in the process achieve greatness.

Partly to dispel doubts about his health, Roosevelt set forth on a grueling campaign tour in 1932. He blamed the depression on Hoover and the Republicans, and began to define his New Deal. Like Hoover, Roosevelt made the requisite pledge to balance the budget, but he left open the loophole that he would incur deficits to prevent starvation. He was evasive on the tariff, and on farm policy he offered several options pleasing to farmers but ambiguous enough not to alarm city dwellers. He did come out unequivocally for strict regulation of utilities, and he consistently stood by his party's pledge to repeal the prohibition amendment. He also announced that a mature economy would require more imaginative national planning. "The country needs, and, unless I mistake its temper, the country demands bold, persistent experimentation." What came across to voters, however, was less the content of his speeches than the confidence and irrepressible buoyancy of the man.

The dour Hoover, by contrast, had no confidence. He could turn a neat phrase, but many elegant passages suffered from the pedestrian manner of his delivery. Democrats, he argued, ignored the international

Governor Franklin D. Roosevelt, the Democratic nominee, campaigning in Topeka, Kansas. Roosevelt's confidence inspired voters.

causes of the depression. Roosevelt's reckless proposals, Hoover warned, "would destroy the very foundations of our American system." But few were listening. Mired in the persistent depression, the country wanted a new course, a new leadership, a new deal.

Many thoughtful voters took a dim view of both candidates. Those who believed that only a truly radical departure would suffice went over to the Socialist Norman Thomas, who polled 882,000 votes, and some went on to support the Communist candidate, who won 103,000 votes. The wonder is that a desperate people did not turn in greater numbers to such radical alternatives. Instead they swept Roosevelt into office by a whopping margin.

THE INAUGURATION   For the last time the country waited four long months, until March 4, for a new president and Congress to take office. The Twentieth Amendment, ratified on February 6, 1933, provided that the president would thereafter take office on January 20 and the newly elected Congress on January 3. Amid spreading destitution and misery, unemployment continued to rise during the bleak winter of 1932–1933, and panic struck the banking system. Depositors played it safe by taking their cash out and squirreling it away. When the Hoover administration left office, four-fifths of the nation's banks were closed, and the country was on the brink of economic paralysis.

The profound crisis of confidence that prevailed when Roosevelt took the oath of office on March 4, 1933, gave way to a mood of expectancy. The new president exploited both with a spirit of assurance that conveyed a new sense of vigorous action. First, he asserted "that the only thing we have to fear is fear itself." He would not merely exhort, he promised: "This nation asks for action, and action now!" It was exactly what a distraught nation wanted to hear. One citizen wrote Roosevelt that the speech was "the finest thing this side of heaven. It seemed to give the people, as well as myself, a new hold on life."

Roosevelt's willingness to act, to be decisive, and to experiment with new programs and policies set his presidency apart from most others. Nevertheless, for all his energy and daring, Roosevelt brought to the White House no concrete agenda or long-range plan. He was a pragmatist rather than an ideologue. As he once explained, "Take a method and try it. If it fails admit it frankly and try another." The new president compared himself to a football quarterback: he could not call the next play until he knew the results of the previous one. Roosevelt's "New Deal," therefore, would take the form of a series of trial-and-error actions. Soon Roosevelt was in action on more than a dozen fronts.

STRENGTHENING THE MONETARY SYSTEM   The first order of business for the new administration was to free up the channels of finance. On his second day in office, Roosevelt called for a special session of Congress, and he then declared a four-day banking holiday. It took Congress only seven hours to pass the Emergency Banking Relief Act, which permitted sound banks to reopen and provided managers for those still in trouble. On March 12, 1933, in the first of his radio "fireside chats," the president told his audience that it was safer to "keep your money in a reopened bank than under the mattress." The following day, deposits in reopened banks exceeded withdrawals, and by March 15 banks controlling nine-tenths of the nation's banking resources were once again open. In rapid order Roosevelt next slashed military pen-

The Galloping Snail. *A vigorous Roosevelt drives the Congress to action in this* Detroit News *cartoon, March 1933.*

sions and government payrolls and then urged Congress to pass the Twenty-first Amendment, ending prohibition.

These measures were but the beginning of an avalanche of executive and legislative action. During the session from March 9 to June 16, the so-called Hundred Days, Congress passed more than a dozen of Roosevelt's major proposals, legislation whose scope was unprecedented in American history. Said one dizzied legislator, Roosevelt's New Deal "reads like the first chapter of Genesis."

With the banking crisis over, there still remained an acute debt problem for farmers and homeowners and a lingering distrust of the banks, which might be aroused again. By executive decree, Roosevelt reorganized all farm credit agencies into the Farm Credit Administration (FCA). Congress confirmed that action and authorized the extensive refinancing of farm mortgages at lower interest rates. The Home Owner's Loan Act (June 13) provided a similar service to city dwellers through the new Home Owner's Loan Corporation (HOLC)—something which, incidentally, Hoover had vainly urged on Congress in 1931. The HOLC refinanced mortgage loans at lower monthly payments for strapped homeowners. This helped slow the rate of foreclosures. The Glass-Steagall Banking Act (June 16) further shored up confidence in the banking system by creating the Federal Deposit Insurance Corporation (FDIC) to insure bank deposits up to $5,000. It also required commercial banks to separate themselves from investment brokerages.

Roosevelt and Congress then turned their attention to tightening the regulation of Wall Street. The Federal Securities Act required that new stock and bond issues register with the Federal Trade Commission and later with the Securities and Exchange Commission (SEC), a new agency that regulated the stock and bond markets.

Throughout 1933 Roosevelt tinkered with devaluation of the currency as a way to raise stock and commodity prices and ease the debt burden on strapped investors and farmers. On April 19 the government achieved this by officially abandoning the gold standard, which infuriated fiscal conservatives. One fumed that Roosevelt's decision "can't be defended except as mob rule." Yet the consequent decline in the value of the dollar increased the prices of commodities and stocks at home.

RELIEF MEASURES   Another urgent priority in 1933 was relieving the widespread personal distress caused by the depression. As Roosevelt once remarked, the "test of our progress is not whether we add to the abundance of those who have much. It is whether we provide enough for those who have too little." Congress took a first step toward such relief with the creation of the Civilian Conservation Corps (CCC), which was designed to provide useful jobs for young men aged eighteen to twenty-five. Beginning in 1933 nearly 3 million men took to the woods to work at a variety of jobs in forests, parks, recreational areas, and soil conservation projects. Directed by army officers and foresters, they worked under military discipline and provided perhaps the most direct analogue of war in the whole New Deal. Like the military at the time, the CCC camps were racially segregated. In Texas, African Americans were initially told that the camps were for whites only, and this falsehood helps explain the low number of blacks enrolled. Only 400 black Texans, less than 5 percent of the total number of men enrolled, participated in the program.

The Federal Emergency Relief Administration (FERA) addressed the broader problems of human distress. Harry L. Hopkins, a tireless social worker from Iowa who had earlier directed Roosevelt's state relief program in New York, headed the new effort and became the second most powerful figure in the administration. He pushed the FERA with a boundless nervous energy, spending $5 million within two hours of taking office. FERA funds supported state construction of over 5,000 public buildings and 7,000 bridges, organized adult literacy programs, financed college education for poor students, and set up day-care centers for low-income families. The agency also provided direct cash payments to the chronically unemployed.

The first large-scale experiment with federal work relief, which put people directly on the government payroll at competitive wages, came with the formation of the Civil Works Administration (CWA). Created in 1933, when it had become apparent that the state-sponsored programs under the FERA would not prevent widespread privation, the CWA provided federal jobs and wages to those unable to find work that winter. It was hastily conceived and implemented, but during its four-month existence, it put to work over 4 million people. It spent over $900 million (mostly in wages) for a variety of useful projects, from making highway repairs to constructing or improving more than 1,000 airports and 40,000 schools, to providing 50,000 teaching jobs that helped keep rural schools open. The CWA, unlike the FERA, which financed state projects, was a wholly federal operation. As the numbers it employed soared, the program's costs skyrocketed to over a billion dollars. Roosevelt balked at such high expenditures and, feeling the CWA had served its purpose of helping many unemployed people weather the winter, he ordered the agency dissolved in the spring of 1934. By April some 4 million workers were again unemployed.

Roosevelt, however, continued to favor work relief over direct cash payment to individuals; he thought the dole was "a narcotic, a subtle destroyer of the human spirit." In 1935 he asked Congress for an array of new federal job programs, and it responded by passing a $4.8 billion bill providing work relief for the jobless. To manage these programs, Roosevelt created the Works Progress Administration (WPA), headed by Harry L. Hopkins, to replace the FERA. Hopkins was told to provide millions of jobs quickly, and as a result some jobs appeared to be make-work or mere "leaning on shovels." But before the WPA died during

World War II, it left permanent monuments on the landscape in the form of buildings, bridges, hard-surfaced roads, airports, and schools.

The WPA also employed a wide range of talents in the Federal Theatre Project, the Federal Art Project, and the Federal Writers' Project. Talented writers such as Ralph Ellison, John Cheever, and Saul Bellow found work writing travel guides to the United States, and Orson Welles directed Federal Theatre productions. The National Youth Administration (NYA), under the WPA, provided part-time employment to students, set up technical training programs, and aided jobless youth. Twenty-seven-year-old Lyndon Johnson was director of an NYA program in Texas, and Richard Nixon, a penniless Duke University law student, found work through the local NYA at thirty-five cents an hour. Although the WPA took care of only about 3 million out of some 10 million jobless at any one time, in all it helped some 9 million clients weather desperate times before it expired in 1943.

RECOVERY THROUGH REGULATION

In addition to rescuing the banks and providing relief for the unemployed, Roosevelt and his advisers promoted the recovery of the agricultural and industrial sectors. Roosevelt's so-called "brain trust" of university-trained experts, lawyers, and professors initially felt that the trend toward economic concentration was inevitable. They also believed that the mistakes of the 1920s showed that the only way to operate an integrated economy at full capacity and in the public interest was through stringent regulation and organized central planning, not through trust-busting. The success of centralized economic planning on a national scale during World War I reinforced such ideas. New farm and recovery programs sprang from their beliefs and experiences.

AGRICULTURAL RECOVERY: THE AAA The Agricultural Adjustment Act of 1933 provided a plan to compensate farmers for voluntary cutbacks in production. The money for the benefit payments made to farmers would result from a tax levied on the businesses that processed farm products for sale, such as cotton gins, flour mills, and meat-packing plants.

By the time Congress acted, the growing season was already advanced, and the prospect of another bumper cotton crop created an urgent problem. The AAA reluctantly sponsored a plow-under program. To destroy a growing crop was a "shocking commentary on our civilization," Agriculture Secretary Henry A. Wallace lamented. "I could tolerate it only as a cleaning up of the wreckage from the old days of unbalanced production." In addition to plowing under ripening crops, the AAA encouraged farmers to destroy young livestock as a means of raising prices. Critics thereafter labeled Wallace the "assassin of little pigs." As a complement to the AAA, Roosevelt created the Commodity Credit Corporation (another CCC!), which extended loans based on the value of cotton and other crops kept in storage and off the market. In principle, if not in form, it was a revival of the old Farmers' Alliance–Populist subtreasury plan.

THE DUST BOWL   For a while these farm measures worked. By the end of 1934 Wallace could report significant declines in wheat, cotton, and corn production and a simultaneous increase in commodity prices. Farm income increased by 58 percent between 1932 and 1935. The AAA, however, was only partially responsible for such gains. The devastating drought that settled over the plains states between 1932 and 1935 played a major role in reducing production and creating the epic "Dust Bowl" migrations so poignantly evoked in John Steinbeck's *Grapes of Wrath*. Many of these migrant families had actually been driven off the land by AAA benefit programs that encouraged large farmers to take the lands worked by tenants and sharecroppers out of cultivation first.

This process of displacement particularly affected Mexican Americans and African Americans. Because many Mexican Americans were unable to prove their citizenship, either out of ignorance of the regulations or because their migratory work hampered their ability to meet residency requirements, they were denied access to the many new federal relief programs under the New Deal. They also were the targets of deeply ingrained racial prejudice. "The Mexicans are trash," declared a California state government official. "They have no standard of living. We herd them like pigs." American labor unions, distressed at high rates of unemployment among their membership, protested against the presence of Mexican workers in the United States. During the 1930s fed-

The Great Blow of 1934. *Severe drought and soil erosion created conditions for the dust storms that plagued the Middle West in the mid-1930s. This photograph is by Dorothea Lange.*

eral officials deported some 400,000 Mexican aliens and Mexican Americans to Mexico. Most of those deported lived in Texas or California, but significant numbers of Mexican Americans were also relocated from Colorado, Indiana, and Illinois.

Like Mexican Americans, the blacks who farmed during the Great Depression were typically tenants or sharecroppers working the marginal lands that owners decided to take out of cultivation in order to earn federal payments. During the 1930s the number of black tenant farmers in Texas decreased from 65,000 to 32,000, while the number of landless black farm laborers rose by 25,000. Some 20,000 other blacks left the state in search of better economic opportunities in other regions of the country. It is estimated that over 200,000 black tenant farmers nationwide were displaced by the AAA. These and other displaced farmers joined a migratory stream rushing from the South and Midwest toward California, buoyed by currents of hope and desperation. One couple claimed they had heard "how much money a man could make out there and we wanted to go."

Although frequently lumped together as "Okies," the Dust Bowl refugees were actually from cotton-belt communities in Arkansas, Texas, and Missouri, as well as Oklahoma. During the 1930s and 1940s, some 800,000 people left those four states and headed west. Not all were farmers; many were professionals, white-collar workers, retailers, and farm implement salesmen whose jobs had been tied to the health of the agricultural sector. Most of the Dust Bowl migrants were white, and most were young adults in their twenties and thirties who relocated with spouses and children. Some traveled on trains or buses, others hopped a freight or hitched a ride; most rode in their own cars, the trip taking four to five days on average.

Most of the Dust Bowl migrants who had come from cities gravitated to California's urban areas—Los Angeles, San Diego, or San Francisco. Half of the newcomers, however, moved into the San Joaquin Valley, the agricultural heartland of the state. There they discovered that California was no paradise. Only a few of the migrants could afford to buy land. Most (men and women) found themselves competing with local Hispanics and Asians for seasonal work as pickers in the cotton fields or orchards of large corporate farms. Living in tents or crude cabins and frequently on the move, they suffered from exposure and from poor sanitation.

They also felt the sting of social prejudice. Steinbeck explained that "Okie us'ta mean you was from Oklahoma. Now it means you're a dirty son-of-a-bitch. Okie means you're scum. Don't mean nothing in itself, it's the way they say it." Such hostility drove a third of the "Okies" to return to their home states. Most of the farm workers who stayed tended to fall back upon their old folkways rather than assimilate themselves into their new surroundings. These gritty "plain folk" brought with them their own prejudices against blacks and ethnic minorities as well as a potent tradition of evangelical Protestantism and a distinctive style of music variously labeled "country," "hillbilly," or "cowboy." This "Okie" subculture remains a vivid part of California society today.

Although it created unexpected problems, the AAA achieved real successes in boosting the overall farm economy. Then the Supreme Court in *United States v. Butler* (1936) ruled the AAA's processing tax unconstitutional because farm production was intrastate and thus beyond the reach of federal power. The administration hastily devised a new plan to achieve crop reduction indirectly in the Soil Conservation and Domestic Allotment Act (1936), which it pushed through Congress in six weeks. The new act omitted processing taxes and acreage quotas, but provided benefit payments to farmers who engaged in soil conservation practices and cut back on soil-depleting staple crops.

The act was an almost unqualified success as an engineering and educational project because it went far to heal the scars of erosion and the plague of dust storms. But soil conservation nevertheless failed as a device for limiting production. With their worst lands taken out of production, farmers cultivated their fertile acres more intensively. In response, Congress passed the second Agricultural Adjustment Act (1938), which reestablished the earlier programs but left out the processing taxes. Benefit payments would now come from general funds. Increasingly, federal farm programs came to dominate the nation's agricultural economy. As the novelist William Faulkner recognized, "Our economy is not agricultural any longer. Our economy is the federal government. We no longer farm in Mississippi cotton fields. We farm now in Washington corridors and Congressional committee rooms."

INDUSTRIAL RECOVERY: THE NRA   The industrial counterpart to the AAA was the National Industrial Recovery Act (NIRA), passed in 1933. The NIRA had two major components. One part created the Public Works Administration (PWA) with $3.3 billion for public buildings, highway programs, flood control, bridges, tunnels, and aircraft carriers. The purpose was to "prime the pump" of business with new expenditures and provide jobs for the unemployed. Under the direction of Interior Secretary Harold L. Ickes, the PWA indirectly served the purpose of work relief, although Ickes directed it toward well-planned permanent improvements rather than the provision of hasty make-work jobs, and he used private contractors rather than placing workers directly on the government payroll. PWA workers built Virginia's Skyline Drive, New York's Triborough Bridge, the Overseas Highway from Miami to Key West, and Chicago's subway system.

The more controversial and ambitious part of the NIRA created the National Recovery Administration (NRA), headed by General Hugh S. Johnson. Its purposes were essentially twofold: first, to stabilize business with codes of "fair" competitive practice, and second, to generate more purchasing power by providing jobs, defining labor standards, and raising wages. The NRA also enlisted trade union hopes for protection of basic hour and wage standards and raised liberal hopes for comprehensive planning.

In each industry, committees representing management, labor, and government drew up the fair practice codes. The labor standards were quite progressive. Every code set a forty-hour week and minimum weekly wages of $13 ($12 in the South, where living costs were considered lower), which more than doubled earnings in some cases. Child labor under the age of sixteen was prohibited.

As the drafting of other codes governing particular industries began to drag, the NRA launched a crusade to whip up popular support for its efforts. The public responded, proudly displaying the NRA symbol of compliance, the "Blue Eagle," on signs and in stores. Some 2 million employers signed a much-publicized pledge affirming their support for the NRA codes.

For a time the NRA worked, perhaps because a new air of confidence had overcome the depression blues and the downward spiral of wages and prices had subsided. But as soon as recovery began, the honeymoon ended. Charges mounted that the larger companies dominated the code negotiations, that they used the codes to stifle competition by dividing up markets and entrenching their own positions, and that price-fixing robbed small producers of the chance to compete. The NRA wage codes also excluded agricultural and domestic workers—occupations involving three out of every four employed blacks. The effort to develop codes for every industry in the nation proved an administrative nightmare, and the daily annoyances of code enforcement inspired growing hostility among business executives.

By 1935 the NRA had developed more critics than friends. When it died in 1935, struck down by the Supreme Court as unconstitutional, few mourned. Yet, while generally deemed a failure, the NRA experiment left an enduring mark. With dramatic suddenness, the codes had set new standards, such as the forty-hour week and the end of child labor, from which it proved hard for management to retreat. The NRA's endorsement of collective bargaining also spurred union growth.

REGIONAL PLANNING: THE TVA   The wide-ranging philosophy of the New Deal embraced more than the restrictive approaches of the

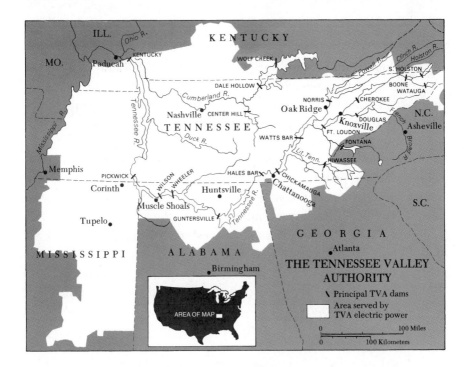

THE TENNESSEE VALLEY AUTHORITY

\ Principal TVA dams

☐ Area served by TVA electric power

0   100 Miles

0   100 Kilometers

AREA OF MAP ■

NRA. The creation of the Tennessee Valley Authority (TVA) was a truly bold venture, the product neither of a single imagination nor of a single concept, but of an unfolding progression of purposes. In 1916 the government started power and nitrate plants at Muscle Shoals, Alabama, to strengthen national defense. New objectives unfolded in succession: the plants could produce nitrate fertilizers as well as nitrate explosives, promote general industrial development, and provide cheap public power to be used as a "yardstick" for private utility rates. Waterpower development led in turn to improved flood control, and to conservation of soil and forests to prevent silting. The chain of connections led ultimately to the concept of overall planning for an entire watershed, which included a total drainage area in the southeast of 41,000 square miles overlapping parts of seven states.

Through the 1920s Nebraska senator George W. Norris had fought off efforts to sell the Alabama project to private developers, but he never marshaled sufficient support for his goal of a federal project to provide electricity for the public. In 1932, however, Norris won the new president's support for a vast enlargement of the Muscle Shoals project.

On May 18, 1933, Congress created the TVA as a multipurpose public corporation. By 1936 the TVA board had six dams completed or under way, and a master plan to build nine high dams on the Tennessee

River, which would create the "Great Lakes of the South," and other dams on the tributaries. The agency, moreover, opened the rivers for navigation, fostered soil conservation and forestry, experimented with fertilizers, drew new industry to the region, and sent cheap power pulsating through the valley.

TVA's success at generating greater power consumption and lower rates awakened private utilities to the mass consumer markets. It also transported farmers of the valley from the age of kerosene to the age of electricity. "The women went around turning the switches on and off," reported a Farm Bureau man who witnessed the transition. "The light and wonder in their eyes was brighter than that from the lamps." Through loans of more than $321 million to rural cooperatives, the Rural Electrification Administration (REA) paved the way to the electrification of the nation's farms.

LAUNCHING THE SECOND NEW DEAL

During Roosevelt's first year in office his programs and his personal charms aroused massive support. The president's travels and speeches, his twice-weekly press conferences, and his "fireside chats" over the radio generated vitality and warmth from a once-remote White House. In the congressional elections of 1934 the Democrats actually increased their strength in both House and Senate, an almost unprecedented midterm victory for the party in power. When it was over, only seven Republican governors remained in office throughout the country.

Criticism of the New Deal during 1933 was muted or reduced to helpless carping. But as the sense of crisis passed, the spirit of unity relaxed. The depression's downward slide had been halted, but prosperity remained elusive. Even more unsettling to some was the dramatic growth of executive power. In 1934 a group of conservative businessmen and politicians, including Al Smith and John W. Davis, two previous Democratic presidential candidates, formed the American Liberty League to oppose New Deal measures as violations of personal and property rights.

THUNDER ON THE LEFT   More potent threats to Roosevelt came from the hucksters of social nostrums, old and new. The most flamboyant of the group by far was Louisiana's "Kingfish," Senator Huey P. Long, Jr. A short, strutting man, Long sported pink suits and pastel shirts, red ties, and two-toned shoes. He seemed like a clown to some observers and loved to make people think he was a country bumpkin. But underneath all the carefully designed hoopla was a shrewd lawyer and consummate politician. First as Louisiana governor, then as political boss of the state, Long had delivered to its citizens tax favors, roads, schools, free textbooks, charity hospitals, and generally better public services. That he had become a sort of state dictator in the process, using bribery, physical intimidation, and blackmail to achieve his ends seemed irrelevant to many of his ardent supporters.

In 1933 Long joined Roosevelt in Washington as a Democratic senator. He initially supported the New Deal but quickly grew suspicious of the NRA's collusion with big business. He also had grown jealous of Roosevelt's mushrooming popularity, having himself developed aspirations for the Oval Office. Promoting himself as a radical egalitarian, a true, if self-indulgent, friend of the people, Long had his own plan for dealing with the Great Depression.

Long's Share Our Wealth program was tantalizingly generous and simple. In one version he proposed to confiscate large personal fortunes, guarantee every family a cash grant of $5,000, every worker an annual income of $2,500, provide pensions to the aged, reduce working hours, pay veterans' bonuses, and assure a college education for every qualified student. It did not matter to him that his figures failed to add up or that his program offered little to promote an economic recovery. As he told a group of distressed Iowa farmers, "Maybe somebody says I don't understand it. Well, you don't have to. Just shut your damn eyes and believe it. That's all." Whether he had a workable plan or not, by early 1935 the charismatic Long was claiming a file of 7.5 million supporters. He was also successful in arousing the concern and ire of the Roosevelt administration. Interior Secretary Harold Ickes growled that Long suffered from "halitosis of the intellect."

Another popular social scheme was hatched by a California doctor, Francis E. Townsend. Outraged by the sight of three haggard old women raking through garbage cans in Long Beach, Townsend proposed government pensions for the aged. In 1934 he began promoting the Townsend Plan of paying $200 a month to every citizen over sixty who retired from employment and who promised to spend the money within the month. The plan had the lure of providing both financial security for the aged and job openings for the young. As the Townsend Clubs grew, critics noted that the cost of his program for 9 percent of the population would be more than half the national income. "I'm not in the least interested in the cost of the plan," Townsend blandly told a House committee.

A third huckster of panaceas, Father Charles E. Coughlin, the "radio priest," founded the National Union for Social Justice in 1934. In broadcasts over the CBS network, he specialized in schemes for the coinage of silver and in attacks on bankers that carried growing overtones of anti-Semitism.

Coughlin, Townsend, and Long drew support largely from desperate lower-middle-class Americans. Of the three, Long had the widest following. A 1935 survey showed that he could draw 5 to 6 million votes as a third-party candidate for president in 1936, perhaps enough to undermine Roosevelt's chances of reelection.

Beset by pressures from both ends of the political spectrum, Roosevelt hesitated for months before deciding to "steal the thunder" from the left with new programs of reform and social security. Political pressures impelled Roosevelt, but so did the growing influence within the administration of Justices Louis Brandeis and Felix Frankfurter. These advisers urged Roosevelt to be less cozy with big business and to push for restored competition and heavy taxes on large corporations.

LIGHTNING FROM THE COURT   A series of Supreme Court decisions finally galvanized the president into action. On May 27, 1935, the Court killed the National Industrial Recovery Act by unanimous vote. In *Schechter Poultry Corporation v. United States,* quickly tagged the "sick chicken" case, the defendants had been convicted of selling an "unfit chicken" and violating other NRA code provisions. The high court ruled that Congress had delegated too much power to the executive branch when it granted the code-making authority, and had exceeded its power under the commerce clause by regulating *intrastate* commerce. The poultry in question, the Court decided, had "come to permanent rest within the state," although it earlier had been moved across state lines. In a press conference soon afterward, Roosevelt fumed: "We have been relegated to the horse-and-buggy definition of interstate commerce." The same line of reasoning, he warned, might endanger other New Deal programs.

LEGISLATIVE ACHIEVEMENTS OF THE SECOND NEW DEAL   To rescue his program Roosevelt in 1935 ended the stalemate in Congress and launched the so-called Second New Deal with demands for several pieces of "must" legislation, most of which were already pending. During the next two months Congress passed another cluster of significant—and quite controversial—legislation.

The National Labor Relations Act, often called the Wagner Act for its sponsor, New York senator Robert Wagner, gave workers the right to bargain through unions of their own choice and prohibited employers from interfering with union activities. A National Labor Relations Board of five members could supervise plant elections and certify unions as bargaining agents where a majority of the workers approved. The board could also investigate the actions of employers and issue "cease and desist" orders against specified unfair practices.

The Social Security Act of 1935, Roosevelt announced, was the New Deal's "cornerstone" and "supreme achievement." Indeed, it has proven to be the most significant and far-reaching of all the New Deal initiatives. The concept was by no means new. Progressives during the early 1900s had proposed a federal system of social security for the aged, indigent, handicapped, and unemployed. Other nations had already enacted such programs, but the United States remained steadfast to its tradition of individual self-reliance. The Great Depression, however, revived the idea, and Roosevelt masterfully guided the legislation through Congress.

The Social Security Act included three major provisions. Its centerpiece was a pension fund for retired people over 65 and their survivors. Beginning in 1937 workers and employers contributed payroll taxes to establish the fund. Benefit payments started in 1940 and averaged $22 per month, a quite modest sum even for those depressed times. Roosevelt knew this, and stressed that the pension program was not intended to guarantee a comfortable retirement; it was designed to supplement other sources of income and protect the elderly from some of the "hazards and vicissitudes of life." Only later did American voters and politicians come to perceive Social Security as the *primary* source

"Yes, You Remembered Me." *The social legislation of the Second New Deal prompted this depiction of FDR as the friend of "The Forgotten Man."*

of retirement income for most of the aged. By 1995 the average monthly payment was about $900.

The Social Security Act also set up a shared federal-state unemployment insurance program, financed by a payroll tax on employers. In addition, the new legislation committed the national government to a broad range of social welfare activities based on the assumption that "unemployables"—people who were unable to work—would remain a state responsibility, while the national government would provide work relief for the able-bodied. To that end the law inaugurated federal grants-in-aid for three state-administered public assistance programs—old age assistance, aid for dependent children, aid for the blind—and further aid for maternal, child welfare, and public health services.

Relatively speaking the new federal program was quite conservative. It was the only government pension program in the world financed by taxes on the earnings of current workers. Most other countries funded such programs out of general revenues. The Social Security payroll tax was also a regressive tax in that it entailed a single fixed rate for all, regardless of income level. It thus hurt the poor more than the rich, and it also hurt Roosevelt's efforts to revive the economy because it removed from circulation a significant amount of money. The new Social Security tax took money out of workers' pockets and placed it into a trust fund, thus exacerbating the shrinking money supply that was one of the main causes of the depression. By taking discretionary income away from workers, the government blunted the sharp increase in public consumption needed to restore the health of the economy. In addition, the Social Security system initially excluded many of those classes of workers who needed it the most: farm workers, domestics, and the self-employed.

Roosevelt recognized and regretted such limitations, but he knew that they were necessary compromises in order to see the Social Security Act through Congress and to enable it to withstand court challenges. As he replied to an aide who criticized funding the pension program through employee contributions, "I guess you're right on the economics, but those taxes were never a problem of economics. They are politics all the way through. We put those payroll contributions there so as to give the contributors a moral, legal, and political right to collect their pensions and their unemployment benefits. With those taxes in there, no damn politician can ever scrap my social security program."

The last of the major laws passed during this period was the Revenue Act of 1935, sometimes called the Wealth Tax Act, but popularly known as the "Soak-the-Rich" tax. The Revenue Act raised tax rates on incomes above $50,000. Estate and gift taxes also rose, as did the corporate tax on all but small corporations—those with less than $50,000 annual income. By "soaking" the rich, Roosevelt stole much of the thunder from the left, as he claimed, although the results fell short of the promise. The new tax law failed to increase federal revenue significantly, nor did it result in a significant redistribution of income.

Still, the prevailing view was that Roosevelt had moved in a radical direction. Newspaper editor William Randolph Hearst growled that the Wealth Tax was "essentially Communism. This bastard proposal should be ascribed to a composite personality which might be labeled Stalin Delano Roosevelt." But the extent of the new departure taken by the Second New Deal is easy to exaggerate. Such measures as Social Security, utility regulation, and higher taxes on the wealthy had long been in the works in Congress and had already been adopted by most other industrial nations. Roosevelt himself stressed that he had no love for socialism. "I am fighting Communism. . . . I want to save our system, the capitalistic system." Yet he added that to save it from revolutionary turmoil required a more equal "distribution of wealth."

THE HUMAN EFFECTS OF THE DEPRESSION   Although the flurry of New Deal programs helped ease the devastation wrought by the depression, it did not restore prosperity. Nor did it end widespread human suffering. As late as 1939, some 9.5 million workers (17 percent of the labor force) remained unemployed. Prolonged economic hardship continued to create personal tragedies and tremendous social strains. Poverty led desperate people to do desperate things. Petty theft soared during the 1930s, as did street-corner begging and prostitution. In Pittsburgh an unemployed father, desperate to feed his starving children, stole a loaf of bread from a neighbor, was arrested, and hanged himself in shame. Although the divorce rate dropped during the decade, in part because couples could not afford to live separately or pay the legal fees to obtain divorces, all too often husbands down on their luck simply deserted their wives. In 1940 a survey revealed that 1.5 million husbands had left home. A California woman reported to a friend that her husband "went north about three months ago to try his luck. The first month he wrote pretty regularly. . . . For five weeks now we have had no word from him. . . . Don't know where he is or what he is up to."

Many couples decided to postpone marriage because of hard times. Some 800,000 marriages were delayed during the 1930s, and the total number of marriages declined by one-fourth compared to the previous decade. With their own future uncertain, married couples often decided not to have children; the birth rate plummeted during the depression. Those with children sometimes could not support them. In 1933 the Children's Bureau reported that one out of every five children was not getting enough to eat. Often, struggling parents sent their children to live with relatives or friends. Some 900,000 other children simply left home and joined the army of tramps.

CIVIL RIGHTS IN THE 1930S   Like Woodrow Wilson before him, Franklin Roosevelt did not give a high priority to racial issues, but he tolerated people in his administration who did. By 1936 there was a "Black Cabinet" of some thirty advisers in various government departments and agencies, and black voters were fast transferring their political allegiance from the Republicans to the Democrats.

During the 1930s the NAACP's legal campaign gathered momentum. Two important precedents emerged from the controversial Scottsboro case in 1931, in which nine black youths were convicted of raping two white women while riding a freight train in Alabama. The first verdict was thrown out by the Supreme Court in *Powell v. Alabama* (1932). It argued that the trial judge denied the defendants due process when he failed to appoint an attorney to defend them. Three years later, in *Norris v. Alabama* (1935) the Court declared that the systematic exclusion of blacks from Alabama juries had denied the Scottsboro defendants equal protection of the law—a principle that had significant and widespread impact on state courts throughout the nation.

CONSERVATIVE DISCONTENT By 1935, many conservatives in both political parties were thoroughly disgusted with Roosevelt and his New Deal programs. Business leaders fumed over his tax and spending policies. The wealthy resented their loss of status and the growing power of government and labor. They railed against the New Deal and Roosevelt, whom they called "a traitor to his own class." Visitors at the home of J. P. Morgan, Jr., were cautioned not to mention Roosevelt's name lest it raise his blood pressure. But the conservative coalition of business and wealth, by its incoherent rage, made a perfect foil for the confident president, and the voting public rushed to his side. As Roosevelt recognized, businessmen "are unanimous in their hatred for me—and I welcome their hatred."

ELEANOR ROOSEVELT Another key element in Roosevelt's unprecedented popularity with the electorate was his wife, Anna Eleanor Roosevelt, who had increasingly become an enormous political asset and would prove to be one of the most influential and revered women leaders of her time. She had lost both parents by age ten and had been a shy, withdrawn youth, utterly aware that her peers deemed her plain and even ugly. "I was a solemn child, without beauty," she recalled. "I seemed like a little old woman entirely lacking in the spontaneous joy and mirth of youth." But the ungainly Eleanor grew into a tall, willowy, outgoing woman, and in the White House she became a more public figure than any previous First Lady.

Eleanor channeled her energies into social service. As a teen she had volunteered in a New York settlement house, and she remained ardently concerned about issues of human welfare and rights for women and blacks. As her secretary recalled, Eleanor Roosevelt "lived to be kind." Compassionate without being maudlin, more stoical than sentimental,

Eleanor Roosevelt and Civil Rights Leader A. Philip Randolph. *The 1936 election marked the first time black voters cast a majority of their votes for a Democratic president.*

she exuded warmth and sincerity, and she challenged the complacency of the affluent. "No woman," observed a friend, "has ever so comforted the distressed or so distressed the comfortable."

One of Eleanor Roosevelt's key functions was to keep the president from being isolated from the public. She served, he said, as his "eyes and ears," as well as his conscience, and she relished traveling around the country, representing him and the New Deal, defying local segregation ordinances, supporting women's causes, highlighting the plight of unemployed youth, and imploring Americans to live up to their egalitarian and humanitarian ideals. She was especially forceful in prodding officials to ease racial discrimination in federal programs. A Maine fisherman described her uniquely endearing qualities: "She ain't stuck up, she ain't dressed up, and she ain't afraid to talk." Eleanor Roosevelt also became her husband's most visible and effective liaison with many liberal groups, bringing labor leaders, women activists, and black spokesmen into the White House after hours, and serving to deflect criticism of the president by taking progressive stands and running political risks he himself dared not. He was the politician, she once remarked, she was the agitator.

THE 1936 ELECTION   The popularity of Eleanor and Franklin Roosevelt, and the New Deal, impelled the Republican convention in 1936 to avoid candidates too closely identified with the "hate-Roosevelt" contingent. The party chose Governor Alfred M. Landon of Kansas, a former Bull Moose Progressive. A fiscal conservative, Landon had nevertheless endorsed many New Deal programs. He was probably more liberal than most of his backers, and clearly more so than the party's platform, which accused the New Deal of usurping power.

The Republicans hoped that the followers of Long, Coughlin, Townsend, and other dissidents would combine to draw enough votes away from Roosevelt to throw the election to them. But that possibility faded when an assassin, the son-in-law of a Louisiana judge whom Long had sought to remove, gunned down the "Kingfish" in September 1935. Coughlin, Townsend, and a remnant of the Long movement did support Representative William Lemke of North Dakota on a Union party ticket, but it was a forlorn effort that polled only 882,000 votes.

In 1936 Roosevelt forged a new electoral coalition that would affect national politics for years to come. While holding the support of most traditional Democrats North and South, FDR made strong gains among beneficiaries of the AAA farm program in the West. In the northern cities he held on to the ethnic groups helped by New Deal welfare measures and afforded greater recognition in government appointments. Middle-class voters, whose property had been saved by New Deal measures, flocked to Roosevelt's support, along with intellectuals stirred by the ferment of new governmental ideas. The revived labor movement threw its support to Roosevelt, and in the most profound new departure of all, black voters for the first time cast the majority of their ballots for a Democratic president. "My friends, go home and turn Lincoln's picture to the wall," a black Pittsburgh journalist told black Republicans. "That debt has been paid in full."

In his acceptance speech to the Democratic convention Roosevelt dropped efforts to reassure corporate leaders. As the Americans of 1776 had sought freedom from political autocracy, he noted, the Americans of 1936 sought freedom from the "economic royalists." Roosevelt campaigned with tremendous buoyancy, and wound up carrying every state except Maine and Vermont, with a popular vote of 27.7 million to Landon's 16.7 million. Democrats would also dominate Republicans in the new Congress, by 77 to 19 in the Senate and 328 to 107 in the House.

SECOND-TERM SETBACKS AND INITIATIVES

As former presidents Jefferson and Jackson had found (and Lyndon Johnson, Richard Nixon, and Ronald Reagan would later discover), a malevolent fate seems to await presidents who win such big victories, and the victorious Roosevelt found himself deluged in a sea of troubles during the next year. His second inaugural address, delivered on January 20, 1937, suggested that he was ready to move toward even more controversial reforms. The challenge to American democracy, he maintained, was that millions of citizens "at this very moment are denied the greater part of what the very lowest standards of today call the necessities of life. . . . I see one-third of a nation ill-housed, ill-clad, ill-nourished." The election of 1936 had been a mandate for even more extensive reforms, he argued, and the overwhelming Democratic majorities in Congress ensured their passage. But one major roadblock stood in the way: the Supreme Court.

THE COURT-PACKING PLAN   By the end of the 1936 term the Court had ruled against New Deal laws in seven of the nine major cases it reviewed. Suits against the Social Security and Wagner Labor Relations Acts were also pending. Given the established trend of rulings, the Second New Deal seemed in danger of being nullified like the first.

For that reason, Roosevelt resolved to change the Court's philosophy by enlarging it, a move for which there was ample precedent and power. Congress, not the Constitution, determined the size of the Court, which at different times had numbered six, seven, nine, and ten justices, and in 1937 numbered nine. On February 5 Roosevelt sent his plan to Congress, without having consulted congressional leaders. He wanted to create up to fifty new federal judges, including six new Supreme Court justices, and to diminish the power of the judges who had served ten or more years or reached the age of seventy.

But the "court-packing" maneuver, as opponents quickly tagged it, backfired on Roosevelt. It was a shade too contrived, much too brazen, and far too political. By implying that some judges were impaired by senility, it affronted the elder statesmen of Congress and the Court, especially Justice Louis D. Brandeis, who was both the oldest and the most liberal of the Supreme Court judges. It also ran headlong into a deep-rooted veneration of the courts and aroused fears that another president might use the precedent for quite different purposes.

As it turned out, unforeseen events blunted Roosevelt's drive to change the Court. A sequence of Court decisions during the spring of 1937 reversed previous judgments in order to uphold the Wagner Act and the Social Security Act. A conservative justice resigned, and Roosevelt named to the vacancy one of the most consistent New Dealers, Senator Hugo Black of Alabama.

Roosevelt later claimed he had lost the battle but won the war. The Court had reversed itself on important New Deal legislation, and Roosevelt was able to appoint justices in harmony with the New Deal. But the episode created dissension in his party and blighted Roosevelt's prestige. For the first time Democrats in large numbers deserted the "champ," and the Republican opposition found a powerful issue. During the first eight months of 1937, the momentum of Roosevelt's great 1936 victory was lost.

A NEW DIRECTION FOR LABOR   Rebellions meanwhile erupted on other fronts. Under the impetus of the New Deal, the labor movement stirred anew. John L. Lewis rebuilt the United Mine Workers from 150,000 members to 500,000 within a year. Spurred by the mine workers' example, Sidney Hillman of the Amalgamated Clothing Workers and David Dubinsky of the International Ladies Garment Workers joined Lewis in promoting a campaign to organize workers in the mass-production industries. As leaders of some of the few industrial unions in the American Federation of Labor (AFL), they found the smaller, more restrictive, craft unions, whose membership was limited to workers in a single skilled trade, to be obstacles to organizing the basic industries.

In 1934 these leaders persuaded the AFL and its president William Green to charter industrial unions in the unorganized industries. But Green and other craft unionists saw these "federal" unions as temporary pools from which to draw members into the crafts. Lewis and the industrial unionists saw them as a chance to organize on a massive scale. In 1935, with passage of the Wagner Act, action began in earnest. The industrial unionists formed a Committee for Industrial Organization (CIO), and craft unionists began to fear submergence by the mass unions. Jurisdictional disputes spread among the unions, and in 1936 the AFL expelled the CIO unions, which then formed a permanent structure called after 1938 the Congress of Industrial Organizations. The rivalry spurred both groups to greater unionizing efforts.

The CIO's major organizing drives in the automobile and steel industries began in 1936, but they were thwarted by management's use of blacklisting, private detectives, labor spies, vigilante groups, and intimidation. Early in 1937 automobile workers spontaneously adopted a new technique, the "sit-down strike," in which workers refused to leave the shop until employers granted the right to collective bargaining rights. Many employers and much of the public saw in such revolutionary tactics a threat to property rights, an alarming gesture of contempt for authority, and further evidence of the New Deal's evil influence. Union leaders, fearing a public opinion backlash, frowned on the tactic, but it brought the first union victory in a major industry. In 1937 General Motors recognized the United Automobile Workers as the bargaining agent for its employees. The following month, United States Steel capitulated to the Steel Workers Organizing Committee (later the United Steelworkers of America), granting it recognition, a 10 percent wage hike, and a forty-hour week.

Having captured two giants of heavy industry, the CIO went on in the next few years to organize much of industrial America: rubber, oil, electronics, and a good part of the textile industry, in which unionists had to fight protracted struggles to organize scattered plants. The laggard pace in textiles denied the CIO a major victory in the South comparable to its swift conquest of autos and steel in the North, but even down South a labor movement appeared that was at last something more than a vehicle for sporadic revolt.

A SLUMPING ECONOMY   Beset by the divisive effects of the Court fight and the sit-down strikes, Roosevelt in the fall of 1937 also faced a renewed depression. The years 1935 and 1936 had seen steady economic improvement, and by the spring of 1937 output had moved above the 1929 level. Then in the late summer the economy suddenly slid into a deep business slump, which the press called a "recession" to distinguish it from the "depression." By the end of 1937, an additional 2 million people had been thrown out of work; grim scenes of the earlier depression reappeared.

In 1937, the "American Way" was out of reach for many. Photograph by Margaret Bourke-White.

The prosperity of early 1937 had been achieved largely through governmental spending. But Roosevelt, worried about mounting deficits and rising inflation, ordered sharp cuts in federal spending. At the same time, the Treasury began to reduce disposable income by collecting $2 billion in Social Security taxes from employee paychecks. Private spending could not fill the gap left by reductions in government spending, and business still lacked the faith to risk large investments. The result was the slump of 1937.

The recession provoked a fierce debate within the administration. One group, led by Treasury Secretary Henry Morgenthau, Jr., favored less federal spending and a balanced budget. The other group, which included Harry Hopkins and Harold Ickes, argued for renewed government spending and stricter enforcement of antitrust laws.

ECONOMIC POLICY AND LATE REFORMS Roosevelt eventually endorsed the ideas of the spenders and antitrusters. In the spring of 1938, he asked Congress to adopt a large-scale spending program, and Congress voted almost $3.3 billion, mainly for public works. In a short time the increase in spending reversed the economy's decline, but the recession and Roosevelt's reluctance to adopt massive and sustained government spending forestalled the achievement of full recovery by the end of the decade. Only the crisis of World War II would return the American economy to full production and full employment.

The 1937 recession helped further erode Roosevelt's prestige and dissipate the mandate of the 1936 elections. Only a few major new reforms were enacted for the benefit of the "ill-housed, ill-fed, and ill-clad." They included the Wagner-Steagall National Housing Act, the Bankhead-Jones Farm Tenant Act, and the Fair Labor Standards Act.

The Housing Act set up the United States Housing Authority (USHA) in the Department of the Interior, which extended long-term loans to local agencies willing to assume part of the cost for slum clearance and public housing. The agency also subsidized rents for low-income residents.

Congress in 1937 also passed the Farm Tenant Act, administered by a new agency, the Farm Security Administration (FSA). The program made available loans to prevent marginal farmers from sinking into tenancy. It also offered loans to tenants for the purchase of their own farms. But the idea of small homesteads by the late 1930s was doomed to failure. American mythology still exalted the family farm, but in reality the ever-larger agricultural unit predominated. In the end the FSA proved to be little more than another relief operation that tided a few farmers over difficult times. A more effective answer to the problem, sadly, awaited mobilization for war, which took many tenants off into the military services or defense industries, broadened their horizons, and taught them new skills.

The Fair Labor Standards Act of 1938 applied to employees in enterprises that operated in or affected interstate commerce. It set a minimum wage of 40¢ an hour and a maximum workweek of forty hours, to be put into effect over several years. The act also prohibited child labor under the age of sixteen, and in hazardous occupations under eighteen. Southern congressmen howled in opposition to the bill because it would have the effect of raising wages in their region and thus increasing employers' expenses. They also feared that higher wage levels would make their region less attractive to northern industries that were considering relocation. A Democratic senator from Georgia denounced the bill as "the wildest dream that was ever presented to the American Congress." It was, he added, a sign of "bureaucracy run mad" under Roosevelt.

*The Farm Tenant Act (1937) and the Agricultural Adjustment Act (1938),
among the last major reforms of the New Deal era, addressed the problem of rural
poverty, which had worsened in the mid-1930s.*

THE LEGACY OF THE NEW DEAL

SETBACKS FOR THE PRESIDENT   Although critics were unable to
defeat the Fair Labor Standards Act, their stiff resistance revealed that
an effective opposition was emerging within the president's own party,
especially in the southern wing. Southern Democrats were at best uneasy bedfellows with organized labor and blacks, and more and more of
them drifted toward closer cooperation with conservative Republicans.
By the end of 1937 a formidable anti–New Deal bloc had developed.

In 1938 the bipartisan conservative opposition stymied a bill granting
Roosevelt authority to reorganize the executive branch amid cries that it
would lead to dictatorship. The House also set up a Committee on Un-
American Activities chaired by Martin Dies of Texas. Dies launched a
crusade against Communists, and soon he began to brand New Dealers
as Red dupes. "Stalin baited his hook with a 'progressive' worm," Dies
wrote in 1940, "and New Deal suckers swallowed bait, hook, line, and
sinker."

As the political season of 1938 advanced, Roosevelt unfolded a new idea as momentous as his Court-packing plan—a proposal to reshape the Democratic party in the image of the New Deal. He announced his purpose to campaign in Democratic primaries as the party leader, "charged with the responsibility of carrying out the definitely liberal declaration of principles set forth in the 1936 Democratic platform." He wanted his own supporters nominated. Instead of succeeding, however, the effort backfired and broke the spell of presidential invincibility, or what was left of it. As in the Court fight, Roosevelt had risked his prestige while handing his adversaries persuasive issues. His opponents tagged his intervention in the primaries an attempted "purge"; the word evoked visions of Adolf Hitler and Joseph Stalin, tyrants who had purged their Nazi and Communist parties in blood.

The elections of November 1938 handed the administration another setback, a result partly of the friction among Democrats. Their majority in the House fell from 229 to 93, in the Senate from 56 to 42. The margins remained large, but the president headed an increasingly divided party. In his State of the Union message in 1939 Roosevelt for the first time proposed no new reforms, but spoke of the need "to *preserve* our reforms." Roosevelt did manage, however, to put through his plan to reorganize the executive branch. Under the Administrative Reorganization Act of 1939 the president could "reduce, coordinate, consolidate, and reorganize" the agencies of government. With that Roosevelt's domestic innovations feebly ended.

A HALFWAY REVOLUTION   The New Deal had lost momentum, but it had wrought several enduring changes. By the end of the 1930s, the power of the national government was vastly enlarged over what it had been in 1932, and hope had been restored to people who had grown fatalistic. But the New Deal entailed more than just bigger government and revived public confidence. It also constituted a significant change from the older liberalism embodied in the progressivism of Theodore Roosevelt and Woodrow Wilson. Those earlier reformers, despite their sharp differences, had assumed that the function of progressive government in the American republic was to ensure through aggressive regulation that the people had equal opportunity to pursue their notions of happiness.

Franklin Roosevelt and the New Dealers, however, went beyond this regulatory-state concept by insisting that the government should not simply *respond* to social crises but take positive steps to *avoid* them. Even more important, the New Deal's various welfare and benefit programs conferred on government the responsibility to ensure a minimum level of well-being for all Americans. The New Deal had established minimum standards for labor conditions and public welfare and helped middle-class Americans hold on to their savings, their homes, and their farms. The protection afforded by deposit insurance, unemployment pay, and Social Security pensions would come to be universally accepted as a safeguard against future depressions. The old progressive formulation of regulation versus trust-busting had finally been superseded by the rise of the "broker state," a government that mediated among major interest groups. Government's role was to act as an honest broker protecting a variety of interests, not just business but workers, farmers, consumers, small business, and the unemployed.

In implementing his domestic program, Roosevelt had steered a zigzag course between the extremes of laissez-faire capitalism and socialism. The first New Deal had experimented for a time with a managed economy under the NRA, but had abandoned that experiment for a turn toward enforcing competition and priming the economy with increased government spending. This finally produced full employment during World War II.

Roosevelt himself, impatient with theory, was indeed a pragmatist in developing policy: he kept what worked and discarded what did not. The result was, paradoxically, both profoundly revolutionary and profoundly conservative. Roosevelt sharply increased the regulatory functions of the federal government and laid the foundation for what would become an expanding welfare state. But his initiatives fell far short of socialism; they left the basic capitalistic structure in place. In the process of such bold experimentation and dynamic preservation, the New Deal represented a "halfway revolution" that permanently altered the social and political agenda.

CULTURE IN THE THIRTIES

THE RETURN OF SOCIAL SIGNIFICANCE   In view of the celebrated—if exaggerated—alienation of writers caught in the materialistic world of the 1920s, one might have expected the onset of the Great Depression to deepen the despair. Instead it brought a renewed sense of militancy and affirmation, as if people could no longer afford the art-for-art's sake outlook of the 1920s. Said one writer early in 1932: "I enjoy the period thoroughly. The breakdown of our cult of business success and optimism, the miraculous disappearance of our famous American complacency, all this is having a tonic effect."

In the early 1930s the "tonic effect" of commitment sometimes took the form of allegiance to revolution. By the summer of 1932 even the "golden boy" of the lost generation, F. Scott Fitzgerald, declared that "to bring on the revolution, it may be necessary to work within the Communist party." But few remained Party followers for long. Writers being a notoriously independent lot, most rebelled at demands to hew to a shifting Party line. And many abandoned Communism upon learning that Soviet leader Joseph Stalin practiced a tyranny more horrible than anything under the czars.

Among the writers who addressed themes of immediate social significance two novelists deserve special notice: John Steinbeck and Richard Wright. The single piece of fiction that best captured the ordeal of the depression, Steinbeck's *The Grapes of Wrath* (1939), avoided political formula to treat workers as people. Steinbeck had taken the trouble to travel with displaced "Okies" driven from the Oklahoma Dust Bowl by bankers and farm combines to pursue the illusion of jobs in the fields of California's Central Valley. The story focused on the Joad family as they made their painful journey west from Oklahoma. Met chiefly with con-

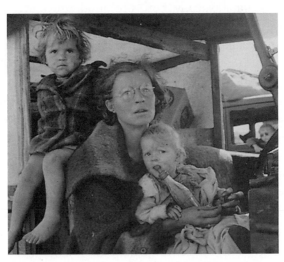

A migrant family on their way west to California.

Richard Wright, author of Native Son *and* Black Boy.

tempt and rejection, Ma Joad strove to keep hope alive. At the end, even as the family was breaking up under the pressure, she grasped at a broader loyalty: "Use 'ta be the fambly was fust. It ain't so now. It's anybody. Worse off we get, the more we got to do."

Perhaps the supreme genius among the new young novelists emerging in the thirties was Richard Wright, a black writer born on a plantation near Natchez, Mississippi. The son of a matriarch whose husband deserted the family, Wright grew up in the course of moving from town to town, ended his formal schooling with the ninth grade (as valedictorian of his class), worked in Memphis, and greedily devoured books he borrowed on a white friend's library card, all the while saving up to go north. In Chicago, where he arrived on the eve of the depression, the Federal Writers' Project gave him a chance to perfect his talent. His period as a Communist from 1934 to 1944 gave him an intellectual framework, Marxism, which did not, however, overpower his fierce independence. His autobiographical *Black Boy* (1945) revealed in its rebellion against racial injustice his ties to the South, for, he wrote, "there had been slowly instilled into my personality and consciousness, black though I was, the culture of the South."

Native Son (1940), Wright's masterpiece, was set in the Chicago he had come to know before moving on to New York. It was the story of Bigger Thomas, a product of the black ghetto, a man hemmed in and finally impelled to murder by forces beyond his control. "They wouldn't let me live and I killed," he says unrepentently at the end. Somehow

Wright managed to sublimate into literary power his bitterness and rage at what he called "The Ethics of Living Jim Crow."

THE SOUTHERN RENAISSANCE   In different ways southern whites had shared the same tragic past as the black writers. Out of the memory and the consciousness of change the best writers among them nurtured a renaissance that burgeoned into one of the most notable literary growths since the flowering of New England a century before.

During the 1920s, the South had reached a historical watershed. It stood between two worlds: the dying world of tradition and the modern, commercial world struggling to be born. The resultant conflict of values, felt more intensely in the South than in the North, aroused the Ku Klux Klan and fundamentalist furies, but had quite another effect on many of the South's most promising young writers. With remarkable speed after 1920, Mencken's supposedly backward South produced a galaxy of literary stars. "One may reasonably argue," wrote one critic in 1930, "that the South is the literary land of promise today."

Just the previous year two vital figures had emerged: Thomas Wolfe, with *Look Homeward, Angel,* and William Faulkner, with *Sartoris* and *The Sound and the Fury.* Fame rushed in first on Wolfe and his native Asheville, North Carolina, which became a classic example of the scandalized community. "Against the Victorian morality and the Bourbon aristocracy of the South," Wolfe had "turned in all his fury," a friend wrote. The reaction was a common response to the works of the south-

William Faulkner.

ern renaissance, created by authors who had outgrown their "provincial" hometowns and looked back from new perspectives acquired in travel and education.

Yet Wolfe never completely severed his roots in the South. *Look Homeward, Angel,* his first novel, remained his most successful; it was the lyrical and searching biography of Eugene Gant's (actually Wolfe's) youth in Altamont (Asheville) and his college days in Pulpit Hill (Chapel Hill). It established him as "the giant among American writers of sensitive youth fiction."

Faulkner's achievement, more than Wolfe's, was rooted in the world that produced him. Born and raised near Oxford, Mississippi, Faulkner passed the postwar decade in what seemed to fellow townspeople an aimless drifting. He briefly attended classes at the University of Mississippi, worked at odd jobs, went to New Orleans, shipped out briefly for Europe, and after knocking around the Gulf Coast, returned to Oxford.

There, in writing *Sartoris* (1929), he began to discover that his "own little postage stamp of native soil was worth writing about" and that he "would never live long enough to exhaust it." In this book a postwar wasteland stood out the more starkly against a legend of past glory in the Sartoris family. With *Sartoris* and the creation of his mythical land of Yoknapatawpha County, Faulkner kindled a blaze of creative energy. Next, as he put it, he wrote his gut into *The Sound and the Fury* (1929), again the story of a demoralized family. Faulkner's creative frenzy continued through the writing of *As I Lay Dying* (1930) and *Light in August* (1932). He began to fill in the early history of Yoknapatawpha and the conflict between tradition and the modern world with *Absalom! Absalom!* (1936).

Most critics at first missed Faulkner's obscure and rankling genius. Some viewed him as the leader in a "cult of cruelty." Others attacked his obscure prose, the slow unfolding of meaning, convoluted syntax, and runaway rhetoric of his novels. Not until the mid-twentieth century did critics generally begin to grasp that Faulkner, in composing his mythical history of Yoknapatawpha, had become also—certainly among Americans—the most skillful creator of modernist style in the novel during the first half of the twentieth century.

THE REDISCOVERY OF AMERICA   In the 1930s America experienced what *Fortune* magazine called "a sort of cultural revolution."

Americans learned that, like it or not, they had a culture and had had one all along—it had simply been overlooked. Now Americans tried to make up for lost time by tracking the culture down, recording, restoring, and celebrating it. They became intrigued with American art of all kinds, and particularly that least influenced by Europe: primitive, folk, or as it was called most often, "popular" art. American writers and artists turned their attention to their homeland. And so the two decades of the 1920s and 1930s, times of unusually creative vitality, began with disillusionment and flight to Europe but ended with the rediscovery of America.

MAKING CONNECTIONS

- In the mid-1930s, just as Roosevelt was getting the New Deal into place, the growing conflict in Europe began to assume more and more of his (and America's) attention: Chapter 28 shows how Roosevelt went from combatting the Depression to leading the United States into World War II.

- Harry Truman, Roosevelt's successor in the White House, tried unsuccessfully to expand the idea of the New Deal into new areas (national health insurance and federal aid to education, for example), a topic covered in Chapter 30.

FURTHER READING

An engaging introduction to the decade of the New Deal is William E. Leuchtenburg's *Franklin D. Roosevelt and the New Deal, 1932–1940* (1963).* Paul Conkin's *The New Deal* (2nd ed., 1975)* is more critical. Alan Brinkley's *The End of Reform: New Deal Liberalism*

---

*These books are available in paperback edition.

in Recession and War (1995)* suggests that the New Deal reformers did not go far enough in their efforts to curb big business.

Works on the critics of the New Deal include T. Harry Williams's *Huey Long* (1969)* and Alan Brinkley's *Voices of Protest: Huey Long, Father Coughlin, and the Great Depression* (1982).* For radical leftist reactions to reform, see Harvey Klehr's *The Heyday of American Communism* (1984). For the cultural impact of the New Deal, consult Richard H. Pells's *Radical Visions and American Dreams: Cultural and Social Thought in the Depression Years* (1973)* and Richard D. McKinzie's *The New Deal for Artists* (1973).*

*These books are available in paperback edition.

28 FROM ISOLATION TO GLOBAL WAR

CHAPTER ORGANIZER

This chapter focuses on:

- isolationism and peace movements between the two World Wars

- America's response to German aggression in Europe

- how events in Asia led to Japan's attack on Pearl Harbor and America's entry into the global war

POSTWAR ISOLATIONISM

THE LEAGUE AND THE UNITED STATES   In the late 1930s the winds of war swept across Asia and Europe, abruptly shifting the focus of American politics from domestic to foreign affairs. Another Democratic president had to turn his attention from social and economic reform to military preparedness and war. But between Woodrow Wilson and Franklin Roosevelt lay two decades of relative isolation from foreign entanglements. The postwar mood of 1920 set the pattern. The voters expressed their resistance to international commitments, and President-elect Harding lost little time in disposing of American membership in the League of Nations. The spirit of isolation found other expressions as well: the higher tariff walls, the Red Scare, the rage for

"100 percent Americanism," and tight immigration laws by which the nation all but shut the door to any more newcomers.

The United States may have felt the urge to insulate itself from a wicked world, but it could hardly stop the world and get off. American business, despite the tariff walls, now had worldwide connections. Investments and loans abroad put in circulation the dollars that purchased American exports. America's overseas possessions, moreover, directly involved the country in world affairs, especially in the Pacific. Even the League of Nations was too great an organization to ignore entirely. After 1924 the United States gradually entered into joint efforts with the League on such matters as policing the international trade in drugs and arms, and on a variety of economic, cultural, and technical conferences.

WAR DEBTS AND REPARATIONS   Probably nothing did more to heighten American isolationism during the 1920s and 1930s—or anti-American feeling in Europe—than the war-debt tangle. When in 1917 the Allies had begun to exhaust their sources of private credit in the United States, the American government advanced them funds, first for the war effort and then for postwar reconstruction. To Americans the repayment of the war debts seemed a simple matter of obligation, but Europeans commonly had a different perception.

The French and British insisted that they could pay America only as they collected reparations from Germany. Twice during the 1920s the resulting strain on Germany brought the structure of international payments to the verge of collapse, and both times the Reparations Commission called in American bankers to work out rescue plans.

The whole structure finally did collapse during the Great Depression. In 1931 President Hoover negotiated a moratorium on both German reparations and Allied payment of war debts. At the end of 1932, after Hoover's debt moratorium ended, most of the European countries defaulted on their war debts to the United States. In retaliation, Congress passed the Johnson Debt Default Act of 1934, which prohibited private loans to any such government.

ATTEMPTS AT DISARMAMENT   Yet for all the isolationist sentiment of the time, Wilsonian internationalism persisted during the 1920s and after. A lingering doubt, tinged with guilt, haunted many Americans about their rejection of the League. Before long the Harding administration hit upon a happy substitute—disarmament. The conviction had grown after World War I that the armaments race had caused the war, and that arms limitation would therefore bring lasting peace. The United States had no intention of maintaining a large army, but under the naval building program begun in 1916, it had constructed a fleet second only to that of Britain.

Neither the British nor the Americans relished a naval armaments race, but both shared a common concern about the alarming growth of Japanese power. Since 1914 Japanese-American relations had grown increasingly strained, as the United States objected to continued Japanese encroachments in Asia. During World War I Japan had quickly taken China's Shantung Peninsula and the islands of Micronesia from its enemy, Germany. In 1917, after the United States entered the war, Viscount Kikujiro Ishii visited Washington to secure American recognition of Japan's expanded position in Asia, dropping hints that Germany had several times tried to get Japan to quit the war. To forestall the loss of an ally in the war, Secretary of State Robert Lansing signed an ambiguous agreement saying that "Japan has special interests in China." Americans were unhappy with the Lansing-Ishii Agreement, but it was viewed as the only way to keep Japan in the war.

After the war ended, Japanese-American relations grew more tense. To address the problem, President Harding invited countries to an armaments conference at which Pacific and East Asian affairs would also be discussed. The Washington Armaments Conference of 1921 opened with a surprise announcement by the American secretary of state, Charles Evans Hughes, who told the delegates that "the way to disarm is to disarm." It was one of the most dramatic moments in American diplomatic history. In less than fifteen minutes, one reporter said, Hughes had destroyed more tonnage "than all the admirals of the world have sunk in a cycle of centuries."

Delegates from the United States, Britain, Japan, France, and Italy signed a Five-Power Naval Treaty incorporating Hughes's plan for tonnage limits and a moratorium of ten years during which no capital ships (battleships and aircraft carriers) would be built. These powers also agreed to refrain from further fortification of their Pacific possessions. The agreement in effect partitioned the world: United States naval power became supreme in the Western Hemisphere, Japanese power in the western Pacific, British power from the North Sea to Singapore.

Two other major agreements emerged from the Washington Conference. With the Four-Power Treaty, the United States, Britain, Japan, and France agreed to respect each other's possessions in the Pacific and to refer any disputes or any outside threat to consultation. The Nine-Power Treaty for the first time formally pledged the signers to support the principle of the Open Door enunciated by Secretary of State John Hay at the turn of the century. The Open Door enabled all nations to compete for trade and investment opportunities in China on an equal footing rather than allow individual nations to create economic monopolies in particular regions of that country. The signers of the Nine-Power Treaty also promised to respect the territorial integrity of China. The powers, in addition to those signing the Five-Power Treaty, were China, Belgium, Portugal, and the Netherlands.

With these agreements in hand, Harding's supporters could boast of a brilliant diplomatic stroke that relieved American taxpayers of the need to pay for an enlarged navy and that defused potential conflicts in the Pacific. Yet the agreements were uniformly without obligation and without teeth. The signers of the Four-Power Treaty agreed only to consult, not to help each other. The formal endorsement of the Open Door in the Nine-Power Treaty was just as ineffective, for the United States remained unwilling to uphold the principle with anything but pious affirmation. Moreover, the naval disarmament treaty set limits only on capital ships; the race to build cruisers, destroyers, submarines, and other smaller craft continued.

THE KELLOGG-BRIAND PACT   In the midst of such wishful thinking, the fanciful ideal of simply abolishing war altogether seized the American imagination. Peace societies thrived, and the glorious vision of ending war by the stroke of a pen culminated in the signing of the Kellogg-Briand Pact in 1928. This unique treaty originated when French Foreign Minister Aristide Briand proposed to Coolidge's secretary of state, Frank B. Kellogg, an agreement that the two countries would never go to war with each other.

The Pact of Paris (its official name) solemnly declared that the signatories "condemn recourse to war . . . and renounce it as an instrument of national policy." Eventually sixty-two powers joined the pact, but all explicitly or tacitly reserved "self-defense" as an escape hatch. The United States Senate included a reservation declaring the Monroe Doctrine necessary to America's self-defense, and then ratified the agreement by a vote of 85 to 1. A Virginia senator who voted for "this worthless, but perfectly harmless peace treaty" wrote a friend that he feared it would "confuse the minds of many good people who think that peace may be secured by polite professions of neighborly and brotherly love."

THE "GOOD NEIGHBOR" POLICY   In Latin America the spirit of peace and noninvolvement helped allay resentments against the United States, which had freely intervened in the Caribbean during the first two decades of the century. In 1924 American marines left the Dominican Republic after an eight-year occupation. The troops left Nicaragua a year later, but returned in 1926 with the outbreak of disorder and civil war. In 1927 the Coolidge administration negotiated an agreement for American-supervised elections, but one rebel leader, César Augusto Sandino, held out, and the marines stayed until 1933. The unhappy legacies of this intervention were public bitterness toward the United States and a Nicaraguan National Guard, created to keep order after the marines left, but used in 1936 to set up the dictatorship of Anastasio Somoza. These legacies continue to have effects to the present day.

The troubles in Nicaragua increased strains with Mexico. Relations were already threatened by repeated Mexican threats to take over American oil properties. In 1928, however, the American ambassador to Mexico so pleased the Mexicans by his gestures of friendship that he was able to get an agreement protecting American economic rights. It lasted until 1938, when the Mexican government expropriated U.S.-owned properties, promising to reimburse American owners.

In 1928 President-elect Hoover improved America's image in Latin America by permitting publication of a memorandum that denied that the Monroe Doctrine justified American intervention in Latin America. It stopped short of repudiating intervention on any grounds, but that fine point hardly blunted the celebration in Latin America. Although Hoover never endorsed this so-called Clark Memorandum, he never ordered military intervention in the area. Before he left office, steps had already been taken to withdraw American forces from Nicaragua and Haiti.

Franklin D. Roosevelt likewise embraced "the policy of the good neighbor" and soon advanced it in practice. In 1933 at the seventh Pan-

American Conference, the United States supported a resolution that affirmed: "No state has the right to intervene in the international or external affairs of another." Under Roosevelt the marines completed their withdrawals from Nicaragua and Haiti, and in 1934 the president negotiated with Cuba a treaty that abrogated the Platt Amendment (1901), which had given America a formal right to intervene in Cuba.

WAR CLOUDS

JAPANESE INCURSIONS IN CHINA   The lessening of irritants in the Western Hemisphere proved an exception in an otherwise dismal world scene, as war clouds darkened over Europe and Asia. Actual conflict erupted first in Asia, where unsettled social and political conditions in China had attracted foreign encroachments since before the turn of the century. In 1929 Chinese nationalist aspirations and China's subsequent clashes with Russia convinced the Japanese that their own extensive rights in Manchuria, including the South Manchurian Railway, were in danger.

Japanese military occupation of Manchuria began with the Mukden Incident of 1931, when an explosion destroyed a section of railway track near that city. The Japanese "Kwantung Army," based in Manchuria to guard the railway, blamed the incident on the Chinese and used it as a pretext to begin its occupation, which it extended during the winter of 1931–1932 to all of Manchuria, including the Russian sphere of influence. In 1932 the Japanese converted Manchuria into the puppet empire of "Manchukuo."

The Manchuria Incident, as the Japanese called their undeclared war, flagrantly violated the Nine-Power Treaty, the Kellogg-Briand Pact, and Japan's pledges as a member of the League of Nations. But when China asked the League and the United States for help, neither obliged. President Hoover refused to invoke either military or economic sanctions.

In early 1932, Japan's indiscriminate bombing of civilians in Shanghai, China's great port city, aroused Western indignation, but provoked no action. When the League of Nations condemned Japanese aggression in 1933, Japan withdrew from the League. Thereafter hostilities in

Manchuria gradually subsided and ended with a truce. An uneasy peace settled upon East Asia for four years, during which Japan's military leaders further extended their political sway at home.

ITALY AND GERMANY   The rise of the Japanese militarists paralleled the rise of warlike dictators in Italy and Germany. In 1922 Benito Mussolini had seized power in Italy after organizing the Fascist movement, which was based on a composite of superheated nationalism and state socialism. The party's program, and above all Mussolini's promise to restore order in a country fragmented by dissension, enjoyed a wide appeal. Once in power, Mussolini largely abandoned the socialist part of his platform and gradually suppressed all opposition. By 1925 he wielded dictatorial power as Il Duce (the leader).

There was always something ludicrous about the strutting Mussolini. Italy, after all, was a minor European power. But Germany was another matter, and most Americans were not amused, even at the beginning, by Il Duce's counterpart, Adolf Hitler. Hitler's National Socialist (Nazi) party duplicated the major features of Italian Fascism, including the ancient Roman salute. Hitler capitalized on the weakness of Germany's postwar government, especially in the face of world depression, and on festering German resentment toward the Versailles treaty.

Mussolini and Hitler in Munich, Germany, June 1940.

Named chancellor on January 30, 1933, Hitler moved swiftly to intimidate the opposition, won dictatorial powers, and in 1934 assumed the title of Reichsfuhrer (national leader) with absolute powers. The Nazi police state cranked up the engines of tyranny, persecuting Jews, whom Hitler blamed for all Germany's troubles, and rearming in defiance of the Versailles Treaty. Hitler flouted international agreements, pulled Germany out of the League of Nations in 1933, and frankly proclaimed that he meant to extend control over all German-speaking peoples. Despite one provocation after another, the European democracies lacked the will to resist.

RUSSIAN RECOGNITION   Isolationist sentiment in the United States grew even more potent during the early 1930s, but one significant exception to American insularity was Roosevelt's decision to favor official recognition of Soviet Russia. By 1933 the reasons for American refusal to recognize the Bolshevik regime had grown stale. Seen as an expansive market for American goods, Russia stirred fantasies of an American trade boom, much as China had at the turn of the century. Japanese expansionism in Asia, moreover, gave Russia and the United States a common foreign policy concern. Given an opening by the shift of opinion, Roosevelt invited the Soviet commissar for foreign affairs to visit Washington. After nine days of talks, a formal exchange of notes on November 16, 1933, signaled the renewal of diplomatic relations. The Soviet commissar promised that his country would abstain from propaganda in the United States, extend religious freedom to Americans in the USSR, and reopen the question of prerevolutionary debts to the United States.

THE MARCH OF AGGRESSION   After 1932 a catastrophic chain of events in Asia and Europe sent the world hurtling toward disaster. In 1934 Japan renounced the Five-Power Naval Treaty. The next year Mussolini commenced Italy's conquest of Ethiopia. That same year a referendum in Germany's Saar Basin, held in accordance with the Versailles Treaty, delivered that coal-rich region into the hands of Hitler. In 1936 Hitler reoccupied the Rhineland with armed forces, in violation of the Versailles Treaty but without any forceful response from the French.

The year 1936 also brought the Spanish Civil War, which began with

AGGRESSION IN EUROPE

Aggressive moves

Axis Powers

an uprising of the Spanish armed forces in Morocco, led by General Francisco Franco, against the democratically elected Spanish Republic. Over the next three years Franco established a fascist dictatorship with help from Hitler and Mussolini while the Western democracies left the Spanish Republic to its fate.

On July 7, 1937, Japanese and Chinese troops clashed at the Marco Polo Bridge near Peking, and the incident quickly developed into a full-scale war. It was the beginning of World War II in Asia, two years before war erupted in Europe. That same year Japan joined Germany and Italy in establishing an alliance known as the Rome-Berlin-Tokyo "Axis."

By 1938 the peace of Europe trembled in the balance. Having rebuilt German military force, Hitler forced the *Anschluss* (union) of Austria with Germany in March 1938. Six months later Germany took the mountainous Sudetenland, largely German in population, which had been given to Czechoslovakia at the Versailles Peace Conference in 1919 because of its strategic importance to that new nation's defense.

Hitler's latest aggression came shortly after the conference at Munich, where Britain and France sought to appease Hitler by agreeing to abandon Czechoslovakia, a country that had probably the second strongest army in central Europe.

After promising that the Sudetenland would be his last territorial demand, Hitler in 1939 brazenly broke his pledge by occupying the remainder of Czechoslovakia. In quick succession the Spanish Republic finally collapsed on March 28, and Mussolini seized the kingdom of Albania on April 7. Finally, on September 1, 1939, Hitler launched his conquest of Poland. A few days before, he had signed a nonaggression pact with Russia. Having deserted Czechoslovakia, Britain and France now honored their commitment to go to war if Poland was invaded.

DEGREES OF NEUTRALITY   During these years of deepening crisis, the Western democracies seemed paralyzed, hoping in vain that each concession would appease the appetites of fascist dictators. Americans retreated more deeply into isolation.

A Senate inquiry into the origins of American involvement in World War I reinforced the desire to stay out of Europe's conflicts. Under Senator Gerald P. Nye of North Dakota, a progressive Republican, the committee sat from 1934 to 1937 and concluded that bankers and munitions makers had made scandalous profits from the war. Although Nye never proved that greed for profit had actually impelled Wilson into war, he did insist that the administration had been duped by the "merchants of death." If the United States wanted to remain neutral in the current crisis, therefore, it would have to keep Americans out of war zones, keep belligerents' vessels out of American ports, embargo arms shipments, and set quotas on the export of contraband. Such ideas became official policy as war enveloped Asia and Europe.

Like generals who are said to be always preparing for the last war, Congress occupied itself with keeping out of the last war. Neutrality laws of the 1930s moved the United States toward complete isolation from the quarrels of Europe. But while Americans wanted to keep out of war, their sympathies were more strongly than ever with the Western democracies, and the eventual triumph of fascist aggression aroused growing fears for national security.

The Neutrality Act of 1935 forbade the sale of arms and munitions to all belligerents whenever the president proclaimed that a state of war existed. Americans who traveled on belligerents' ships thereafter did so at their own risk. Roosevelt would have preferred discretionary authority to levy an embargo only against aggressors, but he reluctantly accepted the act because it was to be effective for only six months, and for the time being met "the need of the existing situation." That is, it would likely be enforced against Italy, which was then threatening war with Ethiopia.

On October 3, 1935, Italy invaded Ethiopia and the president invoked the Neutrality Act. When Congress reconvened in 1936, it fell into a three-cornered debate among the advocates of mandatory embargoes, flexible embargoes aimed only at aggressors, and traditional neutrality. After six weeks Congress simply extended the arms embargo and added a provision forbidding loans to belligerents.

Then in July 1936, while Italian troops mopped up the last resistance in Ethiopia, the Spanish Civil War broke out. Roosevelt now became more isolationist than some of the isolationists. Although the Spanish Civil War involved a fascist uprising against a recognized, democratic government, Roosevelt accepted the French and British position that only nonintervention would localize the fight and keep it from spreading to the rest of Europe. There existed, moreover, a strong bloc of pro-Franco Catholics in America who feared that the liberal Spanish Republic was influenced by the Communists and was a threat to the church. Intrigues by Spanish Communists did prove divisive, and the Soviet Union did supply aid to the Republic, but nothing like the quantity of German and Italian aid to Franco.

Roosevelt asked for a "moral embargo" on the arms trade, and he encouraged Congress to extend the neutrality laws to cover civil wars. Congress did so in 1937 with only one dissenting vote. The Western democracies then stood witness while German and Italian soldiers, planes, and armaments supported Franco's overthrow of Spanish democracy.

In the spring of 1937 isolationist sentiment in the United States peaked. A Gallup poll found that 94 percent of its respondents preferred efforts to keep out of war over efforts to prevent war. That same spring Congress passed yet another neutrality law, which continued restraints on arms sales and loans, forbade Americans to travel on belligerents' ships, and forbade the arming of American merchant ships trading with belligerents. The new law also empowered the president to require that goods other than arms or munitions exported to belligerents be placed on a cash-and-carry basis. This was an ingenious scheme to preserve a profitable trade without running the risk of war.

The new law had its first test in July 1937, when Japanese and Chinese forces clashed at the Marco Polo Bridge. Since neither side declared war, Roosevelt was able to avoid invoking the neutrality law, which would have favored the Japanese, since China had greater need of arms but few means to get supplies past the Japanese navy. A flourishing trade in munitions to China flowed around the world as ships carried American arms across the Atlantic to England, where they were reloaded onto British ships bound for Hong Kong. Roosevelt, by inaction, had challenged strict isolationism.

He soon ventured a step further. In Chicago on October 5, 1937, Roosevelt denounced the "reign of terror and international lawlessness" in which 10 percent of the world's population threatened the peace of the other 90 percent. He called for a "quarantine" against nations "creating a state of international anarchy and instability from which there is no escape through mere isolation or neutrality." On the whole, public reaction to the speech was mixed, but the president nevertheless quickly backed off from its implications and refused to spell out any specific program for dealing with aggression.

The continuing Japanese war against China brought public outrage and protests from Secretary of State Cordell Hull. In 1938, after nearly a year of war in China, the State Department notified domestic aircraft manufacturers and exporters that it opposed sales to those guilty of attacks on civilian populations. To have imposed an outright embargo would have violated a commercial treaty of 1911 with Japan, but after another year, on July 26, 1939, the United States gave six months' notice of the termination of the treaty—thus clearing the way for an embargo on all war materials.

By then Hitler had brought Europe to the brink of war. After the German occupation of Czechoslovakia, Roosevelt no longer pretended impartiality in the impending struggle. He urged Congress to repeal the embargo and permit the United States to sell arms on a cash-and-carry basis to Britain and France, but to no avail. "You haven't got the votes," Vice-President Garner told him, "and that's all there is to it." When the

Germans attacked Poland on September 1, 1939, Roosevelt proclaimed official neutrality, but in a radio talk stressed that he did not, like Wilson, ask Americans to remain neutral in thought because "even a neutral has a right to take account of the facts."

Roosevelt summoned Congress into special session and asked it again to amend the Neutrality Act. "I regret the Congress passed the Act," he confessed. "I regret equally that I signed the Act." Under the Neutrality Act of 1939 the Allies could buy for cash and take away in their own ships arms or anything else they wanted. American ships, on the other hand, were excluded from belligerent ports and from specified war zones. Roosevelt then designated as a war zone the Baltic Sea and the waters around Great Britain and Ireland from Norway south to the coast of Spain. One unexpected effect of this move was to relieve Hitler of any inhibitions against using unrestricted submarine warfare to blockade Britain.

American attitudes continued to vacillate. When the war crisis first developed, an isolationist policy prevailed. Once the great democracies of western Europe faced war, American public opinion, appalled at Hitler's tyranny, came to support measures short of war to help their cause. For a time it seemed that the Western Hemisphere could remain insulated from the war. After Hitler overran Poland in less than a month, the war settled into an uneasy stalemate that began to be called the "Phony War." What lay ahead, it seemed, was a long war of attrition—much like World War I—in which Britain and France would have the resources to outlast Hitler. The illusion lasted from October 1939 through the winter of 1940.

THE STORM IN EUROPE

BLITZKRIEG   In the spring of 1940 the winter's long *Sitzkrieg* suddenly erupted into *Blitzkrieg*—lightning war. At dawn on April 9, without warning, Nazi troops entered Denmark and disembarked along the Norwegian coast. Denmark fell in a day, Norway within a few weeks. On May 10 Hitler unleashed his dive bombers and tank divisions on neutral Belgium and the Netherlands. On May 21 German forces moving down the valley of the Somme reached the English Channel, cutting off a British force sent to help the Belgians and French. A desper-

St. Paul's Cathedral looms above the destruction wrought by German bombs in London during the Blitz. Churchill's response: "We shall never surrender."

ate evacuation from the beaches at Dunkirk enlisted every available boat from warship to tug. Some 338,000 men, about a third of them French, escaped to England.

Having outflanked France's heavily fortified defense perimeter, the Maginot Line, the German forces rushed ahead, cutting the French armies to pieces and spreading panic by strafing refugees in a deliberate policy of terror. On June 10 Mussolini entered the war. "I need only a few thousand dead to enable me to take my seat . . . at the peace table," Il Duce said. On June 14 the swastika flew over Paris.

AMERICA'S GROWING INVOLVEMENT   Britain now stood alone, but Prime Minister Winston Churchill breathed defiance. "We shall go on to the end," he pledged; "we shall never surrender." Despite such grim resolution, America itself seemed suddenly vulnerable as Hitler unleashed his air force against Britain. President Roosevelt, who in his annual budget had requested $1.9 billion for defense, now asked for more, and called for the production of 50,000 combat planes a year. In 1940 Congress had voted more than $17 billion for defense. In response to Churchill's appeal for American military supplies, the War and Navy Departments began releasing stocks of arms, planes, and munitions to the British.

The summer of 1940 brought the desperate Battle of Britain, in which the Royal Air Force finally forced the Germans to give up plans to invade the British Isles. Submarine warfare meanwhile strained the resources of the battered Royal Navy. To relieve the pressure, Churchill urgently requested the transfer of American destroyers. Secret negotiations led to an executive agreement under which fifty "overaged" destroyers went to the British in return for ninety-nine-year leases on naval and air bases in Newfoundland, Bermuda, and islands in the Caribbean. Two weeks later, on September 16, 1940, Congress adopted the first peacetime conscription in American history. All men aged twenty-one to thirty-five were required to register for a year's military service within the United States.

The new state of affairs prompted vigorous debate between "internationalists," who believed national security demanded aid to Britain, and isolationists, who charged that Roosevelt was drawing the United States into a needless war. In 1940 the nonpartisan Committee to Defend America by Aiding the Allies was organized, drawing its strongest support from the East and West Coasts and the South. Two months later, isolationists formed the America First Committee. Before the end of 1941 the committee had about 450 chapters around the country, but probably two-thirds of its members lived within a 300-mile radius of Chicago. The isolationists argued that a Nazi victory, while distasteful, would pose no threat to national security.

A THIRD TERM FOR FDR   In the midst of these profound developments the quadrennial presidential campaign came due. Isolationist sentiment was strongest in the Republican party, yet their nominee took a different stance. Wendell L. Willkie was a former Democrat who had voted for Roosevelt in 1932. An Indiana farm boy whose disheveled charm inspired strong loyalty, he openly supported aid to the Allies.

The Nazi victory also ensured another nomination for Roosevelt. The president cultivated party unity behind his foreign policy and kept a sphinx-like silence about his intentions. The world crisis reconciled southern conservatives to the man whose foreign policy, at least, they supported. At the convention in Chicago Roosevelt won nomination for a third term with only token opposition. For his new running mate, Roosevelt tapped his Secretary of Agriculture, Henry Wallace, a devoted supporter who would appeal to farm voters.

Through the summer Roosevelt assumed the role of a man above the political fray, busy rather with urgent matters of defense and diplomacy. Willkie inspired a more intense personal devotion than any Republican candidate since Theodore Roosevelt, but he had trouble positioning himself since there was little on which he disagreed with Roosevelt. Most New Deal programs were too popular, in any case, to oppose head-on.

Like Alf Landon in 1936, Willkie was reduced to attacking New Deal red tape and promising to run the programs better. A widespread reluctance to violate the tradition against a presidential third term strengthened his argument that new blood was needed in the White House. In the end, however, as his campaign languished, he switched to an attack on Roosevelt's conduct of foreign policy: "If you re-elect him you may expect war in April, 1941." To this Roosevelt responded, "I have said this before, but I shall say it again and again and again: Your boys are not going to be sent into any foreign wars." Three days before the election he declared in Buffalo that "this country is not going to war." Neither man distinguished himself with such hollow claims, since each knew the risk of the all-out aid to Britain, which they both supported.

Roosevelt won the election by a comfortable margin of 27 million votes to Willkie's 22 million, and a wider margin of 449 to 82 in the electoral college. Though the popular vote was closer than any presidential election since 1916, the dangerous world situation convinced a majority of voters to back the Democrats' slogan: "Don't switch horses in the middle of the stream."

THE ARSENAL OF DEMOCRACY Bolstered by the mandate for an unprecedented third term, Roosevelt moved quickly to provide greater aid to Britain. Soon after the election, Churchill informed him that

British credit at American banks was fast running out. Since direct government loans would arouse memories of earlier war-debt defaults—the Johnson Act of 1934 forbade such loans anyway—the president created an ingenious device to bypass that issue and yet supply British needs: the "lend-lease" program.

In a fireside chat, Roosevelt told the nation that it must become "the great arsenal of democracy" to help prevent Britain's fall. In his annual message to Congress on January 6, 1941, he warned that only the British navy stood between America and the peril of attack. Greater efforts to bolster British defenses were therefore in order. The Lend-Lease Bill, introduced in Congress on January 10, authorized the president to sell, transfer, exchange, lend, lease, or otherwise dispose of arms and other equipment and supplies to "any country whose defense the President deems vital to the defense of the United States."

For two months a bitter debate over the bill raged in Congress and around the country. Isolationists saw it as the point of no return. Administration supporters denied that lend-lease would lead to American involvement in the war, but it did indeed increase the risk. Lend-lease became law in early 1941, and Britain and China were the first beneficiaries.

While the nation debated, the war intensified. In late 1940, as the American presidential campaign approached its climax, Mussolini launched attacks on Greece and, from Italian-controlled Libya, assaulted the British in Egypt. But his forces had to fall back in both cases, and in the spring of 1941 Hitler came to his aid. German forces under General Erwin Rommel joined the Italians in Libya, forcing the British, whose resources had been drained to help Greece, to withdraw into Egypt.

In April 1941 Nazi armored divisions overwhelmed Yugoslavia and Greece, and by the end of May airborne forces subdued the Greek island of Crete, putting Hitler in a position to menace the entire Middle East. With Hungary, Romania, and Bulgaria forced into the Axis fold, Hitler controlled nearly all of Europe. Then, on June 22, 1941, he suddenly fell upon Russia, his ally, hoping to eliminate the potential threat on his rear with another lightning stroke. The Nazis moved on a 2,000-mile front from the Arctic to the Black Sea with seeming invincibility until, after four months, the Russian soldiers and civilians rallied in front of Leningrad, Moscow, and Sevastopol. During the winter of 1941–1942, Hitler began to learn the bitter lesson the Russians had taught Napoleon and his French invaders in 1812.

Winston Churchill had already decided to provide British support to Russia in case of such an attack. Roosevelt adopted the same policy, offering American aid two days after the German invasion. Stalinist Russia, so long as it held out, ensured Britain's survival. American aid was now indispensable to Europe's defense, and the logic of lend-lease led to deeper American involvement. To deliver aid to Britain, goods had to be maneuvered through the German U-boat "wolf packs" in the North Atlantic. So on April 11, 1941, Roosevelt informed Churchill that the United States Navy would extend its patrol areas in the North Atlantic nearly all the way to Iceland.

In August 1941 Roosevelt and Churchill held a secret rendezvous in Newfoundland. There they drew up a statement of principles known as the Atlantic Charter. In effect it amounted to a joint declaration of war aims, its eight points a mixture of the idealistic goals of the New Deal and Wilson's Fourteen Points. It called for the self-determination of all peoples, economic cooperation, freedom of the seas, and a new system of collective security. The Soviet Union later endorsed the statement.

Having entered into a joint statement of war aims with the anti-Axis powers, the United States soon became involved in shooting incidents in the North Atlantic. The first attack on an American warship occurred on September 4, when a German submarine fired two torpedoes at a destroyer. A week later the president ordered American ships to "shoot on sight" any German or Italian raiders ("rattlesnakes of the Atlantic") that ventured into American defensive waters. Five days later the United States navy announced it would convoy merchant ships all the way to Iceland.

Further attacks hastened Congress into making changes in the neutrality act already requested by the president. On November 17 Congress removed the bans on arming merchant vessels and allowed them to enter combat zones and belligerent ports. Step by step the United States was giving up neutrality and embarking on naval warfare against Germany. Still, the American people hoped to avoid taking the final step into all-out war. The decision for war would come in an unexpected quarter—the Pacific.

JAPANESE EXPANSION
BEFORE PEARL HARBOR

■ Territory under Japanese
control, Dec. 7, 1941

Dates indicate year of
acquisition or occupation

THE STORM IN THE PACIFIC

JAPANESE AGGRESSION   After the Nazi victories in the spring of
1940, America's relations with Japan also took a turn for the worse.
Japanese militarists, bogged down in the vastness of China, now eyed
new temptations in South Asia. They wanted to incorporate into their
"Greater East Asia Co-Prosperity Sphere" the oil, rubber, and other
strategic materials that their crowded homeland lacked. As it was, they
depended on the United States for important supplies, including 80
percent of their oil.

During the summer of 1940 Japan forced the helpless French government to permit the construction of Japanese airfields in northern Indochina and sever the rail line into South China, thus cutting off Western supplies to the Chinese. The United States responded with a loan
to China and the Export Control Act of July 2, 1940, which authorized
the president to restrict the export of arms and other strategic materials
to Japan. Gradually Roosevelt extended embargoes on aviation gas,
scrap iron, and other supplies to Japan.

On September 27, 1940, the Tokyo government signed a Tripartite Pact with Germany and Italy, by which each pledged to declare war on any nation that attacked any of them. The Germans hoped to persuade Japan to enter Siberia when German forces entered Russia from the west. The Soviet presence in Siberia did inhibit the Japanese impulse to move southward into Indochina, but on April 13, 1941, while the Nazis were sweeping through the Balkans, Japan signed a nonaggression pact with Russia and, once the Nazis invaded Russia in June, the Japanese were freed of any threat from the north.

In July 1941 Japan announced that it was assuming a protectorate over all of French Indochina. Roosevelt froze all Japanese assets in the United States; he restricted exports of oil to Japan; and he took the armed forces of the Philippines into the Army of the United States and put their commander, General Douglas MacArthur, in charge of all American forces in the Far East. By September the oil restrictions had tightened into a complete embargo. Forced to secure oil supplies elsewhere, the Japanese army and navy began to plan attacks on the Dutch and British colonies in Southeast Asia.

Actions by both sides put the United States and Japan on the path to a war neither wanted. In his regular talks with the Japanese ambassador, Secretary of State Cordell Hull insisted that Japanese withdrawal from Indochina and China was the price of renewed trade. A more flexible position might have strengthened the moderates in Japan. Premier Konoye, however, while known as a man of liberal principles who preferred peace, caved in to pressures from the militants. Perhaps he had no choice.

The Japanese warlords, for their part, seriously misjudged the United States. The desperate wish of Americans to stay out of war might still have enabled the Japanese to conquer the British and Dutch colonies before an American decision to act. But the warlords decided that they dared not leave the American navy intact and the Philippines untouched on the flank of their new lifeline to the south.

TRAGEDY AT PEARL HARBOR   Thus a tragedy began to unfold with a fatal certainty mostly out of sight of the American people, whose attention was focused on the war in the Atlantic. Late in August 1941 Premier Konoye proposed a personal meeting with President Roosevelt. Hull advised Roosevelt not to meet unless agreement on fundamentals could be reached in advance. Soon afterward, on September 6, an imperial conference approved preparations for an attack on Hawaii and gave Premier Konoye six more weeks to reach a settlement.

The Japanese emperor's clear displeasure with the risk of an attack afforded the premier one last chance to pursue a compromise, but the presence of Japanese troops in China remained a stumbling block. In October Konoye urged War Minister Hideki Tojo to consider withdrawal while saving face by keeping some troops in North China. Tojo refused. Faced with this rebuff, and Tojo's threat to resign and bring down the cabinet, Konoye himself resigned on October 15; Tojo became premier the next day. The war party was now in complete control.

On the very day that Tojo became premier, a special Japanese envoy conferred with Hull and Roosevelt in Washington. His arrival was largely a cover for Japan's war plans, although neither he nor Japan's ambassador to the United States knew that. On November 20 they presented Tojo's final proposal to Hull: Japan would occupy no more territory if the United States would cut off aid to China, restore trade with Japan, and help the Japanese get supplies from the Dutch Indies. In that case Japan would pull out of southern Indochina immediately and abandon the remainder once peace had been established with China—presumably on Japanese terms. Tojo expected the United States to refuse such demands. On November 26 Hull repeated that Japan must withdraw altogether from China. That same day a Japanese naval force began heading silently across the North Pacific toward Pearl Harbor, Hawaii.

Washington officials already knew that war was imminent. Reports of Japanese troop transports moving south from Formosa prompted Washington to send warnings to Pearl Harbor and Manila, and to the British government. The massive Japanese movements southward clearly signaled attacks on the British and the Dutch. American leaders had every reason to expect war in the southwest Pacific, but none expected that Japan would commit most of its carriers to another attack 5,000 miles away at Pearl Harbor.

On the morning of December 7, 1941, Americans decoded the last part of a Japanese message breaking off the negotiations in Washington. Tojo instructed Japan's ambassador to deliver the message at 1:00 P.M. (7:30 A.M. in Honolulu), about a half hour before the blow fell, but

The Attack on Pearl Harbor. (Above) *The view from a Japanese fighter plane shows American battleships in vulnerable positions.* (Below) *The view from an American airfield shows the destruction and confusion brought on by the surprise attack.*

delays held up delivery until more than an hour later than scheduled. The War Department sent out an alert at noon that something was about to happen, but the message, which went by commercial wire because radio contacts were broken, arrived in Hawaii eight and a half hours later. Even so, the decoded Japanese message did not mention Pearl Harbor specifically, and American military leaders there would probably have assumed the attack was to come in southeast Asia.

It was still a sleepy Sunday morning when the first Japanese planes roared down the west coast and the central valley of Oahu to begin their assault. At 7:53 A.M. the flight commander sounded the cry "Tora! Tora! Tora!" (Tiger! Tiger! Tiger!), the signal that the attackers had taken the American navy by surprise.

For nearly two hours the Japanese planes kept up their fierce attack. Of the eight battleships in Pearl Harbor, three were sunk and the others were badly battered. Altogether nineteen ships were sunk or disabled. At the airfields on the island the Japanese destroyed about 150 planes. Before it was over the raid had killed more than 2,400 American servicemen and civilians.

The surprise attack fulfilled the dreams of its planners, but it fell short of total success in two ways. The Japanese ignored oil storage tanks, without which the surviving ships might have been forced back to the West Coast, and they missed the American aircraft carriers that had fortuitously left port a few days earlier. In the naval war to come, these carriers would be decisive.

Later the same day (December 8 in the western Pacific) Japanese forces began assaults on the Philippines, Guam, and Midway, and on British forces in Hong Kong and the Malay Peninsula. With one stroke the Japanese had silenced America's debate on neutrality, and a suddenly unified and vengeful nation resolutely prepared for the struggle. A Michigan man recalled his reactions to the Japanese attack: "First it was indignation, then it turned to anger, and by the time one went to work the following morning it was determination: 'They can't do that to us.'"

The day after the attack President Roosevelt told Congress that December seventh "will live in infamy," and he asked for a declaration of war. It was approved unanimously, with the sole exception of Representative Jeanette Rankin, who was unable in conscience to vote for war in 1917 or 1941. On December 11 Germany and Italy declared war on the

United States. The separate wars in Asia and Europe had become one global war—and American isolationism was cast aside.

MAKING CONNECTIONS

- The United States tried to stake out a neutral position in the growing world conflict. Compare this to earlier American attempts at neutrality, from the Napoleonic-wars era of Jefferson's administration onward.

- The American alliance with the Soviet Union described in this chapter proved to be temporary: after the war, the Americans and the Soviets would be adversaries in a great Cold War, the beginnings of which are outlined in Chapter 30.

- The Japanese conquest of French Indochina (Vietnam) would play an important role in the events leading to American involvement in the region, a topic discussed in Chapter 32.

FURTHER READING

Robert Dallek's *Franklin D. Roosevelt and American Foreign Policy, 1932–1945* (1979)* covers the foreign policy of the 1930s. For American relations in East Asia during the period, see Akira Iriye's *After Imperialism: The Search for a New Order in the Far East, 1921–1933* (1965) and Jonathan G. Utley's *Going to War with Japan, 1937–1941* (1985).

A good study of America's entry into World War II is Waldo Heinrichs's *Threshold of War: Franklin D. Roosevelt and American Entry into World War II* (1988). Bruce M. Russett's *No Clear and Present Danger*

---

*These books are available in paperback editions.

(1972)* provides a critical account of American actions. On Pearl Harbor, see Gordon W. Prange's *At Dawn We Slept: The Untold Story of Pearl Harbor* (1981)* and John Toland's *Infamy* (1982).*

*These books are available in paperback editions.

29 ✑ THE WORLD AT WAR

CHAPTER ORGANIZER

This chapter focuses on:

- the social and economic effects of World War II, especially in the West

- how the Allied forces won the war

- the efforts of the Allies to shape the postwar world

The Japanese attack on Pearl Harbor ended a period of uneasy neutrality for the United States. Even more important, of course, it launched America into an epochal world event that would transform the nation's social and economic landscape as well as its position in international affairs. In early December 1941, however, few Americans envisioned such seismic consequences. For the moment, all attention was focused on halting the Japanese advance and mobilizing the whole nation for war.

AMERICA'S EARLY BATTLES

SETBACKS IN THE PACIFIC For months after Pearl Harbor the news from the Pacific was "all bad," as President Roosevelt frankly confessed. A string of Allied outposts surrendered in the three months after December 1941: Guam, Wake Island, the Gilbert Islands, Hong Kong, Singapore, and Java. The Japanese capture of Rangoon in March 1942 cut off the Burma Road, the main supply route to China.

In the Philippines, where General Douglas MacArthur abandoned Manila on December 27, the main American forces, outmanned and outgunned, held out tenaciously on Bataan Peninsula until April 9, and then on the fortified island of Corregidor. MacArthur himself slipped away in March, when he was ordered to Australia to take command of Allied forces in the Southwest Pacific. By May 6, when American forces surrendered Corregidor, Japan controlled a new empire that stretched from Burma eastward through the Dutch Indies and on out to Wake Island and the Gilbert island group.

If the Japanese had stopped there, they might have consolidated an almost impregnable empire with the resources they had seized. But the Japanese navy succumbed to what one of its admirals later called "victory disease." The Japanese Supreme Command grew ever more greedy and decided to push on into the South Pacific, isolate Australia, and strike again at Hawaii. Planners hoped to destroy the American navy before the productive power of the United States could be brought to bear on the war effort.

CORAL SEA AND MIDWAY   American forces finally halted the Japanese advances in two decisive naval battles. The Battle of the Coral Sea (May 7–8, 1942) stopped a fleet convoying Japanese troop transports toward the southern coast of New Guinea. Planes from the *Lexington* and *Yorktown* sank one Japanese aircraft carrier, damaged another, and destroyed smaller ships. American losses were greater, and included the carrier *Lexington,* but the Japanese designs on Australia were thwarted.

Less than a month after the Coral Sea engagement Admiral Isoruku Yamamoto, the Japanese naval commander, decided to force a showdown in the central Pacific. With nearly every ship under his personal command, he headed for Midway Island, from which he hoped to render Pearl Harbor helpless. This time it was the Japanese who were the victims of surprise. American cryptanalysts had by then broken the Japanese naval code, and Admiral Chester Nimitz, commander of the central Pacific, knew their plan of attack. He reinforced Midway with planes and the carriers *Enterprise, Hornet,* and *Yorktown.*

The first Japanese foray against Midway, on June 4, severely damaged the American installation on the island, but at the cost of about a third of the Japanese planes. Before another attack could be mounted, American torpedo planes and dive bombers had caught three of the four Japanese carriers in the process of servicing their planes. Dive bombers sank three of them during the first assault. Later the Japanese lost another carrier, but not before its planes disabled the *Yorktown.* The only other major American loss was a destroyer. The Japanese defeat at Midway was the turning point of the Pacific war, a loss they were never able to surmount.

SETBACKS IN THE ATLANTIC   Early Allied setbacks in the Pacific were matched by losses in the Atlantic. Since the *Blitzkrieg* of 1940, German submarine "wolf packs" had wreaked havoc in the North Atlantic. In January 1942, after an ominous lull, German U-boats suddenly appeared off American shores and began to sink coastal shipping, much of it tankers. Nearly 400 ships were lost in American waters before effective countermeasures brought the problem under control. The naval command hastened the building of small escort vessels, meanwhile pressing into patrol service all kinds of surface craft and planes, some of them civilian. During the second half of 1942 these efforts reduced losses to a negligible number.

MOBILIZATION AT HOME

The Pearl Harbor attack ended not only the long debate between isolation and intervention but also the long economic depression of the 1930s. The war effort required all of America's huge productive capacity and full employment of the work force. For 1942 alone the government ordered 60,000 planes, 45,000 tanks, and 8 million tons of merchant shipping. The next year's goals were even higher. Soon after Pearl Harbor, Winston Churchill recalled that someone had compared the United States to a gigantic boiler: "Once the fire is lighted under it, there is no limit to the power it can generate."

Mobilization was in fact already farther along than preparedness had been in 1916–1917. The draft had been in effect for more than a year, and the army had grown to more than 1.4 million men. Congress quickly extended the term of military service to last until six months after the war's end. Men between eighteen and forty-five became subject to service. Altogether more than 15 million American men and women served in the armed forces during the war.

ECONOMIC CONVERSION   The economy, too, was already partially mobilized by lend-lease and defense efforts. Congress authorized the president to reshuffle government agencies and to allot materials and facilities as needed for defense, with penalties for those who failed to comply. The War Production Board (WPB), created in 1942, directed industrial conversion to war production. For a year the WPB oversaw a wild scramble of manufacturers for available supplies. The Office of Scientific Research and Development mobilized thousands of scientists to create and modify radar, sonar, the proximity fuse, the bazooka, and the many other innovations that contributed to the war effort.

The pressure of wartime needs and the stimulus of government spending doubled the gross national product between 1940 and 1945. Government expenditures during the war years soared. The total was about 10 times what America spent in World War I and 100 times the expenditures during the Civil War. The massive infusion of government capital into the economy also encouraged greater centralization and consolidation in private industry. The larger companies tended to win the most government contracts, and the more they won the larger they became. Conversely, those without government contracts withered and died. In 1942 alone 300,000 businesses shut down.

FINANCING THE WAR   To cover the war's huge cost the president preferred taxes to borrowing, but Congress, dominated by fiscal conservatives, feared taxes more than deficits and refused to go more than halfway with Roosevelt's fiscal prudence. The government covered about 45 percent of its 1939–1946 costs with tax revenues; the rest was borrowed from the public. War-bond drives induced citizens to put aside more than $150 billion in bonds. Financial institutions picked up most of the rest of the government's debt. In all, the national debt grew by the end of the war to $260 billion, about six times its size at the time of Pearl Harbor.

America's basic economic problem during the war years was no longer finding jobs but finding workers for the booming shipyards, air-craft factories, and munitions plants. Millions of people, especially women, were brought fully into the economic system who before had lived on its margin. Stubborn poverty did not disappear, but for most civilians the war spelled neither severe hardship nor suffering but a bet-ter life than ever before, despite shortages and rationing. Labor unions benefited directly from the dramatic growth of the civilian work force. Union membership increased significantly during the war years, from about 11 million to 15 million.

ECONOMIC CONTROLS   Increased incomes and spending during the war raised the specter of inflation. Some of the available money went into taxes and war bonds, but even so, more purchasing power was sent chasing civilian goods just as production was converting to war needs. Consumer durables such as cars, washing machines, and nonde-fense housing in fact ceased to be produced at all. Only strict restraints

Mobilization for war deflected many New Deal programs.

would keep prices on other items from soaring out of sight. In 1941 Roosevelt created the Office of Price Administration (OPA), and the following year Congress authorized it to set price ceilings. With prices frozen, goods had to be allocated through rationing, which began with tires and was gradually extended to other scarce items such as sugar, coffee, and gasoline.

At first, however, wages and farm prices were not controlled, and this complicated matters. War prosperity offered farmers a chance to redress the balance from two decades of distress, and farm-state legislators raised both floors and ceilings on farm prices. Higher food prices reinforced worker demands for higher wages. To relieve this inflationary pressure, the president won new authority to control wages and farm prices. Both business and workers chafed at the new controls, and on occasion the government was forced to seize industries threatened by strike. The coal mines and railroads were both nationalized for a short time in 1943. Despite these problems, the government's program to stabilize the war economy succeeded. By the end of the war consumer prices had risen about 31 percent, a far better record than the World War I rise of 62 percent.

To make the economic controls work, the government launched a program to encourage conservation of resources. As one popular slogan had it, "Use it up, wear it out, make it do or do without." The public collected scrap metal and grew their own food in backyard "victory gardens." In 1942, when the war plants faced a rubber shortage, Roosevelt asked citizens to turn in "old tires, old rubber raincoats, old garden hoses, rubber shoes, bathing caps, gloves—whatever you have that is made of rubber."

SOCIAL EFFECTS: WOMEN   The war marked an important watershed in the changing status of women. From 1910 to 1940 the proportion of women working had barely altered, but with millions of men going into military service, the demand for labor shook up old prejudices about sex roles in the workplace—and in the military. Nearly 200,000 women went into the Women's Army Corps (WAC) and the navy's equivalent, Women Accepted for Volunteer Emergency Service (WAVES). Lesser numbers joined the Marine Corps, the Coast Guard, and the Army Air Force.

Even more significant were the 6 million women who entered the

Women workers assembling the tail section of the B17F bomber (the Flying Fortress) at the Douglas Aircraft plant in Long Beach, California, 1942.

work force during the war, an increase in general of over 50 percent and in manufacturing alone of some 110 percent. By 1944 over a third of all American women were in the labor force. Old barriers fell overnight as women put on slacks, gloves, goggles, hairnets, and hard hats to become toolmakers, machinists, riveters, crane operators, lumberjacks, stevedores, blacksmiths, and railroad workers. Desperate for laborers, the government launched an intense publicity campaign to draw women into traditional male jobs. "Do your part, free a man for service," one ad pleaded. "Rosie the Riveter," a beautiful model dressed in overalls, served as the cover girl for the campaign.

One striking feature of the wartime economy was the larger proportion of older, married women in the work force. In 1940 about 15 percent of married women went into gainful employment; by 1945 it was 24 percent. In the work force as a whole, married women for the first time outnumbered single women. There were many vocal opponents to this new trend. One disgruntled legislator asked what would happen to traditional domestic tasks if married women worked in factories: "Who will do the cooking, the washing, the mending, the humble homey tasks to which every woman has devoted herself; who will rear and nurture the children?" Many women, however, were eager to get away from the grinding routine of domestic life. One woman welder remembered that her wartime job "was the first time I had a chance to get out of the kitchen and work in industry and make a few bucks. This was something I had never dreamed would happen." And it was something that many women did not want to relinquish after the war.

SOCIAL EFFECTS: BLACKS   The most volatile issue ignited by the war was that of black participation in the defense effort. From the start black leaders demanded full recognition in the armed forces and defense industries. Eventually about a million African Americans served in the armed forces, in every branch and every theater. But most served in segregated units that mirrored the society from which they came. Every army camp had its separate facilities and its periodic racial "incidents." The most important departure from this pattern came in a 1940 decision to give up segregation in officer candidate schools, except those for air force cadets. A separate flight school at Tuskegee, Alabama, trained about 600 black pilots, many of whom distinguished themselves in combat.

War industries were even less accessible to black influence and pressure, although government policy in theory opposed discrimination. In 1941 A. Philip Randolph, the resolute head of the Brotherhood of Sleeping Car Porters, organized a March on Washington Movement to demand an end to racial discrimination in defense industries. The administration, alarmed at the prospect of a mass descent on Washington, struck a bargain. The Randolph group called off its march in return for an executive order prohibiting discrimination in defense work and training programs by requiring a nondiscrimination clause in defense contracts.

About 2 million blacks were working in war plants by the end of 1944. The demand for black labor revived migration out of the South, which had lagged during the depression, and large numbers of southern blacks now headed for the Far West as well as the North. States with the highest proportionate increases of black population in the 1940s were, in order, California, Michigan, Oregon, Washington, Utah, Colorado, Wisconsin, Illinois, and New York.

Blacks quickly broadened their drive for wartime participation into a more inclusive and open challenge to all kinds of discrimination, in-

Members of the 99th Fighter Group of the U.S. Army Air Force, a unit of black pilots famous for their skill and bravery.

cluding racial segregation itself. Membership in the NAACP soared during the war from 50,000 to 450,000. Blacks could look forward to greater political participation after the Supreme Court, in *Smith v. Allwright* (1944), struck down Texas's whites-only primary on the grounds that Democratic primaries were part of the election process and thus subject to the Fifteenth Amendment.

Growing black militancy aroused antagonism from some whites. Racial violence did not approach the level of that in World War I, but rising tensions on a hot summer afternoon in Detroit sparked two days of fighting in 1943, until federal troops arrived on the second evening to stop it. Twenty-five blacks and nine whites had been killed.

SOCIAL EFFECTS: NATIVE AMERICANS Indians may have supported the war effort more fully than any other group in American society. Almost a third of eligible Native American men, over 25,000 people, served in the armed forces. Another one-fourth worked in defense-related industries. Thousands of Indian women volunteered as nurses or joined the Women's Voluntary Service. As was the case with African Americans, Indians benefited from the broadening experiences afforded by the war. Those who left reservations to work in defense plants or to join the military gained new vocational skills as well as a greater awareness of American society and how to succeed within it.

Why did Native Americans so eagerly fight for a nation that had stripped them of their lands and decimated their heritage? Some felt that they had no choice. Mobilization for the war effort ended many New Deal programs that had provided Indian jobs. Reservation Indians thus faced the necessity of finding new jobs elsewhere. Many viewed the Nazis and Japanese warlords as threats to their own homeland. Others saw in the war an opportunity to revitalize the warrior tradition. Joseph Medicine Crow remembered that, while fighting in Europe, he "never thought" about the traditional requirements for a young Crow male to earn his status as a warrior, but "afterwards, when I came back and went through this telling of the war deeds ceremony, why, I told my war deeds, and lo and behold I completed the four requirements to become a chief." The most common sentiment animating Indian involvement in the war effort, however, seems to have been a genuine sense of patriotism.

Whatever the reasons, Indians distinguished themselves in the military during the war. Unlike their African-American counterparts, Indian servicemen were integrated within the regular units. Perhaps the most distinctive activity performed by Indians was their service as "code talkers." Every military branch used Indians—Oneidas, Chippewas, Sauks, Foxes, Comanches, and Navajos—to encode and decipher messages so as to prevent enemy discovery. The Dineh (Navajo) developed their own specialized dictionary to convey idiomatic military terms. For example, a submarine became an "iron fish" and a machine gun was a "fast shooter."

SOCIAL EFFECTS: JAPANESE-AMERICANS   The record on civil liberties during World War II was on the whole better than that during World War I, if only because there was virtually no opposition to the war effort after the attack on Pearl Harbor. Neither German-Americans nor Italian-Americans faced the harassments meted out to their counterparts in the previous war; few had much sympathy for Hitler or Mussolini. The shameful exception to an otherwise improved record was the treatment given to Americans of Japanese descent. Few, if any, were disloyal, but all were victims of fear and racial prejudice.

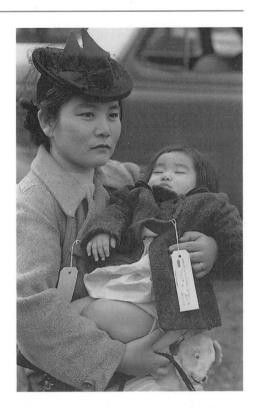

A Japanese-American mother and child await relocation in Washington state, 1942.

This was especially the case in the months following the attack on Pearl Harbor. One California barbershop offered "free shaves for Japs" but noted that it was "not responsible for accidents." Others were even blunter. Idaho's governor declared: "A good solution to the Jap problem would be to send them all back to Japan, then sink the island. They live like rats, breed like rats, and act like rats." Such attitudes were regrettably widespread, and the government finally succumbed to demands that it force all Japanese, citizens or not, into "War Relocation Camps" in the interior. More than 100,000 were eventually removed from their homes and businesses in this sorry episode. As one Japanese-American poignantly complained, "What really hurts most is the constant reference to us evacuees as 'Japs.' 'Japs' are the guys we are fighting. We're on this side and we want to help. Why won't America let us?" Not until 1983 did the government finally acknowledge the injustice of the internment policy. Five years later, Congress voted to give $20,000 and an apology to each of the 60,000 former internees who were still living.

SOCIAL EFFECTS: THE DEVELOPMENT OF THE WEST   The dramatic expansion of defense production after 1940 and the mobilization of millions into the armed forces accelerated economic development and the population boom in the western states. Nearly 8 million people moved into the states west of the Mississippi River between 1940 and 1950. The states witnessing the largest population growth during the war were California, Oregon, Washington, Nevada, Utah, Texas, and Arizona. Most of this expansion occurred in urban centers. Indeed, the Far West experienced the fastest rate of urban growth in the country. Small cities such as Phoenix and Albuquerque mushroomed, while Seattle, San Francisco, Los Angeles, and San Diego witnessed dizzying growth. San Diego's population, for example, increased by 147 percent between 1941 and 1945.

Abundant jobs at high wages enticed people to the western states. California alone garnered 10 percent of all the defense contracts during the war years. In Texas, manufacturing employment almost doubled between 1940 and 1945. Los Angeles, which in 1939 was the seventh largest manufacturing center in the nation, had by 1943 become second only to Detroit in industrial activity. City services could not keep up with the influx of workers and military personnel. Employees at Seattle's shipyards and the Boeing aircraft plant lived in tents because of a housing shortage. To address the problem, Congress passed the Lanham Act, which authorized the federal government to finance over a million new temporary housing units across the country. Yet this federal housing program still did not meet the demand. Some women workers at a San Diego defense plant lived eight to a room in a company dormitory.

The migration of workers to new defense jobs in the West also had significant demographic effects. Communities that earlier had few African Americans witnessed an influx of blacks. Lured by news of job openings and higher wages, blacks from Texas, Oklahoma, Arkansas, and Louisiana headed west. During the war years Seattle's black population jumped from 4,000 to 40,000, Portland's from 2,000 to 15,000. Many of these new arrivals found that the only available housing was that vacated by the Japanese-Americans being relocated to internment camps.

As rural folk moved to the western cities, the farm counties experienced a labor shortage. In an ironic about-face, local and federal government authorities who before the war strove to force Mexican alien laborers back across the border now recruited them to harvest crops. The Mexican government, however, first insisted that the United States ensure certain minimum work and living conditions before it would assist in providing the needed workers. The result was the creation of the *bracero* program in 1942. Mexico agreed to provide seasonal farm workers in exchange for a promise by the American government not to draft them into military service. The workers were hired on year-long contracts that offered wages at the prevailing rate, and American officials provided transportation from the border to their job sites. Under this *bracero* program, some 200,000 Mexican farm workers entered the western United States. At least that many more crossed the border as illegal aliens.

The influx of people created new tensions. The rising tide of Mexican-Americans in Los Angeles provoked a growing stream of anti-Hispanic editorials and incidents. Even though Mexican-Americans fought in the war with great valor, earning seventeen Congressional Medals of Honor, there was constant conflict between servicemen and Mexican-American gang members and teenage "zoot-suiters" in southern California. "Zoot suits" were the flamboyant clothes worn by some young Chicano men. In 1943, several thousand off-duty sailors and soldiers, joined by hundreds of local white civilians, rampaged through downtown Los Angeles streets, assaulting Hispanics, blacks, and Filipinos. The violence lasted a week and came to be labeled the "zoot suit" riots.

DOMESTIC CONSERVATISM   In domestic politics a growing conservatism marked the wartime period. Discontent with price controls, labor shortages, rationing, and a hundred other petty vexations spread, and the 1942 congressional elections registered a national swing against the New Deal. Republicans gained forty-six seats in the House and nine in the Senate, chiefly in the Midwest farm areas. Democratic losses outside the South strengthened the southern delegation's position within the party, and the delegation itself was becoming increasingly conservative. A coalition of Republican and Democratic conservatives gutted "nonessential" New Deal agencies. In 1943 Congress abolished the Works Progress Administration, the National Youth Administration, and the Civilian Conservation Corps.

Organized labor, despite substantial gains during the war, felt the impact of the conservative trend. In the spring of 1943, when John L. Lewis led the coal miners out on strike, widespread public resentment prompted Congress to pass the Smith-Connally War Labor Disputes Act, which authorized the government to seize plants useful to the war effort and forbade unions to make political contributions. In 1943 a dozen states adopted laws variously restricting picketing and other union activities, and in 1944 Arkansas and Florida started a wave of state "right-to-work" laws that outlawed the closed shop (requiring that all employees be union members).

THE ALLIED DRIVE TOWARD BERLIN

In mid-1942 the "home front" began to get news from the war fronts that some of the lines were holding at last. By midyear a fleet of American air and sea sub-chasers was ending six months of happy hunting for U-boats off the Atlantic coast. This was all the more important because war plans called for the defeat of Germany first.

WAR AIMS AND STRATEGY   There were many reasons for giving top priority to defeating Hitler: Nazi forces in western Europe and the Atlantic posed a more direct threat to the Western Hemisphere; German war potential exceeded Japan's, and German science was more likely to come up with some devastating new weapon. Lose in the Atlantic, General George Marshall grimly predicted, and you lose everywhere. Hitler's attack on Russia in June 1941 strengthened the argument. Yet Japanese attacks involved Americans directly in the Pacific war from the start, and as a consequence, during the first year of fighting more Americans went to the Pacific than across the Atlantic.

The Pearl Harbor attack brought Prime Minister Churchill quickly to Washington for long talks about a common war plan that affirmed the priority of first winning the war against Germany. Agreement on war aims, however, did not bring agreement on strategy. When Roosevelt and Churchill met at the White House again in 1942, they could not agree on where to hit first. American strategists wanted to strike directly across the English Channel before the end of 1942. With vivid memories of the last war, the British feared a mass bloodletting in trench warfare if they struck prematurely. The Soviets, bearing the brunt of the German attack in the east, insisted that the Western Allies must do something to relieve the pressure. Finally, the Americans accepted Churchill's proposal to invade French North Africa.

THE NORTH AFRICA CAMPAIGN   On November 8, 1942, Anglo-American forces under the command of General Dwight D. Eisenhower landed in Morocco and Algeria. Completely surprised, French forces under the Vichy government (which collaborated with the Germans) had little will to resist. Farther east the tide had turned and British forces were pushing German armies back across Libya. Before spring, the Germans were caught in a gigantic pincers. By April the British had linked up with American forces. Hammered from all sides, unable to retreat across the Mediterranean, an army of 275,000 Germans surrendered on May 13, 1943, leaving all of North Africa in Allied hands.

While this battle of Tunisia was still unfolding, Roosevelt, Churchill, and the Combined Chiefs of Staff met at Casablanca. Stalin declined to leave beleaguered Russia for the meeting but continued to press for the opening of a second front in western Europe. The Anglo-American planners, however, decided to postpone the cross-Channel invasion further and to carry out Churchill's scheme to attack what he called the "soft underbelly of the Axis" by invading Sicily and then Italy. They also authorized an American offensive in the Pacific islands. Top priority, however, went to an antisubmarine campaign in the Atlantic.

Before leaving Casablanca, Roosevelt announced, with Churchill's endorsement, that the war would end only with the "unconditional surrender" of all enemies. This was designed to reassure Stalin that the Western Allies would not negotiate separately with the Germans. The West desperately needed Soviet cooperation in defeating Germany, and Roosevelt and Churchill were eager to reassure Stalin of their good intentions.

The announcement also reflected Roosevelt's determination to see that "every person in Germany should realize that this time Germany is a defeated nation." This dictum was later criticized for having stiffened enemy resistance, but it probably had little effect; in fact neither the Italian nor Japanese surrender would be totally unconditional. But the decision did have one unexpected result: it virtually assured eventual Soviet control of eastern Europe because it required Russian armies to

WAR IN EUROPE AND AFRICA, 1942-1945

Axis Powers at outbreak of war

Maximum extent of Axis military power

Allies

Neutral countries

Allied offensives

--- Heaviest Allied aerial bombing

.... Inside limit of German U-boat operations

pursue Hitler's forces all the way to Germany. And as they liberated the countries of eastern Europe, the Russians created puppet governments they could easily control.

THE BATTLE OF THE ATLANTIC While fighting raged in North Africa, the more crucial Battle of the Atlantic reached its climax on the high seas. Several factors brought success to the Allied effort. Scientists perfected a variety of new detection devices: radar, which the British had already used to advantage in the Battle of Britain, bounced radio waves off objects above the surface and registered their positions on a screen; sonar gear detected sound waves from submerged U-boats, and sonobuoys, dropped from planes, radioed back their findings; advanced magnetic equipment enabled aircraft to detect objects under water. New escort aircraft carriers ("baby flat-tops") and improvements in depth charges added to the effectiveness of convoys.

By early 1943 there were in the western half of the North Atlantic at any time an average of thirty-one convoys with 145 escorts and 673 merchant ships, and a number of heavily escorted troopships. None of the troopships going to Britain or the Mediterranean was lost, although submarines sank three en route to Greenland and Iceland. The U-boats kept up the Battle of the Atlantic until the war's end; but their commander later admitted that the Battle of the Atlantic was lost by the end of May 1943. He credited the difference largely to radar. What he did not know then was that the Allies had a secret weapon. By early 1943 their cryptanalysts were routinely decoding secret messages and telling their sub-hunters where to look for the German prey.

SICILY AND ITALY   After the Allied victory in the North African campaign, on July 10, 1943, about 250,000 British and American troops landed on Sicily, scoring a complete surprise. General George Patton led his Seventh Army ashore on the southwest coast, and after a fierce battle at the beachhead, the Americans moved swiftly across the island to take Palermo twelve days later. The entire island was in Allied hands by August 17, although some 40,000 Germans escaped to the mainland.

The German-Italian collapse in Sicily ended Mussolini's twenty years of Fascist rule. On July 25, 1943, Italy's king notified the dictator of his dismissal as premier. A new regime startled the Allies when it offered not only to surrender but to switch sides in the war. Unfortunately, mutual suspicions prolonged talks until September 3, while the Germans poured reinforcements into Italy and seized key points. In the confusion the Italian army disintegrated, although most of the navy escaped to Allied ports. A few army units later joined the Allied effort, and many of the soldiers joined bands of partisans who fought behind the German lines. Mussolini, plucked from imprisonment by a daring German airborne raid, became head of a shadowy puppet government in northern Italy.

The Allied assault on the Italian mainland therefore did not turn into an easy victory. The main landing at Salerno on September 9 encountered heavy German resistance. The Americans, joined by British troops, nevertheless secured beachheads within a week and soon captured Naples. Rome was the next objective, but mountainous country stood in the way. Fighting stalled through the winter of 1943–1944 in some of the most miserable, muddy, and frigid conditions of the war. After a five-month siege the Americans finally took Rome on June 4,

1944. Yet they enjoyed only a brief moment of glory, for the long-awaited cross-Channel landing in France began two days later.

STRATEGIC BOMBING OF EUROPE   Behind the long-postponed landings on the Normandy beaches lay months of preparation. While waiting, the United States Army Air Force and the Royal Air Force (RAF) carried the battle into Hitler's "Fortress Europe." By 1943 American strategic bombers were full-fledged partners of the RAF in the effort to pound Germany into submission. Yet despite the widespread damage it caused, the strategic air offensive ultimately failed to cut severely into German production or, as later studies found, to break civilian morale. German war production in fact increased until the last few weeks of the war, and German fighter planes downed more and more Allied bombers. By the end of 1943, however, new jettisonable gas tanks permitted Allied escort fighters to fly as far as Berlin and back. Thereafter, heavy losses of both planes and pilots forced the German Luftwaffe to conserve its strength and cease challenging every Allied mission.

With air supremacy assured, the Allies were free to concentrate on their primary urban and industrial targets, and, when the time came, to provide cover for the Normandy landings. On April 14, 1944, General Dwight D. Eisenhower assumed control of the Strategic Air Forces for use in the Normandy landings, less than two months away. On D-Day he told the troops: "If you see fighting aircraft over you, they will be ours."

THE TEHERAN MEETING   By the summer of 1943 the buildup of American forces in Britain, combined with successes in the Battle of the Atlantic and the strategic bombing of Europe, finally brought Churchill around on the cross-Channel invasion. Late in November he and Roosevelt met with Stalin in Teheran, Iran, to coordinate plans for the invasion of France and a Russian offensive from the east. After Churchill and Roosevelt assured Stalin that a cross-Channel invasion was finally coming, the Russian premier in return promised to enter the war against Japan after Germany's defeat. The Allied leaders also agreed to begin plans for a new international peacekeeping organization and for the occupation of postwar Germany.

Earlier in November 1943, while on the way to the Teheran meeting with Stalin, Churchill and Roosevelt had met with China's Generalissimo Chiang Kai-shek in Cairo, Egypt. The resultant Declaration of Cairo affirmed that war against Japan would continue until Japan's unconditional surrender, that all Chinese territories taken by Japan would be restored to China, and that "in due course Korea shall become free and independent."

D-DAY AND AFTER   In early 1944 General Eisenhower arrived in London to take command at Supreme Headquarters, Allied Expeditionary Forces (SHAEF). Already battle-tested in North Africa and the Mediterranean, he now faced the supreme test of planning and conducting Operation "Overlord," the cross-Channel assault on Hitler's "Atlantic Wall." The Allies had been discussing a large-scale invasion of German-controlled France since early 1942, but debates between British and American strategists caused lengthy delays. Serious planning began in 1943, and by early 1944, over a million American soldiers were training along England's southern coast for the cross-Channel invasion.

Of course, Hitler had been preparing for such an assault as well. German forces using captive Europeans for laborers had created what seemed to be a series of impregnable fortifications along the French coastline. Huge concrete blockhouses protected their artillery, and trenches and camouflage shielded their machine-gun nests. The Germans also sowed the beaches with 4 million mines interlaced with barbed wire and antitank obstacles. The prospect of an amphibious assault against such defenses in a single huge battle unnerved some of the Allied planners. Churchill worried about "Channel tides running red with Allied blood" and "beaches choked with bodies of the flower of American and British manhood." As D-Day approached, Eisenhower's chief of staff predicted only a 50-50 chance of success. Ike had his doubts as well. He kept in his wallet a message for the press in case the invasion failed. It read: "My decision to attack at this time and place was based upon the best information available. If any blame or fault attaches to the attempt, it is mine alone."

On the evening of June 5, Eisenhower visited some of the 16,000 American paratroopers preparing to land behind the German lines to create chaos and disrupt communications. The men noticed his look of grave concern and tried to lift his spirits. "Now quit worrying, General,"

General Dwight D. Eisenhower instructing paratroopers just before they board their airplanes to launch the D-Day assault.

one of them said, "we'll take care of this thing for you." After the planes took off, Eisenhower returned to his car with tears in his eyes. "Well," he said quietly to his driver, "it's on." He knew that many of his troops would die within a few hours.

The day before, Eisenhower's German counterpart, Field Marshal Erwin Rommel, left his headquarters along the French coast to go to Berlin to see his family and meet with Hitler. As he departed, he confidently asserted that "there's not going to *be* an invasion. And if there is, then they won't even get off the beaches." When the American public learned that the invasion had been launched, routine activities gave way to anxious listening over the radio for reports from the front. Stores closed, baseball games and horse races were canceled, and church bells tolled across the country.

Operation Overlord surprised the Germans. Eisenhower fooled Hitler's generals into believing that the invasion would come at Pas de Calais, on the French-Belgian border, where the English Channel was narrowest. Instead, the landings occurred in Normandy, about 200 miles south. Airborne forces dropped behind the beaches during the night while planes and battleships pounded the coastal defenses.

At dawn on June 6, the invasion fleet of some 4,000 ships and 150,000 men (57,000 Americans) filled the horizon off the Normandy coast. Overhead, thousands of Allied planes supported the invasion force. Sleepy German soldiers awoke to see the vast armada arrayed before them. Lieutenant Hans Heinze, a twenty-one-year-old veteran of the Russian front, could not believe his eyes. Wiping off his binoculars, he peered through the lifting fog and shouted to his messenger: *"Sie kommen!"* [They are coming!] He then scribbled a note for his headquarters and handed it to his messenger, thinking "They'll never believe it." Nearby, another German lookout peered through his binoculars and muttered, "That's not possible! That's not possible!" His aide retreated into their bunker to pray.

For several hours, the local German commanders refused to believe that this was the real invasion. They interpreted the Normandy landings as merely a diversion for the "real" attack at Pas de Calais. When Hitler learned of the Allied landings, he boasted that "the news couldn't be better. As long as they were in Britain, we couldn't get at them. Now we have them where we can destroy them."

Despite Eisenhower's meticulous planning and the imposing array of Allied troops and firepower, the D-Day invasion almost failed. Cloud cover and German antiaircraft fire caused many of the paratroopers and glider pilots to miss their landing zones. Oceangoing landing craft delivered their troops to the wrong locations. Low clouds also led the Allied planes assigned to soften up the seaside defenses to drop their bombs too far inland. The naval bombardment was equally ineffective. Rough seas caused many of the soldiers to become seasick and capsized dozens of landing craft. Over a thousand men drowned. Waterlogged radios failed to work, and the deafening noise of the artillery and gunfire made oral communication impossible.

On Utah Beach the American invaders made it in against relatively light opposition, but farther east, on a four-mile segment designated Omaha Beach, bombardment had failed to take out German defenders and the Americans were caught in heavily mined water. They then had to make it across a fifty-yard beach exposed to crossfire from concrete pillboxes before they could huddle under a seawall and begin to root out the defenders. In just ten minutes, one rifle company of 205 men had 197 of them killed or wounded, including every officer and sergeant.

General Omar Bradley, commander of the American invasion force, watched the battle unfold through binoculars aboard one of the naval vessels. His initial reaction was horror. He feared that "our forces had suffered an irreversible catastrophe" and considered halting the attack at Omaha Beach. But at 1:30 P.M. he received word that American troops had made it across the beach and were beginning to scale the bluffs. Still farther east, British forces had less difficulty on Gold, Juno, and Sword beaches, but found themselves subjected to bitter counter-attack by German forces. By nightfall there were some 5,000 killed or wounded Allied soldiers strewn across the sand and surf of Normandy.

The sullen battlefield was a museum of horror. German losses, however, were even more incredible. Entire units were decimated or captured. Operation Overlord was the greatest military invasion in the annals of warfare and the climactic battle of World War II. With the beachhead secured, the Allied leaders knew that victory was now in their grasp. "What a plan!" Churchill exclaimed to the British parliament. Stalin, who had been clamoring for the cross-Channel invasion for years, applauded the Normandy operation and heaped praise on the Allies. He declared that the "history of warfare knows no other like undertaking from the point of view of its scale, its vast conception and its orderly execution."

Within two weeks the Allies had landed a million men, 556,000 tons of supplies, and 170,000 vehicles. They had seized a beachhead sixty miles wide and five to fifteen miles deep. Before the end of June they

The array of Allied forces at Normandy, June 1944.

had swept up the peninsula to the port of Cherbourg, only to find the harbor so completely blocked that it took two months to clear. But they continued to pour men and supplies onto the beaches and to edge inland through the Normandy marshes and hedgerows. On July 19, 1944, General Omar Bradley's troops took St. Lô, a transportation hub for roads and railroads into the heart of France. The German commanders advised withdrawal to defenses behind the Seine River, but a stubborn Hitler issued disastrous orders to contest every inch of land. Field Marshal Erwin Rommel, convinced that all was lost, began to intrigue for a separate peace. Other like-minded German officers, convinced that the war was hopeless, tried to kill Hitler at his headquarters on July 20, 1944, but the Führer survived the bomb blast, and hundreds of conspirators and suspects were tortured to death. Rommel was granted the option of suicide, which he took.

Meanwhile, the Führer's tactics brought calamity to the German forces in western France. On July 25 General Bradley's First Army broke through west of St. Lô and, soon augmented by George Patton's Third Army, the American forces broke out westward into Brittany and eastward toward Paris. Patton moved east and north to link up with British forces coming south from Caen, and the two caught the German forces (twenty-one divisions) in a trap. Only remnants managed to escape across the Seine before the pincers closed.

Meanwhile, on August 15 a joint American-French invasion force landed on the French Mediterranean coast and raced up the Rhône Valley. German resistance in France collapsed. A Free French division, aided by American forces, had the honor of liberating Paris on August 25. German forces retreated pell-mell toward the German border, and by mid-September most of France and Belgium were cleared of enemy troops. By this time the Americans were in Aachen, the old seat of Charlemagne's empire, the first German town to fall.

LEAPFROGGING TO TOKYO

Even in the Pacific, relegated to lower priority, Allied forces had brought the war within reach of the enemy homeland by the end of 1944. The war's first American offensive in fact had been in the southwest Pacific. There the Japanese, stopped at Coral Sea and Midway, had thrust into the southern Solomons, and were building an airstrip on Guadalcanal from which they could attack transportation routes to Australia. On August 7, 1942, two months before the North Africa landings, the First Marine Division landed on Guadalcanal.

This provoked a savage Japanese response. Japanese reinforcements poured in, and the opposing navies challenged each other in a confusing series of night battles that battered both badly. But while the Americans suffered heavy losses, they so devastated the Japanese carrier groups that the Japanese navy remained on the defensive for the rest of the war. The marines, helped by reinforcements, finally cleared Guadalcanal of Japanese soldiers six months later.

MACARTHUR IN NEW GUINEA   Meanwhile, American and Australian forces under General MacArthur had begun to push the Japanese out of their positions on New Guinea's north coast. These costly battles, fought through some of the hottest, most humid and mosquito-infested swamps in the world, secured the eastern tip of New Guinea by the end of January 1943.

At this stage American war planners made a critical decision. MacArthur proposed to advance westward along the northern coast of New Guinea toward the Philippines and ultimately Tokyo. Admiral Chester Nimitz argued for a sweep through the islands of the central Pacific toward Formosa and China. The Combined Chiefs of Staff agreed to MacArthur's plan, but they also ordered Nimitz to undertake his sweep in order to protect MacArthur's northern flank.

A new tactic expedited the movement. During the air Battle of the Bismarck Sea (March 2–3, 1943), American bombers sank eight Japanese troopships and ten warships bringing reinforcements. Thereafter the Japanese dared not risk sending transports to points under siege, making it possible to use the tactic of neutralizing Japanese strongholds with air and sea power, and moving on, leaving them to die on the vine. Some called it "leapfrogging," and Premier Tojo later acknowledged the strategy as a major cause of Allied victory. By the end of 1943 MacArthur's forces controlled the northern coast of New Guinea.

NIMITZ IN THE CENTRAL PACIFIC   Admiral Nimitz's advance through the central Pacific had as its first target Tarawa in the Gilbert Islands. Tarawa was one of the most heavily protected islands in the Pacific. There nearly 1,000 American soldiers, sailors, and marines lost their lives rooting out 4,000 Japanese who refused to surrender. The Gilberts provided airfields from which the Seventh Air Force began softening up strong points in the Marshall Islands to the northwest. Japanese planes completely abandoned the region.

THE WAR IN THE PACIFIC,
1942-1945

Areas controlled by Japan, 1942

⬅ Major Allied offensives

⬅-- Major Allied air offensives

✱ Major battle

In the Battle of the Philippine Sea, fought mostly in the air on June 19 and 20, 1944, the Japanese lost three more carriers, two submarines, and over 300 planes, at the cost of only 17 American planes. The battle secured the Marianas, and soon B-29 bombers were winging their way to the first systematic bombing of the Japanese homeland. Defeat in the

Marianas finally convinced General Tojo that the war was lost. On July 18, 1944, he and his entire cabinet resigned.

THE BATTLE OF LEYTE GULF   With New Guinea and the Marianas all but conquered, President Roosevelt met with General MacArthur and Admiral Nimitz in Honolulu to decide the next major step. Previous plans had marked China as the essential springboard for invading Japan, but a Japanese offensive in April 1944 had taken most of the South China airfields from which American air power had operated. This strengthened MacArthur's opinion that the Philippines would provide a safer staging area. He also had a personal desire to recapture the islands he and his American troops had earlier defended. Sentimental and political considerations, as well as military, tipped the decision his way. MacArthur made his move into the Philippines on October 20, 1944, landing first on the island of Leyte. Wading ashore behind the first landings, he issued an emotional announcement: "People of the Philippines: I have returned."

The Japanese, knowing that loss of the Philippines would cut them off from the essential resources of the East Indies, brought in fleets from three directions. The three encounters that resulted on October 25 came to be known collectively as the Battle of Leyte Gulf, the largest naval engagement in history. The Japanese lost most of their remaining sea power and the ability to defend the Philippines. The battle also included the first use of suicide attacks by Japanese pilots. The "Kamikaze" units, named for the "Divine Wind" that centuries before had saved Japan from Mongol invasion, were able to inflict severe damage on the American navy until the end of the war.

A New Age Is Born

ROOSEVELT'S FOURTH TERM   In 1944, war or no war, the calendar dictated another presidential election. This time the Republicans turned to the former crime-fighter and New York governor, Thomas E. Dewey, as their candidate. Once again no Democratic challenger rose high enough to contest Roosevelt, but a fight did develop over the second spot on the ticket. Vice-President Henry Wallace had aggravated both southern conservatives and northern city bosses who feared his ties with labor, so Roosevelt finally chose the relatively unknown Missouri senator Harry S. Truman.

Dewey ran under the same handicap as Landon and Willkie before him. He did not propose to dismantle Roosevelt's programs, but argued that it was time for younger men to replace the tired old leaders of the New Deal. The problem was that, even though considerably younger than Roosevelt, Dewey showed few signs of vitality. Though blessed with a silky voice and a stylish wardrobe, he was ill at ease in public, stiff, formal, seemingly arrogant, and worst of all—dull. "How can we be expected to vote for a man who looks like the bridegroom on a wedding cake?" one Washington veteran asked. Roosevelt betrayed decided signs of illness and exhaustion, but nevertheless carried the contest to the opposition. On November 7, 1945, he was once again elected, this time by a popular margin of 25.6 million to 22 million and an electoral vote of 432 to 99.

CONVERGING FRONTS   The war was not going as well; final victory remained elusive. After the quick sweep across France, the Allies lost momentum in the fall of 1944 and settled down to slugging it out on the frontiers of Germany. The armies fought along this line all winter.

Then the Germans sprang a surprise in the rugged Ardennes Forest, where the Allied line was thinnest. On December 16, 1944, they advanced along a fifty-mile bulge in Belgium and Luxembourg before they stalled at Bastogne—hence the name: Battle of the Bulge. Reinforced by the Allies just before it was surrounded, Bastogne held out for six days against all the Germans could bring against it. On December 22 American General "Tony" McAuliffe gave his memorable answer to the German demand for surrender: "Nuts." His situation remained desperate until the next day when the clouds lifted, allowing Allied air power to drop in supplies and hit the Germans. On December 26 Bastogne was relieved, but it would be mid-January 1945 before the previous lines were restored.

Germany's sudden thrust upset Eisenhower's timetable and made continued coordination with the Soviet army even more crucial. The Nazi counterattack in the West had weakened their defense of the eastern front, and in January 1945 the Russians began their final offensive. The destruction of Hitler's last reserve units at the Battle of the Bulge also left open the door to Germany's heartland. The western offensives started in February, and by early March Allied forces were pouring across the Rhine. By this time the Russian offensive had also reached Germany itself.

With the British and American armies racing across western Germany and the Russians moving in from the east, the attention of the war planners turned to Berlin. Churchill had grown suspicious of the Russians and worried that if they arrived in Berlin first, they would gain dangerous leverage in deciding the postwar map of Europe. He told Eisenhower of his concerns and urged him to get to Berlin first. Eisenhower, however, refused to mix politics with military strategy. Berlin, he said, no longer was of military significance. His purpose remained the destruction of the enemy's ground forces. Churchill disagreed and appealed to Roosevelt, but the American leader, now seriously ill, left the decision to the Supreme Commander. Eisenhower then asked General Omar Bradley to predict what it would take to liberate Berlin before the Russians. Bradley estimated that it would cost 100,000 Allied casualties, which he described as a "pretty stiff price to pay for a prestige objective." Eisenhower agreed, and they left Berlin for the Russians to conquer.

YALTA AND THE POSTWAR WORLD   As the final offensives got under way, the Big Three leaders met again in early February 1945 at Yalta, a resort in southern Russia. While the focus at Teheran in 1943 had been on wartime strategy, it was now on the shape of the postwar world. Two aims loomed large in Roosevelt's thinking. One was the need to ensure that the Soviet Union join the war against Japan. The other was based on the lessons he drew from the previous world war. Chief among the mistakes to be remedied were the failure of the United States to join the League of Nations and the failure of the Allies to maintain a united front in negotiations with the German aggressors.

The Yalta meeting thus began by calling for a conference to create a new world organization. The conferees also decided that substantive decisions in the new organization's Security Council would require the agreement of its five permanent members: the United States, Britain, Russia, France, and China.

GERMANY AND EASTERN EUROPE   With Hitler's "Thousand-Year Reich" stumbling to its doom, the leaders at Yalta had to make arrange-

The Yalta Conference, February 1945. *Stalin* (right), *FDR* (center), *and Churchill* (left) *confer on the shape of the postwar world.*

ments for the postwar governance of Germany. The war map dictated the basic pattern of occupation zones: Russia would control the east and the Western Allies would control the rich industrial areas of the west. Berlin, isolated within the Russian zone, would be jointly occupied. Churchill and Roosevelt insisted that liberated France receive a zone along its border with Germany and also in Berlin. Austria was similarly divided, with Vienna, like Berlin, under joint occupation within the Russian zone. Russian demands for reparations of $20 billion to the Allies, half of which would go to Russia, were referred to a Reparations Commission. The commission never reached agreement, although the Russians took untold amounts of machinery and equipment from their occupation zone.

With respect to eastern Europe, where Russian forces were advancing on a broad front, there was little the Western Allies could do to influence events. Poland became the main focus of Western concern. Britain and France had gone to war in 1939 to defend Poland, and now, six years later, the course of the war had ironically left Poland's fate in the hands of the Russians. Events had long foreshadowed the outcome.

When they reentered Poland in 1944, the Soviets placed civil administration under a puppet regime in Lublin. The Soviets refused to recognize the legitimacy of Poland's government-in-exile in London, formed by officials who had fled the country following Hitler's invasion in September 1939. With Soviet troops at the gates of Warsaw, the underground resistance in the city rose against the Nazi occupiers. The underground, however, supported Poland's government-in-exile in London. The Russians then stopped their offensive for two months while the Nazis in Warsaw wiped out thousands of Poles, potential rivals to the Russians' Lublin puppet government.

Hope that postwar cooperation could survive such events was a triumph of optimism over experience. The Western Allies found at Yalta that they could do no more than acquiesce or stall. On the Soviet proposal to expand the Lublin Committee into a provisional government together with representatives of the London Poles, they acquiesced. On the issue of Poland's boundaries, they stalled. The Russians proposed to keep eastern Poland, offering land taken from Germany as compensation. Roosevelt and Churchill accepted the proposal, but considered Poland's new western boundary at the Oder–Western Neisse Rivers only provisional. Yet the peace conference at which Poland's western boundary was to be settled never took place because of later disagreements. The presence of the London Poles in the provisional government only lent a tone of legitimacy to a regime dominated by the Communists, who soon ousted their rivals.

The Big Three also promised to sponsor free elections, democratic governments, and constitutional safeguards of freedom throughout the rest of Europe. The Yalta Declaration of Liberated Europe reaffirmed faith in the principles of the Atlantic Charter and the United Nations, but in the end it made little difference. It may have postponed Communist takeovers in eastern Europe for a few years, but before long Communist members of coalition governments had their hands on the levers of power and purged the opposition. Russia, twice invaded by Germany in the twentieth century, was determined to create buffer states between it and the Germans.

YALTA'S LEGACY   Critics later attacked the Yalta agreements for "giving" eastern Europe over to Soviet domination. Some argued that Roosevelt's declining health caused him to buckle under Stalin's insistent demands. But the course of the war shaped the actions at Yalta, not personal diplomacy. The Red Army had the upper hand in eastern Europe. Perhaps the most bitterly criticized of the Yalta understandings was a secret agreement on the Far East, not made public until after the war. The Joint Chiefs of Staff still estimated that Japan could hold out for eighteen months after the defeat of Germany. Costly campaigns thus lay ahead, and the atomic bomb was still an expensive and untested gamble.

So Roosevelt felt that he had no choice but to accept Stalin's demands on postwar arrangements in the Far East, subject technically to later agreement by Chiang Kai-shek. Stalin wanted continued Russian control of Outer Mongolia through its puppet People's Republic there, acquisition of the Kurile Islands from Japan, and recovery of rights and territory lost after the Russo-Japanese War in 1905. Stalin in return promised to enter the war against Japan two or three months after the German defeat, to recognize Chinese sovereignty over Manchuria, and to conclude a treaty of friendship and alliance with the Chinese Nationalists. Roosevelt's concessions would later appear in a different light, but given their geographical advantages in Asia as in eastern Europe, the Soviets were in a position to get what they wanted in any case.

THE THIRD REICH COLLAPSES   The collapse of Nazi resistance was imminent, but President Roosevelt did not live to join the celebrations. All through 1944 his health had been declining, and on April 12, 1945, while he was drafting a speech, a cerebral hemorrhage brought sudden death.

Hitler's Germany collapsed less than a month later. The Allied armies rolled up almost unopposed to the Elbe River, where they met advance detachments of Russians on April 25. Three days later Italian partisans captured and brutally killed Mussolini and his mistress as they tried to flee. In Berlin, which was under siege by the Russians, Hitler married his mistress, Eva Braun, in an underground bunker on the last day of April, just before killing her and himself. On May 2 Berlin fell to the Russians. That same day German forces in Italy surrendered. On May 7 the Germans signed an unconditional surrender in Allied headquarters at Reims. So ended the Thousand-Year Reich, little more than twelve years after its Führer had come to power.

Massive victory celebrations on V-E Day, May 8, 1945, were tem-

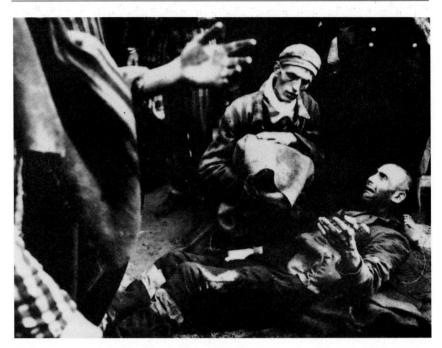

U.S. troops encounter surviving inmates at the Nazi concentration camp at Wobbelin, May 1945.

pered by the tragedies that had engulfed the world: mourning for the lost president and the death and mutilation of untold millions. Most shocking was the revelation of the Nazi Holocaust, scarcely believable until the Allied armies discovered the death camps in which Nazis had sought to apply their "final solution" to the Jewish "problem": the wholesale extermination of some 6 million Jews along with more than 1 million others who had incurred Nazi contempt for one reason or another.

During the war, reports from Red Cross and underground sources had amassed growing evidence of Germany's systematic genocide against European Jews. Stories appeared in major American newspapers as early as 1942, but they were nearly always buried on inside pages. And reports of such horror seemed beyond belief. American government officials, even some Jewish leaders, dragged their feet on the question for fear that relief efforts for Jewish refugees might stir latent anti-Semitism at home. Finally, Roosevelt set up a War Refugees Board in 1944, but with few resources at its disposal. It nevertheless managed to rescue about 200,000 European Jews and some 20,000 others. But more might have been done. The Allies rejected the bombing of rail lines into the largest death camp, Auschwitz in Poland, although American planes hit industries five miles away. Moreover, few refugees were accepted into the United States. The Allied handling of the tragic affair was inept at best and disgraceful at worst.

A GRINDING WAR   The sobering thought that Japan must still be defeated cast a further pall over the victory celebrations. American forces continued to penetrate and disrupt the Japanese Empire in the early months of 1945, but at heavy cost. On February 19, 1945, marine assault forces invaded Iwo Jima, a volcanic island 750 miles from Tokyo. The island was needed to provide fighter escort for bombers over Japan and as a landing strip for disabled B-29s. It took nearly six weeks to secure Iwo Jima from defenders hiding in an underground labyrinth, and the cost was high: more than 20,000 American casualties, including 7,000 dead.

The fight for Okinawa, beginning on Easter Sunday, April 1, was even bloodier. The island was large enough to afford a staging area for invasion of the Japanese islands, and its capture required the largest amphibious operation of the Pacific war, involving some 300,000 troops. Desperate Japanese counterattacks inflicted heavy losses. Kamikaze planes attacked by the hundreds. The battle for Okinawa raged until late June, when the bloody attrition destroyed any further Japanese ability to resist. The fighting brought nearly 50,000 American casualties. The Japanese lost an estimated 140,000 dead. Casualties included about 42,000 Okinawans.

The campaign was significant mainly for wearing down the remaining Japanese defenses. Now American ships could freely roam the coastline of Japan, shelling targets ashore. American planes bombed at will and mined the waters of the Inland Sea. Tokyo and other major cities were devastated by firestorms ignited by incendiary bombs, made all the worse by the prevalence of wooden structures in earthquake-prone Japan. Still, it seemed that ahead lay further beachheads and more bitter fighting against the same suicidal fury that had made Okinawa so costly a conquest. But as the irony of timing would have it, Okinawa was never needed as a staging area. When resistance on the island collapsed, the Japanese emperor instructed the new premier to seek peace terms. Washington had picked this up by decoding Japanese messages that suggested either an effort to avoid unconditional surrender or perhaps just a stall.

THE ATOMIC BOMB   By the summer of 1945, however, word of a new weapon had changed all strategic calculations: President Truman had just learned of the first successful test-firing of an atomic bomb, the result of several years of intensive work. In 1939, Albert Einstein had alerted President Roosevelt to German research on nuclear fission. In 1940 the president diverted some army and navy funds into research that grew ultimately into the $2 billion top-secret Manhattan Project, involving over 120,000 workers.

A group of physicists under Dr. J. Robert Oppenheimer worked out the scientific and technical problems of bomb construction in a laboratory at Los Alamos, New Mexico. On July 16, 1945, the first atomic fireball rose from the New Mexico desert. The test explosion broke windows 125 miles away, and a blind woman saw the flash. The awestruck Oppenheimer said later that in the observation bunker, "A few people laughed, a few people cried, most people were silent." After learning of the successful test, Truman wrote in his diary: "We have discovered the most terrible bomb in the history of the world."

How to use this awful new weapon posed unique problems. Some scientists favored a demonstration in a remote area, but this was vetoed because only two bombs were available, and even those might misfire. The choice of targets received more consideration. Four Japanese cities had been reserved from conventional bombing as potential targets for the new weapon. After Secretary of War Henry Stimson eliminated Kyoto, Japan's ancient capital and repository of many national and religious treasures, priority went to Hiroshima, center of war industries, headquarters of the Second General Army, and command center for the homeland's defenses. This met Truman's guidelines. He had written that, even though "the Japs are savages, ruthless, merciless, and fanatic," only military personnel and installations rather than "women and children" should be targeted. He had no idea that the bomb would destroy virtually an entire city.

On July 25, 1945, President Truman, then at the Big Three Conference in Potsdam, Germany, ordered the bomb dropped if Japan did not surrender before August 3. The next day the heads of the American, British, and Chinese governments issued the Potsdam Declaration de-

A charred watch marks the moment of nuclear confla-gration in Hiroshima, August 6, 1945.

manding that Japan surrender or face "prompt and utter destruction." The deadline passed, and at 9:15 A.M. on a warm August 6, 1945, a B-29 bomber, the *Enola Gay,* dropped an atomic bomb over Hiroshima. A sudden flash wiped out four square miles of the city, wrecked the defense headquarters, destroyed most of the Second General Army, and killed 50,000–100,000 people. Even those who appeared unhurt began mysteriously to sicken and die, the first victims of a deadly radiation that blighted lives and the environment for years to come. In the United States, Americans greeted the first news with elation: it promised a quick end to the long nightmare of war. Only later would people realize that it marked the start of a more enduring nightmare, the nuclear arms race.

Three days later Russia hastened to enter the war, and a few hours after that, about noon on August 9, a second atomic bomb exploded over the port city of Nagasaki, killing 36,000 more. That night the emperor urged his cabinet to accept the inevitable and surrender on the sole condition that he remain as sovereign. The next day the United States government, to facilitate surrender and an orderly transition, announced its willingness to let him keep the throne, but under the authority of an Allied supreme commander. Frantic exchanges ended with Japanese acceptance on August 14, 1945, when the emperor himself broke precedent to record a radio message announcing the surrender to his people. Even then a last-ditch palace revolt had to be squashed. On September 2, 1945, General MacArthur and other Allied representatives accepted Japan's formal surrender on board the battleship *Missouri*.

THE FINAL LEDGER   Thus ended the most deadly conflict in human history. No effort to tabulate a ledger of death and destruction can ever take the full measure of the war's suffering, nor hope to be more than a rough guess as to the numbers involved. One estimate has it that 70 million in all fought in the war, at a cost of some 35 million military and civilian dead. Material costs were also enormous, perhaps $1 trillion in military expenditures and twice that in property losses. The Soviet Union suffered the greatest losses of all, over 6 million military deaths, more than 10 million civilians dead, and at least 25 million left homeless. World War II was more costly for the United States than any other of the country's foreign wars: 292,000 battle deaths and 114,000 other deaths. But in proportion to population, the United States suffered a far smaller loss than any of the major Allies or enemies, and American territory escaped the devastation inflicted on so many other parts of the world.

The war's end opened a new era for the United States. It accelerated the growth of American power while devastating all other world powers, leaving the United States economically and militarily the strongest nation on earth. But the Soviet Union, despite its human and material losses, emerged from the war with much new territory and enhanced influence, making it the greatest power on the whole Eurasian landmass. Just a little over a century after the French observer Alexis de Tocqueville had predicted that western Europe would come to be overshadowed by the power of the United States and Russia, his prophecy had come to pass.

MAKING CONNECTIONS

- Compare the impact of World War II on the home front to that of World War I, especially the effects of war on race and gender relations.

- The growing domestic conservatism of the war years continued into the 1950s, a topic discussed in the next chapter.

- Dwight D. Eisenhower's success as American general and Allied leader led to his nomination and election as president in 1952. Compare to the experience of General Grant in and after the Civil War, and to the political experiences of other American military leaders.

FURTHER READING

Roosevelt's wartime leadership is analyzed in Eric Larrabee's *Commander in Chief: Franklin Delano Roosevelt, His Lieutenants and Their War* (1987). John Keegan's *The Second World War* (1990)* surveys the European conflict in its entirety, while Charles B. MacDonald's *The Mighty Endeavor: American Armed Forces in the European Theatre in World War II* (1969) concentrates on American involvement. For the war in the Far East, see Ronald H. Spector's *Eagle against the Sun* (1984),* John Dower's *War Without Mercy: Race and Power in the Pacific War* (1986),* and Dan van der Vat's *The Pacific Campaign* (1992).*

Overviews of the home front include Michael C. C. Adams's *The Best War Ever: America and World War II* (1993)* and William L. O'Neill's *A Democracy at War: America's Fight at Home and Abroad in World War II* (1993).*

Susan M. Hartmann's *The Home Front and Beyond* (1982)* and Karen Anderson's *Wartime Women* (1981) treat the new working envi-

*These books are available in paperback editions.

ronment for women. Neil Wynn looks at the participation of blacks in *The Afro-American and the Second World War* (1976). The story of the oppression of Japanese-Americans is told in David J. O'Brien and Stephen S. Fugita's *The Japanese American Experience* (1993).*

The issues and events that led to the deployment of atomic weapons are addressed in Martin J. Sherwin's *A World Destroyed: The Atomic Bomb and the Grand Alliance* (1975).* Gar Alperovitz's *Atomic Diplomacy: Hiroshima and Potsdam* (new ed., 1985)* details how the bomb helped shape American postwar policy. Paul S. Boyer's *By the Bomb's Early Light* (1985)* shows American cultural and intellectual responses to the bomb.

*These books are available in paperback editions.

PART SEVEN

THE AMERICAN AGE

Amid the joyous celebrations of the Allied victory in the Second World War, one commentator announced that the "American era was at hand." Such a declaration was filled with chauvinism, and yet it contained a kernel of truth. The United States emerged from World War II the dominant military and economic power on the world stage. Americans had a monopoly over the atomic bomb and enjoyed a commanding position in international trade. While much of Europe and Asia struggled to recover from the horrific physical devastation of the war, the United States emerged virtually unscathed, its economic infrastructure intact and operating at peak efficiency. Jobs that were scarce in the Thirties were now available for the taking. By 1955 the United States, with only 6 percent of the world's population, was producing well over half of the world's goods. American capitalism not only demonstrated its economic strength; it also became a dominant cultural force as well. In Europe, Japan, and elsewhere, American products and forms of entertainment and fashion attracted excited attention.

Yet the specter of a new "Cold War" cast a pall over the buoyant revival of the American economy after World War II. The ideological contest with the Soviet Union and Communist China produced numerous foreign crises and sparked a domestic witch-hunt for Communists that far surpassed earlier episodes of political and social repression in the nation's history. And yet there was widespread acceptance in both major political parties of the geopolitical assumptions embedded in the ideological Cold War with international communism. Both Republican and Democratic presidents affirmed the need to "contain" the spread of communist influence around the world.

This bedrock assumption eventually embroiled the United States in a tragic war in southeast Asia that destroyed Lyndon Johnson's presidency and revived neo-isolationist sentiments. The Vietnam War also was the catalyst for a countercultural movement in which young idealists of the "baby-boom generation" sought alternatives to a government and society that in their eyes had become oppressive and corrupt. The youth revolt provided energy for many overdue social reforms, including the civil rights and environmental movements, but it also contributed to an array of social ills, from street riots to drug abuse. The social upheavals of the 1960s and early 1970s provoked a conservative backlash that overreached itself as well. In their efforts to restore "law and order," mayors overlooked the protection of civil liberties in their cities. Richard Nixon's paranoid reac-

tion to his critics led to the destruction of his presidency as a result of the Watergate investigations.

Through all of this turmoil, however, the basic premises of welfare state capitalism that Franklin Roosevelt had instituted with his New Deal programs remained essentially intact. With only a few exceptions, both Republicans and Democrats after 1945 came to accept the notion that the federal government must assume greater responsibility for the welfare of individual Americans than had heretofore been the case. Even Ronald Reagan, a sharp critic of liberal social welfare programs, recognized the need for federal government programs to provide a "safety net" for those who could not help themselves.

Yet this fragile consensus about public policy began to disintegrate in the late 1980s amid stunning international events and less visible domestic developments. The internal collapse of the Soviet Union and the concomitant disintegration of European Communism stunned observers and sent policy makers scurrying to respond to a post–Cold War world in which the United States remained the only legitimate superpower. After forty-five years, American foreign policy was no longer centered on a single adversary, and world politics lost its bipolar quality. During the early 1990s the European Community finally coalesced, the two Germanies reunited, apartheid in South Africa finally ended, and Israel and the Palestinians signed a heretofore unimaginable peace treaty.

At the same time, American foreign policy began to focus less on military power and more on economic competition and technological development. In those arenas, Japan and a reunited Germany challenged the United States for preeminence. By reducing the public's fear of nuclear annihilation, the ending of the Cold War also reduced public interest in foreign affairs. The presidential election of 1992 was the first since 1936 in which foreign-policy issues played virtually no role. This was an unfortunate development, for post–Cold War world affairs remained dangerous. The implosion of Soviet Communism unleashed a series of ethnic, nationalist, and separatist conflicts. In the face of inertia among other governments and pleas for assistance, the United States found itself being drawn into crises in faraway locations such as Bosnia, Rwanda, Somalia, and Chechnya. As a former CIA director observed, the more fragmented world "is more dangerous" now than during the Cold War.

As the new multipolar world careened toward the end of a century and the start of a new millennium, fault lines began to appear in the American social and economic landscape. A gargantuan federal debt and rising annual deficits threatened to bankrupt a nation that was becoming top-heavy with retirees. Without fully realizing it, much less appreciating the cascading consequences, the American population was becoming dispro-portionately old. Those aged ninety-five to ninety-nine doubled between 1980 and 1990, and the number of centenarians increased 77 percent. The proportion of the population aged 65 and older rose steadily during the 1990s. By the year 2000, half of the elderly population would be over the age of seventy-five. This demographic fact harbored profound social and political implications. It exerted increasing stress on health care costs, nursing home facilities, and the very survival of the Social Security system.

At the same time that the gap between young and old was increasing, so, too, was the disparity between rich and poor. This trend threatened to stratify a society already experiencing rising levels of racial and ethnic tension. Between 1960 and 1990 the gap between the richest 20 percent of the population and the poorest 20 percent doubled. Over 20 percent of all American children in 1990 lived in poverty, and the infant mortality rate rose. The infant death rate in Japan was less than half that in the United States. Despite the much-ballyhooed "war on poverty" programs initiated by Lyndon Johnson and continued in one form or another by all of his successors, the chronically poor in 1996 were more numerous and more bereft of hope than those in 1964.

30 ∽ THE FAIR DEAL AND CONTAINMENT

*N*o sooner did the Second World War end than a new cold war began. The uneasy wartime alliance between the United States and the Soviet Union collapsed completely by the fall of 1945. The two strongest nations to emerge from the carnage of World War II could not bridge their ideological differences over such basic issues as essential human rights, individual liberties, and religious beliefs. Mutual suspicion and a race to gain influence and control over the so-called Third World countries further polarized the two nations. The defeat of Japan and Germany created power vacuums that sucked Russia and America into an unrelenting war of words fed by clashing strategic interests. At the same time, the destruction of Western Europe and the exhaustion of its peoples led to anticolonial uprisings in Asia and Africa that threatened to strip Britain and France of their once-great empires. The postwar world was thus an unstable one in which international tensions shaped the contours of domestic politics and culture as well as foreign adventures.

DEMOBILIZATION UNDER TRUMAN

TRUMAN'S UNEASY START   "Who the hell is Harry Truman?" Roosevelt's chief of staff asked the president in the summer of 1944. The question was on more lips when, after less than twelve weeks as vice-president, Harry Truman took the presidential oath on April 12, 1945. Clearly he was not as charismatic or as magisterial as Franklin Roosevelt and that was one of the burdens he would bear. Roosevelt, a journalist wrote years later, "looked imperial, and he acted that way, and he talked that way. Harry Truman, for God's sake—looked and acted and talked like—well, like a failed haberdasher"—which he was.

Roosevelt and Truman came from different backgrounds. For Truman there had been no inherited wealth, no early contact with the great and near-great, no European travel, no Groton, no Harvard—indeed, no college at all. Born in 1884 in western Missouri, Truman had pioneer grandparents from Kentucky and a Southern Baptist background. He grew up in Independence, outside of Kansas City. Too nearsighted to join in the activities of other boys, Truman became bookish and introverted. After high school, however, he spent a few years working in Kansas City banks and grew into an outgoing young man.

During World War I Truman served in France as captain of an artillery battery. Afterward, he and a partner went into the clothing business, but it failed during the recession of 1922 and Truman then entered politics. Elected county judge in 1922, he was defeated in 1924 and elected once again in 1926. In 1934 Missouri sent him to the United States Senate, where he remained fairly obscure until he became chairman of the committee to investigate corruption in defense industries.

Something about Harry Truman evoked the spirit of Andrew Jackson: his decisiveness, his feisty character, his family loyalty. But that was a side of the man that the American people came to know only as he settled into the presidency. On his first full day as president, as the war in Asia ground on, he remained awestruck. "Boys, if you ever pray, pray for me now," he told a group of reporters. "I don't know whether you fellows ever had a load of hay fall on you, but when they told me yesterday what had happened, I felt like the moon, the stars and all the planets had fallen on me."

Truman's accession heartened the party bosses who had helped engineer his nomination as Roosevelt's vice-president. But as one reporter observed, the men who put Truman in "knew what they wanted but did not know what they were getting." What they were getting was a man who favored much of the New Deal and was even prepared to extend it, but at the same time was uneasy with many of the most ardent New Deal reformers. Within ninety days he had replaced much of the Roosevelt cabinet with his own choices. These included fewer Missourians and "cronies" than his detractors claimed, but on the whole his cabinet was more conservative in outlook and included enough mediocrities to lend credence to the criticism. Truman suffered the further handicap of seeming to be a caretaker for the remainder of Roosevelt's term. Few expected him to run on his own in 1948.

Truman gave one significant clue to his domestic policies on September 6, 1945, when he sent Congress a comprehensive peacetime program that in effect proposed to continue and enlarge the New Deal. Its twenty-one points included expansion of unemployment insurance, a higher minimum wage, a permanent Fair Employment Practices Commission, slum clearance and low-rent housing projects, regional development of the nation's river valleys, and a public works program. "Not even President Roosevelt asked for so much at one sitting," charged the House Republican leader. "It's just a plain case of out-dealing the New Deal." Beset by other problems, Truman failed to set priorities among his demands, and his new domestic proposals soon were mired down in disputes over the transition to a peacetime economy.

CONVERTING TO PEACE   The raucous celebrations that greeted Japan's surrender signaled the habitual American response to victory: a rapid demobilization and a return to more carefree pursuits. The public demanded that the president and Congress bring the boys home as soon as possible. By 1947 the total armed forces were down to 1.5 mil-

The Eldridge General Store, Fayette County, Illinois. *Postwar America quickly demobilized, turning its attention to the pursuit of abundance.*

lion from a wartime high of almost 12 million. In his memoirs Truman termed this "the most remarkable demobilization in the history of the world, or 'disintegration' if you want to call it that." By early 1950 the army had shrunk to 600,000 personnel.

The veterans returned to schools, new jobs, wives, and babies. Population growth, which had dropped off sharply in the Depression decade, now soared: the birth rate per 1,000 of total population grew from 19.4 in 1940 to above 24 per year by 1946, and did not begin to show a decline until the 1960s. Americans born during this postwar period comprised what came to be known as the baby-boom generation.

The end of the war, with its sudden demobilization and reconversion to a peacetime economy, brought sharp dislocations but not the postwar depression that many feared. Several shock absorbers cushioned the economic impact of demobilization: unemployment pay and other Social Security benefits; the Servicemen's Readjustment Act of 1944, known as the "GI Bill of Rights," under which $13 billion was spent for veterans on education, vocational training, medical treatment, unemployment insurance, and loans for building houses or going into business; and, most important, the pent-up demand for consumer goods that was fueled by wartime incomes. Instead of sinking into depression after the war, the economy enjoyed a spurt of private investment in new industrial plants and equipment.

CONTROLLING INFLATION   The economic problem facing Truman was not depression but inflation. Released from wartime restraints, the demands of businesses for higher prices and of workers for higher wages alike conspired to frustrate Truman's efforts to "continue stabilization of the economy." Truman endorsed "reasonable" demands for wage increases, which he thought businesses could absorb without raising prices, and which he considered necessary to sustain purchasing power. Management, however, did not agree. Within six weeks of war's end, corporations refused a wave of union demands for higher wages and better benefits, and a series of strikes followed in the automotive, steel, mine, petroleum, and railroad industries.

Truman, miffed at what he considered to be excessive union demands, including a 30 percent wage boost, responded forcefully, using powers granted the chief executive during wartime to seize the mines and threaten to draft striking railroad workers into the armed forces. In a staff meeting, Truman asked what organized labor "wanted to do—run the country?" A strike in the steel industry finally gave rise to a formula for settling most of the disputes. President Truman suggested a pay raise of 18½¢ per hour, which the Steel Workers accepted but United States Steel refused. To break the logjam, the administration in 1946 agreed to let the company increase its prices. That pattern then became the basis for settlements in other industries, and also set a dangerous precedent of price-wage spirals that would plague consumers in the postwar world.

Into 1946 the wartime Office of Price Administration maintained some restraint on price increases while gradually ending the rationing of most goods, and Truman asked for a one-year renewal of its powers. But during the late winter and spring of 1946 business lobbyists mounted a massive campaign against price controls, and Truman allowed them to end. Congress finally extended controls in July, but by then the cost of living had already risen by 6 percent. After the 1946 congressional elections Truman gave up the battle against inflationary prices, ending all controls except on rents, sugar, and rice.

PARTISAN CONFLICT   As congressional elections approached in the fall of 1946, discontent ran high, most of it directed against the administration. Truman caught the blame for labor problems from both sides. A speaker at the CIO national convention tagged Truman "the No. 1 strikebreaker," while much of the public, angry at striking unions, blamed the White House for the strikes. In 1946 Truman fired Henry A. Wallace as secretary of commerce in a disagreement over foreign policy, thus offending the Democratic left. At the same time, Republicans charged that Communists had infiltrated the government. Critics of the administration had a field day coining slogans. "To err is Truman" was credited to Martha Taft, the wife of Senator Robert Taft. But most effective was the simple "Had enough?" attributed to a Boston ad agency: their message was that the Democrats had simply been in power too long. In the end, Republicans won majorities in both houses of Congress for the first time since 1928.

With momentum building up against organized labor, the new Congress quickly passed the Taft-Hartley Act of 1947, which banned the closed shop (in which nonunion workers could not be hired) but permitted a union shop (in which workers newly hired were required to join the union), except where banned by state law. The legislation included provisions against "unfair" union practices such as "featherbedding" (pay for work not done), refusal to bargain in good faith, and contributing to political campaigns. Unions' political action committees were allowed to function only on a voluntary basis, and union leaders had to take oaths that they were not members of the Communist party. Employers were permitted to sue unions for breaking contracts and to speak freely during union campaigns. The act forbade strikes by federal employees, and imposed a "cooling-off" period of eighty days on any strike that the president found to be dangerous to the national health or safety.

Truman vetoed the bill, which unions called the "slave-labor act." This restored his credit with labor and brought many unionists who had voted Republican in 1946 back to the Democratic fold. But the bill passed over Truman's veto and, as it turned out, had a less than ruinous effect on unions. Its most severe impact probably was on the CIO's "Operation Dixie," a drive to win for unions a more secure foothold in the South. By 1954 fifteen states, mainly in the South, had used the Taft-Hartley Act's authority to pass "right-to-work" laws forbidding the union shop.

Truman clashed with the Republicans on other domestic issues, including a tax reduction measure passed by Congress. The president vetoed the bill on the principle that in times of high production and employment the federal debt should be reduced. In 1948, however, Congress managed to override his veto of a $5-billion tax cut at a time when government debt still ran high.

These conflicts between Truman and Congress obscured the high degree of bipartisan cooperation marking matters of governmental reorganization and foreign policy. After a postwar congressional investigation into the Pearl Harbor disaster made plain a fatal lack of coordination among the armed forces and intelligence services, a bipartisan majority in Congress set out to correct this problem by passing the National Security Act in 1947.

It created a national military establishment, headed by a secretary of defense with subcabinet departments of army, navy, and air force, and a new National Security Council (NSC), which included the president, heads of the defense departments, and the secretary of state, among others. The act made permanent the Joint Chiefs of Staff, which had been a wartime innovation, and established the Central Intelligence Agency (CIA), to coordinate intelligence-gathering abroad. There was at the time no intention to have the CIA engage in covert actions, nor any purpose that it engage in domestic activities. But the act included two gigantic loopholes that would in time allow the CIA to engage in both: authority to perform "such other functions and duties related to intelligence" as the NSC might direct, and responsibility for "protecting intelligence sources and methods."

Congress also adopted the Presidential Succession Act of 1947, which inserted the Speaker of the House and the president pro tempore of the Senate ahead of the secretary of state as replacements for a nonfunctioning president, on the principle that the presidency should first go to elected rather than appointed officers. Congress took the initiative in adopting the Twenty-second Amendment, ratified in 1951, which limited presidents after Truman to two terms—a belated slap at Roosevelt.

THE COLD WAR

BUILDING THE U.N. The hope that the wartime alliance would carry over into the postwar world proved but another great illusion. The pragmatic Roosevelt had shared no such illusion. He expected that the Great Powers in the postwar world would have spheres of influence, but felt he had to temper such *Realpolitik* with an organization "which would satisfy widespread demand in the United States for new idealistic or universalist arrangements for assuring the peace."

On April 25, 1945, two weeks after Roosevelt's death and two weeks before the German surrender, delegates from fifty nations at war with the Axis met in San Francisco to draw up the charter of the United Nations. Additional members could be admitted by a two-thirds vote of the General Assembly. This body, one of the two major agencies set up by the charter, included delegates from all member nations and was to meet annually in regular session to approve the budget, receive annual reports from U.N. agencies, and choose members of the Security Council and other bodies.

The Security Council, the other major charter agency, would remain in permanent session and would have "primary responsibility for the maintenance of international peace and security." Its eleven members included six elected for two-year terms and five permanent members: the United States, Russia, Britain, France, and China. Each permanent member could veto any question of substance. The Security Council might investigate any dispute, recommend settlement or reference to another U.N. body—the International Court of Justice at the Hague, in the Netherlands—and take measures, including a resort to military force. The United States Senate, in sharp contrast to the reception it gave the League of Nations, ratified the U.N. charter by a vote of 89 to 2.

DIFFERENCES WITH THE SOVIETS   Since the end of World War II, historians have debated about which side was more responsible for the onset of the Cold War. The conventional or "orthodox" view declares that the Soviets, led by a paranoid dictator, tried to dominate the globe, and the United States had no choice but to stand firm in defense of democratic capitalist values.

By contrast, those scholars known as "revisionists" argue that Truman and American economic imperialists were the culprits. Instead of maintaining Roosevelt's efforts to collaborate with Stalin and ensure the survival of the alliance after the war, these scholars assert, Truman adopted an unnecessarily belligerent stance and activist foreign policy that itself sought to create American spheres of influence around the world. He and his military advisers exaggerated the Soviet threat, in part to justify an American military buildup. Their provocative policies thus crystallized the tensions between the two countries. Yet such an interpretation fails to recognize that Truman inherited a deteriorating relationship with the Soviets. Events of 1945 made compromise and conciliation more and more difficult, whether for Roosevelt or Truman.

There were signs of trouble in the grand alliance as early as the spring of 1945, as Russia moved to set up compliant governments in eastern Europe, violating the Yalta promises of democratic elections. On February 1 the Polish Committee of National Liberation, a puppet group already claiming the status of provisional government, moved from Lublin to Warsaw. In March the Soviets installed a puppet premier in Romania. Protests against such actions led to Russian counterprotests that the British and Americans were negotiating German surrender in Italy "behind the back of the Soviet Union." A few days before his death, Roosevelt responded to Stalin: "I cannot avoid a feeling of resentment toward your informers . . . for such vile misrepresentations."

Such was the atmosphere when Truman entered the White House. A few days before the San Francisco conference, he gave Soviet Foreign Minister Vyacheslav Mikhaylovich Molotov a dressing down in Washington on the Polish situation. "I have never been talked to like that in my life," Molotov protested. "Carry out your agreements," Truman snapped, "and you won't get talked to like that."

On May 12, 1945, four days after victory in Europe, Winston Churchill sent Truman a telegram: "What is to happen about Europe? An iron curtain is drawn down upon [the Russian] front. We do not know what is going on behind [it]. . . . Surely it is vital now to come to an understanding with Russia, or see where we are with her, before we weaken our armies mortally." Nevertheless, as a gesture of goodwill, and over Churchill's protest, the American forces withdrew from the occupation zone in Germany assigned to Russia at Yalta. Americans still hoped that the Yalta agreements would be carried out, and they were even more eager to have Russian help against Japan.

Although the Russians admitted British and American observers to their sectors of eastern Europe, there was little the Western powers could have done to prevent Russian control of the region even if they had kept up their military strength. The presence of Soviet armed forces frustrated the efforts of non-Communists to gain political influence. Opposition leaders were either exiled, silenced, executed, or imprisoned.

Secretary of State James F. Byrnes, who took office in 1945, struggled on through 1946 with the problems of postwar settlements. In early 1947, the Council of Foreign Ministers finally produced treaties for Italy, Hungary, Romania, Bulgaria, and Finland. The treaties in effect confirmed Soviet control over eastern Europe, which in Russian eyes seemed but a parallel to American control in Japan and Western control over most of Germany and all of Italy. The Yalta guarantees of democracy in eastern Europe had turned out much like the Open Door Policy in China, little more than pious rhetoric sugar-coating the realities of power and national interest.

Byrnes's impulse to brandish the atomic bomb only added to the irritations, intimidating no one. As early as April 1945, he had suggested to Truman that possession of the new weapon "might well put us in a position to dictate our own terms at the end of the war." And after becoming secretary of state, he tried on several occasions to threaten Russian diplomats with America's growing arsenal of nuclear weapons. But they paid little notice, and such attempts at intimidation were soon dropped.

The United States still enjoyed exclusive possession of atomic weapons and, together with Britain and Canada (partners in developing the atomic bomb), proposed in 1946 to internationalize the control of atomic energy. Under the plan presented to the U.N. Atomic Energy Commission, an International Atomic Development Authority would have a monopoly of atomic explosives and atomic energy. The Russians, fearing Western domination of the agency, proposed instead simply to outlaw the manufacture and use of atomic bombs, with enforcement vested in the Security Council and thus subject to a veto. Later they conceded the right of international inspection, but still refused to give up the veto. The American government rejected the arrangement, which it considered a compromise of international control.

CONTAINMENT   By the beginning of 1947 relations with the Soviet Union had become even more troubled. The year before, Stalin had already pronounced international peace impossible "under the present capitalistic development of the world economy." His statement impelled George F. Kennan, counselor of the American Embassy in

Moscow, to send an 8,000-word dispatch in which he sketched the roots of Soviet policy and warned that the Soviet Union was "committed fanatically to the belief that it is desirable and necessary that the internal harmony of our society be disrupted, our traditional way of life be destroyed, the international authority of our state be broken, if Soviet power is to be secure."

More than a year later, Kennan, now back at the State Department in Washington, spelled out his ideas for a proper response to the Soviets in a 1947 article published anonymously in *Foreign Affairs*. He advocated "a long-term, patient but firm and vigilant *containment* of Russian expansive tendencies." Americans, he added, could hope for a long-term moderation of Soviet ideology and policy, so that in time tensions with the West would lessen. There was a strong possibility "that Soviet power, like the capitalistic world of its conception, bears within it the seeds of its own decay, and that the sprouting of those seeds is well advanced."

Kennan's containment strategy lay behind the new departure in foreign policy that America's political leaders had already decided to take. Containment reflected a growing fear that Russian aims reached beyond eastern Europe, posing dangers in the eastern Mediterranean, the Middle East, and western Europe itself. The USSR was indeed looking for a breakthrough into the Mediterranean region, long important to Russia for purposes of trade and defense. After the war the USSR began to press Turkey for territorial concessions and the right to build naval bases on the Bosporus, an important gateway between the Black Sea and the Mediterranean. In 1946 civil war broke out in neighboring Greece between a British-backed government and a Communist-led faction that held the northern part of Greece. In 1947 the British ambassador informed the American government that the British could no longer bear the economic and military burden of aiding Greece and suggested that the United States assume the responsibility. Truman agreed, and on March 12, 1947, he asked Congress for $400 million in economic and military aid to both Greece and Turkey.

THE TRUMAN DOCTRINE AND THE MARSHALL PLAN In his speech to Congress the president announced what quickly became known as the Truman Doctrine. Although intended as a response to a specific crisis, its rhetoric was dangerously universal. "I believe," Truman declared, "that it must be the policy of the United States to support free peoples who are resisting attempted subjugation by armed minorities or by outside pressures." In 1947 Congress passed the Greek-Turkish aid bill, and by 1950 had spent $659 million on the program. Turkey achieved economic stability, and Greece defeated the Communist insurrection in 1949.

But such immediate gains created long-term problems. The Truman Doctrine marked the beginning of a contest that stock market whiz Bernard Baruch labeled "a cold war." Greece and Turkey were but the front lines of an ideological struggle for world power and influence between East and West. That struggle quickly focused on western Europe, where wartime damage had devastated factory production, and a severe drought in 1947, followed by a harsh winter, destroyed crops. Europe had become, in Winston Churchill's words, "a rubble heap, a charnel house, a breeding ground of pestilence and hate." Amid the chaos the Communist parties of France and Italy were flourishing.

In the spring of 1947, the State Department reported to George C. Marshall, who had replaced Byrnes as secretary of state, that the United States had underestimated the extent of wartime damage in Europe. Only a program of massive aid could rescue western Europe from disaster and possible Communist subversion. Late in May, George Kennan developed a plan that Secretary Marshall presented at the Harvard Commencement on June 5. Taking Kennan's lead, Marshall avoided the ideological overtones of the Truman Doctrine. "Our policy," he pledged, "is directed not against country or doctrine, but against hunger, poverty, desperation, and chaos." Marshall offered comprehensive economic aid to all European countries, including Russia. On June 27 the foreign ministers of France, Britain, and Russia met in London to discuss Marshall's overture. Molotov arrived with eighty advisers, but during the talks got word from Moscow to withdraw from this "imperialist" scheme. Two weeks later a meeting of delegates from western Europe formed a Committee of European Economic Cooperation (CEEC), which had a plan ready by September.

In late 1947 Truman submitted his proposal for the European Recovery Program to Congress. Two months later, a Communist coup d'état in Czechoslovakia ended the last remaining coalition government in eastern Europe. The seizure of power in Prague assured congressional

OCCUPATION OF GERMANY AND AUSTRIA

French zone · British zone · U.S. zone · Soviet zone

passage of the Marshall Plan, which from 1948 until 1951 poured $13 billion into European recovery.

DIVIDING GERMANY   The breakdown of the wartime alliance left the problem of postwar Germany unsettled. The German economy had stagnated, requiring the American army to carry a staggering burden of relief. Slowly, occupation zones evolved into functioning governments. In 1948 the British, French, and Americans merged their zones, and the West Germans then elected delegates to a federal constitutional convention.

Soviet reactions to the Marshall Plan and the unification of West Germany were sharp and quickly focused on Berlin, situated deep in the Soviet occupation zone. In April 1948 the Russians began to restrict the flow of traffic into West Berlin; on June 23 they stopped all traffic. The Soviets hoped the blockade would force the Allies to give up either Berlin or the plan to unify West Germany. But the American commander in Germany proposed to stand firm. "If we mean . . . to hold Europe against communism," he told his superiors at the Pentagon, "we must not budge."

Truman agreed, and after considering the use of armed convoys to supply West Berlin, he opted for a massive airlift. At the time this seemed an enormous and perhaps impossible task. By quick work, however, the Allied air forces brought in planes from around the world, and soon they were flying in nearly 5,000 tons of food and coal a day. Altogether, from June 1948 to mid-May 1949, the Berlin Airlift provided more than 1.5 million tons of supplies, or well over a half ton for each of the 2.2 million West Berliners.

Finally, on May 12, 1949, after extended talks, the Russians lifted the blockade. Before the end of the year, the German Federal Republic had a functioning government. At the end of May 1949, a German "Democratic" Republic arose in the Soviet-dominated eastern zone, dividing Germany into two independent states.

BUILDING NATO   As relations between the Soviets and western Europe chilled, transatlantic unity ripened into an outright military al-

The Berlin Airlift. *An American airplane arrives in West Berlin with much-needed supplies, 1948.*

NATO, a hopeful sign for the West.

liance. By March 1948 Britain, France, and the "Benelux" countries (Belgium, the Netherlands, and Luxembourg) had signed a fifty-year treaty of alliance and economic cooperation, the Brussels Pact. That June the Senate passed a resolution authorizing the administration to develop a collective defense pact with its European allies.

On April 4, 1949, diplomats signed the North Atlantic Treaty in Washington. Twelve nations were represented: the five Brussels Pact countries plus the United States, Canada, Denmark, Iceland, Italy, Norway, and Portugal. Greece and Turkey joined the alliance in 1952, West Germany in 1955, and Spain in 1982. The treaty pledged that an attack against any one of the signers would be considered an attack against all, and provided for a council of the North Atlantic Treaty Organization (NATO), which could establish other necessary agencies.

Truman observed at the signing ceremony that NATO would create "a shield against aggression and the fear of aggression—a bulwark which will permit us to get on with the real business . . . of achieving a fuller and happier life." In 1950 the council decided to create an integrated defense force for western Europe. Five years later the Warsaw Treaty Organization appeared as the eastern European counterpart to NATO.

The eventful year 1948 produced one other foreign-policy decision with long-term consequences. Late in 1947 the U.N. General Assembly voted to partition Palestine into Jewish and Arab states. Despite fierce Arab opposition, Jewish leaders proclaimed the independence of the new state of Israel on May 14, 1948. President Truman, who had been in close touch with Jewish leaders, ordered immediate recognition of the new state—the United States became the first nation to so act.

The neighboring Arab states thereupon went to war against Israel, which, however, held its own. U.N. mediators gradually worked out truce agreements with Israel's Arab neighbors that restored an uneasy peace by May 11, 1949, when Israel was admitted as a member of the United Nations. But the hard feelings and intermittent warfare between Israel and the Arab states have festered ever since, complicating American foreign policy, which has tried to maintain friendship with both sides while insisting on the legitimacy of the Israeli nation.

HARRY GIVES 'EM HELL

SHAPING THE FAIR DEAL   The determination Truman projected in foreign affairs did not alter his lackluster image on the domestic front. By early 1948, after three years in the White House, Truman had yet to shake the impression that he was not up to the job. Rather than go with a loser, New Deal stalwarts and party regulars tried to draft General Eisenhower as their presidential candidate for 1948, but in vain. The Democratic party seemed about to fragment: southern conservatives as well as the party's liberal wing had problems with Truman.

Yet Truman had a game plan for 1948. His advisers knew that to win he needed the midwestern and western farm belts, and he enjoyed fairly strong support among farmers. In metropolitan areas he needed to carry the labor and the black vote, which Truman wooed by working closely with unions and pressing the cause of civil rights. Truman's advisers counted on the Solid South to stay in the Democratic column. With the South and West, Truman could afford to lose some New Deal strongholds in the East and still win. This strategy erred chiefly in underrating the rebellion that would take four Deep South states out of Truman's camp.

What provoked the southern defection was Truman's forthright support of civil rights—a politically advantageous issue now that so many blacks had migrated to northern cities in states with large electoral votes. Truman's motivations in embracing civil rights were complex. When in 1946 he appointed the President's Committee on Civil Rights—a panel of distinguished citizens, black and white, North and South—he acted not only in response to the pressures of black organizations but also out of outrage at several recent attacks on blacks. The committee's report, *To Secure These Rights* (1947), touched on virtually every category of racial discrimination and called for the "elimination of segregation based on race, color, creed, or national origin, from American life."

Truman used his State of the Union message in 1948 to set the agenda for an election year. The speech offered something to nearly every group the Democrats hoped to win over. The first goal, Truman remarked, was "to secure fully the essential human rights of our citizens," and promised a special message later on civil rights. "To protect human resources," he proposed federal aid to education, increased and extended unemployment and retirement benefits, a comprehensive system of health insurance, more federal support for housing, and extension of rent controls. As one senator put it, the speech "raised all the ghosts of the old New Deal. . . ." On July 26, 1948, Truman banned racial discrimination in hiring federal employees, and four days later ordered an end to segregation in the armed forces. This last act was truly significant, since it involved the nation's largest single organization.

THE 1948 ELECTION   The Republican majority in Congress for the most part spurned the Truman program, an action it would later regret. Scenting victory in November, Republican delegates again nominated Thomas Dewey, former New York governor. The platform endorsed most of the New Deal reforms as an accomplished fact and approved the administration's bipartisan foreign policy, but as Landon had in 1936, Dewey promised to run things more efficiently.

In July a glum Democratic convention gathered in Philadelphia, expecting to do little more than go through the motions, only to find itself doubly surprised: first by the battle over the civil rights plank, and then by Truman's acceptance speech. To keep from stirring southern hostility, the administration sought a platform plank that opposed discrimination only in general terms. Activists, however, sponsored a plank that called on Congress for specific action and commended Truman "for his courageous stand on the issue of civil rights." Speaking last in favor of the change, Minneapolis Mayor Hubert H. Humphrey electrified the delegates and set off a ten-minute demonstration: "The time has arrived for the Democratic party to get out of the shadow of states' rights and walk forthrightly into the bright sunshine of human rights." Segregationist delegates from Alabama and Mississippi walked, instead, out of the convention.

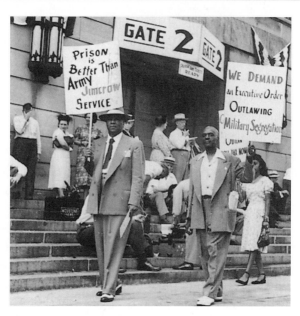

The opening of the 1948 Democratic National Convention is marked by demonstrations against racial segregation, led by A. Philip Randolph (left).

After the convention had nominated Truman, the president appeared on the rostrum during the wee hours of the morning to give his acceptance speech. It was a rousing, combative address, unlike most of his earlier speeches, which he usually read in a flat drone. Near the end he dropped a bombshell. He would call Congress back into session "to get the laws the people need."

A group of rebellious southerners, miffed by the party's civil rights plank, met in Birmingham, Alabama, and nominated South Carolina governor J. Strom Thurmond on a States' Rights Democratic ticket, quickly dubbed the "Dixiecrat" ticket. The Dixiecrats sought to draw enough electoral votes to preclude a majority for either major party, throwing the election into the House, where they might strike a sectional bargain. A few days later the left wing of the Democratic party gathered in Philadelphia to name Henry A. Wallace on a Progressive party ticket. These splits in the Democratic ranks seemed to spell the final blow to Truman. The special session of Congress petered out in futility.

But Truman, undaunted, set out on a 31,000-mile "whistle-stop" train tour during which he castigated the "do-nothing" Eightieth Congress, provoking cries from his audiences: "Pour it on, Harry!" and "Give 'em hell, Harry." Truman responded: "I don't give 'em hell. I just tell the truth and they think it's hell." Dewey, in contrast, ran a restrained campaign designed to avoid controversy. By so doing he may have snatched defeat from the jaws of victory.

To the end the polls and the pundits predicted a sure win for Dewey, and most speculation centered on his cabinet choices. But on election day Truman chalked up the biggest upset in American history, taking 24 million votes (49.5 percent) to Dewey's 22 million (45.1 percent) and winning a thumping 303 to 189 margin in the electoral college. Thurmond and Wallace each got more than a million votes, but the revolt of right and left worked to Truman's advantage. The Dixiecrat rebellion reassured black voters who had questioned the Democrats' commitment to civil rights, while the Progressive movement, which had received support from the Communist party, made it hard to tag Truman as "soft on Communism." Thurmond carried four Deep South states, and his

The Man Who "Done His Damndest." Truman's victory in 1948 was a huge upset.

success started a momentous disruption of the Democratic Solid South. But Truman's victory also carried Democratic majorities into Congress.

Truman viewed the outcome as a vindication for the New Deal and a mandate for liberalism. His State of the Union message repeated the agenda he had set forth a year previously. "Every segment of our population and every individual," he stressed, "has a right to expect from his government a fair deal." Whether deliberately or not, he had invented a tag, the "Fair Deal," to set off his program from the New Deal.

The president won approval of some of his Fair Deal proposals, but they were mainly extensions or enlargements of New Deal programs already in place: a higher minimum wage, bringing more people under Social Security, extension of rent controls, farm price supports, a sizable slum-clearance and public housing program, and more money for the TVA, rural electrification, and farm housing. Despite Democratic majorities in Congress, however, the conservative coalition disdained any drastic new departures in domestic policy. Congress balked at civil rights bills, national health insurance, federal aid to education, and a plan to provide subsidies that would hold up farm incomes rather than farm prices. Congress also turned down Truman's demand for repeal of the Taft-Hartley Act.

THE COLD WAR HEATS UP

Global concerns, never far from center stage in the postwar world, plagued Truman's second term, as they had his first. In his inaugural address he called for foreign policy to rest on four pillars: the United Nations, the Marshall Plan, NATO, and a "bold new plan" for technical assistance to underdeveloped parts of the world, a sort of global Marshall Plan that came to be known simply as "Point Four." This program to aid the postwar world began in 1950 with a modest outlay of $35 million. But it never accomplished its goals, in part because other international problems soon diverted Truman's attention.

"LOSING" CHINA AND THE BOMB   One of the most intractable problems, the China tangle, was fast coming unraveled in 1949. The Chinese Nationalists (Kuomintang) of Chiang Kai-shek had been fighting Mao Tse-tung[†] and the Communists since the 1920s. The outbreak of war with Japan in 1937 halted the civil war, and Roosevelt, and Stalin as well, believed that the Nationalists would organize China after the war.

The commanders of American forces in China during World War II, however, concluded that Chiang's government had become hopelessly corrupt, tyrannical, and inefficient. U.S. policy during and immediately after the war was to promote peace between the factions in China. But when the civil war resumed in 1945, American forces nevertheless ferried nationalist armies back into the eastern and northern provinces as the Japanese withdrew.

It soon became a losing fight for the Nationalists, as the Communists radicalized the land-hungry peasantry. By late 1948 the Communists were in Peking and heading southward. A year later they had taken the port city of Canton, and the Nationalist government had fled to the island of Formosa, which it renamed Taiwan.

From 1945 through 1949 the United States had funneled some $2 billion in aid to the Nationalists, to no avail. Administration critics asked bitterly: "Who lost China?" and a State Department report blamed Chiang for his failure to hold the support of the Chinese people. In fact it is hard to imagine how the United States government could have prevented the outcome short of military intervention, which would have been very risky, quite costly, and exceedingly unpopular. The United States continued to recognize the Nationalist government on Taiwan as the rightful government of China, delaying formal relations with Red China for thirty years. In an effort to shore up friendly governments in Asia, the United States in 1950 recognized the French-supported regime of Emperor Bao Dai in Vietnam and shortly afterward extended aid to the French in their battle against Ho Chi Minh's Vietnamese guerrillas.

As the Communists secured control in China, American intelligence in 1949 found evidence that the Soviets had set off an atomic explosion. The discovery of the Russian bomb provoked an intense reappraisal of the strategic balance in the world, causing Truman in 1950 to

[†]The traditional spellings are used in this text. After Mao's death the Chinese government adopted the "Pinyin" transliterations that are widely used today: Mao Tse-tung became Mao Zedong; and Peking became Beijing.

order the construction of a hydrogen bomb, a weapon far more powerful than the Hiroshima bomb, lest the Russians make one first. Another result was a National Security Council recommendation for rebuilding conventional military forces to provide options other than nuclear war. This represented a major departure from America's time-honored aversion to keeping large standing armies in peacetime, and was an expensive proposition. But the American public was growing more receptive to the nation's role as world leader, and an invasion of South Korea by Communist forces from the north clinched the issue for most.

WAR IN KOREA   The Japanese had occupied Korea during World War II, and after their defeat and withdrawal, the victorious Allies faced the difficult task of creating a new nation. Complicating that task was the fact that Russian troops had advanced into northern Korea and had accepted the surrender of Japanese forces above the 38th parallel, while American forces did the same south of the line. The Soviets quickly organized a Korean government along Stalinist lines while the Americans set up a Western-style regime in the south.

Like the division of Germany, the division of Korea at the 38th parallel in 1945 began as a temporary expedient and ended as a permanent fact. With the onset of the Cold War, it became clear that Soviet-American agreement on unification was no more likely in Korea than in Germany. By the end of 1948, separate regimes had appeared in the two sectors and occupation forces had withdrawn.

American leaders then inadvertently may have given false impressions to the Communists. General MacArthur and Secretary of State Dean Acheson omitted both Korea and Formosa (Taiwan) from an America defense perimeter that included the Philippines and Japan. The weakened state of the demobilizing American military contributed to the impression that South Korea was vulnerable. A growing body of evidence recently gleaned from Russian archives reveals that Stalin encouraged the North Koreans to use force to unify their country and oust the Americans from the peninsula. The Soviets helped design and ultimately approved a war plan that called for North Korean forces to seize Seoul within three days and all of South Korea within a week.

North Korean forces crossed the boundary on June 25, 1950, and swept down the peninsula. President Truman responded decisively. Korea might have been outside America's defense perimeter, but its southern tip was dangerously close to U.S.-occupied Japan. Besides, American policy remained subject to what might be called the "Munich syndrome," or what MacArthur called "history's clear lesson . . . that appeasement but begets new and bloodier war." Failure to act, Truman reasoned, would embolden Communist leaders "to override nations closer to our own shores."

An emergency meeting of the U.N. Security Council quickly censured the North Korean "breach of peace." The Soviet delegate, who held a veto power, was at the time boycotting the council because it would not seat Communist China in place of Nationalist China. On June 27, its first resolution having been ignored, the Security Council called on U.N. members to "furnish such assistance to the Republic of Korea (ROK) as may be necessary to repel the armed attack and to restore international peace and security in the area."

Truman ordered American air, naval, and ground forces into action. Eventually American forces numbered over 350,000 while the South Koreans contributed 400,000. In all, some fourteen other U.N. members sent in military units totaling about 50,000 men. Later, when the U.N. voted a unified command, it put General MacArthur in charge. The defense of South Korea remained chiefly an American affair, and one that set a precedent of profound consequence: war by order of the president rather than by vote of Congress. It had the sanction of the U.N. Security Council, to be sure, and could technically be considered a "police action," not a war. Other presidents had ordered American troops into action without a declaration of war, but never on such a scale.

For three months things went badly for the South Korean and U.N. forces. Soviet pilots battled American planes over South Korea. To mask their identity, the Soviets wore Chinese uniforms and used Chinese phrases over the radio. By September the ROK and U.N. forces were barely hanging on to the Pusan perimeter in the southeast corner of Korea. Then, in a brilliant ploy, on September 15, 1950, MacArthur landed a new force to the North Korean rear at Inchon. Synchronized with a breakout from Pusan, the sudden blow stampeded the enemy back across the border.

At this point MacArthur convinced Truman to allow him to push on and seek to reunify Korea. The Russian delegate was back in the Security Council, wielding his veto, so on October 7 the United States got approval for this course from the U.N. General Assembly, where the veto did not apply. American forces had already crossed the boundary into North Korea by October 1, and now continued northward against minimal resistance. President Truman, concerned over broad hints of Communist Chinese intervention, flew out to Wake Island for a conference with General MacArthur on October 15. There the general discounted chances that the Red Army would act, but if it did, he confidently predicted, "there would be the greatest slaughter."

That same day Peking announced that China "cannot stand idly by." On October 26, U.N. units reached the Yalu River border with China. MacArthur predicted total victory by Christmas, but on the night of November 25, thousands of Chinese "volunteers" counterattacked, and massive "human wave" attacks, with the support of tanks and planes, turned the tables on the U.N. forces, sending them into a desperate retreat just at the onset of winter. It had become "an entirely new war," MacArthur concluded. Soon he was reporting that the war dragged on because the administration refused to let him blockade China and use Taiwanese Nationalists to invade the mainland. MacArthur seemed to have forgotten altogether his one-time reluctance to bog down the country in a major war on the Asian mainland.

Truman opposed leading the United States into the "gigantic booby trap" of war with China, and the U.N. forces soon rallied. By January 1951, U.N. troops under General Matthew Ridgway finally secured their lines below Seoul, and then launched a counterattack that in some places carried them back across the 38th parallel in March. When Truman seized the chance and offered negotiations to restore the boundary, MacArthur undermined the move by issuing an ultimatum for China to make peace or be attacked. Truman decided then that he had no choice but to accept MacArthur's policy or fire him. Civilian control of the military was at stake, Truman later asserted, and he did not let it remain at stake very long. The Joint Chiefs of Staff all backed the decision, and on April 11, 1951, the president removed MacArthur from all his commands and replaced him with Ridgway.

Truman's action set off an uproar across the country, and a tumultuous reception greeted MacArthur upon his return home for the first time since 1937. His dramatic speech to a joint session of Congress provided the climactic event. "Once war is forced upon us," he maintained, "there is no alternative than to apply every available means to bring it to a swift end." A Senate investigation brought out the administration's arguments, best summarized by General Omar Bradley, chairman of the Joint Chiefs of Staff. The MacArthur strategy "would involve us in the wrong war at the wrong place at the wrong time and with the wrong enemy." Americans, nurtured on classic Western showdowns in which good always triumphed over evil, found the logic of limited war hard to swallow, but also found Bradley's logic persuasive.

On June 24, 1951, the Soviet representative at the United Nations proposed a cease-fire and armistice along the 38th parallel. A few days later Secretary of State Acheson accepted in principle. The U.N. China and North Korea responded favorably—at the time General Ridgway's "meat-grinder" offensive was inflicting severe losses. Truce talks started at Panmunjom on July 10, 1951, only to drag out for another two years while the fighting continued. The chief snags were prisoner exchanges and the insistence of South Korea's president on unification.

By the time a truce was finally reached on July 27, 1953, Truman had relinquished the White House to Dwight D. Eisenhower. The truce line followed the front at that time, mostly a little north of the 38th parallel, with a demilitarized zone of 2 1/2 miles separating the forces; repatriation of prisoners would be voluntary, supervised by a neutral commission. No final peace conference ever took place, and Korea, like Germany, remained divided. The war had cost the United States more than 33,000 deaths and 103,000 wounded and missing. South Korean casualties, all told, were about 1 million, and North Korean and Chinese casualties totaled an estimated 1.5 million.

ANOTHER RED SCARE   In calculating the costs of the Korean War one must add in the far-reaching consequences of the second Red Scare, which had grown since 1945 as the domestic counterpart to the Cold War abroad and reached a crescendo during the Korean conflict. Since 1938, a House Committee on Un-American Activities had kept up a barrage of accusations about subversives in government. On March 21, 1947, just nine days after the president announced the Truman Doctrine, he signed an executive order setting up procedures for an employee loyalty program in the federal government. Designed partly to protect the president's political flank, it failed to do so, mainly because of disclosures of earlier Communist penetrations into government that were few in number but sensational in character.

Perhaps the single case most damaging to the administration involved Alger Hiss, president of the Carnegie Endowment for International Peace, who had served in several government departments, including the State Department. Whittaker Chambers, a former Soviet agent and later an editor of *Time* magazine, told the House Un-American Activities Committee in 1948 that Hiss had given him secret documents ten years earlier, when Chambers worked for the Soviets. Hiss sued for libel, and Chambers produced microfilms of the State Department documents he claimed Hiss had passed on to him. Hiss denied the accusation, whereupon he was indicted for perjury and, after one mistrial, convicted in 1950.

Most damaging to the administration was the fact that President Truman, taking at face value the many testimonials to Hiss's integrity, called the charges against him a "red herring." Secretary of State Dean Acheson compounded the damage when, meaning to express compassion, he pledged not "to turn my back on Alger Hiss." The Hiss affair had another political consequence: it raised to national prominence a young California congressman, Richard M. Nixon, who doggedly insisted on pursuing the case and then exploited an anti-Communist stance to win election to the Senate in 1950.

Senator Joseph McCarthy.

More cases surfaced. In 1950 the government disclosed the existence of a British-American spy network that had fed information about the development of the atomic bomb to Russia. These disclosures led to the arrest of, among others, Julius and Ethel Rosenberg. The Rosenbergs, convicted of espionage in wartime, were executed in 1953.

MCCARTHY'S WITCH-HUNT   Such revelations encouraged politicians to exploit public fears. If a man of such respectability as Hiss was guilty, many wondered, who then could be trusted? Early in 1950 the hitherto obscure Republican senator from Wisconsin, Joseph R. McCarthy, suddenly surfaced as the shrewdest and most ruthless exploiter of such anxieties. He took up the cause, or at least the pose, of anticommunism with a vengeance. He began with a speech at Wheeling, West Virginia, on February 9, 1950, in which he claimed that the State Department was infested with Communists and that he held in his hand a list of their names. Later there was confusion as to whether he had said 205, 81, 57, or "a lot" of names, and even whether the sheet of paper carried a list. But such confusion always pursued McCarthy's charges.

Challenged to provide names, McCarthy finally pointed to Owen Lattimore of the Johns Hopkins University, an Asia expert, as head of "the espionage ring in the State Department." A special Senate committee looked into the matter and pronounced McCarthy's charges "a fraud and a hoax." McCarthy then turned, in what became his common tactic, to other charges, other names. McCarthy never uncovered a single Communist agent in government. But with the United States at war with Korean Communists in mid-1950, he continued to mobilize true believers behind his crusade. Republicans encouraged him to keep up the game. By 1951 he was riding so high as to list Generals George C. Marshall and Dwight D. Eisenhower among the disloyal. He kept up his campaign without successful challenge until the end of the Korean War.

Under the influence of the anti-Communist hysteria the Congress in 1950 passed the McCarran Internal Security Act over President Truman's veto. The act required Communist and Communist-front organizations to register with the attorney-general. Aliens who had belonged to totalitarian parties were barred from admission to the United States, a provision that, ironically, also discouraged any temptation for lapsed Communists to defect to the United States.

ASSESSING THE COLD WAR   In retrospect, the onset of the Cold War takes on an appearance of terrible inevitability. America's preference for international principles, such as self-determination and democracy, conflicted with Stalin's preference for international spheres of influence. Russia, after all, had suffered two German invasions in the first half of the twentieth century, and Soviet leaders wanted tame buffer states on their borders for protection. The people of eastern Europe, as usual, were caught in the middle. But the Communists themselves held to a universal principle: world revolution. And since the time of President Monroe, Americans had bristled at the thought of foreign intervention in their own sphere of influence, the Western Hemisphere.

If international conditions set the stage for the Cold War, the actions of political leaders and thinkers set events in motion. President Truman may have erred in suggesting that the United States must intervene anywhere in the world to stop the tide of Communist aggression. His loyalty program, following on the heels of the Truman Doctrine, may have spurred on the anti-Communist hysteria of the times.

The years after World War II were unlike any other postwar era in American history. Having taken on global burdens, the nation had become, if not a "garrison state," at least a country committed to a major and permanent national military establishment. By 1952 this newly entrenched sector of the government included the National Security Council, the Central Intelligence Agency, and the enormous National Security Agency, entrusted with the monitoring of media and communications for foreign intelligence.

The policy initiatives of the Truman years had led the country to abandon its long-standing aversion to peacetime alliances. It was a far cry from the world of 1796, when George Washington in his Farewell Address warned against "those overgrown military establishments which . . . are inauspicious to liberty" and advised his country "to steer clear of permanent alliances with any portion of the foreign world." But, then, Washington had warned only against participation in the "ordinary" combinations and collisions of Europe, and surely the postwar years had seen extraordinary events and unprecedented combinations.

MAKING CONNECTIONS

- The Cold War had a major impact on American society; among other things, it helped create the "conforming culture" described in the next chapter.

- The New Frontier and Great Society programs of Presidents Kennedy and Johnson accomplished much of what Truman tried to do through his Fair Deal policies. See Chapter 33.

- The world seemed a dangerous place at the height of the Cold War, but when seen from the perspective of the post–Cold War world of the 1990s, it had a certain order that discouraged political violence. See Chapter 36.

FURTHER READING

The origins of the Cold War are still hotly debated. Traditional interpretations by John L. Gaddis in *The United States and the Origins of the Cold War, 1941–1947* (1972)* can be balanced with the revisionist view in Walter LaFeber's *America, Russia, and the Cold War, 1945–1980* (1981).* Also see Melvyn P. Leffler's *A Preponderance of Power: National Security, the Truman Administration, and the Cold War* (1992),* Gaddis's *The Long Peace: Inquiries Into the History of the Cold War* (1993),* and Wilson D. Miscamble's *George F. Kennan and the Making of American Foreign Policy* (1992).*

The anti-Communist syndrome is surveyed in David Caute's *The Great Fear: The Anti-Communist Purge under Truman and Eisenhower* (1978).* Thomas C. Reeves's *The Life and Times of Joe McCarthy* (1982)* analyzes McCarthy himself. Allen Weinstein's *Perjury! The Hiss-Chambers Conflict* (1978)* covers that subject well. For a well-documented account of how the Cold War was sustained by superpatriotism, intolerance, and suspicion, see Stephen J. Whitfield's *The Culture of the Cold War* (1990).*

*These books are available in paperback editions.

31 THROUGH THE PICTURE WINDOW: SOCIETY AND CULTURE, 1945–1960

CHAPTER ORGANIZER

This chapter focuses on:

- the economic prosperity of America in the postwar period

- the culture of the 1950s, with its strains of conformity and innovation

- America's burgeoning consumer culture

Americans emerged from World War II elated, proud of their military strength and industrial might. As the editors of *Fortune* magazine proclaimed in 1946, "This is a dream era, this is what everyone was waiting through the blackouts for. The Great American Boom is on." So it was, from babies to Buicks to Admiral television sets. An American public that had known deprivation and sacrifice for the last decade and a half began to enjoy unprecedented prosperity. The postwar era enjoyed tremendous economic growth and seeming social contentment.

Yet in the midst of such rising affluence and optimism, many social critics, writers, and artists expressed a growing sense of unease. Was postwar American society becoming too complacent, too conformist, too materialistic? These questions reflected the perennial tension in American life between idealism and materialism, a tension that arrived with the first settlers and remains with us today. Americans have always struggled to accumulate goods and cultivate goodness. During the postwar era the nation tried to do both, and for a while, at least, it appeared to succeed.

PEOPLE OF PLENTY

The dominant feature of post–World War II American society was its remarkable prosperity. After a surprisingly brief postwar recession, the economy soared to record heights. The gross national product (GNP) nearly doubled between 1945 and 1960, and the 1960s witnessed an even more spectacular expansion of the economy. By 1970 the gap between living standards in the United States and the rest of the world had become a chasm: with 6 percent of the world's population, Americans produced and consumed nearly two-thirds of the world's goods.

Such abundance generated a mood of giddy optimism. During the 1950s government officials assured the citizenry that they should not fear another economic collapse. The leading economists of the postwar era agreed that the New Deal safeguards built into the economy would prevent another dramatic downturn. They and others led the public to believe that perpetual economic growth was possible, desirable, and, in fact, essential. The expectation of unending plenty thus became the reigning assumption of social thought in the two decades after 1945.

Several factors contributed to this sustained economic surge. The massive federal expenditures for military needs during World War II, which had catapulted the economy out of the depression, continued to drive the postwar economy, thanks to the tensions generated by the Cold War and the increase in defense spending provoked by the Korean conflict. Military-related research also helped spawn the new glamour industries of the postwar era: chemicals, electronics, and aviation.

Most of the other major industrial nations of the world—England, France, Germany, Japan, the Soviet Union—had been physically devastated during the war, which meant that American manufacturers enjoyed a virtual monopoly over international trade. In addition, the widespread use of new and more efficient machinery and computers led to a 35 percent jump in the productivity of American workers between 1945 and 1955.

The major catalyst in promoting economic expansion after 1945 was the unleashing of pent-up consumer demand. During the war Americans had postponed purchases of major items such as cars and houses, and in the process had saved over $150 billion. Now they were eager to buy. Likewise, many young adults who had delayed having a family were also intent upon making up for lost time. The United States after World War II experienced both a purchasing frenzy and a population explosion.

THE GI BILL OF RIGHTS   Part of the purchasing frenzy was financed by the federal government. People feared that a sharp drop in military spending and the sudden influx of veterans back into the civilian workforce would send the economy into a downward spiral and produce widespread unemployment. Such concerns led Congress to pass by a unanimous vote the Servicemen's Readjustment Act of 1944. Popularly known as the GI Bill of Rights (GI meant "government issue," a phrase stamped on military uniforms and also slang for a serviceman), it led to the creation of a new government agency, the Veterans Administration. The GI Bill also included provisions for mustering out pay, unemployment pay for one year, preference for civil-service jobs, loans for home construction, access to government hospitals, and generous subsidies for college or professional training.

The infusion of funds into the economy provided by the GI Bill helped fuel the postwar prosperity. Almost 8 million veterans took advantage of $14.5 billion in GI Bill subsidies to attend college. Some 5 million people used additional monies from the GI Bill to buy new suburban homes. These two programs combined to produce a social revolution.

The educational benefits of the GI Bill encouraged many people to consider pursuing higher education for the first time. Before World War II, approximately 160,000 Americans graduated from college each year. By 1950 the figure had more than tripled. In 1949 veterans accounted for 40 percent of all college enrollments, and the United States could boast the world's best-educated work force. The influx of veterans onto campuses caught university administrators by surprise. Classrooms and dormitories overflowed with students, and many of the grizzled war veterans quickly grew impatient with parietal rules intended for traditional students.

The GI Bill also served to democratize higher education. It provided a generation of working-class Americans an opportunity to earn a college degree for the first time. In turn, a college education served as a lever into the middle class and economic security. But while the GI Bill helped erode class barriers, it was less successful in dismantling racial barriers. Many black veterans could not take advantage of the education benefits. Most colleges and universities after the war remained racially segregated, either by regulation or by practice. Almost 80 percent of the black population after the war resided in the southern states.

But racial prejudice was nationwide. Of the 9,000 students enrolled at the University of Pennsylvania in 1946, for example, only 46 were African Americans. Throughout the 1940s, Princeton University debated whether to admit blacks. Those blacks who did manage to gain admission to white colleges or universities were barred from playing on athletic teams, attending dances and other social events, and joining fraternities or sororities.

The historically black colleges, almost all of which were in the South, could not expand quickly enough to meet the demand. In 1940 black colleges enrolled 43,000 students; in 1950 the number had soared to 77,000. Yet over 20,000 were denied admission because of overcrowded facilities. As a result, most black veterans did not get into a college. In 1946 only one-fifth of the 100,000 who had applied for educational benefits had enrolled. In other cases, black veterans were inadequately prepared for college-level work. As late as 1950, some 70 percent of black adults in the southern states had only a seventh-grade education or less.

The return of some 12 million veterans to private life also helped generate a postwar "baby boom," which peaked in 1957. Between 1946 and 1964 America's total population grew by almost 40 million, a whopping 30 percent increase. Such a dramatic growth rate had a host of reverberating effects. Indeed, much of America's social history since the 1940s has been the story of the unusually large baby-boom generation and its progress through the stages of life. Initially the baby boom created a massive demand for diapers, baby food, toys, medicines, schools, books, teachers, and housing. It also spurred the growth of new suburban communities as the burgeoning population moved from the cities into the countryside.

AN EXPANDING CONSUMER CULTURE   American factories soon adjusted to new consumer demands. Native and foreign observers alike marveled at the widespread abundance generated by America's prolific industrial plant. In 1950 almost 37 percent of American homes were deemed substandard, in 1970 only 9 percent. The proportion of homeowners in the population increased by 50 percent between 1945 and 1960. And those new homes were increasingly filled with the latest electrical appliances—refrigerators, washing machines, sewing machines, vacuum cleaners, freezers, and mixers.

By far the most popular new household product was the television set. In 1946 there were only 7,000 primitive black-and-white sets in the country; by 1960 there were 50 million high-quality sets. Nine out of ten homes had one, and by 1970, 38 percent owned new color sets. *TV Guide* was the fastest-growing new periodical of the 1950s, and the new television culture had a transforming effect on the patterns of daily living. Time previously devoted to reading, visiting, playing, or movie-going was now spent in front of the "electronic hearth."

"I Love Lucy," starring Lucille Ball (right), *was one of the most popular television series in the 1950s.*

What differentiated the affluence of the post–World War II era from earlier periods of prosperity was its ever-widening dispersion. Although pockets of rural and urban poverty persisted, destined to explode in the 1960s, during the 1950s few noticed such exceptions to the prevailing prosperity. After being sworn in as head of the AFL-CIO in 1955, George Meany proclaimed that "American labor never had it so good."

To perpetuate such prosperity, economists repeated the basic marketing strategy of the 1920s: the public must be taught to consume more and expect more. Experts knew that people had more money than ever before. The average American had twice as much *real* income in 1955 as in the rosy days of the late 1920s before the crash. Still, many adults who had undergone the severities of the depression and the rationing required for the war effort had to be weaned from a decade and a half of imposed frugality in order to nourish the consumer culture. A motivational researcher told a business group that the fundamental challenge facing the modern capitalist economy was to demonstrate to the consumer that "the hedonistic approach to life is a moral, not an immoral one."

Advertising became a more crucial component of the consumer culture than ever before. TV advertising expenditures increased 1,000 percent during the 1950s. Such startling results led the president of the National Broadcasting Company (NBC) to claim in 1956 that the primary reason for the postwar economic boom was that "advertising has created an American frame of mind that makes people want more things, better things and newer things."

Paying for such "things" was no problem; the age of the credit card had arrived. Between 1945 and 1957, consumer credit soared 800 percent. Where families in other industrialized nations were typically saving 10 to 20 percent of their income, American families by the 1960s were saving only 5 percent. "Never before have so many owed so much to so many," *Newsweek* announced in 1953. "Time has swept away the Puritan conception of immorality in debt and godliness in thrift."

This consumer revolution had far-reaching cultural effects. Shopping, for instance, became a major recreational activity. In 1945 there were only eight shopping centers in the entire country; by 1960 there were almost 4,000. Much as life in a medieval town revolved around the cathedral, life in postwar suburban America seemed to center on the new giant shopping centers and malls.

Young Americans especially participated in this shopping culture. By the late 1950s the baby boom generation was entering its teens, and the disproportionate number of affluent adolescents generated a vast new specialized market for goods ranging from transistor radios, hula hoops, and rock-and-roll records to cameras, surfboards, *Seventeen* magazine, and Pat Boone movies. Most teenagers had far more discretionary income than previous generations. Teens in the postwar era knew nothing of depressions or rationing; they were immersed in abundance from an early age and took the notion of carefree consumption for granted.

THE CRABGRASS FRONTIER   The population increase of the 1950s and 1960s was an urban as well as a suburban phenomenon. Dramatic new technological advances in agricultural production reduced the need for manual laborers and thereby led 20 million Americans to leave the land for the city between 1940 and 1970. Much of the urban population growth occurred in the South, the Southwest, and the West, in an arc that stretched from the Carolinas down through Texas and into California, diverse states that by the 1970s were being lumped together into the "Sunbelt." The dispersion of air conditioning throughout these warm regions dramatically enhanced their attraction to northerners. But the Northeast remained the most densely populated area; by the early 1960s, 20 percent of the national population lived in the corridor that stretched from Boston to Norfolk, Virginia.

While more concentrated in cities, Americans after World War II were simultaneously spreading out within metropolitan areas. In 1950 the Census Bureau redefined the term "urban" to include suburbs as well as central cities. During the 1950s suburbs grew six times faster than cities. By 1970 more Americans lived in suburbs (76 million) than in central cities (64 million). "Suburbia," proclaimed the *Christian Century* in 1955, "is now a dominant social group in American life."

William Levitt, a brassy New York developer, led the suburban revolution. In 1947, on 1,200 acres of flat Long Island farmland, he built 10,600 houses that were immediately sold and inhabited by more than 40,000 people—mostly adults under thirty-five and their children. "Everyone is so young," one Levittowner noted, "that sometimes it's hard to remember how to get along with older people."

Within a few years there were similar Levittowns in Pennsylvania and New Jersey, and other developers soon followed suit around the coun-

Moving Day, 1953. *A new subdivision opens its doors.*

try. The federal government aggressively fostered this suburban revolution. "If it weren't for the government," a San Francisco developer explained, "the boom would end overnight." By insuring loans for up to 95 percent of the value of a house, the Federal Housing Administration made it easy for a builder to borrow money to construct low-cost homes. Military veterans were given added benefits. A veteran could buy a Levitt house with no down payment and monthly installments of $56.

Expanded automobile production and highway construction also facilitated the rush to the suburbs, as more and more people were able to commute longer distances to work. Car production soared from 2 million in 1946 to 8 million in 1955, and a "car culture" soon emerged. As one commentator observed, the proliferation of automobiles "changed our dress, manners, social customs, vacation habits, the shape of our cities, consumer purchasing patterns, and common tastes." Widespread car ownership also necessitated an improved road network. Local and state governments built many new roads, but the guiding force was the federal government. In 1947 Congress authorized the construction of 37,000 miles of highways, and nine years later it funded 42,000 additional miles of interstate expressways.

Such new roads provided access to the suburbs, and Americans— mostly young middle-class white Americans—rushed to take advantage of the new living spaces. Motives for moving to the suburbs were numerous. The availability of more spacious homes as well as greater security and better educational opportunities for children all played a role. Racial considerations were also a factor. After World War II blacks migrated in record numbers from the rural South into the cities of the North, Midwest, and West. And as they moved in, white residents moved out. Those engaged in "white flight" were usually eager to maintain residential segregation in their new suburban communities. Contracts for homes in Levittown, Long Island, for example, specifically excluded "members of other than the Caucasian race." Such discrimination, whether explicit or implicit, was widespread; the nation's suburban population in 1970 was 95 percent white.

THE GREAT BLACK MIGRATION   World War II, like World War I, helped spur a mass migration of rural southern blacks to the cities of other regions. This second great migration was much larger in scope than the first, and its social consequences were much more dramatic. After 1945 more than 5 million southern blacks, mostly farm folk, left their native region in search of better jobs, higher wages, decent housing, and greater social equality. During the 1950s, for example, the black population of Chicago more than doubled. As many as 2,000 migrants a week arrived at the Illinois Central train station. The South Side of Chicago soon became known as the capital of black America. It remains the largest concentration of African Americans in the country. In its scope and effects, this internal migration of blacks from South to North was every bit as significant as the settlement of the West.

Many of these southern blacks were sharecroppers and farm laborers from the Mississippi Delta, the richest cotton-producing land in the world. For over a century the Delta cotton culture had been dependent on black workers, first as slaves and then as sharecroppers and wage laborers. But a more efficient mechanical cotton picker invented in 1944 changed all that. The new machine could do the work of fifty people, thus making many farm workers superfluous. Displaced southern blacks, many of them illiterate and provincial, streamed northward in search of a new promised land, only to see their dreams dashed. The great writer Richard Wright, himself a migrant from the Delta to Chicago, observed that "never in history has a more utterly unprepared folk wanted to go to the city." In northern cities such as Chicago,

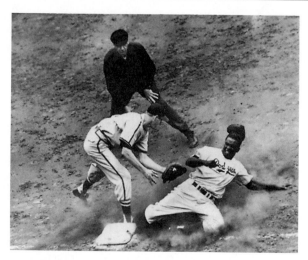

Jackie Robinson, 1949. *Racial discrimination remained widespread through the postwar period. In 1947 Jackie Robinson of the Brooklyn Dodgers became the first black to play major-league baseball.*

Philadelphia, Newark, Detroit, New York, Boston, and Washington, D.C., rural blacks confronted harsh new realities. Slumlords gouged them for rent, employers refused to hire them, and union bosses denied them membership. Soon the promised land had become an ugly nightmare of slum housing, joblessness, illiteracy, dysfunctional families, welfare dependency, street gangs, pervasive crime, and racism.

The unexpected tidal wave of black migrants severely taxed the resources of urban governments and the patience of white urban dwellers. For several nights during 1951, a white mob in a Chicago suburb assaulted a building into which a black family had moved. The National Guard had to quell the disturbance and disperse the crowd. Like other northern cities, Chicago sought to deal with the migrants and alleviate racial stress by constructing massive, all-black public housing projects to accommodate the newcomers. These overcrowded racial enclaves, however, soon came to resemble segregated prisons. To be sure, many black migrants and their children did manage through extraordinary determination and ingenuity to "clear," that is, to climb out of the teeming ghettos and into the middle class. But most did not. As a consequence, the great black migration produced a complex social problem that in the 1960s would burgeon into a crisis.

A CONFORMING CULTURE

In the 1950s, however, white middle-class America mostly ignored people and cultures outside the mainstream. As evidenced in many of the new look-alike suburbs sprouting up across the land, much of middle-class social life during the two decades after the end of World War II exhibited an increasingly homogenized character. Fears generated by the Cold War initially played a key role in encouraging orthodoxy, but suburban life itself encouraged uniformity. In new communities of strangers, people quickly felt a need for companionship and a sense of belonging. "Nobody wants people around who criticize and sit off by themselves and don't take part," observed one resident.

CORPORATE LIFE   Changes in corporate life also played an important socializing role. "Conformity," predicted an editor in 1954, "may very well become the central social problem of this age." During World War II big business grew bigger. The government relaxed antitrust activity, and huge defense contracts tended to promote corporate concentration and consolidation. In 1940, for example, 100 companies were responsible for 30 percent of all manufacturing output; three years later they were providing 70 percent. In such huge companies as well as in similarly large government agencies and universities, the working atmosphere began to take on a distinctive new cast. The traditional notion of the hard-working, strong-minded individual advancing by dint of competitive ability and creative initiative gave way to a new managerial personality and an ethic of collective cooperation and achievement.

WOMEN'S "PLACE"   Increasing conformity in middle-class business and corporate life was mirrored in the middle-class home. A special issue of *Life* magazine in 1956 featured the "ideal" middle-class woman, a thirty-two-year-old "pretty and popular" suburban housewife, mother of four, who had married at age sixteen. Described as an excellent wife, mother, hostess, volunteer, and "home manager" who made her own clothes, she hosted dozens of dinner parties each year, sang in the church choir, worked with the PTA and Campfire Girls, and was devoted to her husband. "In her daily round," *Life* reported, "she attends club or charity meetings, drives the children to school, does the weekly

The Ideal Woman. *A 1956* Life *magazine cover story pronounced the ideal woman a "pretty and popular" suburban housewife who "attends club or charity meetings, drives the children to school, does the weekly grocery shopping, makes ceramics, and is planning to study French."*

grocery shopping, makes ceramics, and is planning to study French." She also exercised on a trampoline in order "to keep her size 12 figure."

Life's ideal of the middle-class woman symbolized a veritable cult of feminine domesticity that witnessed a dramatic revival in the postwar era. The soaring birth rate reinforced the deeply embedded notion that a woman's place was in the home as tender of the hearth and guardian of the children. "Of all the accomplishments of the American woman," the *Life* cover story proclaimed, "the one she brings off with the most spectacular success is having babies."

So even though millions of women had responded to intense wartime appeals and joined "Rosie the Riveter" in the traditionally male work force, afterward they were encouraged—and even forced—to turn their jobs over to the returning veterans and resume their full-time commitment to home and family. An article in *House Beautiful* in 1945 lectured women on their postwar responsibilities. The ex-serviceman was "head man again. . . . Your part in the remaking of this man is to fit his home to him, understanding why he wants it this way, forgetting your own preferences." Women were also to forget any thoughts of continuing their own careers in the workplace. "Back to the kitchen" was the repeated refrain after 1945. Although many married women kept their jobs after the war, more of them, willingly or unwillingly, returned to their traditional domestic roles.

Throughout the postwar era, educators, politicians, ministers, advertisers, and other commentators exalted the cult of domesticity and castigated the few feminists who were encouraging women to broaden their horizons beyond crib and kitchen. Even a liberal politician and self-styled progressive intellectual such as Adlai Stevenson reminded Smith College graduates that their heroic purpose in life was to "influence man and boy" in the "humble role of housewife."

RELIGIOUS REVIVAL Another illustration of the conformist tendencies of middle-class life during the 1950s was the spiraling growth of membership in social institutions. Americans, even more than usual, became joiners; they joined civic clubs, garden clubs, bridge clubs, car pools, and babysitting groups.

They also joined churches and synagogues in record numbers. The postwar era witnessed a massive renewal of religious participation, and the Cold War was a strong impetus behind the awakening. "Since Communists are anti-God," FBI director J. Edgar Hoover advised, "encourage your child to be active in the church." Many American parents heeded his warning. In 1940 less than half of the adult population belonged to churches; by 1960 over 65 percent were official communicants. Bible sales soared, and books, movies, and songs with religious themes were stunning commercial successes. Hollywood glamour girl Jane Russell, hitherto noted more for her buxom bosom and sultry smile than her spiritual intensity, was one of many celebrities who promoted the religious revival. "I Love God," she confessed. "And when you get to know him, he's a livin' doll."

President Eisenhower also promoted a patriotic crusade to bring Americans back to God. "Recognition of the Supreme Being," he declared, "is the first, the most basic, expression of Americanism. Without God, there could be no American form of government, nor an American way of life." Not to be outdone in professing piety, Congress in 1954 added the phrase "one nation under God" to the pledge of allegiance. The following year it made the statement "In God We Trust" mandatory on all American currency.

The prevailing tone of the popular religious revival during the 1950s was upbeat and soothing. Many ministers assumed that people were not interested in "fire-and-brimstone" harangues from the pulpit; they did not want their consciences overly burdened with a sense of personal sin or social guilt over such issues as segregation or inner-city poverty. Instead they wanted to be reassured that their own comfortable way of life was indeed God's will. As the Protestant Council of New York City explained to its corps of radio and television speakers, their messages "should project love, joy, courage, hope, faith, trust in God, good will. Generally avoid condemnation, criticism, controversy. In a very real sense we are 'selling' religion, the good news of the Gospel."

By far the best salesman of this gospel of reassuring "good news" was the Reverend Norman Vincent Peale, the impresario of "positive thinking" and feel-good theology. No speaker was more in demand during the 1950s, and no writer was more widely read. Peale's book *The Power of Positive Thinking* (1952) was a phenomenal best-seller throughout the decade—and for good reason. It offered a simple "how-to" course in personal happiness. "Flush out all depressing, negative, and tired thoughts," Peale advised. "Start thinking faith, enthusiasm, and joy." By following this simple formula for success, he pledged, the reader could become "a more popular, esteemed, and well-liked individual."

Peale's message of psychological security and material success was powerfully reassuring, and many Americans stood in need of reassurance. That tranquilizers were the fastest growing new medication suggested that considerable anxiety accompanied America's much-trumpeted affluence. Many Americans were profoundly anxious about the meaning of their lives and of life in general in the nuclear age. Peale offered them peace of mind and peace of soul, assuring them that everything was fine and for the best as long as they believed in God, the American Way, and themselves. "Stop worrying and start living" was his simple credo.

NEO-ORTHODOXY   But was it too simplistic? The "positive thinking" psychology promoted by Peale and others struck some members of the religious community as shallow and dangerously misleading. Champions of a "neo-orthodox" theology charged that such consoling religiosity lacked genuine conviction and commitment.

The leader of the "neo-orthodox" movement was Reinhold Niebuhr (1892–1970). A brilliant preacher-professor at New York's Union Theological Seminary, Niebuhr repeatedly lashed out at the "undue complacency and conformity" settling over American life in the postwar era. He found the popular religion of self-assurance and the psychology of material success promoted by Peale and his followers woefully inadequate prescriptions for the ills of modern society. "They cannot be taken seriously by responsible religious or secular people," he warned in 1955, "because they do not come to terms with the basic collective problems of our atomic age, and because the peace which they seek to inculcate is rather too simple and neat." True peace, Niebuhr insisted, entailed the reality of pain, a pain "caused by love and responsibility" for the well-being of the entire human race, rather than to be solely concerned with one's tortured self. Self-love, he reminded smug Americans, was the very basis of sin.

CRACKS IN THE PICTURE WINDOW

Niebuhr was one of many impassioned disturbers of the peace who challenged the moral complacency and social conformity that he and others claimed had come to characterize American social life during the 1950s and early 1960s. As the philosopher and editor Joseph Wood Krutch recognized in 1960, "the gap between those who find the spirit of the age congenial and those who do not seems to have grown wider and wider."

THE LONELY CROWD   The criticism of postwar American life and values began in the early 1950s and quickly gathered momentum among intellectuals, theologians, novelists, playwrights, poets, and artists. Social scientists, too, attacked the prevailing optimism of the time. In *The Affluent Society* (1958), for example, economist John Kenneth Galbraith warned that sustained economic growth would not necessarily solve chronic social problems. He reminded readers that for all of America's vaunted postwar prosperity, the nation had yet to confront, much less eradicate, the chronic poverty plaguing the nation's inner cities and rural hamlets.

Postwar cultural critics also questioned the supposed bliss offered by middle-class suburban life. John Keats, in *The Crack in the Picture Window* (1956), launched the most savage assault on life in the huge new suburban developments. He ridiculed Levittown and other such mass-produced communities as having been "conceived in error, nurtured in greed, corroding everything they touch." In these rows of "identical boxes spreading like gangrene," commuter fathers were always at work and "mothers were always delivering children, obstetrically once and by car forever after." Locked into a deadly routine, hounded by financial insecurity, and engulfed by mass mediocrity, suburbanites, he concluded, were living in a "homogeneous, postwar Hell."

Social critics repeatedly cited the huge modern corporation as an equally important source of regimentation in American life. The most comprehensive and provocative analysis of the docile new corporate character was David Riesman's *The Lonely Crowd* (1950). Riesman, a social psychologist, detected a fundamental shift in the dominant American personality from what he called the "inner-directed" to the "other-directed" type. Inner-directed people, Riesman argued, possessed a deeply internalized set of basic values implanted by strong-minded parents or other elders. This core set of fixed principles, analogous to the traditional Protestant ethic of piety, diligence, and thrift, acted, in his words, like an internal gyroscope. Inner-directed people had a built-in stabilizer of fixed values that kept them on course.

Such an assured, self-reliant personality, Riesman claimed, had been dominant in American life throughout the nineteenth century. But during the mid-twentieth century a new, other-directed personality had displaced it. In the huge, hierarchical corporations that abounded in postwar America, employees who could win friends and influence people thrived; rugged individualists indifferent to personal popularity did not. The other-directed people who adapted to this corporate culture had few internal convictions and standards; they did not follow their conscience so much as adapt to the prevailing standards of the moment. They were more concerned with being well liked than being independent.

Riesman amassed considerable evidence to show that the other-directed personality was not just an aspect of the business world; its characteristics were widely dispersed throughout middle-class life. One source of this may have been Dr. Benjamin Spock's influential advice on raising children. Spock's popular manual, *The Common Sense Book of Baby and Child Care,* sold an average of 1 million copies a year between its first appearance in 1946 and 1960. Although Spock never endorsed the anarchic permissiveness attributed to him by later critics, he did insist that parents should foster in their children qualities and skills that would enhance their chances in what Riesman called the "popularity market." Reisman charged that this made the middle-class mother a "chauffeur and booking agent," determined to "cultivate all the currently essential talents, especially the gregarious ones. It is inconceivable to some that a child might prefer his own company or that of just another child."

ALIENATION IN THE ARTS   Many of the best novels and plays of the postwar period reinforced Riesman's image of modern American society as a "lonely crowd" of individuals, hollow at the core, groping for a sense of belonging and affection. Arthur Miller's much-celebrated play *Death of a Salesman* (1949) powerfully explored this theme. Willy Loman, an aging, confused traveling salesman in decline, centers his life and that of his family on the notion of material success through personal popularity, only to be abruptly told by his boss that he is in fact a failure. Loman repeatedly insists that it is "not what you say, it's how you say it—because personality always wins the day," and he tries to raise his sons, Biff and Happy, in his own image, encouraging them to be athletic, outgoing, popular, and ambitious. As he instructs them: "Be liked and you will never want." Happy had followed his father's advice but was anything but happy: "Sometimes I sit in my apartment—all alone. And I think of the rent I'm paying. And it's crazy. But then, it's what I always wanted. My own apartment, a car, and plenty of women. And still, goddammit, I'm lonely."

Such vacant loneliness is the play's recurring theme. Willy, for all his puffery about being well liked, admits that he is "terribly lonely." He has no real friends; even his relations with his family are neither honest nor intimate. "He never knew who he was," Biff sighs. Indeed, when Willy finally realizes that he has been leading a counterfeit existence, he yearns for a life in which "a man is not a piece of fruit," but eventually he is so haunted and dumbfounded by his predicament that he decides he can endow his life with meaning only by ending it.

Death of a Salesman and many other postwar plays written by Arthur Miller, Edward Albee, and Tennessee Williams portray a central theme of American literature and art during the postwar era: the sense of alienation experienced by sensitive individuals in the midst of an oppressive mass culture. In the aftermath of the horrors of World War II and the Holocaust, and in the midst of the nuclear terror, many of the country's foremost writers, painters, and poets refused to embrace the prevailing celebration of modern American life and values. The novelist Philip Roth observed in 1961: "The American writer in the middle of the twentieth century has his hands full in trying to understand, and then describe, and then make credible much of American reality. It stupefies, it sickens, it infuriates, and finally it is even a kind of embarrassment to one's own meager imagination." Roth's gloomy assessment illustrated the revulsion felt by other writers and artists, many of whom were determined to lay bare the conceits and illusions of their times.

While millions were reading heartwarming religious epics such as *The Cardinal* (1950), *The Robe* (1953), and *Exodus* (1957), literary critics were praising the more unsettling and sobering novels of James Baldwin, Saul Bellow, John Cheever, Ralph Ellison, Joseph Heller, James Jones, Norman Mailer, Joyce Carol Oates, J. D. Salinger, William Styron, John Updike, and Eudora Welty. There were few happy endings here—and even fewer celebrations of contemporary American life. J. D. Salinger's *The Catcher in the Rye* (1951) was an unsettling exploration of a young man's search for meaning and self in a smothering society. Holden Caulfield finally decides that rebellion against conformity is useless. "If you want to stay alive," he concludes, "you have to say that stuff, like 'Glad to meet you' to people you are not at all glad to meet."

This brooding sense of resigned alienation dominated the best literature in the two decades after 1945. The characters in novels such as Jones's *From Here to Eternity*, Ellison's *The Invisible Man*, Bellow's *Dangling Man* and *Seize the Day*, Styron's *Lie Down in Darkness*, and Updike's *Rabbit, Run*, among many others, tended to be like Willy Loman—restless, tormented, impotent individuals who are unable to fasten on a satisfying self-image and therefore can find neither contentment nor respect in an overpowering or impersonal world.

Office in a Small City. *Edward Hopper's 1953 painting suggests the alienation associated with white-collar work and a new corporate atmosphere in the 1950s.*

PAINTING   The artist Edward Hopper (1882–1967) adopted a similar outlook in his paintings. From the start of his career at the turn of the century, Hopper had explored the theme of desolate loneliness in urban-industrial American life. But his concern grew more acute in the postwar era. Virtually all of his paintings depict isolated individuals, melancholy, anonymous, motionless. A woman undressing for bed, a diner in an all-night restaurant, a housewife in a doorway, a businessman at his desk, a lone passerby in the street—these are the characters in Hopper's world. The silence of his scenes is deafening, the monotony striking, the alienation absorbing.

A younger group of painters centered in New York City felt that postwar society was so chaotic that it denied any attempt at literal representation. As Jackson Pollock maintained, "the modern painter cannot express this age—the airplane, the atomic bomb, the radio—in the old form of the Renaissance or of any past culture. Each age finds its own technique."

The technique Pollock adopted came to be called Abstract Expressionism, and during the late 1940s and 1950s it dominated not only the American art scene but the international field as well. In addition to Pollock, its adherents included Robert Motherwell, William de Kooning, Arshile Gorky, Clyfford Still, Adolph Gottlieb, and Mark Rothko. "Abstract art," Motherwell declared, "is an effort to close the void that modern men feel."

In practice this meant that the *act* of painting was as important as the final result, and that art no longer had to represent one's visual surroundings. Instead it could unapologetically represent the painter's personal thoughts and actions. Wyoming-born Pollock, for example, placed his huge canvases flat on the floor and then walked around each side, pouring and dripping his paints, all in an effort to "literally be *in* the painting." Such action paintings, with their commanding size, bold form, powerful color contrasts, and rough texture, conveyed the whole spectrum of aesthetic qualities: they were vibrant, frenzied, meditative, disorienting, provocative. Many among the general public found them simply provoking. One wit observed that "I suspect any picture I think I could have made myself."

THE BEATS   The desire to liberate self-expression and reject middle-class conventions also animated a small but highly visible and controversial group of young writers, poets, painters, and musicians known as the Beats. These angry young men—Jack Kerouac, Allen Ginsberg, Gary Snyder, William Burroughs, and Gregory Corso, among others—rebelled against the mundane horrors of middle-class life. The Beats were not lost in despair, however; they strenuously embraced life. But it was life on their own terms, and their terms were shocking to most observers.

The Beats grew out of the bohemian underground in New York's Greenwich Village. Kerouac was a handsome, athletic, working-class kid from Lowell, Massachusetts, who went to Columbia University on a football scholarship. Ginsberg also studied at Columbia, where a perplexed dean directed him to undergo psychotherapy. The moody poet chose William Burroughs as his therapist. Burroughs graduated from Harvard in 1936, then studied medicine in Vienna. Later he would become a heroin addict, kill his wife while trying to shoot an apple off her head, and write the influential experimental novel *Naked Lunch* (1959).

This fervent threesome found its hero in Neal Cassady, a twenty-year-old ex-convict who arrived in New York from Denver hoping to enroll at Columbia. He was in their view a mythic cowboy turned "cool" hipster, utterly free and rootless because he defied both maturity and reason. Soon this quartet attracted others in quest of *real* life, and the Beat culture was born.

Essentially apolitical throughout the 1950s, the Beats sought personal rather than social solutions to their hopes and anxieties. As Kerouac insisted, they were not beat in the sense of beaten; they were "mad to live, mad to talk, mad to be saved." Their road to salvation lay in hallucinogenic drugs and alcohol, sex, a penchant for jazz and the street life of urban ghettos, an affinity for Buddhism, and a restless, vagabond spirit that took them speeding back and forth across the country between San Francisco and New York.

This existential mania for intense experience and frantic motion provided the subject matter for the Beats' writing. Ginsberg's long prose-poem *Howl* (1956) featured an explicit sensuality as well as an impressionistic attempt to catch the color, movement, and dynamism of modern life. In this it bore a marked resemblance to Walt Whitman's *Leaves of Grass*. But *Howl* lacked Whitman's celebratory tone; its mood was bitter and critical. Ginsberg howled at the "Robot apartments! invincible suburbs! skeleton treasuries! blind capitals! demonic industries!" Kerouac published his autobiographical novel *On the Road* a year later. In frenzied prose it portrayed the Beats' life of "bursting ecstasies" and maniacal traveling. At one point Dean Moriarty (Neal Cassady) has the following exchange with Sal Paradise (Kerouac): "We gotta go and never stop going till we get there." "Where we going, man?" "I don't know, but we gotta go."

Howl and *On the Road* provoked angry sarcasm from many reviewers, but the books enjoyed a brisk sale, especially among young people. *On the Road* made the best-seller list, and soon the term "Beat generation" or "beatnik" referred to almost any young rebel who openly dissented from the comfortable ethos of middle-class life. Defiant young actors such as James Dean and Marlon Brando were added to the pantheon of Beat "anti-heroes." In *The Wild One* (1954) a waitress asks Brando what he is rebelling against. He replies: "Whattaya got?" A young folksinger from Minnesota named Bob Dylan was directly inspired by *Howl* and *On the Road*. In this sense the anarchic gaiety of the Beats played an important role in preparing the way for the more widespread youth revolt of the 1960s.

A PARADOXICAL ERA

For all their color and vitality, the Beats had little impact on the prevailing patterns of postwar social and cultural life. The same held for most of the other critics who attacked the smug conformity and excessive materialism they saw pervading their society. The public had become understandably weary of larger social or political concerns in the aftermath of the depression and the war. Instead Americans eagerly focused their efforts on personal and family goals and took great pride in their material achievements.

Yet those achievements, considerable as they were, eventually created a new set of problems. The benefits of abundance were by no means equally distributed, and millions of Americans still lived in poverty. For those more fortunate, unprecedented affluence and security fostered greater leisure and independence, which in turn provided opportunities for pursuing more diverse notions of what the good life entailed. Yet the conformist mentality of the Cold War era discouraged experimentation. During the mid-1960s, however, tensions between innovation and convention would erupt into open conflict. Many members of the baby-boom generation would become the leaders of the 1960s rebellion against the corporate and consumer cultures. Ironically, the person who would warn Americans of the 1960s about the mounting dangers of the burgeoning "military-industrial complex" was the president who had long symbolized its growth—Dwight D. Eisenhower.

MAKING CONNECTIONS

- The culture of the 1950s laid the groundwork for the counterculture of the 1960s. See Chapters 33 and 34.

- There are fruitful comparisons between American culture in the 1950s and the earlier postwar period, the 1920s. See Chapter 25.

- The women's movement of the 1970s, discussed in Chapter 34, was led by women who rejected the cult of domesticity described in this chapter.

- The baby boom of the postwar period would have continuing economic, social, political, and cultural significance as this generation moved through the life cycle. Follow along in coming chapters.

FURTHER READING

There are a number of excellent overviews of social and cultural trends in the postwar era. Among the best are William H. Chafe's *The Unfinished Journey* (1986)* and William E. Leuchtenburg's *A Troubled Feast* (1982).* For fascinating insights into the cultural life of the 1950s, see Jeffrey Hart's *When the Going Was Good: American Life in the Fifties* (1982), and David Halberstam's *The Fifties* (1993).*

The baby boom generation and its impact are vividly described in Paul C. Light's *Baby Boomers* (1988). Readers interested in economic trends should consult Harold Vatter's *The U.S. Economy in the 1950s* (1963). The emergence and impact of the television industry are discussed in Erik Barnouw's *Tube of Plenty* (1982).*

*These books are available in paperback editions.

An excellent comprehensive account of the process of suburban development is Kenneth Jackson's award-winning study *The Crabgrass Frontier* (1985).* Michael Danielson examines racial discrimination in the suburbs in *The Politics of Exclusion* (1976).*

The middle-class ideal of family life in the 1950s is examined in Elaine Tyler May's *Homeward Bound: American Families in the Cold War Era* (1988).* For an overview of the resurgence of religion in the 1950s, see George Marsden's *Religion and American Culture* (1990).

A lively discussion of movies of the 1950s can be found in Peter Biskind's *Seeing Is Believing* (1983).* The origins and growth of rock 'n' roll music are surveyed in Carl Belz's *The Story of Rock* (1972).* Thoughtful interpretive surveys of postwar American literature include Josephine Hendin's *Vulnerable People* (1978)* and Malcolm Bradbury's *The Modern American Novel* (1984).* Developments in American art are assessed in Serge Guibaut's *How New York Stole the Idea of Modern Art* (1983).*

*These books are available in paperback editions.

32   CONFLICT AND DEADLOCK: THE EISENHOWER YEARS

"TIME FOR A CHANGE"

By 1952 the Truman administration had piled up a heavy burden of political liabilities. Its bold stand in Korea had brought a bloody stalemate abroad, renewed wage and price controls at home, reckless charges of subversion and disloyalty, and exposure of corrupt lobbyists and influence peddlers who rigged favors in Washington. The disclosure of government corruption led Truman to fire nearly 250 employees of the Bureau of Internal Revenue. But doubts lingered that he would ever finish the housecleaning.

EISENHOWER'S POLITICAL RISE   It was, in a slogan of the day, "time for a change," and Republicans saw public sentiment turning their way as the 1952 election approached. The Republican field quickly narrowed to two men, Ohio senator Robert A. Taft and General Dwight D. Eisenhower. The party wheelhorses turned instinctively to Taft, "Mr. Republican," long a faithful party worker. For all his experience and ability, however, Taft was a dull public figure. Eisenhower the war hero, on the other hand, had the popular appeal that Taft lacked, and his unpretentious manner inspired widespread support.

Despite his roots in rural Kansas Republican conservatism, Eisenhower had initially supported Roosevelt and the New Deal, and he admired Roosevelt's wartime leadership. But during the Truman years Eisenhower reverted to the political party of his youth. In early 1952 he affirmed that he was a Republican and permitted his name to be entered in party primaries. Bumper stickers across the land announced simply, "I like Ike," and the immensely popular Eisenhower won the nomination on the first ballot. He then balanced the ticket with a youthful Californian, the thirty-nine-year-old Senator Richard M. Nixon, who had built a career on strenuous opposition to domestic "subversives."

THE 1952 ELECTION   The Twenty-second Amendment, ratified in 1951, forbade any president to seek a third term. The amendment exempted the incumbent, but weary of the war in Korea, harassed by charges of subversion and corruption in his administration, and with his popularity declining, Truman chose to withdraw. In a wide-open Democratic race, he supported Illinois governor Adlai E. Stevenson, who aroused the convention delegates with an eloquent speech welcoming them to Chicago. On the third ballot the convention drafted Stevenson.

The campaign matched two of the most magnetic personalities ever pitted against each other in a presidential contest, but the race was uneven from the start. Eisenhower, though a political novice, was a world figure who had been in the public eye for a decade. Stevenson was hardly known outside Illinois.

The genial Eisenhower, who disliked politics and politicians, opened a domestic crusade to clean up "the mess in Washington." To this he added a promise, late in the campaign, that as president-elect he would

Dwight D. Eisenhower (right) *and Richard M. Nixon* (left), *the Republican standardbearers for 1952.*

go to Korea to secure "an early and honorable" peace. Stevenson offered a lofty eloquence spiced with a quick wit, but his resolve to "talk sense" and "tell the truth to the American people" came across as a bit too aloof, a shade too intellectual. The Republicans labeled him an "egghead," in contrast to Eisenhower, the folksy man of the people, the man of decision and action. And Eisenhower's running mate, Richard Nixon, savagely—and clumsily—tried to tar Stevenson with the brush of being "soft" on communism. Can such a man, Nixon asked the voters, be "trusted to lead our crusade against communism?" Stevenson replied: "If the Republicans will stop telling lies about us, we will stop telling the truth about them."

In the end, Stevenson's humor and intellect were no match for Eisenhower's popularity. The war hero triumphed in a landslide of 34 million votes to 27 million. The election marked a turning point in Republican fortunes in the South: for the first time since the heyday of the Whigs in the 1840s the South was moving toward a two-party system. Stevenson carried only eight southern states plus West Virginia; Eisenhower picked up five states in the outer South: Florida, Oklahoma, Tennessee,

Texas, and Virginia. The "nonpolitical" Eisenhower had made it respectable, even fashionable, to vote Republican in the South. Elsewhere, too, the general made inroads into the New Deal coalition, attracting supporters among the ethnic and religious minorities in the major cities.

The voters, it turned out, liked Ike better than they liked his party. Democrats retained most of the governorships, lost control of the House by only eight votes, and broke even in the Senate. The congressional elections two years later would weaken the Republican grip on Congress, and Eisenhower would have to work with a Democratic Congress until he left office.

IKE   Born in Denison, Texas, in 1890, Dwight David Eisenhower grew up in Abilene, Kansas. After finishing West Point he spent nearly his entire adult life in the military service. As a general he took command of American forces in the European theater and directed the invasion of North Africa in 1942. In 1944 he assumed the post of supreme commander of Allied forces in preparation for the invasion of the continent. After the war, by then a five-star general, he became chief of staff and supreme commander of NATO forces, with a brief interlude in between as president of Columbia University.

Eisenhower's inauguration brought a change in style to the White House. The contrast in character between the feisty Truman and the fatherly Ike accompanied a contrast in philosophy and approach to the presidency. Eisenhower's military experience developed in him an instinct for methodical staff work. He met with the cabinet and the National Security Council nearly every week, and relied heavily on them for advice. His chief assistant, former New Hampshire governor Sherman Adams, decreed that any paperwork destined for the Oval Office be digested into single-page summaries.

Such procedures isolated the president from conflicting viewpoints and reduced the policy choices available to him. The public image of Ike confirmed that view, but it endeared him all the more to the people as a man who rose above politics. It was hard not to like the buoyant and modest war hero. Ike was warm, sincere, and unpretentious, an ardent golfer and bridge player, a common man who read little but Western novels, uninformed on the currents of intellectual and artistic life, and given to simple maxims: "Everybody ought to be happy every day.

Play hard, have fun doing it, and despise wickedness." As one diplomat observed: "He was the nation's number one Boy Scout."

Yet those who were close to Ike have presented another side to the man. When provoked he could release a fiery temper and scalding profanity. The scrambled syntax in which he answered reporters' questions was sometimes intentional evasion. He once told his press secretary before a news conference: "Don't worry, Jim. If that comes up, I'll just confuse them."

"DYNAMIC CONSERVATISM" AT HOME   Like Ulysses Grant, however, Eisenhower betrayed a weakness for hobnobbing with rich men. His cabinet, a journalist quipped, consisted of "eight millionaires and a plumber." The plumber, Secretary of Labor Martin Durkin, was gone in eight months, charging that the administration had reneged on a promise to change the Taft-Hartley Act. The president of General Motors became secretary of defense, and two auto distributors were appointed secretary of the interior and postmaster-general. The New Dealers, Adlai Stevenson wryly remarked, "have all left Washington to make way for the car dealers."

Eisenhower called his domestic program "dynamic conservatism," which meant being "conservative when it comes to money and liberal when it comes to human beings." Budget cutting was a high priority. Eisenhower warned repeatedly against the dangers of "creeping socialism," huge bureaucracies, and budget deficits. His administration abolished the Reconstruction Finance Corporation, ended wage and price controls, and reduced farm price subsidies.

But though Eisenhower chipped away at New Deal programs, his presidency in the end served rather to legitimate the New Deal by keeping its basic structure and premises intact during an era of prosperity. In a letter to his brother in 1954, he observed: "Should any political party attempt to abolish social security and eliminate labor laws and farm programs, you would not hear of that party again in our political history." He added that those conservative Republicans who sought to dismantle the New Deal in its entirety were "stupid." Essentially Eisenhower sought to leave the basic structure of the New Deal intact while preventing its costs from rising. This led Republican Senator Barry Goldwater to grouse that Ike was promoting a "Dime Store New Deal."

In some ways, moreover, the administration not only maintained the

New Deal but extended its reach, especially after 1954, when it had the help of Democratic Congresses. Amendments to the Social Security Act in 1954 and 1956 brought coverage to millions in categories formerly excluded: professional people, domestic and clerical workers, farm workers, and members of the armed forces. The federal minimum wage rose in 1955 from 75¢ to $1 an hour. Federal expenditures for public health rose steadily in the Eisenhower years, and low-income housing continued to be built, although on a much reduced scale. Some farm-related aid programs were actually expanded during the Eisenhower years.

Despite Eisenhower's general disapproval of federal electric power programs, he continued to support public works for which he saw a legitimate need. Indeed, two such programs left major monuments to his presidency: the St. Lawrence Seaway and the interstate highways. The St. Lawrence Seaway, opened in 1959 as a joint venture with Canada, made it possible for oceangoing ships to reach the Great Lakes. The Federal Highway Act of 1956 authorized the federal government to put up 90 percent of the cost of building 42,500 miles of limited-access interstate highways to serve the needs of commerce and defense, as well as private convenience. The states provided the remaining 10 percent. It was only afterward that people realized that the huge national commitment to the automobile might have come at the expense of America's railroad system, already in a state of advanced decay.

CONCLUDING AN ARMISTICE   America's new position in the postwar world continued to absorb Eisenhower's attention. The most pressing problem when he entered office was the continuing, painful deadlock in the Korean peace talks. The North Koreans and Red Chinese insisted that all prisoners be returned regardless of their wishes. To break the deadlock, Eisenhower took a bold stand. In mid-May 1953 he stepped up aerial bombardment of North Korea, then had Secretary of State John Foster Dulles warn the Chinese of his willingness to use atomic bombs. Whether for that reason or others, negotiations then moved quickly toward an armistice along the established battle line just above the 38th parallel, and toward a complicated arrangement for prisoner exchange that allowed captives to decide whether to accept or refuse repatriation.

On July 26, 1953, Eisenhower announced the conclusion of the armistice. No one knows if he actually would have forced the issue with atomic weapons. Perhaps the more decisive factors in bringing about a settlement were the size of Chinese Communist losses, which they increasingly found unacceptable, and the new spirit of uncertainty and caution felt by Russian Communists after the death of Joseph Stalin on March 5, 1953—six weeks after Ike's inauguration.

CONCLUDING A WITCH-HUNT   The Korean armistice helped to end another dismal episode: the meteoric career of Senator Joseph R. McCarthy, which had flourished amid the anxieties of wartime. Supposedly convinced that the government was thoroughly infested with Communists and spies, the Wisconsin senator launched a splenetic crusade to root them out. In the process he and his aides lied, falsified evidence, and bullied or blackmailed witnesses. Eventually the logic of McCarthy's unscrupulous tactics led to his self-destruction, but not before he had left many careers and reputations in ruins. The Republicans thought their victory in 1952 would curb his recklessness, but McCarthy actually grew more outlandish in his charges and his investigative methods. Yet many Americans caught up in the anti-Communist hysteria viewed him as a heroic knight doing battle against the forces of darkness.

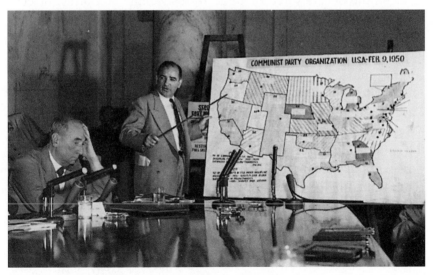

The Army-McCarthy Hearings, June 1954. *Joseph Welch* (head in hand) *listens dejectedly after McCarthy's attempt to smear one of Welch's associates.*

McCarthy finally overreached himself in 1954 when, as chairman of the Senate's Government Operations Committee, he ordered hearings to investigate charges of Soviet espionage at the Army Signal Center in Fort Monmouth, New Jersey, and then tried to peddle the absurdity that the United States Army itself was "soft" on communism.

The televised hearings displayed McCarthy at his capricious worst, scowling at critics, bullying witnesses, dragging out lengthy irrelevancies, repeatedly calling "point of order." He became the perfect foil for the army's gentle but unflappable counsel, Joseph Welch, whose rapier wit repeatedly drew blood. When McCarthy tried to smear one of Welch's young associates, the counsel went into a cold rage: "Until this moment, Senator, I think I never really gauged your cruelty or your recklessness. . . . Have you no sense of decency, sir, at long last?" When the audience, including press corps photographers, burst into applause, the confused and skulking senator was reduced to whispering, "What did I do?"

Perhaps McCarthy never found out, but at that point the house he had thrown together began to crash around his ears. He descended into new depths of scurrility, now directing charges at his own colleagues, calling one senator "senile" and another "a living miracle . . . the only man who has lived so long with neither brains nor guts." On December 2, 1954, the Senate voted 67 to 22 to "condemn" McCarthy for contempt of the Senate. McCarthy was finished and increasingly took to alcohol. Three years later, at the age of forty-eight, he was dead. For all his attacks and inquiries, he had never uncovered one Communist in government.

The witch-hunt was over. McCarthyism, Ike joked, had become McCarthywasm, though not for those whose reputations had been wrecked. To the end Eisenhower kept his resolve not to "get down in the gutter with that guy" and sully the dignity of the presidency. He did work resolutely against McCarthy behind the scenes, but some scholars consider his "hidden hand" approach to have been ineffective at best and cowardly at worst. Eisenhower shared, nevertheless, the widely held conviction that espionage posed a real danger to national security. He denied clemency to Julius and Ethel Rosenberg, who had been convicted of passing atomic secrets to the Russians, on the grounds that they "may have condemned to death tens of millions of innocent people." Although few if any scientists believed that the design principles of the bomb were a secret, the Rosenbergs were electrocuted at Sing Sing Prison in 1953.

INTERNAL SECURITY Even before 1954, Eisenhower stiffened the government security program. In 1953 he issued an executive order broadening the basis for firing government workers. It replaced Truman's criterion of "disloyalty" with the new category of "security risk." Under the new edict federal workers could lose their jobs because of dubious associations or personal habits that might make them careless or vulnerable to blackmail. In 1953 the Atomic Energy Commission removed the security clearance of physicist J. Robert Oppenheimer, the "father of the atomic bomb," on the grounds that he had expressed qualms about the hydrogen bomb in 1949–1950 and had associated with Communists or former Communists in the past. Lacking evidence of any disloyalty or betrayal, the AEC nevertheless branded him a "security risk" because of "fundamental defects in his character."

The Supreme Court, however, modified some of the more extreme expressions of this new Red Scare. In 1953 Eisenhower appointed as chief justice former governor Earl Warren of California, a decision the president later pronounced the "biggest damnfool mistake I ever made." Warren, who had seemed safely conservative while in electoral politics, led an active Court on issues of civil rights and civil liberties. The Warren Court (1953–1969), under the chief justice's influence, became an important agency of social and political change through the 1960s. In connection with security programs and loyalty requirements, the Court veered back in the direction of traditional individual rights.

DULLES AND FOREIGN POLICY The Eisenhower administration promised new foreign policy departures under the direction of Secretary of State John Foster Dulles. Grandson of one secretary of state and nephew of another, Dulles pursued a lifetime career as an international lawyer and sometime diplomat. Son of a minister and himself an earnest Presbyterian, Dulles, in the words of the British ambassador, resembled those old zealots of the wars of religion who "saw the world as an arena in which the forces of good and evil were continuously at war." Tall, spare, and stooped, he gave the appearance of dour sternness and Calvinist righteousness. But he was also a man of immense energy, intelligence, and experience. As Eisenhower once said of Dulles, "There's only one man I know who has seen *more* of the world, and talked with more people and *knows* more than he does—and that's me."

The foreign policy planks of the 1952 Republican platform, which Dulles wrote, showed both the moralist and the tactician at work. Truman's policy of containment was needlessly defensive, Dulles thought. Containment implied contentment with the status quo. He saw no need for the United States to accept a permanent Soviet presence in eastern Europe. Americans instead should promote the "liberation" of sovereign nations from Soviet domination. This conviction meshed nicely with the conventional wisdom of the right wing that the Yalta Conference agreements were perhaps a betrayal, at best a blunder. The 1952 platform, therefore, promised to "repudiate all commitments . . . such as those of Yalta which aid Communist enslavement" and to end "the negative, futile and immoral policy of 'containment' which abandons countless human beings to a despotism and godless terrorism." A new policy of liberation, the platform promised, would help generate independence movements within the Communist bloc.

The policy verged perilously close to proclaiming a holy war, but Dulles stressed that he did not intend forcible liberation. Soon it became apparent that it was less a policy than a web of rhetoric to catch ethnic voters whose homelands had fallen captive to the Russians. This became evident when the administration did nothing but deplore a Russian crackdown on rebellious East German workers in 1953. For three years more Dulles assumed that his rhetoric was undermining the Communist hold on Eastern Europe—until ruthless Russian suppression of the 1956 uprising in Hungary underscored the danger of stirring futile hopes among captive peoples.

Insofar as American interventions occurred abroad, they were covert operations by the Central Intelligence Agency in countries outside the Soviet sphere. Under Eisenhower, Allen Dulles, brother of the secretary of state, rose from second in command to chief of the CIA. A veteran of the wartime Office of Strategic Services, he had already helped enhance the CIA's capacity for cloak-and-dagger operations. In two cases early in the Eisenhower years this capability was actually used to overthrow governments believed hostile to American interests: in Iran (1953) and in Guatemala (1954).

BRINKSMANSHIP   For all his talk of liberation, Dulles made no significant departure from the containment strategy created under Acheson and Truman. Instead he institutionalized containment in the rigid mold of his Cold War rhetoric and extended it into the military strategy of deterrence. Dulles betrayed a fatal affinity for colorful phrases. In addition to "liberation" and "roll back," he added two major new contributions while in office: "massive retaliation" and "going to the brink."

"Massive retaliation" was an effort to get, in the slogan soon current, "more bang for the buck." Budgetary considerations lay at the root of the administration's military plans, for Eisenhower and his cabinet shared the fear that in the effort to build a superior war power the country could spend itself into bankruptcy. During 1953 the Joint Chiefs of Staff designed a new military posture. The heart of their New Look was the assumption that nuclear weapons could be used in limited-war situations, allowing reductions in conventional forces and thus budgetary savings. No longer would "the Communists nibble us to death all over the world in little wars," Vice-President Nixon explained.

By this time both the United States and Russia had exploded hydrogen bombs. With the new policy of deterrence, what Winston Churchill called a "balance of terror" had replaced the old "balance of power." The threat of nuclear holocaust was terrifying, but the notion that the United States would risk such a disaster in response to local wars had little credibility.

Dulles's policy of "brinksmanship" depended for its strategic effect on those very fears of nuclear disaster. He argued in 1956 that in following a tough policy of confrontation with communism, one sometimes had to "go to the brink" of war: "The ability to get to the verge without getting into war is the necessary art. If you cannot master it, you inevitably get into war. . . . We walked to the brink and we looked it in the face." The first occasion on which a firm stand had halted further aggression had been America's threat in 1953 to break the Korean stalemate by using atomic weapons. The second had come in 1954, when aircraft carriers moved into the South China Sea "both to deter any Red Chinese attack against [French] Indochina and to provide weapons for instant retaliation."

INDOCHINA: THE BACKGROUND TO WAR   Like the rest of the old colonial world of Asia and Africa, Indochina experienced a wave of nationalism in the years after World War II, damaging both the power and prestige of the colonial powers. By the early 1950s most of British Asia was independent or on the way: India, Pakistan, Ceylon (now Sri

Lanka), Burma (now Mynamar), and the Malay States (now Malaysia). The Dutch and French, however, were less willing to give up their colonies and thus created a dilemma for American policy makers. Americans sympathized with colonial nationalists who sometimes invoked the example of 1776, but Americans also wanted Dutch and French help against the spread of communism. The Truman administration felt obliged to comply with their pleas for aid in reconquering areas that had passed from Japanese occupation into the hands of local patriots.

French Indochina, created in the nineteenth century out of the old kingdoms of Cambodia, Laos, and Vietnam, offered a variation on Third World nationalism. During World War II, opposition to the Japanese occupation of Indochina was led by the Vietminh (Vietnamese League for Independence), nationalists who fell under the influence of Communists led by the magnetic rebel Ho Chi Minh. At the end of the war the Vietminh controlled part of northern Vietnam, and on September 2, 1945, Ho Chi Minh proclaimed a Democratic Republic of Vietnam, with its capital in Hanoi. American officers were on the reviewing stand in Hanoi and American planes flew over the celebration. Ho had received secret American help against the Japanese during the war, but his bids for further aid after the war went unanswered. Vietnam took low priority in American diplomatic concerns, which at the time were focused on restoring Western Europe and containing the spread of communism there.

Ho Chi Minh.

In 1946 the French government, preoccupied with domestic politics, recognized Ho's new government as a "free state" within the French colonial union. Before the year was out, however, Ho opposed French efforts to establish another regime in the southern provinces, and this clash soon expanded into the First Indochina War.

This was a troubling development for the American government. On the one hand, the United States resented France's determination to restore colonial rule. Yet Truman was even more determined to see France become a bulwark against communism in Europe. As a State Department report concluded in 1948, the United States had an "immediate and vital interest" in supporting the French government in order to further "our aims in Europe," and that goal must "take precedence over active steps looking toward the realization of our objectives in Indochina." As a result the American government acquiesced in France's efforts to crush Vietnamese nationalism.

The Vietminh movement thereafter became more completely dominated by Ho Chi Minh and his Communist associates, and more dependent on Russia and Red China for help. In 1950, with the outbreak of fighting in Korea, the struggle in Vietnam took on the appearance of a battleground in the Cold War. When the Korean War ended, American aid to the French in Vietnam, begun by the Truman administration, escalated dramatically. By the end of 1953 the Eisenhower administration was paying about two-thirds of the cost of the French war effort, or about $1 billion annually.

But even with lavish American aid the French were unable to suppress the well-organized and tenacious Vietminh. In 1954 the United States found itself at the edge of the "brink" to which Dulles later referred. A major French force had been sent to Dien Bien Phu in the northwest corner of Vietnam, near the Laos border, in the hope of luring Vietminh guerrillas into the open and grinding them up with superior firepower. The French instead found themselves surrounded by a superior force that laid siege to their stronghold.

The French government requested an American air strike to relieve the pressure on Dien Bien Phu. Eisenhower seemed to endorse forceful action when he advanced his "domino theory" at a news conference on April 7, 1954. He implied that if Indochina fell to the Communists, the rest of Asia would be next. Eisenhower, however, opposed direct American military action unless the British lent support. When they refused,

Eisenhower backed away from unilateral action, explaining that it would be a "tragic error to go in alone as a partner of France."

THE GENEVA ACCORDS AND U.S. POLICY   America's decision not to intervene sealed the fate of the besieged French garrison at Dien Bien Phu. On May 7, 1954, the Vietminh launched massive attacks and finally overwhelmed the courageous, but vastly outnumbered, French resistance. It was the very eve of the day an international conference at Geneva took up the question of Indochina. Six weeks later, as French forces continued to meet defeats in Vietnam, a new French government promised an early settlement. On July 20 representatives of France, Britain, Russia, the People's Republic of China, and the Vietminh reached agreement on the Geneva Accords, and the next day produced their Final Declaration, which proposed to neutralize Laos and Cambodia and divided Vietnam at the 17th parallel. The Vietminh would take power in the north, and the French would remain south of the line until elections in 1956 should reunify Vietnam. American and South Vietnamese representatives refused either to join in the accord or to sign the Final Declaration.

Dulles then launched an effort to set up mutual defense arrangements for Southeast Asia. On September 8, 1954, at a meeting in Manila, the United States joined seven other countries in an agreement the press quickly labeled the Southeast Asia Treaty Organization (SEATO). The impression that it paralleled NATO was false, for the Manila Defense Accord was neither a common defense organization like NATO nor was it primarily Asian. The signers agreed that in case of an attack on one, the others would act according to their "constitutional practices," and in case of threats or subversion they would "consult immediately."

The members of SEATO included only three Asian countries—the Philippines, Thailand, and Pakistan—together with Britain, France, Australia, New Zealand, and the United States. India and Indonesia, the two most populous countries in the region, refused to join. A special protocol added to the treaty extended coverage to Indochina. The treaty reflected what Dulles's critics called "pactomania," which by the end of the Eisenhower administration had contracted the United States to defend forty-three other countries.

Eisenhower announced that though the United States "had not itself

POSTWAR ALLIANCES: The Far East

Nations having bilateral treaties with U.S.

Members of SEATO

Communist bloc

been party to or bound by the decision taken at the [Geneva] Conference," any renewal of Communist aggression in Vietnam "would be viewed by us as a matter of grave concern." (He failed to note that the United States had agreed at Geneva to "refrain from the threat or use of force to disturb" the agreements.) Ho Chi Minh and his government in Hanoi quickly sought to consolidate control throughout the north. In the hinterlands local Communists held kangaroo courts that tried and executed landowners and confiscated their lands. Residents of the North who wished to leave for southern Vietnam did so with American aid. Over 900,000 refugees, most of them Catholics, relocated to the South, causing staggering logistical problems for the struggling new government there.

Power in the South gravitated to a new premier: Ngo Dinh Diem, a Catholic nationalist who had opposed both the French and the Vietminh. Diem took office during the Geneva talks after returning from exile at a Catholic seminary in New Jersey. In 1954 Eisenhower offered to assist Diem "in developing and maintaining a strong, viable state, capable of resisting attempted subversion or aggression through military means." In return the United States expected Diem to carry out "needed reforms." American aid was forthcoming in the form of CIA and military cadres charged with training Diem's armed forces and police.

Instead of instituting comprehensive reforms, however, Diem tightened his grip on the country, suppressing opposition on both right and left, offering little or no land distribution, and permitting widespread corruption. In 1956 he refused to join in the elections to reunify Vietnam, and the United States endorsed his decision. But Diem's efforts to eliminate all opposition only played into the hands of the Communists, who found more and more recruits among the discontented. By 1957 guerrilla forces in the South, known as the Vietcong, had begun attacks on the government, and in 1960 the resistance formed its own political arm, the National Liberation Front. As guerrilla warfare gradually disrupted the country, Eisenhower was helpless to do anything but "sink or swim with Ngo Dinh Diem."

CIVIL RIGHTS IN THE FIFTIES

If the Eisenhower presidency seems an interlude of relative tranquility between two decades of domestic and foreign strife, it should be remembered that those years also saw the onset of a revolution in race relations. Eisenhower entered office committed to civil rights in principle, and he did push the issue in areas of federal authority. During his first three years, public services in Washington, D.C., were desegregated, as were navy yards and veterans' hospitals. Beyond that, however, two aspects of the president's philosophy inhibited vigorous action in enforcing the principle of civil rights: his preference for state or local rather than federal action, and his doubt that law could really be effective in such matters. "I don't believe you can change the hearts of men with laws or decisions," he stressed. For the time, then, leadership in the civil-rights field came more from the judiciary than from the executive or legislative branches of the government.

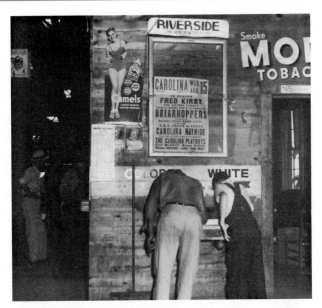

Segregation began to be tested in the courts by the NAACP in the late 1930s.

THE *BROWN* DECISION   In the 1930s the NAACP had resolved to test the "separate but equal" doctrine that had upheld racial segregation since the *Plessy* decision in 1896. But it was not until the 1950s that challenges to segregation in the public schools were rising through the appellate courts. Five such cases, from Kansas, Delaware, South Carolina, Virginia, and the District of Columbia—usually cited by reference to the first, *Brown v. Board of Education of Topeka, Kansas*—came to the Supreme Court for joint argument in 1952.

Chief Justice Earl Warren wrote the opinion, finally handed down on May 17, 1954, in which a unanimous Court declared that "in the field of public education the doctrine of 'separate but equal' has no place." In support of its opinion the Court cited current sociological and psychological findings demonstrating that even if separate facilities were equal in quality, the mere fact of separating people by race engendered feelings of inferiority. A year later, after further argument, the Court directed that compliance with the *Brown* ruling should move "with all deliberate speed."

The white South's first response was relatively calm, deceptively so as it happened. Eisenhower refused to take any part in leading white southerners toward compliance. Privately he maintained "that the Supreme Court decision *set back* progress in the South *at least fifteen years.* The fellow who tries to tell me you can do these things by *force* is just plain *nuts.*" While token integration began as early as 1954 in the border states, hostility mounted in the Deep South and Virginia, led by the newly formed White Citizens' Councils. Before the end of 1955 moderate sentiment in the South gave way to surly reaction. Democratic Senator James Eastland of Mississippi growled that the South would neither "abide by nor obey this legislative decision by a political court."

Virginia's Senator Harry F. Byrd supplied a rallying cry for the growing opposition to the *Brown* decision: "Massive Resistance." State legislatures tried to interpose their power between the courts and the schools. In 1956, 101 southern members of Congress signed a "Southern Manifesto" that denounced the Court's decision as "a clear abuse of judicial power." At the end of 1956, in six southern states not a single black child attended school with whites.

THE MONTGOMERY BUS BOYCOTT   At the end of 1955 the drive for civil rights took a new turn in Montgomery, Alabama, "the cradle of the Confederacy." There, on December 1, 1955, Rosa Parks, a black seamstress weary at the end of a long day, was arrested for refusing to comply with a city ordinance and give up her seat on a city bus to a white man. "I'm going to have you arrested," the driver said. "You may do that," Parks replied. The next night black community leaders met in the Dexter Avenue Baptist Church to organize the Montgomery Improvement Association and launch a massive bus boycott.

The movement found a courageous leader in Dexter Avenue's twenty-six-year-old pastor, Martin Luther King, Jr. Born in Atlanta, the grandson of a slave and the son of a minister, King was endowed with intelligence, energy, courage, and charisma. After attending Morehouse College in Atlanta and then receiving a seminary degree, he earned a Ph.D. in philosophy from Boston College before accepting a call to preach in Montgomery. He brought to the civil rights movement a message of nonviolent, passive resistance compounded from the Gospels, the writings of Thoreau, and the example of Mahatma Gandhi in India. "We must use the weapon of love," he stressed. "We must realize so

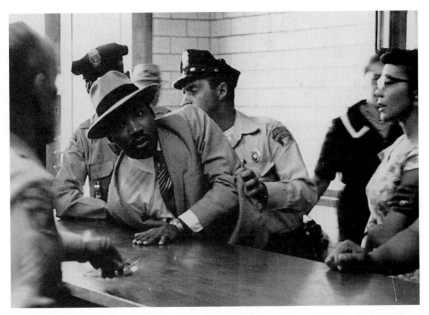

Martin Luther King, Jr., here facing arrest for leading a civil-rights march, advocated nonviolent resistance to racial segregation.

many people are taught to hate us that they are not totally responsible for their hate." To his antagonists he pledged: "We will soon wear you down by our capacity to suffer, and in winning our freedom we will so appeal to your heart and conscience that we will win you in the process." Although racists bombed his home and repeatedly threatened him and his family, King remained steadfast in his nonviolent principles.

The bus boycott achieved a remarkable solidarity. For months blacks in Montgomery got to and from home, work, and school by forming car pools, hitchhiking, or simply walking. The boycotters finally won the case they had initiated in the federal courts against bus segregation, and on December 20, 1956, the Supreme Court affirmed that "the separate but equal doctrine can no longer be safely followed as a correct statement of the law." The next day King and other blacks boarded the buses, but they still had a long way to travel before the Jim Crow system could be laid finally to rest.

To keep alive the spirit of the bus boycott, King and a group of associates in 1957 organized the Southern Christian Leadership Conference (SCLC). They did so in the face of continuing racist threats. Several days later, on a Sunday morning, King found an unexploded dynamite bomb on his front porch. Two hours later he addressed his congregation: "I'm not afraid of anybody this morning. Tell Montgomery they can keep shooting and I'm going to stand up to them; tell Montgomery they can keep bombing and I'm going to stand up to them. If I had to die tomorrow morning I would die happy because I've been to the mountain top and I've seen the promised land and it's going to be here in Montgomery."

Despite Eisenhower's reluctance to take the lead in desegregating schools, he had no problem with supporting the right of blacks to vote. In 1956 Eisenhower proposed legislation that became the Civil Rights Act of 1957, the first civil-rights law passed since Reconstruction. It finally got through the Senate, after a year's delay, with the help of Democratic Majority Leader Lyndon B. Johnson, who won southern acceptance by watering down the act. Still, it established for a period of two years the Civil Rights Commission, which was later extended indefinitely, and a new Civil Rights Division in the Justice Department, which could seek injunctions to prevent interference with the right to vote. The SCLC promptly announced a campaign to register 2 million black voters in the South.

LITTLE ROCK In 1957, Arkansas governor Orval Faubus called out the National Guard to prevent nine black students from entering Little Rock's Central High School under federal court order. A conference between the president and the governor proved fruitless, but on court order Faubus withdrew the Guard. When the students tried to enter the school, an hysterical mob of whites forced their removal for their own safety. At that point Eisenhower, who two months before could not "imagine any set of circumstances that would ever induce me to send federal troops," ordered a thousand paratroopers to Little Rock to protect the students, and mobilized the National Guard. The soldiers stayed through the school year. Thereafter, massive resistance for the most part was confined to the Deep South where five states, from South Carolina west through Louisiana, still held out against even token integration.

A LANDSLIDE FOR IKE In 1956 the Republican convention renominated Eisenhower by acclamation and again named Nixon as the vice-presidential candidate. The party platform endorsed Eisenhower's "modern Republicanism." The Democrats turned again to Stevenson, with a platform that evaded the civil-rights issue and otherwise stuck to party staples: less "favoritism" to big business, repeal of the Taft-Hartley Act, increased aid to farmers, and tax relief for those in low-income brackets.

Neither candidate generated much excitement during the 1956 campaign. The Democrats focused their fire on the heir apparent, Richard Nixon, a "man of many masks." Stevenson aroused little enthusiasm for two controversial proposals: to drop conscription and rely on an all-volunteer army, and to ban H-bomb tests by international agreement. Both involved military questions that put Stevenson at a disadvantage by pitting his judgment against that of a successful general. Voters handed Eisenhower a landslide victory. He lost one border state, Missouri, but in carrying Louisiana became the first Republican to win a Deep South state since Reconstruction; nationally, he carried all but seven states.

A Season of Troubles

CRISIS IN THE MIDDLE EAST   To forestall Russian penetration into the Middle East, the Eisenhower-Dulles foreign policy sought to cultivate Arab friendship, departing from the Truman-Acheson focus on Israel and from the support of British and French economic interests. In 1955 Dulles completed his line of alliances across the "northern tier" of the Middle East. Under American sponsorship, Britain joined Turkey, Iraq, Iran, and Pakistan in the Middle East Treaty Organization (METO), or Baghdad Pact, as the treaty was commonly called. By linking the easternmost NATO state (Turkey) to the westernmost SEATO state (Pakistan), METO had a certain superficial logic. But after Iraq, the only Arab member, withdrew in 1959, METO collapsed. Below the northern tier, moreover, the Arab states remained aloof from the organization. These were the states of the Arab League (Egypt, Jordan, Syria, Lebanon, and Saudi Arabia), which had warred on Israel in 1948–1949 and remained committed to its destruction.

The most fateful developments in the region turned on the rise of Egyptian general Gamal Abdel Nasser, who overthrew King Farouk in

POSTWAR ALLIANCES:
Europe, North Africa, The Middle East

Members of NATO

Members of CENTO

Arab League

Communist bloc
(Warsaw Pact)

1952. Nasser's nationalist regime soon pressed for the withdrawal of British forces guarding the Suez Canal, the crucial link between the Mediterranean Sea and the Indian Ocean. Eisenhower and Dulles supported Nasser's demand, and in 1954 an Anglo-Egyptian treaty provided for British withdrawal within twenty months. Ownership of the canal, however, remained with the Anglo-French Suez Canal Company.

Nasser, like other leaders of the Third World, remained unaligned in the Cold War and sought to play both sides off against each other. The United States in turn courted Egyptian support by offering the prospect of American assistance in building a great hydroelectric plant at Aswan on the Nile River. From the outset the administration's proposal was opposed by Jewish constituencies concerned with Egyptian threats to Israel, and by southern congressmen who feared the competition from Egyptian cotton. When Nasser then increased trade with the Soviet bloc and recognized Red China, Dulles abruptly canceled the loan offer in 1956.

The outcome was far from a triumph of American diplomacy. The chief victims, it turned out, were Anglo-French interests in the Suez. Unable to retaliate against the United States, Nasser nationalized the Anglo-French Suez Canal Company and earmarked its revenues for the Aswan project, thereby enhancing his prestige in the Arab world. The British and French reacted strongly. While negotiations dragged out, Israeli forces invaded the Gaza Strip and Sinai peninsula. Ostensibly their aim was to root out Arab guerrillas, but actually it was to synchronize with the British and French, who jointly began bombing Egyptian air bases and occupied Port Said. The British and French claimed that their actions were meant to protect the canal against the opposing belligerents.

The Suez War put the United States in a quandary. Either the administration could support its Western allies and see the troublesome Nasser crushed, or it could stand on the United Nations Charter and champion Arab nationalism against imperialistic aggression. Eisenhower opted for the latter course, with the unusual result that Russia sided with the United States. Once the threat of American embargoes had forced Anglo-French-Israeli capitulation, the Russians capitalized on the situation by threatening to use missiles against the Western aggressors. This belated bravado won for Russia some of the credit in the Arab world for what the United States had done.

REPRESSION IN HUNGARY All the while, Soviet Premier Nikita Khrushchev was subjugating Hungary. On October 23, 1956, fighting against Hungary's Stalinist leadership broke out in Budapest, followed by the installation of a moderate Communist as head of the government. Seemingly content with these developments, the Russians withdrew their forces from Budapest on October 28, but Hungary's announcement three days later that it would withdraw from the Warsaw Pact brought back the Russian tanks. They installed a more compliant leader, and two years later, the Soviets executed the leader of Hungary's moderates. It was a tragic ending to a liberation movement that, at the outset, promised the sort of moderation that might have vindicated George Kennan's policy of "containment," if not Dulles's notion of "liberation."

SPUTNIK On October 4, 1957, the Soviets launched the first satellite, called *sputnik*, an acronym for the Russian phrase "fellow traveler of earth." Americans, until then complacent about their technical superiority, suddenly discovered an apparent "missile gap." If the Russians were so advanced in rocketry, then perhaps they could hit American cities just as Nazi rockets had hit London in 1944–1945. All along Eisenhower knew that the "gap" was more illusory than real, but he could not reveal that high-altitude American U-2 spy planes were gathering this information. Even so, American missile development floundered, with a tangle of agencies and committees engaged in waste and duplication. The launching of Explorer I, the first American satellite, on January 31, 1958, did not quiet the public outcry.

Russia's success with Sputnik frightened the United States and provoked efforts to enlarge defense spending, to offer NATO allies intermediate-range ballistic missiles (IRBMs) pending development of long-range intercontinental ballistic missiles (ICBMs), to set up a new agency to coordinate space efforts, and to establish a crash program in science education. The "sputnik syndrome," compounded by a sharp recession through the winter of 1957–1958, loosened the purse strings of frugal congressmen, who added to the new budget more than Eisenhower wanted for both defense and domestic programs. In 1958 Congress created the National Aeronautics and Space Agency (NASA) to coordinate research and development in the space program. Before the end of the year NASA had a program to put a manned craft in orbit, but the first manned flight, by Commander Alan B. Shepard, Jr., did not take place until May 5, 1961. Finally, in 1958 Congress enacted the National Defense Education Act, which authorized federal grants especially for training in mathematics, science, and modern languages, as well as for student loans and fellowships.

CORRUPT PRACTICES   During the first two years of Eisenhower's second term, public confidence in his performance, as registered by opinion polls, dropped sharply from 79 percent to 49 percent. Emotional issues such as civil rights and defense policy had compounded his troubles. The president's image was further tarnished when congressional investigations revealed that the administration, which had promised to clean up "the mess in Washington," was itself touched by scandals, one of which involved the White House chief of staff, who had taken gifts of a fur coat and an Oriental rug from a businessman in exchange for favors. In 1958 the president reluctantly accepted his aide's resignation.

Republicans also faced the growing opposition of farmers, angry with cuts in price supports, and organized labor, angry because many Republicans had made "right-to-work" (or open-shop) laws a campaign issue in 1958. The Democrats came out of the midterm elections with nearly two-to-one majorities in Congress: 282 to 154 in the House, 64 to 34 in the Senate. Eisenhower would be the first president to face three successive Congresses controlled by the opposition party. The president thus could manage few new departures in domestic policy, but he did oversee the admission of the first states not contiguous to the continental forty-eight. Alaska became the forty-ninth state on January 3, 1959, and Hawaii the fiftieth on August 21, 1959.

FESTERING PROBLEMS ABROAD   In 1958 the Middle East flared up again. By this time the president had secured from Congress authority for what came to be called the Eisenhower Doctrine, which promised to extend economic and military aid to Middle East nations, and to use armed forces if necessary to assist any such nation against military aggression from any Communist country.

Egypt's President Nasser meanwhile had emerged from the Suez crisis with heightened prestige, and in 1958 he created the United Arab Republic (UAR) by merger (a short-lived one) with Syria. Then a leftist coup in Iraq, supposedly inspired by Nasser and the Russians, threw out the pro-Western government. Lebanon, already unsettled by internal conflict, appealed to the United States for support against a similar fate. Eisenhower immediately ordered 5,000 marines into Lebanon, where they limited themselves to the capital, Beirut, and its airfield. He proposed to go no farther because, he said later, if the government was not strong enough to hold out with such protection, then "we probably should not be there." Once the situation stabilized, and the Lebanese factions reached a compromise, American forces withdrew.

The problem of Berlin being situated in East Germany continued to fester with little chance of a resolution for either side. Premier Khrushchev called it a bone in his throat. West Berlin provided a "showplace" of Western democracy and prosperity in the middle of Communist East Germany, a listening post for Western intelligence, and a funnel through which news and propaganda from the West penetrated what Winston Churchill had called "the iron curtain." Although East Germany had sealed its western frontiers, refugees could still pass from East to West Berlin. On November 10, 1958, Khrushchev threatened to give East Germany control of East Berlin and the air lanes into West

Berlin. After the deadline he set, May 27, 1959, Western occupation authorities would have to deal with the East German government, in effect recognizing it, or face the possibility of another blockade.

But Eisenhower refused to budge from his position on Berlin. At the same time he refused to engage in saber-rattling or even to cancel existing plans to reduce the size of the army. Khrushchev, it turned out, was no more eager for confrontation than Eisenhower. Khrushchev's deadline passed almost unnoticed. In 1959, Premier Khrushchev visited the United States, going to New York, Washington, Los Angeles, San Francisco, and Iowa, and dropping in on Eisenhower at Camp David. In talks there Khrushchev endorsed "peaceful coexistence," and Eisenhower admitted that the Berlin situation was "abnormal." They agreed to hold a summit meeting in the spring.

THE U-2 SUMMIT   The summit meeting, however, blew up in Eisenhower's face. On May 1, 1960, a Soviet rocket brought down an American U-2 spy plane on a mission over the Soviet Union. After a period of international jousting with Khrushchev, Eisenhower finally took personal responsibility for the incident—an unprecedented action for a head of state—and justified the action on grounds of national security. At a summit meeting in Paris five days later, Khrushchev called on the president to repudiate the U-2 flights, which had been going on for more than three years, and "pass severe judgment on those responsible." When Eisenhower refused, Khrushchev left the meeting.

CASTRO'S CUBA   The greatest thorn in Eisenhower's side was the Cuban regime of Fidel Castro, which took power on January 1, 1959, after three years of guerrilla warfare against a right-wing dictator. In their struggle Castro's forces had the support of many Americans who hoped for a new day of democratic government in Cuba. But these hopes were dashed when American television reported trials and executions conducted by the victorious Castro. Staged like a Roman holiday before crowds of howling spectators, the trials offered little in the way of legal procedure or proof. Castro, moreover, opposed the widespread foreign control of the Cuban economy. When he began programs of land reform and nationalization of foreign-owned property, relations with the United States worsened. Some observers believed, however, that by rejecting Castro's requests for loans and other help, the American government lost a chance to influence the direction of the revolu-

Fidel Castro (center) *became Cuba's premier in 1959 after three years of guerrilla warfare against the Batista regime.*

tion. Some thought too that by acting on the assumption that Communists already had the upper hand in his movement, the administration may have ensured that fact.

Castro, on the other hand, eagerly accepted the Communist embrace. In 1960 he entered a trade agreement to swap Cuban sugar for Soviet oil and machinery. One of Eisenhower's last acts as president was to suspend diplomatic relations with Cuba. The president also secretly authorized the CIA to begin training a force of Cuban refugees (some of them former Castro stalwarts) for a new revolution. But the final decision on its use would rest with the next president, John F. Kennedy.

ASSESSING THE EISENHOWER YEARS

Until recent years the Eisenhower administration has not drawn much acclaim. One observer called the Eisenhower terms "the time of the great postponement," during which the president left domestic and foreign policies "about where he found them in 1953." Yet even these critics granted that Eisenhower had succeeded in ending the war in Korea and settling the dust raised by McCarthy. If Eisenhower failed to end the Cold War and in fact institutionalized it as a global confrontation, he had sensed the limits of American power and kept its application to low-risk situations. He also tried to restrain the arms race. If he took few initiatives in addressing the social problems that would erupt in the 1960s, he sustained the major innovations of the New Deal. If he tolerated unemployment of as much as 7 percent at times, inflation remained minimal during his two terms.

Eisenhower's farewell address to the American people showed his remarkable foresight in his own area of special expertise, the military. Like George Washington, Eisenhower couched his wisdom largely in the form of warnings: that America's "leadership and prestige depend, not merely upon our unmatched material strength, but on how we use our power in the interests of world peace and human betterment"; that the temptation to find easy answers should take into account "the need to maintain balance in and among national problems"; and above all that Americans "must avoid the impulse to live only for today, plundering, for our own ease and convenience, the precious resources of tomorrow."

As a soldier, Eisenhower highlighted, perhaps better than anyone else could have, the dangers of a military establishment in a time of peace. "In the councils of government we must guard against the acquisition of unwarranted influence, whether sought or unsought, by the military-industrial complex. The potential for the disastrous rise of misplaced power exists and will persist." Eisenhower confessed that his great disappointment was his inability to affirm "that a lasting peace is in sight," only that "war has been avoided."

MAKING CONNECTIONS

- The civil-rights movement of the 1950s aimed to achieve the racial integration of public services and equal access to political rights. This struggle would continue into the 1960s and then move in several new directions. See Chapter 33.

- American involvement in Vietnam grew in the 1950s, but remained limited to an advisory role. Escalation to an active fighting role came under Lyndon Johnson in 1965, a topic covered in Chapter 33.

- Eisenhower's "hands-off" approach to the presidency was reminiscent of the Gilded Age presidencies and those of the 1920s. See Chapters 17, 21, and 26.

FURTHER READING

Scholarship on Eisenhower is extensive. The best overview is Charles C. Alexander's *Holding the Line: The Eisenhower Era, 1951–1961* (1975).* For the manner in which Eisenhower conducted foreign policy, see Robert A. Divine's *Eisenhower and the Cold War* (1981).

For the buildup of American involvement in Indochina, consult Lloyd C. Gardner's *Approaching Vietnam: From World War II through Dien Bien Phu* (1988) and David L. Anderson's *Trapped by Success: The Eisenhower Administration and Vietnam, 1953–1961* (1991).*

Two introductions to the impact wrought by the Warren Supreme Court during the 1950s are Alexander Bickel's *The Supreme Court and the Idea of Progress* (1970)* and Archibald Cox's *The Warren Court: Constitutional Decision as an Instrument of Reform* (1968).* A masterful study of the important Warren Court decision on school desegregation

---

*These books are available in paperback editions.

is Richard Kluger's *Simple Justice: The History of Brown v. Board of Education and Black America's Struggle for Equality* (1975).*

For the story of the bus boycott in Montgomery, see David L. Lewis's *King: A Critical Biography* (1970)* and Stephen B. Oates's *Let the Trumpet Sound: The Life of Martin Luther King, Jr.* (1982).* William H. Chafe's *Civilities and Civil Rights: Greensboro, North Carolina, and the Black Struggle for Freedom* (1980)* examines how one community dragged its feet on the Brown implementation order.

*These books are available in paperback editions.

33 ∽ NEW FRONTIERS:
KENNEDY AND JOHNSON

CHAPTER ORGANIZER

This chapter focuses on:

- the New Frontier and the Great Society

- the achievements of the civil rights movement and ensuing splinter movements

- America's growing involvement in Vietnam and the rising opposition to it

- Kennedy's efforts to combat communism in Cuba

For those pundits who considered the social and political climate of the 1950s dull, the following decade would provide a striking contrast. The 1960s were years of extraordinary turbulence and innovation in public affairs—as well as sudden tragedy and trauma. Many social ills that had been simmering for decades suddenly forced their way onto the national agenda during the 1960s. At the same time, the deeply entrenched assumptions of Cold War ideology led the country into the longest, most controversial, and least successful war in the nation's history.

The New Frontier

KENNEDY VS. NIXON   In 1960, however, there was little sense of dramatic change on the horizon. The presidential election that year featured two candidates—Richard M. Nixon and John F. Kennedy—who initially seemed to symbolize the becalmed politics of the 1950s. Though better known than Kennedy because of his eight years as Eisenhower's vice-president, Nixon had also developed the reputation of a cunning chameleon, the "Tricky Dick" who concealed his duplicity behind a series of masks. "Nixon doesn't know who he is," Kennedy told an aide, "and so each time he makes a speech he has to decide which Nixon he is, and that will be very exhausting."

But Nixon could not be so easily dismissed. He possessed ability, tenacious energy, and a compulsive love for politics, the more combative the better. Born in suburban Los Angeles in 1913, he grew up amid a Quaker family struggling to make ends meet. Acquaintances remembered young Richard Nixon as an introverted and diligent fellow. "He wasn't a little boy that you wanted to pick up and hug," recalled one family friend.

After law school and service in the Pacific during World War II, Richard Nixon jumped into the political arena in 1946 as a Republican and surprised observers by unseating a popular congressman in southern California. He arrived in Washington eager to reverse the tide of New Deal liberalism. "I was elected to smash the labor bosses," he explained. Four years later he won election to the Senate. In his campaigns, Nixon unleashed scurrilous personal attacks on his opponents, shrewdly manipulating the growing anti-Communist hysteria. Yet Nixon became both a respected and effective member of Congress, and by 1950 he was the most requested Republican speaker in the country. His rapid rise to political stardom led to his being offered the vice-presidential nomination in 1952 and 1956. He was an active, highly visible vice-president.

Kennedy lacked such experience and exposure. Despite an abundance of assets, including a widely publicized record of heroism in World War II, a glamorous young wife, a Harvard education, and a large, wealthy family, the handsome forty-three-year-old Kennedy lacked national prominence and political distinction. Kennedy's record in the Senate was mediocre. Author of a Pulitzer Prize–winning study of political leaders who had "made the tough decisions," entitled *Profiles in Courage* (1956), Kennedy, said the Washington pundits, had shown more profile than courage during the McCarthy witch-hunts of the early 1950s and had a weak record on civil rights. Eleanor Roosevelt declined to endorse Kennedy in 1960, noting that presidential authority should not be vested in "someone who understands what courage is and admires it, but has not quite the independence to have it."

During his campaign for the Democratic nomination, Kennedy had shown that he had the energy to match his grace and ambition. As the first Catholic to run for the presidency since Al Smith, he strove to dispel the impression that his religion was a major political liability. By the time of the convention in 1960, he had traveled over 65,000 miles and made over 350 speeches. Hubert Humphrey, the buoyant liberal senator from Minnesota, was knocked out of the race in the West Virginia primary. In his acceptance speech Kennedy found the stirring rhetoric that would stamp the rest of his campaign and his presidency: "We stand today on the edge of a New Frontier—the frontier of unknown opportunities and perils—a frontier of unfulfilled hopes and threats."

The turning point in the presidential campaign came when Richard Nixon agreed to debate his less prominent opponent on television. During the first of four debates, some 70 million viewers saw Nixon, still weak from a recent illness, perspiring heavily and sporting a five-o'clock shadow. He looked haggard, uneasy, and even sinister before the camera. Kennedy, on the other hand, projected a cool poise that made him seem equal, if not superior, in his fitness for the office. Kennedy's popularity immediately shot up in the polls. Reporters discovered that he had "charisma" and noted the giddy young people who now greeted his arrival at campaign stops. In the words of a bemused southern senator, Kennedy combined "the best qualities of Elvis Presley and Franklin D. Roosevelt."

When the votes were counted, Kennedy and his running-mate, Lyndon B. Johnson of Texas, had won the closest presidential election since 1888. The winning margin was only 118,574 votes out of the 68 million cast. Kennedy's wide lead in the electoral vote, 303 to 219, belied the paper-thin margin in several key states, especially Illinois, where Chicago Mayor Richard Daley's Democratic machine appeared to have lived up to its legendary campaign motto: "In Chicago we tell our people to vote early and to vote often."

John F. Kennedy's poise and precision in the debates with Richard Nixon impressed viewers and voters.

THE NEW ADMINISTRATION Kennedy was the youngest person ever elected president, and his cabinet appointments put an accent on youth and "Eastern Establishment" figures. A self-described "idealist without illusions," Kennedy sought to attract the "best and the brightest" minds available, men who would inject a tough, dispassionate, pragmatic, and vigorous outlook into governmental affairs. To that end he asked Robert McNamara, one of the "whiz kids" who had reorganized the Ford Motor Company with his "systems analysis" techniques, to bring his managerial magic to bear on the Department of Defense. Kennedy appointed Harvard professor McGeorge Bundy, whom he called "the second smartest man I know," as special assistant for national security affairs, and chose as his secretary of state Dean Rusk, a career diplomat and former Rhodes Scholar. When critics attacked the appointment of Kennedy's thirty-five-year-old brother Robert as attorney-general, the president quipped, "I don't see what's wrong with giving Bobby a little experience before he goes into law practice."

The inaugural ceremonies set the tone of elegance and youthful vigor that would come to be called the "Kennedy style." After Robert Frost paid tribute to the administration in verse, Kennedy dazzled listeners with his uplifting rhetoric. "Let every nation know," he proclaimed, "that we shall pay any price, bear any burden, meet any hardship, support any friend, oppose any foe, to assure the survival and success of liberty. And so, my fellow Americans: ask not what your country can do for you—ask what you can do for your country." Spines tingled; Kennedy, one journalist wrote, was the first president to be a Prince Charming.

THE KENNEDY RECORD   But for all of his idealistic and energetic rhetoric, Kennedy had a difficult time launching his New Frontier domestic program. Elected by a razor-thin margin, he enjoyed no popular mandate. Nor did he show much skill in dealing with Congress. Moreover, Congress, although overwhelmingly Democratic, remained in the grip of a conservative southern coalition that blocked Kennedy's effort to increase federal aid to education, provide health insurance for the aged, and create a new Department of Urban Affairs.

Administration proposals, nevertheless, did win some notable victories in Congress. They included a new Housing Act that appropriated nearly $5 billion for urban renewal over four years, a raised minimum wage, and increased Social Security benefits. Just two months into his administration Kennedy launched the celebrated Peace Corps to supply volunteers for educational and technical service in underdeveloped countries. Kennedy also won support for an accelerated program to land Americans on the moon before the end of the decade. Congress readily approved a series of broad foreign aid programs to help Latin American nations, dubbed the "Alliance for Progress." Another important Kennedy initiative was a bold tax-reduction bill intended to accelerate economic growth. Although it was not passed until 1964, after Kennedy's death, it provided a surprisingly potent boost to the economy. Perhaps Kennedy's most significant legislative accomplishment was the Trade Expansion Act of 1962, which eventually led to tariff cuts averaging 35 percent between the United States and the European Common Market.

CIVIL RIGHTS   The most important development in American domestic life during the Kennedy years occurred in the area of civil rights. Kennedy was initially reluctant to challenge conservative southern Democrats on the race issue. He also was never as personally committed to civil rights as his brother Bobby or Hubert Humphrey. Despite a

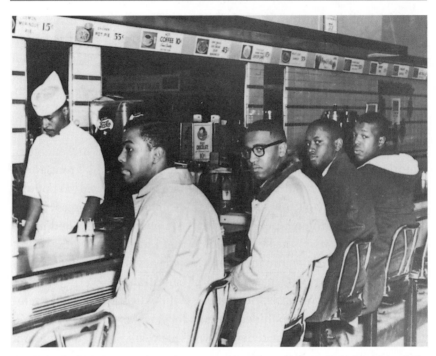

Sit-in at the Woolworth's Lunch Counter in Greensboro, North Carolina, February 1, 1960. *The four protesters, students at North Carolina A & T College, were* (from left) *Joseph McNeil, Franklin McCain, Billy Smith, and Clarence Henderson.*

few dramatic gestures of support toward black leaders, John Kennedy only belatedly grasped the moral and emotional significance of the most widespread reform movement of the decade. Eventually, however, his conscience was pricked by the grassroots civil-rights movement so ably led by Martin Luther King, Jr.

After the Montgomery bus boycott of 1955, King's philosophy of "militant nonviolence" inspired thousands to challenge Jim Crow practices with direct action. At the same time, lawsuits to desegregate the schools activated thousands of parents and young people. The momentum generated the first genuine mass movement in the history of African Americans when four black college students sat down and demanded service at a "whites only" Woolworth's lunch counter in Greensboro, North Carolina, on February 1, 1960. Within a week the "sit-in" movement had spread to six more towns in the state, and within a month to towns in six more states.

In April 1960 the student participants, black and white, formed the Student Nonviolent Coordinating Committee (SNCC), which worked with King's Southern Christian Leadership Conference (SCLC) to spread the movement. The sit-ins at restaurants became "kneel-ins" at churches and "wade-ins" at segregated public pools. And even when struck with clubs, poked with cattle prods, or burned with lighted cigarettes, the protesters refused to retaliate. Not a few paid for such courage and commitment with their lives.

In 1961 the Congress of Racial Equality (CORE) sent a group of black and white "freedom riders" on buses to test a federal ruling that had banned segregation on buses, trains, and their depots. In Alabama, mobs attacked the young travelers, burned one of the buses, and assaulted Justice Department observers, but the demonstrators persisted, drawing national attention and generating new support for their cause. The following year Governor Ross Barnett of Mississippi, who believed that God made "the Negro different to punish him," defied a court order and refused to allow James H. Meredith to enroll at the University of Mississippi. Attorney-General Robert Kennedy thereupon dispatched federal marshals to enforce the law, but they were prevented by a violent white mob. Federal troops had to intervene, and Meredith was finally registered at "Ole Miss," but only after two deaths and many injuries.

Everywhere, it seemed, black activists and white supporters were challenging deeply entrenched patterns of segregation and prejudice. In 1963 Martin Luther King launched a series of demonstrations in Birmingham, Alabama, where Police Commissioner Eugene "Bull" Connor proved the perfect foil for King's tactic of nonviolent civil disobedience. Connor's policemen used dogs, tear gas, electric cattle prods, and fire hoses on the protesters while millions of outraged Americans watched the confrontations on television.

King, who was arrested and jailed during the demonstrations, then wrote his "Letter from a Birmingham Jail," a stirring defense of his nonviolent strategy that became a classic of the civil-rights movement. "One who breaks an unjust law," he stressed, "must do so openly, lovingly, and with a willingness to accept the penalty." He also signaled a shift in his strategy for social change. Heretofore King had emphasized the need to educate southern whites about the injustice of segregation and other patterns of discrimination. Now he focused more on gaining

Eugene "Bull" Connor's police unleash attack dogs on civil-rights demonstrators in Birmingham, Alabama, May 1963.

federal enforcement and new legislation by provoking racists to display their violent hatreds in public. As King admitted in his "Letter," he sought through organized nonviolent protest to "create such a crisis and foster such a tension that a community which has constantly refused to negotiate is forced to confront the issue."

Still, southern traditionalists remained steadfast. In 1963, Governor George Wallace dramatically stood in the doorway of a building at the University of Alabama to block the enrollment of several black students, but he stepped aside in the face of insistent federal marshals. Later the same night NAACP official Medgar Evers was shot to death as he returned home in Jackson, Mississippi.

The high point of the integrationist phase of the civil-rights movement occurred on August 28, 1963, when over 200,000 blacks and whites marched down the Mall in Washington, D.C., toward the Lincoln Memorial singing "We Shall Overcome." The March on Washington was the largest civil-rights demonstration in American history. Standing in front of Lincoln's statue, King delivered one of the memorable public speeches of the century: "Even though we face the difficulties of today and tomorrow, I still have a dream. It is a dream chiefly rooted in the American dream . . . one day . . . the sons of former slaves and the sons of former slave-owners will be able to sit together at the table of brotherhood." That the time for such racial harmony had not yet arrived, however, became clear a little over two weeks later when a bomb exploded in a Birmingham church, killing four black girls who had arrived early for Sunday school.

Yet King's dream—shared and promoted by thousands of other activists—survived. The intransigence and violence that civil-rights workers encountered won converts to their cause all across the country. Persuaded by his brother Robert, a man of passion, compassion, and vision, and by the pressure of events, President Kennedy finally decided that enforcement of existing statutes was not enough; new legislation was needed to deal with the race question. In 1963 he told the nation that racial discrimination "has no place in American life or law," and he then endorsed an ambitious civil-rights bill intended to end discrimination in public facilities, desegregate the public schools, and protect black voters. But southern conservatives quickly blocked the bill in Congress.

THE WARREN COURT The Supreme Court under Chief Justice Earl Warren continued to be one of the strongest and most controversial influences on American domestic life during the 1960s. Its *Brown* decision of 1954 exerted a steady pressure for change in the traditional patterns of race relations, North and South. During the Kennedy-Johnson years, the Court's stand on civil liberties proved equally controversial. In 1962 the Court had ruled that a school prayer adopted by the New York State Board of Regents violated the constitutional prohibition against an established religion. In *Gideon v. Wainwright* (1963) the Court required that every felony defendant be provided a lawyer regardless of the defendant's ability to pay. Three years later, in *Miranda v. Arizona,* the Court confirmed the obligation of police to inform arrested suspects of their rights before questioning.

FOREIGN FRONTIERS

EARLY SETBACKS Kennedy's record in foreign affairs was mixed, more spectacularly so than his domestic record. Upon taking office he discovered that there was in the works a CIA operation designed to prepare 1,500 anti-Castro Cubans for an invasion of their homeland. The Joint Chiefs of Staff endorsed the plan; diplomatic advisers reported that the invasion would inspire Cubans on the island to rebel against Castro. The scheme, poorly conceived and executed, had about as much chance of succeeding as John Brown's raid on Harper's Ferry a little over a century earlier. When the invasion force landed at Cuba's Bay of Pigs on April 19, 1961, it was crushed in three days and 1,200 men were captured. A *New York Times* columnist lamented that the United States "looked like fools to our friends, rascals to our enemies, and incompetents to the rest."

Two months after the Bay of Pigs disaster Kennedy met Soviet Premier Khrushchev in Vienna, Austria. It was a tense confrontation during which Khrushchev tried to bully the young and inexperienced Kennedy. He threatened to limit Western access to Berlin, the divided city located deep within East Germany. Kennedy was shaken by the aggressive Soviet stand, but he returned home determined to demonstrate American resolve—and his own courage. He called up Army Reserve and National Guard units. The Soviets responded by erecting the Berlin Wall, which cut off movement between East and West Berlin and became a symbol of the chill in relations between the Soviet Union and the United States.

THE MISSILE CRISIS   A year later Khrushchev posed another serious challenge, this time just ninety miles south of Florida. Khrushchev granted Castro's request for Russian nuclear missiles in Cuba to protect the island from future American-sponsored invasions, and to redress the strategic imbalance caused by the presence of American missiles in Turkey aimed at the Soviet Union. While such missiles would hardly alter the military balance, they would come from a direction not covered by American radar systems and arrive too quickly for warning. More important to Kennedy was the psychological effect of American acquiescence to a Soviet presence on its doorstep. Khrushchev's purpose was apparently to demonstrate his toughness to both Chinese and Russian critics of his earlier advocacy of peaceful coexistence. But he misjudged the American response.

On October 14, 1962, American intelligence flights discovered that Russian missile sites were under construction in Cuba. The administration immediately decided that they had to be removed; the only question was how. In a series of secret meetings, the Executive Committee of the National Security Council debated between a "surgical" air strike and a blockade of Cuba. They opted for a blockade, but since this would technically represent an act of war, they called it a "quarantine" rather than a blockade. It offered the advantage of forcing the Soviets to shoot first, if it came to that, and it left open further options of stronger action. Monday, October 22, began one of the most anxious weeks in world history. On that day the president announced to Congress and then to the public the discovery of the missile sites in Cuba; he also announced the quarantine.

Tensions grew as Khrushchev blustered that Kennedy had pushed humankind "to the abyss of a world nuclear-missile war." Soviet ships, he declared, would ignore the quarantine. But on Wednesday, October 24, five Soviet supply ships stopped short of the American ships. Two days later an agent of the Russian embassy privately approached a television journalist with a proposal for an agreement: Russia would withdraw the missiles in return for a public pledge by the United States not to invade Cuba. Secretary of State Dean Rusk sent back word that the administration was interested, but told the journalist: "Remember, when you report this, that eyeball to eyeball, they blinked first." On Sunday, October 28, Khrushchev agreed to remove the missiles and added a conciliatory invitation "to continue the exchange of views on the prohibition of atomic and thermonuclear weapons, general disarmament, and other problems relating to the relaxation of international tension."

In the aftermath of the crisis, the United States took several symbolic steps to relax tensions: an agreement to sell surplus wheat to the Soviets, the installation of a "hot line" telephone between Washington and Moscow to provide instant contact between the heads of government, and the removal of obsolete American missiles from Turkey, Italy, and Britain. The United States also negotiated a treaty with Russian and British representatives to stop nuclear testing in the atmosphere. The treaty, ratified in September 1963, did not provide for on-site inspection, nor did it ban underground testing, which continued, but it promised to end the dangerous pollution of the atmosphere with radioactivity. The test-ban treaty was an important move toward greater international cooperation on nuclear proliferation. Kennedy quoted the Chinese sage Confucius to suggest the treaty's significance: "A journey of a thousand miles begins with one step."

KENNEDY AND VIETNAM   As tensions with the Soviet Union were easing, a crisis was growing in Southeast Asia that would become within a decade the greatest American foreign-policy debacle ever. During John Kennedy's "thousand days" in office, the turmoil of Indochina never preoccupied the public mind for any extended period, but it dominated international diplomatic debates from the time the administration entered office.

The Geneva Accords of 1954 had declared the landlocked kingdom of Laos a neutral country, but thereafter a complex power struggle erupted between the Communist Pathet Lao and the Royal Laotian Army. There matters stood when Eisenhower left office and told Kennedy: "You might have to go in there and fight it out." The chairman of the Joint Chiefs of Staff argued in favor of a stand against the Pathet Lao, even at the cost of direct intervention. After a lengthy consideration of alternatives, the Kennedy administration decided to back the formation of a neutralist coalition that would preclude American military involvement in Laos, yet prevent a Pathet Lao victory. The Soviets, who were extending aid to the Pathet Lao, indicated a readiness to negotiate, and in May 1961 talks began in Geneva. After more than a year of tangled negotiations, the three factions in Laos agreed to a neutral coalition.

Meanwhile, North Vietnam kept open the Ho Chi Minh Trail through eastern Laos, over which it supplied its Vietcong allies fighting in South Vietnam. There the situation worsened under the leadership of the Catholic premier Ngo Dinh Diem, despite encouraging reports from the military commander of the American "advisers" in South Vietnam. At the time the problem was less the scattered guerrilla attacks than Diem's failure to deliver social and economic reforms and to rally popular support. His repressive tactics, directed not only against Communists but also against the Buddhist majority and other critics, played into the hands of his enemies.

In 1961 White House assistant Walt Rostow and General Maxwell Taylor became the first in a long line of presidential emissaries to South Vietnam's capital, Saigon. They proposed a major increase in the American military presence, but Kennedy refused, and instead continued to dispatch more military "advisers." When he took office there had been 2,000 American troops in South Vietnam; by the end of 1963 there were 16,000, none of whom had been committed to battle. But the

Diem regime continued to be its own worst enemy. By mid-1963 growing Buddhist demonstrations made the public discontent in South Vietnam more plainly visible. The spectacle of Buddhist monks immolating themselves on Saigon streets in protest of Diem's iron-fisted rule shocked Americans but brought from Diem's sister-in-law only sarcasm about "barbecued monks."

By the fall of 1963 the Kennedy administration had decided that Diem was a lost cause. When dissident Vietnamese generals proposed a coup d'état, American ambassador Henry Cabot Lodge assured them that Washington would not stand in the way. On November 1 the insurgent military leaders seized the government and murdered Diem. Yet the generals provided no more stability than earlier regimes, as successive coups set South Vietnam spinning from one military leader to the other.

KENNEDY'S ASSASSINATION   By the fall of 1963 Kennedy seemed to be facing up to the intractability of the situation in Vietnam. He spoke of the South Vietnamese: "In the final analysis it's their war. They're the ones who have to win it or lose it. We can help them as advisers but they have to win it." Some of his aides later argued that Kennedy would never have allowed a dramatic escalation of American military involvement in Vietnam. Others strongly disagreed.

The answer of course will never be known, for on November 22, 1963, while on a campaign swing through downtown Dallas, Kennedy was shot twice in the throat and head and died almost immediately. A few hours later Dallas police arrested Lee Harvey Oswald, a twenty-four-year-old ex-Marine drifter who had worked in the Texas Book Depository, the building from which the shots were fired at Kennedy. Investigators had several other reasons to suspect Oswald: he had recently returned from a prolonged stay in the Soviet Union, in recent years he had also visited Cuba, and his family had ties to a Mafia member who had made threats to kill Kennedy. Yet before Oswald could be thoroughly interrogated, he too was killed. Two days after Oswald's arrest, as television cameras covered his transfer to another jail, Jack Ruby, a Dallas nightclub owner, stepped from the crowd of onlookers and fatally shot Oswald in the abdomen.

Oswald's death ignited a controversy over the assassination that still simmers today. In December 1963 President Johnson appointed a commission to investigate Kennedy's murder. Headed by Chief Justice Earl Warren, it concluded that Oswald had acted alone. Yet many people were (and are) not convinced, and since 1963 dozens of conspiracy theories have been hatched. Some blame the CIA or the Mafia, others point at Fidel Castro, whom the CIA had once tried to assassinate. Still others insist that Cuban exiles in Miami, angered by Kennedy's failure to rescue their comrades during the Bay of Pigs fiasco, were behind the assassination. In 1979 a House committee reported that more than one person had fired shots at Kennedy in Dallas, but FBI scientists discredited the theory. Books and movies setting forth various conspiracy theories have kept the controversy alive. Whatever the actual story of the assassination, Kennedy's tragic death enshrined him in the public imagination as a martyred leader cut down in the prime of his career.

LYNDON JOHNSON AND THE GREAT SOCIETY

Texan Lyndon Johnson took the oath as president of the United States on board the plane that took John Kennedy's body back to Washington from Dallas. At age fifty-five, Johnson had spent twenty-six years on the Washington scene and had served nearly a decade as Senate

Kennedy's vice-president, Lyndon B. Johnson, takes the presidential oath as Air Force One *returns from Dallas with Jacqueline Kennedy* (right), *the presidential party, and the body of the assassinated president.*

Democratic leader, where he had displayed the greatest gift for compromise since Henry Clay.

Johnson brought to the White House a marked change of style from his predecessor. A truly self-made man who through gritty determination and shrewd manipulation had worked his way out of a hardscrabble rural Texas background to become one of Washington's most powerful figures, he had none of the Kennedy elegance or charisma. Johnson yearned for both political power and public affection. The first southern president since Woodrow Wilson, he harbored a sense of being the perpetual "outsider" despite his long experience with power. And indeed he was so regarded by Kennedy "insiders."

Those who viewed Johnson as a stereotypical southern conservative ignored his long-standing admiration for Franklin Roosevelt, the depth of his concern for poor people, and his heartfelt commitment to the cause of civil rights. The day after the assassination he told an aide: "I am a Roosevelt New Dealer. As a matter of fact . . . Kennedy was a little too conservative to suit my taste." In foreign affairs Johnson was, like Woodrow Wilson, a novice. But in the domestic arena during the 1950s he was unsurpassed in his ability to shepherd legislation through the gauntlet of special-interest lobbyists and Congress. He once bragged that "Ike couldn't pass the Lord's Prayer in Congress without me."

THE LAST FRONTIERSMAN   Lyndon Johnson the man was a baffling paradox, capable of altering himself to fit any occasion. In one of his favorite stories, he told of an applicant for a teaching job who is asked by the school board whether the world is flat or round. The man replies: "I can teach it either way." Likewise, Johnson could assume the guise of a multitude of different characters at will. On the one hand he was a compulsive worker and achiever, animated by greed, ambition, and an all-consuming lust for power, an overbearing man capable of ruthlessness and deceit and driven by inner demons that required him to be the center of attention. As the former secretary of state Dean Acheson once told Johnson, you are "not a very likable person." On the other hand, he could be warm, caring, and gracious. He made friends easily and displayed genuine concern for the welfare of the disadvantaged. Overflowing with passions and self-doubts, eager for affection and attention, Johnson was both a loving husband and a philanderer.

Johnson was a fourth-generation Texan who liked to refer to himself as "the last Frontiersman." His grandfather was a member of the Populist party and his father Sam called himself a "latter-day Populist." Sam Johnson was elected five times to the state legislature, the last congressman who still carried a pistol. When Lyndon was five, his family moved to Johnson City, a desolate village noted for its prickly pears, rattlesnakes, and armadillos. The town had no paved roads, no plumbing or electricity—not even a train station. Illness forced Sam Johnson to resign his legislative post and quit working. The family thereafter lived a hand-to-mouth existence.

Lyndon became an obstreperous son, rebellious and defiant, determined to control others rather than submit to authority himself. He was able to work his way through Southwest Texas State Teachers College. In 1931 he was hired as an assistant to a South Texas congressman and moved to Washington, D.C. Johnson thereafter became an enthusiastic New Dealer and an avid fan of Franklin Roosevelt. In 1935 he returned to Texas to head up the National Youth Administration for the state. He did so well that he was elected to Congress two years later. While visiting Texas, Roosevelt told an aide that he "liked this boy." He liked him so much that when Johnson ran for a vacant Senate seat in 1941, the president made strenuous efforts to assure his victory. But Johnson lost a narrow, fraudulent election. To him the moral of the story was that one needed to bend the rules to get elected a senator in Texas.

After a stint in the navy during World War II, which Johnson, like Kennedy, later exaggerated to appear more heroic than it was, he ran for the Senate again in 1948. This time he played the "Texas game," letting his lieutenants bribe local political bosses to "stuff" ballot boxes in their precincts. At the last minute Johnson was declared the winner by eighty-seven votes. He tried to deflect criticism by jokingly referring to himself as "Landslide Lyndon," but a cloud of suspicion hung over him as he assumed his Senate seat. During the early 1950s Johnson kept his seat by engaging in the required "Red-baiting," catering to the oil and natural gas interests in Texas, and opposing civil-rights legislation. "There's nothing more useless," he once observed, "than a dead liberal." In 1950, at age forty-three, he became the youngest Senate whip in Democratic party history. The next year he became minority leader, again the youngest ever.

After reelection in 1954 Johnson became Senate majority leader when the Democrats recaptured the upper house of Congress. During the next six years he displayed a remarkable ability for manipulating others to get legislation passed, resorting to horse-trading and back-room deals in order to shepherd some 1,300 bills through the Senate. He engineered the censure of Joseph McCarthy and the passage of the Civil Rights Act of 1957. His accomplishments made him a natural candidate for the presidency in 1960, but he was unable to project himself as anything more than a regional candidate. Having done all he could as a legislative leader, he eagerly accepted Kennedy's invitation to join the ticket as his vice-presidential running mate. The invitation resulted not from affection or admiration. Kennedy simply needed Johnson to help carry the South for him.

POLITICS AND POVERTY   Quite naturally, President Johnson established domestic politics as his first priority. He exploited the nation's grief after the assassination by declaring that Kennedy's legislative program, stymied in several congressional committees, would now be passed. The logjam in the Congress that had blocked Kennedy's program broke under Johnson's forceful leadership, and a torrent of legislation poured through.

At the top of Johnson's agenda were the stalled measures for tax reduction and civil rights. He then added to his "must" list a bold new idea that bore the LBJ brand: "This Administration today, here and now, declares unconditional war on poverty in America." The particulars were to come later, the product of an administration task force already at work before Johnson took office.

Americans had suddenly rediscovered poverty in the early 1960s when the social critic Michael Harrington published a powerful exposé titled *The Other America* (1962). Brandishing an impressive array of statistics as well as convincing theories of social psychology, Harrington argued that while most Americans had been celebrating their rising affluence during the postwar era, some 40 to 50 million people were mired in a "culture of poverty" hidden from view and passed on from one generation to the other. Unlike the upwardly mobile immigrant poor at the turn of the century, they were impervious to hope. "To be impoverished," he asserted, "is to be an internal alien, to grow up in a culture that is radically different from the one that dominates the society."

President Kennedy read a review of *The Other America* in 1963 and asked his advisers to investigate the problem and suggest a plan of attack. Upon taking office Johnson announced that he wanted an antipoverty package that was "big and bold that would hit the nation with real impact." Money for the program would come from the economic growth generated by the tax reduction of more than $10 billion passed in 1964.

The administration's Economic Opportunity Bill incorporated a wide range of programs: a Job Corps for inner-city youths, a Head Start program for disadvantaged preschoolers, work-study jobs for college students, grants to farmers and rural business, loans to those willing to hire the chronic unemployed, the Volunteers in Service to America (VISTA, a "domestic Peace Corps"), and the Community Action Program, which would provide "maximum feasible participation" of the poor in directing programs designed for their benefit. Speaking at Ann Arbor, Michigan, Johnson called for a "Great Society" resting on "abundance and liberty for all. The Great Society demands an end to poverty and racial injustice, to which we are fully committed in our time." In theory it was liberalism triumphant; in practice its considerable achievements were accompanied by administrative bungling, corruption, and misguided idealism.

THE 1964 ELECTION As the 1964 election approached, Johnson was conceded the Democratic nomination from the start. He chose as his running mate Hubert H. Humphrey of Minnesota, the prominent liberal senator with the seemingly permanent smile and inexhaustible supply of optimism and energy.

In the Republican party, conservatives charged that the party was falling into the hands of an "Eastern Establishment" that had given in to the same internationalism and big-government policies as liberal Democrats. Ever since 1940, so the theory went, the party nominated "me-too" candidates who merely promised to run more efficiently the programs that Democrats promoted. Offer the voters "a choice, not an echo," they reasoned, and a truly conservative majority would assert itself.

By 1960 Arizona's Senator Barry Goldwater, a millionaire department-store owner, had begun to emerge as the leader of the Republican right. A movement to draft Goldwater began as early as 1961, mobilizing conservative activists to capture party caucuses and contest primaries. In 1964 they took an early lead, and after Goldwater swept the all-important California primary, his forces controlled the Republican convention. "I would remind you," Goldwater told the delegates, "that extremism in the defense of liberty is no vice."

Goldwater displayed an unusual gift for frightening voters. Accusing the administration of waging a "no-win" war in Vietnam, he urged wholesale bombing of North Vietnam and left the impression of being trigger-happy. He also savaged Johnson's War on Poverty and the New Deal tradition. At one stop he called LBJ the "Santa Claus of the free lunch." In Tennessee he proposed the sale of TVA; in St. Petersburg, Florida, a major retirement community, he questioned the value of Social Security. He had voted against both the nuclear test ban and the Civil Rights Act. Republican campaign buttons claimed: "In your heart, you know he's right." Democrats responded: "In your guts, you know he's nuts."

Johnson, on the other hand, appealed to the middle of the political spectrum. In contrast to Goldwater's bellicose rhetoric on Vietnam, he made a pledge that won great applause at the time and much comment later: "We are not about to send American boys nine or ten thousand miles from home to do what Asian boys ought to be doing for themselves."

The election was a landslide. Johnson polled 61 percent of the total vote; Goldwater carried only Arizona and five states in the Deep South. Johnson won the electoral vote by a whopping 482 to 52. In the Senate the Democrats increased their majority by two (68 to 32) and in the House by thirty-seven (295 to 140).

LANDMARK LEGISLATION   Johnson took advantage of his new mandate to launch his Great Society program. It would, he promised, end poverty, renovate the decaying central cities, provide every young American with the chance to attend college, protect the health of the elderly, enhance the cultural life of the nation, clean up the air and water, and make the highways safer.

To accomplish such goals the Johnson administration pushed an array of new legislation through the Congress at a pace unseen since Roosevelt's Hundred Days. "Hurry, boys, hurry," Johnson told aides. "Get that legislation up to Capitol Hill and out. Eighteen months from now ol' Landslide Lyndon will be lame-duck Lyndon." Priority went to health insurance and aid to education, proposals that had languished since President Truman advanced them in 1945. The proposal for a comprehensive plan of medical insurance had long been stalled by the American Medical Association's ardent opposition. But now that Johnson had the votes, the AMA joined Republicans in boarding the bandwagon for a bill serving those over age sixty-five. The act not only created the Medicare insurance program for the aged, but added another program, Medicaid, which provided states with federal grants that would help cover medical payments for the indigent.

Five days after he submitted his Medicare program, Johnson sent to Congress his proposal for $1.5 billion in federal aid to elementary and secondary education. Such proposals had been ignored since the 1940s, blocked alternately by issues of segregation or separation of church and state. Now Johnson and congressional leaders devised a means of extending aid to "poverty-impacted" school districts regardless of their public or parochial character.

The momentum generated by the passage of these measures had already begun to carry others along, and it continued through the following year. Altogether the tide of Great Society legislation carried 435 bills through the Congress. Among them was the Appalachian Regional Development Act of 1966, which allocated $1.1 billion for programs to enhance the standard of living of those in remote mountain coves. The Housing and Urban Development Act of 1965 provided for construction of 240,000 housing units and $2.9 billion for urban renewal. Rent supplements for low-income families followed in 1966, and in that year there began a new Department of Housing and Urban Development, headed by Robert C. Weaver, the first black cabinet member. Johnson had, in the words of one Washington reporter, "brought to harvest a generation's backlog of ideas and social legislation."

THE IMMIGRATION ACT   Little noticed among the legislation flowing from the Congress was a major new immigration bill that had originated in the Kennedy White House. In collaboration with the Anti-Defamation League, John Kennedy had written a pamphlet in 1958 entitled "A Nation of Immigrants," in which he celebrated the role played by immigration in shaping the United States and emphasized the need for revising the immigration regulations. In 1963 he sent to Congress a new immigration bill, but it was languishing in committee when he was assassinated. Johnson used his 1964 State of the Union address to endorse immigration reform in general and the Kennedy bill in particular. A modified version finally passed the Congress in the fall of 1965.

President Johnson signed the Immigration Act of 1965 in a ceremony held on Liberty Island in New York Harbor, with Ellis Island in the background. In his speech, Johnson stressed that the new law would redress the wrong done to those "from southern and eastern Europe" and the "developing continents" of Asia, Africa, and Latin America. It did so by abolishing the discriminatory quotas based on national origins that had governed immigration policy since the 1920s. The old system had favored immigrants from Britain and other countries in western Europe and had effectively shut the door to most people from eastern Europe and Asia.

The new law, whose provisions were to take full effect in 1968, treated all nationalities and races equally. In place of national quotas it created hemispheric ceilings on visas issued: 170,000 for persons from outside the Western Hemisphere, 120,000 for persons from within. It also stipulated that no more than 20,000 people could come from any one country each year. The new act allowed the entry of immediate family members of American residents without limit. For others, the immigration bill provided a revised system of preferences used to decide which applicants qualified for admission. Most of the annual visas were to be given on a first-come-first-served basis to "other relatives" of American residents, and only a small proportion (about 10 percent) were allocated to those with special talents or job skills.

The Immigration Act of 1965 passed with so little opposition in part because no one expected it to generate profound change. Attorney-General Robert Kennedy told the Senate that perhaps as many as 5,000 Asians might come the first year, "after which immigration from that source would virtually disappear." But he was wrong. During the prosperous sixties, few western Europeans sought to emigrate to the United States; those living in Communist-controlled eastern Europe could not leave. But Asians and Latin Americans flocked to American consulates in search of visas. And within a few years the new arrivals in turn used the family-preference system to bring their family members as well. This so-called chain immigration quickly filled the annual quotas for nations such as the Philippines, Mexico, Korea, and the Dominican Republic, and Hispanics and Asians became the largest contingent of new Americans.

THE GREAT SOCIETY: SUCCESSES AND FAILURES The Great Society programs included several genuine success stories. The Highway

Safety Act and the Traffic Safety Act established safety standards for automobile manufacturers and highway design, and the scholarships provided for college students under the Higher Education Act were quite popular. Many Great Society initiatives aimed at improving the health, nutrition, and education of poor Americans, young and old, made headway against these intractable problems. So, too, did efforts to clean up air and water pollution. But several ambitious programs were hastily designed and ill conceived, others were vastly under-funded, and many were mismanaged. Medicare, for example, removed any incentives for hospitals to control costs, and medical bills skyrock-eted. Often funds appropriated for various programs never made it through the tangled bureaucracy to the needy. Widely publicized cases of welfare fraud placed a powerful weapon in the hands of those op-posed to liberal social programs. By 1966 middle-class resentment over the cost and waste of the Great Society programs helped generate a strong conservative backlash.

FROM CIVIL RIGHTS TO BLACK POWER

VOTING RIGHTS   Among the successes of the Great Society were several key pieces of civil-rights legislation. After Kennedy's death, President Johnson called for passage of the long-stalled civil-rights bill as a memorial to the fallen leader. The Civil Rights Act of 1964 was the most far-reaching civil-rights measure ever enacted. It outlawed racial discrimination in hotels, restaurants, and other public accommodations. In addition, the attorney-general could now bring suits for school de-segregation, relieving parents of a painful necessity.

Perhaps equally important, the Civil Rights Act gave new momentum to activists in the cause. Early in 1965 Martin Luther King, the recipi-ent of the Nobel Peace Prize the year before, announced a voter-regis-tration drive aimed at the 3 million blacks in the South who had not registered to vote. On March 7 civil-rights protesters began a march for voting rights from Selma, Alabama, to Montgomery, only to be violently dispersed by state troopers and a mounted posse. A federal judge then agreed to allow the march, and President Johnson provided federal pro-tection. By March 25, when the demonstrators reached Montgomery,

Martin Luther King, Jr. (second from left), and other civil rights leaders at the head of the March on Washington for Jobs and Freedom, August 28, 1963.

they numbered 35,000, and King delivered a rousing address from the steps of the state capitol.

Several days before the march President Johnson went before Congress with a moving plea for voting rights legislation. The resulting Voting Rights Act of 1965, passed to ensure all citizens the right to vote, authorized the attorney-general to dispatch federal examiners to register voters. In states or counties where fewer than half the adults had voted in 1964, the act suspended literacy tests and other devices commonly used to defraud citizens of the vote. By the end of the year some 250,000 blacks were newly registered.

"BLACK POWER"   In the midst of success, however, the civil-rights movement began to fragment. On August 11, 1965, less than a week after the passage of the Voting Rights Act, the predominantly black Watts area of Los Angeles exploded in a frenzy of riots and looting. When the uprising ended, there were thirty-four dead, almost 4,000 rioters in jail, and property damage exceeding $35 million. Liberal commentators were stunned, since the riots occurred in the wake of the greatest legislative victories for black Americans since the first Reconstruction.

But events did not stand still to await white liberal comprehension. The Watts upheaval marked the beginning of four "long hot summers" of racial conflagration. Riots in the summer of 1966 erupted in Chicago and Cleveland, along with forty other American cities. The following summer Newark and Detroit burst into flames. Detroit provided the most graphic example of urban violence, as tanks rolled through the streets and soldiers from the 101st Airborne used machine guns to root out snipers in the tenements.

In retrospect it was understandable that the civil-rights movement would begin to focus on the plight of urban blacks. By the middle 1960s about 70 percent of America's black population lived in metropolitan areas, most of them in central-city ghettos that had been bypassed by the postwar prosperity. It seems clear, also in retrospect, that the nonviolent tactics that had worked in the rural South would not work in the northern cities. In the North, racial problems resulted from segregated residential patterns not amenable to changes in law, and northern white ethnic groups did not have the cultural heritage that southern whites shared with blacks. A special Commission on Civil Disorders noted that, unlike earlier race riots that had been started by whites, the urban upheavals of the middle 1960s were initiated by blacks themselves in an effort to destroy what they could not stomach and what civil-rights legislation seemed unable to change.

In the midst of such violence, a new philosophy of racial separatism began to emerge. By 1966 "black power" had become the rallying cry of young activists. Radical members of SNCC had become estranged from Martin Luther King's theories of nonviolence. When Stokely Carmichael, a twenty-five-year-old graduate of Howard University, became head of SNCC in 1966, he adopted a separatist philosophy of black power, and ousted whites from the organization. "We reject an American dream defined by white people and must work to construct an American reality defined by Afro-Americans," said a SNCC position paper. H. Rap Brown, who succeeded Carmichael as head of SNCC in 1967, even urged blacks to "get you some guns" and "kill the honkies." Meanwhile Carmichael had moved on to the Black Panther party, a self-professed group of urban black revolutionaries founded in Oakland, California, in 1966. Headed by Huey P. Newton and Eldridge Cleaver, the Black Panthers echoed the separatist demands of Marcus Garvey and terrified the public by wearing bandeleros and carrying rifles. Eventually the Panthers fragmented in spasms of violence, much of which the FBI and local police officials helped to provoke.

Malcolm X, influential spokesman for the Black Muslim movement.

The most articulate spokesman for black power was one of the earliest, Malcolm X (formerly Malcolm Little, with the "X" denoting his lost African surname). Malcolm had risen from a ghetto childhood involving narcotics and crime to become the chief disciple of Elijah Muhammad, the Black Muslim prophet who rejected Christianity as "the religion of white devils" and encouraged black culture and black pride. "Yes, I'm an extremist," Malcolm acknowledged in 1964. "You show me a black man who isn't an extremist and I'll show you one who needs psychiatric attention." By 1964 Malcolm had broken with Elijah Muhammad and founded his own organization, which was committed to the establishment of alliances between American blacks and the nonwhite peoples of the world. He also had begun to abandon his earlier separatist agenda and violent tactics. But just after the publication of his *Autobiography* in 1965, Malcolm was gunned down in Harlem by Black Muslim assassins. With him went the most effective voice for urban black militancy. What made the assassination of Malcolm X especially tragic was that he had just months before begun to abandon his strident antiwhite rhetoric and to preach a biracial message of social change.

Although widely publicized and highly visible, the "black power" movement never attracted more than a small minority of African Americans. Only about 15 percent of blacks labeled themselves separatists. The preponderant majority continued to identify with the philosophy of nonviolent integration promoted by Martin Luther King and organizations such as the NAACP. King criticized black separatism and the promotion of violent social change as a "nihilistic philosophy." He reminded his followers that "we can't win violently. We have neither the instruments nor the techniques at our disposal, and it would be totally absurd for us to believe we could do it."

Yet the black power philosophy, despite its hyperbole and violence, had two very positive effects upon the civil-rights movement. First, it helped African Americans take greater pride in their racial heritage. As Malcolm X often pointed out, prolonged slavery and institutionalized racism eroded the self-esteem of many blacks in the United States. "The worst crime the white man has committed," he declared, "has been to teach us to hate ourselves." He and others helped blacks appreciate their African roots and their American accomplishments. In fact, it was Malcolm X who insisted that blacks call themselves African Americans as a symbol of pride in their roots and as a spur to learn more about their history as a people. As the popular singer James Brown urged, "Say it loud—I'm black and I'm proud."

Second, the black power phenomenon forced King and other mainstream black leaders and organizations to launch a new stage in the civil-rights movement that would focus attention on the plight of poor inner-city blacks. Legal access to restaurants, schools, and other public accommodations, King pointed out, meant little to people mired in a culture of urban poverty. They needed jobs and decent housing as much as they needed legal rights. To this end, King began to emphasize the economic plight of the black urban underclass. The time had come for radical measures "to provide jobs and income for the poor." Yet as King and others sought to escalate the war on poverty at home, the war in Vietnam was commandeering more and more of America's resources and energies.

THE TRAGEDY OF VIETNAM

As violence was escalating in America's inner cities, the war in Vietnam reached new levels of intensity and destruction. At the time of President Kennedy's death there were 16,000 American military "advisers" in Vietnam. Lyndon Johnson inherited a commitment to prevent a

CHINA

U.S.
1966-

GULF OF
TONKIN

TH
NAM

GULF OF TONKIN INCIDENT
AUGUST 4, 1964

SOUTH CHINA SEA

LAOS

Vientiane

DMZ 17TH PARALLEL
DEMARCATION LINE
Hue JULY 1954

TET OFFENSIVE
JAN. 30-
FEB., 1968

MASSACRE
H 16, 1968

THAILAND

CAMBODIA

SOUTH
VIETNAM

Phnom Penh

TET OFFENSIVE
JAN. 30-FEB., 1968

GULF OF THAILAND

THE VIETNAM WAR

0   200 Miles

0   200 Kilometers

Communist takeover in South Vietnam along with a reluctance to assume the military burden for fighting the war. One president after another had done just enough to avoid being charged with having "lost" Vietnam. Johnson did the same, fearing that any other course would undermine his influence and endanger his Great Society programs in Congress. But this path took him and the United States inexorably deeper into intervention in Asia.

ESCALATION   The official sanction for America's "escalation"—a Defense Department term coined in the Vietnam era—was the Tonkin Gulf Resolution, voted by Congress on August 7, 1964. Johnson reported in a national television address that two American destroyers had been attacked by North Vietnamese vessels on August 2 and 4 in the Gulf of Tonkin off the coast of North Vietnam. Although he described the attacks as unprovoked, in truth the destroyers had been monitoring South Vietnamese raids against two North Vietnamese islands—raids planned by American advisers. The Tonkin Gulf Resolution authorized the president to "take all necessary measures to repel any armed attack against the forces of the United States and to prevent further aggression."

Three months after Johnson's landslide victory over Goldwater, he and his advisers made the crucial decisions that shaped American policy in Vietnam for the next four years. On February 5, 1965, Vietcong guerrillas killed 8 and wounded 126 Americans at Pleiku. Further attacks on Americans later that week led Johnson to order operation "Rolling Thunder," the first sustained American bombings of North Vietnam, which were intended to stop the flow of soldiers and supplies into the South. Six months later a task force concluded that the bombing had little effect on the supplies pouring down the Ho Chi Minh Trail from North Vietnam through Laos. Still, the bombing continued.

In March 1965 the new American army commander in Vietnam, General William C. Westmoreland, requested and got the first installment of combat troops, ostensibly to defend American airfields. By the end of 1965 there were 184,000 American troops in Vietnam; in 1966 the troop level reached 385,000. As combat operations increased, so did the list of American casualties, announced each week on the nightly news along with the "body count" of alleged enemy dead. "Westy's War," although fought with helicopter gunships, chemical defoliants, and napalm, became like the trench warfare of World War I—a grinding war of attrition.

THE CONTEXT FOR POLICY   Johnson's decision to "Americanize" the war, so ill-starred in retrospect, was entirely consistent with the foreign policy principles pursued by all American presidents after World War II. The version of the containment theory articulated in the Truman Doctrine, endorsed by Eisenhower and Dulles throughout the 1950s, and reaffirmed by Kennedy, pledged United States opposition to the advance of communism anywhere in the world. "Why are we in Vietnam?" Johnson asked rhetorically at Johns Hopkins University in 1965. "We are there because we have a promise to keep. . . . To leave Vietnam to its fate would shake the confidence of all these people in the value of American commitment." Secretary of State Dean Rusk repeated this rationale before countless congressional committees, warning that Thailand, Burma, and the rest of Southeast Asia would fall to communism if American forces withdrew. American military intervention in Vietnam was thus no aberration, but a logical culmination of the assumptions widely shared by the foreign policy establishment and leaders of both political parties since the early days of the Cold War.

Nor did the United States blindly "stumble into a quagmire" in Vietnam, as some commentators maintained. Johnson insisted from the start that American military involvement must not reach levels that would provoke the Chinese or Soviets into direct intervention. He therefore exercised a tight rein over the bombing campaign, once boasting that "they can't even bomb an outhouse without my approval." Such a restrictive policy meant, in effect, that military victory in any traditional sense of the term was never possible. "It was startling to me to find out," the new secretary of defense, Clark Clifford, recalled in 1968, "that we had no military plan to end the war." America's goal was not to win the war in a conventional sense by capturing enemy territory, but to prevent the North Vietnamese and Vietcong from winning. This meant that America would have to maintain a military presence as long as the enemy retained the will to fight.

As it turned out, American public support for the war eroded faster than the will of the North Vietnamese leaders to tolerate casualties. Systematic opposition to the war broke out on college campuses with the escalation of 1965. And in 1966 Senator J. William Fulbright of Arkansas, chairman of the Senate Foreign Relations Committee, began congressional investigations into American policy. George Kennan, the architect of the containment doctrine, told Fulbright's committee that the doctrine was appropriate for Europe, but not Southeast Asia. By 1967 opposition to the war had become so pronounced that antiwar demonstrations in New York and at the Pentagon attracted massive support. Nightly television accounts of the fighting—Vietnam was the first war to receive extended television coverage, and hence has been dubbed the "living room war"—made the official optimism look fatuous. As Secretary of Defense McNamara admitted, "The picture of the world's greatest superpower killing or injuring 1,000 noncombatants a week, while trying to pound a tiny backward nation into submission on an issue whose merits are hotly disputed, is not a pretty one."

In a war of political will, North Vietnam had the advantage. Johnson and his advisers grievously underestimated the tenacity of North Vietnam's commitment to unify Vietnam and expel the United States. Ho Chi Minh had warned the French in the 1940s that "You can kill ten of my men for every one I kill of yours, but even at those odds, you will lose and I will win." He knew that in a battle of attrition, the Vietnamese Communists had the advantage, for they were willing to sacrifice all for their cause. While the United States fought a limited war for limited objectives, the Vietnamese Communists fought a total war for their very survival. Indeed, just as General Westmoreland was assuring Johnson and the American public that his forces in early 1968 were on the verge of gaining the upper hand, the Communists again displayed their resilience.

THE TURNING POINT   On January 31, 1968, the first day of the Vietnamese New Year (Tet), the Vietcong and North Vietnamese defied a holiday truce to launch a wave of surprise assaults on American and South Vietnamese forces throughout South Vietnam. The old capital city of Hué fell to the Communists, and Vietcong units temporarily occupied the grounds of the American embassy in Saigon. Within a few days, however, American and South Vietnamese forces organized a devastating counterattack. General Westmoreland justifiably proclaimed the Tet offensive a major defeat for the Vietcong. But while Vietcong

During the 1968 Tet offensive Vietcong units temporarily took the grounds of the American embassy in Saigon. Here, American military police lead a captured Vietcong guerrilla away from the embassy.

casualties were enormous, the psychological impact of the offensive on the American public was more telling. *Time* and *Newsweek* soon ran antiwar editorials urging American withdrawal. Walter Cronkite, the dean of American television journalists, confided to his viewers that he no longer believed the war was winnable. "If I've lost Walter," Johnson was reported to say, "then it's over. I've lost Mr. Average Citizen." Polls showed that Johnson's popularity had declined to 35 percent, lower than any president since Truman in his darkest days. In 1968 the United States was spending $322,000 on every enemy killed in Vietnam; the poverty programs at home received only $53 per person.

During 1968 Johnson grew increasingly isolated. The secretary of defense reported that a task force of prominent soldiers and civilians saw no prospect for a military victory; the war was hopelessly stalemated. Robert Kennedy was considering a run for the presidency in order to challenge Johnson's Vietnam policy. And Senator Eugene McCarthy of Minnesota had already decided to oppose Johnson in the Democratic primaries. With antiwar students rallying to his candidacy, McCarthy polled 42 percent of the vote to Johnson's 48 percent in New Hampshire's March primary. Though voters had to write in Johnson's name to vote for the president, it was still a remarkable showing for a little-known senator. Each presidential primary now promised to become a referendum on Johnson's Vietnam policy.

Despite Johnson's troubles in the conduct of foreign policy, he remained a master at reading the political omens. On March 31 he announced a limited halt to the bombing of North Vietnam and fresh initiatives for a negotiated cease-fire. Then he added a dramatic postscript: "I have concluded that I should not permit the Presidency to become involved in the partisan divisions that are developing in this political year. Accordingly, I shall not seek, and I will not accept, the nomination of my party for another term as your President." Although American troops would remain in Vietnam for five more years and the casualties would mount, the quest for military victory had ended. Now the question was how the most powerful nation in the world could extricate itself from Vietnam with a minimum of damage to its prestige. It would not be easy. When direct negotiations with the North Vietnamese finally began in Paris in May 1968, they immediately bogged down over North Vietnam's demand for an American bombing halt as a precondition for further discussion.

The Vietnam War sapped the spirit of Lyndon Johnson, who decided not to run for reelection in 1968.

SIXTIES CRESCENDO

A TRAUMATIC YEAR   History seemed to move at a fearful pace throughout the 1960s, but 1968 was a year of extreme turbulence even for that decade. On April 4, only four days after Johnson's announced withdrawal from the presidential race, Martin Luther King was gunned down while standing on the balcony of a motel in Memphis, Tennessee. The assassin had expressed hostility toward blacks, but debate still continues over whether he was a pawn in an organized conspiracy. King's death set off an outpouring of grief among whites and blacks. It also set off riots in over sixty American cities, with the most serious occurring in Chicago and Washington, D.C.

Two months later, on June 6, Robert Kennedy was shot in the head by a young Palestinian who resented Kennedy's strong support of Israel. Kennedy died at the end of the day on which he had convincingly defeated Eugene McCarthy in the California primary, thereby assuming leadership of the antiwar forces in the race for the Democratic nomination for president.

CHICAGO AND MIAMI   In August 1968 Democratic delegates gathered inside the convention hall at Chicago to nominate Vice-President

Hubert Humphrey, while 24,000 police and National Guardsmen and a small army of television reporters stood watch over several thousand diverse protesters herded together miles away in a public park. The Democratic party's liberal tradition was clearly in disarray, a fact that gave heart to the Republicans who gathered in Miami to nominate Richard Nixon.

Nixon's nomination represented a remarkable political comeback. His narrow loss to Kennedy in 1960 had been followed by a disastrous defeat in the California gubernatorial race two years later. In what he labeled his "last press conference," he bitterly lashed out at reporters, claiming that they had cost him the race. "You won't have Nixon to kick around any more," he defiantly pledged. Yet Nixon displayed his remarkable resilience by returning to national politics in 1964, when he crisscrossed the nation in support of Goldwater's candidacy. For the next several years he remained active, and in 1968 Nixon was ready to take advantage of Johnson's crumbling popularity. He offered a vision of stability and order that a majority of Americans—soon to be called "the silent majority"—wanted desperately.

But others were ready as well to challenge the Democratic party regulars. George Wallace, the Democratic governor of Alabama, ran as a third candidate in the campaign on the American Independent party ticket. Wallace had made his political reputation as a brazen defender of segregation, but in his campaign for national office in 1968 he moderated his position on the race issue. And he appealed even more candidly than Nixon to the fears generated by antiwar protesters, the welfare system, and the growth of the federal government. Wallace insisted that "liberals, intellectuals, and long-hairs have run the country for too long," and he pledged that when he took over in Washington, he would "throw all these phonies and their briefcases into the Potomac." Wallace's platform was compelling in its simplicity: rioters would be shot, the war in Vietnam would be won, states' rights and law and order would be restored, open-housing laws would be repealed, and welfare cheats would be jailed.

Wallace's reactionary candidacy generated considerable appeal outside his native South, especially in white working-class communities where resentment against Johnson's Great Society liberalism was rife. Although never a possible winner, Wallace's campaign had to be taken seriously: it held the possibility of denying Humphrey or Nixon an elec-

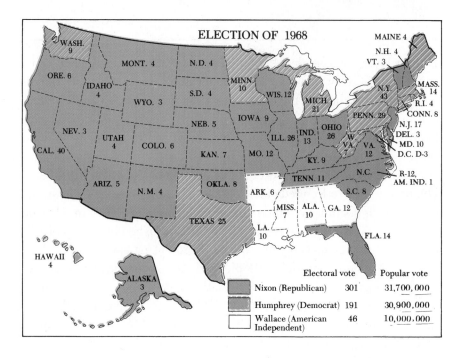

ELECTION OF 1968

	Electoral vote	Popular vote
Nixon (Republican)	301	31,700,000
Humphrey (Democrat)	191	30,900,000
Wallace (American Independent)	46	10,000,000

toral majority and thereby throwing the choice into the House of Representatives, which would have provided an appropriate climax to a chaotic year.

NIXON AGAIN   It did not happen that way. Nixon enjoyed an enormous early lead in the polls, which narrowed as the election approached. Wallace's campaign was hurt by his outspoken running mate, retired Air Force General Curtis LeMay, who spoke approvingly of using nuclear weapons in Vietnam. In October 1968, Humphrey, tainted by his ties to LBJ and the party bosses, announced that he would stop bombing North Vietnam "as an acceptable risk for peace." Eugene McCarthy, who had been strangely silent during the campaign and had even spent some time cloistered in a monastery, eventually endorsed Humphrey.

Nixon and his running mate, Governor Spiro Agnew of Maryland, eked out a narrow victory by roughly 800,000 votes, a margin of about 1 percentage point. The electoral vote was more decisive, 301 to 191. Wallace won 10 million votes, 13.5 percent of the total, the best showing by a third-party candidate since Robert La Follette in 1924. All but one of Wallace's forty-six electoral votes were from the Deep South. Nixon swept all but four of the states west of the Mississippi, while Humphrey's support came almost exclusively from the Northeast.

So at the end of a turbulent year, near the end of a traumatic decade, power passed peacefully to a president who was associated with the superficial stability of the 1950s. A nation that had seemed on the verge of consuming itself in spasms of violence looked to Richard Nixon to provide what he had promised in the campaign: "peace with honor" in Vietnam and a middle ground on which a majority of Americans, silent or otherwise, could come together.

MAKING CONNECTIONS

- The reform movements of the 1960s galvanized the baby-boom generation into a new youth movement, described in the next chapter, that continued through the early 1970s.

- The conflict in Vietnam, America's longest war, would come to a bitter end for American forces, but the divisions it spawned would echo through the rest of the century.

- The Immigration Act of 1965 would have profound and unexpected consequences on American society: see Chapter 35.

- The success of the civil-rights movement in the 1960s led to similar movements for women, gays, Native Americans, and Hispanics, as we see in the next chapter.

FURTHER READING

For the political context of the 1960s, consult first James L. Sundquist's *Politics and Policy: The Eisenhower, Kennedy, and Johnson Years* (1968).* Less favorable assessments come from Thomas C. Reeves's *A Question of Character: The Life of John Kennedy* (1991)* and Bruce Miroff's *Pragmatic Illusions: The Presidential Politics of John F.*

*These books are available in paperback editions.

Kennedy (1976). For details of the assassination, see Gerald L. Posner's *Case Closed: Lee Harvey Oswald and the Assassination of John F. Kennedy* (1993).*

There are fewer works about Kennedy's successor, but many are solidly detailed. The most comprehensive biography is Robert Caro's two-volume work: *The Early Years of Lyndon Johnson* (1982)* and *The Path to Power* (1990).* More sympathetic treatment can be found in Robert Dallek's *Lone Star Rising: Lyndon Johnson and His Times, 1908–1960* (1990).*

On foreign policy, see Richard Walton's *Kennedy's Quest for Victory: American Foreign Policy, 1961–1963* (1989), edited by Thomas G. Paterson. To learn more about Kennedy's problems in Cuba, see *On the Brink: America and the Soviets Reexamine the Cuban Missile Crisis* (1989),* by James G. Blight and David A. Welch.

Policy in Vietnam has received voluminous treatment from all political perspectives. For an overview, see Larry Berman's *Planning a Tragedy: The Americanization of the War in Vietnam* (1982) and *Lyndon Johnson's War: The Road to Stalemate in Vietnam* (1989), as well as Stanley Karnow's *Vietnam: A History* (1983).* The best recent analysis of policy making concerning the Vietnam War is David M. Barrett's *Uncertain Warriors: Lyndon Johnson and His Vietnam Advisors* (1994).* A first-rate treatment of the final phases of the war is Ronald Spector's *After Tet* (1993).* Former secretary of defense Robert McNamara confesses his mistakes in *In Retrospect* (1995).

Many scholars have dealt with various aspects of the civil-rights movement and race relations of the 1960s. On the national politics of civil rights see Carl Brauer's *John F. Kennedy and the Second Reconstruction* (1977).* These treatments of Martin Luther King, Jr., are helpful: David Garrow's *Bearing the Cross* (1986), Adam Fairclough's *To Redeem the Soul of America: The Southern Christian Leadership Conference and Martin Luther King, Jr.* (1987), and David Lewis's *King: A Critical Biography* (1970).* William Chafe's *From Civilities to Civil Rights: Greensboro, North Carolina, and the Black Struggle for Freedom* (1980)* details the original sit-ins.

*These books are available in paperback editions.

34 ⟨⟩ REBELLION AND REACTION IN THE 1960s AND 1970s

CHAPTER ORGANIZER

This chapter focuses on:

- rebellion and struggles for rights in the 1970s.

- ending the war in Vietnam.

- Watergate and Nixon's resignation.

- the Ford and Carter administrations.

THE ROOTS OF REBELLION

By the 1960s the postwar baby boomers were maturing. Now young adults, they differed from their elders in that they had experienced neither economic depression nor a major war. Record numbers of these young people were attending American colleges and universities during the 1960s: college enrollment quadrupled between 1945 and 1970. At the same time, many universities had become sprawling institutions increasingly dependent upon research contracts from giant corporations and the federal government. As these "multiversities" grew more bureaucratic and hierarchical, they unknowingly invited resistance from students wary of involvement in what Eisenhower had called the "military-industrial complex."

The Greensboro sit-ins in 1960 not only precipitated a decade of civil rights activism; they also signaled an end to the supposed apathy that had enveloped college campuses and social life during the 1950s. Although primarily concerned with the rights and status of black people, the sit-ins, marches, protests, principles, and sacrifices associated with the civil-rights movement provided inspiring models for other estranged and excluded groups demanding justice, freedom, and equality.

During 1960–1961 a small but significant number of white students joined the sit-in movement. They and many others were also inspired by President Kennedy's direct appeals to their youthful idealism. Thousands enrolled in the Peace Corps and VISTA. But soon it became clear that politics was mixed with principle in the president's position on civil rights. Later, as criticism of escalating American involvement in Vietnam mounted, more and more young people grew disillusioned with the government and other institutional bastions of the status quo. By the mid-1960s, a full-fledged youth revolt erupted on many campuses, and rebellious students began to flow into two distinct, yet frequently overlapping, movements: the New Left and the counterculture.

THE NEW LEFT   The explicitly political strain of the youth revolt coalesced when Tom Hayden and Al Haber, two student radicals at the University of Michigan, formed the Students for a Democratic Society (SDS) in 1960. Hayden had been inspired during his college years by Jack Kerouac's *On the Road* and Jean-Jacques Rousseau's notion of participatory democracy. Two years later, Hayden drafted what became known as the Port Huron Statement: "We are the people of this generation, bred in at least moderate comfort, housed in universities, looking uncomfortably to the world we inherit."

Hayden's earnest manifesto focused on the absence of individual freedom in modern American life. The country, he insisted, was dominated by huge organizational structures—governments, corporations, universities—all of which conspired to oppress and alienate the individual. Inspired by the example of black activism in the South, Hayden declared that students had the power to restore "participatory democracy" to American life by wresting "control of the educational process from the administrative bureaucracy" and then forging links with other dissident movements. He and others soon adopted the term "New Left" to distinguish their efforts at grassroots democracy from the Old Left of the 1930s, which had espoused an orthodox Marxism and had embraced Stalinism.

In the fall of 1964, students at the University of California at Berkeley took Hayden's program to heart. When Clark Kerr, the university chancellor, announced that sidewalk solicitations for political causes would no longer be allowed, several hundred students staged a sit-in. Soon thereafter over 2,000 more joined in, including even the conservative student members of Youth for Goldwater. After a tense standoff the administration relented. Student groups then formed the Free Speech Movement (FSM).

Led by Mario Savio, a philosophy major and compelling public speaker, the FSM initially protested on behalf of student rights. But it quickly escalated into a more general criticism of the modern university and what Savio called the "depersonalized, unresponsive bureaucracy" infecting all of American life. In 1964 Savio made an impassioned speech on the steps of the main administration building in which he asserted that there comes "a time when the operation of a machine becomes so odious, makes you so sick at heart, that you can't take part— you can't even passively take part, and you've got to put your bodies upon the gears and upon the wheels, upon the levers, upon all the apparatus and you've got to make it stop." When he finished, hundreds of students rushed into the building and organized a sit-in. In the early morning hours, 600 police officers moved in and arrested the protesters.

The program and tactics of the FSM and SDS soon spread to universities throughout the country, but their focus changed as escalating American involvement in Vietnam brought a dramatic expansion of the military draft, and millions of young men faced the grim prospect of participating in an increasingly unpopular war. In fact, however, Vietnam, like virtually every other American war, was a poor man's fight. In 1965–1966, thanks to deferments and exemptions, college graduates made up only 2 percent of all military inductees. Yet several thousand male collegians would flee to Canada or Sweden to escape the draft, while hundreds of thousands engaged in various protests against a war they considered to be immoral.

In the spring of 1967, 500,000 marchers of all ages converged on

New York's Central Park, chanting "Hey, hey, LBJ, how many kids did you kill today?" Dozens of young men ceremoniously burned their draft cards, and the so-called resistance phase of the antiwar movement was born. Thereafter a coalition of protest groups around the country sponsored draft-card burning rallies and sit-ins that led to numerous arrests.

Meanwhile, some SDS leaders were growing even more militant. Inspired by the rhetoric and revolutionary violence of black power spokesmen such as Stokely Carmichael, Rap Brown, and Huey Newton, Tom Hayden abandoned his earlier commitment to participatory democracy and passive civil disobedience. "If necessary," he now could "shoot to kill." As the SDS embraced violence, it also grew more centralized and authoritarian. Rousseau now replaced Lenin as the organization's prophet, and capitalist imperialism replaced university bureaucracy as the primary foe.

During that eventful spring, spreading campus unrest reached a climax with the disruption of Columbia University. Mark Rudd, leader of the campus SDS chapter, and a small group of radicals protested the university's insensitive decision to disrupt a neighboring black community in order to build a new gymnasium. They occupied some campus buildings, and the protest quickly spread. During the following week more buildings were occupied, faculty and administrative offices were ransacked, and classes were cancelled. University officials finally called in New York City police. While arresting the protesters, the police injured a number of innocent bystanders. Their excessive force angered many heretofore unaligned students, who staged a strike that shut down the university for the remainder of the semester. That same spring similar clashes between students, administrators, and eventually police occurred at Harvard, Cornell, and San Francisco State.

At the 1968 Democratic convention in Chicago, the polarization of American society reached a tragic and bizarre climax. Inside the tightly guarded convention hall Democrats were nominating Lyndon Johnson's faithful vice-president, Hubert Humphrey. At the same time, Chicago's streets were filled with the whole spectrum of antiwar dissenters, from the earnest supporters of Eugene McCarthy, through the Resistance and SDS, to the nihilistic Yippies (the Youth International Party). The Yippies were especially determined to provoke anarchy in the streets of Chicago. Abbie Hoffman, one of their leaders, explained that their "conception of revolution is that it's fun."

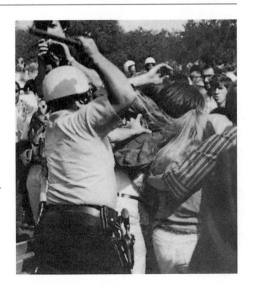

The violence at the 1968 Democratic National Convention in Chicago seared the nation.

The outlandish behavior of the Yippies and other anarchic protesters did not justify the unrestrained response of Chicago's arch-conservative Mayor Richard Daley and his army of 12,000 police. As a national television audience watched, many of the police went berserk, clubbing and gassing demonstrators as well as bystanders caught up in the chaotic scene. The spectacle lasted three days and generated a wave of anger among many middle-class Americans, anger that Richard Nixon and the Republicans shrewdly exploited at their convention in Miami. At the same time, the Chicago riots helped to fragment the antiwar movement.

By 1968 SDS was breaking up into rival factions, the most extreme of which was the Weathermen, a term derived from Bob Dylan's lyrics: "You don't need a weatherman to know which way the wind blows." These hardened young activists decided that revolutionary terrorism was the only appropriate strategy. During 1969 and 1970 the Weathermen launched a campaign of violence and disruption, fire-bombing university and government buildings and killing innocent people—as well as several of themselves. Government forces responded in kind, arresting most of the Weathermen and sending the rest underground.

The mercurial Tom Hayden finally broke with the group, declaring that it was "not the conscience of its generation, but more like its id." By 1971 the New Left was dead as a political movement. In large measure it had committed suicide by abandoning the democratic and pacifist principles that had originally inspired participants and given the movement its moral legitimacy. The larger antiwar movement also began to fade. There would be a final wave of student protests against the Nixon administration in 1970–1971, but thereafter campus unrest virtually disappeared as American troops returned home from Vietnam and the draft ended.

If the social mood was changing during the Nixon years, a large segment of the public still persisted in the quest for personal fulfillment *and* social justice. The burgeoning environmental and consumer movements attested to the continuity of sixties idealism. A *New York Times* survey of college campuses in 1969 revealed that many students were transferring their attention from the antiwar movement to the environment. This ecological conscience would blossom in the 1970s into one of the most compelling items on the nation's social agenda.

THE COUNTERCULTURE   The numbing events of 1968 led other disaffected activists away from radical politics altogether and toward another manifestation of the sixties youth revolt: the "counterculture." Long hair, jeans, tie-dyed shirts, sandals, mind-altering drugs, rock music, and group living arrangements were more important than revolutionary ideology or mass protest to the "hippies," the direct descendants of the Beats of the 1950s and the romantic utopians of the 1830s. These advocates of the counterculture were, like their New Left peers, primarily affluent, well-educated young whites alienated by the Vietnam War, racism, political corruption and parental demands, runaway technology, and a crass corporate mentality that equated the good life with goods. Disillusioned with organized political action, they eagerly embraced the tantalizing credo announced by the Harvard professor Timothy Leary, "Turn on to the scene, tune in to what's happening, and drop out."

For some the counterculture primarily entailed the study and practice of Oriental mysticism. For others it focused on the use of hallucinogenic drugs such as LSD. Collective living in urban enclaves such as San Francisco's Haight-Ashbury district or New York's East Village was the rage for a time among the hippies, until conditions grew so crowded and violent that residents migrated elsewhere.

Rural communes also attracted bourgeois rebels. During the 1960s and early 1970s, thousands of young and inexperienced romantics flocked to the countryside, eager to be liberated from parental and insti-

The Woodstock festival drew nearly half a million people to a New York farm in August 1969.

tutional restraints, to live in harmony with nature, and to coexist in an atmosphere of love and openness. Only a handful of these utopian homesteads survived more than a few months.

Huge outdoor rock music concerts were also a popular source of community for hippies. The largest of these was the Woodstock Music Festival, held in 1969 on a 600-acre farm near the tiny rural town of Bethel, New York. For three days some 500,000 young people reveled in good music and cheap marijuana. According to one journalist, the country had never "seen a society so free of repression." But the Woodstock karma was short-lived. When promoters tried to repeat the scene four months later, this time at a Rolling Stones concert in Altamont, California, members of the Hell's Angels motorcycle gang beat to death a man wielding a knife in front of the stage. Just as the Chicago convention marked the end of the New Left as a vital political force, the violence at Altamont sharply diminished the appeal of the counterculture.

FEMINISM   The logic and lure of liberation that spanned the sixties helped accelerate a powerful women's rights crusade. Like the New Left, the new feminism drew much of its inspiration and initial tactics

Betty Friedan, author of The Feminine Mystique.

from the civil-rights movement. Its aim was to challenge the cult of domesticity that had been touted as the ideal during the 1950s.

The mainstream of the women's movement was led by Betty Friedan. Her influential book, *The Feminine Mystique* (1963), launched a new phase of female protest on a national level. Friedan, a Smith College graduate, had married in 1947. During the 1950s she raised three children in a New York suburb. In 1957 she conducted a poll of her fellow Smith alumnae and discovered that, despite the rhetoric about the happy suburban housewife during the fifties, many were in fact miserable. This revelation led to more research, which culminated in the publication of *The Feminine Mystique*.

Women, Friedan wrote, had actually lost ground during the years after World War II, when many left wartime assembly lines and settled down in suburbia to care for the kids. Advertisers and women's magazines promoted the "feminine mystique" of blissful domesticity. In Friedan's view, the American middle-class home had become "a comfortable concentration camp" where women saw their individual potential suffocated in an atmosphere of mindless consumption and affluent banality.

An immediate best-seller, *The Feminine Mystique* raised the consciousness of many women who had long suffered from a feeling of being trapped in a rut. In 1966 Friedan and a small group of spirited activists founded the National Organization for Women (NOW), whose membership grew rapidly. NOW spearheaded efforts to end job discrimination on the basis of sex, to legalize abortion, and to obtain federal and state support for child-care centers.

Pressured by NOW, Congress and the Supreme Court in the early 1970s advanced the cause of sexual equality. Under Title IX of the Educational Amendments Act of 1972, colleges were required to institute "affirmative action" programs to ensure equal opportunity for women in such areas as admissions, faculty and staff hiring, and athletics. In the same year Congress overwhelmingly approved the Equal Rights Amendment (ERA) to the Constitution. In 1973 the Supreme Court, in *Roe v. Wade,* struck down state laws forbidding abortions during the first three months of pregnancy on the grounds of a constitutional right of privacy. Meanwhile, many bastions of male education, including Yale and Princeton, led a new movement for coeducation that swept the nation. "If the 1960s belonged to blacks," said one feminist, "the next ten years are ours."

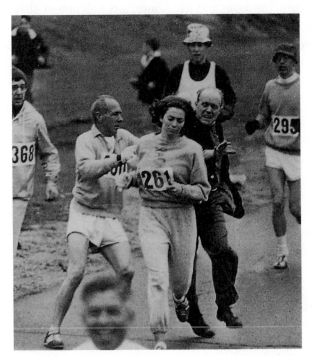

In 1967 Syracuse University student Kathy Switzer challenged the Boston Marathon's men-only tradition. Officials tried to pull her from the course but with the aid of fellow runners she completed the race. Women became official entrants in 1971.

By the end of the 1970s, however, sharp divisions between moderate and radical feminists, as well as the failure of the movement to broaden its appeal much beyond the confines of the white middle class, caused reform efforts to stagnate. In 1982 the Equal Rights Amendment died, several states short of ratification. The very success of NOW's efforts to liberalize abortion laws helped generate a powerful reaction, especially among Catholics and fundamentalist Protestants, who mounted a potent "right to life" crusade.

Yet the success of the women's movement seemed likely to endure despite setbacks. For in fact women were not another minority group pursuing the traditional path of liberal reform. They were a majority: they constituted 51 percent of the population. Their growing political power and expanding presence in the work force combined to become one of the most dramatic developments of the era. By 1976 over half the married women in America and nine of ten women college graduates were employed outside the home, a development that one economist called "the single most outstanding phenomenon of this century." Many career women did not regard themselves as "feminists"; some took jobs because they and their families needed the money to survive or to achieve higher levels of material comfort. Whatever their motives, women were changing traditional sex roles and childbearing practices to accommodate the two-career family, which had replaced the established pattern of male breadwinner and female housekeeper as the new American norm.

HISPANIC RIGHTS   The activism that animated the student revolt, the civil-rights movement, and the crusade for women's rights soon spread to various ethnic minority groups. The labor shortages during World War II had led defense industries to offer Hispanic Americans their first significant access to industrial and skilled-labor jobs in the cities. As was the case with African Americans, service in the military during the war years helped to heighten an American identity among Hispanic Americans and increase their desire for equal rights and opportunities.

But equality was elusive. After World War II Hispanic Americans still faced widespread discrimination in hiring, housing, and education. Poverty was widespread. In 1960, for example, the median income of a Mexican-American family was only 62 percent of the median income of the general population. Hispanic American activists during the 1950s and 1960s mirrored the efforts of black civil-rights leaders such as Martin Luther King. They too denounced segregation, promoted efforts to improve the quality of public education, and struggled to increase Hispanic American political influence and economic opportunities. Like their black peers, Hispanic college students during the 1960s seized upon ways to heighten their sense of ethnic pride and distinctiveness and to bolster their solidarity.

One of the most popular initiatives was the use of the term *Chicano* as an inclusive label for all Mexican immigrants, Spanish Americans in New Mexico, as well as old *californios* (descendants of the inhabitants of California before it was seized by the United States, most of whom were Indians or of mixed ancestry), and *Tejanos* (descendants of the inhabitants of Texas before it became independent). The word *Chicano* was originally a Mexican slang term for a clumsy person. Over the years, Anglo Americans had fastened upon the term as a pejorative reference. Now *Chicano* took on a positive connotation. In southern California, students formed Young Chicanos for Community Action, a social service group designed to promote greater self-reliance and local involvement within Chicano neighborhoods. Wearing brown berets, the members protested the disproportionate number of Hispanics being killed in the Vietnam War and demanded improvements in their neighborhood schools. Others promoted Hispanic Studies as a new academic discipline. In 1968 nearly 10,000 Chicano students walked out of five Los Angeles high schools as a protest against inadequate facilities, racist teachers, and a high dropout rate. Their actions prompted students in other states to stage similar demonstrations.

Unlike their black counterparts, however, *Chicano* leaders faced an awkward dilemma: what should they do about the continuing stream of illegal Mexican aliens flowing across the border? Many Mexican-Americans argued that their own hopes for economic advancement and social equality were put at risk by the influx of Mexican laborers willing to accept low-paying jobs. Mexican-American leaders thus helped to end the *bracero* program in 1964 and to form the United Farm Workers (UFW) in 1962 (originally the National Farm Workers Association) to represent Mexican-American migrant workers.

The founder of the UFW was César Chavez. Born in Yuma, Arizona, in 1927 to Mexican immigrant parents, Chavez moved with his parents

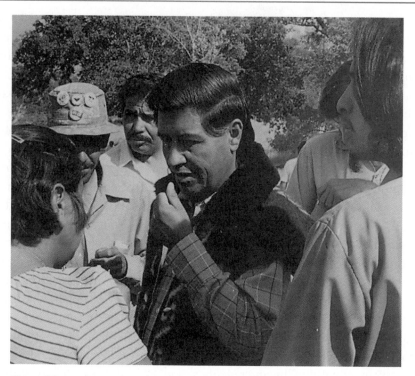

César Chavez (center) *with organizers of the grape boycott.*

and four siblings to California in 1939. There they joined thousands of other migrant farm workers traversing the state, moving from job to job, living in tents, cars, or ramshackle cabins. In 1944, at age seventeen, Chavez joined the navy and served for two years in the Pacific. After the war he married and found work first as a sharecropper raising strawberries and then as a migrant laborer in apricot orchards. In 1952 Chavez joined the Community Service Organization (CSO), a social service group that sought to educate and organize the migrant poor so that they could become more self-reliant. He founded new CSO chapters and was named general director in 1958.

In 1962 Chavez left the organization when it refused to back his proposal to establish a union for farm workers. Other CSO leaders believed that it was impossible to organize migrant workers into an effective union. They were too mobile, too poor, too illiterate, too ethnically diverse, and too easily replaced by *braceros,* Mexican contract day laborers trucked in at harvest time. Moreover, farm workers did not enjoy protected status under the National Labor Relations Act of 1935 (the Wagner Act). Unlike industrial laborers, they were not guaranteed the right to organize or to receive a minimum wage. Nor did federal regulations govern the safety of their workplace.

Despite such obstacles Chavez resolved to organize the migrant farm workers. His intimate contact with the wretched camps, corrupt labor contractors, and virulent racism bolstered his resolve. His fledgling Farm Workers Association gained national attention in 1965 when it joined a strike by Filipino farm workers against the corporate grape farmers in the Delano area of California's San Joaquin Valley. Chavez's personal charisma and Catholic piety, his insistence on nonviolent tactics and his reliance upon college student volunteers, his skillful alliance with organized labor and religious groups, all combined to attract media interest and popular support. Soon the UFW began organizing migrant workers in the lettuce fields of the Salinas Valley.

Still, the strike itself brought no tangible gains. So Chavez organized a nationwide consumer boycott of grapes. Contrary to Chavez's own principles and orders, some of the striking workers used violence to express their frustration at the recalcitrant growers. In an effort to break the impasse and defuse the tension among his followers, Chavez began a personal fast in 1968. He explained that "the truest act of courage, the strongest act of manliness, is to sacrifice ourselves for others in a totally nonviolent struggle for justice." After fasting for three weeks, he had lost thirty-five pounds, and doctors began to fear for his life. A week later he ended his fast by taking communion and breaking bread with Senator Robert F. Kennedy.

Two years later, in 1970, the grape strike and consumer boycott finally succeeded in bringing twenty-six grape growers to the bargaining table. They signed formal contracts recognizing the UFW, and soon migrant workers throughout the West were benefiting from Chavez's strenuous efforts on their behalf. Wages increased and working conditions improved. In 1975 the California state legislature passed a bill that required growers to bargain collectively with the elected representatives of the farm workers. As Robert Kennedy observed, César Chavez was "one of the heroic figures of our time."

But the chief strength of the Hispanic movement lay less in the duplication of the civil-rights strategies than in the sheer growth of the Hispanic population. In 1960 Hispanics had numbered slightly more than 3 million; by 1970 they had increased to 9 million, and by 1990 they numbered over 22 million, making them the largest minority in America after African Americans. The most numerous among the Hispanics were Mexican-Americans, or Chicanos, who were concentrated in California and the Southwest. Next came the Puerto Rican population, most of whom lived in New York City and the Connecticut Valley. Finally, there were the Cubans, many of them refugees from Fidel Castro's Communist regime, concentrated in southern Florida.

During the 1960s four Mexican-Americans—Senator Joseph Montoya of New Mexico and Representatives Elizio ("Kika") de la Garza and Henry B. Gonzales of Texas and Edward R. Roybal of California—were elected to Congress. In 1974 two Chicanos were elected governor—Jerry Apodaca in New Mexico and Raul Castro in Arizona. In 1981 Henry Cisneros of San Antonio became the first Mexican-American mayor of a large city. In 1993 he was appointed the Secretary of Housing and Urban Development in the Clinton administration.

NATIVE AMERICANS   American Indians—many of whom now called themselves Native Americans—also emerged as a new political force in the late 1960s. Two conditions combined to make Indian rights a priority: first, white Americans felt a persistent sense of guilt for the destructive policies of their ancestors toward a people who had, after all, been here first; second, the plight of the Indian minority was more desperate than that of any other minority group in the country. Indian unemployment was ten times the national rate, their life expectancy was twenty years lower than the national average, and the suicide rate was 100 times higher than that for whites. If blacks in the 1960s had extracted a deserved promise of compensation for past injustices from whites, Indians felt that they had an even more compelling claim on white consciences.

In 1965 President Johnson acknowledged the plight of the Indians by establishing the National Council on Indian Opportunity to target federal antipoverty program funds into the reservations. Three years later he became the first president to send a special message to Congress requesting additional federal support for the Indians. By then, however, militants within the Indian community were impatient with the pace of change. They proposed a new name for themselves—Native Americans—and organized protests and demonstrations against local, state, and federal agencies.

At first the Indian militants adopted the tactics of civil-rights and black power activists. In 1968 the American Indian Movement (AIM) was founded on the promise of advancing "red power." The leaders of AIM occupied Alcatraz Island in San Francisco Bay in 1969, claiming the site "by right of discovery." In 1972 an Indian sit-in at the Bureau of Indian Affairs in Washington attracted national attention to their cause. Soon Indian protesters discovered a more effective tactic than direct action and sit-ins. They went into federal courts armed with copies of old treaties and demanded that these become the basis for restitution. In Alaska, Maine, and Massachusetts they won significant settlements that provided legal recognition of their tribal rights and financial compensation at levels that upgraded the standard of living on several reservations.

GAY RIGHTS   The liberationist impulses of the sixties also encouraged homosexuals to organize and assert their own right to equal treatment and common dignity. On June 17, 1969, New York City police raided the Stonewall Inn, a male gay bar in the heart of Greenwich Village. Efforts to close down homosexual gathering places were then commonplace around the country. This time, however, the patrons fought back and the struggle spilled into the streets. Hundreds of other gays and their supporters joined the fracas against the police. Rioting lasted throughout the weekend, and when it ended gays had forged a new sense of solidarity and a new organization called the Gay Liberation Front. "Gay is good for all of us," proclaimed one member. "The artificial categories 'heterosexual' and 'homosexual' have been laid on us by a sexist society. As gays we demand an end to the gender programming which starts when we are born."

As news of the Stonewall riots spread across the country, the gay rights movement assumed national proportions. One of its main tactics was to encourage people to "come out" and make public their homosexuality. This was by no means an easy decision, for professing gays faced social ostracism, physical abuse, exclusion from the military and civil service, and discrimination in the workplace. Yet despite the risks, thousands of homosexuals did "come out." By 1973 almost 800 gay and lesbian organizations had been formed across the country, and every major city had a visible gay community and cultural life. One commentator noticed "an explosion of things gay." Homosexuals started their own newspapers and gained election to public offices. In 1974 gay activists convinced the American Psychiatric Association to remove its classification of homosexuality as a "mental disorder" from its official diagnostic manual. The following year the U.S. Civil Service Commission lifted its ban on the employment of homosexuals.

But as was the case with the civil-rights crusade and the women's movement, the campaign for gay rights soon suffered from internal divisions and a conservative backlash. Gay activists engaged in increasingly fractious disputes over tactics and objectives. Lesbian leaders, for instance, accused male homosexuals of being chauvinists insensitive to issues peculiar to women. One woman radical saw no common ground between the two groups: "Lesbians are feminists, not homosexuals." Even more threatening to the gay community during the seventies was the nationwide counterattack launched by conservative moralists and Christian fundamentalists. They successfully repealed new local laws banning discrimination against homosexuals. True equality had yet to be achieved. By the end of the decade the gay movement had lost its initial momentum and was struggling to salvage many of its hard-won gains, just as an even more ominous threat emerged on the horizon in the form of AIDS (acquired immune deficiency syndrome).

During the early 1980s, public health officials discovered a strange and deadly new disease that primarily struck gay men and intravenous drug users. Those infected with the virus showed signs of fatigue, developed a strange combination of infections, and eventually died. Frustrated by a lack of federal funds, medical researchers struggled to discern the origins of the new virus. Eventually they concluded that it originated in Africa and was most likely spread to the United States via Haiti. People contracted AIDS by coming into contact with the blood or body fluids of an infected person. The threat of AIDS and the initially slow response of the federal government to the disease served to revitalize the gay rights movement. Activists mobilized to raise public awareness of the epidemic and to exert public pressure on government agencies and the medical community to divert more funds to AIDS-related research and treatment. The crisis atmosphere drew new members to the movement and brought it renewed momentum.

NIXON AND VIETNAM

The numerous liberation movements of the 1960s fundamentally changed the tone and texture of American social life. By the early 1970s, however, there were signs that the pendulum of national mood was swinging back toward conservatism. The election of Richard Nixon and Spiro Agnew in 1968 and the rise of George Wallace as a serious political force on the radical right reflected the emergence of the "silent majority"—those white working-class and middle-class citizens who were determined to regain control of a society they felt had run amok in permissiveness and special pleading.

Large as the gap was between the "silent majority" and the varied forces of dissent, they agreed on one thing: that the Vietnam War remained the dominant event of the time. Until the war was ended and all American troops were returned home, the nation would find it difficult to achieve the equilibrium that the new president had promised. In his State of the Union message of 1970, President Nixon called on Americans to pursue "the lift of a driving dream," a memorable phrase that reporters asked him to define. "Well, before we can get the lift of a driving dream," Nixon explained, "we have to get rid of the nightmares we inherited. One of the nightmares is a war without end."

GRADUAL WITHDRAWAL   The Nixon administration promised a new course in Vietnam. Nixon and his special assistant for national security affairs, Henry Kissinger, claimed to have a secret plan to achieve "peace with honor." But peace was long in coming and not very honorable when it came. The Nixon administration, even while withdrawing American forces, held to a policy that it was contrary to the national interest to let the North Vietnamese dominate Indochina. By the time a settlement was finally reached in 1973, another 20,000 Americans had died, the morale of the American army had been shattered, millions of Asians were killed or wounded, and fighting in fact continued in Southeast Asia. In the end, Nixon's policy gained little that he could not have accomplished in 1969.

The administration's new strategy in Vietnam moved along three separate fronts. The first front was at the deadlocked Paris peace talks, where American negotiators demanded the withdrawal of North Vietnamese forces from South Vietnam and the preservation of the American-supported regime of President Nguyen Van Thieu. The North Vietnamese and Vietcong negotiators, however, insisted on retaining a military presence in the South and reunifying the Vietnamese people under a government dominated by the Communists. There was no common ground on which to come together.

Second, Nixon tried to defuse domestic unrest generated by the war. To this end he sought to "Vietnamize" the conflict by turning over most of the combat missions to Vietnamese units and sharply reducing the number of American ground forces. To assuage the South Vietnamese he provided more equipment and training for their troops. From a peak of 540,000 in 1969, American combat units were withdrawn at a gradual and steady pace. By 1973 only 50,000 American troops remained in Vietnam. In late 1969 Nixon had also established a lottery system that clarified the likelihood of being drafted—only those with low lottery numbers would have to go. Nixon was more successful in achieving the goal of reducing antiwar activity than at forcing concessions from the North Vietnamese in Paris.

Third, while reducing the number of American combat troops in Vietnam, Nixon and Kissinger secretly expanded the air war in an effort to persuade the enemy to come to terms. On March 18, 1969, American planes began "Operation Menu," a fourteen-month-long bombing of Communist sanctuaries in Cambodia. Over 100,000 tons of bombs were dropped, four times the tonnage dropped on Japan during World War II. Congress did not learn of these raids until 1970, when Nixon announced what he called an "incursion" by United States troops into supposedly "neutral" Cambodia to "clean out" North Vietnamese staging areas.

DIVISIONS AT HOME   News of the Cambodia "incursion" came on the heels of another incident that rekindled public indignation against the war. Late in 1969 the story of the My Lai massacre broke. During the next two years the public learned the gruesome tale of Army Lieutenant William Calley, who ordered the murder of over 200 Vietnamese civilians in My Lai village in 1968. Twenty-five officers were charged with complicity in the massacre and subsequent cover-up, but only Calley was convicted of murder. Nixon shortly thereafter granted him parole.

"Son . . .!" "Dad . . . !" *The Vietnam War caused vehement divisions between "hawks" and "doves," old and young, even parents and children.*

The loudest public outcry against Nixon's Indochina policy occurred in the wake of the Cambodian "incursion." Campuses across the country witnessed a new wave of protests in 1970. At Kent State University, the Ohio National Guard was called in to quell rioting, during which the campus ROTC building was burned. Pelted by rocks and verbal taunts, the inexperienced Guardsmen panicked and opened fire on the demonstrators, killing four. Eleven days later, on May 15, Mississippi highway patrolmen riddled a dormitory at Jackson State College with bullets, killing two black students. Although an official investigation of the Kent State episode condemned the "casual and indiscriminate shooting," polls indicated that the American public supported the National Guard; students had "got what they were asking for."

The following year, in 1971, the *New York Times* began publishing excerpts from a secret Defense Department study. The so-called Pentagon Papers, leaked to the press by a former Pentagon official, Daniel Ellsberg, confirmed what many critics of the war had long suspected: Congress and the public had not received the full story on the Gulf of Tonkin incident of 1964. Contingency plans for American entry into the war were being drawn up even while Johnson was promising the American people that combat troops would never be sent to Vietnam. The Nixon administration attempted to block publication of the Pentagon Papers, arguing that publication would endanger national security and prolong the war. By a vote of six to three the Supreme Court ruled against the government. Newspapers throughout the country began publication the next day.

WAR WITHOUT END   Although Nixon's decision in the spring of 1970 to use American forces to root out Communist bases in Cambodia did bring a tactical victory, it also served to widen a war he had promised to end. Moreover, his hopes that the South Vietnamese units replacing American forces could hold their own against the North Vietnamese were dashed when they suffered repeated defeats in 1971 and 1972. Disorganized, poorly led, and lacking tenacity, the South Vietnamese soldiers had to call upon American air power to fend off North Vietnamese offensives.

The deteriorating ground war along with mounting social divisions at home and the approach of the 1972 presidential elections combined to produce a shift in the American negotiating position in Paris. In the summer of 1972 Henry Kissinger dropped his insistence on the removal of all North Vietnamese troops from the South before the withdrawal of American troops. On October 26, only a week before the American presidential election, he announced: "Peace is at hand." But the Thieu regime in South Vietnam objected to the plan for a cease-fire, understandably fearful that the continued presence of North Vietnamese troops in the South virtually guaranteed an eventual Communist victory. Hanoi then stiffened its position by demanding that Thieu resign.

The talks broke off on December 16, and Nixon told his military advisers that only a massive show of American air power would make the North Vietnamese more cooperative at the negotiating table. Two days later the United States unleashed furious B-52 raids on Hanoi and Haiphong. The so-called "Christmas bombings" aroused worldwide protest, but Henry Kissinger claimed Nixon's "jugular diplomacy" worked, for the talks in Paris soon resumed.

On January 27, 1973, the United States signed an "agreement on ending the war and restoring peace in Vietnam." The agreement showed that despite the Christmas bombings, the North Vietnamese never altered their basic stance: they kept troops in the South and remained committed to the reunification of Vietnam under one government. What had changed since the previous fall was the willingness of the South Vietnamese to accept these terms, albeit reluctantly, on the basis of Nixon's promise that the United States would respond "with full force" to any violation of the agreement.

On March 29, 1973, the last American combat troops left Vietnam, leaving behind several thousand who were declared "missing in action."

On that same day the last of several hundred American prisoners of war, most of them downed pilots, were released from Hanoi. Within a period of months, however, the war between North and South resumed, and the military superiority and greater political unity of the Communist forces soon became evident. In Cambodia and Laos, where fighting had been more sporadic, Communist victory also seemed inevitable.

In 1975 the North Vietnamese launched a full-scale armored invasion against the South. President Thieu appealed to Washington for assistance, but the Democratic majority in Congress refused, and on April 30 Americans watched on television as North Vietnamese tanks rolled into Saigon, soon to be named Ho Chi Minh City. The scene at the American embassy in Saigon, where thousands of terrified Vietnamese fought to board the last departing helicopters, provided a poignant and tragic ending to America's greatest foreign policy disaster.

The longest war in American history was finally over, leaving in its wake a bitter legacy. The war described as a noble crusade on behalf of

The scramble to board evacuation helicopters on the roof of the American Embassy, Saigon, April 30, 1975.

democratic ideals instead suggested that democracy was not easily transferable to Third World regions, which lacked any historical experience with liberal values and representative government. The war eroded respect for the military so thoroughly that many young Americans came to regard military service as inherently corrupting and ignoble. The war, fought to show the world that the United States was united in its convictions, instead divided Americans more drastically than any event since the Civil War. The Vietnam war cost the nation some 58,000 deaths and $150 billion. Little wonder that the dominant reaction to the war's end was the urge to "put Vietnam behind us" and revert to a non-interventionist foreign policy.

NIXON AND MIDDLE AMERICA

Richard Nixon had been elected in 1968 as the representative of "Middle America," those citizens fed up with the liberal politics and social radicalism of the 1960s. The Nixon cabinet and White House staff reflected the values of this "silent majority." The chief figures were John Mitchell, the gruff attorney-general who had made his fortune as a lawyer in Nixon's old firm, and H. R. Haldeman and John Ehrlichman, advisers on domestic policy whose major experience before their association with the Nixon campaign had been in advertising. The cabinet was all white, all male, all Republican. "There are no blooded patricians in the lot," said *Time* magazine, "just strivers who have acted out the middle-class dream."

DOMESTIC AFFAIRS   Confronting a Congress controlled by Democrats, Richard Nixon focused his energies on foreign policy, where presidential initiatives were less restricted and where he, in tandem with Kissinger, achieved several stunning breakthroughs. The domestic front became a holding action in which Nixon, like Eisenhower before him, found it difficult to stop the march of liberal programs.

Despite the efforts of the Nixon administration, the civil-rights legislation enacted during the Johnson years continued to take effect. Administration officials launched a concerted effort in 1970 to block congressional renewal of the Voting Rights Act and to delay implementation of court orders requiring the desegregation of school districts in

Mississippi. Congress then extended the Voting Rights Act over Nixon's veto. The Supreme Court, in the first decision made under the new Chief Justice Warren Burger—a Nixon appointee—ordered the integration of the Mississippi schools. More schools were desegregated during Nixon's first term than in all the Kennedy-Johnson years combined.

Nixon's attempts to block desegregation efforts in urban areas also failed. The Burger Court ruled unanimously in *Swann v. Charlotte-Mecklenburg Board of Education* (1971) that cities must bus students out of their neighborhoods if necessary to achieve racial integration. Protest over desegregation now began to manifest itself more in the North than in the South, as white families in Boston, Denver, and other cities denounced the destruction of "the neighborhood school." Busing opponents won a limited victory when the Supreme Court ruled in 1974 that requiring the transfer of students from the inner city to the suburbs was unconstitutional. This ruling, along with the *Bakke v. Board of Regents of California* (1978) decision, which restricted the use of quotas to achieve racial balance in university classrooms, marked the transition of desegregation from an issue of simple justice to a more tangled thicket of conflicting group and individual rights.

It also reflected the growing conservatism of the Supreme Court, a trend encouraged by Nixon. The litany of liberal decisions during the 1960s had made the Warren Court a prime target for mostly middle-class Americans who resented what they regarded as the federal government's excessive protection of the "undeserving." Fate and the aging of the justices on the Warren Court gave Nixon the chance to make four new appointments. Only one, William Rehnquist, would consistently support Nixon's conservative interpretation of the Constitution, but overall the tenor of the Court did shift toward a more moderate stance.

Nixon also fervently desired to reverse the welfare state policies of his Democratic predecessors and decentralize responsibility for social programs. To that end he proposed, and got from Congress in 1972, a five-year revenue-sharing plan that would distribute $30 billion of federal revenues to the states for use as they saw fit. But the administration never succeeded in developing a comprehensive domestic agenda acceptable to Congress. Frustrated by the Democratic majority on Capitol Hill, Nixon sent Vice-President Spiro Agnew on a national speaking tour in the fall of 1969 to assault the opposition. Agnew described war protesters as "anarchists and ideological eunuchs," the liberal news media as "an effete corps of impudent snobs" and "nattering nabobs of negativism."

But while Agnew turned phrases, the Democratic Congress moved forward with new legislation: the right of eighteen-year-olds to vote in national elections (1970) and, under the Twenty-sixth Amendment (1971), in state and local elections as well; increases in Social Security benefits tied to the inflation rate; a rise in food-stamp funding; the Occupational Safety and Health Act (1970), and the Federal Election Campaign Act (1972).

During Nixon's first term Americans in large numbers began to lobby for government action to improve and protect the natural environment. In 1970 hundreds of thousands of activists rallied across the country in support of the first "Earth Day." In response, Congress established new programs to control water pollution and passed the Clean Air Act (1970) over Nixon's veto. Congress also created the Environmental Protection Agency (EPA) to oversee federal guidelines for air pollution, toxic wastes, and water quality. The EPA began requiring developers to perform environmental impact studies before new construction could begin. The agency also set fuel efficiency standards for automobiles and required manufacturers to reduce the level of carbon monoxide emissions from car engines.

ECONOMIC MALAISE   The major domestic development during the Nixon years was a floundering economy. The annual inflation rate began to rise in 1967, when it was at 3 percent. By 1973 it reached 9 percent; a year later it was at 12 percent, and it remained in double digits for most of the 1970s. Unemployment, at a low of 3.3 percent when Nixon took office, climbed to 6 percent by the end of 1970 and threatened to keep rising. Somehow the American economy was undergoing a recession and inflation at the same time. Economists coined the term "stagflation" to describe the syndrome that defied the orthodox laws of economics.

The economic malaise had at least three deep-rooted causes. First, the Johnson administration had attempted to pay for both the Great Society and the war in Vietnam without a major tax increase, thus generating larger deficits, a major expansion of the money supply, and rapid price inflation. Second, and more important, by the late 1960s American goods faced stiff competition in international markets from West Germany, Japan, and other emerging industrial powers. This sharply reduced the export of American goods and generated a growing trade deficit.

Third, the American economy had grown heavily dependent on cheap sources of energy. Just as domestic petroleum reserves began to dwindle and dependence on foreign sources increased, the nations in the Organization of Petroleum Exporting Countries (OPEC), centered in the Middle East, combined to use their oil as a political and economic weapon. In 1973, when the United States sent massive aid to Israel during the Yom Kippur War, OPEC announced that it would not sell oil to nations supporting Israel and that it was raising its prices by 400 percent. American motorists thereafter faced long lines at gas stations, schools and offices closed down, factories cut production, and the inflation rate soared.

Another condition leading to stagflation was the flood of new workers—mainly baby boomers and women—entering the labor market. From 1965 to 1980 the work force grew by 40 percent, or almost 30 million workers, a figure greater than the total labor force of France or West Germany. The number of new jobs created could not keep up, leaving many unemployed. At the same time, worker productivity declined, pushing up prices in the face of rising demand.

Stagflation posed a new set of economic problems, but the Nixon administration responded erratically and ineffectively with old remedies. First, it tried to reduce the federal deficit by raising taxes and cutting the budget. When the Democratic Congress refused to cooperate with this approach, the White House encouraged the Federal Reserve Board to reduce the money supply by raising interest rates. But the move backfired as the stock market immediately collapsed, plunging the economy into the "Nixon recession."

A sense of desperation then infected the White House. In 1969, when asked about wage and price controls, Nixon had been unequivocal: "Controls. Oh, my God, no! . . . We'll never go to controls." On August 15, 1971, however, he reversed himself. He froze all wages and prices for ninety days, yet the economy floundered. By 1973 the wage and price guidelines were made voluntary, and therefore almost entirely ineffective. Stagflation continued, and it would plague the economy for the rest of the decade.

NIXON TRIUMPHANT

CHINA   If the economy's ailments proved more than Nixon could remedy, in foreign policy his administration managed to improve American relations with the major powers of the Communist world—China and the Soviet Union—and to shift fundamentally the pattern of the Cold War. In 1971 Henry Kissinger made a secret trip to Peking to explore the possibility of American recognition of China. In 1972, Nixon himself arrived in Peking and made recognition an official and public fact. The irony of the event was overwhelming. Richard Nixon, the former anti-Communist crusader who had condemned the State Department for "losing" China in 1949, accomplished a diplomatic feat his more liberal predecessors could not.

DÉTENTE   China sought the breakthrough in relations with the United States because its rivalry with the Soviet Union, with which it shares a long border, had become increasingly bitter. Soviet leaders, troubled by the Sino-American agreements, were also anxious for an easing of tensions now that they had, as the result of a huge arms buildup following the Cuban missile crisis, achieved virtual parity with the United States in nuclear weapons. Once again the president surprised the world, by announcing that he would visit Moscow in 1972 for discussions with Leonid Brezhnev, the Soviet premier.

President Nixon and the chairman of the Chinese Communist party, Mao Tse-tung, February 1972.

What became known as "détente" with the Soviets offered the promise of a more orderly and restrained competition between the two superpowers. Nixon and Brezhnev signed the Strategic Arms Limitation Talks (SALT) agreement, which set ceilings for each nation on the number of intercontinental ballistic missiles (ICBMs) and sharp limits to the construction of antiballistic missile systems (ABMs). In effect the Soviets were allowed to retain a greater number of missiles with greater destructive power while the United States retained a lead in the total number of warheads. No limitations were placed on new weapons systems, though each side agreed to work toward a permanent freeze on all nuclear weapons.

SHUTTLE DIPLOMACY   The Nixon-Kissinger initiatives in the Middle East were less dramatic and less conclusive than the China or Russia agreements, but did show that America recognized Arab power in the region and its own dependence on the oil from Islamic states fundamentally opposed to Israel. After Israel recovered from the initial shock of the Arab attacks that triggered the Yom Kippur War of 1973, it recaptured the Golan Heights and seized additional Syrian territory. Kissinger initiated the negotiations leading to a cease-fire and exerted pressure to prevent Israel from taking more Arab territory. American reliance on Arab oil led to closer ties with Egypt and its president, Anwar el-Sadat, and more restrained support for Israel. Kissinger, whose "shuttle diplomacy" among the capitals of the Middle East won acclaim from all sides, failed to find a comprehensive peace formula for the troubled region and ignored altogether the problem of establishing a homeland for Palestinian refugees. But his efforts did lay groundwork for the subsequent accord between Israel and Egypt in 1977.

THE 1972 ELECTION   Nixon's foreign policy achievements allowed him to stage the campaign of 1972 as a triumphal procession. The main threat to his reelection came from George Wallace, who had the potential as a third-party candidate to deprive the Republicans of conservative votes and thereby throw the election to the Democrats or the Democratic-controlled Congress. But on May 15, 1972, Wallace was shot and paralyzed below the waist by a deranged man and was forced to withdraw from the campaign.

Meanwhile, the Democrats were further ensuring Nixon's victory by nominating Senator George S. McGovern of South Dakota, a former college history professor and crusading liberal whose antiwar and social welfare positions were associated with the turbulence of the 1960s. At the Democratic convention party reforms helped McGovern's nomination by increasing the representation of women, blacks, and minorities, but these reforms alienated the party regulars. Chicago's Mayor Richard Daley was actually ousted from the convention, and the AFL-CIO refused to endorse the Democratic candidate.

Nixon won the greatest victory of any Republican presidential candidate in history, winning 520 electoral votes to only 17 for McGovern. During the course of the campaign McGovern complained about the "dirty tricks" of the Nixon administration, most especially the curious incident during the summer of 1972 in which burglars were caught breaking into the Democratic National Committee headquarters in the Watergate apartment complex in Washington. McGovern's accusations seemed shrill and biased at the time. Nixon and his staff made plans for "four more years" as the investigation of the fateful Watergate break-in unfolded.

WATERGATE

During the trial of the accused Watergate burglars, the relentless prodding of Judge John J. Sirica led one of the accused to tell the full story of the Nixon administration's complicity in the episode. James W. McCord, a former CIA agent and security chief for the Committee to Re-elect the President (CREEP), was the first of many informers and penitents in a melodrama that unfolded over the next two years. It ended in the first resignation of a president in American history, the conviction and imprisonment of twenty-five officials of the Nixon administration, including four cabinet members, and the most serious constitutional crisis since the impeachment trial of President Andrew Johnson.

UNCOVERING THE COVER-UP   The trail of evidence pursued by Judge Sirica, a grand jury and several special prosecutors, and a televised Senate investigation headed by Samuel J. Ervin, Jr., of North Carolina, led directly to the White House. No evidence surfaced that

Nixon had ordered the break-in or that he had been aware of plans to burglarize the Democratic National Committee. From the start, however, Nixon participated in the cover-up, using his presidential powers to discredit and block the investigation. Perhaps most alarming was that the Watergate burglary proved to be one small part of a larger pattern of corruption and criminality sanctioned by the Nixon White House. Since 1970, Nixon had ordered intelligence agencies to spy on his most outspoken opponents, open their mail, and even burglarize their homes in an effort to uncover compromisng information.

The cover-up unraveled further in 1973 when L. Patrick Gray, acting director of the FBI, resigned after confessing that he had destroyed several incriminating documents. On April 30 Ehrlichman and Haldeman resigned, together with Attorney-General Richard Kleindienst. A few days later Nixon nervously assured the public in a television address, "I'm not a crook." New evidence suggested otherwise. John Dean, whom Nixon had dismissed as presidential counsel, testified before the Ervin Committee and a rapt television audience that Nixon had ap-

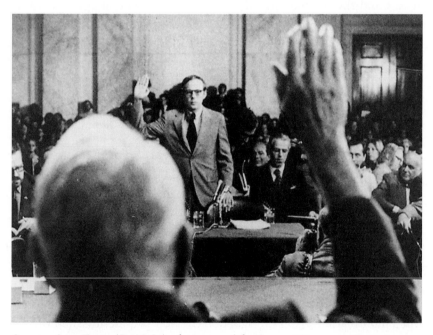

Senator Sam Ervin (D, N.C.), chairman of the Senate Watergate Committee, swears in the ex-White House counsel John Dean, whose testimony linked President Nixon to the cover-up.

proved the cover-up. In another "bombshell" disclosure, a White House aide told the committee that Nixon had installed a taping system in the White House and that many of the conversations about Watergate had been recorded.

A year-long battle for the "Nixon tapes" then began. Harvard law professor Archibald Cox, whom Nixon had appointed as a special prosecutor to handle the Watergate case, took the president to court in 1973 to obtain the tapes. Nixon, pleading "executive privilege," refused to release them and ordered Cox fired. In what became known as the "Saturday Night Massacre," the new attorney-general, Elliot Richardson, and his deputy resigned rather than execute the order. Cox's replacement as special prosecutor, Leon Jaworski, proved no more pliable than Cox, and he also took the president to court.

On July 24, 1974, the Supreme Court ruled unanimously that the president must surrender the tapes. A few days later the House Judiciary Committee voted to recommend three articles of impeachment: obstruction of justice through the payment of "hush money" to witnesses and the withholding of evidence; using federal agencies to deprive citizens of their constitutional rights; and defiance of Congress by withholding the tapes. Before the House of Representatives could meet to vote on impeachment, however, Nixon handed over the complete set of White House tapes. On August 9, 1974, fully aware that the evidence on the tapes implicated him in the cover-up, Richard Nixon resigned from office.

EFFECTS OF WATERGATE Vice-President Spiro Agnew did not succeed Nixon, because Agnew himself had been forced to resign in 1973 when it became known that he had accepted bribes from contractors before and during his term as vice-president. The vice-president at the time of Nixon's resignation was Gerald Ford, the former minority leader in the House from Michigan, whom Nixon had appointed with congressional approval, under the provisions of the Twenty-fifth Amendment (1967). Ford insisted that he had no intention of pardoning Nixon, who was still liable for criminal prosecution. But a month after Nixon's resignation the new president issued the pardon, explaining that it was necessary to end the national obsession with the Watergate scandals. Many suspected that Nixon and Ford had made a deal, though there was no evidence to confirm the speculation.

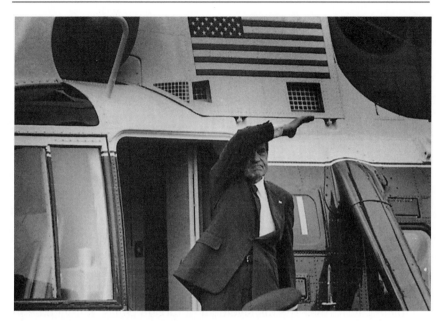

Having resigned his office, Richard Nixon waves farewell outside the White House, August 9, 1974.

If there was a silver lining in Watergate's dark cloud, it was the vigor and resiliency of the institutions that had brought a president down—the press, Congress, the courts, and an aroused public opinion. The Watergate revelations provoked Congress to pass several pieces of legislation designed to curb executive power in the future. The War Powers Act (1973) required presidents to consult with Congress before sending American troops into combat abroad and to withdraw troops after sixty days unless Congress specifically approved their stay. In an effort to correct abuses of campaign funds, Congress enacted legislation in 1974 that set new ceilings on contributions and expenditures. And in reaction to the Nixon claim of "executive privilege" as a means of withholding evidence, Congress strengthened the 1966 Freedom of Information Act to require prompt responses to requests for information from government files and to place on government agencies the burden of proof for classifying information as secret.

The nation had weathered a profound constitutional crisis, but the aftershock of the Watergate episode produced a deep sense of disillusionment with the "imperial presidency." Coming on the heels of the erosion of public confidence generated by the Vietnam War, the Watergate affair renewed public cynicism toward a government that had systematically lied to the people and violated their civil liberties. Said one bumper sticker of the day: "Don't vote. It only encourages them." Restoring credibility and respect became the primary challenge facing Nixon's successors. Unfortunately, a new array of economic and foreign crises would make that task doubly difficult.

An Unelected President

While the Watergate crisis dominated the Washington scene, major domestic and foreign problems received little executive attention. The perplexing combination of inflation and recession worsened, as did the oil crisis. At the same time, Henry Kissinger, who assumed virtually complete control over the management of foreign policy, watched helplessly as the South Vietnamese forces began to crumble before North Vietnamese attacks, attempted with limited success to establish a framework for peace in the Middle East, and supported a CIA role in overthrowing the popularly elected Marxist president of Chile.

THE FORD YEARS   Gerald Ford inherited these simmering problems, as well as the burden of being an unelected president. An amiable, honest man, Ford enjoyed widespread popular support for only a short time. "I am a Ford, not a Lincoln," he candidly recognized upon becoming vice-president. His pardon of Nixon on September 8, 1974, generated a storm of criticism. The *New York Times* called it "an unconscionable act."

As president Ford adopted the posture he had developed as a conservative minority leader in the House: a nay-saying leader of the opposition who believed that the federal government exercised too much power over domestic affairs. In his fifteen months as president, Ford vetoed thirty-nine bills, thereby outstripping Herbert Hoover's veto record in less than half the time. By resisting congressional pressure to reduce taxes and increase federal spending, he succeeded in plummeting the economy into the deepest recession since the Great Depression. Unemployment jumped to 9 percent in 1975, and the federal deficit hit a

record the next year. Ford rejected wage and price controls to curb inflation, preferring voluntary restraints.

In foreign policy, Ford retained Henry Kissinger as secretary of state
and attempted to pursue Nixon's goals of stability in the Middle East,
rapprochement with China, and détente with the Soviet Union. Late in
1974 Ford met with Russia's Leonid Brezhnev and accepted the framework for another arms-control agreement that was to serve as the basis
for SALT II. Meanwhile Kissinger's tireless shuttling between Cairo
and Tel Aviv produced an agreement: Israel promised to return to Egypt
most of the Sinai territory captured in the 1967 war, and the two nations agreed to rely on negotiations rather than force to settle future disagreements.

These limited but significant achievements should have enhanced
Ford's image, but they were drowned in the sea of criticism and carping
that followed the collapse of South Vietnam in 1975. Not only had a
decade of American effort in Vietnam proven futile, but the Khmer
Rouge, the Cambodian Communist movement, had also won a resounding victory, plunging that country into a fanatical bloodbath. And
the OPEC oil cartel was threatening another boycott, while other Third
World nations denounced the United States as a depraved imperialistic
power.

THE 1976 ELECTION   In the midst of such turmoil, the Democrats
could hardly wait for the 1976 election. At the Republican convention
Ford managed to thwart a powerful challenge for the nomination from
the former California governor and Hollywood actor, Ronald Reagan.
The Democrats chose an obscure former naval officer turned peanut
farmer who had served one term as governor of Georgia. Jimmy Carter
capitalized on the post-Watergate cynicism by promising never to "tell a
lie to the American people" and by citing his independence from traditional Washington power politics.

To the surprise of many pundits, Carter revived the New Deal coalition of southern whites, blacks, urban labor, and ethnic groups to win
the election, 41 million votes to Ford's 39 million. Polls showed that the
Carter victory benefited from a heavy turnout of blacks in the South,
where he swept every state but Virginia. Minnesota Senator Walter F.
Mondale, Carter's liberal running mate and a favorite among blue-collar
workers and the urban poor, also gave the ticket a big boost. The real

story of the election, however, was the low voter turnout. Almost half of America's eligible voters, apparently alienated by Watergate and the lackluster candidates, chose to sit out the election.

THE CARTER INTERREGNUM

EARLY SUCCESSES   During the first two years of his term, Carter enjoyed several successes. His administration appointed more blacks, Hispanics, and women than any before. He also offered amnesty to the thousands of young men who had fled the country rather than serve in Vietnam, closing one of the remaining open wounds of that traumatic event. He reformed the civil service to provide rewards for meritorious performance, and he created new cabinet-level Departments of Energy and Education. Carter also pushed significant environmental legislation through Congress, including a bill to regulate strip mining, and a "superfund" to clean up chemical waste sites.

His success was short-lived. Carter's political predicament emerged during the debate over energy policy. Borrowing a phrase from the turn-of-the-century philosopher William James, the president declared that solving the energy problem must become "the moral equivalent of war" for the nation, and he presented the Congress with what he called "a comprehensive energy program" that would ensure victory. Carter's energy bill called for the creation of a cabinet-level Department of Energy, tax incentives and penalties to encourage conservation and new oil and gas production as well as solar power and synthetic fuels, and the increased development of nuclear power as a "last resort." Yet the energy bill passed in 1978 was a gutted version of the original. It focused primarily on new oil and gas production rather than conservation. Carter and his aides lacked the experience and the flexibility to maneuver his proposals around congressional obstacles.

In the summer of 1979, when renewed violence in the Middle East produced a second fuel shortage, motorists were forced to wait in long lines again for limited supplies of gasoline that they regarded as excessively expensive. Soon they directed their frustration at the White House. Opinion polls showed Carter with an approval rating of only 26 percent, lower than Nixon during the worst moments of the Watergate crisis. Faced with such vanishing support, Carter solicited advice from an array of national leaders during an extraordinary retreat at Camp David, Maryland. He emerged ten days later and proclaimed that the nation required "a rebirth of the American spirit." He also announced a "new and positive energy program." It fell on skeptical ears. A Phoenix newspaper editorialized: "The nation did not tune in Carter to hear a sermon. It wanted answers. It did not get them." Congress only partially funded the major feature of his new program—synthetic energy research.

Several of Carter's early foreign policy initiatives also got caught in political crossfires. Soon after his inauguration Carter vowed that "the soul of our foreign policy" should be the defense of human rights abroad. But the human rights campaign provoked attack from two sides: those who feared that it sacrificed a detached appraisal of national interest for high-level moralizing, and those who pointed to the administration's inconsistency in applying the standard.

Similarly, Carter's successful negotiation of treaties to turn over control of the Panama Canal to the Panamanian government in twenty years generated intense criticism. Even though the administration reminded Americans that Theodore Roosevelt himself had admitted "stealing" the Canal Zone for American use, many political conservatives flayed Carter's judicious decision all the same. Republican Ronald Reagan manipulated historical fact by claiming that the Canal Zone was sovereign American soil purchased "fair and square." Carter argued that the limitations on American influence in Latin America, and the deep resentment toward American colonialism in Panama, left the United States with no choice. The Senate ratified the treaties by a paper-thin margin (68 to 32, two votes more than the required two-thirds). The Canal Zone would revert in stages to Panama by 1999.

THE CAMP DAVID ACCORDS   Carter's crowning diplomatic achievement was the arrangement of a peace agreement between Israel and Egypt. In 1978 Carter invited Egypt's President Anwar el-Sadat and Israeli Prime Minister Menachem Begin to Camp David for two weeks of difficult negotiations. The first part of the eventual agreement required Israel to return all land in the Sinai in exchange for Egyptian recognition of Israel's sovereignty. But the second part of the agreement, calling for Israel to negotiate with Sadat a resolution to the Palestinian refugee dilemma, began to unravel soon after the Camp David summit. Still,

Egyptian president Anwar Sadat (left), Jimmy Carter, and Israeli prime minister Menachem Begin at the announcement of the Camp David accords, September 1978.

Carter and Secretary of State Cyrus Vance had orchestrated a dramatic display of high-level diplomacy that, whatever its limitations, made an all-out war between Israel and the Arab world less likely. It also represented a significant first step toward a comprehensive settlement of the region's volatile tensions.

MOUNTING TROUBLES   Carter's crowning failure was his management of the economy. In effect he inherited a bad situation and left it worse. Carter employed the same economic policies as Nixon and Ford to fight stagflation, but he reversed the order of the federal "cure," preferring to fight unemployment first with a tax cut and increased public spending. Unemployment declined slightly, from 8 to 7 percent in 1977, but inflation soared; at 5 percent when he took office, it reached 10 percent in 1978 and kept rising. During one month in 1980 it measured an annual rate of 18 percent. Like previous presidents, Carter then reversed himself to fight the other side of the economic malaise. By midterm he was delaying tax reductions and vetoing government spending programs that he had proposed in his first year. The result, however, was the worst of all possible worlds—a deepened recession with unemployment at 7.5 percent in 1980, mortgage rates at 15 percent, interest rates at an all-time high of 20 percent, and a runaway inflation averaging between 12 and 13 percent.

The signing of a controversial SALT II treaty with the Soviets in 1979 put Carter's leadership to the test just as the mounting economic problems made him the subject of biting editorial cartoons. To quell his conservative critics, who charged that SALT II would give the Soviets a decided advantage in the number and destructive power of land-based missiles, Carter announced that the United States would build the new MX missile system.

But the SALT II treaty became moot in 1979 when the Soviet army invaded Afghanistan in order to extend "fraternal assistance" to the faltering Communist government there, which was being challenged by Muslim rebels. While continuing the MX missile program, Carter immediately shelved SALT II, suspended grain shipments to the Soviet Union, and began a campaign for an international boycott of the 1980 Olympics, which were to be held that summer in Moscow. Zbigniew Brzezinski, Carter's hard-line national security adviser, won out over Cyrus Vance in the behind-the-scenes shuffling for influence and persuaded the president that the Soviet invasion of Afghanistan was only the first step in a Soviet scheme to dominate the oil-rich Persian Gulf. Calling the Soviet invasion "the gravest threat to world peace since World War II," Carter threatened that the United States would oppose by force any further Soviet advances in the Middle East.

IRAN   Then the Iranian crisis exploded in a year-long barrage of unwelcome events that epitomized the inability of the United States to control world affairs. The crisis began in 1979 with the overthrow of the shah of Iran, long a staunch American ally and right-wing dictator. The revolutionaries who toppled the shah rallied around Ayatollah Ruhollah Khomeini, a fundamentalist Muslim leader who symbolized the Islamic values the shah had tried to replace with Western ways. Khomeini's hatred of the United States dated back to 1953, when the CIA had sponsored the overthrow of Iran's Prime Minister Mohammed Mossadegh, an ardent nationalist who sought to rid his country of Western influence and interests. The 1953 coup had restored the shah's regime to power.

Late in 1979, Carter allowed the exiled shah to enter the United States in order to undergo treatment for cancer. A few days later, on November 4, a frenzied mob stormed the American embassy in Teheran and seized the staff. Khomeini applauded the mob action and demanded the shah's return along with all his wealth in exchange for the release of the fifty-three American hostages. In the meantime the Iranian militants staged daily demonstrations, burning the American flag and effigies of Carter for the benefit of worldwide news and television coverage.

Carter was furious, but his options were limited. He appealed to the United Nations, protesting what was a clear violation of diplomatic immunity and international law. But Khomeini scoffed at U.N. requests for the release of hostages. Carter then froze all Iranian assets in the United States and appealed to American allies for a trade embargo of Iran. The trade restrictions were only partially effective—even America's most loyal European allies did not want to lose access to Iranian oil.

So a frustrated Carter, hounded by a public and press demanding "action," authorized a rescue attempt by American commandos in April 1980. The raid, however, was aborted in the Iranian desert because of helicopter malfunctions, and it ended with eight fatalities when another American helicopter collided with a transport plane. Carter's presidency died with them. Secretary of State Cyrus Vance resigned in protest against the risky venture. Meanwhile, nightly television coverage of the taunting Iranian rebels generated a near obsession with the seeming impotence of the United States and the fate of the hostages. The crisis ended after 444 days of captivity when Carter, in his last act as president, released several billion dollars of Iranian assets to ransom the kidnapped hostages.

The turbulent and often tragic events of the 1970s—the conquest of South Vietnam, the Watergate scandal and Nixon's resignation, the energy shortage and stagflation, the Iranian hostage episode—provoked among Americans what Carter labeled a "crisis of confidence." By 1980 American power and prestige seemed to be on the decline, the economy remained in a shambles, and the rights revolution launched in the sixties, with the questions it raised for the family and other basic social and political institutions, had sparked a backlash of resentment among "middle America." With theatrical timing, Ronald Reagan emerged to tap the growing reservoir of public frustration and transform his political career into a crusade to make "America stand tall again." He told his supporters that there was "a hunger in this land for a spiritual revival, a return to a belief in moral absolutes." The United States, he declared, remained the "greatest country in the world. We have the talent, we have the drive, we have the imagination. Now all we need is the leadership."

MAKING CONNECTIONS

- Foreign affairs in the 1970s show the changing patterns of the cold war. The next chapter details the end of both the cold war and the Soviet Union.

- Presidents Nixon and Ford tried, with limited success, to decrease the power of the federal government over domestic affairs. President Reagan was much more successful at advancing the conservative agenda, a topic covered in the next chapter.

- The rebellion and turbulence of the 1960s and 1970s became less apparent in the following decade; as Chapter 36 shows, however, that turbulence reappeared, in a somewhat different form in the 1990s.

- This chapter ends by noting that Ronald Reagan promised to make "America stand tall again." Chapter 35 discusses Reagan's policies to achieve this goal.

FURTHER READING

Engaging overviews of the cultural trends of the 1960s include William L. O'Neill's *Coming Apart* (1972)* and Godfrey Hodgson's *America in Our Time* (1976).* A good assessment of the New Left is

*These books are available in paperback editions.

Irwin Unger's *The Movement: A History of the American New Left* (1974).* A good scholarly analysis of the "hippies" that takes them seriously is Timothy Miller's *The Hippies and American Values* (1991).*

There is a wealth of good books dealing with the women's liberation movement. For the background of the movement in the 1960s and 1970s, see Nancy Cott's *The Grounding of Modern Feminism* (1987) and Cynthia Harrison's *On Account of Sex: The Politics of Women's Issues, 1945–1968* (1988).

The organizing efforts of César Chavez are detailed in Ronald Taylor's *Chavez and the Farm Workers* (1975).* The struggles of Native Americans for recognition and power are sympathetically described in Stan Steiner's *The New Indians* (1968). On the shifting cultural mood of the 1970s, see Christopher Lasch's influential jeremiad, *The Culture of Narcissism* (1978).*

On Nixon see Roger Morris's *Richard Milhous Nixon: The Rise of an American Politician* (1990), Stephen Ambrose's *Nixon: The Triumph of a Politician, 1962–1972* (1989) and *Nixon: Ruin and Recovery, 1973–1990* (1991).* Equally valuable is Herbert S. Parmet's *Richard Nixon and His America* (1990).*

For a solid overview of the Watergate scandal, see Stanley Kutler, *The Wars of Watergate* (1990). For the way the Republicans handled affairs abroad, consult Tad Szulc's *The Illusion of Power: Foreign Policy in the Nixon Years* (1978). The loss of Vietnam and the end of American involvement are traced in A. E. Goodman's *The Lost Peace: America's Search for a Negotiated Settlement of the Vietnam War* (1978) and Gareth Porter's *A Peace Denied: The United States, Vietnam and the Paris Agreement* (1975). The most comprehensive treatment of the antiwar movement in the United States is Tom Wells's *The War Within: America's Battle over Vietnam* (1994).*

To examine the rise of Jimmy Carter, consult Betty Glad's *Jimmy Carter: In Search of the Great White House* (1980). A work critical of the Carter administration is Haynes Johnson's *In the Absence of Power: Governing America* (1980). Gaddis Smith's *Morality, Reason, and Power* (1986) provides an overview of American diplomacy in the Carter years.

*These books are available in paperback editions.

35 ✺ A NEW GILDED AGE

CHAPTER ORGANIZER

This chapter focuses on:

- the demographic, social, and economic reasons for the rise of Ronald Reagan and Republican conservatism.

- changing relations with the Soviet Union, including the end of the cold war.

- the economic and social aspects of the 1980s that gave rise to the phrase "a new Gilded Age."

- the cause and aftermath of the Gulf War.

THE REAGAN RESTORATION

THE MAKING OF A PRESIDENT   As the 1980 election approached, the Republicans eagerly anticipated the contest with a struggling Jimmy Carter. Their candidate, Ronald Reagan, had initially appeared as an even more improbable presidential possibility than Carter had four years earlier. Born in Illinois in 1911, Reagan graduated from tiny Eureka College and then worked as a cheery radio announcer and sportscaster before heading to Hollywood in 1937.

A disciple of New Deal politics, Reagan adopted FDR's confident rhetoric and engaging smile, and he employed both during World War II when he made uplifting patriotic movies. But after the war his movie career stagnated, and Reagan abandoned his New Deal liberalism. He grew enamored of the Republican party's premise that too much government stifled free enterprise.

In 1964 Reagan entered the political limelight when he delivered a rousing speech on behalf of Barry Goldwater at the Republican convention. During two terms as governor of California (1967–1975) he displayed a commitment to conservative principles as well as a political realism capable of compromise. Nevertheless, by the middle 1970s Reagan's brand of free enterprise conservatism still appeared too extreme for a national audience.

THE MOVE TO REAGAN   By the eve of the 1980 election, however, Reagan had become the beneficiary of three developments that made his conservative vision of America much more than a harmless flirtation with nostalgia. First, the 1980 census revealed that the American population (226,505,000) was aging, and was moving in large numbers from the liberal Northeast to the conservative "Sunbelt" states of the South and West. This dual development meant that demographic forces were carrying the electorate toward Reagan's conservative position.

Second, in the 1970s the country experienced a major revival of evangelical religion not unlike the Great Awakenings of the eighteenth and early nineteenth centuries. No longer simply a local or provincial phenomenon, Christian evangelicals and fundamentalists owned their own television and radio stations and operated their own schools and universities. The Reverend Jerry Falwell's "Moral Majority" expressed the political sentiments of countless other fundamentalist groups: free enterprise should remain free, big government should be made little, abortion should be outlawed, evolution should be replaced in schoolbooks by the biblical story of creation, and Soviet expansion should be opposed as a form of pagan totalitarianism. The moralistic zeal and financial resources of the religious right made them effective opponents of liberal political candidates and programs. As defenders of traditional and local values—prayer in schools, families in which women stayed home to care for children, tough criminal laws—the religious right rallied to Reagan.

A third factor contributing to the conservative resurgence was a well-organized and well-financed backlash against the feminist movement. Like all the liberationist crusades spawned during the 1960s, the feminist movement provoked a conservative reaction. During the 1970s women who opposed the social goals of feminism formed counterorganizations with names such as "Women Who Want to Be Women" and "Females Opposed to Equality."

Spearheading such efforts was Phyllis Schlafly, a right-wing Republican activist from Illinois. She orchestrated the campaign to defeat the Equal Rights Amendment and thereafter served as the galvanizing force behind a growing antifeminist movement. She characterized feminists as a "bunch of bitter women seeking a constitutional cure for their personal problems." She instead urged women to embrace their God-given roles as wives and mothers. Feminists, she charged, were "anti-family, anti-children, and pro-abortion."

Many of Schlafly's supporters in the anti-ERA campaign also participated in a mushrooming anti-abortion or "pro-life" movement. By 1980 the National Right to Life committee, created by the National Conference of Catholic Bishops, boasted 11 million members representing all religious denominations. The intensity of their commitment made them a powerful political force in their own right, and the Reagan campaign was quick to highlight its own support for traditional family values, gender roles, and the rights of the unborn.

By 1980 Reagan also benefited from the deep popular disenchantment with Jimmy Carter. His campaign was burdened by the frustrations of the Iranian hostage crisis, a desperately sick economy, and the party divisions created by Senator Edward M. Kennedy's luckless quest for the Democratic nomination. Like Ford before him, Carter proved to be a sincere but lackluster leader who faced an almost insurmountable set of domestic and international problems. He was expected to cure the economic recession and inflation at a time when all industrial economies were shaken by a shortage of oil and confidence. He was expected to reassert America's global power at a time of waning respect for America's international authority. And he was expected to do this, as well as buoy the national spirit, through a set of political institutions in which many Americans had lost faith. In short, Carter was virtually predestined to fail at an impossible task.

By 1980 voters seemed eager to embrace Reagan's cheery promises of

President Ronald Reagan, "the Great Com-municator."

a new era of less government, lower taxes, renewed prosperity, waning inflation, and revived military strength and national pride. His "supply-side" economic proposals, soon dubbed "Reaganomics" by supporters and "voodoo economics" by critics, suggested that stagflation resulted from governmental intrusions into the marketplace and from excessive taxes that weakened the incentive to work, save, and reinvest. The solution was to slash tax rates. For a long-suffering nation, it was, in theory, an alluring economic panacea.

On election day Reagan swept to a decisive victory, with 489 electoral votes to 49 for Carter, who carried only six states. The popular vote proved equally lopsided: 44 million (51 percent) to 35 million (41 percent), with 7 percent going to John Anderson, a moderate Republican who had bolted the party after Reagan's nomination and ran on an independent ticket.

In addition to affirming Reagan's conservative agenda, the election reflected the triumph of what one political scientist called the "largest mass movement of our time"—nonvoting. Almost as striking as Reagan's one-sided victory was the fact that his vote total represented only 28 percent of the potential electorate. Only 53 percent of eligible voters cast ballots in the 1980 election.

Where had all the voters gone? Political analysts noted that most of the nonvoters were working-class Democrats in the major urban centers. Voter turnout was lowest in poor inner-city neighborhoods such as New York's Bedford-Stuyvesant district, which had a 19 percent voter participation rate. Turnout was highest, by contrast, in the affluent sub-urbs of large cities, areas where the Republican party was experiencing a dramatic surge in popularity. Such trends meant that American office-holders were being selected during the 1970s by an electorate increas-ingly dominated by middle- and upper-class white voters.

There were varied explanations for the high levels of voter apathy among working-class Americans. Some stressed the continuing sense of disillusionment with government growing out of the Watergate affair. Others noted that the widespread perception that the Democratic party had alienated its traditional blocs of support among common folk. Democratic leaders no longer spoke eloquently on behalf of those at the bottom of America's social scale. By embracing a fiscal conservatism in-distinguishable from the Republicans, as Carter had done, Democrats lost their appeal among blue-collar workers and ghetto dwellers. When viewed in this light, Ronald Reagan's victory represented less a resound-ing victory for conservative Republicans than a self-inflicted defeat by a fractured Democratic party. For the moment, however, such results were masked by the Republicans' euphoric victory celebrations. Flush with a sense of power and destiny, Ronald Reagan headed toward Washington with a blueprint for dismantling the welfare state.

REAGANOMICS Ronald Reagan brought to Washington the most conservative economic philosophy since Calvin Coolidge, whose pic-ture soon replaced Harry Truman's in the Cabinet Room. "Government is not the solution to our problem," Reagan insisted; "Government is the problem." The new president also brought his polished skills as a public speaker and experienced television performer, which served him well in presenting his views to the American people. And unlike Carter, he seemed to know exactly what ailed the economy and how to restore America's prestige in the world.

Reagan first abandoned price controls on oil, then he ended the wheat embargo on the Soviet Union. He then focused most of his ener-gies on dramatically increasing defense spending, sharply reducing so-cial spending, and passing a sweeping tax reform proposal. Despite loud protests from liberal groups and politicians, Congress passed the entire Reagan economic package by the summer of 1981. Enough Demo-crats—mostly sympathetic southern conservatives dubbed "boll weevils"—supported the measures to pass them by overwhelming majorities. On August 1, 1981, Reagan signed the Economic Recovery Tax Act, which cut personal income taxes by 25 percent, lowered the maximum rate from 70 to 50 percent for 1982, cut the capital gains tax by a third, and offered a broad array of other tax concessions.

The new legislation embodied an idea that went back to Alexander Hamilton: more money in the hands of the affluent would benefit society at large, since the wealthy would engage in productive investment. A closer parallel was Treasury Secretary Andrew Mellon's tax reduction program of the 1920s under Harding and Coolidge. The difference was that the Reagan tax cuts were accompanied by massive increases in defense spending that generated ever-mounting deficits. Reagan's advisers insisted that such unbalanced budgets were only temporary; once the new tax plan began to take effect, the economy would take off and government tax revenues would soar as personal incomes and corporate profits skyrocketed. But it did not work out that way. By the summer of 1983 a major recovery was underway, but the deficits grew ever larger, so much so that the president, who in 1980 had pledged to have a balanced federal budget by 1983, had in fact run up debts larger than those of all his predecessors combined.

BUDGET CUTS   In trying to slash expenditures, Reagan's budget director pushed through $35 billion in budget cuts in educational and cultural programs, housing, food stamps, and school lunches in 1981. Reagan assured critics that despite these cuts he was committed to maintaining the "safety net" of government services for the "truly needy." This meant that aid would remain available only to those who could not work because of disability or child care. New Deal welfare programs had had the same purpose, but the Roosevelt administration had also provided federal jobs for those who could work. This was not a part of "Reaganomics." Cuts in programs to the disadvantaged, when added to the sluggish economy, helped raise the percentage of persons living under the poverty level from 11.7 in 1979 to 15.3 in 1983.

American bankers and investors feared that the rising government debt would send interest rates soaring, a fear expressed in sagging bond and stock markets. A business slump and rising unemployment carried through most of 1982. That same year the federal deficit doubled. Aides finally convinced Reagan that to reassure the public about deficits and the threat of inflation the government needed "revenue enhancements," a euphemism for tax increases. With Reagan's support, Congress passed a new tax bill in 1982 that would raise almost $100 billion.

During the midterm elections, Reagan rarely mentioned the new tax bill. Instead he focused his campaign speeches on the benefits of supply-side economics and rosy economic forecasts. He urged voters to "stay the course" and appealed for more time to let his economic program take effect. Meanwhile, the economic slump persisted through 1982, with unemployment standing at 10.4 percent.

CONFLICTS OF INTEREST   Like Harding and Coolidge in the 1920s, Reagan named people to government positions who frequently were unsympathetic to the regulatory functions for which they were responsible, rendering such regulation less than effective. The most visible early example was Interior Secretary James Watt, who castigated environmentalists for hindering the commercial use of timber and mineral resources. He was finally forced out of office by the uproar over an offensive joke he made.

The Reagan administration also paralleled the Harding administration by finding itself embroiled in charges of conflict of interest, ethical misconduct, and actual criminal behavior. Public outcry forced the administrator of the Environmental Protection Agency to resign for granting favors to industrial polluters. The president's deputy chief of staff obtained a sweetheart loan from a person who was subsequently given a governmental post. Once he left the White House in 1985, he set up a lucrative consulting business that traded upon his connections with high government officials, as another former presidential aide had done earlier. Both men were later indicted.

Although some 200 other Reagan appointees were also accused of unethical or illegal activities, the president himself remained untouched by any hint of impropriety. His personal charisma and aloof managerial style helped shield him from the political fallout associated with the growing scandals and conflicts of interest among his aides and cronies. Public affection for him as a person remained his most enduring asset. This led one member of Congress to label the Reagan White House the "Teflon Presidency," where the buck never stopped because the blame never stuck.

Organized labor encountered severe setbacks during the Reagan years. Presidential appointments to the National Labor Relations Board tended to favor management, and in 1981 Reagan fired members of the Professional Air Traffic Controllers (PATCO) who had participated in an illegal strike. Even more important, Reagan's smashing electoral victories in 1980 and 1984 broke the political power of the AFL-CIO. His criticism of unions seemed to reflect a general trend in public opinion. Although a record number of new jobs was created during the 1980s, union membership steadily dropped. By 1987 unions represented only 17 percent of the nation's full-time workers, down from 24 percent in 1979.

Reagan also went on the offensive against feminism. He ardently opposed the Equal Rights Amendment, abortion on demand, and the legal guarantee of equal pay for jobs of comparable worth. He did name Sandra Day O'Connor as the first woman justice to the Supreme Court, but critics labeled it a token gesture rather than a reflection of any genuine commitment to gender equality.

Blacks and other minorities shared a similar aggravation at the administration's limited support for affirmative action programs in employment. Reagan cut funds for civil-rights enforcement and the Equal Employment Opportunity Commission, and he initially opposed renewal of the Voting Rights Act of 1965, but was overruled by Congress.

THE DEFENSE BUILDUP   Reagan's conduct of foreign policy was governed by the idea that trouble in the world stemmed mainly from Moscow. At one of his first news conferences he charged that the Soviets were "prepared to commit any crime, to lie, to cheat," and do anything necessary to promote world communism. He and Secretary of Defense Caspar Weinberger embarked on a major buildup of nuclear and conventional weapons to close the gap that they claimed had developed between Soviet and American military forces.

Reagan also recovered the rhetoric of Harry Truman, John Foster Dulles, and the Kennedy inaugural to express American resolve in the face of "Communist aggression anywhere in the world." Détente deteriorated even further when the Soviets imposed martial law in Poland during the winter of 1981. The crackdown came after Polish workers, united under the banner of an independent union called Solidarity, challenged the Communist monopoly of power. As with Hungary in 1956 and Czechoslovakia in 1968, there was little the United States could do except register protest and impose economic sanctions against Poland's Communist government.

THE AMERICAS   Reagan's ruling passion, however, was Central America, where he detected the most serious Communist threat. The tiny nation of El Salvador, caught up since 1980 in a brutal struggle between Communist-supported revolutionaries and right-wing extremists, received American commitments of economic and military assistance. Reagan stopped short of sending American troops, but he did increase the number of military advisers and the amount of financial aid to the Salvadoran government. He also abandoned Carter's strident criticism of right-wing Salvadoran militants whose "death squads" engaged in systematic terror and murder. Critics argued that American involvement ensured that the revolutionary forces would emerge as the victorious representatives of Salvadoran nationalism. Supporters countered by warning that American failure to act would allow for a repeat of Communist victories in Nicaragua, and that Honduras, Guatemala, and then all of Central America would eventually enter the Communist camp. By 1984, however, the American-backed government of President José Napoleón Duarte brought a modicum of stability to El Salvador.

Even more troubling was the situation in Nicaragua. The Reagan State Department claimed that the Cuban-sponsored Sandinista government in Nicaragua, which had only recently taken control of the country after ousting a corrupt dictator, was funneling Soviet and Cuban arms to leftist Salvadoran rebels. In response the administration ordered the CIA to train and supply guerrilla bands of disgruntled Nicaraguans, tagged "Contras," who staged attacks on Sandinista bases and officials from sanctuaries in Honduras. In supporting these "freedom fighters," Reagan sought not only to impede the traffic in arms to Salvadoran rebels but also to overthrow the Communist Sandinistas.

Critics of Reagan's anti-Sandinista policy questioned the motives and ethics of the Contras, accusing them of being mostly right-wing fanatics who indiscriminately killed civilians as well as Sandinista soldiers. They also feared that the United States might eventually commit its own combat forces, thus threatening another Vietnam-like intervention. Reagan warned that if the Communists prevailed in Central America, "our credibility would collapse, our alliances would crumble, and the safety of our homeland would be jeopardized."

THE MIDDLE EAST   The Middle East remained a tinderbox of geopolitical conflict throughout the Reagan years. No peaceable end seemed possible to the bloody Iran-Iraq war, which had erupted in 1980, entangled as it was with the passions of Islamic fundamentalism. In 1984 both sides began to attack tankers in the Persian Gulf, a major source of the world's oil. Although the Reagan administration harbored no affection for either nation, it viewed Iranian fundamentalism as the greater threat and funneled aid to Iraq, a policy that produced unforeseen and grave consequences.

American diplomats continued to see Israel as the strongest ally in the region, all the while seeking to encourage moderate Arab groups. Israel's aim in the area was to secure peaceful borders, America's to prevent Russian involvement through its ally Syria. But both objectives ran up against the continuing chaos in Lebanon, where ethnic and religious tensions erupted into an anarchy of warring groups. The capital, Beirut, became a battleground of rival Muslim and Christian factions, the Palestine Liberation Organization (PLO) army, Syrian invaders cast as peacekeepers, and Israelis responding to PLO attacks.

In 1982 Israeli forces pushed the PLO out of southern Lebanon all the way north to Beirut. The United States neither endorsed nor condemned the invasion, but sent a special ambassador to negotiate a settlement. That August, Israel began heavy shelling of PLO strongholds in Beirut, and horrified American reactions led to hurried attempts to negotiate a cease-fire. The combatants finally agreed to allow French, Italian, and American troops to supervise the withdrawal of PLO troops from Beirut. Reagan's new secretary of state, George Shultz, sought to build a broad international settlement, with a homeland for the Palestinians and a guarantee of Israel's borders by its Arab neighbors. It was an admirable goal, but one defeated by age-old hostilities. Israeli troops moved back into Beirut. While they looked the other way, Lebanese Christian militiamen took revenge for the murder of their president by slaughtering women and children left in Palestinian refugee camps.

French, Italian, and American forces thereupon moved into Beirut as "peacekeepers," but in such small numbers as to become targets themselves. On October 23, 1983, an Islamic suicide bomber drove a truck laden with explosives into the U.S. Marine quarters at the Beirut airport. The explosion left 241 Americans dead. Reagan declared that a continued American presence in the city was essential, but he soon began preparations for the withdrawal of the exposed American troops. On February 7, 1984, he announced that the Marines would be rede-

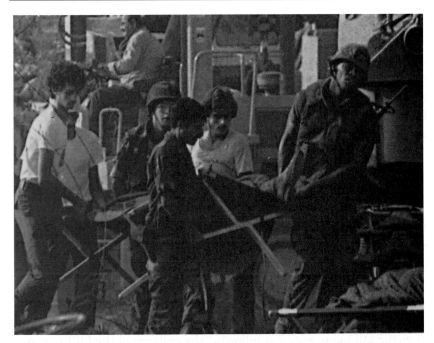

A terrorist bomb attack devastated U.S. Marine headquarters near Beirut International Airport, October 23, 1983—241 Marines were killed, and 80 wounded, in the attack.

ployed on warships offshore. The Israelis pulled back to southern Lebanon, while the Syrians remained in eastern Lebanon and imposed a tenuous peace upon the faction-ridden country.

GRENADA   In a fortunate turn for the Reagan administration, an easy military triumph closer to home eclipsed news of the debacle in Lebanon. On the Caribbean island of Grenada, the smallest independent nation in the Western Hemisphere, a leftist government had admitted Cuban workers to build a new airfield and had signed military agreements with several Communist-bloc countries. In 1983 an even more radical military council seized power.

Appeals from the governments of neighboring islands led Reagan in 1983 to order 1,900 American army paratroopers and marines to invade the island, depose the radical regime, and evacuate a group of American students at Grenada's medical school. Grenadan troops and Cuban workers were easily subdued—although later reports suggested shockingly poor coordination of American forces.

Soviet premier Mikhail Gorbachev (left) and U.S. president Ronald Reagan during a light moment at the Geneva summit, November 1985.

ARMS CONTROL   Meanwhile Reagan, for all his bluff talk about Russia's being "an evil empire," seemed determined to reach an arms control agreement with the Soviet Union. In Geneva in 1985 he met with Mikhail Gorbachev, the innovative new leader of the Soviet Union. The two signed several cultural and scientific agreements and issued a statement on arms limitations talks, but no treaty was in the offing. A major stumbling block was Reagan's refusal to consider any restrictions on his pursuit of the Strategic Defense Initiative (SDI, often called "Star Wars"), which he had announced in 1983. Its objective was to shield the United States from nuclear attack by creating a space-based defense system using futuristic computers, laser beams, and more exotic technology. Critics, many of them scientists, argued that the system was a pipe dream—expensive, far-fetched, and a violation of the Anti-Ballistic Missile Treaty of 1972. Yet SDI generated grave concerns in the Soviet Union and forced them into an arms race they could not afford.

Nearly a year after the Geneva summit, on sudden notice and with limited preparation, Gorbachev and Reagan met in Iceland for two days to discuss arms reduction. Early reports predicted a major break-through, as the two leaders discussed the possibility of a total ban on nuclear weapons, but the talks collapsed in disagreement over SDI. After the Iceland meeting the two nations reduced the scope of their discussions in order to break the impasse. Talks now focused on eliminating short-range nuclear weapons from Europe.

THE IRAN-CONTRA AFFAIR   The year 1986 opened with a terrible tragedy on January 28 when the space shuttle *Challenger* exploded minutes after liftoff, killing its crew members as a horrified nation watched on television. Investigations later revealed evidence of startling failures at NASA to heed warnings about cold-weather launches. Yet such revelations did little to affect Reagan's continuing popularity. In fact, the president's prestige shot up in April when he ordered a daring air raid on Libya, a country responsible for many of the terrorist killings, kidnappings, and hijackings that had become commonplace in the Middle East. The administration also drew praise for its support of the ouster of two corrupt dictators: Ferdinand Marcos of the Philippines and Haiti's "Baby Doc" Duvalier.

During the fall of 1986, however, the Reagan administration suffered a double blow. In the midterm elections the Democrats regained control of the Senate by 55 to 45. For his final two years in office, Reagan would face an opposition Congress. What was worse, on election day, reports surfaced that the United States, with Israeli assistance, had been secretly selling arms to Iran in hope of securing the release of American hostages held in Lebanon by extremist Islamic groups with close ties to Iran. Such action contradicted Reagan's repeated public insistence that his administration would never negotiate with terrorists. It angered America's allies and many Americans who vividly remembered the 1979 Iranian takeover of the American embassy.

Yet there was more to the story. Over the next several months, a series of revelations reminiscent of the Watergate affair disclosed a more complicated series of covert activities carried out by administration officials. At the center of what came to be dubbed "Irangate" was the much-decorated Marine Lieutenant-Colonel Oliver North. An aide to the National Security Council who specialized in counter-terrorism, North had been running secret operations from the basement of the

Lt.-Col. Oliver North testifying before the congressional committee investigating the Iran-Contra affair, July 1987.

White House involving numerous governmental, private, and foreign individuals. His most far-fetched scheme sought to use the profits gained from the secret sale of arms to Iran to subsidize the Contra rebels fighting in Nicaragua, at a time when Congress had voted to ban such aid.

North's activities, it turned out, had been approved by National Security Adviser Robert McFarlane, his successor Admiral John Poindexter, and CIA Director William Casey. Secretary of State George Shultz and Secretary of Defense Caspar Weinberger both had criticized the sale of arms to Iran, but their objections were ignored. Later, on three occasions, Shultz threatened to resign because no one was trying to stop the "pathetic" scheme. As information about the illegal dealings surfaced in the press, McFarlane attempted suicide, Poindexter resigned, and North was fired. Casey, who denied any connection, left the CIA for health reasons. Casey died shortly thereafter from a brain tumor.

The White House, meanwhile, assumed a siege mentality as the president's popularity plummeted. Under increasing criticism and amid growing doubts of his own credibility and ability, Reagan appointed both an independent counsel and a three-man commission, led by former Republican senator John Tower, to investigate the spreading scandal.

The Tower Commission issued a devastating report early in 1987 that placed much of the responsibility for the bungled Iran-Contra affair on

Reagan's loose management style. The report portrayed Reagan as uninformed and forgetful, a leader detached from the inner workings of his own administration.

Worse was yet to come. During the spring and summer of 1987, a joint House-Senate investigating committee began holding televised hearings into the Iran-Contra affair. The sessions dominated public attention for months and revealed a tangled web of inept financial and diplomatic transactions, the shredding of incriminating government documents, crass profiteering, and misguided patriotism. The hearings confirmed Reagan's insistence that he had not known about the diversion of funds to the Contras, but testimony also contradicted his earlier claim that the sale of arms to Iran was intended to open up new diplomatic channels rather than buy the freedom of American hostages.

The Iran-Contra affair left support for the Nicaraguan Contras badly eroded in the Congress, and it undermined much of Reagan's popularity. The investigations of the independent counsel led to six indictments in 1988. A Washington jury found Oliver North guilty of three relatively minor charges but innocent of nine more serious counts, apparently reflecting the jury's reasoning that he had acted as an agent of higher-ups. His conviction was later overturned on appeal. Of those involved in the affair, only John Poindexter got a jail sentence—six months for his conviction on five felony counts of obstructing and lying to Congress.

TURMOIL IN CENTRAL AMERICA   The Iran-Contra affair showed the lengths to which members of the Reagan administration would go to support the Nicaraguan Contras. Fearing heightened Soviet and American involvement in Central America, neighboring countries pressed during the mid-1980s for a negotiated settlement to the fighting in Nicaragua. In 1987 Costa Rican president Oscar Arias received the Nobel Peace Prize for designing an ambitious new regional peace plan signed by five Central American presidents.

In the spring of 1988 negotiations produced a cease-fire agreement, ending nearly seven years of fighting in Nicaragua. Secretary of State Shultz called the pact an "important step forward," but it surprised and disappointed hardliners within the Reagan administration who saw in it a Contra surrender. The Contra leaders themselves, aware of the eroding support for their cause in the United States Congress, saw the truce as their only chance for tangible concessions such as amnesty for political prisoners, the return of the Contras from exile, and "unrestricted freedom of expression."

Meanwhile, in neighboring El Salvador, the administration's attempt to shore up the centrist government of José Napoleón Duarte through economic and military aid was dealt a body blow when the far-right ARENA party scored an upset victory at the polls during the spring. Further embarrassment to the administration's Latin American policies occurred when a federal grand jury in Miami indicted Panama's military ruler, General Manuel Antonio Noriega, for drug trafficking. After Noriega refused to resign, the Reagan administration applied economic sanctions in the hope of sparking a domestic rebellion, only to see Noriega turn to Cuba for military aid and tighten his iron-fisted control of the country. Everywhere in Central America, it seemed in 1988, events conspired to highlight the limits of American power and the ineptness of administration initiatives.

THE ECONOMY   During the 1980s, all kinds of debt—personal, corporate, and governmental—increased dramatically. Whereas in the 1960s, Americans on average saved 10 percent of their income, in 1987 they saved less than 4 percent. The Reagan budget deficits also reached record levels. Between 1981 and 1987 the federal debt totaled $1.4 trillion, a figure half again larger than the entire debt for the previous two centuries. This statistic led some economists to refer to the nation's "charge card" economic recovery. Caught up in the exhilarating momentum of such prolonged prosperity and what had become a roaring bull market, however, few observers recognized the cost of such carefree spending.

A seeming epidemic of greed and self-absorbed materialism had spread through the country. Wall Street witnessed a rash of arrests and convictions for trading in securities on inside information unavailable to the public. Television ministries were embarrassed by revelations of sexual misconduct and intramural power plays. And more government officials, including Attorney-General Edwin Meese, became entangled in the web of corruption. Commentators talked of a compulsive materialism energizing those young, upwardly mobile urban professionals dubbed "Yuppies." Caught up in the race for money, goods, and status, these post–World War II baby boomers in the fast lane captured the tone and mood of affluent life in the 1980s.

Then, on October 19, 1987, the bill collector suddenly arrived at the nation's doorstep. On that "Black Monday," Wall Street, already buffeted by sharp declines the previous week, experienced a tidal wave of selling reminiscent of the 1929 crash. The Dow Jones industrial average plummeted 508 points, or an astounding 22.6 percent. The market plunge was almost double the record 12.8 percent fall on October 28, 1929. Almost $560 billion in paper value disappeared, an amount larger than the gross national product of France. With cyclonic suddenness the nation's financial mood went from boom to gloom during the fall of 1987. Several smaller brokerage houses went under amid the speculative whirlpool, thousands of investment bankers and stockbrokers were fired, and consumer confidence took a beating. Wall Street's selling frenzy reverberated throughout the capitalist world, sending stock prices plummeting in Tokyo, London, Paris, and Toronto.

What caused such a goring of the bull market? The reasons were complex and long in developing. Some analysts argued that the runaway market of the 1980s had become artificially high, driven by greed and hope rather than by any relation to the economy's actual performance. Others blamed new computerized trading programs that distorted market activity and misled individual investors. But most agreed that the fundamental problem was the nation's spiraling indebtedness and chronically high trade deficits. Americans were consuming more than they were producing, importing the difference, and paying for it with borrowed money and a dollar sharply declining in value. Foreign investors had lost confidence in Reaganomics and were no longer willing to finance America's spending binge. As the editors of *Business Week* declared, "The Message of the Crash is clear: Americans have spent too much, borrowed too much, and imported too much. Now it has to stop."

In the aftermath of the calamitous selling spree on Black Monday, President Reagan tried to reassure the nation that there was no need for panic. He insisted that the "underlying economy remains sound," an unsettling echo of Herbert Hoover's equally sunny assurances in 1929. Few observers actually feared a depression of the magnitude of the 1930s; there were too many safeguards built into the system to allow that. But there was real concern of an impending recession, and within a few weeks the White House began to take some action. Reagan agreed to work with Congress in developing a deficit-reduction package, and for the first time indicated that he was willing to include increased taxes in such a package. Yet the eventual compromise plan was so modest that it did little to restore investor confidence. As one Republican senator lamented, "There is a total lack of courage among those of us in the Congress to do what we all know has to be done."

A HISTORIC TREATY In the midst of a shaky, unpredictable economic situation, the main prospect for positive achievement before the end of Reagan's second term seemed to lie in arms reduction agreements with the Soviet government. Under Mikhail Gorbachev the Soviets promoted renewed détente in order to free their energies to address pressing domestic problems. The logjam impeding the arms negotiations suddenly broke in 1987, when Gorbachev announced that he was willing to deal separately on a medium-range missile treaty. After nine more months of strenuous, highly technical negotiations, Reagan and Gorbachev met amid much fanfare in Washington on December 9, 1987, and signed a treaty to eliminate intermediate-range (300–3,000 miles) nuclear forces (INF).

It was an epochal event, not only because it marked the first time that the two nations had agreed to destroy a whole class of weapons systems but because it represented a key first step toward the eventual end of the arms race altogether. Under the terms of the treaty, the United States would destroy 859 missiles and the Russians would eliminate 1,752. Provision was also made for on-site inspections by each side to verify compliance. Still, this winnowing of weapons would represent only 4 percent of the total number of nuclear missiles on both sides. Arms-control advocates thus looked toward a second and more comprehensive treaty eliminating long-range strategic missiles.

But virtually all Kremlin watchers were heartened by continuing evidence that General Secretary Gorbachev was successfully liberalizing Soviet domestic life and aggressively improving East-West foreign relations. The Soviets suddenly began stressing cooperation with the West in dealing with "hot spots" around the world. They urged the Palestine Liberation Organization to recognize Israel's right to exist and advocated a greater role for the U.N. in the volatile Persian Gulf. Perhaps the most dramatic symbol of a thawing Cold War was the phased withdrawal of 115,000 Soviet troops from Afghanistan, which began in 1988.

THE REAGAN LEGACY As Ronald Reagan prepared to leave office, his legacy remained problematic. Would he be remembered as the architect of revitalized military spending, lower tax rates, sharply reduced inflation and unemployment, a prolonged economic recovery, and an unprecedented arms-reduction treaty? Or would history find an administration rife with corruption and policies that had weakened American credibility abroad and bequeathed an economic time bomb to the 1990s?

Only time would tell, but the herd of aspiring Democratic candidates for the 1988 election thought they knew the answer. Said Jesse Jackson, "We must fundamentally reject the lie of Reaganomics." He and other aspirants knew that history was on their side. Few two-term presidents had left office with greater popularity than when they entered it. Thus the stage was set for a tempestuous campaign year.

THE 1988 ELECTION Scenting victory in November, a gaggle of eight Democratic presidential candidates entered a wild scramble for their party's nomination. However, as the primary season progressed, it soon became a two-man race between Massachusetts governor Michael Dukakis and Jesse Jackson, the black civil-rights activist who had been one of Martin Luther King, Jr.'s chief lieutenants. Dukakis eventually won out, and managed a difficult reconciliation with the Jackson forces that left the Democrats unified and confident as the fall campaign began. As in 1960, they envisioned a popular president and his tired presidency giving way to a cool, poised politician from Massachusetts.

The Republicans nominated Reagan's two-term vice-president, George Bush, who after a bumpy start had easily cast aside his rivals in the primaries. As Reagan's handpicked heir, Bush claimed credit for the administration's successes, but like all dutiful vice-presidents, he also faced the challenge of defining and asserting his own political identity. Although he was a veteran government official, having served as a Texas congressman, envoy to China, ambassador to the U.N., and head of the CIA, Bush projected none of Reagan's charisma, charm, or rhetorical skills. Cartoonists caricatured the patrician vice-president, the son of a rich Connecticut senator, schooled at Andover and Yale, as a well-heeled "wimp," and one Democrat described him as a man born "with a silver foot in his mouth." Early polls showed Dukakis with a surprisingly wide lead.

Yet at the Republican convention Bush delivered a forceful address that sharply enhanced his stature. Although pledging to continue the Reagan agenda, he also recognized that "things aren't perfect" in America, an admission his boss rarely acknowledged. Bush promised to use the White House to fight bigotry, illiteracy, and homelessness. The most memorable line was a defiant statement on taxes: "Congress will push me to raise taxes, and I'll say no, and they'll push, and I'll say no, and they'll push again. And all I can say to them is, read my lips: *no new taxes.*"

Bush's convention performance gave his heretofore sluggish campaign a jump-start. The Republicans also enjoyed two real advantages. In 1988 the United States basked in peace and prosperity, and the Republican party benefited from its continuing demographic advantages. During the 1980s, population growth was most rapid in the Republican-dominated Sunbelt states. Throughout the nation, population during the decade had continued to shift from Democratic cities to Republican suburbs. In addition, the leftward tilt of the Democratic party in 1984 had led many moderate and conservative Democrats as well as the growing number of "independents" to vote for Reagan.

In a campaign given over to mudslinging, the Bush campaign leaders fastened on an effective strategy: they attacked Dukakis as a camouflaged liberal in the mold of McGovern, Carter, and Mondale who would increase federal spending, raise taxes, gut the defense program, refuse to intervene against Communist aggression abroad, and oppose the pledge of allegiance to the flag. Perhaps the most inflammatory—and scurrilous—Republican tactic against Dukakis was an advertisement that preyed upon the prejudices and anxieties of middle-class whites by showing the picture of a convicted black murderer who brutally raped a woman after he had been let out of a Massachusetts prison on a weekend furlough. Dukakis chose not to respond to the Republican attacks. Studiously informed on the issues, he had a Jimmy Carter–like trust in the force of sweet reason. Dukakis was, in Bush's words, "the Iceman," cool, rational, in control of his emotions, blind to the emotional power that trivial issues could exert.

The Republican onslaught took its toll against the less organized, less focused Dukakis campaign. Dukakis took ten states plus the District of Columbia, with clusters in the Northeast, Midwest, and Northwest. Bush carried the rest, with a margin of about 54 percent to 46 percent in the popular vote and 426 to 111 in the electoral college—one Democratic elector voted for Lloyd Bentsen, the Texas senator Dukakis had chosen as his running mate.

THE BUSH YEARS

Although Bush's inaugural address lacked specific calls to action, it did invite national unity and bipartisan harmony. The American people had a purpose, he said, "to make kinder the face of the nation and gentler the face of the world." The new president acknowledged the sufferings of the homeless, "the children who have nothing," the addicted, the unwed mothers, but pleaded: "We have a deficit to bring down. We have more will than wallet, but will is what we need." In short, he looked to voluntary associations and individuals, not government, to take the lead on such issues.

During eight years as vice-president, Bush had loyally embraced the Reaganism he had once called "voodoo economics." His own administration, one commentator now said, would be "déjà voodoo." But there would be subtle differences. Whereas Reagan had hung Coolidge's portrait in place of Truman's on a White House wall, Bush now installed one of Theodore Roosevelt. The symbolism suggested two things. An eastern patrician with a Western patina, like Teddy Roosevelt, Bush would preside over an administration drawn mostly from the upper crust or career public servants. And in foreign policy he would go much further than TR in wielding the big stick. The parallels vanished, though, in Bush's lack of interest in domestic policy, noted by *Time* magazine when it named the president its "Men of the Year" for 1990, attributing to him a double image: "a foreign policy profile that was a study in resoluteness and mastery, the other a domestic visage just as strongly marked by wavering and confusion."

DOMESTIC INITIATIVES   The Reagan administration left some issues that demanded immediate attention from the Bush White House. In 1989 Bush tackled the most pressing of these, the savings and loan crisis. One effect of the Reagan administration's efforts to eliminate "unnecessary" federal regulations in the economic sector was a debacle in the savings and loan industry. To enable savings and loan institutions (also called S&Ls or "thrifts") to compete with commercial banks, Reagan pushed through a congressional bill that allowed them to invest depositors' funds in commercial real estate and junk bonds as well as in the traditional single-family housing market.

The result was catastrophic. Knowing that the federal government insured deposits up to $100,000, incompetent or corrupt lenders engaged in a frenzy of speculative high-risk investments and freewheeling personal expenditures. By 1989 hundreds of thrifts had failed, and Bush responded with a rescue plan to close or sell ailing thrifts and bail out the depositors. Congress responded the following August by consolidating the insurance fund for savings and loan deposits with the fund covering banks, the Federal Deposit Insurance Corporation (FDIC). A new agency, the Resolution Trust Corporation (RTC), was created to sell off failed thrifts—or at least their assets. At the time, the cost to taxpayers of the bailout was put at $300 billion over thirty years, although in 1990 the General Accounting Office estimated the cost at $500 billion.

The biggest hangover from the 1980s was the national debt, which stood at $2.6 trillion by the time Bush was elected, nearly three times its 1980 level. Bush's taboo on tax increases (meaning mainly income taxes) made it more difficult to reduce the deficit or trim the debt.

By early 1990, according to one political writer, the country faced "a horrendous fiscal mess." Bipartisan budget talks between administration and congressional leaders, begun in May, were characterized by "rancorous partisanship [and]deep divisions within the two parties." Eventually, on June 26, Bush issued a statement: "It seems clear to me that both the size of the deficit problem and the need for a package that can be enacted" required a number of measures, including "tax revenue increases." Congress finally reacted to mounting public anger at the continued indecision and approved a settlement with the Bush administration in October, although most Republicans still opposed it. Through a combination of tax hikes and spending cuts, the measure promised to reduce the budget deficit by $43.1 billion in 1991 and by $331.4 billion in 1991–1995.

SOCIAL CRISES   Perhaps the most discussed and feared social crisis of the 1990s was the spread of AIDS (Acquired Immune Deficiency Syndrome). By June 1991, AIDS had claimed over 110,000 American lives, and nearly 1.5 million Americans were carrying the deadly virus. Almost 90 percent of the AIDS cases were men, and infections were disproportionately common among intravenous drug users, homosexuals, African Americans, and Hispanic Americans. But during the nineties the number of women with the virus increased dramatically and was projected to pass the rate of men by the year 2000, and the number of cases traced to heterosexual contact was also on the rise. With no prospect for an early cure and with skyrocketing treatment costs, AIDS became during the 1990s one of the nation's most horrifying—and frustrating—problems.

The issue of what constitutes free speech aroused emotions when the Supreme Court ruled by a 5–4 vote in 1989 that burning an American flag as a form of protest was protected as free speech under the First Amendment of the Constitution. Bush led the Right in a call for a constitutional amendment to permit laws against desecrating the flag. Congress instead overwhelmingly passed legislation to make it a crime to desecrate the flag by burning or defacing it. When the high court struck down that law too, in 1990, the call for an amendment was renewed, but Congress again declined to tinker with the Bill of Rights on the eve of its 200th anniversary.

There was more symbolism than substance in the Bush administration's plans to deal with the deadly matter of drug abuse. During the 1980s, cocaine addiction had spread through sizable segments of American society, luring those with money to spend and, in its smokable form, known as crack, those with little money to spare. Bush vowed to make drug abuse his number-one domestic priority, and appointed William J. Bennett, former education secretary, as "drug czar," or head of a new Office of National Drug Control Policy, with cabinet status but no department.

Bush's war on drugs was planned along three fronts: more stringent law enforcement, drug testing in the workplace, and heightened efforts to cut off the supply of drugs coming from Colombia and Peru. Although drug-related arrests increased 20 percent from 1988 to 1989, "crack" cocaine remained readily available and immensely popular. In 1989 some 375,000 American babies were born addicted to cocaine or heroin. Equally sobering was the connection between the drug subculture and the street gangs terrorizing inner cities across the country. Like Reagan before him, Bush chose to focus on arrests and interdiction, which failed to address the basic question: why were so many young people attracted by illegal drugs?

The answer involved many factors, but the disproportionate incidence of drug and alcohol abuse among poor people pointed to the culture of poverty as a primary culprit. The United States had clearly lost its thirty-year war on poverty. Statistics illuminate the tragic realities of what sociologists called America's hidden "underclass." In 1992 10 percent of whites were classified as "poor," compared to 26 percent of Hispanics and 30 percent of blacks. More than 60 percent of all black children were born to unwed mothers (five times the rate for whites) and 23 percent of Hispanic families were headed by single women. Everyone agreed that education was a necessary lever to catapult people out of such desperate circumstances, but few members of the underclass made it through the school system. Almost 40 percent of black male high school dropouts were unemployed. Only 4 percent of black males and 6 percent of black females attended college.

Most members of the American underclass subsisted on government welfare checks and lived in rundown, crime-ridden government housing projects and deteriorating ghettos, what one black minister called America's "brand of apartheid." A government official observed that these inner-city dwellers made up a "caste of people almost totally dependent on the state, with little hope of breaking free." Those living amid such squalor and stunted hopes constituted both a tragic refutation of the American dream of upward mobility and a ticking time bomb of anger and frustration waiting to explode.

"THE COLD WAR IS NOW BEHIND US" Bush entered the White House with more foreign policy experience than most presidents, and he found the spotlight of the world stage more congenial than wrestling with the intractable problems of the inner cities or the deficit. Within two years of his inauguration, George Bush would lead the United States into two wars, a record unequaled by any of his predecessors. Throughout most of 1989, however, he merely had to sit back and observe the dissolution of one totalitarian or authoritarian regime after another. For the first time in years, democracy was suddenly on the march in a sequence of mostly bloodless revolutions that took the world by surprise.

Although in China a suddenly risen democracy movement came to a tragic end in 1989, when government forces mounted a deadly assault on demonstrators in Peking's Tiananmen Square, Eastern Europe had an entirely different experience. Mikhail Gorbachev set events in motion by responding to Soviet economic problems with policies of *perestroika* (restructuring) and *glasnost* (openness), a loosening of central economic planning and censorship. His foreign policy sought rapprochement with the West, to encourage trade and relieve the Soviet economy of burdensome military costs.

Gorbachev backed off from Soviet imperial ambitions. Early in 1989, Soviet troops left Afghanistan, after nine years bogged down in civil war there. Then in July, in Paris, Gorbachev repudiated the "Brezhnev doctrine," which had asserted the right of the Soviet Union to intervene in the internal affairs of Communist countries. The days when Soviet tanks would roll through Warsaw and Prague were over, and hard-line leaders in the East-bloc countries found themselves beset by demands for reform. With opposition strength building, the old regimes fell in rapid order, and with surprisingly little bloodshed. Communist party rule ended first in Poland and Hungary, then in hard-line Czechoslovakia and in Bulgaria. In Romania, the year of peaceful revolution ended in a bloodbath when the Romanian people in December were joined by the army in a bloody uprising against the brutal dictator Nicolae Ceausescu. He and his wife were captured, tried, and then executed on Christmas Day. But lacking experienced opposition leaders, as did all the Eastern European countries, the new government fell under the control of members of the old Communist establishment.

The most spectacular event in the collapse of the Soviet empire in Eastern Europe came on November 9, when the chief symbol of the Cold War—the Berlin Wall—fell, and the East German government succumbed to popular pressures for change. With the borders to the West fully open, the Communist government of East Germany collapsed, a freely elected government followed, and on October 3, 1990, the five states of East Germany were united with the West. The reunified German nation remained in NATO, and the Warsaw Pact alliance was dissolved.

In 1990, Gorbachev visited Washington, where on June 1 he and Bush signed more than a dozen documents. These included an agreement to reduce long-range nuclear weapons to a limit of 1,600 delivery rockets and 6,000 warheads; another agreement requiring both countries to give up the manufacture of chemical weapons; and a treaty that would loosen trade restrictions between the countries. A few days later, speaking at Stanford University, Gorbachev said: "The Cold War is now behind us. Let us not wrangle over who won it."

The democratic movement reached other parts of the world. During

West Germans chipping away at the Berlin Wall on November 11, 1989, two days after all crossings between East and West Germany were opened.

1990, the Communist party of Mongolia—a country strategically located on the borders of the Soviet Union and China—voted to give up its monopoly on power, and in Nicaragua, where the ruling Sandinista party avowed Marxism, President Daniel Ortega was defeated in a presidential election in February. Even in isolated Albania, the ruling party yielded to demands for a free election in 1991.

Democratic change overtook authoritarian regimes of a different stripe as well. In Chile, Augusto Pinochet, who had become military dictator in a bloody coup of 1973, yielded to a popular vote against continuing him in office, and was defeated in presidential elections in 1989. In South Africa, to which Congress had applied trade sanctions in protest of its apartheid (racial segregation) policies since 1986, a new prime minister, Frederik W. DeKlerk, came to office in 1989. In early 1990 he released black nationalist Nelson Mandela from twenty-seven years in prison and announced plans to abandon apartheid gradually. By early 1992 DeKlerk had pushed through a constitution ending apartheid and setting up procedures for the full integration of blacks into government and society.

The reform impulse that Gorbachev helped unleash in the East-bloc countries began to career out of control at home. Gorbachev proved unusually adept at political restructuring. While yielding to the Communist monopoly of government, he built a new presidential system that gave him, if anything, increased powers. His skills, however, did not extend to an antiquated economy that resisted change. The revival of old ethnic allegiances added to the instability. Although Russia proper included slightly over half the Soviet Union's population, it was only one of fifteen constituent republics, most of which began to seek autonomy, if not independence. Along the fringes of the Russian republic, to the west and south, lay a jigsaw puzzle of about a hundred nationalities and languages.

Gorbachev's popularity in the Soviet Union shrank as it grew abroad. It especially eroded among the Communist hard-liners, who saw in his reforms the unraveling of their bureaucratic and political empire. On August 18, 1991, a cabal of political and military leaders suddenly tried to seize the reins of power. They accosted Gorbachev at his vacation retreat in the Crimea and demanded that he sign a decree proclaiming a state of emergency and transferring his powers to them. He replied: "Go to hell," whereupon he was placed under house arrest. Twelve hours later the Soviet news agency reported to the world that Gorbachev was "ill" and had temporarily transferred his powers to his vice-

Mikhail Gorbachev and Boris Yeltsin before the Soviet parliament in the days following the failed coup of late August 1991.

president and an eight-member emergency committee. Political parties were suspended, newspapers were silenced, a curfew was announced, and street demonstrations were banned. Tanks and armored vehicles surrounded strategic installations and government buildings in Moscow. The new leadership promised to end the "chaos and anarchy" they claimed were bedeviling the country.

But the coup was doomed from the start. Poorly planned and clumsily implemented, it lacked effective coordination. The plotters failed to arrest popular leaders such as Boris Yeltsin, the populist president of the Russian republic, and they neglected to close the airports or cut off telephone and television communications. Most important, the plotters failed to recognize the strength of the democratic idealism unleashed by Gorbachev's reforms. Upon learning of the attempted overthrow, tens of thousands of Muscovites poured into the streets outside Yeltsin's headquarters to act as human shields against efforts to arrest him. Three were killed in the process.

A crescendo of indignation welled up from foreign leaders around the world. On August 20 President Bush, after a day of indecision, responded favorably to Yeltsin's request for support and convinced world leaders to join him in refusing to recognize the legitimacy of the new government. Siberian coal miners went on strike to oppose the coup. The next day word began to seep out that the plotters had given up and were fleeing. Several committed suicide, and a newly released Gorbachev ordered the others arrested. But his freedom did not bring a restoration of his power. By courageously clambering atop a menacing tank and publicly defying the conspirators, Yeltsin had emerged as the most popular political figure in the country. Gorbachev reclaimed the title of president, but was forced to resign as head of the Communist party and admit that he had made a grave mistake in appointing the men who had turned against him.

What began as a reactionary coup turned into a powerful accelerant for stunning new changes in the Soviet Union. No sooner had the plotters been arrested than most of the fifteen republics proclaimed their independence, with the Baltic republics of Latvia, Lithuania, and Estonia regaining the status of independent nations. The Communist party apparatus was dismantled, prompting celebrating crowds to topple statues of Lenin and other Communist heroes.

By the end of 1991, the Soviet Union had dissolved into a new—and

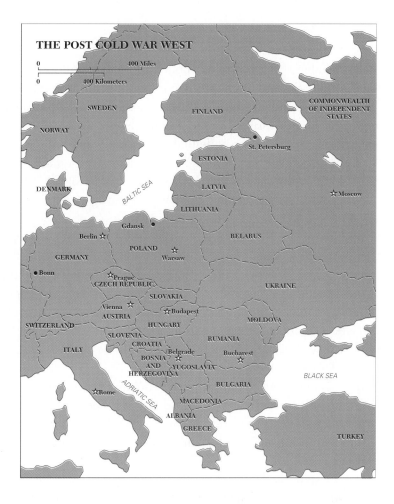

THE POST COLD WAR WEST

0   400 Miles

0   400 Kilometers

SWEDEN

FINLAND

COMMONWEALTH
OF INDEPENDENT
STATES

NORWAY

St. Petersburg

ESTONIA

DENMARK

BALTIC SEA

LATVIA

☆Moscow

LITHUANIA

Gdansk

Berlin ☆

POLAND

BELARUS

GERMANY

☆
Warsaw

● Bonn

☆Prague
CZECH REPUBLIC

UKRAINE

SLOVAKIA

Vienna ☆

☆Budapest

AUSTRIA

SWITZERLAND

HUNGARY

MOLDOVA

SLOVENIA

CROATIA

RUMANIA

ITALY

Belgrade
☆

Bucharest
☆

BOSNIA
AND
HERZEGOVINA

YUGOSLAVIA

BLACK SEA

☆Rome

ADRIATIC SEA

BULGARIA

MACEDONIA

ALBANIA

GREECE

TURKEY

fragile—Commonwealth of Independent States made up of twelve autonomous republics. Held together by little other than historic ties and contiguous borders, the federated republics soon suffered outbreaks of ethnic tensions and separatist movements. For his part, Mikhail Gorbachev found himself out of a job. With the Communist party dissolved, the Soviet Union dismantled, and continuing economic woes raising objections to his leadership, Gorbachev resigned as president at the end of 1991. Yeltsin, now a national hero, replaced him. The democratic reforms Gorbachev had set in motion to save the Union of Soviet Socialist Republics proved inadequate to the task.

The aborted coup accelerated Soviet and American efforts to reduce the stockpiles of nuclear weapons. In 1991 President Bush stunned the world by announcing that the United States would destroy all its tactical nuclear weapons on land and at sea in Europe and Asia, take its long-range bombers off twenty-four-hour alert status, and initiate discussions with the Soviet Union for the purpose of instituting sharp cuts in ICBMs with multiple warheads. Bush explained that the prospect of a Soviet invasion of Western Europe was "no longer a realistic threat," and this presented an unprecedented opportunity for reducing the threat of nuclear holocaust. President Gorbachev responded by announcing reciprocal Soviet cutbacks. As Joint Chiefs of Staff Chairman Colin Powell remarked, the Cold War "has vaporized before our eyes."

The dilution of the Russian military threat led the Defense Department in 1992 to withdraw large numbers of military personnel from bases in Asia and Europe. The Pentagon also announced a plan to shrink the armed forces by 500,000 troops over the next five years. In 1992 Bush and Yeltsin announced their intention to reduce their combined arsenals of nuclear weapons from about 22,500 to no more than 7,000 by the year 2003. All land-based multiple-warhead missiles would be destroyed.

Drastic cuts in military spending pushed defense contractors into the sharpest cutbacks since the end of World War II. "The world is becoming a friendlier place," noted one industry analyst, and American defense and aerospace firms faced a painful period of adjustment.

PANAMA   Despite the hopes of many, the end of the Cold War did not spell the end of international tensions and conflicts. Indeed, before the end of 1989, American troops were engaged in battle in Panama, where General Manuel Noriega, as chief of the Panamanian Defense Forces since 1983, was head of the government in fact if not in title. Years earlier Noriega had worked secretly with the CIA, providing information about developments in Central America. At the same time, however, he got involved in the lucrative—and illegal—drug trade. In 1988, federal grand juries in Miami and Tampa, Florida, indicted him and fifteen others on charges of international drug smuggling, gun running, and laundering the money through Panamanian banks.

In 1989 Panama's National Assembly named Noriega head of the government and proclaimed that Panama "is declared to be in a state of war" with the United States. The next day, December 16, 1989, four off-duty American servicemen were stopped at a roadblock and one marine was shot and killed. President Bush responded by ordering an invasion of Panama with the purpose of capturing Noriega for trial on the American indictments and installing a government headed by opposition leaders who had been chosen in an election nullified by Noriega earlier that year.

The 12,000 American military personnel in Panama were quickly joined by 12,000 more, and in the early morning of December 20, five military task forces struck at strategic targets in the country. They quickly disabled and seized the headquarters of the Panamanian Defense Forces, but Noriega vanished. Resistance collapsed when Noriega took refuge in the Vatican embassy on Christmas Eve. After intense negotiations, Noriega surrendered to American forces a week later. Twenty-three American servicemen were killed in the action, and estimates of Panamanians killed and wounded ranged up to 4,000, including many civilians caught in the crossfire. Noriega was detained in a U.S. federal jail well over a year after his surrender, before his trial began in late 1991. He was convicted in 1992 on eight counts of racketeering and drug distribution.

THE GULF WAR   Months after Panama had moved to the background of public attention, another former American client, Saddam Hussein, dictator of Iraq, focused attention on the Middle East when his army suddenly fell upon his tiny, wealthy neighbor Kuwait on August 2, 1990. A decade earlier, when Saddam attacked Iran hoping to exploit its revolutionary turmoil for territorial concessions, the United States and most Arab countries "tilted" toward Iraq as a regional buffer against Iran, which was then holding American diplomats hostage. From 1985 to 1990, Iraq received about $500 million worth of American technology—advanced computers, lasers, and specialized machine tools related to the development of missiles.

Saddam's war against Iran meanwhile bogged down in a bloody stalemate, until the U.N. finally arranged a truce on August 8, 1988. The next day the neighboring oil-rich enclave of Kuwait raised its production of oil contrary to agreements with the Organization of Petroleum Exporting Countries (OPEC). The resultant drop in oil prices offended Saddam, deep in debt and heavily dependent on oil revenues. Complaining of "economic aggression" against Iraq, he demanded that Kuwait reduce its production and, with Saudi Arabia, cancel Iraqi debts of $30 million. He also revived boundary disputes that had simmered

THE GULF WAR
1990–1991

Key:
○ Allied troops
⬭ Iraqi troops
△ Allied air bases
▲ Iraqi air bases
☐ U.S. Naval forces
→ Gound attack, Feb. 24–28, 1991

since a post–World War I settlement had created the current map of the Gulf region. Saddam seemed to nurture hopes of unifying the Arab lands and dominating the region's oil resources.

As tensions heightened, American officials remained focused on events in Europe and on Iraq's value as a counterweight to Iran. A meeting on July 25, 1990, between Saddam Hussein and the American ambassador to Iraq, April Glaspie, failed to resolve the mounting crisis. A text of the meeting later released by Iraq pictured Glaspie as deferential and conciliatory, assuring Saddam that the United States would not get involved in a dispute between Arab neighbors. Glaspie, a career expert on the Middle East and fluent in Arabic, later testified to Congress: "I told him orally we would defend our vital interests, we would support our friends in the Gulf, we would defend their sovereignty and integrity." The main American mistake, she said, was not to "realize he was stupid." On August 2, the Iraqi army occupied Kuwait.

Saddam did not expect the firestorm of world indignation he ignited. The U.N. Security Council quickly voted 14–0 to condemn the invasion and demand withdrawal. Secretary of State James Baker and Soviet foreign minister Edouard Shevardnadze issued a joint statement of condemnation. The Security Council then endorsed Resolution 661, an embargo on trade with Iraq, by a vote of 13–0, with Cuba and Yemen abstaining. Such unanimity, of course, would have been unlikely during the Cold War.

On August 2 President Bush condemned Iraq's "naked aggression" and said he was not ruling any options out. On August 6–7, the United States dispatched planes and troops to Saudi Arabia on a "wholly defensive" mission—to protect Saudi Arabia. British forces soon joined in, as did Arab troops from a half dozen nations. On August 22, Bush began to order the mobilization of American reserve forces for the operation dubbed "Desert Shield."

On November 8, Bush announced that he was doubling American forces in the Middle East from about 200,000 to 400,000, to build up "an adequate offensive military capability." Bush asserted that he already had authority to take such action under the Security Council resolutions. Bush's position was strengthened on November 29 by U.N. Resolution 678, which authorized the use of force to dislodge Iraq from Kuwait, and set a deadline for Iraqi withdrawal of January 15, 1991.

A flurry of peace efforts sent diplomats scurrying all over, but without result. Saddam refused to yield. On January 10 Congress began to debate a resolution authorizing the use of U.S. armed forces. The outcome was uncertain to the end, but on January 12 the resolution for the use of force passed the House by 250–183, and the Senate by 52–47.

By January 1991, a twenty-eight-nation allied force was committed to Operation Desert Storm when the first missiles and planes began to hit Iraq at about 2:30 A.M., January 17, Baghdad time. The Persian Gulf War, the "mother of all battles" in Saddam Hussein's words, was intense but short, ending with an allied cease-fire just six weeks later, and leaving consequences to be played out far into the future.

War has long been a popular spectator sport, in the age of television literally so, and Americans derived their impressions of the Gulf conflict largely from that source. With the allies in control of the air from the beginning, Saddam's only recourse was to fire off lumbering Soviet-made SCUD missiles, which he aimed from the first day into Israel with the hope of provoking Israeli retaliation and undermining the coalition against him. But the resulting damage and casualties were light, and the Israelis showed remarkable restraint in the face of the continuing attacks. The Iraqis responded with desperation moves, which did more damage to the environment than to enemy forces: releasing oil into the Persian Gulf from tankers and loading platforms in Kuwait—and setting fire to hundreds of Kuwaiti oil wells.

Saddam concentrated his forces in Kuwait, expecting an allied attack northward into Kuwait and a landing on the coast. But the Iraqis were outflanked when 200,000 allied troops, largely American, British, and French, vanished with much of their heavy armor and turned up on the undefended border with Saudi Arabia 100–200 miles to the west. The allied ground assault began on February 24, and lasted only four days. Iraqi tanks were smashed in the largest armored battle, probably, since the Battle of the Bulge. Thousands of Iraqi soldiers surrendered, and there was a quick breakthrough into Kuwait.

On February 28, President Bush called for a cease-fire, the Iraqis accepted, and the shooting ended. American fatalities were 137. The lowest estimates of Iraqi fatalities, civilian and military, were around 100,000. The coalition forces occupied about one-fifth of Iraq.

The Middle East, as it had for centuries, resisted any quick fix. The Persian Gulf War was far from a reprise of Vietnam, but it ended with what conceivably could turn into a longer hangover. There was an understanding—details to be worked out—that the United States would maintain a military presence in the Persian Gulf. Secretary of State Baker succeeded in organizing a conference to address the tough problems between Israel and its Arab neighbors, but any settlement remained far off. It was, ironically, an American missionary who said to one of the British planners carving up the former Ottoman territory after World War I: "You are flying in the face of four millenniums of history." The words retain their haunting quality.

MAKING CONNECTIONS

- As the chapter title indicates, much of what happened in the 1980s, from economic and social policy to presidential leadership style, was reminiscent of the late nineteenth century. The chapter also draws parallels between the 1980s and the 1920s and 1950s.

- Another parallel between the late nineteenth century and the 1980s was a rise in immigration and a change in immigration patterns. This is discussed in the next chapter.

- Chapter 36 shows how the economic and political conservatism of the 1980s became much more ideological in the early 1990s.

FURTHER READING

On Reaganomics, see David Stockman's *The Triumph of Politics: How the Reagan Revolution Failed* (1986). For Reagan's foreign policy in Central America, see James Chace's *Endless War: How We Got Involved in Central America and What Can Be Done* (1984)* and Walter LaFeber's *Inevitable Revolutions: The United States in Central America* (rev. ed., 1984).*

Several books of essays collect varying assessments of the Reagan years. Among these are *The Reagan Revolution* (1988), edited by B. B. Kymlicka and Jean V. Matthews; *The Reagan Presidency: An Incomplete Revolution* (1990), edited by Dilys M. Hill et al., and *Looking Back on the Reagan Presidency* (1990), edited by Larry Berman. A good overview of the Reagan years is Michael Schaller's *Reckoning with Reagan: America and Its President in the 1980s* (1992).*

On the Bush presidency, see Ryan J. Barilleaux and Mary E. Stuckey's *Leadership and the Bush Presidency: Prudence or Drift in an Era of*

---

*These books are available in paperback editions.

Change (1992), and Charles Tiefer's *The Semi-Sovereign Presidency: The Bush Administration's Strategy for Governing without Congress* (1994).

On the banking and other scandals, see Kathleen Day's *S&L Hell: The People and Politics Behind the $1 Trillion Savings & Loan Scandal* (1993).

*These books are available in paperback editions.

36 &ↄ CULTURAL POLITICS

CHAPTER ORGANIZER

This chapter focuses on:

- the growth of cultural politics.

- the Democratic resurgence of the early 1990s and the Republican landslide of 1994.

- demographic patterns from the 1990 census.

- the "new immigrants" of the 1980s and 1990s.

ince the end of World War II American politics has been largely concerned with issues of economic policy and foreign relations. In the late 1960s, however, political debate became morally charged, especially on the divisive issue of American involvement in Vietnam. Political differences began to form a cultural chasm. In the 1970s, a cultural conservatism coalesced, with people professing old-time virtues and eternal verities expressing rising fears that the nation had lost its moral bearings.

Cultural conservatives helped elect Reagan and Bush in the 1980s, but many were disappointed in the results. Once in office, neither president had, in their eyes, adequately addressed their moral agenda. By the 1990s a new generation of young conservative activists, mostly political independents or Republicans, began to emerge as a force to be reckoned with in national affairs. They were more ideological, more libertarian, more partisan, and more impatient than their predecessors.

This new breed of cultural conservatives steadfastly rejected the excesses of liberalism. They not only lamented the disappearance of basic forms of decency and propriety; they also believed that fundamental liberties were at risk. Affirmative action programs designed to redress historic injustices against women and minorities came under increasing attack. Prominent black conservatives supported such efforts, arguing that racially based preferences were demeaning and condescending remedies. As Shelby Steele argued in his runaway bestseller, *The Content of Our Character* (1990), preferential governmental treatment of blacks raised doubts in the minds of both blacks and whites about the inherent worth of any black achievement. Blacks, he contended, needed to free themselves of their preoccupation with viewing themselves as "victims" and demonstrate to a skeptical world that they were perfectly capable of achieving the American dream on their own.

THE RELIGIOUS RIGHT   Although quite diverse, cultural conservatives tended to be evangelical Christians or orthodox Catholics who joined together to exert increasing pressure on the political process. In the decades after the end of World War II those Americans identifying themselves as "fundamentalist Christians" increased almost sevenfold. In 1979 conservative political activists had convinced the Baptist television evangelist Jerry Falwell to form the Moral Majority to exert pressure on political candidates to support prayer in public schools and oppose abortion. Ten years later, television evangelist Pat Robertson organized the Christian Coalition to replace the now-defunct Moral Majority as the flagship organization of the resurgent religious right. Robertson had no doubts about the righteousness of his own positions. "When I pray, I get answers," he claimed.

A similar sense of self-righteous conviction galvanized the Christian Coalition. Its 1.6 million members were led by a charismatic young executive director named Ralph Reed. Robertson and Reed encouraged religious conservatives to vote, run for public office, and support candidates who shared the organization's views. Christian Coalition members often professed a "holier-than-thou" insistence that their values

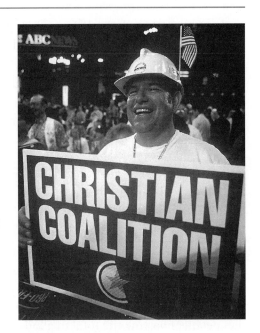

Christian Coalition supporter at the 1996 Republican National Convention in San Diego, California.

were the only correct values for the United States to embrace. The Oklahoma state chairman declared, "Only we can restore this nation. Only the people here today, and people like us, can turn this around . . . only Christian believers doing the work . . . in the thick of battle."

The Christian Coalition chose the Republican party as the best vehicle for transforming its profamily campaign into new public policies. Reed encouraged his supporters to withhold their political support from any candidate who did not provide an ironclad promise to support the Coalition's school prayer, anti-abortion, anti–gay rights positions. In addition to promoting "traditional family values," Reed urged politicians to "radically downsize and relimit government." The conservative commentator turned presidential candidate Patrick Buchanan wholeheartedly agreed. He explained his desire "to return to their places of honor the Republican beliefs, cultural norms, and moral values they were raised with. These are the conservatives of the heart."

As a centrist professional politician, George Bush initially tried to keep the cultural conservatives at arm's length, only to find himself the target—and victim—of their in-your-face attacks and take-no-prisoners tenacity. His Democratic successor, Bill Clinton, also underestimated the growing strength of organized groups such as the Christian Coalition. In the 1994 congressional elections, religious conservatives went to the polls in record numbers, and 70 percent of them voted Republican tickets. A third of the voters identified themselves as "white, evangelical, born-again Christians." In many respects, these cultural conservatives took control of the political and social agendas in the nineties. As one journalist acknowledged in 1995, "the religious right is moving toward center stage in American secular life."

AMERICA'S CHANGING FACE: THE 1990 CENSUS

AGE, GENDER, RACE   In 1990 an army of census workers roamed the streets and byways of the United States, counting heads and accumulating data about the American people. The 1990 census revealed several dramatic changes in the country's demographic profile. During the 1980s the nation's population grew by 10 percent, or some 23 million people, boosting the total to almost 250 million. The median age of the quarter-billion Americans rose from thirty to thirty-three, and the much-discussed "baby boom" generation—the 43 million people born between 1946 and 1964—entered middle age. Because of its disproportionate size, the baby-boom generation magnifies changes in American society as it moves through the life cycle. Political analysts suggested that this generation's maturation and preoccupation with practical concerns such as raising families and buying houses helped explain the surge of political conservatism during the 1980s. Surveys revealed that baby-boomers wanted stronger family and religious ties in the eighties and promoted a greater respect for authority. Yet having come to maturity during the turbulent sixties and early seventies, the baby-boomers also displayed more tolerance of social and cultural diversity than their parents.

The census revealed that the fastest-growing age groups, however, were the oldest ones. Americans in their nineties more than doubled during the 1980s, and those over a hundred years old grew by 77 percent. How was the nation to care for so many old people? To finance an ever-growing group of retirees, American workers had to contribute an ever-higher portion of their paycheck to the Social Security system. During the 1980s, supposedly a time of lower taxes, Social Security payroll taxes increased 14 percent.

The 1990 census uncovered a nation on the move, as the "Sunbelt" states of the South and West continued to lure residents from the Midwest and Northeast. Fully 90 percent of the nation's total population growth during the 1980s occurred in southern or western states. California gained more people than any other state during the eighties, boosting its total to 30 million, 5 million more than in 1980. Texas and Florida each added more than 3 million new residents, while West Virginia, Iowa, and the District of Columbia experienced a net loss of residents. The Northeast became the least populous region of the country. These population shifts forced a massive redistricting of the House of Representatives, with Florida and California gaining three more seats each and Texas two, while states such as New York lost seats.

By the end of the twentieth century, the average American lived in twelve different residences during a lifetime, roughly twice as many as the average person in Britain or France, and four times as many as the typical Irish citizen. Why were Americans so mobile? A major factor was the high divorce rate in the United States, one of the highest in the world. In addition, economic opportunity in the United States is more geographically dispersed than in other countries. Upwardly mobile people can choose among many different locales to strike out in search of new jobs or careers. In smaller countries, however, the economy is often dominated by a single metropolitan area.

As they moved during the 1980s, Americans tended to settle in large communities. Almost 90 percent of the decade's population growth occurred in large metropolitan areas. The number of cities with 100,000 people or more increased by 29 to a total of 195, with 18 of the new metropolises in California alone. In 1990 some 78 percent of the population lived in a metropolitan urban area and, for the first time, a majority of Americans lived in cities of a million or more people. This move to the cities largely reflected trends in the job market, as the economy continued to shift from manufacturing to professional service industries, particularly those specializing in telecommunications and information processing. Of course the migration to large cities meant that large numbers of Americans continued to leave rural areas. During the 1980s more than a million people moved from their farms to cities or suburbs. By 1990 fewer than 5 million people out of a total population of 250 million—or 2 percent—lived on farms.

The 1990 census also showed that women continued to enter the work force in large numbers. Indeed, one of the most significant socio-logical developments in American life since 1970 was the accelerated entry of women into the world of work outside the home. In 1970, 38 percent of the work force was female; in 1990 the figure was almost 50 percent. Women workers accounted for 60 percent of labor force growth since 1980, and fully 58 percent of all adult women were gain-fully employed. A third of the new medical doctors during the eighties were women (4 percent in 1970); 40 percent of new lawyers were fe-male (8.4 percent in 1970); and 23 percent of new dentists were women (less than 1 percent in 1970). Such advances in the professions indicated that women were also better educated than ever. During the 1980s the educational gap between men and women continued to nar-row. Among people aged forty-five to fifty-four, the share of men with college degrees was 10 points higher than the share of women. But among people aged twenty-five to thirty-four the difference was less than 1 percent.

The decline of the traditional family unit—two parents with chil-dren—continued during the 1980s. The proportion of the nation's households in that category dropped from 31 percent in 1980 to 26 per-cent in 1990. And more people were living alone than ever before, largely as a result of high divorce rates or a growing practice of delaying marriage until well into the twenties. One out of every four households in 1990 was made up of a person living alone, a 26 percent increase over 1980. The number of single mothers increased 35 percent during the decade. The rate was much higher for African Americans: in 1990 less than 38 percent of black children lived with both parents, down from 67 percent in 1960.

Young blacks burdened by the absence of one or both parents also faced shrinking economic opportunities in the 1980s. The 1990 census documented a slight rise in the proportion of Americans living in pov-erty but a substantially heightened inequality in the distribution of in-come. By 1992, roughly 14.5 percent of the American people were liv-ing at or below the official poverty level, pegged at $14,335 in annual income for a family of four. The urban poor were particularly victimized by a developing underclass culture, with young black males suffering the most. In 1990 the leading cause of death among black males be-tween the ages of fifteen and twenty-four was homicide. Twenty-five percent of black males aged twenty to twenty-nine were in prison, on parole, or on probation, while only 4 percent were enrolled in college. Forty percent of black adult males were functionally illiterate.

THE NEW IMMIGRANTS   The Census Bureau reports also revealed that the racial and ethnic composition of the country changed rapidly during the 1980s, with nearly one in every four Americans claiming African, Asian, Hispanic, or American Indian ancestry. Among an overall population of 250 million, blacks represented 12 percent of the total, Hispanics 9 percent, Asians about 3 percent, and American Indians almost 1 percent. The rate of increase among those four groups was twice as fast as it had been during the 1970s.

The primary cause of this dramatic change in the nation's ethnic mix was a surge of immigration. During the 1980s, legal immigration into the United States totaled over 7 million people, 30 percent higher than the previous decade and more than in any other decade except 1901–1910. Between 1990 and 1996 another 6 million newcomers arrived, most of them from Mexico and Asia. These figures do not include the hundreds of thousands of illegal aliens, mostly Mexicans and Haitians.

RESIDENT POPULATION DISTRIBUTION FOR THE UNITED STATES BY RACE AND HISPANIC ORIGIN: 1990 AND 1980

	1990		1980		
	Number	%	Number	%	Increase
Total population	248,709,873	100.0	226,545,805	100.0	9.8
White	199,686,070	80.3	188,371,622	83.1	6.0
Black	29,986,060	12.1	26,495,025	11.7	13.2
American Indian, Eskimo, or Aleut	1,959,234	0.8	1,420,400	0.6	37.9
Asian or Pacific Islander	7,273,662	2.9	3,500,439	1.5	107.8
Other race	9,804,847	3.9	6,758,319	3.0	45.1
Hispanic origin	22,354,059	9.0	14,608,673	6.4	53.0

Source: Bureau of the Census, 1991.

IMMIGRANTS ADMITTED BY
TOP 15 COUNTRIES OF BIRTH
IN FISCAL YEAR 1990

Country of Birth	1990
Total	**656,111**
Mexico	56,549
Philippines	54,907
Vietnam	48,662
Dominican Republic	32,064
Korea	29,548
China (mainland)	28,746
India	28,679
Soviet Union	25,350
Jamaica	18,828
Iran	18,031
Taiwan	13,839
United Kingdom	13,730
Canada	13,717
Poland	13,334
Haiti	11,862
Other	248,265

Source: U.S. Immigration and Naturalization Service, 1991.

In 1990 the United States welcomed more than twice as many immigrants as all other countries in the world put together. The magnetic attraction of the United States to foreigners during the 1980s was vividly revealed in 1987, when the Immigration Service opened a special "visa lottery" for citizens in those countries historically short-changed by annual immigration quotas. Officials allotted 10,000 such visas and assumed that would meet the demand, but 1.4 million people applied.

Even more significant than the overall number of newcomers were their places of origin. For the first time in the nation's history, the majority of immigrants came not from Europe but from other parts of the world. The percentage of European immigrants to the United States declined from 53 percent of the total in the 1950s to 12 percent in the 1980s and 1990s. Asian-Americans were the fastest-growing segment of the population in the eighties, with numbers increasing by 80 percent, a rate seven times as great as the general population. Among the legal immigrants during the decade, Mexicans made up the largest share, averaging about 60,000 a year. The second-highest number came from the Philippines (46,000), and immigrants from mainland China,

Taiwan, and Hong Kong totaled 45,000 annually. The next largest groups were Vietnamese and Koreans, followed by Dominicans, Asian Indians, Jamaicans, Iranians, Cubans, Cambodians, and Laotians.

Heightening the social impact of these new immigrants was their tendency to cluster in a handful of states and cities. Most of them gravitated to New York, Illinois, and New Jersey, as well as Florida, Texas, Hawaii, California, and other Sunbelt states. By 1990, California harbored 64 percent of the Asian-Americans in the country and 34 percent of the Hispanics. The population of Miami, Florida, was 64 percent Hispanic, and San Antonio, Texas, boasted 55 percent. Los Angeles contained 2 million Mexican-Americans, more than any other city except Mexico City itself. Preferring their own ethnic enclaves and bringing with them distinctive languages, cuisine, clothes, dress, and folkways, the immigrants from Asia, Latin America, and the Caribbean quickly became an insistent cultural presence.

The wave of new immigration brought rising conflict between old and new ethnicities. African-American leaders such as the Reverend Calvin Butts of the Abyssinian Baptist Church in Harlem worried that the newcomers were gaining an economic foothold at the expense of poor blacks. And many native whites resented the influx of newcomers into their communities.

Such reactions recall earlier chapters in American immigrant history, a story marked from the start by ambivalence about the nation's tradition of inclusiveness. With rhetoric reminiscent of the nativist movement a century earlier, critics of the new tide of immigration charged that America was being "overrun" with foreigners; they questioned whether Hispanics and Asians could be "assimilated" into American culture. In 1986 California voters passed a referendum ending bilingual education. Florida soon followed suit. In 1994 a large majority of California voters approved Proposition 187, a controversial initiative that denied the state's estimated 4 million illegal immigrants access to public schools, nonemergency health care, and other social services. It also required teachers, doctors, and government officials to report anyone suspected of being an undocumented immigrant. Proponents of the new measure claimed it would save taxpayers billions of dollars. Critics labeled Proposition 187 racist in motive and effect. Initially, at least, the measure had no practical impact because a federal judge barred the state government from implementing the measure because it conflicted with federal authority.

The bitter irony of this new nativism was that it targeted recent immigrants for bringing with them to the United States virtues long prized by Americans—hope, energy, persistence, and an aggressive work ethic. Like most of their predecessors who braved tremendous hardships to make their way to America, they toiled long and hard for a slice of the American dream, and most economic studies concluded that their presence was beneficial to the nation. They created more wealth than they consumed, and many of them compiled an astonishing record of achievement. The median household income of Asian-Americans, for example, exceeded every other group, including native whites, and Asian-Americans were disproportionately represented in the nation's most prestigious colleges and universities. Yet the very success of the new immigrants contributed to the resentment they encountered from other groups.

In this turbulent atmosphere of mounting ethnic strife and political confrontation, some observers worried that the social fabric was being stretched to the breaking point. There seemed to be evidence of this in the fall of 1995 with the racially polarized response to the acquittal of football star O. J. Simpson on murder charges. Moreover the nation seemed awash in "special-interest groups," highly organized, well financed, and politically savvy organizations designed to promote single issues: corporate tax breaks, gun ownership, prayer in schools, abortion, animal rights, and environmentalism, to name just a few. It was becoming increasingly difficult to recognize the common good. Said a prominent law professor: "We are witnessing a gradual decline in the legal and social significance of community interests."

Indeed, the most potent challenge facing Americans during the 1990s came not from abroad but from within: how could they find a "common ground" of shared civic values that nourished both cultural pluralism and individual rights? How could Americans live up to their national motto—*E pluribus unum,* One out of many?

BUSH TO CLINTON

For months after the Gulf War, George Bush seemed unbeatable. In the polls his approval rating rose to 91 percent. But the aftermath of Desert Storm was mixed, with Saddam Hussein's grip on Iraq still intact. The Soviet Union meanwhile, stumbled on to its surprising end. On December 25, 1991, the Soviet flag over the Kremlin came down and the flag of the Russian Federation went up. The Cold War had ended with not just the collapse but the dismemberment of the Soviet Union into its fifteen constituent republics. As a result, the United States was now the world's only superpower.

"Containment" of the Soviet Union, the bedrock of American foreign policy for more than four decades, had lost its reason for being. Bush, the ultimate Cold War careerist—ambassador to the U.N., envoy to China, head of the CIA, vice-president under Reagan—struggled to interpret the fluid new international scene. He spoke of a "New World Order" but never defined it. By his own admission he had trouble with the "vision thing."

The situation, in fact, did not lend itself to a simple vision—unless the answer was to drift into isolation, a great temptation, with foreign dangers seemingly lessened. By the end of 1991 Bush faced a primary challenge from the Republican commentator and former White House aide Patrick Buchanan, who adopted the slogan "America First" and called on Bush to "bring home the boys." As the victory euphoria wore off, a popular bumper sticker reflected the growing public frustration with the Bush administration: "SADDAM HUSSEIN STILL HAS HIS JOB. WHAT ABOUT YOU?"

THE GREAT COMPRESSION   In 1988, a few days after George Bush was elected president, a journalist observed that the most important issue to be addressed by the new administration was the nation's deepening financial debt. "It is the issue that probably will determine the fate of the President. Indeed, it could also be his ultimate undoing."

It was a prescient prediction. For the Bush administration and for the nation the most devastating development in the early nineties was a prolonged economic recession that began in 1990. The first economic setback in more than eight years, it grew into the longest, if not the deepest, since the Great Depression. By early 1992 over 2 million jobs had dried up. During 1991, 25 million workers—about 20 percent of the labor force—were unemployed at some time.

What made this recession unusual was that its victims included large numbers of white-collar workers. In the corporate world, terms such as "restructuring" and "downsizing" ruled the day. Companies began reducing personnel, switching employees to part-time status to reduce benefits, using temporary workers (providing "temps" became a growth industry), hiring independent contractors for certain work ("outsourcing"), and finding other ways to cut labor costs.

The nationwide shrinkage of the work force led some analysts to label the trend the "Great Compression." Prosperity gave way to firings, growing unemployment, declining sales and profits, the continuing imbalance in foreign trade, and the lack of a plan for the demobilization of the military-industrial complex after the Cold War. With soaring expenditures on defense and social entitlement programs, a $150 billion annual deficit had become a $450 billion shortfall during 1991.

A long-term cause of the economic slump was America's low rate of investment compared to that of its major trading partners. While Japan invested 31 percent of its Gross Domestic Product (GDP) into new machinery, equipment, and production technologies, the United States committed only 15 percent of its GDP.

A Senate committee analysis of the stagnant economy confirmed a chilling fact: under the Bush administration "the average standard of living has actually declined." Some critics with a historical bent compared Bush to Hoover: both presidents and their aides initially denied that there was a problem with the economy and then assured the nation that the recession would be short and self-correcting. The euphoria over the Allied victory in the Persian Gulf quickly gave way to anxiety and resentment generated by the depressed economy. In 1991 Bush confessed that he had not "been able to sort out exactly why there has been this degree of pessimism." With his domestic policies in disarray and his foreign policy abandoned, George Bush tried a clumsy balancing act in addressing the recession, on the one hand acknowledging that "people are hurting" while on the other urging Americans that "this is a good time to buy a car."

THE COURT VEERS RIGHT   Other developments affected the president's popularity, among them the retirement in 1991 of the first black Supreme Court justice, Thurgood Marshall, after twenty-four years on the bench. To succeed him Bush named Clarence Thomas, a black federal judge who had been raised in poverty in the segregated South and educated in Catholic schools. After graduating from Yale Law School,

Thomas had worked as an aide to a Republican senator before serving as chairman of the Equal Employment Opportunity Commission (EEOC) from 1982 to 1990. Then, after sixteen months on the U.S. Court of Appeals, he was tapped for the Supreme Court.

Despite Thomas's limited time in the judiciary, his views commended him to conservative senators. He had questioned the wisdom of the minimum wage, school busing for desegregation, and affirmative-action hiring programs, and he had preached "black self-help," once declaring that all civil rights leaders ever did was "bitch, bitch, bitch, moan, and whine."

Such opinions promised trouble in the Democratic Senate, but the real explosion occurred when Anita Hill, a soft-spoken law professor at the University of Oklahoma, charged that Thomas had sexually harassed her when she worked for him at the EEOC. "He talked about pornographic materials" and "various sex acts," she said. Pro-Thomas senators orchestrated an often savage and sometimes absurd cross-examination of Hill. Some accused her of mental instability. An indignant Thomas denied her charges and implied that Hill had fabricated the charges at the behest of civil rights groups determined to thwart his confirmation. "I would have preferred an assassin's bullet to this kind of living hell," he said the next day, but he added that he "would rather die than withdraw."

The televised hearings revealed that either Hill or Thomas had lied, and the committee's tie vote reflected the doubt: seven to recommend and seven against. The full Senate then narrowly confirmed Thomas by a 52–48 margin.

The hearings marked a new surge in the women's movement. Before the galvanizing effects of Anita Hill's rough treatment at the hands of male senators, feminism as an organized political movement was in disarray. As early as 1975 Betty Friedan had broken away from NOW, the organization she had started less than a decade before, claiming that radical leaders had abandoned the core constituency of working women. By 1992 many claimed that NOW had reached a dead end. Columnist Sally Quinn charged that "many women have come to see the feminist movement as anti-male, anti-child, anti-family, anti-feminine. And therefore it has nothing to do with us."

In the ambiguous aftermath of the Thomas hearings, many women grew incensed at the treatment of Hill, and an unprecedented number of women ran for national and local offices in 1992. The Thomas confirmation struggle thus widened the gender gap for a Republican party already less popular with women than with men. The feminist rallying cry became: "You just don't get it." As one political commentator put it: "The war with Anita Hill was not a war Bush needed."

REPUBLICAN TURMOIL   The president, moreover, had set a trap for himself when he declared in his 1988 convention address: "Read my lips. No new taxes!" Then, fourteen months into his term, he decided that ignoring the deficit was a greater risk than violating his "no tax" pledge. After intense negotiations with congressional Democrats, Bush announced that the deficits now required "tax revenue increases." He did not exactly say "new taxes," but as one House Democrat put it, "the charade is over." Bush's backsliding set off a revolt among House Republicans, but a bipartisan majority (most Republicans opposing) finally approved a tax measure raising the top personal rate from 28 to 31 percent, disallowing certain deductions to the upper brackets, and raising various excises—an estimated increase of about $165 billion. Conservative Republicans would not let George Bush forget his abandoned pledge.

Social issues had been one of the adhesives in the Reagan coalition, keeping the focus away from divisive economic issues, but as hardships crowded in on workers, attention on the economy surged to the fore. Moreover, social issues strengthened the force of the new "Christian Right" and grated on traditional Republicans. Reagan had been adept at exploiting moral issues, especially abortion, while doing little or nothing about them in practice. Bush's efforts to talk up such issues eventually ran out of control when right-wing militants seized the podium and the attention of the TV cameras at the 1992 Republican convention.

Patrick Buchanan, who had consistently won about a third of the votes in the Republican primaries, used the occasion for a defense of "family values." Pat Robertson, the television evangelist, insisted that the proposed Equal Rights Amendment represented "a socialist, anti-family political movement that encourages women to leave their husbands, kill their children, practice witchcraft, destroy capitalism and become lesbians."

DEMOCRATIC RESURGENCE

In contrast to such strident rhetoric, the Democrats presented an image of centrist forces in control. For several years the Democratic Leadership Council (DLC), in which Arkansas governor William Jefferson Clinton figured prominently, had pushed the party in that direction.

THE COMEBACK KID   Clinton strove to move the Democrats closer to the mainstream of political opinion. A graduate of Georgetown University, he had won a Rhodes scholarship to Oxford and then earned a law degree from Yale, where he met and married the brightest woman in the class, Hillary Rodham. By 1979, at age 32, he was back in his native Arkansas as the youngest governor in the country. He served three more terms as governor and in the process emerged as a dynamic young leader within the national Democratic party committed to winning back the middle-class white voters who had voted Republican during the eighties.

A self-described moderate, Clinton promised to cut the defense budget, provide tax relief for the middle class, and send a massive economic aid package to the former republics of the Soviet Union. He was less precise about how such initiatives would be funded. Handsome, witty, intelligent, and a compelling speaker, Clinton reminded many political observers of John F. Kennedy.

But underneath the veneer of Clinton's charisma were several flaws. He made extensive use of polls to shape his stance on issues, pandered to special interest groups, and flip-flopped on controversial issues, leading critics to label him "Slick Willie." Said one former opponent in Arkansas, "He'll be what people want him to be. He'll do or say what it will take to get elected." Even more enticing to the media and more embarrassing to Clinton were unending reports that he was an adulterer and that he had used political pull during the Vietnam war to avoid the draft. Clinton's denials of both allegations could not dispel a lingering distrust of his personal character.

After a series of bruising party primaries, Clinton emerged the front-runner by the time of the nominating convention in the summer of 1992. The Clinton forces dominated the convention in New York, where

Clinton chose Albert Gore, Jr., of Tennessee as his running mate. So the Democratic candidates were two southern Baptists from adjoining states.

Flushed with their convention victory, sporting a ten-point lead in the polls, the Clinton-Gore team stressed economic issues to win over working-class white and black voters. The formula worked. Exit polls showed that the most important issue had been the economy. Clinton won with 370 electoral votes and about 43 percent of the votes; Bush had 168 electoral votes and 39 percent; and off-and-on independent candidate H. Ross Perot of Texas garnered 18 percent of the popular vote but no electoral votes. A feisty billionaire, Perot found a big audience for his simplified explanations of public problems and his offers to just "get under the hood and fix them." Yet during the Democratic convention, Perot withdrew, explaining that the Democratic party had "revitalized itself." Later he got back in the race and stayed for a surprisingly strong finish, one that suggested a widespread disillusionment with politics as usual.

THE CLINTON PRESIDENCY Clinton's presidency suffered from promises made during the campaign. One was a middle-class tax cut, which Clinton decided would have to yield to keeping down the deficit. The others had to do with restrictions on federal bans on abortions and on homosexuals in the military. Clinton erased the federal bans on abortions by executive order right away. His attempt to accept professed homosexuals in the military provoked strong opposition among military commanders and in Congress. Faced with the possibility that a gay ban might be written into law, Clinton backed down nine days into office and postponed a new order for six months. Later, he announced a new policy for gays in the military that came to be summed up in the words "Don't ask, don't tell." These actions at the start of the new administration had an effect on public impressions of the president, whom opponents accused on the one hand of putting a leftist agenda first and on the other hand of being too quick to cave in. In Clinton's first two weeks in office his favorability standings dropped 20 percent in the polls.

Clinton also encountered trouble with his major appointments. Two nominees for attorney-general were forced to withdraw when they admitted employing illegal aliens in their households. Clinton turned fi-

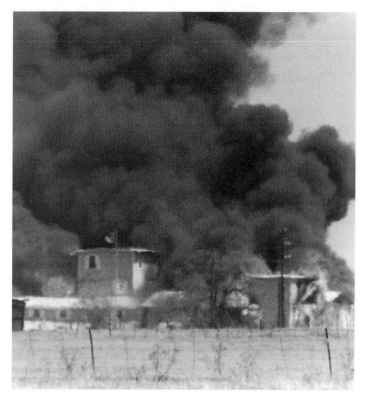

The Branch Davidian compound ablaze in Waco, Texas.

nally to Janet Reno, the first woman to serve as attorney-general. She took office twelve days after an ill-fated siege began near Waco, Texas, at the Mt. Carmel compound of an apocalyptic sect, the Branch Davidians, an offshoot of the Seventh Day Adventists. Their leader, David Koresh (a.k.a. Vernon Howell), a high-school dropout, rock musician, habitué of gun shows, a spellbinding speaker, and a polygamist prophet, styled himself the messiah. Reports flourished about the group's stockpiling arms, abusing children, violating immigration laws, engaging in false imprisonment. On February 28, 1993, a force of agents from the Treasury Department's Bureau of Alcohol Tobacco and Firearms (BATF) were met with gunfire when they tried to enter the compound. Soon four agents and two Branch Davidians were dead, and twenty or so people were injured.

The FBI then took over the siege from the BATF. After fifty days of psychological warfare against the compound without result, the FBI yielded to frustration and to hints of child abuse in the compound and on the fifty-first day attacked with armored vehicles and tear gas. Amid the commotion the compound caught fire, and blazes spread by prairie winds consumed it. Searches of the rubble yielded the body of Koresh, a bullet hole through his forehead. At least seventy-seven died in the inferno.

Janet Reno immediately took responsibility for the decision to assault the compound, as did President Clinton. The bloodshed at Waco had lasting repercussions among elements of the radical right, and would become the touchstone for further acts of violence, particularly the deadly bombing of the federal building in Oklahoma City in spring 1995.

THE RISE OF MILITIAS   The tragedy at the Branch Davidian compound near Waco helped accelerate a burgeoning "militia" or "patriot" movement across the country. It represented a paranoid and populist strain in the cultural politics of the 1990s. Convinced that the federal government was conspiring against individual liberties (especially the right to bear arms), thousands of people joined well-armed militia organizations. Some militias harkened back to the origins of the Ku Klux Klan and fomented racial and ethnic hatred. Others aligned themselves with right-wing Christian groups, particularly the militant wing of the anti-abortion movement. In the far West, several of the militias challenged the federal control of public lands, refused to pay taxes, and threatened to arrest and execute local government and judicial officials.

Most Americans were unaware of the militia movement until April 19, 1995, the second anniversary of the Waco incident. On that day a massive truck bomb exploded in front of the federal office building in Oklahoma City, Oklahoma. The entire front portion of the nine-story building collapsed, killing 168 people, nineteen of them children in a day-care center. Six hundred others were injured.

Within days the FBI arrested Timothy McVeigh and Terry Nichols and charged them with the bombing. A third man pleaded guilty to separate charges of conspiring to produce explosives. All three men were militia members with a virulent hatred for the federal government and for the way in which the BATF and FBI had dealt with the Branch Davidians at Waco.

CLINTON AND THE ECONOMY   During the campaign Clinton had promised to submit within 100 days an economic program and a health-care plan. On February 17, he laid out a program of tax hikes and spending cuts that added up to a $493 billion deficit reduction. He proposed higher taxes for corporations and for individuals in higher tax brackets. Clinton also called for an economic stimulus package of $16 billion for "investment" in public works (transportation, utilities, and the like) and in "human capital" (education, skills, health, and welfare). This was his program's first casualty. By focusing on deficit reduction, he helped the opposition picture the "stimulus package" as a "budget buster" that would fail to pep up the economy.

The Republican minority in the Senate filibustered to block the stimulus package. Four times the Democrats tried and failed to get the sixty votes (three-fifths of the Senate) needed to cut off debate. On April 2 they gave up the effort, killing the economic stimulus package. Over the next two years a united Republican party repeatedly used this stratagem to frustrate the administration.

The Clinton administration ran into a crossfire again when it sent to Congress its deficit-reduction package of spending cuts and tax hikes on upper incomes. The Republican "spin doctors" defined the package as solely a tax increase. Clinton also aroused the ire of conservative Democrats who favored deeper spending cuts. With the final bill holding to Clinton's effort to get $500 billion in deficit reduction, the vote, in August 1993, turned into another cliffhanger. The bill passed by 218–216 in the House and 51–50 in the Senate, with Vice-President Gore breaking the tie.

The narrow victory allowed critics to say that the president had failed to organize an effective campaign for the legislation, letting the opposition define it as a tax increase, that he bargained away parts of the original plan (and left the impression that he could be intimidated by hard bargainers), and that he had failed to cultivate moderate Republicans, who might have been brought around by timely attention.

NAFTA   The major scuffle of the fall 1993 season was over approval of the North American Free Trade Agreement (NAFTA), which the Bush administration had negotiated with Canada and Mexico. The debate repeated once more time-honored arguments on the tariff, pro and con. Over the years Republican support for a high tariff had eroded as large corporations went abroad looking for bigger markets and smaller expenses. The party, in fact, had harbored supporters of reciprocal tariff reductions since the days of James G. Blaine, who had hoped for a pan-American customs union in the 1870s. Growth, it seemed, might be better served by free trade than by tariff protection. Moreover, American consumers might benefit in both quality and prices from the greater competition. The Democratic free-trade citadel in the agricultural South, however, had been breached by labor-intensive industries such as textiles, which favored barriers against cheaper foreign products. And factory workers had always wanted to bar the products of cheaper labor abroad. Free trade, therefore, incurred the opposition of organized labor.

Clinton stuck with his party's tradition of low tariffs and came down on the side of growth and competition. He urged approval of NAFTA, which would make North America the largest free trade area in the world. He and his supporters argued that tariff reductions would open foreign markets to American industries. Ross Perot, who thrust himself into the forefront of the opponents, said that with NAFTA the country would hear a "giant sucking sound" of American jobs being drawn to Mexico. Yet Clinton prevailed with solid Republican support while losing a sizable minority of Democrats, mostly from the South. The final vote in the House was 234–200, with 102 Democrats and 132 Republicans making up the majority. The Senate approved NAFTA on November 21, 1993.

HEALTH-CARE REFORM   The previous September, Clinton had gone before Congress to present his health-care plan. Government-subsidized health insurance was not a new idea. Other industrial countries had long since started national health insurance programs, Germany as early as 1883, Britain in 1911. The idea had been a subject of political discussion in the United States off and on throughout the twentieth century—endorsed by the Progressive party of 1912, by the American Medical Association (and then rejected), by Presidents Truman, Johnson, and Nixon. After 1965 Medicare provided coverage for people sixty-five and older, and Medicaid funded state programs to help the indigent. These programs had grown enormously in the years since, as had business spending on private health insurance.

Sentiment for health-care reform spread as annual costs approached the trillion-dollar mark, and some 39 million Americans went without insurance either by choice or necessity. The Clinton administration endorsed universal medical coverage. Employers and employees would share the cost, 80 to 20 percent. Government would subsidize all or part of the payments for small businesses and the poor, the latter from funds that formerly went to Medicaid, and would collect a "sin tax" on tobacco and perhaps on alcohol to pay for the program. The plan was projected to cost the federal government $350 billion over seven years.

Clinton chose to lay health-care reform before Congress on September 22, 1993. The president vowed that he would veto any measure that fell short of universal coverage. Hillary Clinton, who chaired the health-care plan task force, became the administration's lead witness on the plan before congressional committees.

But the bill aroused opposition from vested interests, especially the pharmaceutical and insurance industries. Drug companies insisted that they needed large profits to support research. Small-business groups attacked the "employer mandates," requirements that business share the cost of medical insurance (already a common practice in old-age, unemployment, and health insurance), even though government would provide subsidies to small business. These "mandates" came to domi-

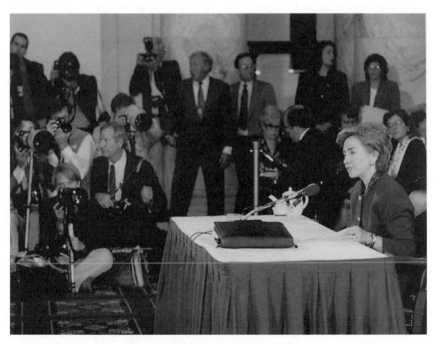

Hillary Clinton testifying before a Congressional committee on the administration's health-care legislation, September 1993.

nate much of the discussion in Congress at the expense of concerns about the overall cost of health care or its quality. Apparently few people grasped—or even heard—the administration's argument that universal coverage would bring lower health costs overall.

WHITEWATER   Whitewater involved a 1978 Clinton investment in a resort project on the White River in northern Arkansas—a losing proposition. The promoter, James McDougal, later took over a small S&L, Madison Guaranty, and turned it into one of the go-go ventures in the flush years of wildcat banking in the eighties. It collapsed in 1989. There were reports that Madison Guaranty had misused funds in the Clinton campaign and that Madison money had gone into the foundering Whitewater project. Charges of a conspiracy and a White House cover-up swirled around Clinton.

With repeated news stories about the Whitewater scandal popping up in the press, the health-insurance plan was pretty well doomed by midsummer 1994. Then a crime bill, which Clinton had called for in his State of the Union message, suddenly emerged as the issue of the day. The bill, held over from 1993, had passed both houses earlier, but when a conference committee reported back a compromise bill, a coalition of unlikely bedfellows voted 225–210 to postpone consideration: black Democrats who objected to enlarging the death penalty, pro-gun Democrats who objected to a ban on assault weapons, and Republicans out to embarrass the administration.

At a crucial time in the health-care debate the administration was distracted for ten days in finally winning approval of the crime bill by 235–195. Republicans dismissed crime prevention programs as "pork." When the Senate passed the bill, people characterized it as one of Clinton's biggest victories, but, ironically, it damaged the chances for health-care legislation. Lacking the votes to overcome a Republican filibuster in the Senate, the Democrats acknowledged defeat.

FOREIGN POLICY CHALLENGES   Foreign policy under Clinton took the same low priority it had reached under Bush—and changed little. Like Woodrow Wilson, Lyndon Johnson, and Jimmy Carter before him, Clinton was a Democratic president who came into office determined to focus on the nation's domestic problems, only to find himself mired in foreign entanglements that had no easy resolution. In the search for a new rationale or paradigm of foreign policy, the Clinton administration faced a more complex situation than before.

Attention focused on Eastern Europe. With the collapse of Communist power, old ethnic and religious enmities quickly resurfaced in Eastern Europe and elsewhere, often involving groups that few Americans had heard of, with infinite variations in detail. In 1993 Clinton's national security adviser, Anthony Lake, announced that "the successor to a doctrine of containment must be a strategy of . . . enlargement of the world's free community of market democracies."

One place to expand democratic capitalism was in Russia itself. On this, as on other issues, Clinton continued the Bush administration policy of support for Russian president Boris Yeltsin. Yet American aid continued to be centered on the exchange of goods, expertise, and training instead of financial assistance. The administration stuck with Yeltsin right on through his brutal invasion of Chechnya, a crime-ridden ethnic region on the Caucasus border with Georgia, to prevent its secession.

THE MIDDLE EAST   Clinton also continued the Bush policy of sponsoring patient negotiations between Arabs and Israelis. After the Gulf War an Arab-Israeli peace initiative with American and Russian sponsorship led to an ongoing conference in Madrid attended by most Arab countries. In a new departure, the Palestine Liberation Organization also participated, accepted by Israel as part of Jordan's delegation. The meetings were dogged by bloody incidents between Israelis and Palestinians. But none of the parties deemed it wise to abandon the talks.

On August 30, 1993, the world learned that secret talks had been going on between Israeli and Palestinian representatives in Oslo with the Norwegian foreign minister as intermediary. A draft agreement between Israel and the PLO provided for the restoration of Palestinian self-rule in the occupied Gaza Strip and in Jericho on the West Bank, in an exchange of land for peace as provided in U.N. Security Council resolutions. A formal signing was quickly arranged at the White House. On September 13, with President Clinton presiding, Prime Minister Yitzhak Rabin and PLO leader Yasir Arafat exchanged handshakes and their foreign ministers signed the agreement.

In the aftermath of this dramatic agreement, talks continued by fits and starts, punctuated by violent incidents provoked by extremist Jewish settlers and Palestinian factions. But a movement toward peace seemed to be proceeding deliberately when on October 26, 1994, Israel and the kingdom of Jordan signed an agreement at ceremonies on their border, which were graced by the presence of President Clinton.

The Middle East peace process suffered a terrible blow in early November 1995 when Yitzhak Rabin was assassinated at a peace rally in Tel Aviv. The gunman was a right-wing Jewish zealot who resented Rabin's efforts to negotiate with the Palestinians.

Some observers feared that the assassin had killed the peace process as well, when seven months later conservative hard-liner Benjamin Netanyahu narrowly defeated the U.S. backed–Shimon Peres in the election for a new prime minister. Netanyahu campaigned against the Rabin-Peres peace efforts, arguing that returning land to Arab control endangered Israeli security. In the face of a flurry of suicide bombings conducted by Islamic extremists against Israelis, he promised to slow the peace process, build new Jewish settlements along the West Bank, block the creation of a Palestinian state in the West Bank and Gaza, and retain control of the Golan Heights, captured from Syria in 1967.

Arab leaders responded to Netanyahu's election by threatening to reconsider the concessions they had made over the previous five years. In 1996 Netanyahu offered to resume negotiations "on all outstanding matters" with Syria, but officials in Damascus dismissed this offer because the Israeli prime minister refused to reaffirm the principle of trading land for peace. Stability in the Middle East thus remained a dream.

Clinton also continued the Bush administration's intervention in Somalia, on the northeastern horn of Africa, where collapse of the government early in 1991 had left the country in anarchy, prey to tribal marauders. The televised scenes of starvation horrified American viewers, many of whom demanded action. President Bush in late 1992 gained U.N. sanction for a military force led by American troops to relieve hunger and restore peace. In early 1993, U.S. troop levels peaked and began to shrink with the arrival of international forces. Clinton inherited this situation.

The Somalia operation proved successful at its primary mission, but never solved the political problems that lay at the root of the starvation. The most serious attempt at political intervention—an effort to capture one clan leader, October 3–4, 1993—left eighteen U.S. soldiers dead and three hundred Somalis killed. This in turn brought American withdrawal in 1994 and, a year later, after failure to set up a stable government, a total withdrawal of U.N. forces, leaving Somalia to its own devices.

Bush had gone into Somalia in part to counter criticism that he had failed to act decisively in the former Yugoslavia, now a volatile mixture of warring ethnic groups, chiefly Orthodox Serbs, Catholic Croats, and Bosnian Muslims. When Yugoslavia imploded in 1991, fanatics and tinpot tyrants set out to stir ethnic conflict as four of its six republics seceded. Serb minorities, backed by Serbia itself, stirred up civil wars in Croatia and Bosnia. In Bosnia especially, the war involved "ethnic cleansing"—driving Muslims from their homes and towns—and mass rape of Muslim women. The options facing the United States were sobering: to ignore the butchery, to accept the refugees, to use American airpower, or to risk introducing ground troops.

Once in the White House, Clinton backed off from his hawkish campaign statements about using force in Yugoslavia. Western European countries dispatched "peacekeeping" forces and put an embargo on arms shipments—which favored Serbs who had fallen heir to the equipment of the Yugoslav army. Clinton settled for dropping food and medical supplies to besieged Bosnians and sending planes to retaliate a few times for attacks on places designated "safe havens" by the United Nations. Serb forces soon learned that by alternating defiance and parleys, they could avoid any real deterrence except by Bosnian forces. Peacemakers came and went, including former president Jimmy Carter, who won a four-month cease-fire at the end of 1994—just enough to last out the winter.

Despite the cease-fire agreement, fighting continued in many parts of the faction-ridden country. In September 1995 American negotiators finally succeeded in getting the foreign ministers of Croatia, Bosnia, and Yugoslavia to agree to a comprehensive peace plan. Bosnia would remain a single nation but would be divided into two states: a Muslim-Croat federation controlling 51 percent of the territory and a Bosnian-Serb republic controlling the remaining 49 percent. Basic human rights would be restored and free elections held to appoint a parliament and joint presidency. To enforce the agreement, 20,000 American troops would be dispatched to Bosnia as part of a 60,000-person NATO peacekeeping operation. A cease-fire went into effect in October, and a final agreement confirming these provisions was signed in Paris in December 1995.

The Congress gave only grudging support to the use of American forces in the Balkans. "I was opposed" to the Bosnian policy, explained Senator John McCain, an Arizona Republican and Vietnam veteran. "But if the president made a commitment and if we reversed it, it would be a terrible blow to the credibility of the United States."

The most successful new departure in foreign policy for the Clinton administration came in Haiti. The end of the Cold War had removed any threat of Soviet infiltration in the Caribbean and brought a new emphasis on Wilsonian themes of democracy. Haiti had emerged suddenly from a cycle of coups with a rebellion in the army rank and file and a democratic election in 1990, which brought to the top a popular priest, Jean-Bertrand Aristide. Old habits returned, however, with his ouster by General Cédras. The United States immediately announced its intention to bring back Aristide and welcomed the U.N. to the process.

Another new element in the situation was the appearance of thousands of Haitian refugees desperate to reach Florida in leaky wooden boats. Coast Guard vessels began to take them back to Haiti or to Guantanamo Bay in Cuba, denying that they were refugees. Public reaction to the flood of new immigrants put the Clinton administration under even greater pressure to address the desperate situation. Some American conservatives, however, still in Cold War mode, found Aristide too radical for their taste.

With drawn-out negotiations leading nowhere, Clinton eventually moved in 1994 to get a U.N. resolution authorizing force as a last resort. A reluctant Senate resolved that military action would require an advance vote of Congress. At this juncture, former president Carter asked permission to negotiate personally with Cédras. Together with Senator Sam Nunn of Georgia and retired General Colin Powell, Carter went to Port-au-Prince and convinced Cédras to quit by October 15. The first American forces were already in the air and landed September 19, without opposition and with a cordial welcome from the people.

Clinton had promised that the bulk of American forces would be quickly withdrawn and replaced by an international force of peacekeepers, and in November the American withdrawal began. Aristide returned to Haiti. On March 31, 1995, the occupation was turned over to a U.N. force commanded by an American general. Only about 2,400 American troops remained to retrain Haitian military and police in orderly procedures. They had a tough assignment, maybe an impossible one, but there was occasion for hope. Aside from Haiti, the status of

American foreign policy remained in 1995 without drastic change from that of 1992.

THE REPUBLICAN AGENDA

REPUBLICAN LANDSLIDE   During 1994 Clinton began to see his young presidency unravel. Unable to get either health-reform or welfare-reform bills through the Democratic Congress, and having failed to carry out his campaign pledge for middle-class tax relief, he and his party found themselves the target of bitter criticism.

In the midterm elections of 1994, the administration and the Democratic party suffered a humbling defeat across the board. It was the first election since 1952 in which Republicans captured both houses of Congress at the same time. In both houses the Republican majority was solid: 52–48 in the Senate, a majority that soon increased when two Democrats switched parties, and 230–204 in the House. Not a single Republican incumbent was defeated. Republicans also won a net gain of eleven governorships and in fifteen chambers in state legislatures.

There could be little question that the returns signaled a repudiation of Clinton and the Democratic Congress. The administration's recklessness had weakened Democratic candidates. Squabbling between the president and congressional Democrats did not help matters. Nor did Clinton's response to the Republican takeover of Congress endear him to party loyalists. Initially, he and his aides decided to adopt a passive role, letting the Republicans initiate policies and programs and then hope that they would be decimated by the affected interest groups. He offered no deficit reduction plan, no welfare reform proposal, no new health reform initiative.

Clinton's waffling on major issues began to convince many in his own party that he was a politician rather than a leader, someone who thrived as a campaigner but was bereft of genuine convictions. Said Democratic Congressman David Obey: "I think most of us learned some time ago that if you don't like the president's position on a particular issue, you simply need to wait a few weeks." In 1995 liberal Democrats especially felt betrayed by Clinton's efforts to work with Republicans in developing new fiscal and social policies. When Clinton joined the chorus of conservatives calling for a scaling back of affirmative-action plans de-

*Georgia Congressman and House
Speaker Newt Gingrich.*

signed to remedy historic patterns of racial discrimination in hiring and the awarding of government contracts, liberals felt betrayed.

Georgia congressman Newton Leroy Gingrich had mounted the most effective efforts to discredit Democratic leadership in Congress. In 1988 he began a line of ethical charges that caused Speaker Jim Wright and Democratic Whip Tony Coelho to resign. He then challenged operations of the House bank and post office, which members (including some Republicans) had been abusing to their financial gain.

Another important factor explaining the Republican victory was the impact of religious and social conservatives associated with the Christian Coalition. Coalition members excelled at grassroots organization, right down to the precinct level, and for several years they had been working in local elections, "flying under the radar," barely noticed by the media.

JUDICIAL CONSERVATISM   The conservative mood during the mid-1990s also manifested itself in the Supreme Court. For over a decade the philosophical center of gravity on the Court had been shifting to the right. In a series of cases the Court restricted federal affirmative action programs, called into question the legality of election districts redrawn ("gerrymandered") to create black or Hispanic majorities, and limited the legal remedies for racially segregated public schools.

All of these cases were decided by the same five-to-four vote, with five conservatives (Chief Justice William Rehnquist, Anthony Kennedy, Sandra Day O'Connor, Antonin Scalia, and Clarence Thomas) voting against four moderates (Stephen Breyer, Ruth Bader Ginsburg, David Souter, and John Paul Stevens). And all of them pointed toward the Court's growing skepticism toward race-based government policies and programs.

In the case of *Adarand Constructors v. Pena* (1995) the Court assessed a program that gave preferential treatment to businesses owned by "disadvantaged" minorities. A Hispanic-owned firm had won a contract even though a white-owned company had submitted a lower bid for the same work. The white-owned company sued on the grounds of reverse discrimination. In writing the majority opinion, Justice O'Connor contended that any government program based on racial preferences, even though intended to redress historical inequities, was unconstitutional unless it was narrowly designed to serve a "specific, compelling interest." This requirement was necessary, she explained, to assure "that the legislative body is pursuing a goal important enough to warrant the use of a highly suspect tool (reverse racial discrimination)." O'Connor did not define what the Court meant by "compelling interest," but the implication of her language was clear: the Court had come to embrace the growing public suspicion of the value and legality of such race-based programs. Civil rights leaders such as Jesse Jackson castigated the Court's ruling as a "major setback." Yet the Clinton administration seemed to endorse the majority opinion when a White House spokesperson noted that the president "was asking many of the questions the court focused on."

In July 1995, a month after the Court released the *Adarand* decision, the University of California Board of Regents scrapped all affirmative action programs related to the admission of students. At the same time, Governor Pete Wilson abolished all state government affirmative action regulations. In 1996 a federal appeals court decision, *Hopwood v. Texas,* rejected the use of race as a factor in college admissions, even for the "wholesome practice" of producing racially balanced student bodies.

By the mid-1990s the rightward-leaning Supreme Court was only one of many indications that the movement of social and political conservatism had gained considerable power. The raging popularity of radio and TV talk shows, most hosted by outspoken conservatives, reflected the groundswell of popular resistance to an activist government. That these programs featured such a negative and strident tone reflected a heightening of social and cultural tensions as the nation careened toward the end of the century. America was becoming more fractious as it was becoming more diverse.

CONTRACT WITH AMERICA   The new Republican majority in Congress immediately set about assaulting the "welfare state" and restoring conservative values and principles. Said the House Majority Whip, Tom Delay, "You've got to understand, we are ideologues. We have an agenda."

The insurgent Republicans' agenda was embodied in what Gingrich called a "contract with America" consisting of ten initiatives. Within the first 100 days of the 104th Congress, Gingrich promised, he would bring to the House bills providing for: a balanced budget amendment and a presidential line-item budget veto; stricter penalties for violent criminals; welfare reforms intended to "encourage people to work, not to have children out of wedlock"; programs to strengthen families by giving parents greater control over education, enforcing child-support payments and getting tough on child pornography; tax cuts for families; increased defense spending; reduced government regulations; legal reforms to stop excessive liability claims, frivolous suits and "overzealous lawyers"; and congressional term limits so as to "replace career politicians with citizen legislators."

True to their word, the Republicans in the House brought all ten initiatives to the House for a vote within 100 days, but only two items became law. Congress agreed to stop imposing mandated programs on local and state governments without footing the bill, and Congress agreed that laws passed by the House must apply to House members as well as ordinary Americans.

Thereafter the much-ballyhooed GOP revolution and the "Contract with America" fizzled out. Its collapse resulted from several factors. President Clinton shrewdly moved to the political center and co-opted much of the Republican agenda. His distinctive strength—at least in the eyes of his supporters—resided in his agile responsiveness to an ever-changing public mood. To him the Republican victory in the 1994

Congressional elections bore a simple message: he must recapture the political center by radically changing his message and agenda.

To help him in this new purpose, Clinton assembled a new team of advisers. The intensely partisan Democrats who engineered his election victory—James Carville, Stanley Greenberg, Paul Begala, and Mandy Grunwald—gave way to a politically ambidextrous group led by Dick Morris, a Democrat turned Republican turned Democrat. Throughout 1995 and 1996 Clinton and Morris stressed that the Democratic party, embroiled in the upheavals of multiple rights revolutions, had allowed special-interest liberalism to become a constrictive orthodoxy. Their objective was now to demonstrate their liberation from such fragmenting forces. To do so they moved closer to the Republican positions on the budget deficit, welfare reform, and governmental regulation.

In this regard the Republicans' "Contract with America" succeeded in focusing public and presidential attention on basic questions of governmental philosophy. At the same time, however, ineffective leadership among the Republican insurgency also contributed to the demise of the "Contract with America." Ironically, Newt Gingrich, who had risen to power by exposing scandals among the Democratic House leadership, became the subject of ethics investigations into possible campaign violations. (He was ultimately cleared of all charges.) And his strident rhetoric alienated rather than excited public support. During 1995 he saw his own approval ratings in the polls plummet. By the time the 1996 Republican national convention was held in San Diego, Gingrich had become such a liability to the Republican Party that he was relegated to a non–prime time slot, giving his speech before party loyalists only.

Gingrich and other House Republican insurgents had overestimated the public's interest in dismantling the federal government and many of its social programs. To be sure voters wanted to reduce the size and intrusiveness of the Washington bureaucracy, but they did not want to return to the laissez-faire approach of Calvin Coolidge and Herbert Hoover. Even Senate Republican leaders refused to go along with key elements of the "Contract with America."

Likewise, Clinton and his advisers sensed the limits of the antigovernment sentiment among the public and deftly used vetoes and shutdowns of federal government offices to thwart the efforts of House Republicans to make draconian cuts in popular federal programs such as

Medicare and Medicaid. Said one contrite Republican freshman in 1996: "We scared too many people last year talking with such revolutionary fervor. I think we showed more guts than brains sometimes."

LEGISLATIVE BREAKTHROUGH   In the late summer of 1996, as lawmakers were preparing to adjourn and participate in the presidential nominating conventions, the 104th Congress broke through its partisan gridlock and passed a flurry of important legislation that President Clinton quickly signed.

Two of the bills increased the minimum wage and broadened access to health insurance. The $4.25 per hour minimum wage was increased by ninety cents over thirteen months. In exchange for their support of the wage increase, Republicans obtained $21 billion in tax cuts over ten years for small businesses. The health-care measure, sponsored by senators Nancy Kassebaum, a Kansas Republican, and Edward Kennedy, a Massachusetts Democrat, allowed workers to keep their insurance coverage even if they change jobs. The Kennedy-Kassebaum bill also made it harder for insurers to deny coverage to patients with a history of illness.

Even more significant was a comprehensive welfare reform measure that ended the federal government's open-ended guarantee of aid to the poor, a guarantee that had been in place since 1935. The Personal Responsibility and Work Opportunity Act turned over the major federal welfare programs to the states. In exchange the states would receive federal grants to fund the programs. The bill also limited the amount of time a person could receive welfare benefits funded by federal money and required that at least half of a state's welfare recipients have jobs or be enrolled in job-training programs by the year 2002. Those states failing to meet the deadline would have their federal funds cut.

The Republican-sponsored welfare reform legislation passed the Senate by a vote of 74–24. It had the effect of cutting $56 billion over six years from Aid to Families with Dependent Children, food stamps, and other programs, several of which dated back to Franklin Roosevelt's New Deal. Senator Patrick Moynihan, the New York Democrat who had been a champion of federal social welfare programs since the 1960s, bitterly characterized the bill as "the most regressive social legislation of the century." He predicted that over 3.5 million children would be thrown into poverty as a result of the bill. Clinton, Moynihan and

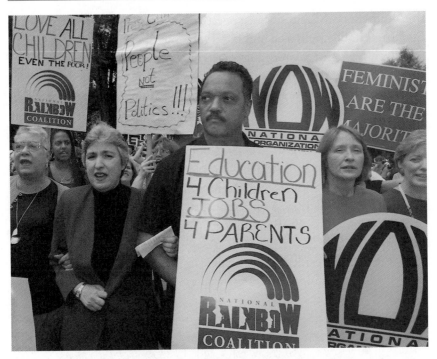

Eleanor Smeal of the Feminist Majority, Rev. Jesse Jackson, and National Organization for Women President Patricia Ireland outside the White House protesting welfare reform legislation, which President Clinton later passed.

other liberals charged, was abdicating Democratic social principles in order to gain reelection amid the conservative climate of the times. Senator Chris Dodd called the president's action "unconscionable."

Clinton and his centrist advisers, however, dismissed such criticisms. With his reelection bid at stake, he was determined to live up to his 1992 campaign pledge to "end welfare as we know it." Clinton also knew that most voters in both parties were eager to see major cuts in federal entitlement programs.

THE 1996 CAMPAIGN   After clinching the Republican nomination in March 1996, Majority Leader Bob Dole resigned his Senate seat in order to devote his attention to defeating Bill Clinton. Born in Kansas in 1923, the product of a hardscrabble existence in a small prairie town, he enrolled at the University of Kansas in 1941, only to be drawn into military service during World War II. During a battle in Italy, a piece of shrapnel shattered his right shoulder and fractured his neck. It took thirty-nine months and seven separate operations before he could leave the hospital. His right arm and hand remained permanently paralyzed.

Driven by a gritty determination to succeed despite his physical setback, Dole graduated from college and law school and then entered local politics. By 1960 he was a member of the House of Representatives, and nine years later he gained election to the Senate. In 1976 Dole served as Gerald Ford's running mate, only to return to the Senate after the Carter-Mondale victory. Dole developed a reputation as a brilliant legislative tactician and a tough, smart, and honest leader known for his ability to build consensus and forge coalitions. An unsuccessful candidate for the presidential nomination in 1980 and 1988, Dole was officially nominated at the Republican Convention in San Diego in mid-August.

As the 1996 presidential campaign unfolded, Clinton maintained a large lead in the polls. With a generally healthy economy and with no

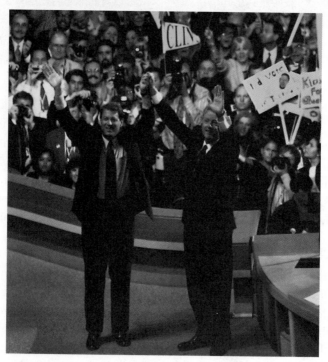

President Clinton and Vice President Gore at the 1996 Democratic National Convention in Chicago.

major foreign policy crises to confront, cultural and personal issues surged into prominence. Concern about Dole's age (seventy-three) and his acerbic manner, as well as rifts in the Republican party between economic and social conservatives over issues such as abortion and gun control, hampered Dole's efforts to generate widespread support.

In an effort to jump start his lagging campaign, Dole announced a surprise choice for his running mate: Jack Kemp, the former pro football star, congressman, secretary of Housing and Urban development under Bush, and presidential candidate himself. On economic issues they were poles apart. Dole represented the Eisenhower wing of the Republican party in promoting deficit reduction and a balanced budget. By contrast, Kemp was a Reaganite in his commitment to supply-side economic theory, with its emphasis on large tax cuts. During the 1988 Republican primary, when they both sought the presidential nomination, Kemp lambasted Dole as the "candidate of pain, austerity, and sacrifice." For his part, Dole dismissed Kemp as a brash upstart with little respect for or knowledge of practical politics. They made for an odd couple but one that attracted public interest.

At the same time that Dole was tapping the charismatic but unpredictable Kemp as his running mate, he unveiled his long-anticipated economic proposal. Its centerpiece was a 15 percent across-the-board income tax cut coupled with child tax credits and capital gains tax cuts and a balanced budget. This supply-side fiscal program assumed that people would spend the $600 billion they saved from the tax cuts over the following six years and thereby generate record economic growth that in turn would raise tax revenues. Most economists, however, greeted the plan with rude skepticism. Said one economist at the University of Texas: "This is worse than voodoo economics. It is doodoo economics."

Yet the announcement of the tax cut plan and the Kemp appointment generated great interest and excitement among the media and the party faithful, providing the boost that Dole's anemic campaign needed. Whether it was enough momentum to oust an incumbent president remained doubtful. The politics of the 1990s remained volatile. With continuing revelations about Clinton's role in the Whitewater affair a possibility and the likelihood of Ross Perot running again as a third-party candidate, any outcome remained possible as the election approached.

FURTHER READING

The early months of the Clinton presidency are most thoroughly covered in Elizabeth Drew's *On the Edge: The Clinton Presidency* (1994). Bob Woodward's *The Agenda: Inside the Clinton White House* (1994) focuses on finance and the economy.

On social and cultural problems and issues of the times a good man-in-the-street account is Haynes Johnson's *Divided We Fall: Gambling with History in the Nineties* (1994). Collections of magazine and newspaper columns are in John Leo's *Two Steps Ahead of the Thought Police* (1994), Molly Ivins's *Nothin' But Good Times Ahead* (1993), and George F. Will's *The Leveling Wind: Politics, Culture, and the Other News* (1994). The onset and growth of the AIDS epidemic are traced in essays edited by historians Elizabeth Fee and Daniel M. Fox, *AIDS: The Burdens of History* (1988) and *AIDS: The Making of a Chronic Disease* (1992).

Fundamentalist and apocalyptic movements are the subject of Paul L. Boyer's *When Time Shall Be No More: Prophecy and Belief in Modern American Culture* (1992), George M. Marsden's *Understanding Fundamentalism and Evangelicalism* (1991), and Ralph Reed's *Politically Incorrect: The Emerging Faith Factor in American Politics* (1994).

Aspects of recent cultural debates can be found in Richard Bolton, ed., *Culture Wars: Documents from the Recent Controversies in the Arts* (1992), Gerald Graff's *Beyond the Culture Wars: How Teaching the Conflict Can Revitalize American Education* (1992), and Darryl Gless and Barbara Herrnstein Smith, eds., *The Politics of Liberal Education* (1992).

Corporate restructuring and downsizing are the subject of Bennett Harrison's *Lean and Mean: The Changing Landscape of Corporate Power in the Age of Flexibility* (1994). The story of the Whitewater affair is the subject of Martin L. Gross's *The Great Whitewater Fiasco: An American Tale of Money, Power, and Politics* (1994).

For further treatment of the end of the Cold War, see Michael R. Beschloss's *At Highest Levels: The Inside Story of the End of the Cold War* (1993).

APPENDICES

THE DECLARATION
OF INDEPENDENCE

WHEN IN THE COURSE OF HUMAN EVENTS, it becomes necessary for one people to dissolve the political bands which have connected them with another, and to assume the Powers of the earth, the separate and equal station to which the Laws of Nature and of Nature's God entitle them, a decent respect to the opinions of mankind requires that they should declare the causes which impel them to the separation.

We hold these truths to be self-evident, that all men are created equal, that they are endowed by their Creator with certain unalienable rights, that among these are Life, Liberty, and the pursuit of Happiness. That to secure these rights, Governments are instituted among Men, deriving their just powers from the consent of the governed. That whenever any Form of Government becomes destructive of these ends, it is the Right of the People to alter or to abolish it, and to institute new Government, laying its foundation on such principles and organizing its powers in such form, as to them shall seem most likely to effect their Safety and Happiness. Prudence, indeed, will dictate that Governments long established should not be changed for light and transient causes; and accordingly all experience hath shown, that mankind are more disposed to suffer, while evils are sufferable, than to right themselves by abolishing the forms to which they are accustomed. But when a long train of abuses and usurpations, pursuing invariably the same Object evinces a design to reduce them under absolute Despotism, it is their right, it is their duty, to throw off such Government, and to provide new Guards for their future security.— Such has been the patient sufferance of these Colonies; and such is now the necessity which constrains them to alter their former Systems of Government. The history of the present King of Great Britain is a history of repeated injuries and usurpations, all having in direct object the establishment of an absolute Tyranny over these States. To prove this, let Facts be submitted to a candid world.

He has refused his Assent to Laws, the most wholesome and necessary for the public good.

He has forbidden his Governors to pass Laws of immediate and pressing importance, unless suspended in their operation till his Assent should be obtained; and when so suspended, he has utterly neglected to attend to them.

He has refused to pass other Laws for the accommodation of large districts of people, unless those people would relinquish the right of Representation in the Legislature, a right inestimable to them and formidable to tyrants only.

He has called together legislative bodies at places unusual, uncomfortable, and distant from the depository of their public Records, for the sole purpose of fatiguing them into compliance with his measures.

He has dissolved Representative Houses repeatedly, for opposing with manly firmness his invasions on the rights of the people.

He has refused for a long time, after such dissolutions, to cause others to be elected; whereby the Legislative powers, incapable of Annihilation, have returned to the People at large for their exercise; the State remaining in the mean time exposed to all dangers of invasion from without, and convulsions within.

He has endeavoured to prevent the population of these States; for that purpose obstructing the Laws of Naturalization of Foreigners; refusing to pass others to encourage their migrations hither, and raising the conditions of new Appropriations of Lands.

He has obstructed the Administration of Justice, by refusing his Assent to Laws for establishing Judiciary powers.

He has made Judges dependent on his Will alone, for the tenure of their offices, and the amount and payment of their salaries.

He has erected a multitude of New Offices, and sent hither swarms of Officers to harass our People, and eat out their substance.

He has kept among us, in times of peace, Standing Armies without the Consent of our legislature.

He has affected to render the Military independent of and superior to the Civil Power.

He has combined with others to subject us to a jurisdiction foreign to our constitution, and unacknowledged by our laws; giving his Assent to their Acts of pretended Legislation:

For quartering large bodies of armed troops among us:

For protecting them, by a mock Trial, from Punishment for any Murders which they should commit on the Inhabitants of these States:

For cutting off our Trade with all parts of the world:

For imposing taxes on us without our Consent:

For depriving us of many cases, of the benefits of Trial by jury:

For transporting us beyond Seas to be tried for pretended offences:

For abolishing the free System of English Laws in a neighbouring Province, establishing therein an Arbitrary government, and enlarging its Boundaries so as to render it at once an example and fit instrument for introducing the same absolute rule into these Colonies:

For taking away our Charters, abolishing our most valuable Laws, and altering fundamentally the Forms of our Governments:

For suspending our own Legislatures, and declaring themselves in vested with Power to legislate for us in all cases whatsoever.

He has abdicated Government here, by declaring us out of his Protection and waging War against us.

He has plundered our seas, ravaged our Coasts, burnt our towns, and destroyed the lives of our people.

He is at this time transporting large armies of foreign mercenaries to compleat the works of death, desolation, and tyranny, already begun with circumstances of Cruelty & perfidy scarcely paralleled in the most barbarous ages, and totally unworthy the Head of a civilized nation.

He has constrained our fellow Citizens taken Captive on the high Seas to bear Arms against their Country, to become the executioners of their friends and Brethren, or to fall themselves by their Hands.

He has excited domestic insurrections amongst us, and has endeavoured to bring on the inhabitants of our frontiers, the merciless Indian Savages, whose known rule of warfare, is an undistinguished destruction of all ages, sexes, and conditions.

In every stage of these Oppressions We have Petitioned for Redress in the most humble terms: Our repeated Petitions have been answered only by repeated injury. A Prince, whose character is thus marked by every act which may define a Tyrant, is unfit to be the ruler of a free people.

Nor have We been wanting in attention to our British brethren. We have warned them from time to time of attempts by their legislature to extend an unwarrantable jurisdiction over us. We have reminded them of the circumstances of our emigration and settlement here. We have appealed to their native justice and magnanimity, and we have conjured them by the ties of our common kindred to disavow these usurpations, which, would inevitably interrupt our connections and correspondence. They too must have been deaf to the voice of justice and of consanguinity. We must, therefore, acquiesce in the necessity, which denounces our Separation, and hold them, as we hold the rest of mankind, Enemies in War, in Peace Friends.

WE, THEREFORE, the Representatives of the UNITED STATES OF AMERICA, in General Congress, Assembled, appealing to the Supreme Judge of the world for the rectitude of our intentions, do, in the Name, and by Authority of the good People of these Colonies, solemnly publish and declare, That these United Colonies are, and of Right ought to be FREE AND INDEPENDENT STATES; that they are Absolved from all Allegiance to the British

Crown, and that all political connection between them and the State of Great Britain, is and ought to be totally dissolved; and that as Free and Independent States, they have full Power to levy War, conclude Peace, contract Alliances, establish Commerce, and to do all other Acts and Things which Independent States may of right do. And for the support of this Declaration, with a firm reliance on the Protection of Divine Providence, we mutually pledge to each other our Lives, our Fortunes, and our sacred Honor.

The foregoing Declaration was, by order of Congress, engrossed, and signed by the following members:

John Hancock

NEW HAMPSHIRE
Josiah Bartlett
William Whipple
Matthew Thornton

MASSACHUSETTS BAY
Samuel Adams
John Adams
Robert Treat Paine
Elbridge Gerry

RHODE ISLAND
Stephen Hopkins
William Ellery

CONNECTICUT
Roger Sherman
Samuel Huntington
William Williams
Oliver Wolcott

NEW YORK
William Floyd
Philip Livingston
Francis Lewis
Lewis Morris

NEW JERSEY
Richard Stockton
John Witherspoon
Francis Hopkinson
John Hart
Abraham Clark

PENNSYLVANIA
Robert Morris
Benjamin Rush
Benjamin Franklin
John Morton
George Clymer
James Smith
George Taylor
James Wilson
George Ross

DELAWARE
Caesar Rodney
George Read
Thomas M'Kean

MARYLAND
Samuel Chase
William Paca
Thomas Stone
*Charles Carroll, of
   Carrollton*

VIRGINIA
George Wythe
Richard Henry Lee
Thomas Jefferson
Benjamin Harrison
Thomas Nelson, Jr.
Francis Lightfoot Lee
Carter Braxton

NORTH CAROLINA
William Hooper
Joseph Hewes
John Penn

SOUTH CAROLINA
Edward Rutledge
Thomas Heyward, Jr.
Thomas Lynch, Jr.
Arthur Middleton

GEORGIA
Button Gwinnett
Lyman Hall
George Walton

Resolved, That copies of the Declaration be sent to the several assemblies, conventions, and committees, or councils of safety, and to the several commanding officers of the continental troops; that it be proclaimed in each of the United States, at the head of the army.

ARTICLES OF
CONFEDERATION

To all to whom these Presents shall come, we the undersigned Delegates of the States affixed to our Names send greeting.

Whereas the Delegates of the United States of America in Congress assembled did on the fifteenth day of November in the Year of our Lord One Thousand Seven Hundred and Seventy-seven, and in the Second Year of the Independence of America agree to certain articles of Confederation and perpetual Union between the States of Newhampshire, Massachusetts-bay, Rhodeisland and Providence Plantations, Connecticut, New York, New Jersey, Pennsylvania, Delaware, Maryland, Virginia, North-Carolina, South-Carolina and Georgia in the Words following, viz.

Articles of Confederation and perpetual Union between the States of Newhampshire, Massachusetts-bay, Rhodeisland and Providence Plantations, Connecticut, New-York, New-Jersey, Pennsylvania, Delaware, Maryland, Virginia, North-Carolina, South-Carolina and Georgia.

ARTICLE I. The stile of this confederacy shall be "The United States of America."

ARTICLE II. Each State retains its sovereignty, freedom and independence, and every power, jurisdiction and right, which is not by this confederation expressly delegated to the United States, in Congress assembled.

ARTICLE III. The said States hereby severally enter into a firm league of friendship with each other, for their common defence, the security of their liberties, and their mutual and general welfare, binding themselves to assist each other, against all force offered to, or attacks made upon them, or any of them, on account of religion, sovereignty, trade or any other pretence whatever.

ARTICLE IV. The better to secure and perpetuate mutual friendship and intercourse among the people of the different States in this Union, the free inhabitants of each of these States, paupers, vagabonds and fugitives from justice excepted, shall be entitled to all privileges and immunities of free citizens in the several States; and the people of each State shall have free ingress and regress to and from any other State, and shall enjoy therein all the privileges of trade and commerce, subject to the same duties, impositions and restrictions as the inhabitants thereof respectively, provided that such restrictions shall not extend so far as to prevent the removal of property imported into any State, to any other State of which the owner is an inhabitant; provided also that no imposition, duties or restriction shall be laid by any State, on the property of the United States, or either of them.

If any person guilty of, or charged with treason, felony, or other high misdemeanor in any State, shall flee from justice, and be found in any of the United States, he shall upon demand of the Governor or Executive power, of the State from which he fled, be delivered up and removed to the State having jurisdiction of his offence.

Full faith and credit shall be given in each of these States to the records, acts and judicial proceedings of the courts and magistrates of every other State.

ARTICLE V. For the more convenient management of the general interests of the United States, delegates shall be annually appointed in such manner as the legislature of each State shall direct, to meet in Congress on the first Monday in November, in every year, with a power reserved to each State, to recall its delegates, or any of them, at any time within the year, and to send others in their stead, for the remainder of the year.

No State shall be represented in Congress by less than two, nor by more than seven members; and no person shall be capable of being a delegate for more than three years in any term of six years; nor shall any person, being a delegate, be capable of holding any office under the United States, for which he, or another for his benefit receives any salary, fees or emolument of any kind.

Each State shall maintain its own delegates in a meeting of the States, and while they act as members of the committee of the States.

In determining questions in the United States, in Congress assembled, each State shall have one vote.

Freedom of speech and debate in Congress shall not be impeached or questioned in any court, or place out of Congress, and the members of Congress shall be protected in their persons from arrests and imprisonments, during the time of their going to and from, and attendance on Congress, except for treason, felony, or breach of the peace.

ARTICLE VI. No State without the consent of the United States in Congress assembled, shall send any embassy to, or receive any embassy from, or enter into any conference, agreement, alliance or treaty with any king, prince or state; nor shall any person holding any office of profit or trust under the United States, or any of them, accept of any present, emolument, office or title of any kind whatever from any king, prince or foreign state; nor shall the United States in Congress assembled, or any of them, grant any title of nobility.

No two or more States shall enter into any treaty, confederation or alliance whatever between them, without the consent of the United States in Congress assembled, specifying accurately the purposes for which the same is to be entered into, and how long it shall continue.

No State shall lay any imposts or duties, which may interfere with any stipulations in treaties, entered into by the United States in Congress assembled, with any king, prince or state, in pursuance of any treaties already proposed by Congress, to the courts of France and Spain.

No vessels of war shall be kept up in time of peace by any State, except such number only, as shall be deemed necessary by the United States in Congress assembled, for the defence of such State, or its trade; nor shall any body of forces be kept up by any State, in time of peace, except such number only, as in the judgment of the United States, in Congress assembled, shall be deemed requisite to garrison the forts necessary for the defence of such State; but every State shall always keep up a well regulated and disciplined militia, sufficiently armed and accoutred, and shall provide and constantly have ready for use, in public stores, a due number of field pieces and tents, and a proper quantity of arms, ammunition and camp equipage.

No State shall engage in any war without the consent of the United States in Congress assembled, unless such State be actually invaded by enemies, or shall have received certain advice of a resolution being formed by some nation of Indians to invade such State, and the danger is so imminent as not to admit of a delay, till the United States in Congress assembled can be consulted: nor shall any State grant commissions to any ships or vessels of war, nor letters of marque or reprisal, except it be after a declaration of war by the United States in Congress assembled, and then only against the kingdom or state and the subjects thereof, against which war has been so declared, and under such regulations as shall be established by the United States in Congress assembled, unless such State be infested by pirates, in which case vessels of war may be fitted out for that occasion, and kept so long as the danger shall continue, or until the United States in Congress assembled shall determine otherwise.

ARTICLE VII. When land-forces are raised by any State of the common defence, all officers of or under the rank of colonel, shall be appointed by the

Legislature of each State respectively by whom such forces shall be raised, or in such manner as such State shall direct, and all vacancies shall be filled up by the State which first made the appointment.

ARTICLE VIII. All charges of war, and all other expenses that shall be incurred for the common defence or general welfare, and allowed by the United States in Congress assembled, shall be defrayed out of a common treasury, which shall be supplied by the several States, in proportion to the value of all land within each State, granted to or surveyed for any person, as such land and the buildings and improvements thereon shall be estimated according to such mode as the United States in Congress assembled, shall from time to time direct and appoint.

The taxes for paying that proportion shall be laid and levied by the authority and direction of the Legislatures of the several States within the time agreed upon by the United States in Congress assembled.

ARTICLE IX. The United States in Congress assembled, shall have the sole and exclusive right and power of determining on peace and war, except in the cases mentioned in the sixth article—of sending and receiving ambassadors—entering into treaties and alliances, provided that no treaty of commerce shall be made whereby the legislative power of the respective States shall be restrained from imposing such imposts and duties on foreigners, as their own people are subjected to, or from prohibiting the exportation or importation of and species of goods or commodities whatsoever—of establishing rules for deciding in all cases, what captures on land or water shall be legal, and in what manner prizes taken by land or naval forces in the service of the United States shall be divided or appropriated—of granting letters of marque and reprisal in times of peace—appointing courts for the trial of piracies and felonies committed on the high seas and establishing courts for receiving and determining finally appeals in all cases of captures, provided that no member of Congress shall be appointed a judge of any of the said courts.

The United States in Congress assembled shall also be the last resort on appeal in all disputes and differences now subsisting or that hereafter may arise between two or more States concerning boundary, jurisdiction or any other cause whatever; which authority shall always be exercised in the manner following. Whenever the legislative or executive authority or lawful agent of any State in controversy with another shall present a petition to Congress, stating the matter in question and praying for a hearing, notice thereof shall be given by order of Congress to the legislative or executive authority of the other State in controversy, and a day assigned for the appearance of the parties by their lawful agents, who shall then be directed to appoint by joint consent, commissioners or judges to constitute a court for hearing and determining the matter in question: but if they cannot agree, Congress shall name three persons out of each of the United States, and from the list of such persons each party shall alternately strike out one, the petitioners beginning, until the number shall be reduced to thirteen; and from that number not less than seven, nor more than nine names as Congress shall direct, shall in the presence of Congress be drawn out by lot, and the persons whose names shall be so drawn or any five of them, shall be commissioners or judges, to hear and finally determine the controversy, so always as a major part of the judges who shall hear the cause shall agree in the determination: and if either party shall neglect to attend at the day appointed, without reasons, which Congress shall judge sufficient, or being present shall refuse to strike, the Congress shall proceed to nominate three persons out of each State, and the Secretary of Congress shall strike in behalf of such party absent or refusing; and the judgment and sentence of the court to be appointed, in the manner before prescribed, shall be final and conclusive; and if any of the parties shall refuse to submit to the authority of such court, or to appear or defend their claim or cause, the court shall nevertheless proceed to pronounce sentence, or judgment, which shall in like manner be final and decisive, the judgment or sentence and other proceedings being in either case transmitted to Congress, and lodged among the acts of Congress for the security of the parties concerned: provided that every commissioner, before he sits in judgment, shall take an oath to be administered by one of the judges of the supreme or superior court of the State where the case shall be tried, "well and truly to hear and determine the matter in question, according to the best of his judgment, without favour, affection or hope of reward:" provided also that no State shall be deprived of territory for the benefit of the United States.

All controversies concerning the private right of soil claimed under different grants of two or more States, whose jurisdiction as they may respect such lands, and the states which passed such grants are adjusted, the said grants or either of them being at the same time claimed to have originated antecedent to such settlement of jurisdiction, shall on the petition of either party to the Congress of the United States, be finally determined as near as may be in the same manner as is before prescribed for deciding disputes respecting territorial jurisdiction between different States.

The United States in Congress assembled shall also have the sole and exclusive right and power of regulating the alloy and value of coin struck by their own authority, or by that of the respective States—fixing the standard of weights and measures throughout the United States—regulating the trade and managing all affairs with the Indians, not members of any of the States, provided that the legislative right of any State within its own limits be not infringed or violated—establishing and regulating post-offices from one State to another, throughout all of the United States, and exacting such postage on the papers passing thro' the same as may be requisite to defray the expenses of the said office—appointing all officers of the land forces, in the service of the United States, excepting regimental officers—appointing all the officers of the naval forces, and commissioning all officers whatever in the service of the United States—making rules for the government and regulation of the said land and naval forces, and directing their operations.

The United States in Congress assembled shall have authority to appoint a committee, to sit in the recess of Congress, to be denominated "a Committee of the States," and to consist of one delegate from each State; and to appoint such other committees and civil officers as may be necessary for managing the general affairs of the United States under their direction—to appoint one of their number to preside, provided that no person be allowed to serve in the office of president more than one year in any term of three years; to ascertain the necessary sums of money to be raised for the service of the United States, and to appropriate and apply the same for defraying the public expenses—to borrow money, or emit bills on the credit of the United States, transmitting every half year to the respective States an account of the sums of money so borrowed or emitted,—to build and equip a navy—to agree upon the number of land forces, and to make requisitions from each State for its quota, in proportion to the number of white inhabitants in such State; which requisition shall be binding, and thereupon the Legislature of each State shall appoint the regimental officers, raise the men and cloath, arm and equip them in a soldier like manner, at the expense of the United States; and the officers and men so cloathed, armed and equipped shall march to the place appointed, and within the time agreed on by the United States in Congress assembled: but if the United States in Congress assembled shall, on consideration of circumstances judge proper that any State should not raise men, or should raise a smaller number of men than the quota thereof, such extra number shall be raised, officered, cloathed, armed and equipped in the same manner as the quota of such State, unless the legislature of such State shall judge that such extra number cannot be safely spared out of the same, in which case they shall raise officer, cloath, arm and equip as many of such extra number as they judge can be safely spared. And the officers and men so cloathed, armed and equipped, shall march to the place appointed, and within the time agreed on by the United States in Congress assembled.

The United States in Congress assembled shall never engage in a war, nor grant letters of marque and reprisal in time of peace, nor enter into any treaties or alliances, nor coin money, nor regulate the value thereof, nor ascertain the sums and expenses necessary for the defence and welfare of the United States, or any of them, nor emit bills, nor borrow money on the credit of the United

States, nor appropriate money, nor agree upon the number of vessels to be built or purchased, or the number of land or sea forces to be raised, nor appoint a commander in chief of the army or navy, unless nine States assent to the same: nor shall a question on any other point, except for adjourning from day to day be determined, unless by the votes of a majority of the United States in Congress assembled.

The Congress of the United States shall have power to adjourn to any time within the year, and to any place within the United States, so that no period of adjournment be for a longer duration than the space of six months, and shall publish the journal of their proceedings monthly, except such parts thereof relating to treaties, alliances or military operations, as in their judgment require secresy; and the yeas and nays of the delegates of each State on any question shall be entered on the Journal, when it is desired by any delegate; and the delegates of a State, or any of them, at his or their request shall be furnished with a transcript of the said journal, except such parts as are above excepted, to lay before the Legislatures of the several States.

ARTICLE X. The committee of the States, or any nine of them, shall be authorized to execute, in the recess of Congress, such of the powers of Congress as the United States in Congress assembled, by the consent of nine States, shall from time to time think expedient to vest them with; provided that no power be delegated to the said committee, for the exercise of which, by the articles of confederation, the voice of nine States in the Congress of the United States assembled is requisite.

ARTICLE XI. Canada acceding to this confederation, and joining in the measures of the United States, shall be admitted into, and entitled to all the advantages of this Union: but no other colony shall be admitted into the same, unless such admission be agreed to by nine States.

ARTICLE XII. All bills of credit emitted, monies borrowed and debts contracted by, or under the authority of Congress, before the assembling of the United States, in pursuance of the present confederation, shall be deemed and considered as a charge against the United States, for payment and satisfaction whereof the said United States, and the public faith are hereby solemnly pledged.

ARTICLE XIII. Every State shall abide by the determinations of the United States in Congress assembled, on all questions which by this confederation are submitted to them. And the articles of this confederation shall be inviolably observed by every State, and the Union shall be perpetual; nor shall any alteration at any time hereafter be made in any of them; unless such alteration be agreed to in a Congress of the United States, and be afterwards confirmed by the Legislatures of every State.

And whereas it has pleased the Great Governor of the world to incline the hearts of the Legislatures we respectively represent in Congress, to approve of, and to authorize us to ratify the said articles of confederation and perpetual union. Know ye that we the undersigned delegates, by virtue of the power and authority to us given for that purpose, do by these presents, in the name and in behalf of our respective constituents, fully and entirely ratify and confirm each and every of the said articles of confederation and perpetual union, and all and singular the matters and things therein contained: and we do further solemnly plight and engage the faith of our respective constituents, that they shall abide by the determinations of the United States in Congress assembled, on all questions, which by the said confederation are submitted to them. And that the articles thereof shall be inviolably observed by the States we respectively represent, and that the Union shall be perpetual.

In witness thereof we have hereunto set our hands in Congress. Done at Philadelphia in the State of Pennsylvania the ninth day of July in the year of our Lord one thousand seven hundred and seventy-eight, and in the third year of the independence of America.

THE CONSTITUTION OF
THE UNITED STATES

WE THE PEOPLE OF THE UNITED STATES, in order to form a more perfect Union, establish Justice, insure domestic Tranquility, provide for the common defence, promote the general Welfare, and secure the Blessings of Liberty to ourselves and our Posterity, do ordain and establish this Constitution for the United States of America.

ARTICLE. I.

Section. 1. All legislative Powers herein granted shall be vested in a Congress of the United States, which shall consist of a Senate and House of Representatives.

Section. 2. The House of Representatives shall be composed of Members chosen every second Year by the People of the several States, and the Electors in each State shall have the Qualifications requisite for Electors of the most numerous Branch of the State Legislature.

No Person shall be a Representative who shall not have attained to the Age of twenty five Years, and been seven Years a Citizen of the United States, and who shall not, when elected, be an Inhabitant of that State in which he shall be chosen.

Representatives and direct Taxes shall be apportioned among the several States which may be included within this Union, according to their respective Numbers, which shall be determined by adding to the whole Number of free Persons, including those bound to Service for a Term of Years, and excluding Indians not taxed, three fifths of all other Persons. The actual Enumeration shall be made within three Years after the first Meeting of the Congress of the United States, and within every subsequent Term of ten Years, in such Manner as they shall by Law direct. The Number of Representatives shall not exceed one for every thirty Thousand, but each State shall have at Least one Representative; and until such enumeration shall be made, the State of New Hampshire shall be entitled to chuse three, Massachusetts eight, Rhode-Island and

Providence Plantations one, Connecticut five, New-York six, New Jersey four, Pennsylvania eight, Delaware one, Maryland six, Virginia ten, North Carolina five, South Carolina five, and Georgia three.

When vacancies happen in the Representation from any state, the Executive Authority thereof shall issue Writs of Election to fill such Vacancies.

The House of Representatives shall chuse their Speaker and other Officers; and shall have the sole Power of Impeachment.

Section. 3. The Senate of the United States shall be composed of two Senators from each State, chosen by the legislature thereof, for six Years; and each Senator shall have one Vote.

Immediately after they shall be assembled in Consequence of the first Election, they shall be divided as equally as may be into three Classes. The Seats of the Senators of the first Class shall be vacated at the Expiration of the second Year, of the second Class at the Expiration of the fourth Year, and of the third Class at the Expiration of the sixth Year, so that one third maybe chosen every second Year; and if Vacancies happen by Resignation, or otherwise, during the Recess of the Legislature of any State, the Executive thereof may make temporary Appointments until the next Meeting of the Legislature, which shall then fill such Vacancies.

No Person shall be a Senator who shall not have attained to the Age of thirty Years, and been nine Years a Citizen of the United States, and who shall not, when elected, be an Inhabitant of that State for which he shall be chosen.

The Vice President of the United States shall be President of the Senate, but shall have no Vote, unless they be equally divided.

The Senate shall chuse their other Officers, and also a President pro tempore, in the Absence of the Vice President, or when he shall exercise the Office of President of the United States.

The Senate shall have the sole Power to try all Impeachments. When sitting for that Purpose, they shall be on Oath or Affirmation. When the President of the United States is tried, the Chief Justice shall preside: And no Person shall be convicted without the Concurrence of two thirds of the Members present.

Judgment in Cases of Impeachment shall not extend further than to removal from Office, and disqualification to hold and enjoy any Office of honor, Trust or Profit under the United States: but the Party convicted shall nevertheless be liable and subject to Indictment, Trial, Judgment and Punishment, according to Law.

Section. 4. The Times, Places and Manner of holding Elections for Senators and Representatives, shall be prescribed in each State by the Legislature thereof; but the Congress may at any time by Law make or alter such Regulations, except as to the Places of chusing Senators.

The Congress shall assemble at least once in every Year, and such Meeting shall be on the first Monday in December, unless they shall by Law appoint a different Day.

Section. 5. Each House shall be the Judge of the Elections, Returns and Qualifications of its own Members, and a Majority of each shall constitute a Quorum to do Business; but a smaller Number may adjourn from day to day, and may be authorized to compel the Attendance of absent Members, in such Manner, and under such Penalties as each House may provide.

Each House may determine the Rules of its Proceedings, punish its Members for disorderly Behaviour, and, with the Concurrence of two thirds, expel a Member.

Each House shall keep a Journal of its Proceedings, and from time to time publish the same, excepting such Parts as may in their Judgment require Secrecy; and the Yeas and Nays of the Members of either House on any question shall, at the Desire of one fifth of those Present, be entered on the Journal.

Neither House, during the Session of Congress, shall, without the Consent of the other, adjourn for more than three days, not to any other Place than that in which the two Houses shall be sitting.

Section. 6. The Senators and Representatives shall receive a Compensation for their Services, to be ascertained by Law, and paid out of the Treasury of the United States. They shall in all Cases, except Treason, Felony and Breach of the Peace, be privileged from Arrest during their Attendance at the Session of their respective Houses, and in going to and returning from the same; and for any Speech or Debate in either House, they shall not be questioned in any other Place.

No Senator or Representative shall, during the Time for which he was elected, be appointed to any civil Office under the Authority of the United States, which shall have been created, or the Emoluments whereof shall have been encreased during such time; and no Person holding any Office under the United States, shall be a Member of either House during his Continuance in Office.

Section. 7. All Bills for raising Revenue shall originate in the House of Representatives; but the Senate may propose or concur with Amendments as on other Bills.

Every Bill which shall have passed the House of Representatives and the Senate shall, before it become a Law, be presented to the President of the United States; If he approve he shall sign it, but if not he shall return it, with his Objections to that House in which it shall have originated, who shall enter the Objections at large on their Journal, and proceed to reconsider it. If after such Reconsideration two thirds of that House shall agree to pass the Bill, it shall be sent, together with the Objections, to the other House, by which it shall likewise be reconsidered, and if approved by two thirds of that House, it shall become a Law. But in all such Cases the Votes of both Houses shall be determined by yeas and Nays, and the Names of the Persons voting for and against the Bill shall be entered on the Journal of each House respectively. If any Bill shall not be returned by the President within ten Days (Sundays excepted) after it shall have been presented to him, the Same shall be a Law, in like Manner as if he had signed it, unless the Congress by their Adjournment prevent its Return, in which Case it shall not be a Law.

Every Order, Resolution, or Vote to which the Concurrence of the Senate and House of Representatives may be necessary (except on a question of Adjournment) shall be presented to the President of the United States; and before the Same shall take Effect, shall be approved by him, or being disapproved by him, shall be repassed by two thirds of the Senate and House of Representatives, according to the Rules and Limitations prescribed in the Case of a Bill.

Section. 8. The Congress shall have Power To lay and collect Taxes, Duties, Imposts and Excises, to pay the Debts and provide for the common Defence and general Welfare of the United States; but all Duties, Imposts and Excises shall be uniform throughout the United States;

To borrow Money on the credit of the United States;

To regulate Commerce with foreign Nations, and among the several States, and with the Indian Tribes;

To establish an uniform Rule of Naturalization, and uniform Laws on the subject of Bankruptcies throughout the United States;

To coin Money, regulate the Value thereof, and of foreign Coin, and fix the Standard of Weights and Measures;

To provide for the Punishment of counterfeiting the Securities and current Coin of the United States;

To establish Post Offices and Post Roads;

To promote the Progress of Science and useful Arts, by securing for limited Times to Authors and Inventors the exclusive Right to their respective Writings and Discoveries;

To constitute Tribunals inferior to the supreme Court;

To define and punish Piracies and Felonies committed on the high Seas, and Offences against the Law of Nations;

To declare War, grant Letters of Marque and Reprisal, and make Rules concerning Captures on land and Water;

To raise and support Armies, but no Appropriation of Money to that Use shall be for a longer Term than two Years;

To provide and maintain a Navy;

To make Rules for the Government and Regulation of the land and naval Forces;

To provide for calling forth the Militia to execute the Laws of the Union, suppress Insurrections and repel Invasions;

To provide for organizing, arming, and disciplining, the Militia, and for governing such Part of them as may be employed in the Service of the United States, reserving to the States respectively, the Appointment of the Officers, and the Authority of training the Militia according to the discipline prescribed by Congress.

To exercise exclusive Legislation in all Cases whatsoever, over such District (not exceeding ten Miles square) as may, by Cession of Particular States, and the Acceptance of Congress, become the Seat of the Government of the United States, and to exercise like Authority over all Places purchased by the Consent of the Legislature of the State in which the Same shall be, for the Erection of Forts, Magazines, Arsenals, dock-Yards, and other needful Buildings;—And

To make all Laws which shall be necessary and proper for carrying into Execution the foregoing Powers, and all other Powers vested by this Constitution in the Government of the United States, or in any Department or Officer thereof.

Section. 9. The Migration or Importation of such Persons as any of the States now existing shall think proper to admit, shall not be prohibited by the Congress prior to the Year one thousand eight hundred and eight, but a Tax or duty may be imposed on such Importation, not exceeding ten dollars for each Person.

The Privilege of the Writ of Habeas Corpus shall not be suspended, unless when in Cases of Rebellion or Invasion the public Safety may require it.

No Bill of Attainder or ex post facto Law shall be passed.

No Capitation, or other direct, Tax shall be laid, unless in Proportion to the Census or Enumeration herein before directed to be taken.

No Tax or Duty shall be laid on Articles exported from any State.

No Preference shall be given by any Regulation of Commerce or Revenue to the Ports of one State over those of another: nor shall Vessels bound to, or from, one State, be obliged to enter, clear, or pay Duties in another.

No Money shall be drawn from the Treasury, but in Consequence of Appropriations made by Law; and a regular Statement and Account of the Receipts and Expenditures of all public Money shall be published from time to time.

No Title of Nobility shall be granted by the United States: And no Person holding any Office of Profit or trust under them, shall, without the Consent of the Congress, accept of any present, Emolument, Office, or Title, of any kind whatever, from any King, prince, or foreign State.

Section 10. No State shall enter into any Treaty, Alliance, or Confederation; grant Letters of Marque and Reprisal; coin Money; emit Bills of Credit; make any Thing but gold and silver Coin a Tender in Payment of Debts; pass any Bill of Attainder, ex post facto Law, or Law impairing the Obligation of Contracts, or grant any Title of Nobility.

No State shall, without the Consent of the Congress, lay any Imposts or Duties on Imports or Exports, except what may be absolutely necessary for executing its inspection Laws: and the net Produce of all Duties and Imposts, laid by any State on Imports or Exports, shall be for the Use of the Treasury of the United States; and all such Laws shall be subject to the Revision and Controul of the Congress.

No State shall, without the Consent of Congress, lay any Duty of Tonnage, keep Troops, or Ships of War in time of Peace, enter into any Agreement or Compact with another State, or with a foreign Power, or engage in War, unless actually invaded, or in such imminent Danger as will not admit of delay.

Article. II.

Section. 1. The executive Power shall be vested in a President of the United States of America. He shall hold his Office during the term of four Years, and, to-gether with the Vice President, chosen for the same Term, be elected, as follows:

Each State shall appoint, in such Manner as the Legislature thereof may direct, a Number of Electors, equal to the whole Number of Senators and Rep-resentatives to which the State may be entitled in the Congress: but no Sena-tor or Representative, or Person holding an Office of Trust or Profit under the United States, shall be appointed an Elector.

The Electors shall meet in their respective States, and vote by Ballot for two Persons, of whom one at least shall not be an Inhabitant of the same State with themselves. And they shall make a List of all the Persons voted for, and of the Number of Votes for each; which List they shall sign and certify, and transmit sealed to the Seat of the Government of the United States, directed to the President of the Senate. The President of the Senate shall, in the Presence of the Senate and House of Representatives, open all the Certificates, and the Votes shall then be counted. The Person having the greatest Number of Votes shall be the President, if such Number be a Majority of the whole Number of Electors appointed; and if there be more than one who have such Majority, and have an equal Number of Votes, then the House of Representatives shall im-mediately chuse by Ballot one of them for President; and if no Person have a Majority, then from the five highest on the List the said House shall in like Manner chuse the President. But in chusing the President, the Votes shall be taken by States, the Representation from each State having one Vote; A quo-rum for this Purpose shall consist of a Member or Members from two thirds of the States, and a Majority of all the States shall be necessary to a Choice. In every Case, after the Choice of the President, the Person having the greatest Number of Votes of the Electors shall be the Vice President. But if there should remain two or more who have equal Votes, the Senate shall chuse from them by Ballot the Vice President.

The Congress may determine the Time of chusing the Electors, and the Day on which they shall give their Votes; which Day shall be the same throughout the United States.

No Person except a natural born Citizen, or a Citizen of the United States, at the time of the Adoption of this Constitution, shall be eligible to the Office of President; neither shall any Person be eligible to that Office who shall not have attained to the Age of thirty five Years, and been fourteen Years a Resident within the United States.

In Case of the Removal of the President from Office, or of his Death, Resignation, or Inability to discharge the Powers and Duties of the said Office, the Same shall devolve on the Vice President, and the Congress may by Law provide for the Case of Removal, Death, Resignation or Inability, both of the President and Vice President, declaring what Officer shall then act as President, and such Officer shall act accordingly, until the Disability be removed, or a President shall be elected.

The President shall, at stated Times, receive for his Services, a Compensation, which shall neither be encreased or diminished during the Period for which he shall have been elected, and he shall not receive within that Period any other Emolument from the United States, or any of them.

Before he enters on the Execution of his Office, he shall take the following Oath or Affirmation:—"I do solemnly swear (or affirm) that I will faithfully execute the Office of President of the United States, and will to the best of my Ability, preserve, protect and defend the Constitution of the United States."

Section. 2. The President shall be Commander in Chief of the Army and Navy of the United States, and of the Militia of the several States, when called into the actual Service of the United States; he may require the Opinion, in writing, of the principal Officer in each of the executive Departments, upon any Subject relating to the Duties of their respective Offices, and he shall have Power to grant Reprieves and Pardons for Offences against the United States, except in Cases of Impeachment.

He shall have Power, by and with the Advice and Consent of the Senate, to make Treaties, provided two thirds of the Senators present concur; and he shall nominate, and by and with the Advice and Consent of the Senate, shall appoint Ambassadors, other public Ministers and Consuls, Judges of the supreme Court, and all other Officers of the United States, whose Appointments are not herein otherwise provided for, and which shall be established by Law;

but the Congress may by Law vest the Appointment of such inferior Officers, as they think proper, in the President alone, in the Courts of Law, or in the Heads of Departments.

The President shall have Power to fill up all Vacancies that may happen during the Recess of the Senate, by granting Commissions which shall expire at the End of their next Session.

Section. 3. He shall from time to time give to the Congress Information of the State of the Union, and recommend to their Consideration such Measures as he shall judge necessary and expedient; he may, on extraordinary Occasions, convene both Houses, or either of them, and in Case of Disagreement between them, with Respect to the Time of Adjournment, he may adjourn them to such Time as he shall think proper; he shall receive Ambassadors and other public Ministers; he shall take Care that the Laws be faithfully executed, and shall Commission all the Officers of the United States.

Section. 4. The President, Vice President and all civil Officers of the United States, shall be removed from Office on Impeachment for, and Conviction of, Treason, Bribery, or other high Crimes and Misdemeanors.

ARTICLE. III.

Section. 1. The judicial Power of the United States, shall be vested in one supreme Court, and in such inferior Courts as the Congress may from time to time ordain and establish. The Judges, both of the supreme and inferior Courts, shall hold their Offices during good Behavior, and shall, at stated Times, receive for their Services, a Compensation, which shall not be diminished during their Continuance in Office.

Section. 2. The judicial Power shall extend to all Cases, in Law and Equity, arising under this Constitution, the Laws of the United States, and Treaties made, or which shall be made, under their Authority;—to all Cases affecting Ambassadors, other public Ministers and Consuls;—to all Cases of admiralty and maritime Jurisdiction;—the Controversies to which the United States shall be a Party;—to Controversies between two or more States;—between a State and Citizens of another State;—between Citizens of different States;—between Citizens of the same State claiming Lands under Grants of different States, and between a State, or the Citizens thereof, and foreign States, Citizens or Subjects.

In all cases affecting Ambassadors, other public Ministers and Consuls, and those in which a State shall be Party, the supreme Court shall have original Jurisdiction. In all the other Cases before mentioned, the supreme Court shall have appellate Jurisdiction, both as to Law and Fact, with such Exceptions, and under such Regulations as the Congress shall make.

The Trial of all Crimes, except in Cases of Impeachment, shall be by Jury; and such Trial shall be held in the State where the said Crimes shall have been committed; but when not committed within any State, the Trial shall be at such Place or Places as the Congress may by Law have directed.

Section. 3. Treason against the United States, shall consist only in levying War against them, or in adhering to their Enemies, giving them Aid and Comfort. No Person shall be convicted of Treason unless on the Testimony of two Witnesses to the same overt Act, or on Confession in open Court.

The Congress shall have Power to declare the Punishment of Treason, but no Attainder of Treason shall work Corruption of Blood, or Forfeiture except during the Life of the Person attainted.

ARTICLE. IV.

Section. 1. Full Faith and Credit shall be given in each State to the public Acts, Records, and judicial Proceedings of every other State. And the Congress may by general Laws prescribe the Manner in which such Acts, Records and Proceedings shall be proved, and the Effect thereof.

Section. 2. The Citizens of each State shall be entitled to all Privileges and Immunities of Citizens in the several States.

A Person charged in any State with Treason, Felony, or other Crime, who shall flee from Justice, and be found in another State, shall on Demand of the executive Authority of the State from which he fled, be delivered up, to be removed to the State having Jurisdiction of the Crime.

No Person held to Service or Labour in one State, under the Laws thereof, escaping into another, shall, in Consequence of any Law or Regulation therein, be discharged from such Service or Labour, but shall be delivered up on Claim of the Party to whom such Service or Labour may be due.

Section. 3. New States may be admitted by the Congress into this Union; but no new State shall be formed or erected within the Jurisdiction of any other State; nor any State be formed by the Junction of two or more States, or Parts of States, without the consent of the Legislatures of the States concerned as well as of the Congress.

The Congress shall have Power to dispose of and make all needful Rules and Regulations respecting the Territory or other Property belonging to the United States; and nothing in this Constitution shall be so construed as to Prejudice any Claims of the United States, or of any particular States.

Section. 4. The United States shall guarantee to every State in this Union a Republican Form of Government, and shall protect each of them against Invasion; and on Application of the Legislature, or of the Executive (when the Legislature cannot be convened) against domestic Violence.

ARTICLE. V.

The Congress, whenever two thirds of both Houses shall deem it necessary, shall propose Amendments to this Constitution, or, on the Application of the Legislatures of two thirds of the several States, shall call a Convention for proposing Amendments, which, in either Case, shall be valid to all Intents and Purposes, as Part of this Constitution, when ratified by the Legislatures of three fourths of the several States, or by Conventions in three fourths thereof, as the one or the other Mode of Ratification may be proposed by the Congress; Provided that no Amendment which may be made prior to the Year One thousand eight hundred and eight shall in any Manner affect the first and fourth Clauses in the Ninth Section of the first Article; and that no State, without its Consent, shall be deprived of its equal Suffrage in the Senate.

ARTICLE. VI.

All Debts contracted and Engagements entered into, before the Adoption of this Constitution, shall be as valid against the United States under this Constitution, as under the Confederation.

This Constitution, and the Laws of the United States which shall be made in Pursuance thereof; and all Treaties made, or which shall be made, under the Authority of the United States, shall be the supreme Law of the Land; and the Judges in every State shall be bound thereby, any Thing in the Constitution or Laws of any State to the Contrary notwithstanding.

The Senators and Representatives before mentioned, and the Members of the several State Legislatures, and all executive and judicial Officers, both of the United States and of the several States, shall be bound by Oath or Affirmation, to support this Constitution; but no religious Test shall ever be required as a Qualification to any Office or public Trust under the United States.

ARTICLE. VII.

The Ratification of the Conventions of nine States, shall be sufficient for the Establishment of this Constitution between the States so ratifying the Same.

Done in Convention by the Unanimous Consent of the States present the Seventeenth Day of September in the Year of our Lord one thousand seven hundred and Eighty seven and of the Independence of the United States of America the Twelfth. In witness thereof We have hereunto subscribed our Names,

G^{o}. WASHINGTON—Presd^{t}.
and deputy from Virginia.

New Hampshire	John Langdon Nicholas Gilman		

		Delaware	Geo: Read Gunning Bedford jun John Dickinson Richard Bassett Jaco: Broom

Massachusetts { Nathaniel Gorham, Rufus King

Connecticut { Wm Saml Johnson, Roger Sherman

Maryland { James McHenry, Dan of St Thos Jenifer, Danl Carroll

New York: . . . Alexander Hamilton

Virginia { John Blair—, James Madison Jr.

New Jersey { Wil: Livingston, David A. Brearley., Wm Paterson., Jona: Dayton

North Carolina { Wm Blount, Richd Dobbs Spaight., Hu Williamson

Pennsylvania { B Franklin, Thomas Mifflin, Robt Morris, Geo. Clymer, Thos FitzSimons, Jared Ingersoll, James Wilson, Gouv Morris

South Carolina { J. Rutledge, Charles Cotesworth Pinckney, Charles Pinckney, Pierce Butler.

Georgia { William Few, Abr Baldwin

AMENDMENTS TO THE CONSTITUTION

Articles In Addition to, and Amendment of the Constitution of the United States of America, proposed by Congress, and ratified by the Legislatures of the several States, pursuant to the fifth Article of the original Constitution.

Amendment I.

Congress shall make no law respecting an establishment of religion, or prohibiting the free exercise thereof; or abridging the freedom of speech, or of the press; or the right of the people peaceably to assemble, and to petition the Government for a redress of grievances.

Amendment II.

A well regulated Militia, being necessary to the security of a free State, the right of the people to keep and bear Arms, shall not be infringed.

Amendment III.

No Soldier shall, in time of peace be quartered in any house, without the consent of the Owner, nor in time of war, but in a manner to be prescribed by law.

Amendment IV.

The right of the people to be secure in their persons, houses, papers, and effects, against unreasonable searches and seizures, shall not be violated, and no Warrants shall issue, but upon probable cause, supported by Oath or affirmation, and particularly describing the place to be searched, and the persons or things to be seized.

Amendment V.

No person shall be held to answer for a capital, or otherwise infamous crime, unless on a presentment or indictment of a Grand Jury, except in cases arising in the land or naval forces, or in the Militia, when in actual service in time of War or public danger; nor shall any person be subject for the same offence to be twice put in jeopardy of life or limb; nor shall be compelled in any criminal case to be a witness against himself, nor be deprived of life, liberty, or property, without due process of law; nor shall private property be taken for public use, without just compensation.

Amendment VI.

In all criminal prosecutions, the accused shall enjoy the right to a speedy and public trial, by an impartial jury of the State and district wherein the crime shall have been committed, which district shall have been previously ascertained by law, and to be informed of the nature and cause of the accusation; to be confronted with the witnesses against him; to have compulsory process for obtaining witnesses in his favor, and to have the Assistance of Counsel for his defence.

AMENDMENT VII.

In Suits at common law, where the value in controversy shall exceed twenty dollars, the right of trial by jury shall be preserved, and no fact tried by a jury, shall be otherwise re-examined in any Court of the United States, than according to the rules of the common law.

AMENDMENT VIII.

Excessive bail shall not be required, nor excessive fines imposed, nor cruel and unusual punishments inflicted.

AMENDMENT IX.

The enumeration in the Constitution, of certain rights, shall not be construed to deny or disparage others retained by the people.

AMENDMENT X.

The powers not delegated to the United States by the Constitution, nor prohibited by it to the States, are reserved to the States respectively, or to the people. [The first ten amendments went into effect December 15, 1791.]

AMENDMENT XI.

The Judicial power of the United States shall not be construed to extend to any suit in law or equity, commenced or prosecuted against one of the United States by Citizens of another State, or by Citizens or Subjects of any Foreign State. [January 8, 1798.]

AMENDMENT XII.

The Electors shall meet in their respective states, and vote by ballot for President and Vice-President, one of whom, at least, shall not be an inhabitant of the same state with themselves; they shall name in their ballots the person voted for as President, and in distinct ballots the person voted for as Vice-President, and they shall make distinct lists of all persons voted for as President, and of all persons voted for as Vice President, and of the number of votes for each, which lists they shall sign and certify, and transmit sealed to the seat of the government of the United States, directed to the President of the Senate;—The President of the Senate shall, in the presence of the Senate and House of Representatives, open all the certificates and the votes shall then be counted;—The person having the greatest number of votes for President, shall be the President, if such number be a majority of the whole number of Electors appointed; and if no person have such majority, then from the persons having the highest numbers not exceeding three on the list of those voted for as President, the House of Representatives shall choose immediately, by ballot, the President. But in choosing the President, the votes shall be taken by states, the representation from each state having one vote; a quorum for this purpose shall consist of a member or members from two-thirds of the states, and a majority of all the states shall be necessary to a choice. And if the House of Representatives shall not choose a President whenever the right of choice shall devolve upon them, before the fourth day of March next following, then the Vice-President shall act as President, as in the case of the death or other constitutional disability of the President.—The person having the greatest number of votes as Vice-President, shall be the Vice-President, if such number be a majority of the whole number of Electors appointed, and if no person have a majority, then from the two highest numbers on the list, the Senate shall choose the Vice-President; a quorum for the purpose shall consist of two-thirds of the whole number of Senators, and a majority of the whole number shall be necessary to a choice. But no person constitutionally ineligible to the office of President shall be eligible to that of Vice-President of the United States. [September 25, 1804.]

AMENDMENT XIII.

Section 1. Neither slavery nor involuntary servitude, except as a punishment for crime whereof the party shall have been duly convicted, shall exist within the United States, or any place subject to their jurisdiction.

Section 2. Congress shall have power to enforce this article by appropriate legislation. [December 18, 1865.]

AMENDMENT XIV.

Section 1. All persons born or naturalized in the United States, and subject to the jurisdiction thereof, are citizens of the United States and of the State wherein they reside. No State shall make or enforce any law which shall abridge the privileges or immunities of citizens of the United States; nor shall any State deprive any person of life, liberty, or property, without due process of law; nor deny to any person within its jurisdiction the equal protection of the laws.

Section 2. Representatives shall be apportioned among the several States according to their respective numbers, counting the whole number of persons in each State, excluding Indians not taxed. But when the right to vote at any election for the choice of electors for President and Vice President of the United States, Representatives in Congress, the Executive and Judicial officers of a State, or the members of the Legislature thereof, is denied to any of the male inhabitants of such State, being twenty-one years of age, and citizens of the United States, or in any way abridged, except for participation in rebellion, or other crime, the basis of representation therein shall be reduced in the proportion which the number of such male citizens shall bear to the whole number of male citizens twenty-one years of age in such State.

Section 3. No person shall be a Senator or Representative in Congress, or elector of President and Vice President, or hold any office, civil or military, under the United States, or under any State, who, having previously taken an oath, as a member of Congress, or as an officer of the United States, or as a member of any State legislature, or as an executive or judicial officer of any State, to support the Constitution of the United States, shall have engaged in insurrection or rebellion against the same, or given aid or comfort to the enemies thereof. But Congress may by a vote of two-thirds of each House, remove such disability.

Section 4. The validity of the public debt of the United States, authorized by law, including debts incurred for payment of pensions and bounties for services in suppressing insurrection or rebellion, shall not be questioned. But neither the United States nor any State shall assume or pay any debt or obligation incurred in aid of insurrection or rebellion against the United States, or any claim for the loss or emancipation of any slave; but all such debts, obligations and claims shall be held illegal and void.

Section 5. The Congress shall have power to enforce, by appropriate legislation, the provisions of this article. [July 28, 1868.]

Amendment XV.

Section 1. The right of citizens of the United States to vote shall not be denied or abridged by the United States or by any State on account of race, color, or previous condition of servitude—

Section 2. The Congress shall have power to enforce this article by appropriate legislation.—[March 30, 1870.]

AMENDMENT XVI.

The Congress shall have power to lay and collect taxes on incomes, from whatever source derived, without apportionment among the several States, and without regard to any census or enumeration. [February 25, 1913.]

AMENDMENT XVII.

The Senate of the United States shall be composed of two senators from each State, elected by the people thereof, for six years; and each Senator shall have one vote. The electors in each State shall have the qualifications requisite for electors of the most numerous branch of the State legislature.

When vacancies happen in the representation of any State in the Senate, the executive authority of such State shall issue writs of election to fill such vacancies: *Provided,* That the legislature of any State may empower the executive thereof to make temporary appointments until the people fill the vacancies by election as the legislature may direct.

This amendment shall not be so construed as to affect the election or term of any senator chosen before it becomes valid as part of the Constitution. [May 31, 1913.]

AMENDMENT XVIII.

After one year from the ratification of this article, the manufacture, sale, or transportation of intoxicating liquors within, the importation thereof into, or the exportation thereof from the United States and all territory subject to the jurisdiction thereof for beverage purposes is hereby prohibited.

The Congress and the several States shall have concurrent power to enforce this article by appropriate legislation.

This article shall be inoperative unless it shall have been ratified as an amendment to the Constitution by the legislatures of the several States, as provided in the Constitution, within seven years from the date of the submission thereof to the States by Congress. [January 29, 1919.]

Amendment XIX.

The right of citizens of the United States to vote shall not be denied or abridged by the United States or by any State on account of sex.

The Congress shall have power by appropriate legislation to enforce the provisions of this article. [August 26, 1920.]

Amendment XX.

Section 1. The terms of the President and Vice-President shall end at noon on the twentieth day of January, and the terms of Senators and Representatives at noon on the third day of January, of the years in which such terms would have ended if this article had not been ratified; and the terms of their successors shall then begin.

Section 2. The Congress shall assemble at least once in every year, and such meeting shall begin at noon on the third day of January, unless they shall by law appoint a different day.

Section 3. If, at the time fixed for the beginning of the term of the President, the President-elect shall have died, the Vice-President-elect shall become President. If a President shall not have been chosen before the time fixed for the beginning of his term, or if the President-elect shall have failed to qualify, then the Vice-President-elect shall act as President until a President shall have qualified; and the Congress may by law provide for the case wherein neither a President-elect nor a Vice-President-elect shall have qualified, declaring who shall then act as President, or the manner in which one who is to act shall be selected, and such person shall act accordingly until a President or Vice-President shall have qualified.

Section 4. The Congress may by law provide for the case of the death of any of the persons from whom the House of Representatives may choose a President whenever the right of choice shall have devolved upon them, and for the case of the death of any of the persons from whom the Senate may choose a Vice-President whenever the right of choice shall have devolved upon them.

Section 5. Sections 1 and 2 shall take effect on the 15th day of October following the ratification of this article.

Section 6. This article shall be inoperative unless it shall have been ratified as an amendment to the Constitution by the legislatures of three-fourths of the several States within seven years from the date of its submission. [February 6, 1933.]

Amendment XXI.

Section 1. The eighteenth article of amendment to the Constitution of the United States is hereby repealed.

Section 2. The transportation or importation into any State, Territory or possession of the United States for delivery or use therein of intoxicating liquors, in violation of the laws thereof, is hereby prohibited.

Section 3. This article shall be inoperative unless it shall have been ratified as an amendment to the Constitution by convention in the several States, as provided in the Constitution, within seven years from the date of the submission thereof to the States by the Congress. [December 5, 1933.]

Amendment XXII.

Section 1. No person shall be elected to the office of the President more than twice, and no person who has held the office of President, or acted as President, for more than two years of a term to which some other person was elected President shall be elected to the office of the President more than once. But this Article shall not apply to any person holding the office of President when this Article was proposed by the Congress, and shall not prevent any person who may be holding the office of President, or acting as President, during the term within which this Article becomes operative from holding the office of President or acting as President during the remainder of such term.

Section 2. This article shall be inoperative unless it shall have been ratified as an amendment to the Constitution by the legislatures of three-fourths of the several states within seven years from the date of its submission to the States by the Congress. [February 27, 1951.]

Amendment XXIII.

Section 1. The District constituting the seat of government of the United States shall appoint in such manner as the Congress may direct:

A number of electors of President and Vice-President equal to the whole number of Senators and Representatives in Congress to which the District would be entitled if it were a State, but in no event more than the least populous State; they shall be in addition to those appointed by the States, but they shall be considered, for the purposes of the election of President and Vice-President, to be electors appointed by a State; and they shall meet in the District and perform such duties as provided by the twelfth article of amendment.

Section 2. The Congress shall have the power to enforce this article by appropriate legislation. [March 29, 1961.]

AMENDMENT XXIV.

Section 1. The right of citizens of the United States to vote in any primary or other election for President or Vice President, for electors for President or Vice President, or for Senator or Representative in Congress, shall not be denied or abridged by the United States or any State by reason of failure to pay any poll tax or other tax.

Section 2. The Congress shall have power to enforce this article by appropriate legislation. [January 23, 1964.]

AMENDMENT XXV.

Section 1. In case of the removal of the President from office or of his death or resignation, the Vice President shall become President.

Section 2. Whenever there is a vacancy in the office of Vice President, the President shall nominate a Vice President who shall take office upon confirmation by a majority vote of both Houses of Congress.

Section 3. Whenever the President transmits to the President pro tempore of the Senate and the Speaker of the House of Representatives his written declaration that he is unable to discharge the powers and duties of his office, and until he transmits to them a written declaration to the contrary, such powers and duties shall be discharged by the Vice President as Acting President.

Section 4. Whenever the Vice President and a majority of either the principal officers of the executive departments or of such other body as Congress may by law provide, transmit to the President pro tempore of the Senate and the Speaker of the House of Representatives their written declaration that the President is unable to discharge the powers and duties of his office, the Vice President shall immediately assume the powers and duties of the office as Acting President.

Thereafter, when the President transmits to the President pro tempore of the Senate and the Speaker of the House of Representatives his written declaration that no inability exists, he shall resume the powers and duties of his office unless the Vice President and a majority of either the principal officers of the executive departments or of such other body as Congress may by law provide, transmit within four days to the President pro tempore of the Senate and the Speaker of the House of Representatives their written declaration that the President is unable to discharge the powers and duties of his office. Thereupon Congress shall decide the issue, assembling within forty-eight hours for that purpose if not in session. If the Congress, within twenty-one days after receipt of the latter written declaration, or, if Congress is not in session, within twenty-one days after Congress is required to assemble, determines by two-thirds vote of both Houses that the President is unable to discharge the powers and duties of his office, the Vice President shall continue to discharge the same as Acting President; otherwise, the President shall resume the powers and duties of his office. [February 10, 1967.]

Amendment XXVI.

Section 1. The right of citizens of the United States, who are eighteen years of age or older, to vote shall not be denied or abridged by the United States or by any State on account of age.

Section 2. The Congress shall have power to enforce this article by appropriate legislation [June 30, 1971.]

Amendment XXVII.

No law, varying the compensation for the services of the Senators and Representatives shall take effect, until an election of Representatives shall have intervened. [May 8, 1992.]

PRESIDENTIAL ELECTIONS

Year	Number of States	Candidates	Parties	Popular Vote	% of Popular Vote	Electoral Vote	% Voter Participation
1864	36	**ABRAHAM LINCOLN**	Republican	2,206,938	55.0	212	73.8
		George B. McClellan	Democratic	1,803,787	45.0	21	
1868	37	**ULYSSES S. GRANT**	Republican	3,013,421	52.7	214	78.1
		Horatio Seymour	Democratic	2,706,829	47.3	80	
1872	37	**ULYSSES S. GRANT**	Republican	3,596,745	55.6	286	71.3
		Horace Greeley	Democratic	2,843,446	43.9		
1876	38	**RUTHERFORD B. HAYES**	Republican	4,036,572	48.0	185	81.8
		Samuel J. Tilden	Democratic	4,284,020	51.0	184	
1880	38	**JAMES A. GARFIELD**	Republican	4,453,295	48.5	214	79.4
		Winfield S. Hancock	Democratic	4,414,082	48.1	155	
		James B. Weaver	Greenback-\Labor	308,578	3.4		
1884	38	**GROVER CLEVELAND**	Democratic	4,879,507	48.5	219	77.5
		James G. Blaine	Republican	4,850,293	48.2	182	
		Benjamin F. Butler	Greenback-\Labor	175,370	1.8		
		John P. St. John	Prohibition	150,369	1.5		
1888	38	**BENJAMIN HARRISON**	Republican	5,477,129	47.9	233	79.3
		Grover Cleveland	Democratic	5,537,857	48.6	168	
		Clinton B. Fisk	Prohibition	249,506	2.2		
		Anson J. Streeter	Union Labor	146,935	1.3		
1892	44	**GROVER CLEVELAND**	Democratic	5,555,426	46.1	277	74.7
		Benjamin Harrison	Republican	5,182,690	43.0	145	
		James B. Weaver	People's	1,029,846	8.5	22	
		John Bidwell	Prohibition	264,133	2.2		

Year	Number of States	Candidates	Parties	Popular Vote	% of Popular Vote	Electoral Vote	% Voter Participation
1896	45	**WILLIAM McKINLEY**	Republican	7,102,246	51.1	271	79.3
		William J. Bryan	Democratic	6,492,559	47.7	176	
1900	45	**WILLIAM McKINLEY**	Republican	7,218,491	51.7	292	73.2
		William J. Bryan	Democratic;\ Populist	6,356,734	45.5	155	
		John C. Wooley	Prohibition	208,914	1.5		
1904	45	**THEODORE ROOSEVELT**	Republican	7,628,461	57.4	336	65.2
		Alton B. Parker	Democratic	5,084,223	37.6	140	
		Eugene V. Debs	Socialist	402,283	3.0		
		Silas C. Swallow	Prohibition	258,536	1.9		
1908	46	**WILLIAM H. TAFT**	Republican	7,675,320	51.6	321	65.4
		William J. Bryan	Democratic	6,412,294	43.1	162	
		Eugene V. Debs	Socialist	420,793	2.8		
		Eugene W. Chafin	Prohibition	253,840	1.7		
1912	48	**WOODROW WILSON**	Democratic	6,296,547	41.9	435	58.8
		Theodore Roosevelt	Progressive	4,118,571	27.4	88	
		William H. Taft	Republican	3,486,720	23.2	8	
		Eugene V. Debs	Socialist	900,672	6.0		
		Eugene W. Chafin	Prohibition	206,275	1.4		
1916	48	**WOODROW WILSON**	Democratic	9,127,695	49.4	277	61.6
		Charles E. Hughes	Republican	8,533,507	46.2	254	
		A. L. Benson	Socialist	585,113	3.2		
		J. Frank Hanly	Prohibition	220,506	1.2		
1920	48	**WARREN G. HARDING**	Republican	16,143,407	60.4	404	49.2
		James M. Cox	Democratic	9,130,328	34.2	127	
		Eugene V. Debs	Socialist	919,799	3.4		
		P. P. Christensen	Farmer-Labor	265,411	1.0		

Year	Number of States	Candidates	Parties	Popular Vote	% of Popular Vote	Electoral Vote	% Voter Participation
1924	48	**CALVIN COOLIDGE**	Republican	15,718,211	54.0	382	48.9
		John W. Davis	Democratic	8,385,283	28.8	136	
		Robert M. La Follette	Progressive	4,831,289	16.6	13	
1928	48	**HERBERT C. HOOVER**	Republican	21,391,993	58.2	444	56.9
		Alfred E. Smith	Democratic	15,016,169	40.9	87	
1932	48	**FRANKLIN D. ROOSEVELT**	Democratic	22,809,638	57.4	472	56.9
		Herbert C. Hoover	Republican	15,758,901	39.7	59	
		Norman Thomas	Socialist	881,951	2.2		
1936	48	**FRANKLIN D. ROOSEVELT**	Democratic	27,752,869	60.8	523	61.0
		Alfred M. Landon	Republican	16,674,665	36.5	8	
		William Lemke	Union	882,479	1.9		
1940	48	**FRANKLIN D. ROOSEVELT**	Democratic	27,307,819	54.8	449	62.5
		Wendell L. Willkie	Republican	22,321,018	44.8	82	
1944	48	**FRANKLIN D. ROOSEVELT**	Democratic	25,606,585	53.5	432	55.9
		Thomas E. Dewey	Republican	22,014,745	46.0	99	
1948	48	**HARRY S. TRUMAN**	Democratic	24,179,345	49.6	303	53.0
		Thomas E. Dewey	Republican	21,991,291	45.1	189	
		J. Strom Thurmond	States' Rights	1,176,125	2.4	39	
		Henry A. Wallace	Progressive	1,157,326	2.4		
1952	48	**DWIGHT D. EISENHOWER**	Republican	33,936,234	55.1	442	63.3
		Adlai E. Stevenson	Democratic	27,314,992	44.4	89	
1956	48	**DWIGHT D. EISENHOWER**	Republican	35,590,472	57.6	457	60.6
		Adlai E. Stevenson	Democratic	26,022,752	42.1	73	

Year	Number of States	Candidates	Parties	Popular Vote	% of Popular Vote	Electoral Vote	% Voter Participation
1960	50	**JOHN F. KENNEDY**	Democratic	34,226,731	49.7	303	64.0
		Richard M. Nixon	Republican	34,108,157	49.5	219	
1964	50	**LYNDON B. JOHNSON**	Democratic	43,129,566	61.1	486	61.7
		Barry M. Goldwater	Republican	27,178,188	38.5	52	
1968	50	**RICHARD M. NIXON**	Republican	31,785,480	43.4	301	60.6
		Hubert H. Humphrey	Democratic	31,275,166	42.7	191	
		George C. Wallace	American\ Independent	9,906,473	13.5	46	
1972	50	**RICHARD M. NIXON**	Republican	47,169,911	60.7	520	55.5
		George S. McGovern	Democratic	29,170,383	37.5	17	
		John G. Schmitz	American	1,099,482	1.4		
1976	50	**JIMMY CARTER**	Democratic	40,830,763	50.1	297	54.3
		Gerald R. Ford	Republican	39,147,793	48.0	240	
1980	50	**RONALD REAGAN**	Republican	43,901,812	50.7	489	53.0
		Jimmy Carter	Democratic	35,483,820	41.0	49	
		John B. Anderson	Independent	5,719,722	6.6		
		Ed Clark	Libertarian	921,188	1.1		
1984	50	**RONALD REAGAN**	Republican	54,451,521	58.4	525	52.9
		Walter F. Mondale	Democratic	37,565,334	41.6	13	
1988	50	**GEORGE H. BUSH**	Republican	47,917,341	54.0	426	48.6
		Michael Dukakis	Democratic	41,013,030	46.0	112	
1992	50	**BILL CLINTON**	Democratic	43,728,375	43.0	370	54.0
		George H. Bush	Republican	38,167,416	38.0	168	
		H. Ross Perot	Independent	19,237,247	19.0	0	

Candidates receiving less than 1 percent of the popular vote have been omitted, so the percentage of popular vote for any election year may not total 100. Before the passage of the Twelfth Amendment in 1804, the Electoral College voted for two presidential candidates; the runner-up became vice-president.

ADMISSION OF STATES

Order of Admission	State	Date of Admission	Order of Admission	State	Date of Admission
1	Delaware	December 7, 1787	26	Michigan	January 26, 1837
2	Pennsylvania	December 12, 1787	27	Florida	March 3, 1845
3	New Jersey	December 18, 1787	28	Texas	December 29, 1845
4	Georgia	January 2, 1788	29	Iowa	December 28, 1846
5	Connecticut	January 9, 1788	30	Wisconsin	May 29, 1848
6	Massachusetts	February 7, 1788	31	California	September 9, 1850
7	Maryland	April 28, 1788	32	Minnesota	May 11, 1858
8	South Carolina	May 23, 1788	33	Oregon	February 14, 1859
9	New Hampshire	June 21, 1788	34	Kansas	January 29, 1861
10	Virginia	June 25, 1788	35	West Virginia	June 30, 1863
11	New York	July 26, 1788	36	Nevada	October 31, 1864
12	North Carolina	November 21, 1789	37	Nebraska	March 1, 1867
13	Rhode Island	May 29, 1790	38	Colorado	August 1, 1876
14	Vermont	March 4, 1791	39	North Dakota	November 2, 1889
15	Kentucky	June 1, 1792	40	South Dakota	November 2, 1889
16	Tennessee	June 1, 1796	41	Montana	November 8, 1889
17	Ohio	March 1, 1803	42	Washington	November 11, 1889
18	Louisiana	April 30, 1812	43	Idaho	July 3, 1890
19	Indiana	December 11, 1816	44	Wyoming	July 10, 1890
20	Mississippi	December 10, 1817	45	Utah	January 4, 1896
21	Illinois	December 3, 1818	46	Oklahoma	November 16, 1907
22	Alabama	December 14, 1819	47	New Mexico	January 6, 1912
23	Maine	March 15, 1820	48	Arizona	February 14, 1912
24	Missouri	August 10, 1821	49	Alaska	January 3, 1959
25	Arkansas	June 15, 1836	50	Hawaii	August 21, 1959

POPULATION OF THE UNITED STATES

Year	Number of States	Population	% Increase	Population per Square Mile
1790	13	3,929,214		4.5
1800	16	5,308,483	35.1	6.1
1810	17	7,239,881	36.4	4.3
1820	23	9,638,453	33.1	5.5
1830	24	12,866,020	33.5	7.4
1840	26	17,069,453	32.7	9.8
1850	31	23,191,876	35.9	7.9
1860	33	31,443,321	35.6	10.6
1870	37	39,818,449	26.6	13.4
1880	38	50,155,783	26.0	16.9
1890	44	62,947,714	25.5	21.1
1900	45	75,994,575	20.7	25.6
1910	46	91,972,266	21.0	31.0
1920	48	105,710,620	14.9	35.6
1930	48	122,775,046	16.1	41.2
1940	48	131,669,275	7.2	44.2
1950	48	150,697,361	14.5	50.7
1960	50	179,323,175	19.0	50.6
1970	50	203,235,298	13.3	57.5
1980	50	226,504,825	11.4	64.0
1985	50	237,839,000	5.0	67.2
1990	50	250,122,000	5.2	70.6
1995	50	263,411,707	5.3	74.4

IMMIGRATION TO THE UNITED STATES, FISCAL YEARS 1820–1990

Year	Number	Year	Number	Year	Number	Year	Number
1820–1989	**55,457,531**	**1871–80**	**2,812,191**	**1921–30**	**4,107,209**	**1971–80**	**4,493,314**
1820	8,385	1871	321,350	1921	805,228	1971	370,478
1821–30	**143,439**	1872	404,806	1922	309,556	1972	384,685
1821	9,127	1873	459,803	1923	522,919	1973	400,063
1822	6,911	1874	313,339	1924	706,896	1974	394,861
1823	6,354	1875	227,498	1925	294,314	1975	386,914
1824	7,912	1876	169,986	1926	304,488	1976	398,613
1825	10,199	1877	141,857	1927	335,175	1976	103,676
1826	10,837	1878	138,469	1928	307,255	1977	462,315
1827	18,875	1879	177,826	1929	279,678	1978	601,442
1828	27,382	1880	457,257	1930	241,700	1979	460,348
1829	22,520	**1881–90**	**5,246,613**	**1931–40**	**528,431**	1980	530,639
1830	23,322	1881	669,431	1931	97,139	**1981–90**	**7,338,062**
1831–40	**599,125**	1882	788,992	1932	35,576	1981	596,600
1831	22,633	1883	603,322	1933	23,068	1982	594,131
1832	60,482	1884	518,592	1934	29,470	1983	559,763
1833	58,640	1885	395,346	1935	34,956	1984	543,903
1834	65,365	1886	334,203	1936	36,329	1985	570,009
1835	45,374	1887	490,109	1937	50,244	1986	601,708
1836	76,242	1888	546,889	1938	67,895	1987	601,516
1837	79,340	1889	444,427	1939	82,998	1988	643,025
1838	38,914	1890	455,302	1940	70,756	1989	1,090,924
1839	68,069	**1891–1900**	**3,687,564**	**1941–50**	**1,035,039**	1990	1,536,483
1840	84,066	1891	560,319	1941	51,776		
1841–50	**1,713,251**	1892	579,663	1942	28,781		
1841	80,289	1893	439,730	1943	23,725		
1842	104,565	1894	285,631	1944	28,551		
		1895	258,536	1945	38,119		
		1896	343,267	1946	108,721		

Year	Number	Year	Number	Year	Number
1843	52,496	1897	230,832	1947	147,292
1844	78,615	1898	229,299	1948	170,570
1845	114,371	1899	311,715	1949	188,317
1846	154,416	1900	448,572	1950	249,187
1847	234,968	**1901–10**	**8,795,386**	**1951–60**	**2,515,479**
1848	226,527	1901	487,918	1951	205,717
1849	297,024	1902	648,743	1952	265,520
1850	369,980	1903	857,046	1953	170,434
1851–60	**2,598,214**	1904	812,870	1954	208,177
1851	379,466	1905	1,026,499	1955	237,790
1852	371,603	1906	1,100,735	1956	321,625
1853	368,645	1907	1,285,349	1957	326,867
1854	427,833	1908	782,870	1958	253,265
1855	200,877	1909	751,786	1959	260,686
1856	200,436	1910	1,041,570	1960	265,398
1857	251,306	**1911–20**	**5,735,811**	**1961–70**	**3,321,677**
1858	123,126	1911	878,587	1961	271,344
1859	121,282	1912	838,172	1962	283,763
1860	153,640	1913	1,197,892	1963	306,260
1861–70	**2,314,824**	1914	1,218,480	1964	292,248
1861	91,918	1915	326,700	1965	296,697
1862	91,985	1916	298,826	1966	323,040
1863	176,282	1917	295,403	1967	361,972
1864	193,418	1918	110,618	1968	454,448
1865	248,120	1919	141,132	1969	358,579
1866	318,568	1920	430,001	1970	373,326
1867	315,722				
1868	138,840				
1869	352,768				
1870	387,203				

Source: U.S. Immigration and Naturalization Service, 1991.

IMMIGRATION BY REGION AND SELECTED COUNTRY OF LAST RESIDENCE, FISCAL YEARS 1820–1989

Region and Country of Last Residence[1]	1820	1821–30	1831–40	1841–50	1851–60	1861–70	1871–80	1881–90
All countries	8,385	143,439	599,125	1,713,251	2,598,214	2,314,824	2,812,191	5,246,613
Europe	7,690	98,797	495,681	1,597,442	2,452,577	2,065,141	2,271,925	4,735,484
Austria-Hungary	—[2]	—[2]	—[2]	—[2]	—[2]	7,800	72,969	353,719
Austria	—[2]	—[2]	—[2]	—[2]	—[2]	[3]7,124	63,009	226,038
Hungary	—[2]	—[2]	—[2]	—[2]	—[2]	[3]484	9,960	127,681
Belgium	1	27	22	5,074	4,738	6,734	7,221	20,177
Czechoslovakia	—[4]	—[4]	—[4]	—[4]	—[4]	—[4]	—[4]	—[4]
Denmark	20	169	1,063	539	3,749	17,094	31,771	88,132
France	371	8,497	45,575	77,262	76,358	35,986	72,206	50,464
Germany	968	6,761	152,454	434,626	951,667	787,468	718,182	1,452,970
Greece	—	20	49	16	31	72	210	2,308
Ireland[5]	3,614	50,724	207,381	780,719	914,119	435,778	436,871	655,482
Italy	30	409	2,253	1,870	9,231	11,725	55,759	307,309
Netherlands	49	1,078	1,412	8,251	10,789	9,102	16,541	53,701
Norway-Sweden	3	91	1,201	13,903	20,931	109,298	211,245	568,362
Norway	—[6]	—[6]	—[6]	—[6]	—[6]	—[6]	95,323	176,586
Sweden	—[6]	—[6]	—[6]	—[6]	—[6]	—[6]	115,922	391,776
Poland	5	16	369	105	1,164	2,027	12,970	51,806
Portugal	35	145	829	550	1,055	2,658	14,082	16,978
Romania	—[7]	—[7]	—[7]	—[7]	—[7]	—[7]	11	6,348
Soviet Union	14	75	277	551	457	2,512	39,284	213,282
Spain	139	2,477	2,125	2,209	9,298	6,697	5,266	4,419
Switzerland	31	3,226	4,821	4,644	25,011	23,286	28,293	81,988
United Kingdom[5,8]	2,410	25,079	75,810	267,044	423,974	606,896	548,043	807,357
Yugoslavia	—[9]	—[9]	—[9]	—[9]	—[9]	—[9]	—[9]	—[9]
Other Europe	—	3	40	79	5	8	1,001	682

Asia	6	30	55	141	41,538	64,759	124,160	69,942
China[10]	1	2	8	35	41,397	64,301	123,201	61,711
Hong Kong	—[11]	—[11]	—[11]	—[11]	—[11]	—[11]	—[11]	—[11]
India	1	8	39	36	43	69	163	269
Iran	—[12]	—[12]	—[12]	—[12]	—[12]	—[12]	—[12]	—[12]
Israel	—[13]	—[13]	—[13]	—[13]	—[13]	—[13]	—[13]	—[13]
Japan	—[14]	—[14]	—[14]	—[14]	—[14]	186	149	2,270
Korea	—[15]	—[15]	—[15]	—[15]	—[15]	—[15]	—[15]	—[15]
Philippines	—[16]	—[16]	—[16]	—[16]	—[16]	—[16]	—[16]	—[16]
Turkey	1	20	7	59	83	131	404	3,782
Vietnam	—[11]	—[11]	—[11]	—[11]	—[11]	—[11]	—[11]	—[11]
Other Asia	3	—	1	11	15	72	243	1,910
America	387	11,564	33,424	62,469	74,720	166,607	404,044	426,967
Canada & Newfoundland[17,18]	209	2,277	13,624	41,723	59,309	153,878	383,640	393,304
Mexico[18]	1	1	6,599	3,271	3,078	2,191	5,162	1,913[19]
Caribbean	164	3,834	12,301	13,528	10,660	9,046	13,957	29,042
Cuba	—[12]	—[12]	—[12]	—[12]	—[12]	—[12]	—[12]	—[12]
Dominican Republic	—[20]	—[20]	—[20]	—[20]	—[20]	—[20]	—[20]	—[20]
Haiti	—[20]	—[20]	—[20]	—[20]	—[20]	—[20]	—[20]	—[20]
Jamaica	—[21]	—[21]	—[21]	—[21]	—[21]	—[21]	—[21]	—[21]
Other Caribbean	164	3,834	12,301	13,528	10,660	9,046	13,957	29,042
Central America	2	105	44	368	449	95	157	404
El Salvador	—[20]	—[20]	—[20]	—[20]	—[20]	—[20]	—[20]	—[20]
Other Central America	2	105	44	368	449	95	157	404
South America	11	531	856	3,579	1,224	1,397	1,128	2,304
Argentina	—[20]	—[20]	—[20]	—[20]	—[20]	—[20]	—[20]	—[20]
Colombia	—[20]	—[20]	—[20]	—[20]	—[20]	—[20]	—[20]	—[20]
Ecuador	—[20]	—[20]	—[20]	—[20]	—[20]	—[20]	—[20]	—[20]
Other South America	11	531	856	3,579	1,224	1,397	1,128	2,304
Other America	—[22]	—[22]	—[22]	—[22]	—[22]	—[22]	—[22]	—[22]
Africa	1	16	54	55	210	312	358	857
Oceania	1	2	9	29	158	214	10,914	12,574
Not specified[22]	300	33,030	69,902	53,115	29,011	17,791	790	789

Region and Country of Last Residence[1]	1891–1900	1901–10	1911–20	1921–30	1931–40	1941–50	1951–60	1961–70
All countries	3,687,564	8,795,386	5,735,811	4,107,209	528,431	1,035,039	2,515,479	3,321,677
Europe	3,555,352	8,056,040	4,321,887	2,463,194	347,566	621,147	1,325,727	1,123,492
Austria-Hungary	592,707[23]	2,145,266[23]	896,342[23]	63,548	11,424	28,329	103,743	26,022
Austria	234,081[3]	668,209[3]	453,649	32,868	3,563[24]	24,860[24]	67,106	20,621
Hungary	181,288[3]	808,511[3]	442,693	30,680	7,861	3,469	36,637	5,401
Belgium	18,167	41,635	33,746	15,846	4,817	12,189	18,575	9,192
Czechoslovakia	—[4]	—[4]	3,426[4]	102,194	14,393	8,347	918	3,273
Denmark	50,231	65,285	41,983	32,430	2,559	5,393	10,984	9,201
France	30,770	73,379	61,897	49,610	12,623	38,809	51,121	45,237
Germany	505,152[23]	341,498[23]	143,945[23]	412,202	114,058[24]	226,578[24]	477,765	190,796
Greece	15,979	167,519	184,201	51,084	9,119	8,973	47,608	85,969
Ireland[5]	388,416	339,065	146,181	211,234	10,973	19,789	48,362	32,966
Italy	651,893	2,045,877	1,109,524	455,315	68,028	57,661	185,491	214,111
Netherlands	26,758	48,262	43,718	26,948	7,150	14,860	52,277	30,606
Norway-Sweden	321,281	440,039	161,469	165,780	8,700	20,765	44,632	32,600
Norway	95,015	190,505	66,395	68,531	4,740	10,100	22,935	15,484
Sweden	226,266	249,534	95,074	97,249	3,960	10,665	21,697	17,116
Poland	96,720[23]	—[23]	4,813[23]	227,734	17,026	7,571	9,985	53,539
Portugal	27,508	69,149	89,732	29,994	3,329	7,423	19,588	76,065
Romania	12,750	53,008	13,311	67,646	3,871	1,076	1,039	2,531
Soviet Union	505,290[23]	1,597,306[23]	921,201[23]	61,742	1,370	571	671	2,465
Spain	8,731	27,935	68,611	28,958	3,258	2,898	7,894	44,659
Switzerland	31,179	34,922	23,091	29,676	5,512	10,547	17,675	18,453
United Kingdom[5,8]	271,538	525,950	341,408	339,570	31,572	139,306	202,824	213,822
Yugoslavia	—[9]	—[9]	1,888[9]	49,064	5,835	1,576	8,225	20,381
Other Europe	282	39,945	31,400	42,619	11,949	8,486	16,350	11,604

Asia	74,862	323,543	247,236	112,059	16,595	37,028	153,249	427,642
China[10]	14,799	20,605	21,278	29,907	4,928	16,709	9,657	34,764
Hong Kong	—[11]	—[11]	—[11]	—[11]	—[11]	—[11]	15,541[11]	75,007
India	68	4,713	2,082	1,886	496	1,761	1,973	27,189
Iran	—[12]	—[12]	—[12]	241[12]	195	1,380	3,388	10,339
Israel	—[13]	—[13]	—[13]	—[13]	—[13]	476[13]	25,476	29,602
Japan	25,942	129,797	83,837	33,462	1,948	1,555	46,250	39,988
Korea	—[16]	—[16]	—[16]	—[16]	—[15]	107[15]	6,231	34,526
Philippines	30,425	157,369	134,066	33,824	528[16]	4,691	19,307	98,376
Turkey	—[11]	—[11]	—[11]	—[11]	1,065	798	3,519	10,142
Vietnam	—[11]	—[11]	—[11]	—[11]	—[11]	—[11]	335[11]	4,340
Other Asia	3,628	11,059	5,973	12,739	7,435	9,551	21,572	63,369
America	38,972	361,888	1,143,671	1,516,716	160,037	354,804	996,944	1,716,374
Canada & Newfoundland[17,18]	3,311	179,226	742,185	924,515	108,527	171,718	377,952	413,310
Mexico[18]	971[19]	49,642	219,004	459,287	22,319	60,589	299,811	453,937
Caribbean	33,066	107,548	123,424	74,899	15,502	49,725	123,091	470,213
Cuba	—[12]	—[12]	—[12]	15,901[12]	9,571	26,313	78,948	208,536
Dominican Republic	—[20]	—[20]	—[20]	—[20]	1,150[20]	5,627	9,897	93,292
Haiti	—[20]	—[20]	—[20]	—[20]	191[20]	911	4,442	34,499
Jamaica	—[21]	—[21]	—[21]	—[21]	—[21]	—[21]	8,869[21]	74,906
Other Caribbean	33,066	107,548	123,424	58,998	4,590	16,874	20,935[21]	58,980
Central America	549	8,192	17,159	15,769	5,861	21,665	44,751	101,330
El Salvador	—[20]	—[20]	—[20]	—[20]	673[20]	5,132	5,895	14,992
Other Central America	549	8,192	17,159	15,769	5,188	16,533	38,856	86,338
South America	1,075	17,280	41,899	42,215	7,803	21,831	91,628	257,954
Argentina	—[20]	—[20]	—[20]	—[20]	1,349[20]	3,338	19,486	49,721
Colombia	—[20]	—[20]	—[20]	—[20]	1,223[20]	3,858	18,048	72,028
Ecuador	—[20]	—[20]	—[20]	—[20]	337[20]	2,417	9,841	36,780
Other South America	1,075	17,280	41,899	42,215	4,894	12,218	44,253	99,425
Other America	—[22]	—[22]	—[22]	31[22]	25	29,276	59,711	19,630
Africa	350	7,368	8,443	6,286	1,750	7,367	14,092	28,954
Oceania	3,965	13,024	13,427	8,726	2,483	14,551	12,976	25,122
Not specified[22]	14,063	33,523[25]	1,147	228	—	142	12,491	93

Region and Country of Last Residence[1]	1971–80	1981–89	1984	1985	1986	1987	1988	1989	Total 170 Years 1820–1989
All countries	4,493,314	5,801,579	543,903	570,009	601,708	601,516	643,025	1,090,924	55,457,531
Europe	800,368	637,524	69,879	69,526	69,224	67,967	71,854	94,338	36,977,034
Austria-Hungary	16,028	20,152	2,846	2,521	2,604	2,401	3,200	3,586	4,338,049
Austria	9,478	14,566	2,351	1,930	2,039	1,769	2,493	2,845	1,825,172[3]
Hungary	6,550	5,586	495	591	565	632	707	741	1,666,801[3]
Belgium	5,329	6,239	787	775	843	859	706	705	209,729
Czechoslovakia	6,023	6,649	693	684	588	715	744	526	145,223
Denmark	4,439	4,696	512	465	544	515	561	617	369,738
France	25,069	28,088	3,335	3,530	3,876	3,809	3,637	4,101	783,322
Germany	74,414	79,809	9,375	10,028	9,853	9,923	9,748	10,419	7,071,313
Greece	92,369	34,490	3,311	3,487	3,497	4,087	4,690	4,588	700,017
Ireland[5]	11,490	22,229	1,096	1,288	1,757	3,032	5,121	6,983	4,715,393
Italy	129,368	51,008	6,328	6,351	5,711	4,666	5,332	11,089	5,356,862
Netherlands	10,492	10,723	1,313	1,235	1,263	1,303	1,152	1,253	372,717
Norway-Sweden	10,472	13,252	1,455	1,557	1,564	1,540	1,669	1,809	2,144,024
Norway	3,941	3,612	403	386	367	372	446	556	800,672[6]
Sweden	6,531	9,640	1,052	1,171	1,197	1,168	1,223	1,253	1,283,097[6]
Poland	37,234	64,888	7,229	7,409	6,540	5,818	7,298	13,279	587,972
Portugal	101,710	36,365	3,800	3,811	3,804	4,009	3,290	3,861	497,195
Romania	12,393	27,361	2,956	3,764	3,809	2,741	2,915	3,535	201,345
Soviet Union	38,961	42,898	3,349	1,532	1,001	1,139	1,408	4,570	3,428,927
Spain	39,141	17,689	2,168	2,278	2,232	2,056	1,972	2,179	282,404
Switzerland	8,235	7,561	795	980	923	964	920	1,072	358,151
United Kingdom[5,8]	137,374	140,119	16,516	15,591	16,129	15,889	14,667	16,961	5,100,096
Yugoslavia	30,540	15,984	1,404	1,521	1,915	1,793	2,039	2,464	133,493
Other Europe	9,287	7,324	611	719	771	708	785	741	181,064

Asia	1,588,178	2,416,278	247,775	255,164	258,546	248,293	254,745	296,420	5,697,301
China[10]	124,326	306,108	29,109	33,095	32,389	32,669	34,300	39,284	873,737
Hong Kong	113,467	83,848	12,290	10,795	9,930	8,785	11,817	15,257	287,863[11]
India	164,134	221,977	23,617	24,536	24,808	26,394	25,312	28,599	426,907
Iran	45,136	101,267	11,131	12,327	12,031	10,323	9,846	13,027	161,946[12]
Israel	37,713	38,367	4,136	4,279	5,124	4,753	4,444	5,494	131,634[13]
Japan	49,775	40,654	4,517	4,552	4,444	4,711	5,085	5,454	455,813[14]
Korea	267,638	302,782	32,537	34,791	35,164	35,397	34,151	33,016	611,284[15]
Philippines	354,987	477,485	46,985	53,137	61,492	58,315	61,017	66,119	955,374[16]
Turkey	13,399	20,028	1,652	1,690	1,975	2,080	2,200	2,538	409,122
Vietnam	172,820	266,027	25,803	20,367	15,010	13,073	12,856	13,174	443,522[11]
Other Asia	244,783	557,735	55,998	55,595	56,179	51,793	53,717	74,458	940,099
America	1,982,735	2,564,698	208,111	225,519	254,078	265,026	294,906	672,639	12,017,021
Canada & Newfoundland[17,18]	169,939	132,296	15,659	16,354	16,060	16,741	15,821	18,294	4,270,943
Mexico[8]	640,294	975,657	57,820	61,290	66,753	72,511	95,170	405,660	3,208,543
Caribbean	741,126	759,416	68,368	79,374	98,527	100,615	110,949	87,597	2,590,542
Cuba	264,863	135,142	5,699	17,115	30,787	27,363	16,610	9,523	739,274[12]
Dominican Republic	148,135	209,899	23,207	23,861	26,216	24,947	27,195	26,744	468,000[20]
Haiti	56,335	118,510	9,554	9,872	12,356	14,643	34,858	13,341	214,888[20]
Jamaica	137,577	184,481	18,997	18,277	18,916	22,430	20,474	23,572	405,833[21]
Other Caribbean	134,216	111,384	10,911	10,249	10,252	11,232	11,812	14,417	762,547
Central America	134,640	321,845	27,626	28,447	30,086	30,366	31,311	101,273	673,385
El Salvador	34,436	133,938	8,753	10,093	10,881	10,627	12,043	57,628	195,066[20]
Other Central America	100,204	187,907	18,873	18,354	19,205	19,739	19,268	43,645	478,319
South America	295,741	375,026	38,636	40,052	42,650	44,782	41,646	59,812	1,163,482
Argentina	29,897	21,374	2,287	1,925	2,318	2,192	2,556	3,766	125,165[20]
Colombia	77,347	99,066	10,897	11,802	11,213	11,482	10,153	14,918	271,570[20]
Ecuador	50,077	43,841	4,244	4,601	4,518	4,656	4,736	7,587	143,293[20]
Other South America	138,420	210,745	21,208	21,724	24,601	26,452	24,201	33,541	623,454
Other America	995	458	2	2	2	11	9	3	110,126
Africa	80,779	144,096	13,594	15,236	15,500	15,730	17,124	22,485	301,348
Oceania	41,242	38,401	4,249	4,552	4,352	4,437	4,324	4,956	197,818
Not specified[22]	12	582	295	12	8	63	72	86	267,009

Source: U.S. Immigration and Naturalization Service, 1991.

[1] Data for years prior to 1906 relate to country whence alien came; data from 1906–79 and 1984–89 are for country of last permanent residence; and data for 1980–83 refer to country of birth. Because of changes in boundaries, changes in lists of countries, and lack of data for specified countries for various periods, data for certain countries, especially for the total period 1820–1989, are not comparable throughout. Data for specified countries are included with countries to which they belonged prior to World War I.

[2] Data for Austria and Hungary not reported until 1861.

[3] Data for Austria and Hungary not reported separately for all years during the period.

[4] No data available for Czechoslovakia until 1920.

[5] Prior to 1926, data for Northern Ireland included in Ireland.

[6] Data for Norway and Sweden not reported separately until 1871.

[7] No data available for Romania until 1880.

[8] Since 1925, data for United Kingdom refer to England, Scotland, Wales, and Northern Ireland.

[9] In 1920, a separate enumeration was made for the Kingdom of Serbs, Croats, and Slovenes. Since 1922, the Serb, Croat, and Slovene Kingdom recorded as Yugoslavia.

[10] Beginning in 1957, China includes Taiwan.

[11] Data not reported separately until 1952.

[12] Data not reported separately until 1925.

[13] Data not reported separately until 1949.

[14] No data available for Japan until 1861.

[15] Data not reported separately until 1948.

[16] Prior to 1934, Philippines recorded as insular travel.

[17] Prior to 1920, Canada and Newfoundland recorded as British North America. From 1820 to 1898, figures include all British North America possessions.

[18] Land arrivals not completely enumerated until 1908.

[19] No data available for Mexico from 1886 to 1893.

[20] Data not reported separately until 1932.

[21] Data for Jamaica not collected until 1953. In prior years, consolidated under British West Indies, which is included in "Other Caribbean."

[22] Included in countries "Not specified" until 1925.

[23] From 1899 to 1919, data for Poland included in Austria-Hungary, Germany, and the Soviet Union.

[24] From 1938 to 1945, data for Austria included in Germany.

[25] Includes 32,897 persons returning in 1906 to their homes in the United States.

—represents zero.

NOTE: From 1820 to 1867, figures represent alien passengers arrived at seaports; from 1868 to 1891 and 1895 to 1897, immigrant aliens arrived; from 1892 to 1894 and 1898 to 1989, immigrant aliens admitted for permanent residence. From 1892 to 1903, aliens entering by cabin class were not counted as immigrants. Land arrivals were not completely enumerated until 1908. For this table, fiscal year 1843 covers 9 months ending September 1843; fiscal years 1832 and 1850 cover 15 months ending December 31 of the respective years; and fiscal year 1868 covers 6 months ending June 30, 1868.

PRESIDENTS, VICE-PRESIDENTS, AND SECRETARIES OF STATE

President	Vice-President	Secretary of State
17. Andrew Johnson, Unionist 1865		W. H. Seward 1865
18. Ulysses S. Grant, Republican 1869	Schuyler Colfax, Republican 1869 Henry Wilson, Republican 1873	E. B. Washburne 1869 H. Fish 1869
19. Rutherford B. Hayes, Republican 1877	William A. Wheeler, Republican 1877	W. M. Evarts 1877
20. James A. Garfield, Republican 1881	Chester A. Arthur, Republican 1881	J. G. Blaine 1881
21. Chester A. Arthur, Republican 1881		F. T. Frelinghuysen 1881
22. Grover Cleveland, Democratic 1885	T. A. Hendricks, Democratic 1885	T. F. Bayard 1885
23. Benjamin Harrison, Republican 1889	Levi P. Morton, Republican 1889	J. G. Blaine 1889 J. W. Foster 1892
24. Grover Cleveland, Democratic 1893	Adlai E. Stevenson, Democratic 1893	W. Q. Gresham 1893 R. Olney 1895
25. William McKinley, Republican 1897	Garret A. Hobart, Republican 1897 Theodore Roosevelt, Republican 1901	J. Sherman 1897 W. R. Day 1897 J. Hay 1898
26. Theodore Roosevelt, Republican 1901	Chas. W. Fairbanks, Republican 1905	J. Hay 1901 E. Root 1905 R. Bacon 1909

President	Vice-President	Secretary of State
27. William H. Taft, Republican 1909	James S. Sherman, Republican 1909	P. C. Knox 1909
28. Woodrow Wilson, Democratic 1913	Thomas R. Marshall, Democratic 1913	W. J. Bryan 1913 R. Lansing 1915 B. Colby 1920
29. Warren G. Harding, Republican 1921	Calvin Coolidge, Republican 1921	C. E. Hughes 1921
30. Calvin Coolidge, Republican 1923	Charles G. Dawes, Republican 1925	C. E. Hughes 1923 F. B. Kellogg 1925
31. Herbert Hoover, Republican 1929	Charles Curtis, Republican 1929	H. L. Stimson 1929
32. Franklin D. Roosevelt, Democratic 1933	John Nance Garner, Democratic 1933 Henry A. Wallace, Democratic 1941 Harry S. Truman, Democratic 1945	C. Hull 1933 E. R. Stettinius, Jr. 1944
33. Harry S. Truman, Democratic 1945	Alben W. Barkley, Democratic 1949	J. F. Byrnes 1945 G. C. Marshall 1947 D. G. Acheson 1949
34. Dwight D. Eisenhower, Republican 1953	Richard M. Nixon, Republican 1953	J. F. Dulles 1953 C. A. Herter 1959
35. John F. Kennedy, Democratic 1961	Lyndon B. Johnson, Democratic 1961	D. Rusk 1961
36. Lyndon B. Johnson, Democratic 1963	Hubert H. Humphrey, Democratic 1965	D. Rusk 1963

	President	Vice-President	Secretary of State
37.	Richard M. Nixon, Republican 1969	Spiro T. Agnew, Republican 1969 Gerald R. Ford, Republican 1973	W. P. Rogers 1969 H. A. Kissinger 1973
38.	Gerald R. Ford, Republican 1974	Nelson Rockefeller, Republican 1974	H. A. Kissinger 1974
39.	Jimmy Carter, Democratic 1977	Walter Mondale, Democratic 1977	C. Vance 1977 E. Muskie 1980
40.	Ronald Reagan, Republican 1981	George Bush, Republican 1981	A. Haig 1981 G. Schultz 1982
41.	George Bush, Republican 1989	J. Danforth Quayle, Republican 1989	J. A. Baker 1989
42.	William J. Clinton, Democrat 1993	Albert Gore, Jr., Democrat 1993	W. Christopher 1993

CHRONOLOGY OF
SIGNIFICANT EVENTS

1865   Freedmen's Bureau established

1865   Assassination of President Lincoln

1866–1868   Fourteenth Amendment passed and ratified

1867   First Reconstruction Act

1867–1877   Congressional Reconstruction of the South

1867   United States purchases Alaska

1868   Impeachment of President Andrew Johnson

1869   Completion of first transcontinental railroad

1869   National Woman Suffrage Association founded

1870   Standard Oil Company of Ohio established by John D. Rockefeller

1873   Crédit-Mobilier Scandal

1876   Battle of the Little Big Horn

1876   Telephone invented by Alexander Graham Bell

1877   *Munn v. Illinois*

1878   Bland-Allison Act

1879   Terence Powderly becomes president of Knights of Labor

1879   Incandescent bulb invented by Thomas Edison

1881   Helen Hunt Jackson's *A Century of Dishonor*

1882   Chinese Exclusion Act

1883   Pendleton Act

1883   Brooklyn Bridge completed

1884   Mark Twain's *The Adventures of Huckleberry Finn*

1885   Josiah Strong publishes *Our Country*

1886   Haymarket Riot

1886   American Federation of Labor founded

1887   Interstate Commerce Act

1887–1889   National Farmers' Alliance founded

1888   Edward Bellamy's *Looking Backward*

1889   Hull House founded by Jane Addams
1890   Battle of Wounded Knee
1890   Sherman Anti-Trust Act
1890   Jacob Riis's *How the Other Half Lives*
1892   Homestead Massacre
1892   Populist party founded
1893   Panic of 1893
1893   Stephen Crane's *Maggie: A Girl of the Streets*
1893   Chicago World's Fair
1894   Pullman Strike
1895   Booker T. Washington's Atlanta Exposition Speech
1896   *Plessy v. Ferguson*
1898   Spanish-American War
1899–1900   "Open Door" Notes
1899   Thorstein Veblen's *The Theory of the Leisure Class*
1900   Theodore Dreiser's *Sister Carrie*
1900–1917   "Ash Can" school of painting
1901–1917   Progressive movement
1903   Orville and Wilbur Wright's first flight
1903   William E. B. DuBois's *Souls of Black Folk*
1904   *Northern Securities Company v. U.S.*
1904–1905   Roosevelt corollary to Monroe Doctrine
1905   Roosevelt mediates end to Russo-Japanese War
1906   Upton Sinclair's *The Jungle*
1906–1914   Construction of the Panama Canal
1908   Gentlemen's Agreement with Japan
1909   First Model T automobile produced by Henry Ford
1909   National Association for the Advancement of Colored People founded
1909–1910   Ballinger/Pinchot dispute
1910   President Taft's "dollar diplomacy" in Nicaragua
1912   Woodrow Wilson elected president
1913   Underwood-Simmons Tariff Act
1913   Federal Reserve Act
1913–1917   Revolt in Mexico and U.S. intervention
1914   Clayton Anti-Trust Act
1914   Outbreak of World War I
1915   German submarine sinks *Lusitania*
1915   Albert Einstein's general theory of relativity
1917   Russian Revolution
1917   United States enters the war against Germany

1918	Wilson announces Fourteen Points
1919	Treaty of Versailles signed
1919	Boston Police Strike
1919	Volstead Act (Prohibition)
1919	Sherwood Anderson's *Winesburg, Ohio*
1919–1920	United States rejects treaty over League of Nations
1919–1920	Red Scare
1920–1930	Harlem Renaissance
1921	Marcus Garvey's African Zionist Movement
1922	T. S. Eliot's *The Waste Land*
1922	Washington Conference on Disarmament
1924	Harding administration scandals
1924	McNary-Haugen Bill
1925	Scopes trial
1925	F. Scott Fitzgerald's *The Great Gatsby*
1926	Ernest Hemingway's *The Sun Also Rises*
1927	Charles Lindbergh's solo flight to Paris
1927	Sacco and Vanzetti executed
1927	Babe Ruth hits 60 home runs
1928	Kellogg-Briand Peace Pact
1929	William Faulkner's *The Sound and the Fury*
1929	Stock market crash
1929–1933	Great Depression
1932	Bonus Army march on Washington
1932	Franklin Delano Roosevelt elected president
1933	Emergency Banking Act
1933	Unemployment Relief Act
1933	Agricultural Adjustment Act
1933	Tennessee Valley Authority Act
1933	National Industrial Recovery Act
1933	Hitler comes to power in Germany
1935–1936	Second New Deal
1935	National Labor Relations Act
1935	Social Security Act
1935	*Schechter v. United States*
1936	Spanish Civil War
1937	Supreme Court "packing" fight
1938	Munich Conference
1939	Germany annexes Czechoslovakia and invades Poland
1939	John Steinbeck's *The Grapes of Wrath*
1940	Battle of Britain

1940 Richard Wright's *Native Son*
1941 Lend-Lease aid to Allies
1941 Atlantic Charter
1941 Japanese attack on Pearl Harbor
1941 United States enters World War II
1944 Allied invasion of Normandy
1945 Atomic bombs dropped on Hiroshima and Nagasaki
1945 Germany surrenders; Japan surrenders
1945 Yalta Conference
1945 Potsdam Conference
1946 Benjamin Spock's *Baby and Child Care*
1947 Taft-Hartley Labor-Management Relations Act
1947 Truman Doctrine
1947 Marshall Plan
1947 Jackie Robinson becomes first black in major-league baseball
1949 North Atlantic Treaty Organization (NATO) founded
1949 Arthur Miller's *Death of a Salesman*
1950 Internal Security Act
1950–1953 Korean War
1950–1954 McCarthyism
1950 David Riesman's *The Lonely Crowd*
1952 Ralph Ellison's *Invisible Man*
1952 Norman Vincent Peale's *The Power of Positive Thinking*
1954 *Brown v. Board of Education of Topeka*
1954 Geneva Conference on Indochina
1955 Montgomery bus boycott
1955 Dr. Jonas Salk's polio vaccine
1956 Suez crisis
1956 Alan Ginsberg's *Howl*
1957 Dispute over integration in Little Rock, Arkansas
1957 Eisenhower Doctrine
1957 Jack Kerouac's *On the Road*
1957 USSR launches Sputnik satellite
1959 Fidel Castro leads revolution in Cuba
1960 U-2 incident
1960 "Sit-in" movement begins in Greensboro, N.C.
1960 Students for a Democratic Society founded
1961 Bay of Pigs invasion
1962 Cuban missile crisis
1962 Michael Harrington's *The Other America*

1962	Rachel Carson's *Silent Spring*
1963	Nuclear Test Ban Treaty
1963	Assassination of President John F. Kennedy
1963	March on Washington for civil rights
1963	Betty Friedan's *The Feminine Mystique*
1964	Gulf of Tonkin Resolution
1964, 1965	Civil Rights Acts
1965	President Lyndon Johnson's Great Society
1965	U.S. troop buildup begins in Vietnam
1965	Ralph Nader's *Unsafe at Any Speed*
1966	National Organization for Women founded
1967	Arab-Israeli War
1968	Tet Offensive in Vietnam
1968	Martin Luther King assassinated
1968	Robert Kennedy assassinated
1968	Violence at Democratic National Convention in Chicago
1969	Woodstock Festival for Music and Peace
1969	My Lai massacre
1969	Neil Armstrong becomes first man on moon
1970	Violence at Kent State and Jackson State Universities
1972	Earth Day demonstrations
1972	President Nixon visits China
1972–1974	Watergate scandal
1973	Vietnam Peace Agreement
1973–1974	Arab oil embargo
1975	Fall of South Vietnam
1978	Camp David accords between Egypt and Israel
1979	Three Mile Island nuclear accident
1979	SALT II Agreement
1979–1981	Iranian hostage crisis
1983	American marines killed in Lebanon
1986	Tax Reform Act
1986	Iran-Contra affair
1987	Scandals in politics and evangelical movement
1987	Congressional hearings on Iran-Contra affair
1987	Controversy over air traffic safety
1987	"Black Monday" on Wall Street
1987	INF treaty with Soviet Union
1988–1989	S&L crisis and bailout
1989	End of Communist Party rule in East-bloc nations

1989   Fall of the Berlin Wall
1989–1990   U.S. military action in Panama
1990–1991   Persian Gulf crisis
1991   U.S. military action against Iraq
1991   Failed coup in the Soviet Union
1992   Riots in Los Angeles
1992   Conflict in the former Yugoslavia flares with Serbian attack on the U.N.-recognized Bosnian republic
1993–1994   Repeated attempts to legislate national health care reform fail in Congress
1993   Terrorist bombing of the World Trade Center in New York
1993   U.S. commits troops to relieve famine and attempt to halt clan warfare in Somalia
1995   Terrorist bombing of a Federal building in Oklahoma City

ILLUSTRATION CREDITS

CHAPTER 17: p. 539, Library of Congress; **p. 543,** National Portrait Gallery, The Smithsonian Institution/Art Resource, N.Y.; **p. 550,** The National Archives; **p. 553,** Library of Congress; **p. 558,** Library of Congress.

CHAPTER 18: p. 571, The Warder Collection, N.Y.; **p. 574,** Brown Brothers; **p. 580,** Library of Congress; **p. 581,** Brown Brothers; **p. 583,** Denver Public Library; **p. 584,** Library of Congress; **p. 587,** Princeton University Press; **p. 588,** The Smithsonian Institution; **p. 589,** Amon Carter Museum; **p. 594,** The Smithsonian Institution: Solomon D. Butcher Collection, Nebraska State Historical Society.

CHAPTER 19: p. 603, Amon Carter Museum; **p. 606,** University of California at Berkeley, Asian American Studies Library; **p. 611,** Carnegie Library, Pittsburgh; **p. 614,** The Pierpont Morgan Library, N.Y.; **p. 624,** Archives of Labor and Urban Affairs, Wayne State University.

CHAPTER 20: p. 634, Library of Congress; **p. 636,** Museum of the City of New York; **p. 639,** (top) The New York Public Library: Astor, Lenox, and Tilden Foundations, (bottom) The New York Public Library: Astor, Lenox, and Tilden Foundations; **p. 643,** California Historical Society Library; **p. 644,** Library of Congress; **p. 645,** Texas A & M University Archives; **p. 656,** The Salvation Army; **p. 657,** University of Illinois at Chicago, University Library, Jane Addams Memorial Collection; **p. 660,** Nebraska State Historical Society.

CHAPTER 21: p. 665, Library of Congress; **p. 679,** The Bettmann Archive; **p. 684,** Library of Congress; **p. 685,** Kansas State Historical Society, Topeka; **p. 690,** Library of Congress.

CHAPTER 22: p. 701, Public Archives of Hawaii; **p. 710,** National Archives; **p. 712,** Library of Congress; **p. 714,** National Archives; **p. 718,** The Warder Collection, N.Y.; **p. 723,** Library of Congress.

CHAPTER 23: p. 723, Library of Congress; **p. 736,** Library of Congress; **p. 746,** Library of Congress; **p. 751,** Historical Pictures Service; **p. 754,** Library of Congress.

CHAPTER 24: p. 761, Library of Congress; **p. 765,** Princeton University Libraries; **p. 772,** National Archives; **p. 774,** National Archives; **p. 777,** National Archives; **p. 780,** National Archives; **p. 786,** Library of Congress; **p. 789,** The Bettmann Archive; **p. 791,** The New York Public Library: Astor, Lenox, and Tilden Foundations.

CHAPTER 25: p. 796, UPI/Bettmann Newsphotos; **p. 798,** Tennessee State Library and Archives; **p. 800,** Chicago Historical Society; **p. 803,** Library of Congress; **p. 804,** The Bettmann Archive; **p. 806,** University of Chicago Press; **p. 807,** Schomberg Center; **p. 812,** Ramsey Archive.

CHAPTER 26: **p. 821,** Library of Congress; **p. 825,** National Archives; **p. 827,** Library of Congress; **p. 831,** The Warder Collection, N.Y.; **p. 837,** Museum of History and Industry, Seattle; **p. 840,** *New York Daily News.*

CHAPTER 27: **p. 846,** © AP/Wide World Photos; **p. 848,** National Archives; **p. 853,** Library of Congress; **p. 862,** Library of Congress; **p. 866,** UPI/Bettmann Newsphotos; **p. 871,** *Life* Magazine, © 1965; **p. 873,** National Archives; **p. 876,** Library of Congress; **p. 877,** © AP/Wide World Photos; **p. 878,** Library of Congress.

CHAPTER 28: **p. 888,** National Archives; **p. 895,** The Warder Collection, N.Y.; **p. 903,** (top) National Archives, (bottom) National Archives.

CHAPTER 29: **p. 911,** The Granger Collection, N.Y.; **p. 913,** National Archives; **p. 915,** National Archives; **p. 917,** Museum of History and Industry, Seattle; **p. 927,** Library of Congress; **p. 929,** UPI/Corbis-Bettmann; **p. 937,** National Archives; **p. 940,** National Archives; **p. 943,** Yuichiro Sasaki, UN Photo 149443.

CHAPTER 30: **p. 954,** University of Louisville Photographic Archives; **p. 964,** U.S. Information Agency; **p. 965,** *Hartford Courant;* **p. 968,** The Bettmann Archive; **p. 969,** Harry S. Truman Archive; **p. 977,** Library of Congress.

CHAPTER 31: **p. 985,** Culver Pictures; **p. 988,** Life Picture Service; **p. 990,** Life Picture Service; **p. 992,** Joe Steinmetz Studio; **p. 999,** The Metropolitan Museum of Art.

CHAPTER 32: **p. 1007,** UPI/Bettmann Newsphotos; **p. 1011,** The Bettmann Archive; **p. 1016,** The Warder Collection; **p. 1021,** University of Louisville, Standard Oil Collection; **p. 1023,** Black Star Publishing Co., Inc.; **p. 1031,** © AP/Wide World Photos.

CHAPTER 33: **p. 1038,** National Archives; **p. 1040,** National Archives; **p. 1042,** National Archives; **p. 1043,** National Archives; **p. 1057,** National Archives; **p. 1059,** National Archives; **p. 1064,** The Bettmann Archive; **p. 1066,** National Archives.

CHAPTER 34: **p. 1075,** Magnum Photos; **p. 1077,** Library of Congress; **p. 1078,** The Warder Collection; **p. 1079,** The Bettmann Archive; **p. 1082,** © AP/Wide World Photos; **p. 1059,** *Los Angeles Times;* **p. 1091,** The Bettmann Archive; **p. 1096,** The Bettmann Archive; **p. 1099,** The Bettmann Archive; **p. 1101,** © AP/Wide World Photos; **p. 1106,** © AP/Wide World Photos.

CHAPTER 35: **p. 1114,** The Bettmann Archive; **p. 1121,** © AP/Wide World Photos; **p. 1124,** © AP/Wide World Photos; **p. 1126,** UPI/Bettmann Newsphotos; **p. 1138,** Black Star Publishing Co., Inc.; **p. 1139,** © AP/Wide World.

CHAPTER 36: **p. 1151,** © Paul Conklin; **p. 1165,** The Bettmann Archive; **p. 1169,** The Bettmann Archive; **p. 1176,** The Bettmann Archive; **p. 1181,** © AP/Wide World Photos; **p. 1182,** © AP/Wide World Photos.

INDEX

ABC powers (Argentina, Brazil, and Chile), 760
abortion laws, 1079–80, 1164
abortion rights, 1113
Absalom! Absalom! (Faulkner), 879
Abstract Expressionism, 999–1000
abstract painting, 1000
Acheson, Dean, 972, 975, 976, 1014–15, 1025, 1049
Adams, Henry, 561, 663
Adams, Sherman, 1008
Adamson Act (1916), 755
Adarand Constructors v. Pena, 1177
Addams, Jane, 657–58, 768
Administrative Reorganization Act (1939), 873
Adventures of Huckleberry Finn, The (Twain), 651
Adventures of Tom Sawyer, The (Twain), 651
advertising, 986
affirmative action, 1118, 1150, 1175–76, 1177
Affluent Society, The (Galbraith), 995–96
Afghanistan, Soviet invasion of (1979), 1107, 1123, 1130, 1137
African-Americans:
  affirmative action and, 1150
  AIDS and, 1134
  in cabinet, 1054
  in Carter administration, 1104
  disfranchisement of, 575–78, 755
  in Great Depression, 849, 853, 856
  Hoover's policies toward, 833
  immigration of, 1155, 1157
  literature of, 806–7
  New Negro spirit among, 805–8
  northward migration of, 773, 806, 914, 989–90
  political influence of, 806
  poverty among, 1157
  Reconstruction and, 538–41, 542, 546–55, 562–63
  as single parents, 1154
  as soldiers in Civil War, 547
  suffrage for, 538, 541, 544, 549, 556, 752–53, 1056–57
  Truman's policies toward, 966
  as underclass, 1136, 1154–55
  violence against, 542, 552–54, 773–74, 790, 966
  as voters, protection of, 554
  voting patterns of, 864, 867
  in West, 583–84, 590, 683–84
  westward migration of, 918
  Wilson's attitude toward, 752–53
  in World War I, 773, 780
  in World War II, 914–15
  see also civil rights movement; racial riots; segregation
age groups, fastest-growing, 1152
Agnew, Spiro, 1068, 1087, 1093–94, 1100
Agricultural Adjustment Act (1933), 851–55
Agricultural Adjustment Act (1938), 853–55, 867
agriculture:
  in Great Depression, 851–55
  migratory workers in, 1081–83
  in New West, 593–96
  in 1920s, 829–30
  sharecropping in, 548
  in South, 573–74
  technological improvements in, 595, 989
  tobacco, 571–72
  see also cotton production; farmers; sugarcane production
Agriculture Department, U.S., 739, 740
Aguinaldo, Emilio, 709, 713–14
AIDS (Acquired Immune Deficiency Syndrome), 1086, 1134–35
Aid to Families with Dependent Children, 1180
air conditioning, 987
airplanes, 826–27
Alabama, 553, 578, 865, 1056
Alabama, University of, 1042
Alaska, 1029, 1085
  gold rush in, 692
  purchase of, 700
Albania, 891, 1138
Albee, Edward, 998
Albuquerque, N.Mex., 918
Alcatraz Island, AIM occupation of (1969), 1085
alcohol consumption, *see* prohibition movement
Algeciras, Act of (1906), 724
Alger, Horatio, 613, 635
Algeria, 921
Alliance Exchange, 682–83
Alliance for Progress, 1039
Altamont concert (1969), 1077

Altgeld, John Peter, 625
Amalgamated Association of Iron and Steel
    Workers, 623
Amalgamated Clothing Workers, 869
America First Committee, 896
American Anti-Imperialist League, 714
American Birth Control League, 803
American Civil Liberties Union (ACLU), 789
American Federation of Labor (AFL), 775,
    869–70
    formation of, 621–22
American Federation of Labor-Congress of
    Industrial Organizations (AFL-CIO), 986,
    1098, 1118, 1122
American Historical Association, 597
American Indian Movement (AIM), 1085
American Liberty League, 858
American Medical Association (AMA), 1053,
    1168–70, 1180
American Political Ideas (Fiske), 703–4
American Protective Association (APA), 642
American Psychiatric Association, 1086
American Railway Union, 624–25, 626
American Revolution, French aid in, 637–38
American Steel and Wire Company, 592
American Telephone and Telegraph Company
    (AT&T), 608
American Tobacco Company, 572, 738
American Woman Suffrage Association, 659
anarchism, 620, 795
Anderson, John, 1114
Anderson, Sherwood, 802, 812
Andrews, Samuel, 609
Angel Island, 643–44
Anglo-French Suez Canal Company, 1026–27
Anschluss, 890
Anthony, Susan B., 659
anthropology, 810
antiballistic missile systems (ABMs), 1097,
    1124
Anti-Ballistic Missile Treaty (1972), 1124
Anti-Saloon League, 734, 799
antitrust laws:
    Taft's enforcement of, 743
    T. Roosevelt's enforcement of, 735–36
    Wilson's program for, 750–52
    see also Sherman Antitrust Act
Apache Indians, 589
Apodaca, Jerry, 1084
Appalachian Regional Development Act (1966),
    1054
Arabic, 767
Arab League, 1025
Arafat, Yasir, 1171
Arapaho Indians, 586–87
Ardennes Forest, battle in (1944), 935
ARENA, 1128
Arena, 730
Argentina, 760
Arias, Oscar, 1127
Aristide, Jean-Bertrand, 1174
Arizona, 585
    in World War II, 918
Arkansas, 854, 1024

arms control negotiations, 1124–25
Armstrong, Louis, 802
Army, U.S.:
    African-Americans in, 547
    see also draft; specific wars
Army Appropriation Act (1901), 715
Army nurse corps, 774
Army Signal Center, 1012
Arrowrock Dam, 593
Arthur, Chester A., 643, 668, 669–70
arts:
    modernism in, 810, 1000
    see also literature; painting in post-World War
        II era; poetry
Asian-Americans, 1055, 1155–58
    see also specific ethnic groups
Asian Indians, 1157
As I Lay Dying (Faulkner), 879
Aswan Dam, 1026–27
Atchison, Topeka and Santa Fe railroad, 605
Atlanta Compromise, 580–82
Atlantic, battle of the (1943), 922–24
Atlantic Charter (1941), 899
Atlantic Constitution, 570
Atlantic Monthly, 652
atomic bombs, 941–44, 960, 1010–11
    see also nuclear weapons
Atomic Energy Commission, U.N., 960, 1013
Auschwitz, death camp at, 941
Australia, 931, 1018
    in World War II, 908
Austria, 640, 838, 890, 937
Austria-Hungary, in World War I, 762–63, 777,
    779, 780, 783, 787
Autobiography (Carnegie), 612
Autobiography (Malcolm X), 1059
automobiles, 633, 827–28, 988
Averell, James, 592

Babbit (Lewis), 825
baby-boom generation, 954, 984–85, 987,
    1071–72, 1152
backcountry, see frontier
Baer, George F., 737
Baghdad Pact, 1025
Baker, James, 1144, 1146
Bakke v. Board of Regents of California, 1093
Baldwin, James, 998
Ball, Lucille, 985
Ballinger, Richard A., 742
Ballinger-Pinchot controversy (1910), 742
Baltic republics, 1140–41
Baltimore, Md., 640
Bankhead-Jones Farm Tenant Act (1937), 872
banking holidays, 847
Bank of the United States (national bank):
    failure of, in Great Depression, 835
    F. D. Roosevelt's reforms in, 847
    in Great Depression, 838
    Wilson's reforms in, 748–50
    see also Federal Reserve System
Baptists, African-Americans as, 547
barbed-wire, 591–92
Barnett, Ross, 1041

Baruch, Bernard, 773, 962
baseball, 990
Bastogne, battle of (1944), 935
Bataan Peninsula, 908
Bay of Pigs invasion (1961), 1044, 1048
Bedford-Stuyvesant (New York City), 1114
Beecher, Henry Ward, 655
beef trusts, 736
Begala, Paul, 1179
Begin, Menachem, 1105–6
Beirut airport, terrorist attack at (1983), 1120
Belgium, 828, 885, 935, 965
    in World War II, 894
Bell, Alexander Graham, 607–8
Bellow, Saul, 851, 998
Bell Telephone Association, 607
Benedict, Ruth, 810
Bennett, William J., 1135
Bentsen, Lloyd, 1132
Berlin, 936, 1029–30, 1044
Berlin, Irving, 640
Berlin, occupation zones in, 937
Berlin Airlift (1948–1949), 963–64
Berlin Wall, 1044, 1137, 1138
Bessemer, Sir Henry, 612
Beveridge, Albert J., 703, 715
bilingualism, 1157
bills of rights, in U.S. Constitution, 1135
Birmingham, Ala., 633
birthrate, 954
Bismarck Sea, battle of the (1943), 931
Black, Hugo, 869
Black Boy (Wright), 877
Black Friday (1869), 557
Black Monday (1987), 1129
Black Muslims, 1059–60
Black Panther party, 1058
Black Power, 808, 1057–60
blacks, *see* African-Americans
Blaine, James G., 560, 665, 667, 676, 1168
    in presidential elections, 668, 670–72, 675
Bland-Allison Act (1878), 668, 677, 680
Blitzkrieg, 894–95
blockades, of Cuba, 1045
Boa Dai, emperor of Vietnam, 971
Bohemian-Americans, 640
Bolshevik Revolution (1917), 770, 777, 779, 781, 790–92
bonds, junk, 1133
Bonus Expeditionary Force, 839–41, 844
Booth, John Wilkes, 537
Bosnia, 1173
Boston, Mass., 633, 640
Boston Police Strike (1919), 789–90
Boulder (Hoover) Dam, 593
Bourbons, 575–77
Boxer Rebellion (1900), 716–17
boycotts, of Montgomery bus system, 1022–24, 1040
Bradley, Omar, 928–30, 936, 975
Branch Davidians, 1165–66
Brandeis, Louis D., 734, 747, 748, 753, 860, 868
Brando, Marlon, 1001

Braun, Eva, 939
Brazil, 760
Brest-Litovsk, Treaty of (1918), 781
Brezhnev, Leonid, 1096, 1103
Brezhnev doctrine, 1137
Briand, Aristide, 885
brinksmanship, 1014–15
Britain, battle of, 896
British Columbia, 700
Brooklyn Eagle, 770
Brooks, Preston S. "Bully," 540
Brotherhood of Sleeping Car Porters, 914
Brown, H. Rap, 1058, 1074
Brown, James, 1060
Brown v. Board of Education of Topeka, Kansas, 1021–22, 1043
Bruce, Blanche K., 550
Brussels Pact (1948), 965
Bryan, William Jennings, 566, 713, 732, 746, 748, 759
    in presidential elections, 689–92, 729, 738, 740
    in Scopes trial, 797–99
    as secretary of war, 764–65, 766–67
    U.S. neutrality and, 767–68
Bryer, Stephen, 1177
Buchanan, Patrick, 1151, 1159, 1162
budget, *see* debt, national; federal budget
budget deficits, 1116–17, 1128, 1133, 1134, 1173
Buffalo, N.Y., 640
Buffalo Evening Telegraph, 671
Bulgaria, 898, 960, 1137
    in World War I, 780
Bulge, battle of the (1944), 935, 1146
Bull Moose Progressives, *see* Progressive party
Bunau-Varilla, Philippe, 721–22
Bundy, McGeorge, 1038
Bunting v. Oregon, 734
Bunyan, John, 730
Bureau of Alcohol Tobacco and Firearms (BATF), 1165
Bureau of Corporations, 737, 747, 750
Bureau of Immigration, 637
Bureau of Indian Affairs, 1085
Bureau of Internal Revenue, 1005
Bureau of Mines, 743
Bureau of Reclamation, 593
Bureau of Refugees, Freedmen, and Abandoned Lands, 536
Burger, Warren, 1093
Burma (Myanmar), 908, 1000–1001
Burroughs, William, 1000–1001
buses, racial segregation on, 1022–24, 1040–41
Bush, George, 1170
    Christian Coalition and, 1151
    domestic policy of, 1133–36, 1159–60
    economic policies of, 1159–60, 1162, 1167
    foreign policy of, 1133, 1136–46
    income tax increases by, 1132, 1134
    1990–1992 recession and, 1159–60
    Panama invasion and, 1142–43
    Persian Gulf War and, 1143–46, 1158–59
    presidency of, 1133–46

Bush, George (*continued*)
  in presidential elections, 1131–32, 1149,
    1159, 1164
  S&L bailout and budget reduction problems
    of, 1133–34
  Somalia intervention of, 1173
  Soviet Union dissolution and, 1136–42
  Supreme Court nominations of, 1160–62
  symbolism of, 1133, 1135
business:
  Coolidge's support of, 822–24
  entrepreneurship in, 607–15
  Harding's support of, 818–20
  philosophical rationale for, 612–13
  politicians' alliance with, 664–65
  postwar culture of, 991
  see also antitrust laws; regulation,
    governmental; trusts; *specific industries*
busing, 1093
Butts, Calvin, 1157
Byrd, Harry F., 1022
Byrnes, James F., 960

Cable, George Washington, 578, 650
cable cars, 633
Cairo, declaration of (1943), 926
California, 1083, 1177
  dust bowl migration to, 853–54, 876–77
  gold rush in, 585
  immigrants in, 584, 1157
  population growth of, 1153
  in World War II, 918
California, University of:
  at Berkeley, 1073
  Board of Regents of, 1177
californios, 1081
Calley, William, 1088
Call of the Wild (London), 653
Cambodia, 1016, 1018, 1088–89, 1090, 1091,
  1103
  immigrants from, 1157
Camp David Accords (1978), 1105–6
Canada, 584, 692, 700, 960, 965
  NAFTA with, 1167–68
Cane (Toomer), 807
Capone, Al, 800–801
Caribbean immigrants, 1157
Carmichael, Stokely, 1058, 1074
Carnegie, Andrew, 611–13, 623, 714
Carnegie Endowment for International Peace,
  976
carpetbaggers, 551–52
Carranza, Venustiano, 759–60
Carter, Jimmy, 1132, 1170, 1182
  domestic policies of, 1104–5, 1106–7
  economic policies of, 1106–7, 1115
  foreign policy of, 1104–9
  hostage crisis and, 1108
  Middle East policy of, 1104–6
  after presidency, 1173
  in presidential elections, 1103–4, 1111,
    1114
Carville, James, 1179

Casablanca, conference at (1943), 921
Casey, William, 1126
Cassady, Neal, 1001
Castle Garden, 637
Castro, Fidel, 1030–31, 1043–44, 1048, 1084
Castro, Raul, 1084
Catcher in the Rye (Salinger), 998
Catholic Church, 704, 1150
  social doctrine of, 655–57
Catt, Carrie Chapman, 659–60, 768, 803
cattle industry, 594
  barbed-wire introduced into, 591–92
  open-range phase of, 590–91
  range wars and, 592–93
Ceausescu, Nicolae, 1137
Cédras, Raoul, 1174
"Celebrated Jumping Frog of Calaveras County,
  The" (Twain), 651
Celtic immigrants, 637
census of 1990, 1152–58
Central Federated Union of New York, 775
Central Intelligence Agency (CIA), 957, 979,
  1014, 1048
  in Chile, 1102
  in Cuba invasion, 1031, 1043–44
  in Nicaragua, 1119
  in Panama, 1142
Central Pacific railroad, 604–5, 606
Century of Dishonor, A (Jackson), 589
Ceylon (Sri Lanka), 1015–16
Challenger, 1125
Chambers, Whittaker, 976
Chaplin, Charlie, 825
Chase, Salmon P., 545
Chavez, César, 1081–83
Chechnya, 1171
Cheever, John, 851, 998
chemical waste sites, 1104
Cheyenne Indians, 587–88
Chiang Kai-shek, 926, 939, 970–71
Chicago, Ill., 640, 641–42, 773–74, 789,
  989–90, 1058, 1074–75
  Haymarket Affair in (1886), 620–21
Chicago Defender, 773
Chicanos, 1081
child labor, 856, 872
  Progressive campaign against, 733, 754–55
  Children's Bureau, 743
Chile, 760, 1138
China, Imperial:
  Boxer Rebellion in, 716–17
  demise of, 887
  dollar diplomacy with, 762
  Japanese influence in, 723–24
  Open Door policy and, 716–17, 723, 724
China, Nationalist:
  Japanese intervention in, 887–88, 890, 893
  Open Door policy and, 885
  Soviet intervention in, 887
  in World War I, 884
  in World War II, 898, 900, 902, 926, 931,
    939, 970–71
  see also Taiwan

China, People's Republic of, 1044
  creation of, 970–71
  democracy movement in, 1136
  Egypt's recognition of, 1026
  Korean War and, 973–75, 1010–11
  rapprochement with, 1096
  Vietnam and, 1016, 1017–18
Chinese-Americans, 583–84, 605, 642–44,
  723–24, 1156
Chinese Exclusion Act, 642–43
Chippewa Indians, 916
Chiricahua Apache Indians, 589
Chivington, J. M., 589
Christian Century, 987
Christian Coalition, 1150–52, 1176
"Christmas bombings," 1090
Churchill, Winston, 895–96, 909, 936–37, 959,
  962, 1015, 1029
  World War II strategies and, 899, 920–21,
  925
  World War II strategies of, 926
Church of Jesus Christ of Latter Day Saints
  (Mormons), 585
Cincinnati, Ohio, 640
Cisneros, Henry, 1084
cities:
  government and policies in, 634–35
  growth of (1860–1920), 631–34
  immigrants in, 635–36, 640–41
  reform efforts in, 657–58
  tenements in, 634
  transportation in, 633–34
  in World War I, 773–74
  in World War II, 918
city-manager plan, 732
Civilian Conservation Corps (CCC), 849, 919
Civil Rights Act (1886), 541–42
Civil Rights Act (1957), 1024, 1051
Civil Rights Act (1964), 1056
Civil Rights Commission, 1024
civil rights movement, 966–68, 1020–25,
  1039–43, 1118
  Black Power and, 1057–60
  boycotts in, 1022–24
  L. B. Johnson and, 1049, 1050–51
  legislative victories of, 1056–57, 1092–93
  nonviolence and, 1022–24
  in World War II, 914–15
  see also African-Americans; segregation
civil service, 669–70
  reform in, 1104
Civil Service Commission, U.S., 669–70, 1086
Civil War, Spanish (1936–1939), 889–90, 892
Civil War, U.S. (1861–1865):
  African-American soldiers in, 547
  military governors in, 533
  veterans of, 673
  see also Reconstruction
Civil Works Administration (CWA), 850
Clark, Bennett Champ, 745–46
Clark Memorandum (1928), 886
Clayton, Henry D., 750
Clayton Antitrust Act (1914), 750–51

Clean Air Act (1970), 1094
Cleaver, Eldridge, 1058
Clemenceau, Georges, 777–78, 782, 783, 784
Clemens, Samuel Langhorne (Mark Twain),
  572, 651, 663
Cleveland, Grover, 642, 683, 689, 690
  foreign policy of, 702
  in presidential elections, 671–72, 675–76,
  688
  Pullman Strike and, 625
  tariff reforms of, 674–75
Cleveland, Ohio, 640, 1058
Clifford, Clark, 1063
Clinton, Bill, 1163–75, 1182
  background of, 1163
  Christian Coalition and, 1151
  crime bill and, 1170
  economic policies of, 1166–67, 1179
  in election of 1992, 1163–64
  foreign policy of, 1167–68, 1170–71
  Haiti and, 1174–75
  health-care plan of, 1166–67, 1168
  Republican Congress and, 1175–76, 1178–81
  Whitewater case and, 1170, 1183
Clinton, Hillary Rodham, 1163, 1169
clothing, in twenties, 802–3
coal industry, 572, 616–17
coal strike (1902), 737
cocaine, 1135
Code of the West, 596
Coehlo, Tony, 1176
Cold War, 948–49, 951, 957–66, 970–79, 982,
  1130, 1160
  Berlin and, 963–64, 1044
  brinksmanship in, 1014–15
  containment policy in, 1014–15
  Cuban missile crisis and, 1044–45
  détente and, 1096–97
  end of, 1136–42
  Indochina and, 1015–20
  occupied Europe and, 958–59
  Red Scares in, 956, 976–78, 1011–13
  U-2 incident and, 1030
colleges and universities:
  affirmative action and, 1177
  African-Americans in, 984
  graduate studies at, 645–47
  Hispanic Studies in, 1081
  moral revolution at (1920s), 802–4
  professors at, 646
  racial segregation and, 1040–41, 1042
  student activism at, 1071–76, 1089
  veterans in, 983
  for women, 646
Colombia, 721, 1135
Colorado, 585
Colored Alliance, 683
Colored Farmers Alliance, 683–84
Columbia University (King's College), 1008,
  1074
Comanche Indians, 587, 916
Command of the Army Act (1867), 543–44, 545
commerce, *see* trade and commerce

Commerce and Labor, U.S. Department of, 737
Commission on Civil Disorders, 1058
commission system, 732
Committee for Industrial Organization (CIO),
    869–70
Committee of European Economic Cooperation
    (CEEC), 962
Committee on Civil Rights, 966
Committee on Public Information, 775
Committee on Un-American Activities, House,
    873, 976
Committee to Defend America by Aiding the
    Allies, 896
Committee to Re-elect the President (CREEP),
    1098
Commodity Credit Corporation (CCC), 852
Common Law, The (Holmes), 649
Common Sense Book of Baby and Child Care,
    The (Spock), 997
Commonwealth of Independent States, 1141
communications:
    radio broadcasting, 1178
    television, 1178
    see also telephone
Communist party, disintegration of, 1140–41
Communists, American, 840–41
    during Great Depression, 846, 876
    Red Scares and, 790–92, 831, 956, 976–78,
        1011–13
    in State Department, 977–78
    Wallace supported by, 969
    see also Cold War; specific countries
Community Action Program, 1052
Community Service Organization (CSO),
    1082
Compromise of 1877, 560, 561
Comstock Lode, 585
Congress, U.S.:
    election mechanisms for, 201, 204; see also
        elections and campaigns
    war powers of, 973–74
    see also House of Representatives, U.S.;
        Senate, U.S.
Congress of Industrial Organizations (CIO),
    870, 956
Congress of Racial Equality (CORE), 1041
Conkling, Roscoe, 667–68, 669
Connor, Eugene "Bull," 1041
conscription, see draft
conservation movement, see environmental
    movement
"Conservative" (Democratic) parties, 554–55
conservatives, cultural, 1149–50
    religious right, 1150–52
constitutional amendments, U.S.:
    1st, 1135
    13th, 538, 562
    14th, 542, 544, 562–63, 579, 808
    15th, 546, 562–63, 577, 808
    16th, 743, 749
    17th, 743
    18th (prohibition), 734, 799–800, 816, 845
    19th (women's suffrage), 752, 805, 816
    20th, 846–47

21st (repeal of prohibition), 848
22nd, 957, 1006
25th, 1100
26th, 1094
Bill of Rights, 1135
proposed Equal Rights Amendment, 805,
    1079–80, 1118, 1162
consumer culture, 985–87
consumer movement, 1076
consumption ethic, 824–26
containment policy, 960–61, 1014–15, 1027,
    1062
Content of Our Character, The (Steele), 1150
Contract Labor Law, (1864), 618, 637
"Contract with America," 1178–80
Contra rebels, 1119, 1125–26
convicts, leasing of, 575
Cooke, Jay, 559
Coolidge, Calvin, 808, 829, 831–32, 833, 1115,
    1116, 1117, 1133, 1179
    in Boston Police Strike, 789–90
    business and, 820, 822–24
    farm policy of, 829, 830
    foreign policy of, 885
    as vice president, 817, 822
coolies, 605
Cooper, Ella, 552
cooperatives, 681–82, 684, 829–30
copper, 585
Coral Sea, battle of the (1942), 908, 930
corn, 829
Cornell, Alonzo, 668
Cornell University, 1074
Corregidor, 908
corruption, 666–78
Corso, Gregory, 1000
Cosmopolitan, 826
Costa Rica, 1127
cotton, 678–79, 829
cotton picker, mechanical, 989
cotton production, in postbellum economy, 573,
    574
Coughlin, Charles E., 860, 867
Council of National Defense, 772
counterculture, in sixties, 1076–77
country music, 854
Country of the Pointed Firs, The (Jewett), 650
courts, see Supreme Court, U.S.
cowboys, 590–92
Cox, Archibald, 1100
Cox, James, 817
Coxey, Jacob S., 688
crack cocaine, 1135
Crack in the Picture Window, The (Keats), 996
Crane, Stephen, 652–53
credit cards, 986
Crédit Mobilier Company, 557–58, 606
Creel, George, 775
crime, organized, 800–801
Croatia, 1173
Crocker, Charles, 605
Croly, Herbert, 747
Cronkite, Walter, 1065
crop lien system, 574

Cuba, 704–5, 710–11, 1121, 1128, 1145
  Castro's rise to power in, 1030–31
  CIA and, 1031, 1043–44
  immigrants from, 1157
  missile crisis and, 1044–45
  see also Spanish-American War
Cuban-Americans, 1084
Cuban exiles, 1084
Cuban Revolutionary party, 705
Cullen, Countee, 807
cultural conservatives, 1149–50
  religious right, 1150–52
culture:
  broader definition of, 810
  in 1990s, 1152–58
currency:
  devaluation of (1933–1934), 849
  European, 838
  greenbacks, 560, 682
  as issue in 1896 elections, 689–92
  Wilson's reforms of, 750
  see also gold; gold standard; silver coinage
Curry, John, 832
Custer, George A., 587–88
Czechoslovakia, 783, 962–63, 1118, 1137
  German occupation of, 890–91
Czolgosz, Leon, 719

Daley, Richard, 1037, 1075, 1098
Dangling Man (Bellows), 998
Daniels, Josephus, 768
Darrow, Clarence, 798–99
Darwin, Charles, 613, 647, 797
  modernism linked to, 810
Daugherty, Harry M., 818, 821
Davis, Henry Winter, 535
Davis, John W., 823, 858
Dawes Severalty Act (1887), 590
D-Day invasion, 925, 926–30
Dean, James, 1001
Dean, John, 1099
death camps, 940–41
Death of a Salesman (Miller), 997–98
Debs, Eugene V., 624–25, 627, 741, 748, 776, 822
debt, national, 1134
  under Bush, 1160
  after Civil War, 556–57
  under Clinton, 1167
debts, Latin American, as excuse for intervention, 722
defense budgets, 1160
deficits, *see* debt, national
DeKlerk, Frederik W., 1138
de Kooning, William, 1000
de la Garza, Elizio "Kika," 1084
Delay, Tom, 1178
DeLeon, Daniel, 626–27
de Lôme, Depuy, 706
Democratic Leadership Council (DLC), 1163
Democratic National Convention (1996), 1182
Democratic party, 1074–75, 1167
  Bourbons and, 575, 576
  conservatives in, 554–55

cultural analysis of, 666, 1114–15
in elections of 1916, 753
in elections of 1992, 1163–64
farmers' influence in, 684–85, 686
Great Depression-era division of, 872–74
in 1980s, 1132
during Republican dominance (1869–1913), 664
Southern resurgence of, 554–55
see also elections and campaigns
Denmark, 771, 894, 965
Denver, Colo., 633
Dependent Pension Act (1890), 676
Dependent Pension bill (1887), 673
Depression, Great, 697, 843, 845–46
  bank failures in, 847
  Hoover's efforts against, 836–39
  literary trends in, 875–76
  renewed economic slump in, 870–72
  social effects of, 864
  unemployment in, 835, 853, 864
  World War II as end of, 909
  see also New Deal
depressions, of 1893, 688–89
desegregation, *see* civil rights movement; segregation
Desert Shield, Operation, 1145
Desert Storm, Operation, 1145–46, 1158
détente, 1096–97
Detroit, Mich., 1058
Dewey, George, 708–9, 713
Dewey, John, 650
Dewey, Thomas E., 934–35, 967–69
Diaz, Porfirio, 759–61
Diem, Ngo Dinh, 1019–20, 1046–47
Dien Bien Phu, battle of (1954), 1017–18
Dies, Martin, 873
Dingley Tariff (1897), 692
disarmament, after World War I, 883–85
disease, Spanish flu, 788
District of Columbia, 1153
  see also Washington, D.C.
Division of Forestry, 740
divorce, 864, 1154
Dixiecrats, 968, 969
Dodd, Chris, 1181
Dole, Bob, 1181–83
  background of, 1181–82
dollar diplomacy, 762
Dominican Republic, 722–23, 886, 1055
  immigrants from, 1157
  U.S. intervention in (1916–1924), 762
Donnelly, Ignatius, 687
Douglass, Frederick, 533, 535–36
draft:
  in Vietnam War, 1088, 1104
  in World War I, 772
draft-card burning, 1074
Dreiser, Theodore, 635, 653
drug abuse, 1134–35
drugs, 1076–77, 1128, 1142
Duarte, José Napoleón, 1119, 1128
Dubinksy, David, 869
Du Bois, W.E.B., 580–82, 808

"due process," judicial interpretations of, 865
Dukakis, Michael, 1131–32
Duke, James Buchanan "Buck," 572–73
Duke, Washington, 572
Dulles, Allen, 1014
Dulles, John Foster, 1010, 1013–15, 1025–26, 1027, 1062
Durham, N.C., 633
  as tobacco center, 572
Durkin, Martin, 1009
Dust Bowl, 852–55, 876–77
  migrants of, 852–55
Duvalier, Jean-Claude "Baby Doc," 1125
Dylan, Bob, 1001, 1075
dynamic conservatism, 1009
Dynamic Sociology (Ward), 648

Earhart, Amelia, 826–27
Eastern European countries, 1137, 1139
East Indies, Dutch, 902
Eastland, James, 1022
East Village (New York City), 1076
Economic Opportunity Bill (1964), 1052
Economic Recovery Tax Act (1981), 1116
economics, in social criticism, 653–54
economy:
  Bush and, 1159–60
  in 1920, 828–29, 833–35
  in 1970s, 1094–95, 1106–7
  in 1980s, 1153
  post-Civil War, 602–28
  post–World War II growth in, 981–83
  Reagan and, 1115–16, 1128–30
  World War I demobilization and, 788–90
  World War II management of, 910–12
  see also agriculture; Bank of the United
    States; business; debt, national;
    Depression, Great; depressions; industry;
    manufacturing; Panics; recessions; trade
    and commerce
Edison, Thomas Alva, 607–9
Edison Electric Illuminating Company, 608
education:
  of African-Americans, 548
  federal aid to, 1054
  in late 1800s, 644–47
  prayer and, 1151
  professionalism and, 646–47
  progressive, 650
  public, 552, 644–46, 1136
  segregation in, 1021–22, 1024, 1040–41,
    1042–43, 1092–93
  in South, 577
  of women, 646, 1079, 1136, 1154
  see also colleges and universities
Education, U.S. Department of, 1104
efficiency, 731–32
Egypt, 898, 1025, 1029, 1097, 1102–3, 1105–6
  in Suez crisis, 1026–27, 1029
Ehrlichman, John, 1092, 1099
Einstein, Albert, 809, 810, 942
Eisenhower, Dwight D., 840, 966, 975, 978,
    1002
  background of, 1006, 1008–9

cabinet of, 1008–10
civil rights movement and, 1020, 1022,
    1032
corruption under, 1028–29
domestic policy of, 1009–10, 1031–32
farewell address of, 1031
foreign policy of, 1013–15, 1025–31
Korean War and, 1005, 1006, 1010–11
Middle East policy of, 1025–27, 1029
on military-industrial complex, 1031
in presidential elections, 1006–8, 1024–25
religion promoted by, 993–94
security program of, 1013
Soviet relations and, 1029–30
Vietnam and, 1017–20, 1046, 1062
in World War II, 921, 925, 926–28, 935–36
Eisenhower Doctrine, 1029
Elbe River, 939
elections and campaigns:
  of 1866, 543
  of 1868, 555–56
  of 1872, 559
  of 1874, 560
  of 1876, 667
  of 1880, 668–69
  of 1884, 670–72
  of 1888, 675–76
  of 1890, 677
  of 1892, 687–88
  of 1894, 688
  of 1896, 689–92
  of 1898, 717
  of 1900, 717–18, 729
  of 1904, 738–39
  of 1908, 740–41
  of 1912, 743, 745–49, 756
  of 1914, 753
  of 1916, 753, 768–69
  of 1918, 781–82
  of 1920, 816–17
  of 1924, 823–24
  of 1928, 832–33
  of 1930, 837
  of 1932, 843–46
  of 1934, 858
  of 1936, 865–68
  of 1938, 873–74
  of 1940, 896–97
  of 1942, 919–20
  of 1944, 934–35
  of 1946, 955–56
  of 1948, 966, 967–70
  of 1952, 1006–8
  of 1956, 1024–25
  of 1958, 1029
  of 1960, 1035–38, 1050–51
  of 1964, 1052–53, 1112
  of 1968, 1066–69, 1074–75
  of 1972, 1090, 1097–98
  of 1976, 1103–4
  of 1980, 1111–15
  of 1982, 1117
  of 1984, 1122–23, 1132
  of 1986, 1125

of 1988, 1131–32
of 1992, 949
of 1994, 1151–52, 1175–76
of 1996, 1181–83
decided in House of Representatives, 561
funding of, 1101
popular vs. electoral vote in, 561–62, 675–76
senatorial popular vote instituted in, 731
see also suffrage; women's suffrage movement
electricity, 607–8
electrification, 857–58
Elephant Butte Dam, 593
elevators, 633
Eliot, T. S., 811
Elkins Act (1903), 737
Ellis, Samuel, 638
Ellis Island, 637–40, 643
Ellison, Ralph, 851, 998
Ellsberg, Daniel, 1089
El Salvador, 1119, 1128
embargo, against Japan, 901, 902
Emergency Banking Relief Act (1933), 847
Emergency Immigration Act (1921), 795
Employment Service, U.S., 775
Energy, U.S. Department of, 1104
energy bill (1978), 1104–5
energy crisis, 1095
Enforcement Acts (1870–1871), 554
England, *see* Great Britain
English-Americans, 640
English language, new nativism and, 1157–58
Enola Gay, 943
Enterprise, 908
environment, 582–83, 1094
environmental movement, 1076, 1104–5, 1117
   T. Roosevelt's concern for, 740
Environmental Protection Agency (EPA), 1094, 1117
Equal Employment Opportunity Commission (EEOC), 1118, 1161
Equal Rights Amendment (ERA), 805, 1079–80, 1113, 1118, 1162
Erie Railroad, 606, 614
Ervin, Samuel J., Jr., 1098
Espionage Act (1917), 776
Estonia, 1140
Ethiopia, 889, 892
European Community, 949
European immigrants, 1156
European Recovery Program, 962
Evers, Medgar, 1042
evolution, bans on teaching of, 797–99
executive branch, *see* president, presidency
executive privilege, 1101
Exodusters, 684
Explorer I, 1028
Export Control Act (1940), 900

Fair Deal, 966–67, 970
Fair Employment Practices Committee (FEPC), 953
Fair Labor Standards Act (1938), 872–73
Fall, Albert B., 818, 820–21

Falwell, Jerry, 1112, 1150
family unit, traditional, 1154
Farewell to Arms, A (Hemingway), 813
farm bloc, 830
Farm Credit Administration (FCA), 848
farmers:
   currency issues and, 676–77, 679–80, 682
   economic hardships of (1870–1898), 678–79
   in Granger movement, 681–83
   in Great Depression, 839
   loans for, 753–54
   problems of, 677
   Progressive movement and, 729, 751–52
   see also agriculture
Farmers' Alliance, 682–83, 852
Farm Security Administration (FSA), 872
Farm Tenant Act (1937), 872, 873
Farm Workers Association, 1083
Farouk, king of Egypt, 1025
Faubus, Orval, 1024
Faulkner, William, 855, 878–79
Federal Art Project, 851
federal budget:
   defense budget and, 1160
   see also debt, national
Federal Bureau of Investigation (FBI), 993, 1048, 1058, 1165–66
Federal Bureau of Labor Statistics, 621
Federal Communications Commission, 826
federal deficit, 1102–3
Federal Deposit Insurance Corporation (FDIC), 849, 1134
Federal Election Campaign Act (1972), 1094
Federal Emergency Relief Administration (FERA), 850
Federal Farm Loan Act (1916), 753
Federal Highway Act (1956), 1010
Federal Highways Act (1916), 754
Federal Home Loan Bank Act (1932), 838
Federal Housing Administration, 988
Federal Radio Commission, 826
Federal Reserve Act (1913), 750, 752
Federal Reserve System, 820, 838
Federal Securities Act (1933), 849
Federal Theatre Project, 851
Federal Trade Commission, 750, 820, 849
Federal Writers' Project, 851, 877
Feminine Mystique, The (Friedan), 1078
feminism, 1077–80, 1113, 1118, 1161–62
   Equal Rights Amendment and, 1162
   see also women's rights movement
Fence-Cutters' War, 592
Ferguson, Mariam "Ma," 797–98
Ferraro, Geraldine, 1122
fifties, *see* postwar era
Finland, 960
fireside chats, 847, 858, 898
Fish, Hamilton, 556
Fisk, Jim, 557
Fiske, John, 703–4
Fitzgerald, F. Scott, 794, 802, 804, 812, 876
Fitzgerald, Zelda, 812

Five-Power Naval Treaty (1921), 884, 889
Fleming, Julius J., 546–47
Florida, 1142
   immigrants in, 1157
   population growth of, 1153
   real-estate boom in, 834
Flynn, Elizabeth Gurley, 628
Foch, Ferdinand, 784
folk art, 879–80
Food Administration, 773, 828
Foraker Act (1900), 715
Foran Act (1885), 621
Ford, Gerald R., 1113, 1182
   foreign affairs and, 1102–3
   Nixon pardoned by, 1101, 1102
   in presidential elections, 1103
   veto record of, 1102
Ford, Henry, 828
Ford Motor Company, 828
Fordney-McCumber Tariff (1922), 819
Foreign Affairs, 961
Forest Reserve Act (1891), 740
Formosa, *see* China, Nationalist; Taiwan
Fort Riley, 788
Fortune, 879, 981
Four-Power Treaty (1921), 885
Fourteen Points, 779–80, 899
Fox Indians, 916
France, 884–85, 962, 963, 971, 1018, 1120
   Imperial China and, 716
   in Indochina, 1016–18
   in Moroccan crisis (1905–1906), 724
   in NATO, 965
   in Persian Gulf War, 1146
   in Revolutionary War, 637–38
   in Suez War, 1026–27
   Vichy government in, 900, 921
   in World War I, 696–97, 763, 771, 777–78,
      782, 783, 784
   World War I debt of, 883
   in World War II, 889, 893, 894–95, 900, 921,
      925–26, 937
Franco, Francisco, 889–90
Frankfurter, Felix, 640, 860
Franz Ferdinand, archduke of Austria, 762
Freedmen's Bureau, 548
Freedmen's Bureau Bill (1866), 542
Freedom of Information Act (1966), 1101
Free Speech Movement (FSM), 1073
Freud, Sigmund, 802
Frick, Henry Clay, 623, 739
Friedan, Betty, 1078–79, 1161
From Here to Eternity (Jones), 998
frontier:
   closing of, 597–98
   see also Manifest Destiny; West, New; *specific*
      territories
Frost, Robert, 1038
Fuel Administration, 773
Fulbright, J. William, 1063
fundamentalism, 797–99, 1112, 1150

Galbraith, John K., 995
Galveston, Tex., 640, 732

Gandhi, Mohandas K., 1022
Garfield, James A., 562
   assassination of, 669
   presidency of, 668–69
Garner, John Nance, 844, 893
Garvey, Marcus, 807–8, 1058
gas production, 1104
Gates, John W. "Bet-a-Million," 591–92
Gay Liberation Front, 1085
Gay rights, 1085–86
gays and lesbians, in military, 1164
Gaza Strip, 1171–72
General Accounting Office, 1134
General Federation of Women's Clubs, 659–60
General Intelligence Division, 791
General Motors, 870
Geneva Accords (1954), 1018–20, 1046
Geneva Summit (1985), 1124–25
"Gentleman's Agreement" (1907), 724
George, Henry, 653–54
Georgia, 553, 578
German-Americans, 584, 621, 637, 785, 916
German Democratic Republic (East Germany),
   964, 1014, 1029–30, 1044, 1137, 1138
German Federal Republic (West Germany),
   964, 965, 1095, 1137, 1138
German scholarship, 646, 649
Germany, Imperial:
   health care in, 1168
   Imperial China and, 716
   in Moroccan crisis (1905–1906), 724
   Pacific possessions of, 701
   in World War I, 763–64, 765–67, 769–71,
      777–80, 783–84, 787, 789
   see also World War I
Germany, Nazi:
   collapse of, 939
   Hitler's rise to power in, 888
   in prelude to World War II, 889–91
   see also World War II
Germany, occupied, governance of, 937, 959,
   963–64
Germany, Weimar, 780, 883
Geronimo, chief of Chiricahua Apaches, 589
gerrymandering, 1176–77
ghettos, 641, 1136
GI Bill of Rights (1944), 954, 983–85
Gideon v. Wainwright, 1043
Gilbert Islands, 908, 931–32
Gilded Age, The (Twain and Warner), 663
Gingrich, Newt, 1176, 1178–79
Ginsberg, Allen, 1000–1001
Ginsburg, Ruth Bader, 1177
Gladden, Washington, 656
glasnost (openness), 1136
Glaspie, April, 1144
Glass-Steagall Act (1932), 838
Glass-Steagall Banking Act (1933), 849
Glidden, Joseph, 591–92
gold, 585, 692
gold rushes, 585, 632–33, 692
gold standard, 688–92, 738, 838, 849
Goldwater, Barry, 1009, 1052–53, 1062,
   1112

Gompers, Samuel, 618, 714, 751, 790
    union philosophy and tactics of, 621–22
Good Neighbor policy, 886–87
Gorbachev, Mikhail, 1124, 1125, 1130
    failed political/military coup against, 1139–40
    Soviet Union dissolution and, 1136–42
Gore, Albert, Jr., 1164, 1183
Gorky, Arshile, 1000
"Gospel of Wealth, The" (Carnegie), 613
Gottlieb, Adolph, 1000
Gould, Jay, 557, 606–7, 620, 674
government:
    growth of, in Progressive era, 737–38
    limited role for, 647–48, 668, 672
    New Deal's transformation of, 874–75
    Social Darwinists' view of, 647–48
    see also reform movements
Government Operations Committee, 1012
Grady, Henry W., 570
Grand Army of the Republic, 673
Grand Canyon, 740
grandfather clause, 578, 808
Granger Movement, 681–82, 684–85
Grant, Ulysses S., 818
    economic policy of, 556–57, 560
    in presidential elections, 555–56, 668
    in Reconstruction, 544, 545
    scandals and corruption under, 556–59, 560
Grapes of Wrath, The (Steinbeck), 852, 876–77
Gray, L. Patrick, 1099
Great Britain, 655, 699, 700–701, 961, 963,
    1018
    in arms control negotiations, 884–85
    health care in, 1168–70, 1180
    immigrants from, 640
    Imperial China and, 716
    in Middle East, 1025–27
    in NATO, 965
    Panama Canal and, 721
    in Persian Gulf War, 1145–46
    U.S. missiles in, 1045
    in World War I, 763, 764, 765–67, 771, 778,
        782–83, 784, 789
    World War I debt of, 883
    in World War II, 922–24
    see also World War I; World War II
Great Compression, 1159–60
Great Depression, *see* Depression, Great
Great Gatsby, The (Fitzgerald), 812
Great Migration, 806, 989–90
Great Northern railroad, 736, 774
Great Plains, 582, 586
Great Railroad Strike (1877), 617–18, 668
Great Society program, 1052–54, 1055, 1061,
    1067, 1094
Greece, 896, 898, 961, 965
    in World War I, 779
Greek-Americans, 640–41
Greeley, Horace, 559
Green, John Ruffin, 572
Green, William, 869
Greenback party, 682
Greenberg, Stanley, 1179
Greenwich Village (New York City), 1000

Grenada, invasion of (1983), 1121–22
Grunwald, Mandy, 1179
Guadalcanal, battle of (1942), 931
Guam, 904, 908
Guantanamo Bay, U.S. naval base at, 716
Guatemala, 1014, 1119
Guinn v. United States, 808
Guiteau, Charles, 669
Gulf War, *see* Persian Gulf War

Haber, Al, 1072
Haight-Ashbury, San Francisco, 1076
Haiti, 1125
    Clinton policy on, 1174–75
    U.S. intervention in (1915–1934), 762,
        886–87
Haitian-Americans, 1155
Haldeman, H. R., 1092, 1099
Half-Breeds, 667
Halpin, Maria, 671–72
Hamilton, Alexander, 1116
Hanna, Mark, 691, 692, 712, 719
Hardin, John Wesley, 597
Harding, Warren G., 787, 829, 1116, 1117
    appointments of, 818–20
    big business and, 818–20
    corruption and, 820–22
    death of, 821–22
    foreign policy of, 882–83, 884
    "Ohio Gang" of, 818, 820
    in presidential election, 816–17
    shortcoming of, 816–17, 818, 821–22
Harlem Renaissance, 807
Harlem Shadows (McKay), 807
Harper's Monthly, 652
Harriman, E. H., 738
Harrington, Michael, 1051
Harris, Joel Chandler, 650
Harrison, Benjamin, 675–78, 823
    foreign policy under, 702
    in presidential elections, 675, 688
Harvard College (University), 1074
Haugen, Gilbert N., 830
Hawaii, 1029, 1157
    annexation of, 701–2, 713
    in World War II, 901–5, 908
Hawley-Smoot Tariff (1930), 834, 837
Hay, John, 711, 716–17, 721–22
Hayden, Tom, 1072–73, 1074, 1075
Hayes, Lucy, 667
Hayes, Rutherford B., 667–68
    background of, 667
    on Indian wars, 589
    in presidential elections, 560–62
Hay-Herrán Treaty (1903), 721
Haymarket Affair (1886), 620–21
Hay-Pauncefote Treaty (1901), 721
Haywood, William D. "Big Bill," 627–28
Head Start, 1052
health care:
    Clinton plan for, 1166–67, 1168–70, 1180
    insurance and, 1168–70, 1180
health insurance, 1053
Hearst, William Randolph, 705, 706, 863

Heinze, Hans, 928
Heisenberg, Werner, 809
Heller, Joseph, 998
Hell's Angels, 1077
Hemingway, Ernest, 651, 812–13
Hepburn, Peter, 739
Hepburn Act (1906), 739
heroin, 1135
Herrán, Thomas, 721
Hickock, James Butler "Wild Bill," 596
Higher Education Act (1965), 1057
highways, 988, 1010
Highway Safety Act (1966), 1055–56
Hill, Anita, 1161–62
Hill, Joe, 628
Hillman, Sidney, 868
hippies, 1076
Hirohito, emperor of Japan, 902, 940, 944
Hiroshima, nuclear bombing of (1945), 942–43
Hispanic-Americans, 583, 796, 919, 1055,
    1080–84, 1104, 1134, 1136, 1155–57,
    1176–77
Hiss, Alger, 976
history, study of, 649
Hitler, Adolf, 874
    assassination attempt on, 930
    death of, 939
    in rise to power, 888
    see also World War II
Ho Chi Minh, 971, 1016–17, 1019, 1063–64
Ho Chi Minh Trail, 1046, 1062
Hoffman, Abbie, 1074
Holmes, E. P., 547
Holmes, Oliver Wendell, Jr., 649, 776–77, 845
Holocaust, 940
Home Owner's Loan Act (1933), 848
Home Owner's Loan Corporation (HOLC),
    848–49
Homestead Act (1862), 593, 594
Homestead Steel Strike (1892), 623
Homestead Works, 623
homosexuals, in military, 1164
Honduras, 1119
Hong Kong, 904, 908, 1157
Hoover, Herbert, 773, 818, 820, 821, 823,
    828–29, 1102, 1179
    foreign policy of, 883, 886, 887
    Great Depression and, 835–39
    in presidential elections, 832–33, 844–45
Hoover, J. Edgar, 791, 993
Hoover (Boulder) Dam, 593
Hope, Bob, 640
Hopkins, Harry L., 850, 871
Hopkins, Mark, 605
Hopper, Edward, 998
Hopwood v. Texas, 1177
Hornet, 909
House, Edward M., 748, 767, 779
House Beautiful, 992
House of Representatives, U.S.:
    A. Johnson impeached by, 545–46
    Committee on Un-American Activities of,
        873, 976
    presidential elections decided by, 561

housing, 641–42, 985
    federal aid for, 1054
Housing Act (1961), 1039
Housing and Urban Development, U.S.
    Department of, 1054
Housing and Urban Development Act (1965),
    1054
Housing Authority, U.S., 872
Houston, Tex., 633
Howard University, 833
Howe, Julia Ward, 659
Howells, William Dean, 651–52
Howl (Ginsberg), 1001
Hué, 1064
Huerta, Victoriano, 759–60
Hughes, Charles Evans, 732, 768–69, 818, 884
Hughes, Langston, 807
Hull, Cordell, 893, 901, 902
Hull House, 658
Humphrey, Hubert H., 967, 1037, 1039
    in presidential elections, 1052, 1066–68,
        1074
Humphreys, Robert M., 683
Hungarian-Americans, 640–41
Hungary, 787, 898, 960, 1014, 1118, 1137
    uprising in (1956), 1027
Huntington, Collis P., 605
Hurston, Zora Neal, 807
Hussein, Saddam, 1143–46, 1158–59
hydroelectric power, 573
hydrogen bomb, 971–72, 1015

Iceland, 899, 965
Iceland Summit (1986), 1125
Ickes, Harold L., 855, 859, 871
Idaho, 676
Illinois, 1157
"I Love Lucy," 985
immigrants:
    from 1860 to 1910, 631–32
    in 1960s, 1054–55
    in 1980s and 1990s, 1155–58
    "Americanizing" of, 644
    illegal, 1081, 1157
    negative perception of, 666
    in New West, 583–85
    see also specific ethnic groups
immigration:
    through Angel Island, 642–44
    through Ellis Island, 637–40, 643
    in late 1800s, 635–44
    new ethnic sources of, 637, 1155–58
    restrictions on, 642–44, 792, 795–96
    see also nativism
Immigration Act (1965), 1054–55
Immigration Service, 1156
impeachment, 1100
imperialism:
    naval power in, 703
    Open Door Policy and, 716–17, 723, 724,
        885
    opposition to, 713
    in Pacific, 699–702
    philosophical justifications for, 703–4

as quest for markets, 711–12, 715
see also Spanish-American War
income tax, 768, 819, 834
in New Deal, 862–63
India, 1015
Indian Peace Commission, 587
Indians, American, 1155
in Native American movement, 1084–85
reservation policy toward, 587, 1084–85
in World War II, 915–16
see also specific tribes
Indian wars, in Great Plains, 586–90
Indochina, French, 900, 901
Indochina War (1946–1954), 971, 1015–20
see also Vietnam War
Industrial Revolution, 566–67, 632
Industrial Workers of the World (IWW;
Wobblies), 627–28, 776
industry:
in postbellum South, 566–67
post-World War I reconversion of, 789
see also manufacturing; *specific industries*
inflation:
in 1970s, 1094–95, 1102–3, 1106–7
silver coinage and, 679–80, 692
after World War II, 955
Influence of Sea Power on History, 703
In re Debs (1894), 625–26
instrumentalism, 650
insurance, medical, 1168–70, 1180
intercontinental ballistic missiles (ICBMs),
1028, 1097, 1142
intermediate range ballistic missiles (IRBMs),
1028
intermediate range nuclear forces (INF) treaty
(1987), 1130
International Court of Justice, 958
International Harvester, 620–21
International Ladies Garment Workers, 869
Interstate Commerce Act (1887), 673–74
Interstate Commerce Commission (ICC),
673–74, 733, 739, 752, 820
Invisible Man (Ellison), 998
Iowa, 582, 1153
Iran:
CIA activities in, 1014
hostage crisis in (1979–1981), 1107–8, 1143
immigrants from, 1157
in Persian Gulf War, 1144
in pro-Western pacts, 1025
Iran-Contra affair, 1125–27
Iran-Iraq war, 1120, 1143
Iraq, 1025, 1029, 1120
in Persian Gulf War, 1143–46, 1158–59
Ireland, Patricia, 1181
Irish-Americans, 640, 672, 785
iron curtain, 1029
Ishii, Viscount Kikujiro, 884
isolationism, 882–87
war-debt tangle and, 883
isolationism, World War I participation and,
889, 893–94
Israel, 965–66, 1097, 1102–3, 1105–6, 1125,
1130

Lebanon invaded by (1982), 1120–21
Palestinian accord with, 1171–72
in Persian Gulf War, 1145–46
in Suez War, 1027
Italian-Americans, 640–41, 785, 916
Italy, 783, 962, 965, 1045, 1120
Ethiopia invaded by (1934), 889, 892
Mussolini's rise to power in, 888–89
treaties with, 884
in World War I, 763, 777, 779, 782–83
in World War II, 892, 898, 921, 924–25, 960
Iwo Jima, battle of (1945), 941

Jackson, Andrew:
Indian policy of, 586
Truman compared with, 952
Jackson, Frankie "Half Pint," 812
Jackson, Helen Hunt, 589
Jackson, Jesse, 1131, 1177, 1181
Jackson, "Shoeless Joe," 789
Jackson State College, 1089
Jamaica, immigrants from, 1157
James, Henry, 631, 652
James, William, 649–50, 652, 714, 1105
Japan, 783, 1095
Imperial China and, 716, 717
pre-World War II treaties with, 724, 884–85
Russian war with (1904–1905), 723–24
U.S. immigration restrictions and, 724
in World War I, 763
in World War II, 900–905, 920, 925–26,
930–34, 936, 960, 971, 972, 1016
see also World War II
Japanese-Americans, 643, 724, 918
wartime internment of, 916–17
Java, 908
Jaworski, Leon, 1100
jazz, 802, 812
jazz age, *see* roaring twenties
Jericho, 1171
Jewett, Sarah Orne, 650
Jewish immigrants, 637
Jews, 641
Israel and, 965–66
Nazi persecution of, 889, 940–41
Jim Crow system, 578–79, 1023, 1040
Job Corps, 1052
Johns Hopkins University, 1062
Johnson, Andrew, 555, 700, 1098
background of, 537
congressional conflicts with, 540–45
impeachment and trial of, 545–46
Reconstruction plan of, 537–38
Johnson, Hiram, 732
Johnson, Hugh S., 855
Johnson, James Weldon, 807
Johnson, Lyndon B., 948, 1037, 1074, 1168,
1170
American Indian policy of, 1084
background of, 851, 1049–50
civil rights and, 1024, 1049, 1050–51,
1056–57, 1092
inauguration of, 1047–49
in presidential elections, 1052–53, 1066–67

Johnson, Lyndon B. (*continued*)
  presidential style of, 1049, 1051
  tax program of, 1051–52
  Vietnam War and, 1060–61, 1062–66
  war on poverty of, 1051–52, 1053–54
Johnson, Sam, 1049–50
Johnson Debt Default Act (1934), 883, 898
Joint Chiefs of Staff, 957, 975, 1015, 1044, 1046
Joint Committee on Reconstruction, 540, 542
Jolson, Al, 640
Jones, James, 998
Jordan, 1025, 1171
Joseph, chief of Nez Perce, 588
journalism, yellow, 705, 706
J. Pierpont Morgan and Company, 614
judiciary, *see* Supreme Court, U.S.
Julian, George W., 540
Jungle, The (Sinclair), 739

Kamikaze pilots, 934, 941
Kansas, 582, 584, 683–85
Kansas City, Mo., 633
Kansas Pacific Railroad, 591
Kassebaum, Nancy, 1180
Keating-Owen Child Labor Act (1916), 755
Keats, John, 996
Kelley, Florence, 734
Kelley, Oliver H., 681
Kellogg, Frank B., 885
Kellogg-Briand Pact (1928), 885–86, 887
Kemp, Jack, 1183
Kennan, George F., 960–61, 962, 1027, 1063
Kennedy, Anthony, 1177
Kennedy, Edward M., 1113, 1181
Kennedy, Jacqueline, 1048
Kennedy, John F., 1051, 1054, 1163
  assassination of, 1047–48
  background of, 1036–37
  Bay of Pigs invasion and, 1031, 1043–44
  cabinet of, 1038
  civil rights movement and, 1039–43
  Cuban missile crisis and, 1044–45
  domestic programs of, 1039, 1043
  inauguration of, 1038–39
  in presidential elections, 1036–38
  Vietnam and, 1046–47, 1062
Kennedy, Robert F., 1038, 1039, 1041, 1043, 1055, 1065, 1083
  assassination of, 1066
Kent State University, 1089
Kerouac, Jack, 1000–1001, 1072
Kerr, Clark, 1073
Keystone Studios, 825
Khmer Rouge, 1103
Khomeini, Ayatollah Ruhollah, 1107–8
Khrushchev, Nikita, 1027, 1029–30, 1044–45
King, Martin Luther, Jr., 1041–43, 1056–57, 1058, 1060, 1081, 1131
  assassination of, 1066
  Montgomery bus boycott led by, 1022–24, 1040
Kiowa Indians, 587

Kissinger, Henry, 1092, 1096, 1097, 1102
  Vietnam and, 1087, 1088, 1090
Kleindienst, Richard, 1099
Knights of Labor, 618–20, 621, 622
Konoye, Fumimaro, 901, 902
Korea, 926, 1055
  division of, 972
  Russo-Japanese rivalry over, 723–24
Korean-Americans, 724, 1157
Korean War, 972–76, 982, 1005, 1006, 1017
  armistice in, 1010–11
Koresh, David (Vernon Howell), 1165–66
Krutch, Joseph Wood, 995
Ku Klux Klan (KKK), 553–54, 752, 1166
  revived after World War I, 796–97
Kuomintang, 887, 970
Kurile Islands, 939
Kuwait, 1143–46
Kwantung Army, 887
Kyoto, 942

labor:
  disorganization of, 616–17
  Great Railroad Strike and, 617–18, 668
  immigrant, 615–16, 618, 636–37, 1081–82
  in 1990s, 1159
  ten- and eight-hour days won by, 618, 734, 755
  women and, 912–14
  working conditions of, 615–16, 733–34
  in World War II, 1080
  see also child labor
labor laws:
  in Great Depression, 856, 869–70
  after World War II, 956, 1028–29
labor unions, 616–28, 751–52
  coal strike and (1902), 737
  decline of, under Reagan, 1118
  emergence of, 618–22
  Great Depression-era growth of, 869–70
  migratory workers in, 1082–83
  NAFTA opposed by, 1168
  secrecy in, 618–19
  socialism and, 626–28
  violence attributed to, 620–21, 623–25
  women in, 774–75
  World War I demobilization and, 775, 789–90, 792, 830–32
  World War I expansion of, 775
  after World War II, 955–56
  World War II restrictions on, 919–20
La Follette, Robert M. "Fighting Bob," 732, 743, 768, 824, 1068
Lake, Anthony, 1171
Landon, Alfred M., 867
land policies:
  in New West, 569–70
  range wars and, 592–93
  during Reconstruction, 535–36, 541
Lanham Act, 918
Lansing, Robert, 767, 884
Lansing-Ishii Agreement (1917), 884
Laos, 1016, 1018, 1091, 1157

Lathrop, Julia, 658
Latin America, 722, 1157
    Alliance for Progress programs for, 1039
    Good Neighbor policy and, 886–87
    Monroe Doctrine and, *see* Monroe Doctrine
    Reagan's policy in, 1119, 1125–28
    see also specific countries
Latin immigrants, 637, 642
Lattimore, Owen, 977
Latvia, 1140
Lazarus, Emma, 638
League of Nations, 782–83, 882–83, 887,
    889
Leary, Timothy, 1076
Lease, Mary Elizabeth, 685–86
Leaves of Grass (Whitman), 1001
Lebanon, 1025, 1029, 1120–21
LeMay, Curtis, 1068
Lemke, William, 867
Lend-Lease Bill (1941), 898
Lenin, V. I., 626, 777, 781, 790, 1074, 1140
Leningrad, 899
Leo XIII, Pope, 657
lesbians and gays, 1085–86
    in military, 1164
"Letter from a Birmingham Jail" (King), 1041
Levitt, William, 987–88
Lewis, John L., 869, 920
Lewis, Sinclair, 801–2, 825
Lexington, 908
Leyte Gulf, battle of (1944), 934
Liberty Loan Act (1917), 771–72
Libya, 898, 921, 1125
licensing laws, 646–47
Lie Down in Darkness (Styron), 998
Life, 991–92
Life on the Mississippi (Twain), 651
light bulb, 608
Light in August (Faulkner), 879
Liliuokalani, queen of Hawaii, 701–2
Lincoln, Abraham, 538
    assassination of, 537
    Reconstruction policy of, 534–36
Lindbergh, Charles A., Jr., 826–27
literature:
    in Great Depression, 875–76
    in late 1800s, 650–54
    local color movement in, 650–52
    modernist, 810–13, 1114–18
    naturalism in, 652–53
    in postwar era (1945–60), 997–98,
        1000–1002
    realism in, 652
    southern, 877–79
Lithuania, 640, 1140
Little Big Horn River, battle of (1874), 587–
    88
Little Rock, Ark., 1024
livestock, *see* cattle industry
Lloyd, Henry Demarest, 654, 730
Lloyd George, David, 782, 784
local colorists, 650–52
Lochner v. New York, 734

Lodge, Henry Cabot, 642, 703, 783, 785–86,
    820, 1047
    on elective courses, 646
London, Jack, 653
Lonely Crowd, The (Riesman), 996–97
Long, Huey P., Jr., 859, 860, 867
Longstreet, James A., 551
Longview, Tex., 790
Longworth, Alice Roosevelt, 818
Look Homeward, Angel (Wolfe), 878–79
Los Alamos, N.Mex., 942
Los Angeles, Calif., 632, 854, 918, 919, 1157
    riots in (1965), 1057–58
Los Angeles Times, 628
lost generation, 794
Louisiana, racial segregation in, 579
"Love Song of J. Alfred Prufrock, The" (Eliot),
    811
Lowell, James Russell, 532–33
LSD, 1076
Lublin Committee, 938
Ludendorff, Erich, 780
lumber industry, 573
Lusitania, 767–68
Luxembourg, 935, 965
Lynch, John R., 550
lynchings, 579, 808

MacArthur, Douglas:
    bonus marchers dispersed by, 840
    in Korean War, 972, 973–75
    in World War II, 901, 908, 931, 934, 944
McAuliffe, Anthony C., 935
McCain, John, 1174
McCarran Internal Security Act (1950), 978
McCarthy, Eugene, 1065, 1066, 1068, 1074
McCarthy, Joseph R., 977–78, 1011–13
McClure's Magazine, 730
McCord, James W., 1098
McCoy, Joseph G., 591
McFarlane, Robert, 1126
McGovern, George S., 1098, 1132
machine politics, 664
McKay, Claude, 807
McKinley, William, 566–67, 677, 720, 818
    assassination of, 719
    in presidential elections, 689–92, 718–19
    Spanish-American War and, 705–8, 709,
        711–13, 715
McKinley Tariff (1890), 676–77, 701
McNamara, Robert, 1038, 1063
McNary, Charles L., 830
McNary-Haugen bill, 830, 832
McTeague (Norris), 652
Macune, Charles W., 683
McVeigh, Timothy, 1166
Madero, Francisco I., 759
Mafia, 1047, 1048
Maggie: A Girl of the Streets (Crane), 652–53
Maginot Line, 895
Mahan, Alfred Thayer, 703
Mailer, Norman, 998
Maine, 1085

Maine, 706
Main Street (Lewis), 801–2
Malay Peninsula, 904
Malaysia, 1016
Malay States, 1016
Malcolm X, 1059–60
Manchuria, 887–88, 939
    Russian interests in, 717, 724
Manchuria Incident (1932), 887
Mandela, Nelson, 1138
Manhattan Project, 942
Manifest Destiny, 582, 700, 703–4
    see also imperialism
Manila Bay, capture of (1898), 708–9
manufacturing, 703, 1153
    technological advances in, 607–8
    see also industry; tariffs; textile manufacturing
Mao Tse-tung, 971, 1096
March on Washington (1963), 1042–43, 1057
Marco Polo Bridge, battle at (1937), 890, 893
Marcos, Ferdinand, 1125
Mariana Islands, 933–34
Marne, second battle of the (1918), 778
marriage:
    among African-Americans, 548
    divorce and, 864
Marshall, George C., 920, 961–63, 978
Marshall, Thurgood, 1160
Marshall Plan, 961–62
Marx, Karl, 810
Massachusetts, 1085
Meany, George, 986
Meat Inspection Act (1906), 739
meat-packing industry, regulation of, 739
    see also cattle industry
Medicaid, 1054, 1168, 1169, 1180
Medicare, 1054, 1056, 1168, 1180
Medicine Creek Lodge, conference at (1867), 587
Medicine Crow, Joseph, 916
Meese, Edwin, 1128
Mellon, Andrew W., 818–19, 820, 833, 834, 836, 1116
Memphis, Tenn., 542
Mencken, H. L., 798, 822, 878
Menu, Operation, 1088
Meredith, James H., 1041
Meuse-Argonne offensive (1918), 778–79
Mexican-Americans, 583–84, 592, 773, 852–53, 1055, 1081–82, 1084, 1155–56
Mexico:
    insurrection in (1911–1917), 759–62
    NAFTA with, 1167–68
    seasonal worker agreement with, 919
    U.S. economic interests in, 886
Michigan, University of, 1072
Micronesia, 884
Middle East, 1171–72
    Carter's policy in, 1104–6, 1107–8
    Eisenhower's policy in, 1025–27, 1029
    Kissinger's shuttle diplomacy in, 1097
    Persian Gulf War in, 1143–46
    Reagan's Marine deployment in, 1119
Middle East Treaty Organization (METO), 1025

Midway, 904, 930
    battle of (1942), 908–9
migratory workers, 1081–83
Military Reconstruction Act (1867), 543–44
militias, 1167
Miller, Arthur, 997–98
Milwaukee, Wis., 640
minimum wage, 1039
mining:
    copper, 585
    gold rushes in, 585, 632–33, 692
    labor and, 616
    regulation of, 1104
    silver, 585
Minneapolis, Minn., 633
Minnesota, 685
minorities, 1080–85
    see also immigrants; immigration; *specific minorities*
Mint Act (1792), 680
Miranda v. Arizona, 1043
missionaries, U.S. imperialism and, 704, 712–13
Mississippi, 1093
    African-Americans disfranchised in, 577–78
Mississippi, University of, 1041
Missouri, 854
Missouri, 944
Missouri-Pacific railroad, 620
Mitchell, John, 1092
Model T, 828
modernism, in literature, 810–13
Mohammed Reza Pahlavi, shah of Iran, 1107–8
Molly Maguires, 616–17
Molotov, V. M., 959, 962
Mongolia, 1138
    Outer, 939
Mongrel Tariff (1883), 670
Monroe Doctrine, 716, 783, 978
    Clark Memorandum and, 886
    Kellogg-Briand Pact and, 885–86
    Roosevelt Corollary to, 722–23
Montana, 585
Montgomery Improvement Association, 1022
Moral Majority, 1112, 1150
Morgan, J. P., 608, 614–15, 736, 738, 742
Morgan, J. P., Jr., 865
Morgenthau, Henry, Jr., 871
Mormons, 585
Morocco, 921
Morocco crisis (1905–1906), 724–25
Morris, Dick, 1179
Morton, Jelly Roll, 802
Moscow, 899
Mossadegh, Mohammed, 1107
Motherwell, Robert, 1000
movies, 825
Moynihan, Daniel Patrick, 1180–81
muckrakers, 730–31
Mugwumps, 671, 673, 729
Muhammed, Elijah, 1059
Mukden Incident (1931), 887
Muller v. Oregon, 734

Mulligan, James, 560
Munich, conference at (1938), 891
Munn v. Illinois, 681
Mussolini, Benito, 888–89, 895, 924
  death of, 939
  see also World War II
MX missiles, 1107
Myanmar (Burma), 908, 1016
My Lai massacre (1968), 1088

Nagasaki, nuclear bombing of (1945), 943
Naked Lunch (Burroughs), 1000
Nash, Beverly, 549
Nashville, 722
Nasser, Gamal Abdel, 1025–27, 1029
National Aeronautics and Space Agency
    (NASA), 1028, 1125
National American Woman Suffrage
    Association, 659, 804
National Association for the Advancement of
    Colored People (NAACP), 808, 864, 915,
    1060, 1122
national banks, *see* Bank of the United States
National Bell Telephone Company, 607
National Broadcasting Company (NBC), 986
National Child Labor Committee, 733
National Conference of Catholic Bishops, 1113
National Consumers League, 660
National Council on Indian Opportunity, 1084
National Defense Act (1916), 768
National Defense Education Act (1958), 1028
National Greenback party, 560
National Industrial Recovery Act (NIRA),
    (1933), 855, 860
nationalism, economy and, 566
National Labor Relations Act (Wagner Act)
    (1935), 861, 1083
National Labor Relations Board, 861, 1118
National Labor Union, 618
national military establishment, 957, 979
National Organization for Women (NOW),
    1078–79, 1080, 1122, 1161, 1181
National Recovery Administration (NRA),
    855–56, 859, 875
National Right to Life committee, 1113
National Security Act (1947), 957
National Security Agency, 979
National Security Council (NSC), 957, 972,
    979, 1008, 1045, 1125
National Suffrage Association, 804–5
National Union for Social Justice, 860
National Woman Suffrage Association, 659
National Youth Administration (NYA), 851, 919,
    1050
"Nation of Immigrants, A" (Kennedy), 1054
Native Americans, *see* Indians, American
Native Son (Wright), 877–78
nativism, 640–42, 666
  of Klan, 796–97
  in 1980 and 1990s, 1158
  after World War I, 795–96
NATO, *see* North Atlantic Treaty Organization
naturalism, 652–53
natural selection, 647–48

Navajo Indians, 916
Naval Construction Act (1916), 768
Naval War of 1812, The (T. Roosevelt), 719
Navy, U.S.:
  building for, 884
  economic importance of, 703
  world tour of (1907), 725
Nazi Germany, *see* Germany, Nazi
Nazi (National Socialist) party, 888–89
Nebraska, 582, 584, 685
Negroes, *see* African-Americans
Neo-orthodoxy, 994–95
Netanyahu, Benjamin, 1172
Netherlands, 885, 894, 965, 1016
Neutrality Act (1935), 892
Neutrality Act (1939), 894
Neutrality laws, 894
Nevada, 585
  in World War II, 918
Newark, N.J., 1058
New Deal, 697, 843–75, 899, 949, 1180
  agricultural recovery programs in, 851–55
  Eisenhower and, 1009–10
  industrial recovery program in, 855–56
  labor legislation in, 856
  labor unions and, 869–70
  legacy of, 873–75
  monetary system reformed in, 847–49
  opposition to, 858–60, 865, 873–74, 919
  regional planning in, 856–58
  relief measures in, 849–51
  renewed depression during, 870–72
  Second, 858–67, 869
  Supreme Court opposition to, 854–55, 856,
      860–61, 868–69
  as trial-and-error effort, 847
  Truman and, 953
  see also Roosevelt, Franklin D.
New England Free Trade League, 674
New England Women's Club, 659
New Freedom, 747, 750
New Frontier domestic program, 1039
New Guinea, 908, 931
New Jersey, 637, 744, 1157
Newlands, Francis G., 593
Newlands Reclamation Act (1901), 593
New Left, 1072–76
New Mexico, 585
New Nationalism, 747
New Orleans, La., 640, 803
  racial riots in (1866), 542
Newsweek, 986, 1065
Newton, Huey P., 1058, 1074
Newton, Sir Isaac, 809–10
New York, 1157
New York, N.Y., 561, 608, 633–34, 671,
    1076–77, 1085, 1114
  arts in, 999, 1000–1001
  immigration through, 637–40
New York Central railroad, 607
New York Consumers League, 660
New York Journal, 705, 706
New York Sun, 738, 783
New York Times, 802, 1044, 1076, 1089

New York Tribune, 691
New York World, 705
New Zealand, 1018
Nez Perce Indians, 588
Nicaragua, 1123, 1138
  Reagan's policy in, 1119, 1126–27
  U.S. interventions in, 762, 886–87
Nicaraguan National Guard, 886
Nichols, Terry, 1166
Niebuhr, Reinhold, 995
Nietzsche, Friedrich, 653
Nile River, 1026
Nimitz, Chester, 908, 931–34
Nine-Power Treaty (1921), 885, 887
Nixon, Richard M., 1015, 1076, 1123
  background of, 851, 1036
  cabinet and staff of, 1092
  domestic policy of, 1092–96, 1168
  foreign policy of, 1097–98
  Hiss affair and, 976
  in presidential elections, 1006, 1007,
    1024–25, 1036–37, 1067–69, 1075, 1087
  resignation of, 1100
  Vietnam War and, 1087–92
  Watergate and, 1098–1102
Nixon tapes, 1100
Nobel Peace Prize, 724–25, 1056, 1127
nominating conventions, *see* Democratic party;
  elections and campaigns; Republican party
Noriega, Manuel Antonio, 1128, 1142–43
Normandy invasion (1944), 925, 926–30
Norris, Frank, 652
Norris, George W., 857
Norris v. Alabama, 865
North, Oliver, 1125–26, 1127
North American Free Trade Agreement
  (NAFTA), 1167
North Atlantic Treaty Organization (NATO),
  964–66, 1008, 1025, 1028, 1137
North Carolina, 578, 1173
North Dakota, 584, 585, 683
Northern Pacific railroad, 614, 736
Northern Securities Company, 736
Norway, 640, 771, 894, 965
Norwegian-Americans, 584
nuclear weapons, 1044–45
  agreements on, 1045, 1097, 1103, 1107,
    1130–31, 1141–42
  atomic bombs, 941–44, 960, 1010–11
  Japanese cities destroyed by, 941–44
Nye, Gerald P., 891–94

Oates, Joyce Carol, 998
Obey, David, 1175
Occupational Safety and Health Act (1970),
  1094
O'Connor, Sandra Day, 1118, 1177
Office of National Drug Control Policy, 1135
Office of Price Administration (OPA), 912, 955
Office of Scientific Research and Development,
  910
oil, imported, 1095, 1097
oil industry, 573, 828, 1104–5
  Rockefeller's dominance of, 609–11

Okies, 854
Okinawa, battle of (1945), 941
Oklahoma, 578, 585, 808
  Dust Bowl exodus from, 854, 876–77
  Indian lands in, 587
Oklahoma City bombing (1995), 1166
older Americans, 1168
Oliver, James, 595
Oliver, King, 802
Olmsted, Frederick Law, 633
Olney, Richard, 625
Omaha, Neb., 633
Omaha Beach invasion (1944), 928
Oneida Indians, 916
On the Origin of Species (Darwin), 647
On the Road (Kerouac), 1001–2, 1072
Open Door Policy, 716–17, 723–24, 885
Oppenheimer, J. Robert, 942, 1013
Oregon, 731
  in World War II, 918
Organization of Petroleum Exporting Countries
  (OPEC), 1095, 1103, 1122, 1123, 1143
Orlando, Vittorio, 782
Ortega Saavedra, Daniel, 1138
Oswald, Lee Harvey, 1047–48
Other America, The (Harrington), 1051
Otis Elevator Company, 633
Ottoman Empire, 1146
*Our Country: Its Possible Future and Its Present
  Crisis* (Strong), 704
Overlord, Operation, 926–29
Owen, Robert, 626

painting, in post-World War II era, 999–1000
Pakistan, 1016, 1018, 1025
Palestine, 965
Palestine Liberation Organization (PLO), 1120,
  1130, 1171
Palestinians, 1097, 1105, 1120
Palmer, A. Mitchell, 790–91
Panama, 720–22, 1128
  invasion of (1989), 1142–43
Panama Canal, 720–22
Panama Canal Treaty (1978), 1105
Panamanian Defense Forces, 1142, 1143
Pan-American Conference (1933), 886–87
Panics:
  of 1873, 559–60, 617
  of 1893, 614
  of 1907, 749
Paris, Pact of (Kellogg-Briand Pact) (1928), 885,
  887
Paris, Treaty of (1898), 711–13
Paris peace conference (1919), 781–83
Paris peace talks (1968–1973), 1087–88, 1090
parity, 830
Parker, Alton B., 738
Parks, Rosa, 1022
Patent Office, U.S., 607
Pathet Lao, 1046
patriot movement, 1166
patronage, *see* civil service
Patton, George S., Jr., 840, 924
Paul, Alice, 804–5

Peace Corps, 1039
Peale, Norman Vincent, 994
Pearl Harbor, Hawaii, 701, 908
    Japanese attack on (1941), 901–5, 957
Peking, Tiananmen Square demonstrations in, 1136
Pendleton, George H., 556, 669
Pendleton Civil Service Act (1883), 669, 672
Pennsylvania, University of, 984
Pennsylvania Railroad, 617
Pentagon Papers, 1089
People's party, 678
Peres, Shimon, 1172
perestroika (restructuring), 1136
Perot, H. Ross, 1164, 1168, 1183
Perry, Matthew, C., 716
Pershing, John J., 761, 771–72
Persian Gulf, 1107, 1120, 1130
Persian Gulf War, 1143–46, 1158–59, 1160, 1171
Personal Responsibility and Work Opportunity Act, 1180
Peru, 1135
petroleum, *see* oil industry
Ph.D. revolution, 646–47
Philadelphia, Pa., 633, 640
Philadelphia railroad, 614
Philippine Government Act (1902), 715
Philippines, 724, 972, 1018, 1055, 1125
    American annexation of, 711–14, 718
    immigrants from, 1156
    Spanish-American War in, 708–9
    World War II fighting in, 901, 904, 931, 933–34
Philippine Sea, battle of the (1944), 933–34
Phoenix, Ariz., 918
phonograph, 608
"Phony War" (1939–1940), 894
physics, 808–10
Pilgrim's Progress (Bunyan), 730
Pinchback, Pinckney B. S., 550
Pinchot, Gifford, 740, 742
Pinkerton agents, 620, 623
Pinochet, Augusto, 1138
Pittsburgh, Pa., 640
Planck, Max, 809
Platt Amendment (1901), 715, 887
Plessy v. Ferguson, 579, 1021
poetry, of beat generation, 1000–1002
Poetry: A Magazine of Verse, 811
Poindexter, John, 1126, 1127
Point Four, 970
Poland, 783, 937–38, 959, 1118, 1137
    German conquest of (1939), 894
Polish-Americans, 640–41
Polish Committee of National Liberation, 959
Pollock, Jackson, 1000
popular art, 879–80
population growth:
    in 1980s, 1132, 1152, 1153
    postwar baby boom and, 954, 984–85, 987
    see also immigration
populism, 749
    progressivism as successor of, 727–29

Populist (People's) party, 830, 852
    African-American vote sought by, 577
    in elections of 1892, 687–88
    in elections of 1896, 690–92
    Farmers' Alliances as antecedents of, 685
Port Huron Statement, 1072
Portsmouth, Treaty of (1905), 723
Portugal, 885, 965
positive thinking, 994
postwar era (1945–60):
    arts in, 997–1002
    civil rights in, 1020–25
    consumer culture in, 985–87
    economy and business in, 981–83, 991, 996–97
    loneliness of, 996–97
    religious revival in, 993–95
    suburbs in, 986–89
    women in, 991–93
Potsdam Conference (1945), 942
Potsdam Declaration (1945), 942
Pound, Ezra, 811
poverty:
    under Bush, 1135–36, 1154
    in 1980 and 1990s, 950
    under Reagan, 1116
    war on (1960s), 1051–52
Powderly, Terence V., 619, 621
Powell, Colin, 1142, 1174
Powell v. Alabama, 865
Power of Positive Thinking, The (Peale), 994
pragmatism, 649–50
prayer, school, 1151
president, presidency, weakness of (1869–1913), 664–65
Presidential Succession Act (1947), 957
price controls, 911–12
Princeton University, 744, 745, 984
Proclamation of Amnesty (1865), 538
Proclamation of Amnesty and Reconstruction (1863), 534
Professional Air Traffic Controllers, 1118
professionalism, 646–47
professional service industries, 1153
Profiles in Courage (Kennedy), 1037
Progress and Poverty (George), 653
Progressive party, 744, 968, 969
progressivism, 697, 727–56
    antecedents to, 729–30
    conservatism of, 728
    democracy sought by, 731
    efficiency gospel of, 731–32
    Harding's dismantling of, 818–20
    muckraking in, 730–31
    post-World War I transformation of, 815–16
    regulatory efforts of, 732–33
    social justice espoused by, 733–34
    of T. Roosevelt, 727–28, 734–38
    of Wilson, 744–55
prohibition movement:
    bootlegging and, 800–801
    constitutional amendment and, 734, 799, 816
    in elections of 1928, 832
Promise of American Life, The (Croly), 747

Proposition 187 (California), 1157
Protestant Council of New York City, 994
Protestantism, 854
    missionaries of, 704
    social gospel movement in, 655–56
    see also religion; specific churches
public works, 837
Public Works Administration (PWA), 855
Puerto Ricans, in continental U.S., 1084
Puerto Rico, U.S. annexation of, 711, 715
Pulitzer, Joseph, 705
Pullman Palace Car Company, 624
Pullman Strike (1894), 623–26
Pure Food and Drug Act (1906), 739

quantum theory, 809
Quinn, Sally, 1161

Rabbit, Run (Updike), 998
Rabin, Yitzhak, 1171–72
racial riots, 542, 990
    in 1960s, 1057–58
    in World War I, 773–74
    after World War I, 790
    in World War II, 915
racism, see African-Americans; nativism
radar, 922–23
Radical Republicans, see Republicans, Radical
radio, 825–26
    talk shows on, 1178
radioactivity, 809
railroads:
    cattle and beef transported on, 591
    decay of, 1010
    financing of, 606–7
    New West shaped by, 594–95
    oil industry and, 609–10
    racial segregation in, 578–79
    regulation of, 660, 673–74, 732–33, 739
    strikes against, 617–18, 619–20
railroads, transcontinental, construction of,
    569–70, 604–7
Rainey, Joseph H., 550
Randolph, A. Philip, 866, 914, 968
range wars, 592–93
Rankin, Jeanette, 904–5
Rapier, James T., 550
rationing, 912
Reading Railroad, 614, 737
Reagan, Ronald, 1105, 1108–9
    appointees of, 1117–18
    arms control negotiated by, 1124–25
    background of, 1111–12
    economic program of, 1115–16
    feminists opposed by, 1118
    foreign policy of, 1118–19, 1124–25,
        1126–27, 1129
    labor setbacks under, 1117–18
    minorities and, 1118
    popularity of, 1117
    in presidential elections, 1103, 1111–15,
        1122–23, 1149
    savings and loan industry and, 1133–34
    scandals under, 1117, 1125–27, 1131

Reagan Doctrine, 1123
Reaganomics, 1115–16
realism, 649–54
recessions:
    of 1957–1958, 1028
    of 1970s, 1094–95, 1102–3
    of 1990–1992, 1159
    see also Panics
Reconstruction:
    African-American politicians in, 549–50
    carpetbaggers and scalawags in, 551–52
    civil rights legislation in, 544, 549, 552
    collapse of Republican control in, 554
    corruption and abuses in, 552
    end of, 562–63
    Johnson's plan for, 537–38
    land policy in, 535–36, 541
    Lincoln's program for, 534–36
    military rule in, 544–45
    pardons in, 534, 538
    Radicals' program for, 535, 540–41, 558–59
    repressive Black Codes in, 538–40, 541
    southern intransigence in, 538–40
    state governments reorganized in, 538–39
    Wade-Davis plan for, 535
    white terror in, 552–54
    see also South
Reconstruction Finance Corporation (RFC),
    838, 839, 1009
Red Badge of Courage, The (Crane), 652–53
Red River War (1874–1875), 587
Red Scares:
    in Cold War, 956, 976–78, 1011–13
    after World War I, 790–92, 831
Reed, Ralph, 1150
reform movements, 666–68, 669–70, 671
    see also labor laws; progressivism; prohibition
        movement; women's rights movement;
        women's suffrage movement
regulation, governmental:
    business support for, 727–28
    Harding's reduction of, 819–20
    progressivism and, 732–33
    of railroads, 660, 673–74, 732–33, 739
    see also antitrust laws; Interstate Commerce
        Commission; labor laws; Sherman Antitrust
        Act
Rehnquist, William, 1093, 1177
religion:
    fundamentalist movement in, 797–99, 1112
    government support of, 993–94
    literature on, 998
    postwar revival of, 993–95
    schools and, 1043
    see also Catholic Church; missionaries;
        Protestantism; specific churches
religious right, 1150–52, 1162
Reno, Janet, 1165, 1166
reparations, after World War I, 783–84, 883,
    937
Reparations Commission, 883, 937
Report on the Condition of the Indian Tribes, 587
Republican National Convention (1996), 1179,
    1182

Republican party, 697, 1162
  agenda of, 1175–83
  Clinton and, 1167–68
  cultural analysis of, 666, 1115
  cultural conservatives in, 1149–52
  domination of (1869–1913), 664
  in elections of 1994, 1175–76
  in 1980s, 1132
  see also elections and campaigns
Republicans, Liberal, 559
Republicans, Radical, 537
  accomplishments of, 551–52
  African-American suffrage and, 541
  electoral success of, 543–45
  Johnson's removal sought by, 545–46
  presidential candidates of, 555–56
  Reconstruction program of, 535, 540–41,
    558–59
  in Southern politics, 551–54
Rerum novarum (Leo XIII), 657
Resistance, 1074
Resolution Trust Corporation (RTC), 1134
Resumption Act (1875), 560
Revels, Hiram, 550
Revenue Act (1916), 768
Revenue Act (1926), 819
Revenue Act (1935), 863
Rhineland, 889
Richardson, Elliot, 1100
Richmond Times, 579
Ridgway, Matthew, 975
Riesman, David, 996–97
right-to-work laws, 1029
roaring twenties, 801–4
  moral values in, 802–4
  women's fashions in, 802–3
Robertson, Pat, 1150, 1162
Robinson, Jackie, 990
Rockefeller, John D., 609, 648, 835
  organizational innovations of, 609–11
Rockne, Knute, 640
Roe v. Wade, 1079
Rogers, Will, 782, 823
Rolling Stones, 1077
Rolling Thunder, Operation, 1062
Romania, 783, 898, 960, 1137
  in World War I, 779
Rome, battle of (1944), 924–25
Rommel, Erwin, 898, 927, 930
Roosevelt, Eleanor, 845, 865–66, 1037
Roosevelt, Franklin D., 697, 828, 957, 958, 971,
    1049, 1180
  at Allied conferences, 921, 926, 936–37,
    938–39
  atomic bomb and, 942
  background of, 844–45
  court-packing plan of, 868–69
  declining health and death of, 938, 939
  fireside chats of, 847, 858, 898
  Hundred Days of, 848
  inaugural addresses of, 847, 868
  L. B. Johnson's admiration for, 1050
  in presidential elections, 817, 843–46,
    867–68, 896–97, 934–35

Prohibition and, 845
racial issues and, 864
U.S. neutrality and, 891–94
World War II and, 896, 901–2, 904, 934
  see also New Deal
Roosevelt, Theodore, 740, 741, 785, 844,
    874–75, 1133
  background of, 718–20
  coal strike and, 737
  conservation movement and, 740
  as imperialist, 703
  Monroe Doctrine extended by, 722–23
  Moroccan crisis and, 724–25
  New Nationalism of, 742–43
  in presidential elections, 717–18, 738–39,
    743–44, 746–48
  progressivism of, 727–28, 734–38
  regulatory legislation sought by, 738–40
  in Rough Riders, 710–11
  in Spanish-American War, 706, 707
  Taft criticized by, 742–44
  as trustbuster, 735–36
  U.S.-Japanese relations and, 724
  World War I and, 765, 767, 768
Roosevelt Corollary, 722–23
Roosevelt Dam, 593
Root, Elihu, 724
Root-Takahira Agreement (1908), 724
Rosenberg, Ethel, 977, 1012–13
Rosenberg, Julius, 977, 1012–13
"Rosie the Riveter," 992
Rostow, Walt, 1046
Roth, Philip, 998
Rothko, Mark, 1000
Roughing It (Twain), 651
Rough Riders, 710–11
Rousseau, Jean Jacques, 1072, 1074
Royal Air Force (RAF), 925
Roybal, Edward R., 1084
Ruby, Jack, 1047
Rudd, Mark, 1074
Rural Electrification Administration (REA), 858
Rusk, Dean, 1038, 1045, 1062
Russell, Jane, 993
Russia, Imperial, 640
  Imperial China and, 716
  North American claims of, 700
  in World War I, 763, 770, 777, 779, 781
  see also Soviet Union
Russian-Americans, 640
Russian Federation, 1159
Russian Republic, 770, 777, 1139–41
Russian Revolution (1917), 770, 777, 779, 781,
    790–92
Russo-Japanese War (1904–1905), 723–24, 939

Saar Basin, 889
Sacco, Nicola, 795
Sackville-West, Sir Lionel, 675
Sadat, Anwar el-, 1097, 1105–6
Saigon, 1064, 1091
St. Lawrence Seaway, 1010
St. Lô, battle of (1944), 930
St. Louis, Mo., 640, 773

St. Paul, Minn., 633
Salinger, J. D., 998
Salvation Army, 655
Samoa, 700–701
San Diego, Calif., 854, 918
Sandino, César Augusto, 886
San Francisco, Calif., 632, 643, 854, 918, 1076
    United Nations Charter Conference in
        (1945), 958
San Francisco State University, 1074
Sanger, Margaret, 803
Santa Fe Railroad, 632
Sartoris (Faulkner), 878–79
satellites, 1027–28
"Saturday Night Massacre," 1100
Saudi Arabia, 1025
    in Persian Gulf War, 1145, 1146
Sauk Indians, 916
savings, 986
savings and loan industry, bailout of, 1133–34
Savio, Mario, 1073
scalawags, 551–52
Scalia, Antonin, 1177
Schechter Poultry Corporation v. United States,
        860–61
Schenck v. United States, 776–77
Schlafly, Phyllis, 1113
school prayer, 1043
Schurz, Carl, 558
science, 808–10
    see also physics; technology
Science, 788
Scopes, John T., 798–99
Scottsboro case (1931), 864–65
SCUD missiles, 1145
Seattle, Wash., 632, 789, 918
Sea Wolf, The (London), 653
Sedition Act (1918), 776
segregation, 578–79, 967, 968, 1067
    of buses and trains, 1022–24, 1040–41
    of Hispanic-Americans, 1081
    in housing, 1058
    of schools, 1021–22, 1024, 1040–41,
        1042–43, 1092–93
    see also African-Americans; civil rights
        movement
Seize the Day (Bellow), 998
Selective Service Act (1917), 772
Senate, U.S.:
    A. Johnson acquitted by, 545
    see also Congress, U.S.
Sennett, Mack, 825
Serbia, 1173
Servicemen's Readjustment Act (1944), 954,
        983–85
settlement houses, 657–58, 733
Sevastopol, 899
Seventeen, 987
Seward, William H., in foreign affairs, 700
sex:
    frankness about, in 1920s, 802–4
    premarital, 802–4
sexual harassment, 1161–62
Seymour, Horatio, 556

Shame of the Cities, The (Steffens), 730
Shantung Peninsula, 884
sharecropping, 573–74
Share Our Wealth program, 859
Shaw, Anna Howard, 659
sheepherders, 592
Shepard, Alan B., Jr., 1028
Sheridan, Philip H., in Indian wars, 587
Sherman, John, 664, 668, 675, 676
Sherman Antitrust Act (1890), 611, 733, 735
Sherman Silver Purchase Act (1890), 676–77,
        680, 689
Shevardnadze, Edouard, 1144
Shipping Board, U.S., 772–73
Shultz, George P., 1120, 1126, 1127
shuttle diplomacy, 1097
Siberia, 901
Sicily, invasion of (1943), 924–25
"Significance of the Frontier in American
        History, The" (Turner), 597
silent majority, 1087
silver coinage, 668, 676–77, 680, 687, 688–92
    see also currency
silver mining, 585
Simmons, William J., 796
Simpson, O. J., 1158
Simpson, "Sockless" Jerry, 686, 691
Sinclair, Upton, 739
Singapore, 908
Sino-Japanese War (1894–1895), 716
Sioux Indians, 587–88
Sirica, John J., 1098
Sister Carrie (Dreiser), 635, 653
sit-ins, 1072, 1073, 1074, 1085
Slavic immigrants, 637, 640, 642
Slovak-Americans, 640
Smeal, Eleanor, 1181
Smith, Alfred E., 832–33, 858
Smith College, 646
Smith-Connally War Labor Disputes Act
        (1943), 920
Smith-Hughes Act (1917), 754
Smith-Lever Act (1914), 754
Smith v. Allwright, 915
Snyder, Gary, 1000
social criticism, 653–54
social Darwinism, 647–49, 741–42
Social Democratic party, 626
social gospel, 654–57
socialism, progressivism spurred by, 730
Socialist Labor party, 626
Socialist party, 791
    presidential candidates of, 626, 740–41, 748,
        846
Social Security, 868–69, 871, 954, 1039, 1094
Social Security Act (1935), 861–63, 1010
social structure, in 1980s, 1177–78
Soil Conservation and Domestic Allotment Act
        (1936), 855
Solidarity, 1118
Solomon Islands, 931
Somalia, 1172–73
Somoza, Anastasio, 886
Sound and the Fury, The (Faulkner), 878, 879

Souter, David, 1177
South:
African-Americans disfranchised in, 575–78, 755
African-Americans introduced into politics in, 547
agriculture in, 573–74
Bourbons of, 575–77
decline of Democratic dominance of, 1007–8
economic growth of, in postbellum era, 570–73
literature of, 877–79
New, 570–82
Republican groups established in, 546
segregation in, 578–79, 1022–24, 1040–43, 1092
see also Civil War, U.S.; Reconstruction
South Africa, 692, 1138
South Carolina, 553, 731
South Dakota, 585, 683, 685, 731
Southeast Asia Treaty Organization (SEATO), 1018, 1025
Southern Christian Leadership Conference (SCLC), 1023–24, 1041
Southern Manifesto (1956), 1022
Southern Pacific Railroad, 605, 632
Southern Power Company, 573
Southern Railway, 614
South Improvement Company, 609
South Manchurian Railway, 887
Soviet Union, 790–92, 1017–18, 1128
Afghanistan invaded by (1979), 1107
China and, 887
containment strategy and, 960–61
Cuba and, 1044–45
détente with, 1096–97
disintegration of, 1136–42
dismantling of, 949, 951, 1159
in Eastern Europe, 921–23, 958–60, 1027, 1171
Hungary invaded by (1956), 1027
Korean War and, 972–73, 974
Middle East and, 1027
Nazi nonaggression pact with, 891
nuclear arsenal of, 971–72, 1015, 1044–45
space program of, 1027
in Spanish Civil War, 892
U.S. defense buildup and, 1118–19
U.S. recognition of, 889
U.S. treaties with, 1097, 1103, 1130–31
in World War I, 777
in World War II, 898–99, 901, 925, 935–38, 944
see also Russia, Imperial; Russian Republic; Russian Revolution
space programs:
American, 1027–28, 1039, 1125
Soviet, 1027–28
Spain, Spanish Empire, 965
cattle industry and, 590
in Cuba, 394; *see also* Spanish-American War
Spanish-American War (1898), 704–16, 720
annexation debate in, 711–14
Cuban campaign in, 709–11
Cuban insurrection leading to, 704–5
governments established in acquisitions from, 715–16
Maine incident and, 706
Manila Bay taken in, 708–9
Philippine insurrection and, 708–9, 713–14
war declaration and, 707–8
yellow journalism and war frenzy in, 704–5, 706
Spanish Civil War (1936–1939), 889–90, 892
Spanish flu, 788
speech, freedom of, 1135
Spencer, Herbert, 613, 647–48
Spindletop gusher, 828
Spock, Benjamin, 997
spoils system, 666–67, 669, 729
sports, baseball, 990
Spotted Tail, chief of Sioux, 588
Sputnik, 1027–28
Sri Lanka (Ceylon), 1015–16
stagflation, 1094–95
Stalin, Joseph, 873–74, 876, 921, 925–26, 930, 936–37, 959, 960, 971, 1011
Stalwarts, 667, 668, 669
Standard Oil Company, 609–11, 730, 738
Stanford, Leland, 605
Stanton, Edwin M., 544, 545
Stanton, Elizabeth Cady, 659
Starr, Ellen, 658
Star Wars (Strategic Defense Initiative), 1124–25
statehood, *see specific states*
States' Rights Democrats, 968, 969
Statue of Liberty, 637–38
Staunton, Va., 732
Steele, Shelby, 1150
steel industry, 572–73, 612, 615
Steel Workers Organizing Committee, 870
Steffens, Lincoln, 730
Stein, Gertrude, 810, 811–12
Steinbeck, John, 852, 876
Stephens, Alexander H., 538
Stephens, Uriah S., 618–19
Stevens, John Paul, 1177
Stevens, Thaddeus, 540, 555
Stevenson, Adlai E., 993, 1006–7, 1009, 1025
Stieglitz, Alfred, 603
Still, Clyfford, 1000
Stimson, Henry L., 942
stock market, 834–35, 1128–29
Stone, Lucy, 659
Stonewall Inn, 1085
Strategic Arms Limitation Talks (SALT), 1097, 1103, 1107
Strategic Defense Initiative (SDI; Star Wars), 1124–25
streetcars, 573, 633
Strong, Josiah, 704
Student Nonviolent Coordinating Committee (SNCC), 1041, 1058
Students for a Democratic Society (SDS), 1072, 1073–74, 1075
Styron, William, 998
submarines, 766–67, 769–70

submarine warfare, in World War II, 922–24
sub-treasury plan, 852
suburbs, 986–89, 996
Sudetenland, 890–91
Suez Canal, 1026–27
Suez War (1956), 1027, 1029
suffrage:
  for African-Americans, 538, 541, 544, 549,
    556, 752–53, 1056–57
  see also women's suffrage movement
sugarcane production:
  in Hawaii, 701–2
  tariffs and bounties in, 701–2
Sugar Trust, 735
Sumner, Charles, 540
Sumner, William Graham, 566, 648, 741
Sun Also Rises, The (Hemingway), 813
Sunbelt, 987
Supreme Court, U.S.:
  abortion issue and, 1079–80
  under Burger, 1093
  civil rights decisions of, 1021–22, 1023
  F. D. Roosevelt court-packing plan for,
    868–69
  free speech and, 1135
  government secrecy and, 1089
  New Deal programs and, 854–55, 856,
    860–61, 868–69
  in 1990s, 1176–78
  Reconstruction issues and, 545
  Thomas nomination for, 1160–62
  under Warren, 1013, 1043, 1093
  Watergate and, 1100
Supreme Headquarters, Allied Expeditionary
  Forces (SHAEF), 926
Surratt, Mary, 537
Swann v. Charlotte-Mecklenburg Board of
  Education, 1093
Sweden, 771
Swedish-Americans, 584
Swift and Company v. United States, 736
Switzer, Kathy, 1079
synthetic energy research, 1105
Syria, 1025, 1029, 1120–21, 1172

Taft, Helen "Nellie," 741
Taft, Martha, 956
Taft, Robert A., 956, 1006
Taft, William Howard, 642, 724
  accomplishments of, 743
  background of, 741
  as chief justice, 741, 748, 818
  Philippine government organized by, 715
  in presidential elections, 740, 743–44, 746
Taft-Hartley Act (1947), 956, 970, 1009, 1025
Taft-Katsura Agreement (1905), 724
Taiwan (Formosa; Republic of China), 716, 902,
  931, 972, 974
  immigrants from, 1157
  Nationalists' flight to, 971; see also China,
    Nationalist
Talmage, De Witt, 655
Tammany Hall, 671

Tarawa, battle of (1943), 931–32
Tarbell, Ida M., 730
tariffs, 664
  Cleveland's annual message on, 674–75
  Dingley (1897), 692
  farmers disadvantaged by, 678–79
  Fordney-McCumber (1922), 819
  Hawley-Smoot (1930), 834, 837
  as issue in election of 1888, 675
  McKinley (1890), 676–77
  Mongrel (1883), 670
  NAFTA reductions in, 1166–67
  Taft's attempted reduction of, 741–42
  Underwood-Simmons (1913), 749
taxation:
  under Bush, 1132, 1134, 1162
  under Clinton, 1167–68
  on increasing land value, 653–54
  under L. B. Johnson, 1051–52
  under Reagan, 1123
  for Social Security, 861–63
  see also income tax
Tax Reform Act (1986), 1123
Taylor, Frederick W., 731
Taylor, Maxwell, 1046
Taylor, Zachary, 555
Teapot Dome scandal, 820–21
technology, in agriculture, 989
Teheran meeting (1943), 925–26
Tejanos, 1081
telephone, 607–8
television, 985–86, 1178
Teller Amendment (1898), 707
  see also prohibition movement
temperance movement, see prohibition
  movement
temporary workers, 1160
tenant farmers, 573–74
tenement houses, dumbbell, 641
Tennessee, 798–99
Tennessee Valley Authority (TVA), 856–58
Tenure of Office Act (1867), 543–44
terrorism, 1120–21, 1125
test-ban treaty (1963), 1045
Tet offensive (1968), 1064–65
Texas, 569, 597, 797, 853–54
  immigrants in, 1157
  population growth of, 1153
  in World War II, 918
Texas Alliance, 682–83
Texas v. White, 545
textile manufacturing, in South, 573
Thailand, 1018
Theory of the Leisure Class, The (Veblen),
  654
Thieu, Nguyen Van, 1088, 1090
This Side of Paradise (Fitzgerald), 802, 812
Thomas, Clarence, 1160–62, 1177
Thomas, Norman, 846
Thoreau, Henry David, 1022
thrift institutions, bailout of, 1133–34
Thurmond, J. Strom, 968, 969
Tiananmen Square demonstrations, 1136

Tilden, Samuel J., 561, 667
Time, 1065, 1092, 1133
Title IX of the Educational Amendments Act (1972), 1079
tobacco, in postbellum economy, 571–72
Tocqueville, Alexis de, 944
Tojo, Hideki, 902, 931, 934
Tonkin Gulf Resolution (1964), 1061–62
Toomer, Jean, 807
To Secure These Rights, 966–67
Tower, John, 1126
Tower Commission, 1126–27
Townsend, Francis E., 859–60, 867
trade and commerce:
  illegal drugs, 1142
  imperialism and, 703, 716–17
  NAFTA and, 1168
  in 1970s, 1094–95
  with South Africa, 1138
  after World war II, 1039
  see also blockades; tariffs; *specific foreign powers*
trade-association movement, 828–29
trade deficits, 1128–29
Trade Expansion Act (1962), 1039
Traffic Safety Act (1966), 1056
transportation:
  in early 1900s, 826–28
  racial segregation in, 578–79, 1022–24, 1040–41
  urban, 633–34
  see also railroads
Triangle Shirtwaist Company, 734
Tripartite Pact (1940), 901
Truman, Harry S., 1005, 1006, 1015, 1017, 1025, 1133
  atomic bomb and, 942
  background of, 952–53
  domestic program of, 953–57, 966–67, 970, 1168
  foreign policy of, 970
  Israel and, 965–66
  military reform under, 957
  in presidential elections, 935, 966–70
  Red Scare and, 976
  Roosevelt compared with, 952
Truman Doctrine, 961–62, 976, 978, 1062
trusts:
  in oil industry, 610–11
  T. R. Roosevelt's policies on, 735–36
  see also antitrust laws; Sherman Antitrust Act
Tunisia, battle of (1943), 921
Turkey, 960–61, 965, 1025, 1044, 1045
  in World War I, 763, 780
Turner, Frederick Jackson, 597, 702
Tuskegee Institute, 644
TV Guide, 985
Twain, Mark (Samuel Langhorne Clemens), 572, 651, 663
Tweed Ring, 561
twenties, *see* roaring twenties
Tydings-McDuffie Act (1934), 715

U-2 incident, 1030
U-boats, 766–67, 769–70
  see also submarine warfare, in World War II
Underwood-Simmons Tariff (1913), 749
unemployment:
  under Bush, 1136
  in Great Depression, 835, 847, 853, 864
  in 1970s, 1094, 1102, 1106
  under Reagan, 1117
unemployment insurance, 861–63
Union Leagues, 549, 551
Union of Russian Workers, 791
Union Pacific Railroad, 557, 604, 605–6, 619
unions, *see* labor unions
Union Theological Seminary, 995
United Arab Republic (UAR), 1029
United Automobile Workers, 870
United Farm Workers (UFW), 1081–83
United Mine Workers (UMW), 737, 869
United Nations (U.N.), 965–66, 1122, 1130, 1143
  creation of, 936, 957–58
  Korean War and, 973–75
  Persian Gulf War and, 1144–45
  Resolution 661 of, 1145
  Resolution 678 of, 1145
  Somalia and, 1172
United Negro Improvement Association, 807
United States Steel, 870
United States v. Butler, 854–55
United States v. E. C. Knight and Company, 735
United States v. Northern Securities Company, 736
United Steelworkers of America, 870
universities, *see* colleges and universities
Updike, John, 998
Utah, in World War II, 918

Vance, Cyrus, 1106, 1108
Vanderbilt, Cornelius, 607, 632
Vanzetti, Bartolomeo, 795
Vassar College, 646
Veblen, Thorstein, 654
V-E Day, 939–40
Veracruz incident (1914), 760–61
Versailles Peace Conference (1919), 890
Versailles Treaty (1919), 781–87
  Hitler's violation of, 889
  League of Nations formed by, 782–83
  reparations in, 783–84
  U.S. rejection of, 785–87
veterans:
  of Civil War, 673
  of World War I, bonuses for, 839–41
Veterans Administration, 983
Veterans Bureau, 820
Victor Emmanuel III, king of Italy, 924
Vienna Conference (1961), 1044
Vietcong, 1020, 1062, 1063, 1064–65, 1088
Vietminh, 1016–18
Vietnam, Democratic Republic of, 1015–20
Vietnamese-Americans, 1157

Vietnam War, 948, 1060–65, 1087–92
  bombing of North in, 1062, 1065, 1090
  Cambodian bombing in, 1088
  casualties in, 1062, 1092
  conscription in, 1088, 1104
  Diem leadership and, 1046–47
  escalation of, 1061–62
  Hispanic-Americans in, 1081
  as issue in presidential elections, 1066–69
  opposition to, 1073–74, 1075–76, 1088
  origins of, 1046–47
  peace talks in, 1087–88, 1090
  social and economic costs of, 1065
  Tet offensive in, 1064–65
  U.S. withdrawal from, 1087–88, 1103
  Vietnamization of, 1088
  see also Indochina War
Villa, Pancho, 760–61
Virginia, 578
Volunteers in Service to America (VISTA), 1052, 1072
voter participation, 665–66, 1114–15
voting rights, see suffrage
Voting Rights Act (1965), 1057, 1092, 1118

Wabash Railroad v. Illinois, 673
Waco, Tex., Branch Davidian standoff near, 1165–66
Wade, Benjamin, 535, 537, 540
Wade-Davis Bill (1864), 535
Wade-Davis Manifesto, 535
wage controls, 912
Wagner, Robert G., 838, 861
Wagner National Labor Relations Act (1935), 861, 868–69, 1083
Wagner-Steagall National Housing Act (1937), 872
Wake Island, 713, 908
Wald, Lillian, 658
Wallace, George, 1042, 1067–68, 1087, 1097
Wallace, Henry A., 818, 852, 897, 934, 956, 968
Wall Street, 834, 1128–29
Wall Street Journal, 823
war bonds, 911
Ward, Lester Frank, 648–49
Warehouse Act (1916), 753
War Industries Board (WIB), 773, 787
Warner, Charles Dudley, 663
War Powers Act (1973), 1101
War Production Board (WPB), 910
War Refugees Board, 940
War Relocation Camps, 917, 918
Warren, Earl, 1013, 1021, 1043, 1047–48
Warsaw, 938
Warsaw Pact alliance, 1137
Warsaw Treaty Organization, 965, 1027
Washington (state), 585
  in World War II, 918
Washington, Booker T., 580–81
Washington, D.C., March on (1963), 1042–43, 1057
Washington, George, Farewell Address of, 979

Washington Armaments Conference (1921), 884
Washington Post, 704
"Waste Land, The" (Eliot), 811
Watergate scandal, 1098–1102, 1123
Watson, Ella, 592
Watson, Tom, 686
Watt, James (Interior secretary), 1117
Watts, Los Angeles, 1057–58
Wealth Against Commonwealth (Lloyd), 654, 730
Wealth Tax Act (1939), 863
Weathermen, 1075
Weaver, James B., 687, 688
Weaver, Robert C., 1054
Weinberger, Caspar, 1118, 1126
Welch, Joseph, 1011–12
welfare, reform of, 1180–81
welfare state, emergence of, 660–61
Welles, Orson, 851
Wellesley College, 646
Welsh-Americans, 640
Welty, Eudora, 998
West, New, 569–70, 582–98
  agriculture in, 593–96
  cattle and cowboys in, 590–92
  Indians in, 586–90
  migratory stream to, 583–85
  mining in, 585
  range wars in, 592–93
  violent culture of, 596–97
West Bank, 1172
Western Federation of Miners, 627
Western Union, 607–8
Westinghouse, George, 608
Westinghouse Electric Company, 608
Westmoreland, William C., 1062, 1064
West Virginia, 1153
Weyler, Valeriano "Butcher," 705
wheat, 593, 596, 678–79, 829
White, William Allen, 728, 768, 817
White Citizens' Councils, 1022
Whitewater case, Clinton and, 1170, 1183
Whitman, Walt, 1001
Wild One, The, 1001
Wilhelm II, kaiser of Germany, 724, 780
Williams, Tennessee, 998
Willkie, Wendell L., 896–97
Wilson, Henry, 540
Wilson, Pete, 1177
Wilson, Woodrow, 642, 663, 697, 816, 874, 1049, 1170
  antitrust program of, 750–52
  background of, 744–45
  banking and currency reform under, 748–50
  Caribbean interventions and, 762
  Fourteen Points of, 779–80
  League of Nations championed by, 782–83, 785–87
  Mexican insurrection and, 758–62
  neutrality and mediation efforts of, 765–68, 769–70
  in presidential elections, 745–49, 769, 815

progressivism of, 753–55
social justice issues and, 752–53
stroke and paralysis of, 785–87
tariff reform under, 748–49
Versailles Treaty and, 781–87
women's suffrage and, 752, 804–5
Wobbelin concentration camp, 940
Wobblies (Industrial Workers of the World),
627–28, 776
Wolfe, Thomas, 878–79
women:
in agrarian movement, 682
AIDS and, 1134–35
clothing and undergarments for, 802–3
domestic duties of, 991–93
education of, 646, 1079, 1136, 1154
employment of, 774–75, 805, 912–14, 1104,
1153
in labor unions, 618
in 1920s, 802–5
in 1940s and 1950s, 991–93
in politics, 1162
as single mothers, 1154
in social reform, 657–58, 1181
in West, 595–96
working conditions of, 734
Women Accepted for Volunteer Emergency
Service (WAVES), 912
Women's Army Corps (WAC), 912
Women's Christian Temperance Union, 734,
799
women's clubs, 659–60
women's rights movement, 1113, 1118
resurgence of (1960s-1970s), 1077–80
suffrage victory and, 804–5
Thomas-Hill hearings and, 1161–62
women's suffrage movement, 658–60, 752, 775,
804–5
Nineteenth Amendment and, 752
splits in, 659
state referenda and, 769
Women's Trade Union League, 774
Women's Voluntary Service, 915
Woodstock Music Festival (1969), 1077
workers, working class, see labor; labor unions
work programs, 850
Work Projects Administration (WPA), 850–51,
919
World War I, 891
Americans' sympathies in, 763–64
civil liberties curtailed in, 776–77
debt from, 883
economic planning in, 851
economic readjustment after, 789–90
European alliances in, 763–64
German-Mexican alliance in, 770
isolationism after, 882–87
labor movement in, 775
labor unrest after, 789–90
mobilization for, 772–75, 777–78
neutral rights issue in, 766–67
opposition to, 776–77
outbreak of, 762–63

Paris Conference in, 1076–80; see also
Versailles Treaty
propaganda in, 764, 771, 775–76
racial riots after, 790
Red Scare after, 790–92, 831
reparations after, 783–84, 883
U.S. entry into, 696–97, 770–77
U.S. neutrality in, 764–65
U.S. preparedness for, 767–68
U.S. troops in, 777–79
veterans of, bonuses for, 839–41
World War II:
African-Americans in, 914–15
air warfare in, 896, 902–5, 925
alliances and pacts in, 889–91, 899–901
Allied advances in, 921–22, 924–25, 926–30,
935–36
Allied conferences in, 920–21, 925–26,
936–37
Allied military strategy in, 920–21, 924–25,
930–34
American Indians in, 915–16
Atlantic shipping and, 909, 920
atomic bomb in, 941–44
casualties of, 903–4, 940–41, 943–44
debate over U.S. involvement in, 896, 904–5
demobilization after, 953–55
domestic mobilization for, 1080
economic conversion in, 910–12
European developments leading to, 888–95
European theatre in, 894–96, 922–25,
926–30, 935–41
financing of, 910–11
foreign assets frozen in, 901
German advances in, 889–91, 895, 898–99,
901, 935
Italian advances in, 898
Italian expansionism and, 889–91, 892
Italian front in, 924–25
Japanese aggression leading to, 887–88,
889–91, 893
Japanese-Americans interned in, 918
Japanese strategy in, 908–9
lend-lease program and, 898
North African campaign in, 898, 921–23
Pacific theatre in, 900–905, 907–8, 930–34,
941–44, 960, 972
Pearl Harbor attack in, 901–5
"Phony War" and, 894
reparations after, 937
Russian front in, 901
submarine warfare in, 899, 909, 920, 922–24
U.S. aid in, 898, 900, 902
U.S. declaration of war in, 904–5
U.S. defense spending in, 896
U.S. dominance after, 948
U.S. mobilization for, 909–20
western states in, 918–19
women's role in, 912–14
Worth, Jonathan, 563
Worthington, Amanda, 533
Wright, Jim, 1176
Wright, Orville, 826

Wright, Richard, 878, 989
Wright, Wilbur, 826
Wyoming, 592, 676

Yale College (University), 648
Yalta Conference (1945), 936–37, 938–39, 959, 960
Yalta Declaration of Liberated Europe (1945), 938
Yamamoto, Isoruku, 908
yellow journalism, 705, 706
Yellowstone National Park, 740
Yeltsin, Boris, 1139–42, 1171
Yemen, 1145

Yippies (Youth International Party), 1074–75
Yom Kippur War (1973), 1095, 1097
Yorktown, 908–9
Young Chicanos for Community Action, 1081
Young Men's Christian Association, 655
Young Women's Christian Association, 659
Youth for Goldwater, 1073
Yugoslavia, 783, 898, 1171, 1173
Yuppies, 1128

Zimmermann, Arthur, 770
Zimmermann Telegram, 770
"zoot suit" riots (1943), 919